# Lord Salisbury

# Lord Salisbury

*A Political Biography*

David Steele

ALLEYN'S SCHOOL

THE FENNER LIBRARY

CLASSIFICATION  942.081

First published in 1999
By UCL Press

First published in paperback in 2001
by Routledge
11 New Fetter Lane, London EC4P 4EE

Simultaneously published in the USA and Canada
by Routledge
29 West 35th Street, New York, NY 10001

*Routledge is an imprint of the Taylor & Francis Group*

© 1999, 2001 David Steele

Typeset in Hong Kong by Graphicraft Ltd
Printed and bound in Great Britain by
TJ International Ltd, Padstow, Cornwall

All rights reserved. No part of this book may be reprinted or reproduced or
utilised in any form or by any electronic, mechanical, or other means, now
known or hereafter invented, including photocopying and recording, or in
any information storage or retrieval system, without permission in writing
from the publishers.

*British Library Cataloguing in Publication Data*
A catalogue record for this book is available from the British Library

*Library of Congress Cataloging in Publication Data*
A catalog record for this book has been requested

ISBN 0-415-23947-8 (hbk)
ISBN 0-415-25761-1 (pbk)

# Contents

# CONTENTS

*Maps*

*Map 1   Africa at the close of the Salisbury era*

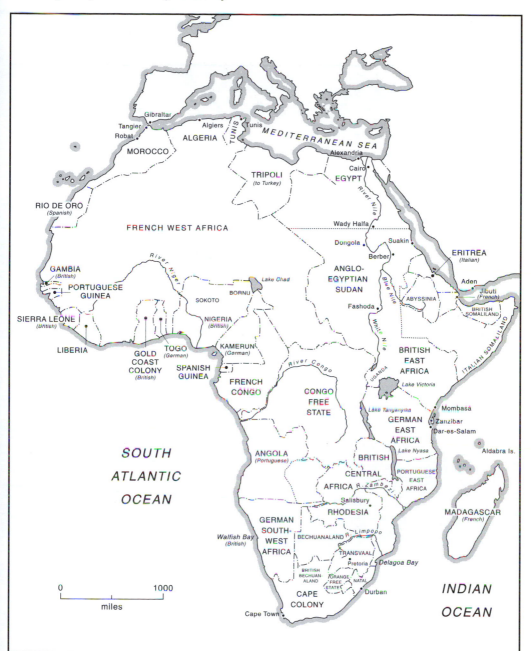

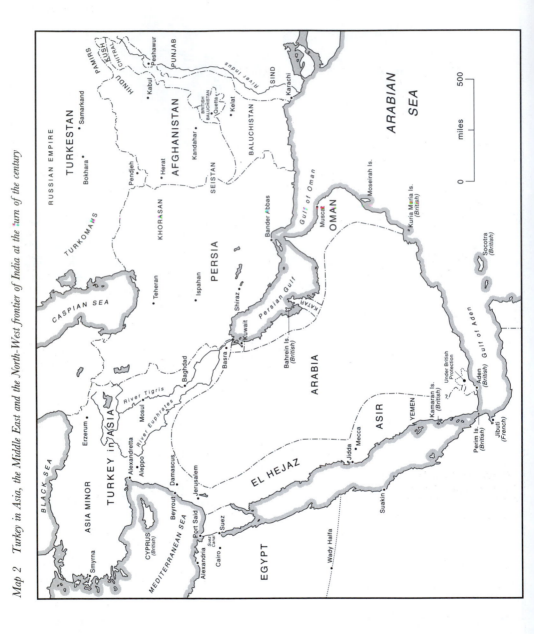

Map 2   Turkey in Asia, the Middle East and the North–West frontier of India at the turn of the century

*Map 3   The Balkans after the Congress of Berlin, 1878*

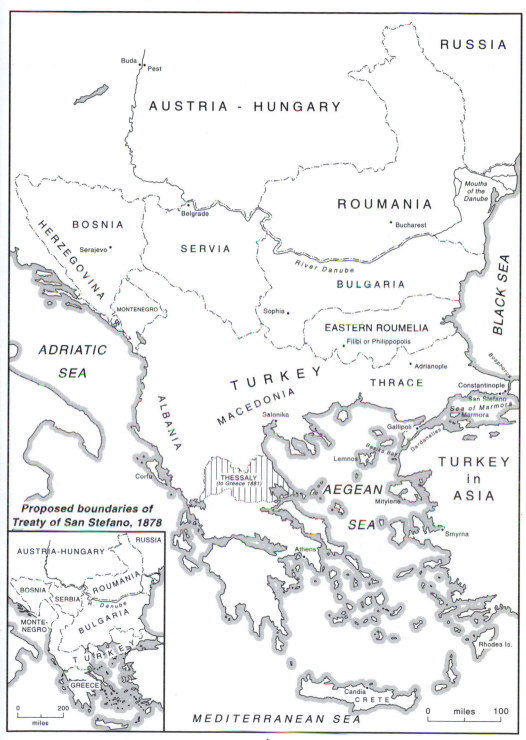

RUSSIA

AUSTRIA - HUNGARY

Buda
Pest

ROUMANIA

Mouths
of the
Danube

Belgrade

BOSNIA

Serajevo

SERVIA

• Bucharest

River Danube

BULGARIA

HERZEGOVINA

MONTENEGRO

Sophia

BLACK SEA

EASTERN ROUMELIA

Filibi or Philippopolis

ADRIATIC

SEA

Bosphorus

• Adrianople

T U R K E Y

THRACE

Constantinople

ALBANIA

MACEDONIA

San Stefano
Sea of Marmora
Marmora

Salonika

Gallipoli
Besita Bay
Dardanelles

Corfu

Lemnos

THESSALY
(to Greece 1881)

TURKEY
in
ASIA

AEGEAN

Mitylene

SEA

Smyrna

Athens

**Proposed boundaries of
Treaty of San Stefano, 1878**

AUSTRIA-HUNGARY          RUSSIA

BOSNIA                ROUMANIA

SERBIA

R. Danube

MONTE-
NEGRO          BULGARIA

T U R K E Y

Rhodes Is.

GREECE

Candia
C R E T E

0          200
miles

0     miles   100

*MEDITERRANEAN SEA*

# *Preface*

I have to acknowledge the gracious permission of Her Majesty the Queen to quote from Queen Victoria's correspondence and journal and from the papers of Edward VII in the Royal Archives. I am deeply grateful to the Marquess of Salisbury for allowing me to make full use of his ancestor's papers, and to the owners and custodians of the other manuscripts listed at the back of this book: the Trustees of the Chatsworth Settlement and the Duke of Devonshire; the Duke of Richmond and Gordon and the West Sussex Record Office; the Earl of Cranbrook and the Ipswich and East Suffolk Record Office; the Earl of Derby and the Liverpool Record Office; Earl St Aldwyn and the Gloucestershire Record Office; Viscount Chilston and the Kent Record Office; Viscount Hambleden and Messrs W. H. Smith and Son Ltd; Earl Cadogan and the House of Lords Record Office; the University Libraries of Birmingham, Bristol and Cambridge, and the Bodleian Library, Oxford; Balliol College, Oxford; Corpus Christi and Trinity Colleges, Cambridge; the Lambeth Palace Library; Liddon House; the National Army Museum and the School of Oriental and African Studies in London. I have also drawn extensively on the great public collections in the Department of Manuscripts at the British Library, the former India Office Library and Records, now absorbed by the British Library, and the Public Record Office. I have benefited from the willing assistance given by their staffs.

I owe a considerable debt of gratitude to Mr Robin Harcourt Williams, the Archivist and Librarian at Hatfield, for his help and seemingly infinite patience; to Hugh Cecil, whose invitation to contribute to *Salisbury: The Man and His Policies* (1987) led on to this book; and to Andrew Roberts, who generously found time to read through my manuscript. John Chartres induced my then employer to grant a sabbatical year which enabled me to do much of the writing. Over the years, two colleagues, Roy Bridge and Keith Wilson, enlightened me about the fields which they adorn. Feroze Yasamee's recently published study of Ottoman diplomacy in the opening years of Sultan Abdul Hamid II and my conversations with him were of the greatest value.

Steven Gerrard encouraged me to think of the book when he was at UCL Press, and commissioned it. After him, Luciana O'Flaherty, Aisling Ryan, Clare Hart and Kate Oldfield saw it through to publication. I wish to thank them all, and Mr Ian Agnew who drew the maps. My daughter Ursula searched the bookshops, successfully, for badly needed sources, long out of print. My wife has sustained the undertaking all along. Nothing I can say is adequate to thank her for devoted labours which transformed barely legible drafts into a neat text.

David Steele
8 December 1998

# Biographical Note

Robert Arthur Talbot Gascoyne-Cecil, born 3 February 1830; known as Lord Robert Cecil until June 1865 and thereafter as Viscount Cranborne until his succession as the third Marquess of Salisbury in April 1868. Educated at Eton, 1840–45, and Christ Church, Oxford, BA 1850; Fellow of All Souls by examination, 1853. MP for Stamford, Lincolnshire, 1853–68. Secretary of State for India, July 1866 to March 1867 and February 1874 to April 1878. Foreign Secretary April 1878 to April 1880. Prime Minister and Foreign Secretary, June 1885 to February 1886. Prime Minister, June 1886 to August 1892, and Foreign Secretary from January 1887. Prime Minister, July 1895 to July 1902 and Foreign Secretary to November 1900; afterwards Lord Privy Seal until his retirement from the premiership. Married, July 1857, Georgina Charlotte (d. 1899), daughter of Sir Edward Alderson, a Baron of the Court of the Exchequer, with whom he had eight children. Died 22 August 1903.

# Introduction

## A "Complex and Mysterious"[1] Figure

This is a study of a notably cerebral politician, who revealed the qualities necessary for success and survival in a career to which he appeared unsuited at the start. No prime minister was less inclined to accept conventional wisdom at face value, or to succumb to the routines of office. The first two chapters take the young Robert Cecil to 1866, through the formative influences of home, school, university and a taste of colonial life, parliament, marriage, his rise in the Tory party, an extraordinary output as a journalist and painful experience of the City. His ideas were evolving and his attitudes changing. Chapters 3 to 6 (1866–80) cover the losing battle in cabinet and the Commons for safeguards to accompany household suffrage, his emergence as the conscience of the party, the time at the India Office spent learning the limitations of power, and the events that led from the Constantinople conference of 1876–7 to the Foreign Office. From 1880 he was a leader in waiting and in 1885–6 at the head of a minority government: half a dozen years that made him a worthy antagonist for Gladstone. After these two chapters (7 and 8) the remaining six are devoted to his achievements with the Unionist alliance that gave him the indispensable parliamentary majority in 1886 and again in 1895 and 1900: 9 and 12 to domestic politics, including Ireland; 10 and 13 to the foreign policy of an expanding but vulnerable empire; 11 to a spell of opposition in 1892–5; and 14 to the last years after he gave up the Foreign Office in 1900.

For nearly seventy years biographers have been attracted to the third Marquess of Salisbury, and have subsequently retreated from a large-scale undertaking. Two brief lives have come out, in 1953 and 1975,[2] and an authorized biography was commissioned a few years ago to replace the four volumes by Salisbury's daughter, Lady Gwendolen Cecil, which stopped short at 1892. The nature of the sources has been a deterrent. The Hatfield archive contains a mass of correspondence addressed to Salisbury but relatively little from him. A glance at the list of manuscript sources at the end of this book will show how much work has had to be done in other

1

archives across the country. There is no comprehensive edition or adequate selection of the speeches, most of which have to be disinterred from the faded columns of *Hansard* and the newspapers. These are not obstacles to discourage a modern professional biographer with a large advance and a research assistant. The real difficulty lies in the man himself. Superficially, at any rate, Peel, Palmerston, Gladstone, even Disraeli, conform to their legends. A few months spent on Salisbury should convince anyone that he is in the historical presence of a very unusual person.

For one thing, there is much about Salisbury that is not particularly Victorian. Gladstone was dated in his lifetime, and knew it. Salisbury, endowed with an almost frightening ability to predict the future of Britain and Europe, was not. His thinking and his language often suggest someone now living: a characteristic libertarianism was qualified by his realization of increasing restraints upon its action in an industrial society; and with maturity he subscribed to Bentham's conviction that "security" – property and order – and a measure of equality were compatible at a certain point in a nation's development.[3] A hereditary Tory, he lacked any sentimental attachment to the House of Lords, an institution that had signally failed to evolve, and viewed members of the reigning house with some distaste, although he came to appreciate Queen Victoria's limited strengths. "If we are doomed for ever to have German royalties", he remarked on the marriage of one of her daughters in the 1860s, "it is better to have such as have learned the use of a tub by residence in this country".[4] His lifelong championship of the Established Church went with a perception of her failings so sharp that one primate suspected him of being indifferent to her survival. He did indeed care more for religion than for its institutional expression.

The vein of mockery in his utterances, including self-mockery, has helped posterity to see in him one who thought, and sometimes seemed to be saying, "*après nous le déluge*". This is not the impression left by a careful reading of Lady Gwendolen's classic work, but it has become the conventional wisdom.[5] Biographers, it does appear, have been put off by the inconsistencies between his opinions, old Toryism and the dominant liberalism; he cannot be made to fit the preconceptions with which writers commonly start. What follows immediately below is a brief reflection on a historical reputation and the case for its revision.

Robert Cecil, Lord Salisbury, may not have been the greatest of British prime ministers: but he was, perhaps, the wisest and remains one of the least known. The longest serving Conservative holder of the post since the Great Reform Bill is set down as a formidable pessimist. His achievements were, apparently, negative ones: he frustrated Irish Home Rule; kept the Liberals out of office for nearly twenty years with one short interval; and, combining the Foreign Office with the premiership, allowed the empire to grow while distancing Britain from Europe. His political philosophy was reactionary and defeatist, as was natural in a landed magnate afraid of what the future held for his order. His deepest concern was for another lost cause: the national influence of the Church of England. His pessimism went, as it usually does, with an enervating cynicism; he is remembered for an irony that was wounding as well as diverting. If it is not easy to understand how a politician without hope, the servant of vested interests whose time had passed, could have led his alliance of Tories and anti-Gladstonian Liberals to victory at three general elections, Salisbury's critics are ready with an answer. The mass electorate created after 1867 required inspiration, which they sought in Gladstone, while Salisbury, in a classical conservative role, played on fears and prejudices. This is not to say that historians have found Salisbury personally unsympathetic: like his contemporaries, they have been drawn to a man so intelligent, articulate and amusing. Their difficulty is that they cannot classify him as "progressive", in the Victorian meaning of the term: someone who believed in the evolutionary politics of the age. It applies to almost everybody of note in political life: the followers of Gladstone and Peel, those of Derby and Disraeli and the radicals – Cobden, Bright and Chamberlain – who were household names. They differed over the pace of change, and not over its ultimately benign character. Salisbury is the great exception.[6]

That portrait of an enigma is made up of half-truths. Even in his high Tory period, before the late 1860s, he was always "progressive", in the sense just described. In line with educated opinion, he was concerned that progress should be safe, as and when parliament added to the electorate. After his defeat at the hands of Disraeli on the 1867 reform bill, which drove him to resign from the Tory cabinet, he adjusted more quickly to the resulting changes than most of those who had voted for unqualified household suffrage. "I am close to the great democracy we all have to obey", he would say: and he was.[7] As much as any radical, he wanted to teach the enlarged political nation its responsibilities. A politically literate democracy, instructed by the methods of the new mass parties as well as by churches and schools, was the best security for individual freedom and property rights, and the best weapon at the disposal of conservatives. His reply to the populism of Gladstone and Chamberlain in the first half of the 1880s was to mobilize opinion in the lower middle and working classes against them, with an unexpected vigour that commanded his rivals' respect. Removed to the Lords by his father's death in 1868, he had little confidence in the Upper House as a check on a radicalizing majority in the Commons. So well was this known that Gladstone suspected him, at one point, of wishing to see the Lords swept away: he could then return to the Commons which he had been reluctant to leave. The impression that with his advent they faced a Tory leader readier than Derby and Disraeli in 1867 to steal their clothes was to be confirmed by his decisive part in the next extension of democracy under the legislation of 1884–5. What was worse for Gladstone, whose obstinate social conservatism offset his increasing political radicalism, Salisbury displayed a tendency that made the great Liberal accuse him – quite seriously and in private – of "socialism".[8]

To thoughtful contemporaries Salisbury was a more radical figure than he seems in his daughter's unfinished biography or in later studies. It is doubtful whether the developing partnership with Joseph Chamberlain would have been possible without the genuine, if limited, social radicalism they had in common. For Chamberlain, too, stood convicted in Gladstone's mind of "socialism". The beginnings of the welfare state are traceable to the measures that Salisbury and Chamberlain got on to the statute book in the 1890s. Unionism, originally the association of Tories and seceding Liberals to defeat Home Rule, became something more than that with positive attitudes and policies at home. Abroad, the leader of the Liberal Unionists, the eighth Duke of Devonshire, Chamberlain, their commanding personality, and Salisbury were all imperialists. So too were Gladstone and nearly all his adherents, who saw Home Rule as an alternative, and not as a prelude, to Irish independence. They were grateful to Salisbury for curbing Chamberlain's characteristic aggression. The growth and prosperity of the Victorian empire, formal and informal, were founded on peace with the European great powers and the United States of America. Salisbury's strongest claim on the gratitude of opponents and supporters alike was the undoubted success of his foreign policy.

The combination of the premiership and the Foreign Office, only possible because the Lords made few demands on his time and strength, gave him a freer hand in making policy than any foreign secretary before or since, Palmerston included. He used that freedom to build the diplomatic system caricatured as "splendid isolation". Isolation was dangerous when it was not impracticable. Gladstone put his trust in the "Concert of Europe", the collective action of the powers. Salisbury preferred to attach Britain to the dominant European power: Germany was central to his policy, as France had been to Palmerston's. Britain's strength at sea might be imposing, but accelerating changes in technology fed national anxiety about the element of uncertainty in naval warfare. Invasion scares were recurrent in nineteenth-century Britain: with the highest per capita expenditure on defence among the great powers, she could not afford a sufficient force of regular troops to defend these shores if the navy let her down; nor would the libertarianism of her people tolerate conscription. The "alliance", as Salisbury called the Anglo-German relationship, reduced the threat from the Continent. Britain, the Germans complained, enjoyed the security conferred by a formal pact without its obligations: Salisbury was unwilling to enter into a binding commitment that would have made his country the fourth member of the Triple Alliance. As international tensions grew towards the end of the century, this semi-detached position in Europe called for stronger nerves than Salisbury's colleagues possessed. His authority, however, was strong enough to dissuade them from modifying Britain's stance except by the literally peripheral Anglo-Japanese treaty of 1902. The Liberals appreciated a policy that kept her relatively independent of a continent divided into two armed camps. On his side, he came to recognize that the Gladstonian approach to Britain's neighbours was not outdated when he spoke in 1897 of an "inchoate federation of Europe" as the only hope of avoiding the catastrophic general war he foresaw clearly.[9]

Germany exacted a price for her co-operation: Salisbury drove hard bargains, but he paid in territory. The expansion of European empires went forward largely by agreement between the powers, and he was a past master of the negotiating process. His horror of war was something he was impelled to express at the height of the conflict with the Boer republics in South Africa: he accepted the inevitability of the small wars that marked the spread of empire. His imperial apprenticeship was served at the India Office in 1866–7 and 1874–8. If, like other secretaries of state, he was unable to change very much in India, he learnt a great deal. The experience reinforced an unusual sympathy with subjugated peoples. Repression of nationalities, he had said in one of his earliest Commons speeches, was as typical of the British as of the Russians with whom they were then at war. The advance of the West was unstoppable but the British yoke ought to be light. He was an advocate of indirect rule wherever Britain found a structure that would support it. Even so, he once referred, publicly, to the Egyptian government as "our luckless puppet". Imperial expansion brought liabilities in its wake, and he warned the public against acquiring territory "simply because it may look well to paint it red upon the map". Unpromising stretches of Africa and remote Pacific islands were bargaining counters, if nothing else, to secure British interests in Europe and elsewhere. Humanitarianism – the peculiarly British cause of anti-slavery – was a powerful incentive to go on adding to the empire: but he naturally stressed "business objects", the provision of new markets for an industrial democracy worried about intensifying foreign competition.[10]

His greatest diplomatic victory, over Fashoda in 1898, drew together the various strands in his moderate, rational imperialism: the cultivation of prestige, as a factor in international relations that governments neglect at their peril; the careful moves to ensure that France was isolated from the other powers; a bigger and better fleet than he had inherited from the Liberals in the 1880s; and a public opinion that needed to be satisfied, and not merely contained, on the subject of empire. That striking success was soon overshadowed by the setbacks of the South African war. Although the Boers were eventually overcome, the damage to Britain's international standing and her self-confidence was considerable. When age, health and the pressure of colleagues induced him to relinquish the Foreign Office, he lost much of his unique authority. He had long anticipated a trial of strength in South Africa between Afrikaner nationalism and a British population increasing in numbers and wealth; but, although well aware of the late Victorian army's deficiencies, he did not give its reform a high enough priority. Nor did he have the temperament of a war premier. That said, his was a steadying influence at a time of national humiliation without precedent in living memory.

The Boer republics fell to the British, but the most ambitious project in the whole of his foreign policy ended in disappointment. For over twenty years, he envisaged a controlled partition of Turkey in Europe and Asia. His inspiration was religious: he looked on Islam as "a false religion", whose contemporary revival would be checked by the break-up of the greatest Muslim state. On a lower plane, he argued that a distribution of the Sultan's lands among the Christian powers would go far to reduce European tensions: they would all be more or less "satisfied" powers for many years to come, occupied in digesting their gains. He obtained Cyprus as Britain's initial share at the time of the Berlin congress in 1878. He had just replaced a foreign secretary who objected both to the spoliation of Turkey and to championing her against Russia until the moment came to put an end to her imperial existence. When it seemed to have arrived in 1895, Salisbury was thwarted by the opposition of the Continental powers and by the resurgence of Turkey under Abdul Hamid II. The Germans, and others, saw his grand design as calculated to inflame the rivalries it was supposed to counteract. Anglo-Ottoman relations in the Salisbury era rate a separate study: here they may be said to demonstrate that he was no isolationist. His contribution to the fraught diplomacy of 1878, when an Anglo-Russian war threatened, established his credentials as a European statesman.[11]

Salisbury redefined the domestic content of Toryism to give it the edge over Liberalism in his day as prime minister.[12] His foreign policy, criticized within the government from the close of the 1890s, was hardly changed by the Anglo-Japanese treaty of 1902. While a Liberal foreign secretary, Sir Edward Grey, was soon driven to contemplate what Salisbury ruled out – a large-scale British military commitment to a Continental power – there was no rejection of his legacy before 1914. There were, however, three areas of policy where the main body of Liberals always differed from him. One was Ireland: but there, too, they were not so far apart. Salisbury did not believe that the Celtic Irish were assimilable; there is a reference in his correspondence for 1890 with a trusted colleague to "the Irish Republic of the future". He had explored the possibility of Home Rule in 1885 – perhaps his boldest initiative – before concluding that it was *"now"* out of the question. His Irish policy was, in effect, a prolonged holding operation; one that elicited his bleakest pronouncements. He had no time in that, or any other, context for "flabby optimism which disdains history and experience".[13] He was equally scathing about the Liberals' dogmatic attachment to free trade against the background of agricultural decline and the impending loss of industrial leadership. Never intellectually convinced of free trade's merits, he incited mass audiences to doubt them. At the same time he guarded himself against breaching the political consensus that upheld this economic orthodoxy since the repeal of the Corn Laws. He contrived to win votes on the issue for years without losing many, if any, of his existing supporters.

Lastly, the religious dimension of Victorian politics provided Salisbury with one of his greatest strengths as a politician; particularly after he learnt to confine his attacks on Nonconformity to the militants bent upon disestablishment. He defended the Church of England with better arguments than the appeal to historic rights. He was a man of the Anglican recovery that gathered pace in his lifetime. Dwelling on the Church's vital achievements in expanding pastoral care and denominational education, he claimed for her the same right to flourish that Nonconformists had demanded of the state: for they were now on the offensive, exploiting their disproportionate and growing influence within Liberalism. He also knew how to make the most of popular dislike for the puritanism of the Nonconformists, turning the argument for individual freedom against the temperance lobby which they dominated. The electoral benefits were clear, as Toryism reaped where the Church had sown. It was a political debt that Salisbury repaid by his services to her in another connection: he probably did more than anyone to prevent the latent "civil war" between High Churchmen and the rest from erupting. Patiently, he furthered reforming ecclesiastical legislation for which MPs could not feel much enthusiasm.[14]

It is harder to describe Salisbury's personality than his policies. The nervous depressions to which he was prone as a very young man have been cited as evidence of continuing instability, which cannot otherwise be substantiated. He struck most people as utterly sane: rational, controlled and well able to take the strain of adversity. "He loves to laugh", wrote a foreign diplomat who came to admire him, as did the other long-serving ambassadors of the great powers. The play of his humour lightens the documentary record today, as it lightened his speeches in and out of parliament. It is quite difficult to find someone who had much to do with Salisbury and disliked him: one who did was the fifteenth Earl of Derby, son of the prime minister, on personal and political grounds. This former friend and cabinet colleague usually put the worst construction upon the motives of his successor at the Foreign Office after they parted company in 1878. Successive Liberal leaders – Gladstone, Rosebery and the cantankerous Sir William Harcourt – were admirers of Salisbury, grateful for the skill and firmness with which he restrained the "Jingoes" on his own side. There seems to have been more criticism of Salisbury personally among his own ministers than on the opposition front bench. Yet he inspired a remarkable loyalty. With him, as with Gladstone, the respect and affection in which he was held were political advantages denied to lesser men. His integrity, like Gladstone's, did not go unquestioned. Derby and another old friend in that cabinet, Carnarvon, told themselves that ambition was the only explanation for his conduct in abandoning them for Disraeli when the cabinet was split over the Eastern question in 1878. That episode was the equivalent of Gladstone's positioning of himself on Home Rule a few years later.[15]

"All men are liars", says the Psalmist. Few tell the whole truth in ordinary life, fewer still in political battles, at whatever level. Not many people in either sphere can stand too much of the undiluted truth. Nor will someone rise to the top and stay there when the political landscape is shifting without an element of ruthlessness in their make-up. Thoroughly civilized and considerate in personal relations, Salisbury was more than a match for a *frondeur* such as Randolph Churchill, whose soaring ascent he cut short – with every help from Churchill. It is sometimes forgotten how fully he indulged a brilliant lieutenant, whose immaturity and irresponsibility he understood very well; their letters show how he got the best out of an impossible colleague until he finally overreached himself. The same qualities – courtesy, wit and intelligence – are to be seen in Salisbury's handling of a far stronger man. "*Chamberlainism*", warned the Duke of Argyll, who had sat with the radical in Gladstone's cabinet, "is . . . an image which may require 'bloody sacrifices'". Inclined at first to think that Chamberlain had no convictions, Salisbury realized that those he had could never again be contained, more or less, within the framework of Gladstonian Liberalism. There is a qualitative difference in their exchanges, compared with the Churchill correspondence. Tory and radical were engaged in constructive politics. There were to be no "bloody sacrifices" to Chamberlainism, not even in South Africa. If the erstwhile demagogue was invaluable to Unionism, the association with Salisbury presented him with greater opportunities than his old party would have allowed him. To some extent, this was a question of personal chemistry: Chamberlain was at ease with Salisbury, as he had never been with Gladstone.[16]

Both men were star performers in the golden age of platform oratory. As Salisbury advised the son who was entering politics in 1881, power was passing from the House of Commons to the platform. Liberalism, Toryism and Unionism were political churches: Salisbury employed religious as well as military metaphors in urging his audiences to organize. The Primrose League, which sought to transcend social class in the furtherance of Tory ideals, were "If I may say so without irreverence . . . the preaching friars of the message": and he likened the struggle for the popular mind, best conducted by working-class Tories and Unionists, to "Inkerman, a soldier's battle". Naturally, his popular speeches did not always reflect the fastidiousness of the private man; their partisanship was unashamed, and effective. But he deliberately assumed that he was addressing a mature democracy: his successful purpose was to elicit its support for aims which he summed up very simply: "What we need above all in this country is peace, and a close attention to the terrible social problems which beset us" – a good summary of the relationship between his foreign and domestic policies. Although the Left in Britain was extremely weak by Continental standards and hardly represented in parliament, Salisbury took it seriously, claiming a legitimate socialism for the Unionist parties. The speeches are a comparatively neglected source, partly because not enough of his social rhetoric, and Chamberlain's, was translated into legislation. They were ahead of their followers, of the Liberal opposition, and of the public opinion they were seeking to inform. The politically conservative late Victorian working class was conservative with a small "c":[17] but the rhetoric served to persuade those plebeians who needed convincing that Tories and Unionists were not their class enemies. It was an antidote to the propaganda of the Left, and, more importantly, to Gladstone's carefully limited attacks on rank and wealth.

The speeches he made in what did not long remain Liberal strongholds, are possibly the most striking expression of Salisbury's personality. Early in his career, he dispensed with notes for greater effect. Scarcely any survive; evidently nothing was committed to paper beforehand. His innate distrust of collective emotion seemed to disappear on the platform: he evoked and responded to it. He left an impression of complete sincerity, and never talked down to the "very unwashed and enthusiastic persons" he encountered in the big towns.[18] His feats of unscripted speechmaking across the country in 1880–85 helped to win him the undivided leadership of his party, and the premiership. Paradoxically, the House of Lords supplied the Tories with the answer to Gladstone's populism.

Salisbury was a religious man in the deepest sense. His Tractarian churchmanship, which ceased to be factional after his youth, was the basis of a profound understanding of human nature. His antagonism to Islam did not stop him from perceiving its resilience, and the stamina of other Oriental religions that had created civilizations. His support for the huge Victorian investment in missionary enterprise went with the realization that it was often flawed: "They have a proverb in the East", he informed the Society for the Propagation of the Gospel " – first the missionary, then the consul, then the general". Similarly, he was sympathetic, not of course to social revolution, but to the nature of the impulse behind the rise of the Left on the Continent, quoting a contemporary description of the Parisian workers in the Commune as "the most truly religious class in Europe".[19] Their secular faith aspired to the redemption of mankind; a vision derived from the Christianity that had failed them. An incipient threat from the Left in Britain was to be countered by making capitalism work rather better than it was doing; hence his encouragement of a flexible protectionism, and his persistent advocacy of other forms of state intervention. But whatever adjustments were made to the economic system, they would not avert the "social war" prefigured by the great strikes of the 1880s and 1890s without constant effort to sustain the religious beliefs on which, in the last resort, the mutual respect of British classes depended. That was one reason, if not the most important in his eyes, why Salisbury fought so hard for authentic religious teaching, as he considered it, in elementary schools. No "mechanical wire-pulled democracy" could preserve that "conservatism in its highest sense" which both parties in the Victorian state embodied.[20]

# CHAPTER ONE

# *Formative Influences*

## Family and School

In a surprising lapse from his usual good taste Mr Gladstone brought up, in private, the old story that Salisbury, then prime minister, was really the son of a Whig predecessor, Lord Melbourne. A noted Tory hostess, his mother was one of the attractive and intelligent women linked with that charming and gifted man.[1] The point of the anecdote is that by then Salisbury's reputation was second only to Gladstone's: Melbourne seemed a more likely father than the second Marquess of Salisbury, whose membership of two cabinets left no mark on British politics. In fact, the future prime minister owed a great deal to his Cecil inheritance, in every sense. Rank and wealth provided a solid foundation for a political career starting in the mid-nineteenth century, when the prestige of the aristocracy had never stood higher in his lifetime, wrote one of the greatest of contemporary radicals, looking back on nearly fifty eventful years.[2] Like other forgotten magnates, the second marquess was a considerable figure in the localities which he dominated. He combined strong Toryism and resistance to the state's modest encroachments on the independence of county government with a zeal for improvement that his opponents acknowledged. Boys directly employed by him on his property at Hatfield were fined if they failed to attend the night school he established for them in the village: half a century later only his son's determination got the abolition of fees for elementary schooling through a reluctant cabinet. The father exploited the coming of the railways to his wide estates, took a keen interest in canals and went in for agricultural innovation. The son accepted the chairmanship of the ailing Great Eastern Railway and oversaw its recovery. He, too, was a conscientious and improving landlord in the intervals of politics. His father was notoriously intolerant of political dissent among his dependants, but a perceptive, and witty, local obituarist – a Liberal – allowed that he was a kind patron, a good employer, and a hero even to his valet.[3]

The quasi-feudal surroundings of Hatfield were not a guarantee of security and happiness for the young Lord Robert Cecil, as he was known until 1865. Although

10

he was the third son, born in 1830, it was soon clear that he might expect to succeed his father or brother in the title: a second son died in infancy, and the heir was from an early age the victim of a degenerative disease which blinded him before he grew up. Robert was oppressed by the misery of his schooldays and by a tendency to depression which, according to expert medical opinion in his early manhood, seemed likely to shut him out from a life of action. The loss of his mother when he was nine must have affected him, though there is no direct evidence of emotional damage on that score. Five years separated him from the younger of the two older sisters, and four years from the brother, Eustace, who was his junior; he was never close to any of his siblings. He inherited her charm from his mother, Frances Gascoyne, as well as, in due course, her substantial contribution to the Cecil fortune. At six, when he was sent away to school, his nature was passionate and sensitive; since he was not physically robust, it exposed him to taunts that ended only with his schooldays. His memory of "an existence among devils" at that first carefully chosen preparatory school was unfading. He refused to send his own sons away until they were old enough for Eton, several years older than himself when he went there at ten, to an Eton that retained a good deal of its eighteenth-century brutality, vice and anarchic freedom. The experience of his first school was repeated, and his troubles were compounded by the exceptional promise of his work. Promoted into a form with boys who were his seniors, he proceeded to defy the custom which dictated that he should help his less talented and lazier elders with their exercises.[4]

That obstinacy was significant. He told his father, at fourteen, that he would not "sacrifice my liberty at the bidding of one lower than myself". The language may amuse in its context, but he meant what he said. His prolonged unpopularity and wretchedness are traceable to a dogged refusal to conform to Etonian *mores* in several important respects. He avoided the playing fields and the river, and had, it appears, no close friends. In quietly pathetic letters home, he wrote that he was "bullied from morning to night without ceasing" when out of the form master's or the housemaster's sight; literally kicked out of meals and forced to spend the evenings in a corner until the house was asleep. Robert's claim that his work had fallen off as a result was not borne out by his school reports. The housemaster, who enjoyed a good reputation, found it hard to believe that the boy was so badly treated. Highly strung and solitary, Robert may have exaggerated his ill treatment. In later life, he related how in the holidays he shunned the streets of the West End and kept to its byways, in dread of encountering the schoolfellows he loathed. Eventually, the second marquess, always a concerned if formidable parent, took him away after five years. Until he went up to Oxford in 1848, he remained at Hatfield with a tutor. Eton left him with an acute sense of the intolerance and irrationality that are more often than not the reward of independent spirits. His school contemporaries had demonstrated that no social class could claim to be exempt from those failings. Authority, in the persons of his father and housemaster, had been found wanting. To the end of his days, Robert Cecil was a sceptic and a libertarian in purely secular matters, though with a conservative bent.[5]

In retrospect, at thirty, Cecil rationalized his experience of boys and masters. The value of public schools lay not in their inadequate academic education but in the introduction they provided to adult realities at every level. He compared them favourably with those private schools where masters supervised the pupils closely. The essential nature of a school like Eton as a schoolboy republic prepared youth for the conditions of life in "a free country". He likened the difference between the two kinds of school to that between English constitutionalism and the governments of the Continent. "The analogy", he maintained, ". . . is very close". Schoolmasters were seldom superior in intelligence and judgement to their charges. Reliance upon them for guidance and protection, as upon government in a larger world, "fatally weakens the fibre of . . . character". The great strength of public schools was that "a salutary neglect" of the boys enabled them to learn how to survive by their unsupported efforts, and to do so without paying the price of failure in an adult environment. Bullying and fagging inculcated the social truth that, while the strong prevail, submission has its limits. Boys discovered for themselves "how bullies are to be resisted, and . . . the decoy ducks of vice . . . detected and foiled". They lived, as they would do when grown men, within the framework of a public opinion to which they contributed. Cecil did not forget that Eton's public opinion had all but broken his spirit. Revisiting the school for the first and last time, when he took his two elder sons for their first term, plunged him into black depression, so painful were his memories. His intellect might be satisfied with the theory that a public school was the making of a man, but the reminder of the personal cost was too much for him.[6]

His sons' Eton, he was careful to ascertain, was a much improved place, academically and in other ways. Through his association with the Reverend Nathaniel Woodard, the founder of the eponymous schools, Cecil became, a little reluctantly, an advocate of taking public school education to a level of the middle classes unused to it. In the speeches which Woodard induced him to deliver in that cause, he dwelt on the need to surround and check the influence of the schoolmaster "on his solitary throne" by the independent opinion of the school as a whole, "which scrutinized, and criticized, and judged all actions". The idea reflected the values and practice of Etonian youth; the humbler institutions whose establishment he encouraged had a different atmosphere. His mature reflections suggest that the lessons he drew from five unhappy years helped to form a successful political philosophy. The realistic democrat of the 1880s and 1890s had learnt the importance of consensus, and the penalties of defying it, in a thoroughly English setting. In the short term however, his schooldays had turned a highly strung and promising child into a nervous, depressive young man, socially ill at ease. Underneath there were reserves of toughness: it must not be forgotten that he had invited his persecution. As happened in similar cases, Oxford went far to heal his open wounds.[7]

## Oxford and Tractarianism

The highly intelligent and vulnerable youth who went up to Christ Church in 1848 had made good the "scandalous deficiency" of his Eton education.[8] His father had engaged a Cambridge don as a tutor in the holidays, and saw that between school and home the boy acquired a command of French and German. After Eton the

same tutor took a receptive pupil forward in mathematics. Botany was an enthusiasm of those days, and Cecil was later to be an amateur of physics and chemistry,
corresponding with scientists and conducting experiments in his laboratory at
Hatfield. He was already, and remained, very well read. His teachers at Eton had
been struck by the precocity of his work in divinity: wide reading only fortified a
natural religious faith. The logical and experiential weakness of Christian apolo-
getics was plain to his young mind: so were those of its radical critics. But he had
yet to satisfy his religious needs. Politics was an absorbing interest from childhood,
and coloured by his father's high Toryism. Oxford was a time of self-discovery in
those and other respects. The solitary boy at Eton and Hatfield made friends and
attracted admirers. He found he had a talent for speaking and writing; there were
forecasts of political distinction. It did not matter that he was entered for a pass
degree, as his father and the Dean of Christ Church decided in accordance with
common practice for young men of his rank. His studies, it has been shown, reached
a standard well above that expected for passmen, in recognition of which he was
awarded honours in mathematics with his degree. In 1853, four years after his early
graduation, he sat for and obtained a fellowship at All Souls; his standing there as
founder's kin did not exempt him from a stiff competitive examination. Successes
masked the nervous cost of his transformation in someone who had yet to develop
the mastery of himself that subsequently impressed observers.[9]

His circle at Oxford mixed aristocrats – the fourth Earl of Carnarvon, Frederick
Lygon, later the sixth Earl Beauchamp, and the eighth Marquess of Lothian, who
died comparatively young – with intending clergymen. There was no repetition of
Cecil's humiliations at school. In an adult world, people courted a magnate's son
and likely heir; "his toadyism chills me", he wrote of one unwelcome acquaintance.[10] The bloods for whom Christ Church was famous had roughed up Gladstone
during his time there; they hardly troubled Cecil: perhaps because, unlike Gladstone,
he did not have an aura of priggishness. Conspicuous in a set that combined social
prestige and intellectual liveliness, Cecil was chosen as prime minister when the
members amused themselves by distributing cabinet office in some distant future
among their leading figures. The more perceptive thought he would outgrow his
Toryism and appear on the Whig side. A surviving example of his oratory in the
Oxford Union, where he was elected secretary and treasurer, is unremarkable.
Tories were still pledged to restore the Corn Laws effectively abolished in 1846 and
deemed essential to the well-being of the landed interest, and therefore to England's
political health: "I cannot agree to destroy the institutions on which this country
rests . . . in order to conciliate any class", he announced. Yet there was a note of
conviction in the performance for an undergraduate audience. He could not forgive
Peel for breaking up his party and, on a less public occasion, spoke of him as
condemned to lie in "the grave of infamy which his tergiversation had dug". He
was at his best in a college essay club – "the Pythic Club" – founded by Lord
Dufferin, who was to serve Cecil as ambassador at St Petersburg, Rome and Paris,
and viceroy of India. In that setting Cecil shone; the papers he read were superior
to the rest. They evinced lasting dislike and scepticism of the economic orthodoxy
to which old-fashioned Tories were deferring in spite of themselves. His views on

social subjects seemed "rather perilous" to his hearers. That youthful sensitivity to the casualties of the Victorian economic miracle was characteristic.[11]

A letter written by a coming lawyer-politician, Roundell Palmer, lord chancellor under Gladstone in the 1870s and 1880s, affords a glimpse of Cecil's quality at twenty-one. Palmer, whose brother Horsley was an Oxford friend of Cecil, described him as able and high-minded with an urge to give practical expression to his ideals: he was animated by "a desire to do something for mankind in his time".[12] That aspiration, which informed his politics, was rooted in his religious faith. Dissatisfaction with the Church of England as he knew her turned him towards the Tractarians who rivalled the Evangelicals in their strenuous efforts to regenerate the Establishment. The new High Churchmanship of the Oxford Movement was the strongest tie with his university friends. He scorned old High Churchmen with their "ignorant horror" of Roman Catholicism and their "shallow, hazy" understanding of Christian truth. They were incapable of effective resistance to the contraction of belief in the face of radical theology and the secularizing tendency of the age; he dismissed them as "the squeezable High and Dry". For the Low Church he felt active hostility. The fundamentals of their position were unacceptable: the emphasis on justification by faith rather than by faith and works, and on Scripture interpreted without adequate reference to tradition. An unfortunate bishop whom he encountered was condemned as "a thoroughgoing Bibliolater"; a man "much tainted" by a leaning to justification by faith alone. At this period of his religious history, Cecil embraced "High Church truths" with few reservations, deploring "Protestant latitude". A follower of Newman's replacement at the head of the Catholic revival in Anglicanism, he was proud to call himself a Puseyite, despite, or even because of, the opprobrium attached to the name.[13]

The cornerstone of Cecil's Tractarian faith was its emphasis on the Eucharist in a Catholic sense, as offering in perpetuity the sacrifice of Christ upon the Cross for suffering humanity; in line with the teaching of John Keble and Pusey he rejected the Roman doctrine of transubstantiation for giving too materialistic an idea of the tremendous change in the elements of bread and wine. For the rest of his life Cecil was a notably devout and regular communicant. In this crucial respect, Tractarianism met his spiritual needs without offending an intellect that recoiled from other features of Catholicism. Never, apparently, tempted to go over to Rome, he maintained, like most of those who adhered to the Oxford Movement, that the Church of England had preserved more of early Christianity than the Roman church had succeeded in doing. His religion was patristic, and the medieval church suspect. He considered the Papal claims intolerable, and shrank from popular Marian devotions as requiring him to "worship the Virgin".[14] Some Tractarians were drawn to the practice of sacramental confession: he was typical of his countrymen in objecting to it as an invasion of conscience and subversion of individual responsibility. Nor did he care for the Tractarian propensity to an unctuous clericalism alien to the Establishment; to him, as to a Protestant public, the prelate who embodied that trend, Samuel Wilberforce, was "Soapy Sam". The temper of Cecil's churchmanship differed significantly from that of his fellow Tractarian Gladstone, who was altogether more ecclesiastical in outlook. Nor would Gladstone have faulted another bishop for taking "too charitable a view of the characters of those whom he has to oppose".[15]

The self-confidence of his immature pronouncements on politics and religion was deceptive. His outward prosperity – the recognition of ability and promise in his fashionable college and at the Union – hid uncertainties that fed the depressions to which he was prone; an affliction that may have been hereditary and was complicated by fussiness over his health, a lifelong trait. The desire to leave the world a better place than he found it fought with a sense of his inadequacy that was real to the sufferer. The worst period of doubt and anxiety occurred in 1849–50 and shortened his time at Oxford. The decision to remove him in 1849 was taken on the insistence of Henry Acland, a young physician with a distinguished career before him. There followed a year spent attempting to read for the Bar. It seems that his illness was psychosomatic; as his daughter remarked, contemporary medicine had much to learn in that area. However, Acland arrived at what was evidently the right diagnosis, and prescribed a conventional remedy in such cases: an extended sea voyage. Cecil always regarded him as his saviour, and they were to form an enduring friendship. Nearly two years of travel in 1851–3 to South Africa, Australia and New Zealand, and home again round Cape Horn, did not effect a permanent cure. On his return he again succumbed to "nerve storms", as he termed them, which prostrated him. Nevertheless, his colonial experiences, recounted in letters to his family and to a clerical friend and Oxford contemporary, the Reverend Charles Conybeare, were important for his personal, and also for his political, development.[16]

## Colonial Impressions

The traveller's letters can be supplemented by a journal kept for about a year. These sources show that Cecil enjoyed the understanding and support of his family; there is no trace of distrust and resentment on either side. His father's concern for him was not lessened by remarriage in 1847 to a woman little older than his son, or by the birth of their five children. Relations between stepmother and stepson were friendly. The new marchioness, Lady Mary Sackville-West, daughter of the fifth Earl de la Warr, was socially ambitious with a taste for politics. She attracted the friendship of able men, and through her Cecil was brought into closer contact with the ruling circles to which the Cecils had belonged for centuries. The security his family provided could not remove the uncertainty about his future, which aggravated, if it did not cause, Cecil's condition. He was someone in search of a settled purpose; a reading of his journal suggests that he might well have ended by taking holy orders, as he contemplated doing. Intensely interested in the prospects for Anglicanism in the colonies, he sought out its leaders, who were gratified by this unusual solicitude in an aristocratic visitor. While there is some political comment in his diary and correspondence, he judged the transplanted civilization of white settlers by the society they had created, and above all by their receptiveness to religion. The last was his final test, as a statesman, of a country's health. His observations would be worth reading even if one were unaware of the writer's destiny. Though he lacked the subtlety that came later, the lightness of touch, the distinguishing irony and the ability to delineate character and motive in a quite secular fashion were all present in his early twenties.[17]

The expatriate clergy who ministered to the colonists reflected the influence of the Oxford Movement which, Cecil noted, could make "a very decent Puseyite" of a typical churchman with his "caution and complaisance, especially to those above him". He never cared much for moderate men in religion or politics, and in his youth was intolerant of them. As a very young man he was inclined to share the apocalyptic vision of a changing world common to ardent Tractarians and Evangelicals in the middle of the century: they believed themselves to be facing a concerted assault by the forces of heresy and unbelief. He was particularly concerned to discover how the Church of England was faring in South Australia, where, exceptionally for the empire then, she did not have the support of the state. To his dismay, he found in the Bishop of Adelaide a prelate who actually said that the Church was "neither High nor Low but Broad". Cecil thought this stance "a logical absurdity . . . a grand practical excuse for cowardice". The organization of the unestablished church in South Australia – "Protestant and plutocratic with a vengeance" – might have been designed to promote everything the Tractarians feared. The house of laity in its governing body consisted of one delegate for every hundred members of the church qualified to vote by the seats they rented for worship. Clergy, though licensed by the bishop, were at the mercy of their congregations, while vesting church property in trustees gave the colonial courts power to rule on doctrinal disputes. There is no doubt that his insight into what disestablishment might mean for the church at home, and for the "Catholic" minority within her, made a deep impression on Cecil. Tractarians aspired to a revised partnership between church and state on the pre-Reformation pattern and, failing that, to independence at the cost of disestablishment. High Churchmen would certainly be the losers if congregational power and the authority of trustees replaced the complex distribution of rights that made for the more or less orderly co-existence of rival parties in the Church.[18]

Another strong objection to Anglicanism on the South Australian model was its social character, "a Church of the rich, not of the poor", in the sense that it made little provision for non-paying members. "Rich" in the colonial context meant the middle classes, whose ascendancy in the nascent democracies of the Antipodes elicited some interesting reflections from the visitor. It was the tractability of the population rather than its already legendary roughness that he noticed. The moral and legal framework of society withstood the uncontrollable influx of newcomers following the discovery of gold in the late 1840s. Travelling with an Irish baronet, Sir Montagu Chapman, whom he had met at sea, Cecil went up to the supposedly turbulent goldfields of Victoria, a magnet for adventurers and masterless men. The shifting communities he saw proved to be astonishingly submissive to authority in the shape of isolated magistrates backed by a handful of mounted policemen. People on the diggings conformed to the Anglo-Saxon origins of the majority, accustomed to a large freedom under the law. The energetic commissioner whom

Cecil accompanied could not have kept the peace and enforced mining regulations as strictly as he did without the co-operation of those whom he was policing. Cecil contrasted what he had seen with the reported disorder and violence of the contemporary Californian gold rush. Attributing the difference to republican America's impatience of traditional restraints, he predicted that they would cease to operate in Australia, and in Britain too, by the end of the century. The agents of this change "as well as [of] every other evil temper of this evil age" would be the middle classes. The position of the Australian "squattocracy" – large pastoralists – was under attack. New South Wales and Victoria adopted manhood suffrage before the end of the 1850s, two generations ahead of the mother country. Cecil's assumption, then, that democracy and destructive radicalism went hand in hand ought to have been shaken by popular respect for law and property in these settler colonies.[19]

The legacy of this colonial tour is discernible in his thinking over the next half century. The Puseyite zealot saw the Anglican church in a novel environment that was not particularly favourable to her. He returned more than ever convinced of her indispensability but more conscious of the gap between the medievalism of the Tractarians and reality. The biting observation of clerical deficiencies in the diary and letters exhibit, besides an innate loathing of humbug and moral cowardice, a growing realisation of what was possible for a friend of the church anxious for her renewal. He had met too few clergymen in those new countries who, like Bishop Gray and Archdeacon Merriman at the Cape, resembled "the saints of antiquity".[20] His political ideas were similarly tested against the knowledge he had acquired. The Australian colonies and New Zealand were poised to become "monarchical republics", as John Bright approvingly described them in 1858.[21] There the egalitarianism of the settlers did not threaten all property and order, partly because land was very cheap and its ownership widely diffused. Cecil's objections to democracy when it was not revolutionary – though the pastoralists had reason to fear for their rights under legislators elected on manhood suffrage – were twofold. It must subvert the power and responsibility of the wealthy and educated to provide leadership; and it would not long tolerate the establishment of religion. That natural leadership and the fundamental importance of an established church comprised the essentials of Cecil's political philosophy, which he adapted to the changes of his long career. It was a philosophy shared by the majority of Victorian politicians, irrespective of party. "I suppose the Church may be disestablished, but I should expect to see a republic in ten years", wrote Lord John Russell in this decade, a past and future premier whose liberalism Cecil professed to find dangerous at the time.[22]

Yet British politicians were virtually all liberals, by Continental standards. There is no vestige of his undergraduate cult of Strafford in Cecil's sensible remarks about the desire of settlers from the Cape to New Zealand for the substantial autonomy already conceded to several of the Canadian colonies. If fact, he sounded very much like radical critics of the Colonial Office at home and in the dependencies he had visited. In New South Wales and Tasmania there was talk of complete separation from Britain and even of resorting to arms. Dismissive of the "rants about rebellion and the rights of man", Cecil sympathised with what he thought were real grievances: the remoteness of Whitehall and the absurdity of its detailed control over appointments and business so far away. Predisposed to dislike bureaucracy where he came across it, he echoed the settlers' rather unfair complaints of "useless clerks" in London. "Responsible government", as extensive self-rule for the settler colonies was designated, would maintain an evolving relationship with Britain.[23] The reflections of a very young man are significant because Cecil was both more consistent and more liberal in his outlook than has been supposed. The classic rationalization of his position is to be located in Burke, whose pervasive influence struck that recent immigrant in Britain, Karl Marx: the eighteenth-century Irishman, he remarked in 1856, was "the man who is held by every party in England as the paragon of British statesmen".[24] Change was inescapable and blind resistance to it self-destructive: that Burkean truth was always in Cecil's mind, and in the minds of his contemporaries. Seeing life on the Australian goldfields for himself reinforced another truth at the heart of Burke's teaching. People's behaviour in society was governed more by inherited assumptions than by conscious reasoning or legislation. The art of government lay in preserving and contriving to adapt those associations in conditions undreamt of not long before.

## Ambition and Self-doubt

His journey round the world had improved Cecil's health and self-confidence, for the time being. He discussed the future in a long letter to his father, written before he sailed for home. The attraction of politics was very strong – "The House of Commons is undoubtedly the place in which a man can be the most useful" – but he claimed that he had no hope of finding a seat. Then there was the Church: "The profession I should place next . . . in usefulness" – a revealing, and typically English, view of holy orders. Beneath his Tractarianism Cecil responded to the spirit of the age: utility was the test of all things. However, he believed himself lacking in the personal qualities that made a good clergyman. That left the Bar, for which he had been intended before his breakdown. Like some Benthamite legal reformer, he viewed that honourable profession as "a public nuisance", living off the unintelligibility of the law. If his father did not choose a career for him, he thought he might supplement his younger son's income by writing for the newspapers. Openings for a gentleman with little money were very few, and he was resigned to "doing nothing in particular". Continual worry about his health, which he persisted in regarding as precarious while telling of fifty mile rides through the wilds of New Zealand, was accompanied by the kind of self-deception to which talented young men are liable. Afraid that they will not be able to demonstrate the ability of which they are conscious, they seek solace in assuring themselves, as Cecil did, that "all modes of life are equally uninviting".[25]

Shortly after reaching England, he sat for the fellowship at All Souls, successfully, after announcing that "my . . . chance . . . never high has sunk to zero". At the same time Lord Salisbury settled his son's future. Acting on Robert's clear preference, he got him into parliament at a by-election for Stamford. Their kinsman, the second Marquess of Exeter, arranged an unopposed return for the small Lincolnshire borough adjacent to his great house at Burghley and largely in his ownership. Returned in December 1853, Cecil was immediately approached to stand for one of the prestigious university seats at Oxford. The invitation showed how wrong he was to fear that he did not have it in him to succeed. His election at All Souls reminded Oxford of his undergraduate fame. His High Church piety, Tory politics, intellect and rank qualified him to fill the vacancy on the retirement of a celebrated reactionary, Sir Robert Inglis. A requisition addressed to Lord Salisbury by the more conservative element in a stronghold of conservatism received the wise reply that his son was untried and, by implication, unequal to the honour. His constituents at Oxford would have expected much more of Cecil than Lord Exeter's tame voters; the senior member for the university was none other than W.E. Gladstone, then chancellor of the exchequer. The paternal caution was justified: his son's first years as an MP were passed in the shadow of his old trouble. Acland advised that Robert was unsuited to an active life and parliament's late hours: constitutionally feeble and liable to "excessive nervous exhaustion", he was in danger of becoming a confirmed hypochondriac. Medical advice had been sought when he alluded, in an exchange with his father, to "nervous attacks" and the "sham" they were making of his political career at its start. Frantic to escape the command of the Middlesex militia, pressed on him by Lord Salisbury as lord lieutenant of that county, Robert dwelt on his unfitness for what was, in the eyes of his class, an obligation and a privilege: "Your proposition gave me a stomach-ache all . . . morning . . . I detest . . . soldiering . . . I would sooner be at the treadmill . . . my wretched health . . . exposes me to these . . . attacks"; the protest reads like that of a neurotic, someone whose emotional development was hopelessly retarded.[26]

It is plain that Salisbury was deeply disappointed in his eventual heir, despite strong signs of genuine promise in the House before and not long after that childish letter. Understandably, the marquess could not believe, as late as 1858, in his son's ability to cut "some figure in the political world". On the formation of a Tory administration that year, the first since Robert entered the Commons, there was no under-secretaryship for him. Again a cabinet minister, and mindful of the demands of a second family on his fortune, Salisbury proposed to give his son one of the well paid clerkships of the Privy Council in his gift as lord president. In the event, the cabinet, keen to impress the electorate with its zeal for economy, decided to abolish the vacant post. Cecil, now married with children, had wanted the financial security the appointment offered. It was not certain that he would inherit anything more than the £10 000 he had from his mother, the interest on which furnished the greater part of his income. His elder brother was the last life in the entail on the estate; though blind and an invalid, it was conceivable that he might marry, or leave all he possessed away from his junior. Cecil referred to these worrying possibilities in a letter of 1857 to his father. Chance rescued him from salaried obscurity. He went on to earn political recognition, in the first instance by his pen. The road to the cabinet lay through the pages of the *Quarterly Review*, the heavyweight of the Tory press.[27]

# CHAPTER TWO

## *The Rising Politician*

### Georgina Alderson

His wife was probably the making of Robert Cecil. The incidence and severity of his depressions lessened until they occurred only very rarely. She brought to the marriage an absolute and intelligent devotion which enabled him to rise to the mental and physical challenges of a political life that was unusually arduous. He displayed such self-command and powers of work that hardly anyone could imagine what he had once suffered from his "nerve storms". Clever, articulate and cultured, Georgina Alderson was well known in Tractarian circles and might be described as a handsome, lively, Puseyite bluestocking. As often happens in a perfect match, she possessed qualities that compensated for her husband's shortcomings. She made the transition to being a politician's wife, and later the mistress of Hatfield, without difficulty. He claimed to dislike the social round: her charm, buoyancy and sociability made it tolerable for him. Her London receptions and the hospitality she dispensed at Hatfield gave a minister frequently accused of remoteness the advantages of being married to a popular hostess. She saw to it that his desire for privacy was satisfied within reasonable limits. Their relationship should be seen in the light of the high Victorian ideal of marriage: for a couple as intelligent and devoted as they were, there was no inequality in its allocation of roles. They gratefully accepted each other within the religious framework of their lives.[1]

Georgina cared nothing for politics, she liked to say in private, except in so far as they occupied her husband. For all that, she was a natural partisan, while he was too independent and critical to be a good party man in church or state. She transmitted her ardently High Church and Tory sympathies to their children, but never allowed her own views to affect a total commitment to their father. She brought up her sons and daughters – a precocious brood – with good humour and good sense; their family circle was remarkable for the freedom of speech and enquiry enjoyed by its younger members. Her influence with Robert was exerted wholly in support of his thinking: she did not try to shape it. He had complete confidence in her, and talked to her with a lack of reserve not shown to anyone else; that is clear from their surviving correspondence. The change she worked in him is apparent from the circumstances of their union and early married life. The resolution and stamina he discovered with her at his side became permanent features of his character.[2]

Poverty is relative, and the young couple deliberately chose what seemed uncomfortably like it to Robert Cecil. Lord Salisbury objected to his choice of a wife, and intimated that he would have to face "privations" if he married her. At risk were a paternal allowance of £100 a year, the expenses of representing Stamford, and the succession to the estates. Agreeing to a six months' separation from his intended, during which they were not to communicate with each other, Cecil warned Salisbury that nothing would make him give her up. The income from his mother – £300 a year – was enough for a lover who had convinced himself of "incompatibility between my tastes and habits and the duties of a great proprietor". It is hard not to feel for the marquess, whose misgivings about the marriage were not groundless. He had married money himself and Georgina Alderson, in those days of substantial dowries, had very little from her family; moreover, she was older than his son, nearly thirty. Worst of all, this strong-minded woman was a Tractarian, and Tractarianism was too often a halfway house on the path to Rome. The thought of his title and lands passing to a Catholic convert was understandably disturbing to the descendant of Lord Burghley. His son strove to reassure him on that point: "the idea of a Romanizing tendency – of which I have as great a horror as any man – is a pure misconception". Salisbury did not attend the wedding in July 1857, but confined his sanctions to leaving the allowance he gave Robert unchanged after marriage. The couple had a friend in the bridegroom's stepmother, who sought to demonstrate her belief in them by committing to paper the wish that Georgina should have the "personal care" of her young children by the marquess, should they be left motherless.[3]

Nevertheless, Lord Salisbury's displeasure was real. It was seven years before Robert Cecil and his wife were asked to Hatfield, when they appeared "nervous and ill at ease". Yet the father settled medical bills and continued to watch over his son's career, if without optimism. The young Cecils lived modestly in Fitzroy Square, near Regent's Park, then in Duchess Street, Portland Place, and did not keep a carriage; but they moved in Society, rented, from 1864, a small house in the Surrey countryside, and went abroad every year. The children born to them at regular intervals increased the pressure on their income. Journalism paid well, but not enough; Robert also took advantage of openings in the City created by the Stock Exchange boom of the time. The limits to the help he could expect from Hatfield tested his nerve. Salisbury's attempt to get him a clerkship in the Privy Council Office was preceded by a request from Robert, addressed to the incoming Tory premier, Lord Derby, for a civil appointment at home or in the colonies. Not even considered for minor office in the new government, and "in difficulty about . . . means", he was ready to abandon politics. He was subsequently offered the governorship of Moreton Bay, the future Queensland, which he declined after calculating the unavoidable expenses. The Tories' expulsion from government in June 1859 removed the temptation for father and son to write off the latter's hopes of parliamentary distinction. What he owed to his wife may be gathered from a routine of their early life together. She sustained his political apprenticeship by sitting nightly in the gallery of the Commons until the House rose and they could leave together. Her silent presence was indicative of the relationship that literally transformed her husband within a few years.[4]

## Parliament and Party: War and Peace, 1854–65

The Toryism of the 1850s and early 1860s was both stronger and weaker than it seemed. Almost half the MPs elected in 1852 and 1859, and well over a third of those returned in 1857, were Tories. In England and Wales those three general elections confirmed the party's hold on the counties and its relative weakness in the boroughs; in Scotland it won less than a third of the seats, doing better in Ireland, for reasons special to that country. Although Liberals' divisions enabled their rivals to form short-lived minority governments in 1852 and 1858–9, the Tories plainly lacked confidence. Their leader, Derby, was a hereditary Whig, converted after departing from Lord Grey's reforming cabinet on a point of religious principle raised by Irish policy. Disraeli, his lieutenant in the Commons, had started as a radical. In 1855 Derby openly told his followers that in his opinion they could not furnish him with the men he needed to fill a cabinet. His candour incensed Disraeli, described as being "in a state of disgust beyond all control".[5] The paucity of talent was only partly due to the Peelite secession of 1846. The ablest men fought shy of Toryism. Continuing aristocratic primacy in the running of an ever more industrial and urban nation depended on the willingness and ability of landed politicians to present themselves as, and to be, "progressive". This fundamental truth was perhaps best stated by the Whig authority, Erskine May, whose *Constitutional History* first appeared in 1861.[6] While they recognized the necessity, the Tories naturally found it harder than the Liberal aristocracy to be progressive. When their leader brought in the first Tory reform bill in 1859 it was designed not merely to safeguard the landed interest and rural Toryism but actually to increase their influence. Nothing else would then have been tolerated by the party. Their religious attitudes earned them the reputation of being positively illiberal and not just resistant to change. From Derby downwards, with too few exceptions, they disliked Palmerston's efforts, so important politically and socially, to foster mutual understanding between Church and Dissent. In foreign and imperial policy insularity was the dominant note of Toryism at this period. The party was uncomfortable with the Anglo-French co-operation central to Palmerston's generally successful policies, his mistrust of French rulers notwithstanding; and it was unenthusiastic about, when it did not oppose, the expansion of formal and informal empire.[7]

Real differences, therefore, separated the historic parties, though it is easy to find contemporaries who thought they were minimal, or non-existent. This was the setting of Robert Cecil's entry into politics. Derby's son and heir, Lord Stanley, whose diary is a major source for this study, classed Cecil as "a strong High Churchman and Tory of the bitter intolerant school", and he was widely seen as such. The diarist, who knew him well and helped to reconcile him with Lord Salisbury, encouraged the slightly younger man to think of himself as a candidate for office.[8] A cabinet minister in 1858–9, Stanley advised Cecil against leaving parliament for financial reasons: his prospects were better than he or the marquess believed.[9] A very liberal Tory, who ended by serving in a Gladstone cabinet, Stanley looked for an intelligent appreciation of current trends in an aspiring politician, and he was not to be disappointed in this case. While he often sounded reactionary in his speeches and journalism, Cecil was, at the same time, cautiously progressive. Taking up positions that appealed to the authentic reactionaries in the party, he did not stay outside the mainstream of politics. By the beginning of 1864 Derby, who liked to make lists of ministers against the eventuality of a return to government, had his name down for the under-secretaryship at the Foreign Office. From that year Cecil attended meetings of what would later be called a "shadow cabinet". His scathing assaults of 1859–60 on Disraeli, whom he blamed for the Tories' unsatisfactory performance during their brief spell in office, were apparently a thing of the past. Those attacks, in articles whose anonymity was quickly penetrated, had established him as a significant figure. Thereafter, in classical fashion, he took his place in the circle of former and future ministers round Derby: he had carefully refrained from direct criticism of the leader in his journalism.[10]

Cecil first came to notice on the backbenches as a critic of British policy during the Crimean War. He was one of the small number of pro-Russian Tories headed by General Peel, the statesman's brother, and Lord Granby, who articulated the wider unease in their party at its backing for British involvement in the conflict. There was friendly contact between Peel's group and those radicals, the following of Cobden and Bright, who were also opposed to the war. Their youthful Tory ally initially used language more outspoken even than those moralistic radicals employed. He not only attacked Anglo-French intervention to halt Russia's advance into the Ottoman lands but disputed the condemnation in the West of her rule over subject peoples. Britain was "alike guilty and hypocritical" in turning on her old friend of the Revolutionary and Napoleonic wars. The British and Russian empires were expanding by "the same process of aggression"; the "repression of . . . nationalities" was common to both. Russia's methods of subjugation in Poland did not differ in kind from those to which his country had lately resorted in Ceylon and the Ionian islands, where her authority had been reasserted by martial law and the lash. Britain was no more entitled to seek the restoration of Polish independence – one of the unofficial war aims entertained by Napoleon III and Palmerston – than she was to call for the abolition of negro slavery in the United States. As for Turkey, Russia's supposedly innocent victim, Britain was only helping her to "rivet the chains" upon the oppressed Christians of her empire. This intemperate speech in March 1855 – the first of so many, mostly very different in tone, on foreign affairs – is that of a very young man, wanting in judgement and experience; no one seems to have taken it seriously. However, its rejection of liberal ideology as a basis for foreign policy in general and an Anglo-French alliance in particular, formed part of his later diplomacy. He never ceased to regard the Crimean War as a mistake, alienating Russia for the rest of the century to Britain's disadvantage in the European balance of power. The Ottoman dynasty and empire ought to have been left to the fate they deserved.[11]

The war was popular in the country, but MPs on both sides were unconvinced that there was "a real national interest in supporting Turkey", commented Sir George Cornewall Lewis, the Liberal chancellor of the exchequer.[12] Derby threatened to overthrow Palmerston's administration, which appeared to be extremely weak for some months after its formation in February 1855. At first General Peel and those who acted with him preferred to keep Palmerston in as the best defence against a noisy but superficial radical agitation inspired by the wartime failures of aristocratic government. In July Cecil seconded Peel's amendment to the motion which helped ministers to dispose of a vote of censure supported by the Tories. Palmerston's underlying strength was revealed later that month when a combination of foes, Cecil among them, reduced his majority to three on the loan urgently needed to save Turkey from collapse. The Tories and their allies of the moment were, in fact, voting to present Russia with victory. So sharp was the reaction outside the House that the loan's opponents were cowed and its passage expedited. By the end of that session Cecil had made a certain impression by speeches more calculated to influence votes than his efforts of March. Disraeli's weekly, *The Press*, actually spoke of this political novice as "a future chief" when parliament resumed next year, such was the shortage of promise on the Tory benches.[13] But the man who was to be perhaps the greatest of British foreign secretaries did not again debate a European question in the House for another eight years. The steady growth of his parliamentary standing reflected his readiness to speak and write with effect on a range of other topics.

His subjects included the aspects of empire that excited controversy, and the implications of the American Civil War for Britain and her place in the world. He did not spare Palmerston's two governments of 1855–8 and 1859–65, their clients, and the public opinion behind them. He went with the majority of his party in voting for Cobden's motion of March 1857 censuring British policy in China. The *Arrow* incident at Canton in October 1856 was exploited to intensify Western, and not solely British, pressure for wider access to the Chinese market. On other occasions, Cecil was critical of the approach to international relations that is labelled Cobdenite: it struck him as quite unrealistic to suppose that trade could be left to do the work of diplomacy and of the force that every state needed to have in reserve for the protection and assertion of its interests. Cobden himself was far too intelligent to hold such a simplistic view. He and Cecil agreed in thinking that it was neither right nor sensible to separate the national interest from the morality of action taken in its name, the issue on which the debate of March 1857 turned. Unlike the leaders of his party, Cecil blamed the national temper rather than the government for armed intervention which, on legal facts, looked like "a buccaneering expedition". Foreigners had good grounds for regarding Britain and her traders as unscrupulous and aggressive: the wars with Burma and Persia as well as China in the lifetime of that parliament could have been avoided. Oriental states attempted to keep Britain out because they feared the escalation of her demands. A double standard characterized her dealings with other countries: appeasement of the strong, currently of the United States, and ill treatment of the weak. These strictures figured in the speeches of contemporaries; they are worth citing to show that his dislike of "Jingoes", as they were later known, went back to his political beginnings. He advocated not so much a change of policy as a change of heart to build a new reputation, for honour, patience and truthfulness. The actions of proconsuls who indulged in "unauthorized aggression" should be disowned. The colonial opinion that incited them – the merchants of Hong Kong and the settlers whose eagerness to set about their African and Maori neighbours he recalled – was always ready to embark upon a war with the bill footed by the British taxpayer.[14]

In the 1860s when he had definitely become someone to reckon with, he returned to his criticism of imperialism and its methods. There was no stopping the spread of an empire, "whose law is growth", he said, then as later.[15] "I shrewdly suspect that we are – as usual – in the wrong", he told his wife on the renewal of hostilities in China.[16] Such suspicions were normal as a healthy Christianity reacted to the motives driving expansion. The abuse of power, wrong in itself, must erode the "moral influence" that counted for much in the informal empire. With Cobden, he protested at the blockade of Rio de Janeiro to resolve a dispute with Brazil which, on the face of it, might have been settled otherwise. Replying, the Foreign Office spokesman in the Commons, A.H. Layard, made a good case, and Cobden was unwilling to vote against the government. In countries where the rule of law was imperfectly understood, the gunboat was a requisite of diplomacy, one that Cecil, when at the Foreign Office himself, used skilfully. His protests were no more successful, if morally convincing, when directed at the inexorable dispossession of Maori tribesmen by the settlers in New Zealand: an irreversible process once the colony was self-governing. Far from sharing the Cobdenite disapproval of empire, however, he rejected suggestions that the nearly independent settler colonies should be left to defend themselves. He opposed the withdrawal and reduction of British garrisons in those colonies, asserting that a formal proposal to leave them to the mercy of Britain's enemies would be "hooted out of the House". Moreover, the deployment of British troops in campaigns against the Maoris or the "Kaffirs" in South Africa allowed the home government to exercise a certain control of the settlers' ruthlessness.[17]

"A sort of tariff of insolence" was Cecil's description of the contrasts between official policy towards China or Brazil, on the one hand, and European powers and the United States, on the other. It is an example of the memorable phrases that marked his rise in politics and journalism. By their appeasement, as he saw it, of Washington in the American Civil War, the Palmerston government departed from Britain's practice of according recognition to breakaway regimes once they had established a separate identity, like Spain's South American colonies or Belgium. Negro slavery was not an obstacle to recognition, on the widespread assumption that it would gradually disappear in an independent South responsive to the sentiments of the civilized world. In long articles for the *Quarterly Review* he championed the Confederacy's right to free its member states from the tyranny of the Northern majority. In the Commons he emphasized another line of argument: Britain and the United States could never be friends, "for this simple reason . . . we were rivals . . . politically and . . . commercially . . . We aspired to the same position . . . to the government of the seas . . . We were both manufacturing peoples". An irresistible logic dictated their antagonism everywhere. Conversely, the Confederacy was Britain's natural ally; the two economies were complementary, exchanging manufactures for the raw material on which Lancashire's mills depended. His deliberate appeal to self-interest and fear ignored the different conclusions that were drawn from the same facts. The Liberal government and Derby at the head of the Tory opposition were afraid that Britain had too much to lose if she recognized the Confederacy: the latter did not like to contemplate "the anger in the North". The size of Britain's trade with the Northern states, the value of her investments there, the vulnerability of Canada to attack, and awe at the scale and speed of the North's mobilization for the first modern war – all these considerations inhibited the British political class from giving more practical expression to their sympathy for the South, where, in Gladstone's words, "a kind of aristocracy" existed.[18]

Cecil's advocacy of the Southern cause, and Gladstone's, implied eventual recourse to armed intervention, if Washington did not come to terms with the rebels. The judgement of both was suspect as a result. Doubts about Cecil were not lessened by his contribution to debate on the other question that compelled government and opposition to acknowledge what Britain could not do, this time in Europe. When he was mentioned as a possible foreign secretary in 1866, Disraeli said he was "too young and too vehement . . . he had tried to lead the country on the American and Danish questions, would have led it wrong, and had failed".[19] While Disraeli was talking of a competitor for the Tory leadership on Derby's retirement, the summary was fair. In their struggle to retain the duchies of Schleswig and Holstein ruled by their king, the Danes had been encouraged by the prospect of British help. Liberals and Tories were strongly pro-Danish, although the treatment of the German element in Schleswig did not help Denmark's case. Cecil pointed to Britain's treaty obligations, reinforced by the premier's verbal promise, apparently of more than merely diplomatic aid. His reproaches, vehement indeed, now put him in the front rank of parliamentary orators. He assailed ministers for pursuing a policy that deprived British diplomacy of the strength that came from being in earnest. "This loss of dignity and honour", he said in July 1864 when the opposition endeavoured to oust Palmerston from a humiliating failure to avert the military defeat of Britain's protégé, "is not a sentiment. It is a loss of power which will have to be bought back . . . some . . . day . . . by . . . blood and treasure".[20] At the very least, reprisals might have been taken against Prussian shipping when Denmark proper was invaded, for Prussia drove Germany's united front in the conflict. Only by such action could Britain have rehabilitated herself in the eyes of Europe.

Earlier, at a Tory conclave summoned by Derby, he had been "warlike", and his language in a debate on 6 May strengthened that impression. As he assured Stanley, he realized that it was already "too late and useless" for any attempt to succour Denmark.[21] He had done enough, however, to make people think that the Tories were readier than the government to go to war, isolated in Europe. This was what the party's chiefs wanted to avoid, believing, rightly, that it would harm their electoral chances. When Cecil spoke in the trial of strength between the parties on this question in July, he did so "under constraint, lest he should say something rash, and incur the charge of supporting a war policy". He was thought to have displayed considerable skill in skirting round the danger. Seizure of the aggressor's shipping, he suggested, would have been an appropriate measure, falling short of open war. Long afterwards, in a similar situation, he remembered that Palmerston's refusal to fight had been understood and rewarded by the voters, who increased his party's majority handsomely at the 1865 election. At the time, he was deeply ashamed of his countrymen. He ridiculed them savagely in the *Quarterly Review* under cover of a supposed anonymity. "Cheap war", he wrote, "is the cry with which, if our age were not too respectable, members would return to their constituents". Such a war as the voters had enjoyed when fought in the distant Crimea; one that "does not send the Funds down and stimulates the iron trade".[22]

Brilliantly unfair, the *Quarterly Review* articles were polemic of a high order. Palmerston's conduct of foreign affairs with Russell at the Foreign Office had been "essentially a policy of cowardice",[23] and "a portentous mixture of bounce and baseness". In the 1880s, criticizing Gladstonian policies, he discovered the merits of those which Palmerston had pursued at home and abroad, never forgetting his public.[24] They liked Britain to be seen playing a role on the Continent commensurate with their inflated idea of her importance in Europe. But they had no wish to submit to the conscription and the level of taxation necessary to maintain land forces of the required size. As it was, a navy in need of periodical modernization and a volunteer army kept the cost per capita of defence above the average for a Continental power. A writer ignored these contradictory desires at his peril. While Britain was not yet a democracy, she was well on her way to becoming one. Palmerston's comment on a contemporary statesman is applicable to himself, with a change of tense: "he might by going along with public opinion have guided and governed it".[25] He gave Britain what she wanted: and his mishandling of the Schleswig-Holstein question was forgiven; the London crowd cheered him when he came out of the House during the censure debate in July 1864. "Peace is . . . paramount", Cecil recognized. He saw, too, that no government could last long – longer than three months, he said – if public opinion was hostile. Distrust of an emergent democracy led him to insist on the Commons' responsibility as "the supreme controller of national policy".[26]

Cecil's criticisms of Palmerstonian foreign policy obscured the extent of his agreement with it, even then. He credited the government with "the best intentions" in Italy at the decisive stage of the Risorgimento in 1859–60, but observed that neither geography nor trade really warranted the British interest in Italy's future. Speaking against the background of the invasion scare at that date, he applauded the premier's determination to enjoy good relations with France from a position of strength. Adequate defences, said Cecil, were "a matter of business . . . a question of insurance", and nothing else. Eschewing "talk of the flag that waved over every sea, or of the honour which had never been sullied", he invited the electors of Stamford and newspaper readers to reflect on the consequences, "so frightful", of invasion. Yet, for all his dislike of bombast, he was susceptible to popular emotion evoked by the thought of allowing an invader "to pollute our shores . . . to injure an empire to which they are proud to belong, or to diminish the value of the institutions they loved so well".[27] This was pure Palmerstonianism, identifying national survival with freedom and order at home as much as with an expanding empire. Three years afterwards he owned to "the greatest respect" for the Palmerston government, though apprehensive of its tendency to interfere increasingly overseas. But he chose to consider, from the abandonment of Denmark and from developments in domestic politics, that in his last couple of years Palmerston was no longer in effective control of his colleagues, and especially not of Gladstone. By conviction and temperament, Cecil favoured an active foreign policy: Palmerston's was more congenial than that of his party in the person of Stanley, foreign secretary under Derby and Disraeli in 1866–8. Stanley was content to be "simply a spectator of events" in Europe.[28]

## Domestic Politics: The First Decade

Foreign policy and empire held the attention of the public for much of Cecil's time on the backbenches. But he gave more of his mind to the defence of the Established Church and to the reform of parliamentary representation generally admitted to be overdue. In the spirit of the intelligent conservatism that inspired him, he also interested himself in a number of other questions. He struck a constructive note on the state's discharge of its growing responsibilities: simple negation was not characteristic of his utterances. They exemplify the dialectic between "Order" and "Progress" that J. S. Mill saw at work in the collective thought of the age.[29] Cecil told his constituents that he was "not sorry" the war of parties had cooled on Palmerston's return to power in 1859. Party was not an end in itself: "he valued party feeling as a means of carrying on the government of the country". As "a party man", he welcomed Derby's tactics under the renewed Liberal ascendancy. His leader envisaged a discriminating support for the ministry that should give the Tories more influence than they could hope to exercise by governing without a majority in the event of another transient split in the Liberal ranks. Cecil dwelt on the failure that attended the Tories' last experience of office without power: they were going into opposition "with broken arms and standards soiled". Their demoralization was "a historical fact".[30] In articles that caused a stir in 1859–60, he depicted Disraeli as the evil genius of Toryism who had induced his colleagues to sacrifice principle for place. The exodus of Peelite talent from the party had confided its direction to "a scratch crew", likened, more offensively, to "damaged goods of unprepossessing appearance" remaindered on the political market. The language was arresting – not such as gentlemen used of one another – and served its purpose. Cecil was noticed as someone whose legitimate aim was to restore credibility to Tory politics.[31]

He answered the continuing protests which these slashing attacks drew from his father and Lord Exeter, among others, by reminding them of the facts. He had raised his objections to Disraeli when invited to sit for Stamford, and his articles – "much praised by very high Tories" – said no more than the party was saying.

When Exeter intimated that he might be jeopardizing his seat, he pointed out that he had never voted against the Tory leader in the Commons, except on the admission of Jews to parliament. The running fire he had directed at Disraeli would stop, he explained, because the delinquent – "I dislike and despise the man" – had mended his ways.[32] His *bête noire*'s flirtations with radicals and the representatives of Irish Catholic nationalism were known to the whole political world, and his loyalty to Derby was at best doubtful. "I could never lift up my head after such an act – it would destroy me", replied John Bright to a suggestion from Disraeli that they might one day be colleagues. Stanley, who was Disraeli's friend, thought the defects of his striking personality would always deny him people's confidence, in and out of parliament.[33] Devious Disraeli undoubtedly was, but it was the open commitment of this childhood convert from Judaism to ending parliament's exclusion of professing Jews that disturbed many Tories. Derby, Stanley and some others in the Tory cabinet of 1858–9 accepted – reluctantly in most cases – the need to do away with a barrier which the Commons had repeatedly voted to remove. The Lords' prolonged resistance to this reform provided uncomfortable evidence of Tory slowness to adapt to the prevailing climate. Cecil was one of the numerous Tories who held that the admission of a single professing Jew to parliament must undermine the Christian state whose preservation was fundamental to his outlook. The compromise embodied in the legislation of 1858 empowered either House to admit a religious Jew by passing a resolution to that effect in every parliament. In the Commons three cabinet ministers voted for the bill, which it was not possible to bring forward as a government measure, and four opposed it.[34]

Cecil joined three of the bill's opponents from the cabinet in the last ditch: they resisted the motion that allowed Baron Lionel de Rothschild to take his seat for the City of London, which had returned him at successive elections since 1847. He argued that a sincere Jew, whom he termed "a peculiar animal", was bound by his beliefs to work for the subversion of Christianity. This was not ignorant prejudice but genuine apprehension based on an abstract knowledge of rabbinical teaching, which condemned Christianity as false and blasphemous. It should not be forgotten that before substantial Jewish immigration later in the century, anti-Semitism in Britain was more religious than racial. Popular respect for the Christian faith would be diminished by the surrender of principle, Cecil contended, and the House lowered in the estimation of those "earnest in religion".[35] The Act of 1858 unquestionably dealt a heavy blow to the Tories' morale. Nothing, perhaps, did more to disillusion them with minority government; they lost caste with friends and enemies. The Peelite Sidney Herbert expressed a general feeling about his old party when he deplored the spectacle of "Jews let in by men who think their own measure destructive of Christianity".[36]

Unashamedly reactionary on that question, Cecil did not oppose the Tories' first attempt at reforming parliament, although he considered it "very ill-advised". The bill of 1859 went too far for the two members of the cabinet who resigned, but it was the proof of Derby's resolve to show that Toryism was not "stationary", as Liberals liked to claim. His government's proposals left the £10 borough franchise unchanged; removed the urban forty shilling freeholders from the counties; brought the rural occupation franchise into line with that in the boroughs; extended plural voting for the middle class by a variety of new qualifications; and redistributed a mere fifteen seats. Stanley, who had drafted a larger scheme with Disraeli, threatened resignation but stayed. The bill, he complained, "upheld the *status quo* . . . I neither think it can succeed, nor that it ought to . . .". With his customary agility, Disraeli made the best of the situation by asserting that a reduction of the £10 franchise in the boroughs would endanger "the social system". He solemnly warned the House against "sentimental assertions of the good qualities of the working class. The greater their good qualities, the greater the danger". The country gentlemen behind him thought it "a magnificent speech". Cecil made a more serious contribution to the debates. He concentrated on the composition of a future electorate and the absolute necessity of balancing social classes within it, including the working-class voters whose numbers were rising with industrial prosperity. A rough balance of that kind had been a preoccupation of electoral reformers since 1832, and earlier. Whatever happened to the Tory bill, there was no stopping another instalment of reform in the next few years.[37]

Cutting the key borough franchise from £10 to something less, as was inevitable, would reflect changes that were spreading through the working class and would make it impossible to hold that franchise at £5 or £6: "at the rate at which education was going on, everybody would soon be worthy of it".[38] The advent of democracy in this evolutionary fashion as the working class achieved political maturity was foreseen by those of Cecil's class who understood what was happening, by the Tory philanthropist, Lord Shaftesbury, for one, and the diarist Charles Greville, for another. As far back as 1837 Palmerston had looked ahead to household suffrage and shorter parliaments before many years had passed. "*All* countries . . . are, and always have been, in a state of transition": that insight of the now veteran statesman was one shared by Cecil and most thinking men and women.[39] But unlike Palmerston he wanted to erect a permanent barrier to working-class domination of an electorate that was already being enlarged. The preponderance of one class, he proceeded to argue, was wrong in principle and would be harmful in practice: "No matter what the class, if it were . . . to rule another class . . . such was the selfishness of mankind, tyranny was almost sure to result". It was a doctrine, or rather a dogma, to which he adhered until the next parliament swept it aside. However, the weight of the evidence that there was no need to fear the working-class vote was not lost on him before then. His speech at Stamford in October 1862 registered the wider significance of the flourishing Volunteer movement: it was immensely reassuring that the population could be trusted "unreservedly" with arms; the Volunteers were an impressive manifestation of the social union underlying party divisions.[40] By the middle of the decade even J.W. Henley, one of the resigning Tory cabinet ministers in 1859, was letting it be known that he was not frightened of household suffrage, while E.B. Pusey, the high priest of Tractarianism, believed the Church would be safe with *manhood* suffrage.[41]

As Cecil noted in that Stamford speech, party politics in the early 1860s had little life in them, so successfully had Palmerston's policies consolidated the position of a government with a tiny majority. Relations between Church and Dissent, which coloured political activity throughout the Victorian era, were better than they had ever been, largely owing to the premier's actions. The more or less Evangelical prelates who figured prominently in his bishop-making were selected with an eye to conciliating Dissenters, who were approving. Although the abolition of church rates was an open question in his second cabinet, he voted with the Liberation Society's supporters on that hotly disputed issue. The removal of legal irritants to Dissent, outdated securities for Anglican pre-eminence, was an integral part of his religious policy, designed to promote a measure of convergence between the Establishment and the sects. In an area of policy bedevilled by tensions between Church and Chapel his government trod very carefully in moves towards undenominational primary education in the spirit of Lord John Russell's plan of 1856 and the Newcastle Commission's report five years later. Administrative action by the Education Department withheld building grants from Church schools with a monopoly of parochial teaching unless Dissenting parents were allowed to remove their child from religious instruction to which they objected. The responsible minister, Robert Lowe, suggested that these schools, containing three-quarters of the children whose education was aided by the state, might confine such instruction to the Ten Commandments, the Lord's Prayer and the Apostles' Creed, leaving specifically Anglican teaching for pupils in Confirmation classes. Palmerston also expressed guarded sympathy with Dissenting aspirations to equality with Anglicans in university government after degrees at Oxford and Cambridge had been opened to them in the 1850s. A sizeable body of Anglican opinion, particularly in the ruling party, supported these initiatives, but they alarmed a great many Churchmen besides Tractarians like Cecil. Whig Erastianism, political Dissent's increasing awareness of its strength and the rise of theological liberalism with friends in high places constituted a triple threat to the Church as she was.[42]

Searching for a means of reviving his party's morale and its fortunes, Disraeli tried to exploit the reaction of good Churchmen to these developments. His emergence as a champion of orthodoxy and an ally of the High Church was the cause of some amusement: "I am beginning to believe that he really has been baptized", said Cecil.[43] The Tories were able to check the parliamentary progress of the Liberationists' church rates bill; otherwise Disraeli's discovery that "there is only one question now . . . the Church" failed to help either his party or the Church. Raising the historic cry of "the Church in danger" at the 1865 election, he was contradicted on the hustings by his friend and front bench colleague, Stanley, who did not believe that "the Establishment in England . . . is in any danger whatsoever". Cecil did not doubt that there was indeed a threat, not to the Establishment as such, but to the religion it existed to teach. In a *Quarterly Review* article on the eve of the election, he represented the ecclesiastical ideal of Palmerstonian Liberalism as a church "purged of dogma, disembarrassed of belief", a state agency for policing and educating the masses. He accused the "latitudinarian assailants of the Church" of reducing her sacred functions to the provision of schools as utilitarian in their purpose as the mechanics' institutes dear to the secularizing radicals. In proposals like that to amend the Act of Uniformity in the interests of religious harmony, he saw only the erosion of old certainties: "the foundations of faith were shaken and men's minds were casting about for something to believe". It was the sincerely held and deeply felt differences between its adherents that gave Christianity its vitality; without which it was merely "sustained hypocrisy". Step by step, comprehension, the goal of the Whigs since they confronted Tories in the seventeenth century, was coming into sight. By assimilation of doctrine, rather than the disestablishment sought by the militants of the Liberation Society, Dissent would invade the Church: the real loser must be religion itself.[44]

In Cecil's Tractarian vision, doctrine was all important. Seen in that light, every derogation from the Church's privileged status had to be examined for its theological implications, and resisted if they were significant. Church rates; the burial of Dissenters with their own rites in parish churchyards; the Anglican monopoly of university government; the oath required of Dissenters in parliament and local government, pledging them to respect the Establishment – Cecil persisted in regarding these subjects of controversy and attempted legislation as episodes in the struggle for "the supremacy of Dissent", aided by "*quasi* Churchmen".[45] Sir John Trelawny, the Anglican sponsor of the Liberationist church rates bills could not believe that his Tory opponents were sincere in their horror of the Liberation Society. His genuinely restricted aim was to get rid of an obstacle to friendly relations between Church and Dissent. As he said, a large minority of Dissenters were "highly favourable" to the Establishment: Conference Methodism, the biggest of the sects, was closer to the Church than to other Dissenters. Bishop Jackson of Lincoln had explained the affinity to Cecil when he became MP for Stamford; Wesleyans were not "altogether Dissenters". Thus divided, the sects had neither the will nor the strength to overturn the Church. Cecil, however, was not inclined to capitalize on this goodwill. He stiffly informed a Wesleyan minister in the constituency that his subscription to a bazaar, initially withheld, was given because he had satisfied himself that it did not subsidize one of the "agencies obstructive to the progress of the Established Church".[46] He did not appreciate the extent to which Palmerston had disarmed leading political Dissenters. Edward Baines the younger, the Leeds MP and newspaper editor who spoke for moderate Liberationists, declared at the 1865 election that he was not prepared to vote for "anything that would diminish the . . . Church . . . as a religious institution": if disestablishment ever came about, it should be with the assent of Church people as well as of parliament.[47]

Cecil gave more time and energy than he could well afford to promoting education under the aegis of the Church. He was associated from the mid-1850s with the Reverend Nathaniel Woodard, and his schools, whose motives, like his own, were as much religious and political as educational. A letter from Cecil to another MP, C.B. Adderley, is a specimen of his appeals on Woodard's behalf for money and patronage. The fate of the Establishment lay with the middle and "lower middle" classes, far too many of whom were unfriendly or indifferent to the Church. On present trends, some of her political enemies confidently predicted disestablishment before the end of the century. Woodard's planned network of inexpensive public schools was intended to remedy the Church's "utter neglect" of education at the lower levels of the middle class. If it could be remedied, Cecil believed she would be strong enough to survive the greatest challenge to her influence and authority.

Speaking at a public meeting in Brighton in aid of Woodard's foundation at Lancing, he emphasized that the middle classes were the real rulers of the country, its "mainstay and sinews". His openness to modernization appeared in the call for a scientific element to be introduced into the education provided. He was concerned at the suspicions that Woodard's devout Tractarianism aroused and urged him not to provoke the Protestant zealots who disrupted the Brighton meeting. Where there was some difference between Tractarian and Roman doctrine hard to explain to an anti-Catholic public, he counselled "a simple, sure, point-blank disclaimer" of any Romanizing tendency. It was partly through the connection with Woodard that he realised the limitations of the Tractarians. He warned Woodard against giving his educational work "irretrievably . . . a sectional character" within Anglicanism.[48]

Woodard's enterprise belonged to a larger movement that helped to attach the bulk of the middle classes more firmly to the Establishment. The Church, said Cecil in 1859, had cared for the aristocracy "possibly too much", and had not neglected the poor: but "there was no hope for . . . her . . . as a temporal institution unless . . . the . . . middle classes could be brought to support her".[49] While his involvement with Woodard continued, popular education attracted more of everybody's attention than the extension of public schools. From Palmerston downwards, politicians were looking for a new franchise, or franchises, that would admit "some of the best and most intelligent of the working classes" without immediately swamping its middle-class majority.[50] Cecil's speech to the mechanics' institute at Stamford in 1856 shows he was not the thoroughgoing young reactionary of legend. National greatness, he affirmed like any advanced Liberal, was founded on collective intelligence and its development: "In a day when thought, not force, is the ruler of mankind . . . when . . . numbers are more powerful than wealth, it is of the most vital importance to the stability of our institutions that . . . thought should be sound and . . . those numbers enlightened". As Marx was to observe, the unenfranchised could make themselves felt; "*pressure from without*" was well understood by their betters. "Real education", Cecil went on, was not imparted in schools but in the family and through religion. The feature of the existing system of state-aided, predominantly denominational and Anglican, schools that he valued most was its religious instruction. He was completely opposed to anything on the lines of Russell's plan, which would dilute that teaching. In another speech in his constituency a year later, he declared that it would be "absolute madness" to introduce a popular franchise until education, in the broadest sense, had made the unskilled labourer fit to vote. He compared the Maoris he had encountered favourably with this numerous element in British society. The "tide of ignorance" which flowed on must be turned; "all the benefits of civilization" were at risk.[51]

The elevation of the working classes, as a whole, was central to his idea of a viable and progressive society. He was not alone, of course, in seeing that self-improvement would be decisive. It was a truism that he discussed in an appropriate setting, a county union of mechanics' institutes in the West Midlands, some years after his Stamford speeches. The endless pursuit of economy by government and parliament restricted Treasury grants and, as a rule, the struggle for existence terminated formal education at eleven or twelve at the latest. Working men had to be induced to practise self-help through adult education. Religion did not suffice for the cultural change necessary to raise the working class: the diffusion of knowledge inculcated the increasing responsibility and sobriety which had transformed the behaviour of the speaker's own class in recent generations. "It was nothing visionary", Cecil considered, "to say that what had been done with one class could be done with the other". He advised against undue optimism; something would be gained if working men preferred reading a "sensational novel" to frequenting a public house. As that last remark indicates, Cecil did not yet possess the sureness of touch, or the insight into the popular mind, evident in his speeches outside parliament at the height of his powers. Devout and fastidious, he felt "an extreme and growing aversion to platform talking on these semi-religious subjects".[52] The experience was good for him, and not only because it provided a foretaste of an activity that was to be indispensable to his political leadership. The partisanship he displayed in the House of Commons was out of place in his labours for middle- and working-class causes transcending party politics. He could not say, as he once did in the Commons on the controversial question of church rates, "I do not think a man can be a good Churchman who is not a good Conservative".[53]

In the House or on the platform, Cecil fought against the disabling weakness which nearly ended his career before it had really begun: "in spite of many strenuous efforts at self-steeling", he confessed in 1855, "I care too much for other people's contempt".[54] He knew the painful cure for the want of self-confidence: he had to brave the contempt he dreaded. This frame of mind helps to account for the acerbity which distinguished his parliamentary oratory, and his journalism, in these early years. His bearing and conversation were quite different in private when, unlike many intellectuals, he was notably considerate. Stanley thought his friend's style in the House was "disagreeable and his opinions exaggerated". Palmerston, who was tolerant of members' foibles, remarked that Cecil "never loses an opportunity of saying or doing an unhandsome thing".[55] Cecil stood out as the opposition concentrated its attacks on Bright and Gladstone; the one represented as an extreme radical, the other as leaning towards the radicals. The tactic was to unsettle, without toppling, the Palmerstonian coalition of Whigs or Liberals, Peelites and radicals put together in 1859, the foundation of the party that Gladstone was to lead. Cecil was predictable on the 1860 reform bill, which Palmerston and his cabinet were not going to drop. Its reduction of the borough franchise to £6 rental instead of rating was "truly dangerous". The new voters could not be trusted with ultimate control over taxation. He did not suppose their gratitude would be proof against those – he singled out Bright – "who made it their business to disparage and defame the aristocracy". Furthermore, the current problem of bribery at elections would worsen with the enfranchisement of a large, and uncertain, number of poor electors.[56]

As a bridging measure, Gladstone lifted income tax to ten pence in the pound when he cut indirect taxes in his great budget of 1860. Cecil accused him of embarking on a permanent shift from indirect to direct taxation, and from the poor to the rich. According to the chancellor's Tory critic, "every principle of sound finance" prescribed fiscal equality between social classes in the total amounts raised from each. The trend in this budget imperilled "the stability of the state".[57] Gladstone himself did not think otherwise: but such charges obliged him to deny any intention of "effecting . . . a considerable alteration in the relative position of classes". By 1865 he had brought income tax down to four pence in the pound and repudiated the idea of graduating the tax, sure that to do so would force "that source of all evils, discord between class and class". Moreover, he was at pains to dispel fears, which Cecil articulated, of an assumed similarity between his thinking on the taxation of capital and that of Bright, who had advocated an annual levy on the value of real property at the very low rate of eight shillings in £100.[58] Well might Cecil say at Stamford in 1862 that party politics had virtually been suspended.[59] In the pages of the *Quarterly Review* he played the worried conservative: it was good journalism to perceive the emergence of threats, political and religious, to the order of things which Palmerston had maintained and adapted. Neither Cecil's writing nor his successes in the House endeared him to many. He was thought to have been ungenerous in his reception of Robert Lowe's too honourable resignation over the exposure of bureaucratic disingenuousness in school inspectors' reports, after a campaign in which Cecil had combined with a leading radical. His speeches on the fate of Denmark were not quite what his party wanted to hear. He made a natural moderate like Sir Stafford Northcote uncomfortable. Northcote, his colleague in the representation of Stamford and shortly in the cabinet, noted in his diary the Liberal *Daily Telegraph*'s comment on a parliamentarian whose abilities were now acknowledged: "Blessed are they who sneer, for they shall have the ear of the House".[60]

## The Journalist's Trade

Robert Cecil's journalistic output between 1856 and 1866 has been put at over 1 500 000 words. He wrote because he was, by his standards, "as poor as a church mouse".[61] He did not seriously try to preserve the conventional anonymity of his long *Quarterly Review* articles. The authorship of his short pieces in the *Saturday Review* between these dates was not well established until long after his death. Students of his politics have naturally gone to this legacy for enlightenment about a statesman whose later opinions have been considered elusive. They have found what a friendly historian calls Cecil's "extreme views"; more reactionary, ironical and pessimistic than in his contemporary speeches. He himself explained the difference simply: he wrote to get and hold the attention of readers who were not to be captured by studied fairness. The substantial earnings from journalism were literally indispensable to his solvency and independence. Lady Gwendolen, who grew up after her father had stopped being a regular contributor to periodicals, recorded his aversion to any mention of his former activity within the family circle. It was understood that no one should refer even to the best known articles as his; other politicians who wrote anonymously were less sensitive. Cecil had outgrown the opinions of his twenties and thirties; the recollection of them embarrassed and irritated him. There was a persistent rumour that he had also written for the newspapers: the Tory *Standard* in the later 1850s and early 1860s, and the Peelite *Morning Chronicle* before 1855. The evidence that he was more than an occasional contributor, if that, is slight. The assertions to the contrary of T.H.S. Escott many years afterwards are suspect.[62]

Surprisingly, Cecil disliked writing; his style does not smell of the lamp. Lengthy letters and memoranda, familiar to workers in the Gladstone archive, are rare with him. Brevity and humour are the hallmarks of a Cecil letter; but the irony that informed the pieces of between ten and fifteen thousand words for the *Quarterly Review* sustained the clarity and verve that made their pick classics of English political journalism. The notion of supplementing a modest private income by his pen had occurred to him before parliament and marriage. The weekly *Saturday Review*, owned by his Tractarian brother-in-law, the Tory MP, A.J.B. Beresford-Hope, opened its columns to him from 1856. Its requirement was for very short articles, generally of two thousand words or less, that would be highly readable and provocative, frequently serious but never solemn. The first of his longer essays to be published appeared in *Oxford Essays* in 1858, an annual publication designed to introduce the educated public to some of the best minds among younger Oxford men. "Theories of Parliamentary Reform" attracted only passing notice, unlike his subsequent attacks on recent Tory policy and Disraeli's influence upon it in successive numbers of *Bentley's Quarterly Review*, which shared an editor, J.D. Cook, with the *Saturday Review*. *Bentley's* expired in January 1860 after four numbers. Cecil was at once taken up by the *Quarterly Review*, still the most prestigious of Tory journals. The quarterlies were losing ground to less ponderous competitors: in Cecil one of them secured an apparently tireless contributor of guaranteed readability. From April 1860 to July 1866 he provided full commentaries on political developments at home and abroad.[63] The opinions he offered before 1866 represented a stage in his political evolution; they did not set out positions which, on a theoretical level, he never abandoned.

His contribution to *Oxford Essays* employed a definition of the state to be found in Burke at his most utilitarian: "a joint stock company to all intents and purposes ... for ... the preservation of life and property". British institutions, as modified by the 1832 settlement, displayed undeniable anomalies and weaknesses: they nevertheless made for "a greater amount of individual happiness" than any that had been devised elsewhere. He noted how "the secret machinery of obstruction" disposed of the reform bills brought in during the 1850s to lower the £10 borough franchise. His unoriginal conclusion was that the figure of £10 marked "exactly" the point beyond which enlargement of the electorate would entail its deterioration.[64] The nearer manhood suffrage came, the greater the temptation to graduate income tax, the nightmare of the propertied in Victorian Britain, not realized until the 1900s. His first article for *Bentley's*, in March 1859, was altogether livelier than this academic discussion of the pros and cons of further electoral reform. "English Politics and Parties" recognized that the majority of industrial working men had "lost their faith in mere political arithmetic" since Chartist days, were content to accept the expression of the "national will" on reform, and valued their tangible liberties above an abstract liberalism. What concerned him, and registered with others, was the unsatisfactory condition of the Tory party. The health of the political process required the conservative party to be conservative. At present it lacked proper leadership and, even more, a grasp of principle. As Gladstone had done in a well known article of 1856, Cecil complained of "anarchy" in the Commons where the parties could not easily be distinguished. If Toryism had any meaning at all, "it means anti-Radical": but in order to keep the current minority administration in being, Disraeli had courted the radicals.[65]

Immobility was not Toryism, either. Cecil favoured an infusion of businessmen in the Lords, an initiative already proposed by Palmerston and rejected by landed politicians all round. This method of gratifying the bourgeois desire for equality would counter Bright's exertions to unite middle and working classes against the land. The second article for *Bentley's* in July, "The Faction Fights", renewed the insults to Disraeli in the first. He was "the grain of dirt that clogs the whole machine" of British politics. Without him, Cecil argued, Tories and conservative Whigs or Liberals might form a new and dominant party. No one on the other side, he rightly held, would join forces with Disraeli, "that soldier of fortune". He was quite wrong, however, in assuming that Palmerston's reunification of the Liberals, with two cabinet places for Bright's associates in June/July 1859, was "a lame and impotent" combination. Liberals of all shades had more in common with each other than with Tories.[66] Cecil, like Disraeli, saw Palmerston as more Tory than Liberal, and praised him accordingly. Cecil's aim was nothing less than to make Disraeli's position impossible by exposing widespread dislike among the Tories for the man and his methods. "I have . . . never concealed my opinion that his influence with Lord Derby in the management of the party has been prejudicial", he told his father.[67] Disraeli survived because he had made himself indispensable to a leader in the Lords, and to Tories in the Commons who could not find a better and more assiduous parliamentarian to replace him. He was also the scapegoat for resentment stirred up by Derby's cautious experiments with new policies in 1858–9, without which the Tories could not be a credible alternative government. It has to be said that the feeling against Disraeli ran right through the party: Lord Malmesbury, foreign secretary under Derby, a shrewd and tolerant man of the world, was infuriated by Disraeli's pursuit of a separate foreign policy for distinctly mixed motives, telling the Whig Lord Clarendon that his colleague *"always lied"*.[68]

Disraeli was a Derbyite, so too was Cecil. There was no alternative to Derby, and Derby's policies. When he consented to stop persecuting Disraeli, Cecil had a more difficult task, even with the benefit of journalistic licence, in depicting the Palmerston government as anything other than intelligently conservative and prudently progressive. Palmerston's cabinet contained no fewer than three dukes and seven holders of lesser hereditary titles, quite as concerned as Cecil to defend "the patient and helpless squire" from fiscal depredations inspired by Bright. Memories of the struggle over the succession duty which Gladstone introduced in 1853 imparted a certain plausibility to fears, on which Cecil played, that Palmerston's chancellor of the exchequer was "deeply tainted with the manias [of] . . . Mr Cobden and Mr Bright". The premier himself was under that impression. Cecil devoted his first *Quarterly Review* article in April 1860 to the case for supporting Palmerston against the chancellor and the chancellor's radical allies – Derby's stated policy. Like his leader, he was, in effect, endorsing Palmerston's policy of controlling the radicals through their presence in "the citadel of power" at his invitation, for

Thomas Milner Gibson sat in the cabinet as representing Cobden and pledging him to its support. Cecil attacked the desire of Gladstone and the radicals for defence economies when a Bonaparte ruled in France: "no self-delusion, however resolute, can really convert the Channel into an Atlantic". He criticized the Anglo-French commercial treaty of that year for its concessions to a potentially hostile country; and tried to link Gladstone's finance, to which the treaty was integral, with a reform bill described as an "approximation to democracy". These points, for what they were worth, were eclipsed by biting sketches of the author's seniors on both sides of the House, where Lord John Russell complained of having been memorably caricatured by "this obscure writer".[69]

If Cecil had been an obscure journalist, his attacks, even in the *Quarterly Review*, would have had a smaller impact. The aristocrat succeeded in what was then a plebeian métier, and was sufficiently confident to assure his father that if forced to decide between continuing in parliament and writing for the reviews, "I am afraid the choice would leave me little room for hesitation".[70] But journalism was now a help with his political ambitions, as well as with his household bills: it built up his reputation as a keeper of the Tory conscience. Russell, like Disraeli, was targeted because he had played politics with a question – parliamentary reform – which Cecil maintained ought to have been above it: "Woe to the blind that lead; woe to the blind that follow!"[71] The contention that he had done "real service" to the Tory party, and even to Disraeli personally, by his candour was not merely special pleading in the argument with his father and Lord Exeter: the Tory press was less given than the Liberal papers to criticizing party leaders. Answering Russell and *The Times*, which had come to Disraeli's defence, Cecil declined to accept that office ever warranted the sacrifice of principle: "It is a doctrine born of mere selfish greed, and reeking of corruption". From the moral high ground, he praised Derby's "usual unhesitating directness" in refusing a chance to overthrow Palmerston when his government and party were divided over Gladstone's repeal of the paper duties.[72] He laid about him vigorously: Gladstone's ten pence on income tax was "galling, corrupting, grossly unjust"; Bright had "a sinister reputation" that scared the middle classes. He capitalized upon militant Dissent's hostility to the Establishment; although there was not, as he alleged, "a compact phalanx" of Liberationists in parliament, eager to see the Church, if not disestablished, broadened under its pressure until Anglicans became "a motley throng of religionists" without piety or zeal.[73] As his correspondence with clerical friends shows, he certainly believed that his was "the policy which alone can protect the . . . Church".[74]

The Cecil of the 1860s was apt to read alarming statements of principle into policies to which he took exception. It was the *déformation intellectuelle* of the ideologue that he was in danger of becoming. One may cite his reaction to Gladstone's pragmatic admission in March 1865 that the position of the Establishment in Ireland, as the church of a small minority, was difficult to justify. Cecil interpreted this in a private letter to an old friend as a declaration of war "against one-half of the Established Church upon principles that will destroy the whole of it".[75] A keen student of the French Revolution, he understood how much more powerful ideas are, at certain junctures, than apparently impregnable political and social structures.

He was a prey, literally, to contemporary nightmares about the possibility of new and more terrible upheavals in a Europe which had not forgotten the June Days of 1848 in Paris and was soon to witness the savagery of the Commune. The democracy of the settler colonies he had visited was restrained by their British traditions: democracy in the United States seemed, and not only to Robert Cecil, as ogreish as Parisian revolution, at least during the terrible Civil War of 1861–5. Nothing in his political life, in his wife's experience, made him more anxious and depressed than that war and its outcome.[76] His thoughts and fears were set out at length in the *Quarterly Review*. A partisan of the South, he agreed with those who identified the North with the future of democracy, although the Confederate states were white democracies, too. He appreciated the moral appeal of democracy: its operation in America was in truth "a great experiment", he wrote in the first of the American articles, significantly entitled "Democracy on its Trial". American conditions, outside the slave states, had been ideal for a prolonged test of democratic institutions: a thriving, racially homogeneous population had access to an almost limitless supply of cultivable land and was free from the aristocratic inheritance that Europe had not shaken off. The failure of those institutions in America, peopled by the same stock as Britain and shaped by much the same respect for law and private rights, was "full of warning". If democracy proceeded to devour itself in America, what hope was there for Britain and her Continental neighbours?[77]

He charged Bright and, quite wrongly, Gladstone with wanting to reproduce "the dead democratic level" on the other side of the Atlantic; though he added that Gladstone, whom he had known since childhood as a visitor to Hatfield, might not be "*consciously*" working to that end. Cecil was less interested in the fate of democracy in America than in its European impact. In the eyes of the world, victory for the North and the restoration of American unity would rehabilitate democracy, understandably taken to have broken down with secession and war, and increase its attraction. But in Europe the event would precipitate "the real political struggle of our age . . . between the classes who have property and the classes who have none". Britain might escape a revolutionary upheaval: but the natural leadership of wealth and education must give way before "a mob's choice" at elections, as in the Northern states. In his country, where social inequality was so marked, fiscal discrimination against the defeated classes would follow inexorably. Writing in October 1862, he hoped its recent successes in the field would secure the existence of the Confederacy, where racial solidarity led the poor whites to align themselves with the planter class. The acceptance of a natural leadership made Southern democracy into something else, in his widely shared view. American slavery, he remarked, "produces a very effective – though on many accounts a very objectionable – form of aristocracy".[78] For similar reasons, Gladstone now sided publicly with the South. The abolition of slavery before its time, he and Cecil held, was not worth the blood shed in such profusion, or the hardship inflicted upon Lancashire cotton operatives in the course of the war.[79]

The South was ruled by "an aristocracy [which] has borne the . . . braggart democracy to the ground"; so it appeared as the Confederate armies advanced deep into Northern territory. The "delusive optimism" about the future of mankind that America had inspired would recede with the Union's fortunes in battle.[80] The recovery of the North and its certain triumph dismayed Cecil in proportion to his earlier confidence in its defeat. He did not think in 1864 that Gladstone contemplated manhood suffrage in his unguarded welcome for an extension of the franchise to working men not disqualified by "personal unfitness or . . . political danger"; the moderation of his finance had become very clear. Even so he foresaw a momentous conflict over parliamentary reform – "the great issue on which hopes of freedom . . . order and civilization depend" – but the prospect did not loom large at the last election that Palmerston fought in 1865.[81] The *Quarterly Review*'s leading contributor made more of the government's errors in foreign policy, expanding on points in his parliamentary speeches. As readers expected, those essays sought to score off ministers: they are still helpful for his later philosophy of international relations.

The articles of 1863–5 on Palmerstonian policy abroad were preceded by pieces on Castlereagh and the Younger Pitt. The latter used reviews of new biographies to reflect on the lessons of past statecraft for Britain in a European context. Castlereagh's reputation did not stand as high as it has done since Sir Charles Webster studied him in depth.[82] Cecil approved a Tory statesman's disinclination to preach constitutionalism to foreigners, as Palmerston could not resist doing. The essence of Castlereagh's policy lay in the concern for peace, social order and freedom from the scourge of war and revolution: conservative aims that gave the masses such chance as they had of happiness. Intervention in the affairs of other countries, to which great powers were prone while deploring the habit, seldom improved matters: the battle of Navarino had resulted in the appearance of another "sick man of Europe" – Greece – beside the ailing Ottoman empire.[83] Castlereagh was one of the Younger Pitt's political heirs: the two essays on Lord Stanhope's life of Pitt placed Cecil in the same tradition. The ambiguity of that tradition ought not to lessen respect for it, "whether his [Pitt's] memory be claimed by Reformers or anti-Reformers". Castlereagh's strength derived from his master Pitt, who was "far too practical a politician to be given to abstract theories"; who undertook reforms at home and in the empire when to do so was "wholesome" and who resisted them when the political climate changed. His flexible mercantilism laid the basis of Britain's economic grandeur. Of the failure of the Irish policy Cecil observed presciently: "The problem was in truth insoluble". Cecil's was not the "untheoretic mind" which he admired in Pitt: but he found the great man's virtues ever topical. They illustrated "the political value of a character", for incorruptible patriotism. Whig by origin, Pitt realised the old Tory ideal of a minister able to rise above party and enlist support from every quarter, "monarchical, aristocratic, agricultural, commercial".[84]

In his writing, more especially on foreign affairs, Cecil was sensitive to the tension between ethics and policy. There was, he felt moved to say, "nothing abiding in political science but the necessity of truth, purity and justice", a requirement that involved unending compromise with the demands of particular situations.[85] Helpless sympathy was Britain's reaction to the Polish rising of 1863 and Russian disregard for nationality and its rights accorded European recognition at the Congress of Vienna. The eighteenth-century partitions of Poland were no more immoral than the British conquest of Bengal at the same period. The facts of power might preclude an independent Poland, but he was not comfortable with the *realpolitik* he applied in this instance.[86] As practised by the Palmerston ministry in Schleswig-Holstein and further afield, such realism shamed his country. He denounced "peace without honour", bought by acquiescing in the surrender of the Danish duchies to German nationalism: but, as he was obliged to concede outside the *Quarterly Review,* there was no alternative. Nationalism, he had written in *Bentley's,* was not a condition of progress, unlike freedom. It was not less powerful for that, but by bowing to it Palmerston had not served Europe well.[87]

Cecil's very short articles in the *Saturday Review* do not rate the attention paid to his essays in the *Quarterly Review.* They were journalism of a kind familiar now: knowing and often impertinent; thumbnail sketches of people and events written to divert as much as to inform. It was a novel approach in its day, and gave the review a real, if limited, influence. It often acted as a scout for the leading newspapers, whose praise or dispraise was taken to be the voice of public opinion. Although he attended what are today called editorial conferences, he continued to preserve his anonymity in this case; the house style, lightly disrespectful, made it hard to pick out his contributions.[88] Enjoying this cover, he freely indulged his detestation of Disraeli. Pilloried as "the artless dodger", Disraeli was said to have reached "the *delirium tremens* stage of trickery" as the Tories struggled to stay in office after the 1859 election by modifying their policies. Other statesmen who incurred Cecil's displeasure were similarly insulted: the Peelite Sir James Graham had "a taste for the puddles and the gutter", and Russell exhibited "moral meanness without . . . a particle of eloquence or talent".[89] This personal abuse ceased when he began to work his passage into a future Tory administration. Subsequent political comment from him in the review tended to be general rather than particular. A late specimen is the earnest hope that his generation, or the next, would recover the confidence of the past that there was no necessary connection between progress and democracy. The belief of Englishmen that they were progressive at their own pace and in their own way constituted "a very salutary element in our national self-respect". He was good at philosophizing in a couple of paragraphs, and got better.[90]

A lot of what he wrote for the *Saturday Review* dealt with other topics than the British political scene. German literature was a speciality: he noticed a tract by Marx for the vigour of its invective, and the insight it afforded into refugee politics. Changing fashions in Society, and their absurdity, furnished material for the irony he perfected in the review. On a more serious level again, he served up assured little commentaries on world events from East to West.[91] They encapsulate opinions expressed at greater length in the quarterlies or *Hansard.* He was a reliable and valued member of J.D. Cook's talented team, able to turn in the requisite number of words on whatever caught his or the editor's eye. The personal note is clearest in the frequent items on religion. Significantly, he grew more tolerant: the harassment of Benjamin Jowett at Oxford and the persecution of contributors to *Essays and Reviews* was ascribed to "an Anglican camorra" uniting High and Low Churchmen. Yet he was conscious that the unchecked development of Broad Church views might end by making them "a mere cloak for the negation of all belief". He disliked the Broad Church's Evangelical critics more, a section of the Church then at the height of their power. They had revolutionized public morals – that he conceded – at the price of fastening upon the country an "incubus of narrow-mindedness and spiritual tyranny". He loathed the resurgent Puritanism which Trollope was assailing in fiction. In the guise of a *Saturday* reviewer, Cecil seized on the failings of one or two prelates to assert that the Evangelical bishops whom Palmerston made with Lord Shaftesbury's help were "a proverb for ignorance and jobbery".[92]

An intense but reasoned animosity explains why a deeply religious man availed himself of journalistic licence in this way: he saw in the central Evangelical doctrine of election to salvation a distortion of true humanity with damaging social effects. The elect, and respectable, were saved: consequently religion bore on its countenance "the very commercial character of our social standard". Two pages on "Poverty" summarize the eternal contradiction between the Church and the world as he experienced it. Christianity, once the religion of slaves, now that of the "powerful and rich", had plainly lost the moral force which enabled it to conquer the Roman Empire from the lowest levels of society. In urban and industrial Britain the degradation of the poor was such that institutional religion, though backed by education and the public opinion of the newspapers, did not have the strength to make the same impression at those levels. This article followed a meditation on Providence unfolded in history, a "vast drama"; he warned against "the arrogant idea that our own planet, our own race, our own generation, our own corner of the earth, is the culmination of the Creator's work". Lesser breeds, supposedly Red Indians or Mexicans, were not to be regarded as legitimate victims of manifest destiny, America's or Britain's. History was littered with tremendous setbacks to progress: he instanced the Muslim subjugation of the Near East.[93]

Robert Cecil was blessed with an inability to be dull. He was ashamed of his journalism because he outgrew many of the opinions embarrassingly preserved in print. Such writing seemed superficial to a fastidious intellect, and unworthy in the servitude it entailed to readers who were usually seeking confirmation of their own prejudices and fears. The desire to publish, never very strong in him, faded once he had enough money to dispense with an activity he did not relish, and had proved, above all to himself, that he could make his mark in politics. While historians ought to be grateful for his output over years so thinly covered in the archives, they need to use the material with caution.

## The City and its Lessons

Cecil's partial estrangement from his father and desire for independence took him into the City as it had taken him into journalism. The proliferation of companies after the coming of limited liability increased the demand for titled directors and MPs on the boards of new ventures. His services were given to the International Land Credit Company, and the Adelaide (North Arm) Railway. He also speculated with his small capital. The Australian company's liquidation cost him, as director, a share of its flotation expenses. Far more serious was the downfall of Overend and Gurney, the leading discount house in which he was a shareholder. Its crash in May

1866 plunged the City into one of its periodic crises.[94] By then his elder brother was dead, and he could count on his father's help. Even so, it was painful to have to admit that he had been found wanting in the qualities necessary for survival in the market-place: "but for this unlucky failure, I was doing very well", he sought to explain in the time-honoured fashion of someone in his predicament. The losses, several times his income, were overshadowed by potential liabilities little short of £20 000, or about one-third of the gross annual receipts from the family estates. Struggling to get out of collapsing shares in more than one company, he was forced into revisions of the figure put upon his needs. The five or six thousand of May – "I want £1500 very badly now – the rest . . . [in] three months" – had almost doubled in a month as he met inescapable commitments. It was, he confessed, "a horrid mess. My only consolation is that much wiser men . . . have been much more heavily hit".[95]

The experience completed Cecil's business training. A financial innocent, he had listened to a bad adviser in his brother-in-law, E.P. Alderson. The wariness that disaster inculcated stood him in good stead as chairman of the big, loss-making Great Eastern Railway for a time after 1868. Memories of the City ensured a cool reception when he was prime minister and foreign secretary for grandiose, under-capitalized projects requiring government's blessing or a subvention. What he saw of their world, culminating in the panic of 1866, strengthened a distrust of "'our enlightened middle class'" in business and politics, who took good care of them-selves and lost nothing for want of asking.[96] Nor did the City increase his respect for the prevailing economic liberalism. No natural harmony of interests was apparent there. Human nature obeyed its selfish impulses, until the criminal law, or the Bank of England, intervened. As an investor in later years, he understandably preferred gilt-edged, or the colonial equivalents, to tempting yields elsewhere. When an aristo-cratic cabinet colleague's directorships got him into difficulties in the 1890s he was warmly sympathetic; it did not seem a resigning matter to him.[97] On the other hand, when he wished to express his bitter resentment of their political trickery, as he considered it, he compared the manoeuvres of his leaders over the 1867 reform bill to those of the partners in Overend and Gurney trying to stave off insolvency, whose judicial condemnation was couched "in terms stronger than we care to reprint".[98]

# CHAPTER THREE

# *The Second Reform Act*

## The Front Rank of Politics

Cecil's admirers were at first confined to the small group of high Tories who detested Disraeli. In an obscure backbench conspiracy, they had picked him out in 1863 to be their leader in the Commons under a duke substituted for Derby. Cecil may not have been aware of the plot, and if he was, appears to have ignored it. By the beginning of 1866, when moves were afoot to replace a Liberal ministry divided over reform with a coalition of the centre, he was being mentioned as a possible premier, with a cross-party appeal, though too young. Loyally, he rejected the idea of serving under anyone but Disraeli, if the ailing and, it was assumed, less flexible Derby made way for him. Disraeli repaid him by letting it be known that there might not be room for him in a cabinet selected on the principle of "fusion" between the moderates of both parties. In the event, the Liberals approached, after the Russell government fell on reform, refused office with the Tories, and Cranborne, as he was known from 1865, entered the cabinet as secretary of state for India. All that can be said in this chapter about his brief responsibility for India is that his marked ability as a minister was generally recognized.[1]

His stand against the second reform bill of Derby and Disraeli made Cranborne a national figure. The great majority of their followers believed the Tory leaders were right to take up household suffrage, after considerable hesitation. Disraeli publicly likened him to a man who thought everybody else insane. By their handling of the party, the leadership isolated a rebel who, at the time of his resignation with two other members of the cabinet in March 1867, seemed to have dealt a fatal blow to a weak government and its bill. Cranborne made no more than half-hearted attempts to organize a cave. Disraeli had the better of their exchanges in the Commons; behind him stood Derby, without whom the Tories would never have accepted such a large instalment of reform. Cranborne despaired of his party for a while: but the Tories saw in him someone who must not be lost to them. Friends endeavoured to draw him out of continued isolation. Disraeli sought to bring him back into the cabinet when Derby handed the premiership to his lieuten-ant in February 1868. With few exceptions, Tories were not proud of the political somersault they had performed since their objections to the Liberal reform bill of 1866 as setting the borough franchise too low to be healthy. Though unconvinced by Cranborne's arguments against household suffrage without built-in checks, they felt with him that self-styled Conservatives should not have outstripped their oppon-ents on a question of fundamental constitutional importance. Divested, as Cranborne predicted, of supposedly essential safeguards by the Commons, where the Tories were a minority, household suffrage did not look like a Conservative achievement in any sense.[2] At the 1868 election the Liberals improved slightly on their habitual lead over the Tories among English voters, and made substantial gains in seats on the Celtic fringe. The Tory government's determination to be seen to be more "progressive" than their rivals had not helped them with the electorate. Cranborne's strong position as a result was enhanced by the character of his opposition to the Derby–Disraeli bill. Unlike his colleague General Peel, who resigned with him, he was no reactionary and had never objected to more working-class voters, only to their preponderance on a revised roll.

## The Liberal Reform Bill

In the last summer of Palmerston's life there was some inconclusive discussion of parliamentary reform among cabinet ministers following their handsome victory in the general election of July 1865. Public opinion, largely indifferent to the succes-sion of reform bills since the mid-1850s, gave signs of stirring at last. The new prime minister, Russell, and Gladstone tried to devise a measure, introduced in March 1866, that would create a working-class majority in the urban electorate. They adopted a £7 rental franchise, equivalent to £5.10s on the old basis calculated from the rate books. Estimates of the probable enfranchisement, compiled by the Poor Law authorities under central direction, were shown to have a wide margin of error. Dissident Liberals and the Tories used the uncertainty to carry an amend-ment in June substituting rating for rental in the operative clause. The cabinet's resignation put the Tories into office to face a popular agitation for reform which, though mild compared with the excitement at the time of the Great Reform Bill, was better supported and more vocal than anything seen since the peak years of Chartism. To some, the Hyde Park disturbances in July 1866 portended a worrying change of atmosphere from the relative social calm to which the country had grown accustomed. While Stanley dismissed the trouble in the park as "more mischief than malice . . . and more of mere larking than either", another cabinet minister, Gathorne Hardy, thought it was not simply the work of what he called "a refuse population". If the angry crowds protesting at the exclusion of the Reform League from the park gave the political class and property generally an unwelcome jolt, the meetings addressed by John Bright in the big towns were more significant. Gladstone had sensed a movement of opinion reaching down into the literate, respectable working class, and responded to it in language that critics in his own party and many Tories construed as minatory.[3]

In front of several thousand people at Liverpool in April, he warned the bill's aristocratic opponents on the Liberal benches that "but one thing . . . can make this country democratic in its feeling", the failure of their order to give leaders to legitimate change. The bill was "an act of justice to the . . . community".[4] When he had talked to the Commons in the same vein, Cranborne accused him of "sentimental rant". The Tory was really afraid that such language would generate expectations out of all proportion to the likely effects of the government bill. His more alarming prophecies of what might flow from enfranchising too many working-class voters were aimed at apprehensive Liberals. He had called in his *Quarterly Review* article of January 1866 for "fusion" in the face of an anticipated radical measure of reform, but no one seriously believed that the new voters, however numerous, were going to demand the erection of national workshops for the unemployed on the Parisian model of 1848.[5] The "two great faults" of the Russell–Gladstone bill, he said, speaking in earnest, were that it must increase electoral corruption and add to the power of ignorance. "The Reform Bill" in the *Quarterly Review* for April 1866 examined the available statistics to establish that the working class would dominate some forty per cent of English and Welsh boroughs. He insisted on "the absolutely experimental character of this undertaking"; in so far as American and Australian experience was relevant, it was "far from reassuring". Tackling a point on which government speakers had dwelt, that the working class did not act as a class, united in pushing its distinctive interests, he argued that it was vulnerable to coercion by organized minorities within it. He made the most of recent publicity given to the intimidation and violence apt to surface in mid-Victorian trade unionism.[6]

Cranborne and those whose doubts and fears he articulated shut their eyes to the clearest evidence that something much less than a £7 rental qualification was safe. A Gladstonian Liberal, the attorney-general Sir Roundell Palmer, was the first outside the small group of decided radicals to advocate household suffrage in the debates of 1866, on 30 May, as the goal "to which we must ultimately advance and to which, on conservative principles, I . . . should be well pleased to advance now".[7] Palmer followed Gladstone a month earlier, who in a telling passage in his speech on the reform bill's second reading, cited the municipal franchise. Operative since 1835, this qualified every ratepaying householder, and had produced "no explosion of class feeling, nor any attempt to confiscate property" such as the Tories had forecast then.[8] Only in one town, Sheffield, had the low franchise permitted the Chartists to win as many as half the seats on a council. Gladstone stopped short of proposing the adoption of the municipal qualification for parliamentary elections, but the thought was implicit in his repeated references to ties of kinship and religion between the classes, and Palmer spelt it out. Despite the substitution of rating for rental in June, the argument was not being won by the government's critics. Cranborne gave ground quite early on when he offered his "confession of faith on the subject of the working-classes". At Liverpool Gladstone had charged his parliamentary assailants with seeing working men as "an invading army": it was wrong, Cranborne admitted, to consider them "different from other Englishmen". They were, however, exposed to greater temptations: invested with the franchise, they would sell their votes to the highest bidder, for cash and election treats. In contrast, he spoke highly of their "natural leaders", the ablest of the artisans, fitter to represent them in the House than middle-class radicals who, "for reasons best known to themselves", sought to identify with the masses.[9]

The temptation for this working-class élite, "more deeply interested" than their followers with a limited understanding of politics, was to seek to impose new fiscal burdens upon other classes and to encroach upon their property rights. Nevertheless, he agreed with J.S. Mill, then briefly a Liberal MP, in thinking it desirable that there should be some working-class MPs. Though an authentic radical, Mill was very close to Cranborne in his distrust of a mass electorate. The latter invoked the sage's authority, pointing out that Mill, too, was opposed to a working-class majority of voters as uneducated for such responsibility. In conclusion, he touched on a question that intensified Tory resistance to the reform bill: the redistribution of seats to accompany the new borough franchise and the less contentious changes in the county franchise.[10] They were convinced that the government's combination of redistribution and franchise would hit their kind at the next election. Now that the long postponed revision of the 1832 settlement was bound to be undertaken sooner or later in the altered climate of opinion, the Tories had a strong incentive to ensure that they, again in office, had as large a say in the admission of new voters and the shaping of constituencies as the Liberal opposition which outnumbered them would allow. Derby's third ministry did not have the option of dropping reform for the duration of its uncertain life.

The *Quarterly Review* for July carried an article in which Cranborne put the case for a Tory reform bill, after some pages spent on Gladstone's mishandling of his party during the session. "The process of self-deceit goes on in his mind without the faintest self-consciousness or self-suspicion", he observed of the Gladstonian propensity to sound conservative and radical at the same time.[11] This was turning the knife in the wound: the victim was uncomfortably aware of an increasingly criticized tendency. He had reacted angrily to Cranborne's strictures in the April *Quarterly Review* on his courtship of the radicals, quoting Shakespeare against his tormentor, "These lies are like the father that begot them, Gross as a mountain, open, palpable". Cranborne alluded in July to this passage in the Liberal's second reading speech on the reform bill, proof of the effectiveness of his writing. The dissident Liberals who had brought down the outgoing government were reminded that the logic of Gladstone's pronouncements pointed to a bill "that shall build up his future power on . . . the Trades Unions of the great towns and . . . rid him for ever of aristocratic opposition". Cranborne's strategy envisaged a Tory bill passed with the help of those Liberals, whose political destiny continued to be "fusion". The necessity for parliamentary reform proceeded from the operation of organic change understood by every intelligent person: "to say that . . . any party . . . is opposed to the admission of the working-man to the polling-booth is studiously to falsify the facts". The only constant was the requirement for balance between social classes in the electorate. Additional votes for the educated and propertied, a feature of Liberal and Tory bills in the past, were to be considered with the downward extension of the franchise.[12]

How far that downward extension went must depend, he wrote, "on the tone in which it is claimed by those who are to benefit". Cranborne was not frightened of widespread popular violence, but of traditional rulers capitulating to demonstrations got up by radical pressure groups. In the final paragraph of this article entitled "The Change of Ministry", he saw that "the public apathy . . . [which] is profound" had effectively left parliamentary reform to be decided by "a score or so of influential politicians of various schools". The Hyde Park disturbances late in July and the enthusiasm at the rallies that Bright addressed through the autumn modified his perception of the national mood. He was still right to maintain, as he persisted in doing, that the Tory cabinet in which he sat and the Liberal opposition were not compelled to concede household suffrage. What most of them perceived as a question of judgement, encouraged by the absence of an agitation resembling that of 1832, was to him a question of principle. His cabinet colleagues had gone on record in its recent debates as upholding the imperative need for social balance in an expanded electorate. He meant to keep them to that: "our system may fairly be said to be on its trial", he declared in July. "The virtue of our public men" was at stake: but they refused to be confined by his notions of political integrity.[13]

## The Tory Cabinet and Household Suffrage

Behind the scenes the Tories were moving towards household suffrage during the recess of 1866–7. Cranborne's friend, and ally in the cabinet, Lord Carnarvon noted in October the conversion of the Earl of Hardwicke, twice a cabinet minister and the epitome of traditional Toryism, who in 1859 thought his party's reform bill went too far. Carnarvon found Disraeli "obviously" undecided at that point, waiting for public opinion to give him a clear lead. He complained that Cranborne was against a Tory bill, and had failed to send him a promised memorandum detailing his objections.[14] On his side, Cranborne was being told, and believed, that Disraeli contemplated a large measure of reform, "possibly household suffrage", with safeguards, "all manner of cunning dodges", which would be discarded under pressure.[15] Looking back, Carnarvon was unsure whether to credit the insistence of Cranborne's stepmother, Lady Salisbury, with her wide circle of informants, that Disraeli had deliberately misled the cabinet about his objectives. One of the most capable Tories, Sir Hugh Cairns, who knew Disraeli well, told Carnarvon, in carefully chosen words, that there had been "no predetermined deception". As late as the end of December 1866 Disraeli assured Cranborne of his opposition, "throughout", to legislating on reform. This is difficult to reconcile with Carnarvon's account of his thinking in October when he suggested a plan to draw the Liberals into criticizing the omission of reform from the Queen's Speech at the start of the 1867 session, and thereby showing their hand, before an announcement of ministerial intentions. Carnarvon demurred: it was "a dodge from which nothing could be gained". Disraeli's stated idea of their intentions was to test opinion by resolutions in favour of reform that should not commit the government to specific provisions. He also mentioned the appointment of a commission, which Cranborne had pressed on him in September. Its recommendations might enable a weak government and the perplexed Liberal majority to advance on an agreed basis.[16]

That was the situation when the cabinet began to consider the whole question at its autumn meetings from 31 October. At the opening discussion, everyone concurred, "however reluctantly", that reform must be tackled. Beyond that, there was little agreement. Derby read out letters from the Queen's private secretary and from the Liberal peer, Lord Grey, urging, respectively, action to resolve a problem that perturbed the monarch, and a commission to inquire and report, the latter being the outcome of consultation among the Liberals whose rebellion had defeated the Russell–Gladstone bill.[17] Notwithstanding his desire to work with that section of the Liberals, Cranborne said on 8 November that no bill could succeed that was not "new and bold": but he put to the cabinet preliminary resolutions excluding "a numerical class ascendancy". With that all important reservation, household suffrage came up almost at once; although Carnarvon was overruled when he proposed it, accompanied by "Conservative" safeguards.[18] Stanley, foreign secretary under his father and initially absorbed in the work of his department, doubted the value of their discussions: the Liberal opposition would never sanction a Tory bill. Resolutions drawn up on 8 November were so general as to be of little help in developing the question.[19] There he was mistaken. As Cranborne had perceived in September, Derby wanted to legislate. It is not always realized that the prime minister was very much in charge of his administration's policy. Disraeli could not move on reform without him, and kept in step with him. From the resolutions considered on 8 November Derby had progressed by the beginning of December to favouring household suffrage, with additional votes for the middle classes, after a precautionary inquiry by the commission.[20]

Derby's Liberal allies of the past session did not anticipate this movement. Robert Lowe, the most eloquent of them, supposed the Tories were "judicially blinded" on reform, by their history, like "the aristocratic party in the French Revolution &c." He and his associates counselled delay, and suggested an electoral pact which would secure their seats and rule out a reform bill. "Simple insanity" was Cranborne's reaction to intimations of Tory and radical co-operation at the expense of Lowe and his friends. He objected to the introduction of specific proposals, "such as household suffrage" into the resolutions they were trying to frame.[21] The mere mention of household suffrage brought a threat of resignation from one member of the cabinet, General Peel. Accordingly, Disraeli informed the House on 11 February of the government's intention to bring in very broad resolutions on reform published the next day. Gladstone replied, asking for legislation: and three days later, without, it seems, consulting the cabinet, Disraeli announced that there were to be more specific proposals. His better than expected reception on the 11th and the attitude of the Liberal leadership determined him, and of course Derby, to force the pace in cabinet. Over the next few days they and their colleagues came close to household suffrage, agreeing on £5 rating in the boroughs with an array of checks: up to four votes each for the educated and propertied. Cranborne approved, but General Peel's resignation was only averted by royal intervention. Gladstone's promise of support on the 18th for an acceptable reform bill strengthened the position of

Derby and Disraeli, who obtained from the cabinet the substitution of household suffrage for £5 rating, with the number of additional votes restricted to two per person.[22]

On the evening of 21 February, Cranborne and Carnarvon talked over these developments in a quiet corner of the House of Lords library. Believing the safeguards with household suffrage to be adequate, Cranborne was nevertheless uneasy and resentful, sure that "Disraeli has played us false . . . is attempting to hustle us into his measures, that Lord Derby is in his hands, and that the present form which the question has . . . assumed has been long planned by him". Carnarvon was sufficiently concerned – "it certainly looks suspicious" – to conclude with his friend "a sort of offensive and defensive alliance . . . in the cabinet", regretting that they had not done so before. Cranborne had been immersed in India Office business. In future they would be in constant touch, and believed that together they could stop their colleagues from pursuing "any very fatal course".[23] They were wrong: on the 23rd a redistribution of thirty seats went through despite their protests at being rushed: "Cranborne muttered his discontent in very audible tones".[24] The following day the latter turned his attention to the statistics furnished by the cabinet's Tory expert, R.D. Baxter, and discovered that the reduced "counterpoise" – no more than two votes for each elector – was not enough to offset the weight of those qualified only as householders. He hurried round to Carnarvon's London house to reveal "a complete revolution . . . in the boroughs" lying concealed in the figures. His ally persuaded him not to resign at once but to ask for a meeting of the cabinet. General Peel, got out of bed, agreed to resign with his two colleagues, if necessary. Another nocturnal visit, by Carnarvon, to Gathorne Hardy, had a significantly different result. Taken to Cranborne, Hardy found him in a "very disturbed state of mind". This strongly Tory lawyer from a family of Yorkshire industrialists, a rising man, advised Cranborne to see Derby or Disraeli, and afterwards wrote to Carnarvon that they must all "stick to the ship". The cabinet had allowed their leader to tell parliament that proposals on reform were imminent, and "our personal honour" was involved in going through with them.[25]

It was the reaction of nearly all their colleagues and of the party. At the meeting of the cabinet on the 25th for which Cranborne had asked, a "very angry discussion" took place. Disraeli did not dispute Cranborne's interpretation of the figures that Baxter had supplied: he simply said that "the influence of land and wealth would be supreme", in the new constituencies as in the old. Cranborne wanted to be able to resign, and urged the cabinet to adhere, without him, to what they had decided.[26] The advice came strangely from someone who had written to Derby the previous evening that, if unchanged, their plan of a bill must mean the destruction of the party at the polls. Cranborne felt compromised by having agreed to so much before making a stand at the last minute. The casual abandonment of social balance in the reformed electorate was intolerable, as was the acquiescence of most of his colleagues in Disraeli's dismissal of its importance. It is plain that Cranborne's overpowering wish was to regain his political independence: "if I consent to this scheme now that I know what its effect will be, I could not look in the face those whom last year I urged to resist Mr Gladstone". The antagonism that Disraeli inspired in him could no longer be disguised, or contained: "That is at the bottom of it", commented Hardy in his diary.[27]

Cranborne, Carnarvon and Peel were made to feel their isolation: "None of the cabinet stood by us", recorded Carnarvon. In the last quarter of an hour of a meeting described by Derby as "of a most unpleasant character", the prime minister gave way to the minority and secured their assent to a £6 rating franchise in the boroughs, proposed by Stanley, with the extra votes for education and property. The principle of social balance, on which Cranborne had refused to yield, was restored.[28] No one there doubted that Carnarvon and the General would have fallen into line without his example and influence. Glad of the retreat from household suffrage – "I think we have had an escape" – Stanley estimated that two-thirds of the cabinet continued to prefer it. His father, "much mortified", left the meeting for one arranged beforehand with Tory MPs, where his announcement disappointed the large number of his followers who had been expecting him to confirm the reported adoption of household suffrage, with compensating franchises. How large that element was became clear in the course of an eventful week. Disraeli presented the cabinet's hastily revised proposals to the Commons, and the preliminary resolutions were dropped: "they . . . have served their purpose", observed Stanley, in moving the discussion between ministers and within the party forward as the need for definition grew. The Liberals were divided: household suffrage, with the built-in compensation, received the support of Liberals hostile to Gladstone who were now interested in a lasting settlement of the question and in denying him the credit for it. He himself entertained genuine reservations about going further than his bill of the last session: it was his style to give moderation the aura of radicalism. A hundred and fifty Tory backbenchers met at the Carlton Club on 28 February, to call, with Disraeli's encouragement, for a return to household suffrage as the basis of legislation. Evidence was accumulating that, as Disraeli contended, Cranborne and the other two ministers had been left behind by opinion in the party and the country.[29]

Carnarvon's diary shows how the three ministers were forced into resigning five days after their victory on 25 February. Not a strong personality, the diarist was oppressed by the atmosphere in cabinet on the 26th, when tactics for implementing the reluctant decision of the day before were discussed: "Great gloom and personal irritation. Cranborne and I said very little. General Peel nothing." On the 27th he was aware of "the greatest irritation" in the party with the three of them. On the 28th – the day of the Carlton Club meeting – newspaper predictions of the pressure to be applied to them decided Cranborne and Carnarvon to send to the premier their version of the struggle over reform inside the cabinet.[30] It was too late to counter the manipulation of the party against them. Derby hinted to his son a day earlier that he was preparing to revert to household suffrage and accept the threatened resignations. Stanley and Disraeli reviewed the situation in one of many such conversations that week. A £6 rating was all very well, but the Liberals were bound to substitute £5, as nearer the £7 rental rejected in 1866. The Tories could not submit to the change "with honour", that is, without losing face in their own eyes and before the political nation. Household suffrage, little different in practice from £5 rating, as Stanley had noted, would yet be sufficiently different to give the Tory reform bill a distinctive character. Stanley's doubts about household suffrage were stilled by the reflection that it was "evidently . . . safer [and] . . . more popular than the alternatives". The turn-out at London radical demonstrations in December and February had been much smaller than the organizers hoped but large enough, and displaying the "good humour, no excitement" that would be content with less than the manhood suffrage advocated by the Reform League in the knowledge that there was no real demand for it.[31]

The conviction prevailed among ministers that they had made a bad mistake in surrendering to Cranborne and the others; the Liberal opposition would not fail to take advantage of the blunder. "The political situation is horrible but can we retrace our steps?" Gathorne Hardy asked himself on 2 March. He got his answer the same day: the cabinet went back to household suffrage as the heart of the reform bill after more than two hours spent in trying to preserve unity.[32] Cranborne was obdurate, and carried Carnarvon and Peel with him in resigning, although they were clearly reluctant. Stanley set down what everyone round the cabinet table felt: "we are bound . . . not to effect a real transfer of power to the working class, which would be equally opposed to our interests and ideas".[33] The retention of a high, though reduced, qualification for the county occupation franchise, and a minimal redistribution were to help sustain the existing order, reinforced by exclusion from the borough electorate of nearly half a million ratepaying householders, it was calculated, whose rates were collected with the rent by their landlords. Denying the vote to "compound householders", usually, but not invariably, the poorer occupiers, was crucial to Disraeli's argument that household would be limited to the respectable working class characterized by "general trustworthiness of life". He was not similarly attached to the "fancy franchises" for the middle classes, by far the most important of which was a second vote for borough electors paying at least twenty shillings a year in direct taxation. Once Cranborne and his allies had gone, he tried to persuade the cabinet to drop that second vote for the middle classes. With or without it, he had convinced himself, "the measure has really no spice of democracy"; the institutions that Tories cherished were not in jeopardy. He had an assurance from Earl Grosvenor, a leader of the dissentient Liberals in 1866, that such a bill, with "some compensatory arrangement against the possible influx of compound householders", would be supported by him and his friends.[34]

When the Tory bill was introduced on 18 March, Cranborne described the second vote for direct taxpayers as inadequate for its purposes, and forecast that the exclusion of compound householders would be shortlived, if only because it was full of anomalies. He took his stand, however, on "a simple proposition of political morality", which, to him, mattered more than any reform bill: the party that resisted £7 rental in 1866 was not the party to propose household suffrage twelve months later. In his view, the Tories were committing political suicide: they would find that they had forfeited the voters' respect. Lastly, he challenged ministers to admit the meaning of their bill "openly and boldly". Disraeli was not ready to make the admission. "The Government", he said in answer to Cranborne, "will never introduce household suffrage pure and simple".[35] Yet that, Stanley had noted the previous week, was exactly what he had in mind. After this initial exchange,

Cranborne was driven to seek the co-operation of Gladstone, whose radical tendencies he had denounced, in overthrowing the Tory ministry, "if possible". The maintenance of party discipline and loyalty to Derby, he argued in his speech, could not avert the Tories' extinction at an election: but he knew those qualities might get a bill on to the statute book.[36]

## The Passing of the Conservative Bill

The Toryism that rejected Sir Robert Peel possessed a cohesion remarkable before the advent of the late Victorian mass parties. Derby's judgement was sometimes questioned: his leadership was unassailable. His followers grumbled about Disraeli's tactics for twenty years, but as Palmerston observed, "when it comes to a division, they will go together into the same lobby like sheep through a gap".[37] So it was in 1867. Derby's unswerving commitment to it sustained the reform bill, while Disraeli's agility in amending the measure to satisfy Liberals whose votes he needed eased its passage. The latter, despite his father's standing as the squire of Bradenham, was the "Jew adventurer" that Cranborne designated him in private.[38] Derby, by contrast, was the exemplar of a functional aristocracy, accorded as much deference in the industrial North West, where his property was concentrated, as any magnate in the agricultural South. His responsibility for the bill constituted a guarantee of its acceptability. It was hard for Cranborne to make headway against a statesman whose personality and authority had held the party together after the Peelite secession, and who had been a member of the cabinet which framed the 1832 Reform Act, that triumph of evolutionary conservatism, with a small "c". Disraeli was pleased to see that his bitterest opponent remained silent in the meeting of the party's MPs on 15 March at which the premier outlined the bill before its introduction.[39] There was little criticism from those present. Disraeli's subsequent moves were made in the knowledge that Tories, having accepted the principle of household suffrage from Derby, would be loath to withhold their support on another part of the bill if by doing so they threatened its prospects and the survival of Derby's government. It did not follow that they relished Disraeli's readiness to give up provisions intended to strengthen the middle-class element in the new electorate and to keep out the poorer householders. Cranborne did what he could, in conjunction with the Liberal opposition, to exploit the tensions within his party.

The bill's reception by the party and the Commons, and the divided Liberals' decision not to oppose the second reading, led Disraeli to try again for the abandonment of "duality", the second vote for the middle classes. Several of his cabinet colleagues objected to dropping what had so recently been represented as important for the stabilizing effect anticipated. With Derby behind him, he overrode the preoccupation with a "point of honour", which he termed "mere foolishness and euphuism". His desire to erode the commitment to excluding compound householders provoked Hardy to exclaim, though only in his diary, "It is one thing to break up a ministry, but how could I again serve under so unscrupulous a man as Disraeli?"[40] Writing to Carnarvon at the beginning of April, Cranborne was not optimistic of stopping Disraeli's progress. He approached Gladstone and voted with him on 12 April to replace household suffrage by £5 rating, when the Liberal leader experienced, in his own words, "a smash perhaps without example", deserted by a sizeable minority of his party.[41] Only a handful of Tories went with Cranborne into the opposition lobby. The impetus of that victory by a margin of twenty-one votes carried the reform bill through its remaining stages in the Commons. Gladstone contemplated retiring from the Liberal leadership in the Commons: but in reality his long-term position was strengthened by a principled stance. Whigs who had been suspicious of supposedly "democratic" leanings drew closer to him, and radicals courted by Disraeli in the lobbies could not permanently take his side. Furthermore, as Cranborne pointed out on the third reading, most of the changes in the bill that Gladstone required were conceded, one after another.[42] Apart from the failure of his April motion on £5 rating, Gladstone was seriously discomfited only when Disraeli beat him again in May on the compound householder issue, and then went further than his rival had ventured to do in accepting the radical Grosvenor Hodgkinson's amendment to enfranchise all householders who paid their rates.

The real loser appeared to be Cranborne, wilfully blind in his speeches to the maturity of the politically aware working-class voters and the innate conservatism of the rest. Even the most timid of his former colleagues, Spencer Walpole, convinced that the bill went too far, and humiliated as home secretary by popular radicals defying his closure of the Royal Parks to reform demonstrations, told the Queen that he retained great confidence in "the good sense and loyalty of the people". "The lower orders" he explained to an uneasy monarch, "are becoming so well educated that they will push on".[43] Disraeli laid more emphasis on the vigour of traditional influences than on rising expectations. The institutions that Toryism existed to perpetuate were not in danger. Aristocracy in Britain would never fall to an assault from below, only to "internal decrepitude" manifested in a loss of confidence in its ability to lead the country. The message of Gladstone's speeches, it should be remembered, was no different. As for democracy, what was it? "Is it household suffrage? I suppose it is." Cranborne, to whom he was replying, appealed to "irrational feelings" with his denunciations of the reform bill as subverting the British constitution. It was "most extraordinary" to see the increase of the electorate in that light: "who are these people to whom you are offering the franchise?", he enquired. "They are Englishmen born and bred under the influence of the laws, manners and customs . . . of the country", which must be far more effective than sentimental talk of "flesh and blood" – a reference to Gladstonian rhetoric – in controlling political behaviour.[44] There were hard-headed politicians who found this complacency alarming: Lowe was privately "in despair", advising any one with money to send it abroad before a working-class ascendancy taxed the rich heavily and legislated for the compulsory division of landed property. Delane of *The Times*, the greatest of Victorian editors, recalled how such prophets of doom were confounded after 1832.[45]

Cranborne worked with Carnarvon and their friend Sir William Heathcote, the Tractarian member for Oxford University, in his unavailing fight against the bill. They had the help of a tiny group of Tory MPs, led by G.M.W. Sandford, known from his former name of Peacocke as "the Peacock's tail".[46] The only powerful voice was Cranborne's, heard with growing respect. Disraeli spoke of the "monstrous and unfounded propositions" in his speeches, but they expressed anxieties which few of his listeners could entirely suppress.[47] Cranborne did not then believe that a working-class majority in the electorate was ready to be educated by responsibility. Its collective self-interest would prevail in "any great social question", and first of all in deciding taxation. A House still predominantly drawn from landed families and elected by open voting was susceptible to another argument which he developed at length. The class "to which I have the honour to belong" might be rich in assets but did not dispose of the liquid resources available to wealthy businessmen; they would be priced out of borough elections and under pressure in the counties, where the occupation franchise was being sharply reduced. Moreover, the unruly behaviour that accompanied open voting already kept respectable voters away from the poll: with many more voters that tendency must increase. Agreeing with the thoughtful radicalism of J.S. Mill on the other side, he predicted that large employers as well as landowners would be unable to compete under those conditions with the speculative fortunes of City men who used membership of the House to promote their financial interests. In Britain's evolving constitution the monarchy had "speaking practically . . . died" and "a large tinge of democracy" was present, which with the passing of the bill would efface aristocracy in a matter of years from the national scene it had dominated for so long. Like many conservatives then, he envisaged democracy as a steam-roller, levelling everything before it. "The principle of the bill", he said, "was that those who lived in hovels should be in the position of holding political power".[48]

Cranborne damaged his case by the "abundant bitterness" of which the last quotation is an example.[49] To his fellow MPs it now seemed obvious that the Derby–Disraeli bill, with its Liberal amendments, was the logical conclusion of the Palmerstonian approach to democracy. The Commons' third reading of the bill in July saw Disraeli's apotheosis; like the second, it was unopposed. It was, wrote Gladstone, "a remarkable night"; he did not speak for fear of inflaming the Liberals' self-inflicted wounds.[50] Reviewing the measure's history and its significance, Cranborne entered a last protest against the imagined destruction of a political system that had ensured ordered change as Britain became an industrial and urban nation with a teeming population. He unquestionably thought his career in the Tory party, and perhaps in active politics, was over. The bill being sent up to the Lords had been transformed in deference to Gladstone's "imperious language". Implacably, Cranborne rehearsed what had been demanded and conceded: a £10 lodger qualification in the boroughs; the removal of "obnoxious distinctions" between personal payment of rates and compounding, secured by complete assimilation of the two categories; the abolition of duality and fancy franchises; a reduction of the occupation franchise in the counties and a redistribution of seats increased by half. This was miscalled "a Conservative triumph". J.W. Henley had excused un-Conservative legislation by alluding to the popular interest in reform, unprecedented since 1831–2: "the pot was boiling over". For Cranborne, Henley's candour encapsulated the "somewhat ignoble" policy of his party: inflexibility until panic supervened.[51]

This contained an element of truth. More uncomfortable still was his assertion that "we are . . . absolutely in the dark" about the likely response of working men to being presented with the franchise. The trade unions of the day practised intimidation and the old freeman voters who survived for a generation after 1832 were notoriously venal: but the great majority of the new electors were an unknown quantity. The apparent confidence in all parts of the House that they would be amenable, like the existing voters, to the influence of wealth and rank was unjustified: it would not suffice to say with Disraeli, "they are Englishmen". They might well continue to return candidates from the upper and middle classes: but whenever the political temperature rose, those members would be found to "care more for their seats than for their class . . . men with Conservative instincts . . . steeped to the lips in radical pledges". He did not fear working-class voters on questions of foreign policy; he, too, trusted to their innate patriotism. There was too much reason to be afraid of the time, not distant, when they would pursue their class interests to the point of conflict with other classes. Disraeli's "fancy statistics", which Cranborne rightly derided, underestimated the size of the final enfranchisement by a factor of three or more and had led party and parliament into the half-understood creation of a mass electorate undreamed of only months before. He had warned Tories that the still very limited redistribution of seats, leaving the urban voter in thickly populated areas grossly underrepresented, could not be a permanent defence against the ill-effects of a democratic franchise.[52]

Conscious that the House viewed him as "something like . . . a champion of a forlorn cause", he ended with a scathing attack on his front bench. He selected for special mention, besides Disraeli, those colleagues – Stanley, Northcote and Hardy – whose opinions on reform were, or had been, closest to his; he professed himself unable to understand the "sophistry" that had induced them to endorse the bill and its transformation. If they, and the overwhelming majority of Tory MPs, did not renounce the political ethos borrowed from an adventurer, he was utterly convinced that "the whole of your representative institutions will crumble beneath your feet". Quite as much as Gladstone, whose earnestness sometimes attracted his mockery, Cranborne was a moralist in politics. England's greatness depended upon her internal achievement: the "mutual trust" eroded, perhaps fatally, by the Tories' conduct in that eventful session. Disraeli thought the "universal sympathy" with which the Commons sent the reform bill on its way diminished this bitter remonstrance at "a political betrayal which has no parallel in our Parliamentary annals".[53]

## The Future of a Rebel

Cranborne had spoken of the "contempt" that greeted his warnings in the House. In fact, he had earned the respect across politics which makes a man someone to reckon with in his generation. On the day following his speech on the third reading of the reform bill, a friend, the historian Dean Milman, called him "the Abdiel of Conservatism", after the seraph in *Paradise Lost* who stood alone against the rebel hosts of Lucifer: "You have at least been faithful found". An Oxford contemporary had presumed upon an old friendship to urge him not to imperil brilliant prospects by cutting himself off from the party: he was "its probable leader".[54] Cranborne turned away from temptation, as he evidently regarded this advice; his "primary duty" was to act upon his political and religious beliefs. He despaired of Toryism: its partisans had been untrue to their deepest convictions on protection, the admission of Jews to parliament and now the franchise. They had not yet betrayed the Church, the Ark of the Tory Covenant, but they were, it seemed to him, "lukewarm" in her defence. He had cared about the franchise, a battle irretrievably lost, and he was determined to fight for the Church, beset by real or imagined dangers: "beyond these two there is nothing, so far as I know, of which the Conservatives are in any special way the protectors".[55] This last remark is essential for an understanding of his career, and of the "good legislation" which he said here was its purpose. The historic parties were, both of them, "progressive" and conservative, committed to evolutionary change. In the aftermath of the reform bill there were those Liberals, in the centre and on the radical wing, too, of their party, who intimated to Cranborne that he might have a future on that side of the House. He himself inclined to the idea of a third party, though alive to the inherent difficulties.

He was bent, it appeared, on severing his ties with the party of Derby and Disraeli. His *Quarterly Review* article of 1867, "The Conservative Surrender", accused its leaders of deliberate political fraud in the course of many pages devoted to repeating his strictures in the recent debates. In a peculiarly offensive comparison, he likened the premier, his lieutenant in the Commons and their colleagues to the defaulting partners in Overend and Gurney, who had issued a highly misleading prospectus. As for the rank and file, they had, at best, displayed the credulity of the Catholics who tamely submitted to the dogmas thrust upon them by the Pope: for the Immaculate Conception in 1854, read household suffrage in 1867.[56] After thus comprehensively insulting the Tories, he wondered where to find a new political home. Talking over the situation with Carnarvon at Highclere, the latter's Hampshire seat, he mentioned overtures from Gladstone and Mill, which he had "neither accepted nor rejected". It would not be easy for them to emulate the Peelites, who had been "a *central* party", while they were cast, by the public at any rate, as reactionaries for their resistance to the reform bill. If a third party occupying the middle ground, their best hope of establishing a distinctive identity and some real influence, were ruled out, Cranborne was weighed down by "the utter uselessness of doing or attempting anything". It was his animosity to Disraeli, which did not cool, that revived his fighting spirit. He mapped out for himself and a tiny band of adherents a course to put them in the centre: "not to hold for a while untenable posts but to decide clearly what we are to stand upon".[57]

Resuming their discussion a couple of days later, Cranborne and Carnarvon were joined by Heathcote from the Commons. Their immediate aim was to dispel the Tory leadership's aura of success, "getting rid of Lord Derby's and Disraeli's supremacy". They were too few to expose themselves to ridicule by announcing a "distinct programme"; and to be effective, their attacks on the Tory chiefs should not give the impression of settled opposition. Behind the personalities in their sights lay the issues which Derby and Disraeli could not be trusted to address constructively, and one issue above all others. "The English Church is a great problem", these three High Churchmen agreed. Her position, menaced by Erastian Whigs and Nonconformist radicals, exemplified the need to clarify what was worth fighting for: "all collateral questions that only raise dust" should be got out of the way. The most important of such questions was the fate of the sister church in Ireland; the Liberals were preparing to reunite around her disestablishment and partial disendowment. The three were ready for large measures in this area of the Irish question when the time came.[58] Cranborne did not share the uneasiness of some Whigs, much more conservative than he was, at the prospect of a Gladstone ministry that allowed the parliamentary radicals a greater influence than they had yet exercised: "My impression is that it is not only inevitable but on the whole not undesirable. It will strip the [popular] agitators of all their leaders." He spelt out in the House his own commitment to the same pragmatism that informed Gladstonian policy: "bound to look at both sides of the question, and not to content myself with stolid opposition . . . then giving way to an unreasonable panic", he accepted the practical abolition of church rates which Gladstone carried in the session of 1868. It was a marked change from his attitude to the Liberation Society's bills earlier in the decade.[59]

The Tories did not hold his animadversions on their intelligence and morals against Cranborne. If Disraeli was accorded a novel respect among them, he still did not enjoy their confidence. The spectacle of Cranborne upbraiding them for unworthy, and possibly self-destructive tactics, filled the party with guilt and admiration; he was the voice of conscience. When Disraeli succeeded to the premiership on Derby's retirement in February 1868, he sought to bring Cranborne back into the cabinet, employing Northcote as an intermediary. The offer, prompted by realism rather than magnanimity, was declined; his honour, he told Carnarvon, would not be safe with Disraeli.[60] His loathing and distrust of the new prime minister pervaded the speech he delivered on Gladstone's Irish church resolutions in March. The Liberals demonstrated their restored unity, and Gladstone his authority, by securing a majority of sixty-one for disestablishment in Ireland. Cranborne spoke from the heart when he said that his church "exercises a hold over me that I regard as sacred". The unsuccessful government amendment, moved by Stanley, made no reference to the principle of establishment, recommending postponement of redistribution of temporalities until the electors had pronounced on the question. Stanley's diary shows that the cabinet, as a whole, had no enthusiasm for the defence of a church to which under twelve per cent of the Irish population adhered: "the general wish seemed to be to commit ourselves as little as possible". For Cranborne the principle which ministers omitted to mention in their amendment had lost none of its worth, commingling "the sacred springs of human feeling and the most important interests of society". Reminding the House of Tory tactics on the two reform bills, he condemned the wording of Stanley's motion, "too clever by half". Cranborne exhorted his former colleagues to "come forward and fight in the light, and not shelter yourselves behind ambiguous phrases".[61] His speech angered not only the new premier but also authentic Tories like Hardy who found it "sneering as regards us all, venomous and remorseless as against Disraeli". Hastily put up to counteract this assault upon the ministry from its own benches, Hardy saw the effect of his bravely orthodox reply dissipated by Disraeli, "obscure, flippant, and impudent" when he wound up for the government.[62]

Hardy felt that a divided and "powerless" ministry might do better to throw in its hand, if Stanley, who made no secret of his belief that the Establishment in Ireland was almost indefensible, decided on resignation. Even Carnarvon thought his friend was rash to insist on the unbreakable bond between the churches of England and Ireland, written into the Act of Union in 1801.[63] Cranborne was so despondent about the course of events that, despite pleas from his admirers on both sides, he did not persist in trying to find a loophole in peerage law when faced with removal to the Lords in April 1868. But for the gloom that enveloped him when he contemplated the future, he would have tried to stay in the Commons. The "Palace of the Dead", as a peer in one of Palmerston's cabinets described the second chamber, had no attraction for him.[64] In his worst moments he regarded himself, still in his thirties, as belonging to the past: "the new principles in politics should be worked by those who sympathize with them heartily", he replied to encouragement from a Gladstonian Liberal MP. All his solicitude for the Church could not draw him out of his tent in the election of 1868 when household suffrage was put to the test. His Tory neighbours in Hertfordshire were refused the expected help from Hatfield. He provided one of them, R.W.G. Gaussen, the squire of Brookman's Park, with the fullest explanation of an attitude which they found difficult to understand. His detestation of Disraeli was unconstrained in private: the premier's origins and social standing did not identify him with "the Conservative classes in the country"; he had no definite programme and, "as I have too good cause to know, he is without principles and without honesty".[65]

If it was said of the new Lord Salisbury, and it was, that he had made a serious error in letting his aversion to Disraeli drive him out of political life, he would not be moved by any representations: "in this matter the personal question is the whole", he maintained. The premier's "great talent and singular power of intrigue" had delivered the Tories to him, body and soul. The conversion of cabinet and party to household suffrage showed "there was nothing strong enough in either to resist his will". As a nominally conservative leader with an unchallenged ascendancy, he was in a unique position to carry forward "Radical changes . . . he alone can silence and paralyze the forces of Conservatism".[66] Brooding on his defeat at Disraeli's hands, Salisbury imputed to him the qualities of a political magician whose mesmerized followers accepted the dismantling of the old order of society as a series of pragmatic adjustments to a new age. It is not clear whether he believed Disraeli to be a radical by conviction, or merely someone who had concluded that the drift towards democracy and all that it implied was unstoppable. Salisbury's defiance of the Tory leadership and resolve to stand aside at the elections when they came had had his father's entire approval: the old marquess' passing was "a bitter blow" to his son politically as well as personally. Only when Disraeli had been replaced would the son be prepared to put his influence in the county behind the Tories.[67]

Salisbury's pessimism was lightened by his intelligence and humour. He was able to poke fun at his propensity to think that everything was going to the dogs: but he noted how many people agreed with his sombre picture of what lay ahead, and "seem to take it very much to heart".[68] There were very few who did not feel apprehensive at the suddenness and completeness of the change embodied in the legislation of 1867. Derby famously spoke of "a leap in the dark". The misgivings that Disraeli's sanguine exterior hid may be glimpsed in his remark to the Queen as the parties got ready to do battle over the Irish church: "It is, perhaps, providential that this religious controversy should have arisen to give a colour to the character, and a form to the action of the newly enfranchised constituencies".[69] The 1868 election was fought largely on that issue, which really belonged to the deliberately limited political warfare of the period between the first two Reform Acts, and not on questions which might have opened the dreaded era of class politics. Sensible men with strong views tried to read the omens. Typically, the Earl of Kimberley, who sat in all Gladstone's cabinets and considered himself a radical among Whig peers, was afraid of "a wild spirit of change taking possession of everyone and destroying Lords and Church and monarchy all together". Robert Lowe, visiting Hatfield in December 1868, defended the use of a vivid simile to describe what parliament had done in enacting the reform bill: "It is just like Niagara. Exactly where the rapids begin there is a strip of dead water through which a child might row a skiff".[70] Salisbury continued to anticipate radical, not revolutionary, developments in the foreseeable future. In that uneasy climate, his speeches were remembered for their prescience as well as for their courage.

*The Times* marked his departure to the Lords with an editorial that saw in him not the rebel now lost to politics but the convinced exponent of Tory ideas and feelings "in all their purity and strength". He had exceeded the modest hopes of his influential family: at the India Office he showed that he had vision in a post where bureaucracy usually subdued its political masters. Resignation from the Derby ministry and the duel with Disraeli in the House, where his strictures on the premier's conduct had been "excusably bitter . . . perhaps a little out of proportion", had made him a major figure on the political scene: "The sudden translation of such a statesman to the Lords must influence the course of our future history". Had he remained an MP he would have possessed a magnetic attraction for the "very large" element on the Tory benches who were dissatisfied with Disraeli. While the move to the upper House reduced his chances of leading the party, they had certainly not been extinguished. *The Times* emphasized the broadening of his outlook since he first entered the Commons.[71] There was no Tory who could match his eloquence, or his political courage. When Disraeli's stock fell sharply after household suffrage had delivered a Liberal victory at the polls, it was not only a high Tory like his friend Lord Bath who believed that Salisbury was destined to be the party's "eventual leader", if not many were yet willing to trust his judgement. Even as he denied Hertfordshire Tories his support, Salisbury was looking ahead to his role in the new parliament: telling Bath that, until Disraeli had ceased to lead the party, the Tory majority in the Lords should decide their tactics "without much reference" to their brethren in the other House.[72] He used speeches which he was invited to give at Manchester in October 1868 to let the public know how he viewed politics after the Reform Act. They were the first of numerous audiences he addressed in the great industrial towns over the next thirty years.

The Tory who had ventured to characterize the monarchy in parliamentary debate as politically dead was not afraid to think aloud about the fate of other institutions that were no longer sacrosanct. Describing himself as "a politician who, by the accident of politics, stands aside from the contests of the day",[73] he said of the Lords that the chamber did not deserve to survive if it could not hold its own in "the free and fair discussion of its merits". As for the Commons, he hoped that the impending election would see the return of independently minded MPs, "not mere supple slaves" of party and the voters.[74] A further speech was devoted to popular education from a political angle, and struck the note of urgency heard on all sides at that point, when it was a matter of educating the working-class electors in their responsibilities. English libertarianism, he felt, was too deeply ingrained for compulsory school attendance to be feasible. Nor could working-class families easily afford to lose the earnings of children taken from fields and factories and sent to school. Persuasion was a better method, and perhaps the only one: voluntary attendance really amounted to "self-education" on the part of those whom it was imperative to reach. The spread of education, meaning basic literacy and simple religious and moral instruction, was vital in a society "when all that is old is being questioned, and when . . . classes are being, as it were . . . set up . . . to judge of each other, to question each other's claims, and often to . . . array themselves against each other". It might not be long before the working classes were assailed by doctrines subversive of received political economy. Salisbury did not know whether those doctrines would prevail: but he contended that the ability of the masses to understand conflicting arguments at a popular level was the best prophylactic.[75]

More serious than any political unrest was a "far deeper disturbance", the exposure of Christian beliefs to the growing doubts of educated men, communicated to those with little or no education. There, too, the issue would ultimately be decided by the convictions of the national majority, formed anew by the diffusion of literacy and a greater familiarity with fundamental religious truths.[76] If this was Toryism, it took full account of changing conditions. The Manchester speeches foreshadowed the Salisbury of the 1880s, whose platform oratory inspired and directed a popular Conservatism which owed little to Disraelian opportunism. Salisbury sounded very like Gladstone in conservative mode. Neither spoke of the "alienation" of the masses, but it was clearly what they were concerned to prevent. Temperament and experience made Gladstone the more optimistic of the two – a legacy of his fruitful, if sometimes grudging, co-operation with Palmerston. Salisbury always considered that Gladstone was too inclined to quicken the pace of change unnecessarily in response to trends the development of which could be influenced by intelligent and determined resistance, as the history of Britain had demonstrated since the proclamation of American and French notions of equality. When, only a few years earlier, Cobden thought the Established Church and the landed class were "great realities" that would endure for another two generations, at least, there was every reason not to be rushed into making concessions at their expense.[77] From the Lords, Salisbury strove to moderate the Liberal legislation of 1869–70 on the Irish church and land, holding that it gave away more than the situation required to Irish nationalists and their British radical sympathizers.

61

# CHAPTER FOUR

## *The Conscience of the Party*

### The Master of Hatfield

On his father's death Salisbury came into an inheritance of 20 000 acres spread over a number of English counties, including valuable urban property in London and Liverpool; two-thirds of this acreage lay in Hertfordshire. He put his gross income in 1873 at £70 000 p.a.; it has been estimated at about £60 000 towards the end of his life. In the interval, agricultural rents fell heavily, by at least twenty per cent in Hertfordshire after the mid-1870s, while the income from urban holdings rose, yielding over £20 000 in London and £10 000 in Liverpool. There were also stock exchange investments: in correspondence with a family trustee, the ninth Earl Waldegrave, Salisbury expressed a preference for the bonds issued by the governments of settler colonies, as safe as Consols and offering another one per cent or more. His disposable income after encumbrances, allowing for an official salary of £5000 in most years from 1874, is impossible to calculate exactly from the surviving accounts, but was around £53 000 in 1873.[1] In the 1890s he still described his income as "largely agricultural", and therefore uncertain in view of the decline in farm rents.[2] It sufficed to maintain him in the style associated with a Victorian magnate; besides Hatfield his houses included a London residence, 20 Arlington Street, in the heart of the West End, rebuilt at a cost of £60 000 after his succession; and a Continental retreat, first at Dieppe, the Chalet Cecil, and then on the Riviera above Beaulieu. Salisbury's political independence rested in part on the wealth that buttressed the prestige of his high rank and historic name. The "upper ten thousand" who constituted the social world in which politicians moved and by which they were influenced, often in spite of themselves, treated landed magnates with respect unless they forfeited it by outrageous or absurdly eccentric behaviour.

It was not unusual for railways to have aristocratic chairmen. Salisbury accepted the chairmanship of the troubled Great Eastern Railway shortly before his father died: the annual salary of £700 was then attractive: the board's appointment of a former cabinet minister was meant to reassure restive shareholders who were going without their dividends. He stayed on until 1872 and played a leading part in the line's recovery. Whatever Edward Watkin, the entrepreneurial figure who brought him in, may have intended, Salisbury filled an executive, and not an ornamental role. Within a week of his arrival, he had given individual board members responsibility for one of six operating divisions under committees chaired by himself. He helped to arrange desperately needed finance from City brokers; he negotiated with rival companies, and acquired a thorough understanding of railway operations, on which he drew in later years at the India Office and the Foreign Office. The Great Eastern soon returned to the dividend list, although Salisbury did not get all his salary. It is evident that he enjoyed the challenge of restoring a large concern to financial health. His confident and successful performance was a far cry from the doubts and fears of early manhood when it seemed that his destiny was a country parsonage, or a life spent dabbling in literature and journalism. He left the company with a considerable reputation in railway boardrooms, one that contributed to the public impression of ability waiting for the opportunity to realize its full potential.[3]

Yet the moral climate of business filled him with distaste. His resignation was ostensibly submitted because politics, the Church and his responsibilities as a great landowner made increasing demands upon his time. In reality, he told Carnarvon, the chairmanship had become intolerable. It forced him to live "in an atmosphere of money, intrigue and corruption which he had no power to check and in which he dreaded, and indeed knew, that his name was continually used for personal ends and not very creditable interests".[4] This is an aspect of his involvement with the railways which has not been stressed by those who have written about it. As he was to argue from the platform in the 1890s, capitalism, subject to a degree of social control, exercised by the state and, more importantly, by the teachings of institutional religion, was always preferable to a socialism that must extinguish liberty. But the Great Eastern reinforced the impressions of his years in the City: while activities driven by profit above all other considerations might be indispensable to the economic growth that underpinned the most stable and the freest society in Europe, they were difficult to reconcile with Christian and aristocratic values. These were the misgivings of someone who had succeeded in business, not of a failure in that alien environment.

He was less successful in the management of his estates; unlike the railways, agriculture was not blessed with dynamic growth, and convention restricted a landlord in his dealings with tenants who, in law, might be subject to six months' notice to quit under the commonest form of tenure. The letter of tenancy-at-will concealed, in his words, "a sort of embryo tenant-right": on many estates, if not on all, an occupier's rent was fixed for life, and raised only with the advent of a new tenant, though reduced in bad seasons and the prolonged depression of the later nineteenth century. Moreover, it was customary to eschew a rack rent, in the proper sense. Such hereditary restraint on the part of landlords was the price of the deference they enjoyed from a rural middle class, the tenant farmers who resisted the overtures of urban radicals from the Anti-Corn Law League to Joseph Chamberlain in his "advanced Liberal" phase. It was an almost universal practice for landlords to bear the cost of the major items of capital expenditure on farms – another reason for the tenantry's attachment to the old order. Salisbury, an authority on English landownership has written, was a good landlord, but in no way exceptional; in ten years after 1868 he spent nearly £10 000 on farm buildings and cottages for labourers on his main property, the Hatfield estate; besides paying for a new church school in Hatfield itself. Like other good landlords, he was anxious to do what he could for the agricultural labourers, mostly employed by the big farmers; their condition troubled the contemporary social conscience. Radical criticism was directed not at the farmers for whom they worked, but at the landlords who let both farms and cottages.[5]

As someone in the public eye, Salisbury had a stronger motive than less politically active proprietors to tackle problems of rural housing. With due circumspection, the investigators of a royal commission in the late 1860s reported unfavourably in this respect on his Hertfordshire and Dorset property. He responded by investing substantially for a generation in the provision of utilitarian and sanitary cottages across the estate, let at rents that did not repay his expenditure. In Hatfield village, or town, where he rebuilt and developed, the rents of three-bedroom cottages, though still uneconomic, were too high for mere labourers; they were paid by his own estate workers on higher wages. The authority cited earlier concludes, a little unfairly, that his efforts represented "an attenuated or parsimonious philanthropy". Salisbury was a slum landlord on a small scale in London, too, and there he resolved the problem by clearing the sites or selling. At Liverpool building leases on farm land made him little more than a receiver of ground rents. Naturally, he and his wife took a close interest in the town at his gates; Salisbury's planning and benefactions shaped its growth. His urban resources – rents and land sales – went far to offset falling agricultural income; they were indispensable to the enlightened landlord and *grand seigneur*. It is a pattern familiar to historians of his class in that age.[6]

The suggestion that Salisbury was "largely indifferent" to the well-being of the working class and the under class on his urban property is mistaken.[7] If he was generally distanced from them by the leases of head tenants, he did not close his mind to the moral challenge and, in the mass, the political danger they represented. He had always been aware of the millions left behind in want and destitution by the Victorian economic miracle. The spectacle of "huge masses of toiling, hopeless poverty covered . . . by a thin crust of gorgeous luxury" oppressed him.[8] From the early 1870s he contemplated some kind of state intervention to save the responsible working class from being forced into the worst housing with the inevitable consequences for them and their children. On his small Essex property at Barking, in the process of being submerged by metropolitan expansion, he parted with some of it under conditions of sale which specified the erection of workmen's dwellings to be offered freehold by the builders.[9] At times the cares of ownership weighed heavily on him: he confessed, not altogether seriously, to dreaming of becoming a rentier, pure and simple, with his entire fortune invested in government stock. Such irresponsibility was not an option, even if it had been legally possible.

The maintenance of his inherited position absorbed a large slice of his income. The upkeep of Hatfield House was functional. His wife, dedicated to furthering her husband's career, entertained for him in Hertfordshire and London on a scale commensurate with his rank and political standing. Weekends at Hatfield, dinners and receptions at Arlington Street, attracted the more serious members of London society; there they met guests from overlapping worlds. The county also made its demands upon Salisbury's time and energy. Neighbouring squires were frequent visitors to Hatfield. Salisbury chaired the local bench and for years was prominent in the transaction of county business, without equalling his father's devotion to it. Husband and wife sought recreation abroad in their full lives when parliament was not sitting, and sometimes when it was. He built the Continental houses for them both. Typically English in their inconsistency, they combined suspicion of France as a European neighbour and a global rival with a fondness for holidays there, when they saw little of the French. A growing family and servants travelled with them. At home Salisbury had a laboratory for his amateur researches and installed electric light in the historic mansion, a pioneering innovation. In common with other men of professedly simple tastes, he found that his were not cheap. The library at Hatfield, to which he added considerably, was among his smaller expenses.[10]

He shunned, or was bored by, the conventional pastimes of his time and class. What this most intellectual of English grandees saved on horseflesh and gambling was needed to meet the family claims on his income. The heaviest of those was the £5000 a year secured to his father's widow, married again in 1870 to her longstanding admirer, Stanley, who had become one of the richest men in England on succeeding as the fifteenth Earl of Derby. She had by 1886 drawn £100 000 from the estates. Beset by falling rents, Salisbury let his strong feelings appear in the draft of a letter to his half-sister, Lady Galloway. Selling land to pay off mortgages dating from an era of agricultural prosperity, he was not inclined to do more than he had to under his father's will for Lady Derby's children, his half-brothers and half-sister. His attitude may have been influenced by the break with her second husband after Derby left the Foreign Office in 1878, believing that Salisbury had worked to force him out. As his sons grew up, each received £1000 a year and the younger ones entered the profession of their choice, the Bar, the army, and the Church. He had earlier had his half-brothers trained in engineering at the Great Eastern's workshops.[11] His impatience with the snobbery that worshipped rank for its own sake, divorced from its traditional functions, led his immediate family to call him "Citizen Salisbury". With the passage of time, he was more and more disposed to think that the peerage, as distinct from socially responsible wealth, had outlived its usefulness.[12]

## The House of Lords

Salisbury took his seat in the Lords as a Tory estranged from his party and doubtful whether it could ever again be a vehicle for the high-minded conservatism he embodied. Gladstone thought him "good and manly" in the midst of their conflict over the Irish church in 1869.[13] It is a specimen of the tributes that Salisbury elicited from opponents by his intelligent defence of interests which he recognised were ripe for reform. From 1869 it was to him that Tory peers looked for guidance rather than to their official leaders. He did not join the latter on the front bench until the beginning of 1870: the leadership might have been his soon after he arrived in the Lords but for his invincible objection to co-operating with Disraeli. Lord Cairns and the sixth Duke of Richmond, who in turn led the party in that House, had in practice to share their position with Salisbury. After, as before, he sat on their front bench, he refused to be tied to a party line. His stature was enhanced by his clarification in 1869 of the constitutional doctrine that encouraged the Lords to play a more dignified and effectual role than would otherwise have been theirs following the 1867 Reform Act. If he strained the doctrine in its application, the influence he wielded over the peers confirmed and extended the perception of him as the conscience of his party.[14] However, his inclusion in the Tory government formed after the 1874 election depended upon an accommodation with a triumphant Disraeli, which was not easily contrived. Possessing a comfortable majority, Disraeli did not have to find room for Salisbury, although his omission would have provided malcontents with a dangerously attractive figure round whom to rally. It says much for Disraeli's judgement that he resisted the temptation he undoubtedly felt to leave Salisbury out.

The powers of the Lords were effectively diminished by the constitutional crisis of 1831–2.[15] For that reason no statutory reform was necessary before the Parliament Act of 1911. The Duke of Wellington acknowledged the Chamber's weakness in the face of a Commons majority and the public opinion of a new industrial England when he advised the peers in 1846 not to throw out Peel's bill repealing the Corn Laws: they would be compelled to submit when it was sent up to them again with the minimum of delay. In his days as a *Saturday* reviewer, Salisbury had more than once echoed the widespread view of the upper House as dying of inanition. Attendances were often tiny – an uncomfortable fact disguised to some extent by the use of proxies in divisions. The atmosphere of quite important debates was lifeless, and proceedings were sometimes a travesty. Supporters of the hereditary principle like himself "must resist the voluntary abdication of those who represent it . . . The peerage must survive a deliberate condemnation by the peers". The country's political health required an active, genuinely independent second chamber.[16] It was in this spirit that he took his seat in the Lords; its rationale and composition were overdue for reconsideration. He spoke and voted for Earl Russell's life peerages bill in April 1869: "We belong too much to one class", he told his order, ". . . with respect to a large number of questions we are all too much of one mind"; a bourgeois element, judiciously selected, would do the House nothing but good. He followed this up in June with one of his major speeches, in which he framed a coherent, updated theory of the peers' constitutional function that was generally acceptable. In doing so, he almost certainly secured an extended lease of life for the unreformed Lords, and won recognition of a statesmanship he had not been thought to possess outside Indian affairs.[17]

Explaining his decision to vote for the second reading of the Gladstone government's bill disestablishing the Irish church, he depicted the Lords as trustee for the nation and not subordinate to the Commons. He had already conceded in 1868, on the precedents, that the House must give way "on those rare and great occasions on which the national mind has fully declared itself", when he argued that the question of Irish disestablishment had not yet been decided in that conclusive fashion. The electorate delivered its verdict at the end of the year: and he used his opening speech on the subsequent legislation to turn an admission of defeat into a vindication of the Lords' continuing relevance to the political process. Ninety-nine times out of a hundred the nation as a whole took no interest in the politics of Westminster, he said sweepingly. In those circumstances their chamber had complete discretion to accept or reject measures passed by the other House. But when the voters of Scotland, Ireland and Wales, and "more doubtfully and languidly" those of England where the Liberal majority was small, had ruled on the question of the hour, "it is no courage . . . no dignity to withstand the real opinion of the nation . . . to delay an inevitable issue . . . to invite . . . discontent, and possibly . . . worse than discontent". He had so defined the Lords' obligation to defer to the electorate, not to the Commons, as to leave the peers a very wide freedom: only a government mandated by the voters to enact a specific measure could summon the House to yield. Moreover, he reserved to the Lords an indeterminate right to amend the detail of such legislation.[18]

On this second reading of the Irish church bill, Salisbury's eloquence saved the peers and his party from certain humiliation. He and Carnarvon, with Bath as their unofficial whip, had prepared the ground carefully. They led nearly forty Tories into the government lobby to give the measure a majority of thirty-three, implementing the flexible approach to unwelcome change discussed between them in their conversations of 1867. Now it was Disraeli who fought, or professed to fight, in the last ditch. The "foul fetish worship"[19] – Carnarvon's description – with which the party rewarded his success in carrying the reform bill had been replaced by continuous speculation about his future as leader. So weak was his authority after losing the 1868 election that his close associate, Lord Cairns, asked to take over the leadership in their House, enquired of Salisbury whether he would be willing to assume it.[20] Although Salisbury declined to fill a position which would force him to work closely with Disraeli, he and Carnarvon did not dissociate themselves from Cairns. The official Tory resistance to the Irish church bill was more apparent than real: a consciously futile, if prolonged, protest in the Commons, one which Disraeli, Cairns, Stanley and others hesitated to repeat in the Lords. It was the former leader, Derby, old and failing, who came out strongly against the second reading; his prestige drew the official leadership after him. Some Tories in the Lords entertained a death wish: "[they] say . . . , not wholly without reason", wrote Stanley, "that they may as well be abolished as live under a perpetual threat of extinction".[21] Salisbury and Carnarvon had argued their case unsuccessfully at a meeting of Tory peers: but while their opponents voted to throw out the bill, they were plainly relieved to be rescued by the organized defection to the government side. The Liberals, too, were grateful for Salisbury's "admirable" speech and the action of his group. Apart from a handful of radicals, they did not want to have recourse to an agitation against the Lords which might take them further than they wished to go.[22]

Ministers had counted on Salisbury to avert a constitutional crisis at that stage of the bill's progress through the Lords. They were well aware that a divided opposition would unite to press amendments in committee unacceptable to Liberals and their Irish allies. Through his stepmother, they sounded Salisbury; she had opined that he might respond positively. He insisted on absolute secrecy for the resulting interview with Gladstone, and was not satisfied with what he learnt. In equally confidential exchanges with Granville, the Liberal leader in the Lords, he let it be known that his hopes and those of his friends centred on an amendment (Carnarvon's) to increase substantially the capital sum available to the disestablished and partly disendowed Church from compulsory commutation of the annuities payable to her beneficed clergy. Salisbury and Carnarvon worked with Cairns, Archbishop Tait of Canterbury, and some dissentient Liberal peers on this and other amendments that salvaged much more of the establishment's wealth than the government was pre-pared to allow. He also supported giving their glebes to the clergy while using the Church's resources to make similar provision for Catholic priests and Presbyterian ministers. He was scathing about the appropriation of endowments for secular purposes, such as the building of lunatic asylums, when enlightened opinion across the political divide favoured a modest concurrent endowment of all the major Irish denominations. This was not one of the amendments on which the Lords voted to insist on the Commons' rejection of changes, which would have restored, Gladstone calculated, nearly ninety per cent of the sum at stake.[23]

The prime minister wished to drop the bill for that session, and expose the Lords to an agitation against the abuse of their power. They had travestied the measure to which they had consented in principle. The cabinet demurred; even Bright, who had just publicly menaced the peers with the consequences of obduracy, felt, on reflection, that an agitation was "premature, and likely to create social disturbance". Salisbury was for standing firm on Carnarvon's amendment and others that still gave the church an extra £800 000, compared with three to four millions when the Lords sent the bill back to the Commons. Although Cairns had agreed this stance with Salisbury, there was pressure from every quarter to isolate the latter. The Court, the primate and Disraeli were all opposed to a confrontation between the Houses, unwanted by many, if not most, Liberal MPs. In the end, Gladstone and Granville gave away little more than they had envisaged at the start of the argument with the Lords: only £280 000 on their computation; rather more, according to the other side. The settlement was reached without Salisbury, and came as a surprise to him.[24] But he was an unseen presence at Cairns' "marvellous" negotiation with Granville on 22 July, and one to which the Tory leader alluded unhappily. When the Houses were informed later that day, Carnarvon shared the general relief, but Salisbury implied that in Cairns' place he would have held out for better terms. Derby, wholeheartedly behind the man who had left his cabinet over the reform bill, walked out of the Chamber in disgust at the opposition's surrender.[25]

Cairns was a casualty of his success in helping to avert the crisis which Gladstone and Salisbury, left to themselves, would have precipitated. The Lords' right to insist on their amendments had not proved sustainable in a test of strength with the first House of Commons elected on household suffrage in the boroughs. Their leader's circular apologising to Tory peers for failing to consult "all, or even some" of them before he settled with the government, did not silence the criticisms of this middle-class Ulster lawyer. He pleaded anxiety at a deteriorating situation, and inadvertently rubbed salt into his followers' wounds. They associated him with a collective loss of nerve: his response was to give up the leadership in the autumn. Disraeli, and at first Cairns, wanted to fill the vacancy with Stanley, who succeeded to his father's earldom in October 1869 – an old and loyal but not uncritical friend of Disraeli's whom the ex-premier regarded as his destined successor in the party leadership. Salisbury ruled himself out: he could not work with Disraeli; nor was he ambitious for the post. His relations with the new Earl of Derby had cooled since the reform bill divided them politically: but he was willing to second Richmond in proposing his election at a meeting of Tory peers on 19 February.[26] At this juncture Derby revealed that he had no stomach for the task: "My habit of mind", he told himself, "is not that of a partisan . . . [and] the Conservative party is in a minority which seems likely to be permanent". The difficulties he feared were real enough: in his supporting speech Salisbury had been careful to say that he would not pledge himself unconditionally "on all points, especially those other than secular"; a refer- ence to Derby's ill-concealed distaste for the religious aspect of Toryism. The sixth Duke of Northumberland, who had held minor office under the elder Derby, spoke for other peers when he referred at the meeting to his profound disillusionment with the party.[27]

While he did not oppose Derby's election, Cairns had already decided that Salisbury was the best choice. It would not be necessary for Disraeli and Salisbury to have much to do with each other: an opinion which, he reminded Carnarvon, should be taken in the context of an earlier discussion between them. Disraeli did not believe he would be prime minister again, and Cairns thought the party in the Commons was "gone for the moment". For the exposition of a distinctive Toryism they must rely on the Lords; that House would supply the next Tory premier. Derby said he was not going to sacrifice himself to others' notions of his duty. Now that his father was dead, he meant to stay "somewhat aloof" from the party and use his influence with Liberals who shared his moderate and secular outlook. There remained Salisbury. Carnarvon was deputed to make another approach to him after conferring with Malmesbury, a former leader in the Lords, Colville, the opposition whip in the House, and Richmond. They went over the arguments that Carnarvon put to Salisbury: he and his front bench would act quite independently of Disraeli; without a strong leader the Tory majority in the Lords was in danger of crumbling, and the Church's interests would suffer severely as a result. Salisbury, and Hardy in the Commons, considered the suggested independence of the Tories in the upper House quite impracticable: the pressure to co-operate with Disraeli and the party in the Commons would be unremitting and irresistible from the force of circumstances. If the singular arrangement could be made to work, it must expose the Tories to Liberal mockery of their palpable disunity. Disraeli with his talent for intrigue would have ample scope for isolating him, again. In the nature of things, the front bench peers' promises to stand by him could not be kept.[28]

If he could never have been described as a good party man, Salisbury's clear- sightedness prevented him from trying to ignore for any length of time the reality that the clash of parties regulated the pace of change in his country. Belonging to the more conservative of the two parties, and perhaps because it was historically the champion of the Establishment's special interests, he was obliged to resume the leading part in its action that was his by common consent. The last sentence of his letter to Carnarvon refusing to stand for the leadership in the Lords, acknowledged a duty to party unity, without which the Tories could not function as a brake on Gladstonian legislation. "The truth of the matter", he concluded, "is that the worst leader who could act with the leader in the . . . Commons would be better than one who could not." He would have liked to see Hardy in Disraeli's place, but there was no immediate prospect of that. When he agreed to propose a reluctant Richmond as leader, the Duke publicly asked him and Carnarvon to sit on the front bench. Salisbury said he sat where he did because there had been no alternative, but nevertheless acceded to Richmond's "earnest and personal request". It was understood that he and Carnarvon were not bound to go with the party against their deepest convictions. This was a turning-point: the author of "The Past and Future of Conservative Policy" in the *Quarterly Review* for October 1869 took the fight against Disraelian tactics into the inner councils of Toryism, from which he had excluded himself in February 1867.[29]

Salisbury correctly surmised, first, that Gladstone's evolving Liberalism might make a not particularly contentious promise of some land reform for Ireland into a radical measure. Secondly, he foresaw that the premier would then bring cabinet colleagues into line by reminding them of Disraeli's indifference to principle when it impeded a parliamentary combination that served his ambition for office and power. "The one great danger the moderate Liberal . . . has to guard against is the radicalism of the Conservative party": Salisbury's purpose on the front bench was to ensure that the moderates in the governing party could rely on the official opposition to defend positions common to them. That was, he insisted, the only policy for Conservatives worthy of the name after a defeat on the scale of 1868. His relations with Richmond were usually good and got better, despite the strain to which they were subjected when he effectively usurped the Duke's leadership, as he did on Irish land, University tests and the ballot in 1870, 1871 and 1872.[30] Richmond, in Derby's opinion, was clearly out of his depth, while Salisbury "destroys by violence the effect of his undoubted ability". Even Carnarvon's loyalty to his friend was sorely tried when Salisbury complained of the "intrigues and diplomacy" by which the two front benches in the Lords arranged the passage of controversial bills with the minimum of amendment. Salisbury's "violence" expressed a rational concern to preserve a significant power to amend legislation in the Lords. With the approval of the majority of Tory peers on the backbenches, he determined to resist the reduction of the House to a "purely decorative" place in the constitution; threatening to join his supporters on those benches if he could not fight the battle from his seat beside Richmond.[31]

Richmond endured the desertion of Tory peers to Salisbury in consecutive sessions. The Commons prevailed in the unequal struggle; but temporary, if repeated, disarray in the Tory ranks was preferable to a permanent split with repercussions for the party in the Commons and the country. However, as a possible successor to Disraeli, or another, Salisbury lost by his inflexible and ultimately futile opposition to a strong Liberal ministry when public opinion did not run against major bills, if it was not enthusiastic for them after 1869. Carnarvon felt that Salisbury's judgement was clouded by "the feeling of extreme irritation at the 'humiliating' position which he thinks we occupy". For peers with expectations of office, which Disraeli encouraged in Carnarvon, the Lords' position, although diminished, held many attractions; they recoiled from the constantly renewed prospect of an unwanted constitutional crisis that might put an end to their hopes, and to other things. But Richmond, and Cairns on whom the Duke leant heavily, could not do without their awkward and brilliant colleague. He might be much too combative: his wish to make the Lords work, in both senses, as a condition of the House's survival, was undoubted. When sitting, the peers should have "some employment . . . beneficial both to us and to . . . legislation", he told Cairns at the start of a session in which they had to wait for a big government bill to come up to them.[32]

The resilience of the mature Salisbury on which Henry Acland commented was evident in the good humour with which he shouldered the burdens of the bench with Richmond and others. There is in the Duke's papers a delicious letter from the last days of the 1872 session, when Salisbury was holding the fort for colleagues who had mostly dispersed for the long recess. "I delivered your firman to Colonsay", he wrote to his leader, "(first pressing it reverently to my forehead): but I regret to say he did not receive it as one of the faithful . . . a majority could not be got together on any terms . . .". An "episcopal ruffian", the combative Tory bishop who wanted to attack the government's treatment of a church school, had perforce been given a similar answer: "All your faithful servants have . . . fled . . . I, only I, remain, and shall get up a quarrel with somebody unless you speedily come back."[33] If the Duke was not devoid of a sense of humour, Salisbury's tone in such private exchanges struck people as unusual, further proof that he lacked "bottom", that quality prized by the cautious mediocrities who gather at the top of political parties. They were apprehensive of his contrasting "wild elephant mood", defiant of friend and foe alike, which took possession of him when Gladstone's first Irish land bill came before the House. Its encroachments upon the rights of landed property were imperfectly concealed by the premier's insistence that they represented the recognition of, or approximation to, the powerful customary tenant-right of Ireland. Derby, who was not easily frightened, saw the measure as "more revolutionary in principle than any . . . which Parliament has yet sanctioned". For that very reason, government and opposition co-operated to avoid giving the principle unwelcome publicity.[34]

The bill passed its second reading in the Lords without a division. Richmond was appallingly frank; rejection was not an option: "Next year we should have to discuss a measure worse, if anything could be worse, than the bill now before us." Salisbury did not seek to force a vote at that stage. To the Irish landlords sitting all round him in the Chamber, he said the government's proposals showed that the Irish landed class had been decisively beaten by their enemies "and are not capable of holding their own in the open fight of politics". Continental experience strongly suggested the wisdom of replacing or supplementing large estates by the peasant proprietors whose emergence was to be encouraged by the land purchase clauses of the legislation. These remarks contain the germ of his later Irish policy in the

1880s and 1890s, and are consequently of great importance.[35] From his days as a *Saturday* reviewer Salisbury had no illusions about the strength of Irish national feeling, and its pervasive influence on the conflict between a Celtic tenantry and their landlords.[36] What he wished to remove from the bill in committee were provisions which might cross the water, and especially that for compensation for disturbance on eviction in the absence of custom entitling the tenant to the value of his occupancy-right. To justify such compensation by pointing to the hardship inflicted furnished an obvious precedent for agitators in the periodic visitations of distress to which industrial Britain was prone. Why should not the British working man receive so many years' wages on being "disturbed" in his employment? "The difference . . . is this . . . in England we put up with loss of bread, and in Ireland they shoot . . . a paternal Parliament therefore compensates the Irish to induce them not to shoot their landlords." It was hard to fault the trenchant reasoning.[37]

Bent, therefore, on limiting the eligibility for compensation for disturbance to the poorest tenants, Salisbury carried an amendment to that effect by 119 votes to 101. Richmond voted with the government, protesting that Salisbury's action was "not judicious": tenants of holdings above the ceiling that Salisbury sought to impose were "a very important class" and would determine the reception of the bill in the countryside. The government was not helped by an admission in debate from a Liberal elder statesman, Lord Halifax, shortly afterwards taken into Gladstone's cabinet as a reward for his loyalty on Irish land in particular: "it was better for the landlords . . . to make some sacrifice . . .", he said, "cheaper to make compensation than to be shot".[38] Salisbury exploited this confirmation of the view he had taken: but Gladstone was unmoved by the Lords' rebellion, "the Commons will stand firm, and if so of course we win". Salisbury's amendment was reversed, as were most of the changes that Richmond supported. The premier and Granville, the Liberal leader in the Lords, did what they could by small concessions to bolster the Duke's authority after the blow Salisbury had dealt it. Salisbury maintained to the last that compensation for disturbance could only be justified as "eleemosynary"; applied to larger holdings, it was "Socialistic".[39]

Tory peers, meeting at the Carlton Club, had reconsidered their amendments – "or, rather, one amendment", Salisbury's – after Richmond, aided by Cairns, had negotiated with ministers. At that gathering, Salisbury argued for continued resistance, while his opponents felt that the point at issue, for all its significance, was not one on which they could appeal to the electorate. The Lords should never try to face down the Commons unless "we had the sense of the country to back us". A majority of the peers went with the Duke and Cairns: Salisbury saw his amendment excised by 130 votes to 48. Yet next year they acted on the constitutional doctrine he had defined for them, and rejected the ballot bill on the ground that it had not been put before the voters in 1868. The government waited until the following session and sent the bill up again. Salisbury persisted with the argument rejected at the Carlton Club in July 1870: it was the Commons, and not the peers, who must have the country at their back: "the nation is our master . . . the House of Commons is not . . . [we] yield . . . only when the judgement of the nation has been challenged at the polls and decidedly expressed".[40]

The Commons could not be expected to submit to this interpretation of the relationship between the Houses, one that, as Salisbury observed, invested the Lords with an almost complete independence such as they had not enjoyed since 1832. Richmond, whose inadequacy as a leader had been "painfully apparent", and, with the exception of Salisbury, the whole front bench abstained on the second reading. The latter protested unavailingly that if the Lords were becoming "a mere copying-machine for the decrees of the Commons", their usefulness was gone. As it was, they had to be content with being a revising chamber which might, if and when public opinion was behind it, venture to defy the other House. That modest function, and the possibility of a moment of decisive importance, were enough for peers who valued their dignified place in the constitution. Even when the Lords were probably in the right, as when they condemned Gladstone's use of the royal prerogative to abolish the purchase system in the army, thus circumventing their obstruction, Salisbury's language disturbed the more thoughtful Tories, although it pleased many peers. To Derby, with the insight derived from personal knowledge, it seemed that he was "rather gratifying his taste in displaying contempt for Parliament and popular institutions than seriously defending an institution in which he had faith".[41] Salisbury was in fact coming to terms with the advent of democracy after 1867, that irreversible change: but to an unusual extent his was a religious perspective in which politics and politicians exhibited their full share of human failings. His religiosity, as critics deemed it, antagonized some Tories and some Liberals, but commended him to others. The Church meant more to him than any secular concern, and much more than the House of Lords.

## The Church and Her Enemies

A High Churchman from his precocious youth, Salisbury was active in the defence of the Establishment, viewed from a Tractarian angle, during the lengthy interval between leaving Derby's cabinet and entering Disraeli's. Sensitive to the intellectual currents flowing away from orthodox Christianity, he took a leading part in resisting the liberalization of Anglican beliefs and attitudes which had exercised him, in common with other staunch Churchmen, for many years. The old latitudinarianism of Whigs and Liberals, to which the Oxford Movement had been a response, was merging with pressures for a modern faith to be reflected in liturgy and doctrine. The advance of Broad Church ideas among the educated sapped the Church's will to fight off the demands of militant Nonconformity, itself affected by a subtly changing religious climate. He was not, however, an extreme High Churchman, disapproving as he did of the provocation offered to Protestant England by the tendency to introduce or revive Catholic ritual in Anglican worship. His fear was that the reaction to an unwise enthusiasm for the externals of religion would expose the essence of the High Church creed, its sacramentalism, to persecution within the Church, and perhaps bring down a divided Establishment. The storm of feeling that carried through the Public Worship Regulation Act in 1874 showed his apprehensions to have been well founded. The ecclesiastics with whom he had most to do

– H.P. Liddon, Malcolm MacColl, Nathaniel Woodard and his young cousin, Edward Talbot – were all High Churchmen. Salisbury opened his heart to no one except his wife, who embraced the High Church cause with a partisan fervour, but his confidences to these four clergymen help to determine where he stood in religious matters. An unobtrusive piety – the weekly Communion he advocated – accompanied realistic assessments of the Church's problems. The weakness of overt anti-clericalism in this country did not mean that the future of religion was secure.[42]

Liddon was a controversial figure; one of the leaders of the High Church and a celebrated preacher.[43] Lady Salisbury, a great admirer of his, brought him to Hatfield, where he became a fairly frequent visitor. Her husband made use of him to counsel moderation to the more combative of their party in the Church, but Salisbury had little sympathy with this eminent clergyman's Romanizing bent. He urged other High Churchmen to shun a feature of Roman Catholicism which attracted Liddon and his kind: "Don't come forward in any way as the champion of confession. It is running your head against the very biggest of stone walls." Few things were more offensive to Protestants, and he shared the public hostility to its adoption reflected in the newspapers. "Thinking men", he told the House of Lords, concurred in objecting to a practice "unfavourable to . . . Christian truth [and] . . . injurious to the moral independence and virility" of peoples amongst whom it prevailed; perhaps nothing had so profoundly influenced national characters. He associated himself with English "abhorrence" of the idea of someone spiritually empowered to come between the head of a family and his wife and children.[44] These robust Protestant sentiments, which set him firmly apart from the High Church represented by Liddon, made Salisbury an effective defender of the larger body of Anglican opinion covered by the term "High". Liddon cultivated him as such; the core of Tractarian belief – the Catholicity of Anglicanism – united them. So did the menace of disestablishment, which Lord Spencer, a younger member of the Gladstone ministry in the classic Whig mould, favoured for England "at the ripe time" after the relatively painless operation in Ireland. Salisbury did not think disestablishment was imminent, but he advised Liddon that where possible the Church's money should be put into trusts devised to fall outside the scope of an English Church Act.[45]

Broad and Low Church combined to press for a contentious change in the liturgy, the omission of the Athanasian Creed, rescued from desuetude by the Tractarians. To Liddon and Pusey this was a question "of vital importance". Salisbury could not agree: the Athanasian Creed lacked authority; no other church gave this sixth-century production the same place in worship.[46] If its revival was an example of the Tractarians' indiscriminate enthusiasm for the past, the dropping of this creed would be interpreted as a victory for the High Church's enemies. Liddon worked on a hesitant Salisbury for two years: High Churchmen were waiting on the outcome of this battle; should it be lost "we shall be very near a disruption, if not actually face to face with it".[47] To the repeated threats of secession from the Establishment, Salisbury replied that they were "hardly consistent with any kind of ecclesiastical order or subordination". He consulted Gladstone as to the course which the two High Churchmen should take. Meetings to support the Athanasian Creed must show up the weakness of High Churchmen and stimulate their foes in parliament, who heavily outnumbered them there, especially in the Commons. It would be much better to rely on the prime minister and a Tractarian lord chancellor to prevent parliament from moving in the matter. Gladstone and Lord Selborne, the former Roundell Palmer, were as good as their word. It was to reassure the High Churchmen who talked of seceding that Salisbury finally consented to speak at a meeting called by Bishop Wilberforce in November 1872 and again at a rally in St James's Hall some weeks later.[48]

The political friends of the High Church at Winchester House, Tories mostly, urged restraint on the clergy present, headed by Pusey. Salisbury warned them not to act independently of the government – in the persons of Gladstone and Selborne – or of the primate, Archbishop Tait, with whom he was in touch. His message to everyone was the imperative need to avoid parliamentary interference. In agreeing to speak at St James's Hall, he took his stand on the impolicy of appearing to call doctrine in question by removing the Athanasian Creed from the liturgical cycle. Once he had decided to speak, he employed language to satisfy the most uncompromising of High Churchmen. He dwelt on "the terrible danger of teaching . . . in the present temper of men's minds, that dogma is of small account, and that men may safely tamper with their faith". Who was to amend the liturgy? The House of Commons was wholly unsuited to the task. The 3000 signatories of Lord Shaftesbury's petition for the removal of this long and detailed creed from the Prayer Book were unrepresentative, "a large assemblage of the rich and educated . . . [although] I am not accustomed in other matters to object to a certain flavour of aristocratic doctrine". The alliance of the Broad Church and the Low in the interests of a more comprehensive religion, attractive to Dissenters and doubters, was thoroughly misguided: "Behind the scrupulous consciences we see the vast forces of unbelief."[49] *The Times* criticized Salisbury for making a difficult situation worse by opposing all change; he, and others like him, would be to blame if there were a "violent" end to the tensions within the Church. Salisbury was equally conscious of external perils to the Church, comparing her to "a beleaguered city" in another speech on the previous day. The besiegers he singled out for mention were the militant Dissenters, whose susceptibility to a new theology he noted.[50]

A sense of duty had driven Salisbury to address the organizations that endeavoured to inform and direct the response of Anglicans to all the problems crowding in upon them. The atmosphere was not congenial to his fastidious spirit: "What a beargarden it was", he wrote feelingly after a visit to the Church congress at Leeds in October 1872 which he hoped he would never have to repeat. There he appealed for tolerance of what might seem to be the excesses of some High Churchmen in ritual. The differences between parties in the Church went deep: they had all to accept responsibility for the "unhappy civil war" that had raged for decades. "Either you must take the line of Alba, or the line of Gamaliel": he invited his hearers to make the choice they thought was consistent with "the mind of Scripture" and the Church's well-being.[51] Their divisions imperilled Christianity itself, as in the University Tests Act of 1871 which ended the Anglican monopoly of teaching posts in Oxford and Cambridge without the stringent reservations that Salisbury tried to insert. Chancellor of Oxford since 1869, he saw himself as fighting to preserve its

Christian character from creeping secularization. It was a losing battle, not least because the bishops were disinclined to prolong it. The Commons had first approved the abolition of university tests in 1862; since then the number of Dissenting MPs had more than doubled to sixty-three, all but one of them Liberals. Salisbury fought a skilful delaying action, emphasizing that Dissenters would not be the real beneficiaries of the reform. If his own faith was unshaken, the development of the physical sciences and a deeper knowledge of Eastern religions were eroding the old religious certainties. Christianity in the universities was already being emptied of its content by clerical dons to whom its central doctrines were at best allegories.[52]

They had to deal, he said, when the university tests bill which the peers rejected in 1869 came up to them again, with "earnest men of clear and powerful intellect, honest, pure in the morality . . . they have derived from the Christianity . . . they repudiate, who seek with all the earnestness of religious propaganda to overturn the religion in which they have been brought up. That is . . . the enemy".[53] He feared the influence of J.S. Mill a great deal more than that of Evangelical Dissent. The bill of 1870 was diverted, on his motion, to a select committee whose inquiries, together with his Oxford correspondence, led him to frame a remarkable amendment to the bill that passed in 1871. He sought to impose a declaration upon lecturers and tutors binding them not to inculcate anything contrary to "the teaching or divine authority of . . . the Old and New Testament". Theological liberalism, well established in English universities, had paved the way for "the most terrible . . . results" on the Continent, and would do so in England unless held back by statutory safeguards. The aim was to deny teachers the principal instrument of subversion, superficially attractive to liberals of every kind, "the idea that all beliefs should be submitted for free selection to the consciences and intelligences of their pupils".[54] Salisbury carried the amendment by only five votes, opposed by the primate and several other prelates. A majority of the bishops voting supported the government when the Commons obliged the peers to remove a clause that offended against the spirit of the legislation. The High Churchmen were divided: the more realistic among them appreciated that Gladstone risked his hold on the party over this bill. With Tory backing, he defied a large majority of Liberals in the Commons to save clerical headships and clerical fellowships from abolition, and forced through a Lords' amendment to ensure that colleges continued to provide religious instruction for their Anglican undergraduates.[55]

Afterwards Salisbury reiterated his fear that Oxford must become "a nucleus and focus of infidel teaching and influence". It was soon clear to him that orthodox religion stood to gain from the climate of opinion – educated opinion, that is – of which the Act was evidence. Discussing Oxford trends with Liddon, he thought the emergence of unbelief into the open "a much healthier state of things . . . people would know where they were going".[56] He did not want their clerical guides to be driven out of the great universities and located exclusively in the theological colleges that had sprung up in his lifetime. Salisbury much preferred "the citizen . . . to the seminary type of clergy"; that was one of the points on which he parted from Liddon. If the clergy were not to be "a separate class", a priestly caste but integrated, as they had been since the Reformation, with the upper and middle classes from which they came, their orthodoxy should be overseen by the state and not consigned to the care of a purely ecclesiastical tribunal. Salisbury was not as keen as were leading Churchmen on reorganizing the work of the ecclesiastical courts: but for the expense of litigation the factions in the Church would "fly at each other's throats".[57] He doubted the wisdom of the argument put to him by Bishop Magee of Peterborough, a Tory in politics but no High Churchman, that "The wine of the nineteenth century cannot be held in the bottles of the sixteenth". Like the bishop, he placed his trust in an appellate jurisdiction in ecclesiastical cases that was secular: the judicial committee of the Privy Council set up by Erastian Whigs in 1833, or the House of Lords in its capacity as the final court of appeal, which, with his approval, was to have replaced the judicial committee under a general reform of the English courts.[58]

Assuming that the Establishment would prove stronger than its factions, Salisbury concerned himself particularly with its educational mission, to which the Acts of 1869 on endowed schools and of 1870 on elementary schooling, posed a threat that he was not inclined to underestimate. He started from the proposition that "the idea of paternal government was not our idea of a free, independent, and self-supporting government". It should not be forgotten that in the previous decade Mill had made a strong libertarian case against state education: but everyone who thought as he did, Tory or radical, had been obliged to accept the 1870 Act which, in Salisbury's words, "degraded us to the level of a paternal government". That speech at Manchester in 1872 reminds us that English Tories were often libertarians too. What Salisbury most disliked about the new legislation was the compromise on religious teaching under school boards that were to supplement the Churches' provision of elementary education. To appease political Nonconformists, and the significant element among Anglican Liberals who favoured comprehension, Gladstone acquiesced in the arrangements for religious instruction on an undenominational basis ironically designated "Board school religion". "Unsectarian religion", said Salisbury when these arrangements had been put into practice, "meant no religion at all". Christianity's tremendous achievements were the work of "intense religious enthusiasm sprung out of an intense and definite belief".[59] Yet he did not then think of upsetting the compromise which his fellow High Churchmen had effected with a view to taking the political pressure off the Church and her schools. As an MP in the mid-1860s, Salisbury had seen in the Education Department under the Vice-President of the Council an enemy to the independence and distinctive identity of Church schools; and its enmity to them remained his preoccupation after 1870. Like Mill again, he thought bureaucracy should be kept out of education and the role of the state confined to providing the subvention necessary if schools were to be accessible to the poor.[60]

"I have a profound distrust of government inspectors, and am generally disposed to find them wrong", he told Woodard.[61] It was a prejudice that never left him; he distinguished between a collectivism recognized, increasingly, as inevitable and desirable, having due regard to liberty and property, and the accompanying growth of officialdom, with an inherent tendency to seek the expansion of its powers. The Education Department was, moreover, biased from its inception against denominationalism. Under the 1870 Act the decision to establish Board schools where the existing denominational provision did not suffice lay with the department. Salisbury expressed *a* Church view when he complained of "the practical oppressiveness" with which officials exercised that power of decision, "though of course I do not mean to impute to them anything but undue routine". Especially where inspectors showed themselves to be "incompetent and imperious" – revealing epithets – managers of Church schools were being denied the opportunity to satisfy the department that they had the resources to meet the estimated demand for places.[62] There were still, in the early 1870s, many more Church than Board schools: but as a method of funding minimal fees the school rate levied by the elective boards possessed a buoyancy wanting in the mixture of Treasury grants and voluntary contributions, clerical and lay, on which the Church relied. Nor were Churchmen united in wishing to maintain the dominant Anglican presence in education, at this and higher levels, without diluting its character. The Broad Church Bishop of Manchester, James Fraser, looked to the convergence of Church and Chapel, through mutually acceptable religious instruction in the schools; it was "the only hope of . . . not only the Church, but even Christianity in this country . . . if men like Lord Salisbury do not succeed in stopping the way, as now". The Conservative party organizer, J.E. Gorst, drew Salisbury's attention to the co-operation of Churchmen and Dissenters on school boards in industrial Yorkshire, making the best of undenominational religion. Those Churchmen were anxious that a partisan spirit should not disturb a working relationship.[63]

Salisbury dismissed Bishop Fraser's arguments as a total surrender of the Anglican position. At the same time he was well aware that the Church militant he seemed to embody was at a permanent disadvantage in controversy. The clericalism of which the High Church stood accused had many enemies and few friends; it elicited an inveterate hostility to so unEnglish a phenomenon. "Politicians were afraid of the Church's curse – they rather like it now", he observed. He had some success in his fight against the Endowed School Commissioners, charged by the Liberals' Act of 1869 to revise the statutes of foundations that were overwhelmingly Anglican. Their tendency was not only to weaken the Church's hold on these schools but to confirm them as middle-class institutions at the expense of the poor scholars favoured by long dead benefactors.[64] Salisbury based his criticism of the Commission's schemes on social as much as religious grounds. The Christians of another age gave away their money: "the philosophic enthusiast of the present" made free with other people's benefactions. While middle-class education, in which he continued to interest himself through the Woodard schools, was undeniably important, "I believe it to be a greater and nobler work to feed the hungry . . . clothe the naked, and . . . educate the poor".[65]

The beginning of the 1870s was peculiarly unsettling for committed adherents of Anglican Christianity who tried, apprehensively, to read the signs of the times. In their minds, the fall of the Establishment in Ireland, the coming of "unsectarian religion" in English schools and the end of university tests, pictured as one of the last bastions of belief, were linked with a more dramatic event, the Paris Commune, the harbinger of the apostasy and revolution forecast by prophets of the Continental

Left. If England was unlikely to see a similar explosion, she was not immune to the inroads of the advancing religion of humanity. "How long do you think they will remain (in a composite sense) Christian?", Salisbury asked Woodard, who had owned to a qualified confidence in the Christianity of the universities. Gathorne Hardy on the Tory front bench in the Commons was no more optimistic. After watching Gladstone, under fire from supporters who considered that the University Tests Bill made too many exceptions in the interests of the Church, Hardy reflected on "Such formidable signs of growing revolutionism. No trusts or endowments are sacred and the appetite for their consumption by the state will grow . . .".[66]

## The Fears of a Modern Conservative

No one on the political scene kept a closer eye on the potential for class warfare on this side of the Channel than Derby in his diary for more than forty years. In May 1871 he noticed ripples of "something like . . . panic" spreading through the educated and propertied, and carefully analysed the origins. First, the really radical nature of the 1870 Irish Land Act, which Gladstone had striven to mask by reference to Celtic custom not transferable to Britain, was evident. Secondly, that legislation strengthened the suspicion, encouraged by his colleagues' talk, that Gladstone's radical inclinations might take his party further than anyone had thought possible in search of a popular cause. Thirdly, the Tories in the Commons were too weak and disorganised to stand up for the threatened interests; moderates in the governing party were consequently deprived of an essential check upon the leadership. Mill's appearance at the head of a movement for British land reform, mild though its initial programme was, added to the unease. Then there were "the supposed existence" in the universities of a body of academic opinion hostile to orthodox belief, and another progressive demand for the extension of political rights to women. The shock of the Paris Commune unified these disparate fears to produce the collective sensation that Derby attempted to describe.[67] Salisbury's *Quarterly Review* article of October 1871 on the Commune and its socialist content was not alarmist: if anything, he underrated the attraction of social revolution in Europe outside France, and especially in Germany. The Commune, however, was a dream, or a nightmare, realized: a violent rejection of the class society which, in one form or another, had always existed. British working men, and, what was more important, those British politicians susceptible to the latest manifestations of progress, would be in some degree influenced by what had happened in Paris. Responsible conservatives must take account of that fact. From this time Salisbury began to rethink his Christian paternalism and, cautiously, to enlarge his idea of the state's legitimate role in attending to the needs and aspirations of an industrial and urban population.[68]

Salisbury devoted his *Quarterly Review* article to an assessment of the Commune's significance for class relations in Britain. He had no doubt of its historic importance, quoting the positivist Frederic Harrison's description of Parisian workers as "the most truly religious class in Europe". Their ill-defined socialism was an affirmation of the secular faith in a new social order to redeem mankind which was to attract massive support in the closing decades of the century, but not in Britain. The excesses of the Communards did not blind Salisbury to the moral force of their shortlived revolt; he quoted Harrison again: it was a "protest against the selfish anti-social independence of wealth".[69] Their British sympathizers included prominent trade unionists, familiar names from the Reform League in the 1860s, and members of the First International's council secured for the International, briefly, a celebrity which it had not previously enjoyed in the country of its foundation. The names of Odger and Lucraft on a defence of the Commune and its actions issued by the British element of the International in June 1871 caused legitimate anxiety to those unaware of the criticism directed against both men from within the movement for their moderation. Salisbury noted that Odger, the International's president, got very few votes when he stood for parliament; although Lucraft was elected to the new London school board. The trade unions led by such men were more interested in higher wages than in a socialist future. So far as Britain was concerned, if the landed Liberals in power and businessmen as a whole combined in resolutely opposing the infant Left, it would expire "harmlessly", too weak for the united front of capital in the virtual absence of the alienation from state and society felt by Continental workers. There was danger, however, in the vulnerability of the ruling Liberal coalition to determined pressure groups: it was conceivable that the adherents of the International and their fellow-travellers would succeed in extracting from Gladstone more of "his present little instalments of socialism" – an allusion to the Irish Land Act.[70]

The incipient threat to property called for a response that was at once firm and constructive. In his article Salisbury cited a suggestion by the historian J.R. Seeley, someone Gladstone was known to admire, that the "great monopoly . . . the right of private property itself" must be reformed to appease what Seeley assumed to be the swelling discontent of those whom it excluded. In fact, Gladstone was unmoved by these portents, fundamentally conservative as he was outside Irish questions. He observed with relish the outcome of discussions between some leading Tories and representatives of the trade unions, with a view to agreement on social legislation in a spirit of industrial partnership. A seven point draft, revealed in October 1871, envisaged a detached house and garden for every working man; the extension of democratic local government to the counties with power to acquire land "for the common good" given to councils in town and country; an eight hour long day at work; technical in addition to elementary schools "for the poor"; together with parks, libraries and continuing education for adults. The provision of public markets selling at wholesale prices was similarly a development of what philanthropists and city fathers were saying and doing: but the idea, lastly, of a great expansion of the state's functions on the model of the Post Office was startling.[71] No attempt seems to have been made to cost these proposals. According to Derby, Disraeli saw in them another chance to outbid the Liberals, "or rather Gladstone". "This manifesto, Internationale or something more, ought to make some sport for us", remarked the premier. It could only serve to demonstrate his rival's opportunism and confirm the Liberals as the party of government. Carnarvon and at least two other former cabinet ministers wanted to make these inchoate ideas Tory policy, despite

Derby's warning that they pointed to "the suppression of the capitalist . . . followed by that of the landowner and fundholder".[72] Salisbury wrote to the Liberal *Daily News* contradicting the report that he had endorsed this new departure in British politics: warmly sympathetic to the general desire to see the working class better housed, he strongly disapproved of several of the seven points.[73]

*The Times* commented that Salisbury's repudiation of the "New Social Movement", as this initiative was designated, was fatal to its prospects of acceptance in anything like its original form. That was an indication of his influence after two years on the opposition front bench in the Lords, still unreconciled to Disraeli. His next contribution to the *Quarterly Review* in October 1872 insisted, once again, that Toryism was incompatible with offering "a rival programme of change". To do so, he said with his old offensiveness, was "to descend from the higher to the lower type of politician". The parties stood, and ought to stand, for "two opposite moods . . . of the English mind".[74] He did not obey this self-denying ordinance himself. His restless intelligence played on issues the timing and development of which could not be entrusted to conflicting forces within the Liberal coalition. *The Times* drew attention to the inconsistencies of his pronouncements: he condemned the trend towards more state intervention while giving a "modified sanction" to the thinking of the "New Social Movement" on working-class housing.[75] Speaking at Bournemouth in November 1872, he deviated noticeably from his line in the previous month's *Quarterly Review*: the scale of poverty, ignorance and crime demanded policies. They must be Tory policies: for those of the Liberals, under radical and Irish pressure, did not strike the right balance between the interests involved.[76] He returned to the subject a year later, in the *Quarterly Review*, and an accompanying speech. The article went over radical aims and suggested that a realignment of political object-ives was needed to prevent them from being imposed on Liberals in the name of party unity. "Shall we never escape from the Party superstition?" he asked. The speech urged Tories to co-operate should conservative Liberals wish "to recast the party structure . . . a blessed consummation".[77]

Yet there could be no halting the stream of legislation, even then: but it might be less contentious. Ideally a requirement for change should be met only after long discussion, "without triumph . . . and without resentment". Salisbury's articles and speeches of the early 1870s veered between exhorting Tories to be true to Toryism, and identifying a conservatism that transcended existing parties. In private, he made it clear that "Dizzyism" – defined for a Liberal cabinet minister as "playing fast and loose" with principle – was the enemy, quite as much as radicalism. He watched for the smallest sign that his nominal leader was renewing the tactics of 1867. "Was it with sanction from headquarters?" he enquired when the Tory candidate at a Scottish by-election surrendered an important position on the land laws.[78] The reconstruction of parties he advocated was designed to marginalize the radicals and eliminate Disraeli; two equally desirable objectives. Nevertheless, Salis-bury's ideas and those of Disraeli on policy and tactics were converging. Disraeli's well known references to social reform in his Manchester speech of April 1872 left him closer to Salisbury than to his old friend and cabinet colleague, Sir John Pakington, an enthusiast for the "New Social Movement". Pakington, wrote Derby disapprovingly, was "intoxicated with the prospect of being one of the regenerators of society, and reconciling the people with the aristocracy". Disraeli's rhetoric did indeed reflect something of that: but the substance of what he said was realistically moderate and cautious. Salisbury's criticisms of Liberal foreign policy were also in line with those that came from Disraeli. Lastly, he was relieved at the Tories' refusal to take office in March 1873 while in a minority in the Commons and without any certainty that the electors would give them a majority. Disraeli had at last risen above the temptation of office for its own sake, to be retained by purchasing Liberal votes with Tory principles. He had not done nearly enough to win Salisbury over.[79]

# CHAPTER FIVE

# *The Making of a Statesman*

## The Return to Office

The lost election of 1868 dispelled the remaining Tory illusions about the Reform Act of the previous year. It confirmed the Whig and Liberal hold on the electorate, broken so rarely since 1832. Gladstone, who had opposed household suffrage, was victorious. His popularity outside parliament gave him a position similar to that enjoyed by Palmerston. Over the next few years he dominated the Commons, holding cabinet and party together under the strain of one controversial piece of legislation after another. Disraeli, for all his parliamentary skills, was quite out-classed during the most brilliant period in his formidable rival's career. The Tories' dissatisfaction with their leader culminated in serious discussion of his replacement at a gathering of party notables before the session of 1872 opened. In the course of this political weekend at Burghley, Lord Cairns suggested to a representative selection of the last Tory cabinet, with the chief opposition whip, G.J. Noel, present, that Disraeli should make way for Derby, whose standing in the North West Noel thought might affect the outcome in as many as fifty constituencies at an election. The objections of Northcote and Lord John Manners, it seems, prevented any further steps in the matter for the time being.[1] It was soon evident that the tide had started to run against Gladstone. In his own cabinet, fears persisted that the Irish Church and Land Acts had undermined the security of those great interests else-where. In Lady Derby's drawing-room, his chancellor of the exchequer, Robert Lowe, forecast the emergence of Gladstone as "the reddest of the red", once freed from the restraints that a cabinet imposed.[2] The prediction revealed more about Lowe and the anxieties of some conservative Liberals than it did about Gladstone. The government's decline was due rather to the reaction against a reforming admin-istration that had exhausted its mandate. Disraeli was the beneficiary of this mood.

As its stock fell, the ministry could no longer maintain party unity. When Gladstone resigned in March 1873 over the failure to carry the Irish university bill through the Commons, Disraeli compelled a fatally weakened government to continue in office until it opted for a dissolution. Their reviving fortunes made the Tories think better of a leader who had waited patiently to claim the middle ground in politics. To many in his party, Salisbury now appeared too angular and partisan to be quite acceptable. Impressive Tory gains in the boroughs in February 1874 vindicated Disraeli's contention down the years that enough working men would prove to be conservative in a party as well as a social sense to give Tories the parliamentary majority which had eluded them for so long. Salisbury's Toryism had an alien quality: too High Church, intellectual, and critical of the vested interests he defended with disconcerting cleverness. What was one to think of a Churchman who considered a bishop's relatively large income and the life-style it supported "nowadays . . . a direct deduction from his influence"?[3] He had, then, no warmer admirer than Gladstone, who when Salisbury was assailing his policies and methods in 1870 paid him a glowing, and private tribute. He described his opponent at forty as "a model of political integrity . . . a most amiable, a most able man".[4] If they were not actually weaknesses to the Tory leadership, his attractions for Gladstone did not recommend him in that quarter. On Salisbury's side, the suspicion of Disraeli was apparently insuperable. Derby believed it would come as a relief to Salisbury were he to be left out of the Tory administration being formed after the election: "my impression is that he will prefer to remain a free lance".[5]

Salisbury had not been a free lance since he was coaxed into sitting on the front bench in the Lords. It was impossible to pass over him, although Derby doubted whether he was "really worth a large price". Their friendship, such as it was, had never recovered from Salisbury's animadversions upon those who had not resigned in 1867. Derby's dislike of strong feelings in politics and religion, but more particularly of the latter in the shape of the High Church, coloured their relationship. His estimate of the mature Salisbury's character was unflattering: "the expression of a desire that he should do a certain thing would probably drive him in the opposite direction". He was disappointed in the hope that Disraeli would refrain from pressing Salisbury to join the government if an unavoidable invitation was not accepted at once. For Salisbury wanted to join if he could do so without losing his self-respect to Disraeli. He hurried home from wintering abroad, dining with Derby on the day after his arrival; when the host, according to his diary, said nothing "as to his joining . . . too delicate a subject to touch upon", and, according to the guest, "hinted much".[6] Intermediaries were at work. Carnarvon had already warned Derby of the danger from Salisbury outside the government as "the involuntary leader" of discontent. Salisbury was politically harder and wiser than he had been when Disraeli worsted him over reform. He dismissed Carnarvon's reflection that they could not trust Disraeli with the remark, "one could trust no prime minister"; the position moulded the occupants to its changing requirements. He attached "little weight" to Carnarvon's further point that serving under Disraeli would be inconsistent with their past. Duty, they agreed, must decide their answer to his offers: a duty to the party, and a duty to themselves; Salisbury, argued Carnarvon, "would certainly waste great powers" by refusing. On balance, Carnarvon was for acceptance and Salisbury for rejection, unable to stomach what he could not help seeing, and feared others would see, as "an act of submission".[7]

He urged Carnarvon not to sacrifice his legitimate ambition to a friend whose predicament he did not share: Disraeli had found Carnarvon willing to resume social relations.[8] The *dea ex machina* in this impasse was Lady Derby, to whom Carnarvon turned. She confirmed that Disraeli and her husband wished to enlist him, but were unenthusiastic about Salisbury. Derby had, however, taken note of the warning he had received against letting Salisbury become the focus of Tory unrest. Mary Derby set herself to rescue her stepson from the political extinction which he thought would be his fate if he did not close with the offer that was going to be made to him. He wanted to be sure that humiliation was not a condition of entering Disraeli's cabinet. Given that assurance, the path was clear. Disraeli was readier to have Salisbury than Derby supposed: he put Lady Derby in charge of the "negotiation" – Salisbury's description of the exchanges that followed. She told him that on the evidence of Tory and Liberal opinion in her influential circle, "the country (I don't mean newspaper articles) . . . Lancashire . . . and Scotland . . . are eagerly looking for you to join". There was really nothing, Salisbury admitted to his wife, but the "intense personal dislike" he felt for Disraeli to keep him out of the government.[9] The Disraeli of 1874 with a comfortable majority at his back was likely to behave more responsibly than "the fortune-hunter in a minority" of previous years. Pressure on Salisbury to drop his objections to working with the new premier was building up: the desire of the *Liberal* press to see him in the cabinet made a strong impression. Sir William Heathcote – "almost the only man in England whose . . . judgement in party questions I much respect" – came up to London at his urgent request to confer with him. Heathcote advised joining, and informed Carnarvon: "his *reason* is really satisfied that it is right . . . his inclinations are still the other way".[10]

Lady Derby divined her stepson's state of mind; she wanted to know whether any offer from Disraeli would be rejected. Replying, he said there would have to be assurances on policy: the "negotiation" had begun.[11] In her presence, Salisbury questioned Derby about the leadership's legislative intentions. Their talk ranged over a bill for a nine hours' working day, mentioned by Salisbury and deemed inapplicable to grown men by Derby; the rate of income tax; the parliamentary franchise and local government reform in the counties; and the, to Salisbury, disturbing possibility of a measure directed against "ritualism", the liturgical revivals and innovations of extreme High Churchmen. It was the last that most interested him – "not in my line", said Derby, typically, referring him to Disraeli. Salisbury summed up their discussion for Carnarvon; joining was in prospect: "The more I look at it, the less I like it but every other alternative seems worse".[12] When they met Disraeli was lavish with reassurances. Though he even professed to be a High Churchman himself, and declared it would be "insanity" for his government to legislate against ritualism, Salisbury was – rightly – unconvinced by the performance. "*Valeat quantum*", he observed grimly. Disraeli told the Queen that Salisbury had made no difficulty about accepting a place in the cabinet, truthfully, if this interview was meant. "I feel . . . *enfoncé*", wrote the reluctant recruit after a couple of days, "and I suspect my colleagues feel it, too". He could not hide from himself the fact of his retirement from the high moral ground which he had occupied *vis-à-vis*

Disraeli for the last eight years.[13] The approval – "puffing", he commented wryly – in the newspapers put a different complexion upon his decision: *The Times* spoke of a man "who could not have excluded himself from active politics without injustice to the public service and to himself". The reality, he told his wife, was a "trying" experiment in the containment of a leader who would not be content to be conservative.[14]

In the short term, he experienced the old Disraeli. The parliamentary session of 1874 was the last in English history mainly devoted to religious controversy. Public hostility to ritualism swept bishops and politicians before it, and Disraeli could not resist the temptation to make political capital out of a nation-wide movement. His relations with Salisbury were further harmed by the abandonment of an endowed schools bill intended to deliver Anglican foundations from an encroaching state. That was, Salisbury realized, "too small a matter to resign upon".[15] The moment for resignation seemed to have arrived when Disraeli made a strong personal attack on him at a critical stage of the Public Worship Regulation Bill. The antagonists drew back from the brink: the premier's political sense and Salisbury's belief in his own indispensability to the Church, and therefore to the party better disposed towards her than its rival, ensured a swift end to their reviving feud. From then on, Salisbury was able to call on Disraeli's help, whenever practicable, in his religious and ecclesiastical concerns. His command of the India Office, where he had been sent in response to newspaper demand, at a time of famine in the sub-continent, impressed the cabinet and its head. The Church and India between them made a statesman of a talented politician.

## The Future of the Church

"I wish party government was at the bottom of the sea. It is only insincerity codified", Salisbury had written disgustedly as he hesitated over his political future after the 1874 election.[16] The Church, as a religious entity, had his absolute loyalty: but at the same time he viewed it as a very human institution. The Anglican ideal might be to position the English Church between the Catholicism of Rome and the Eastern Orthodox, on the one hand, and Protestantism in its proliferating forms, on the other. In practice, her divisions reflected that great divide, and, moreover, the steady, if undramatic, development of a modernist climate of belief among the clergy and educated laity. In a letter of January 1874, Gladstone noted with apprehension the existence of "a certain number" of clergy who not only denied the authority of scripture and the Church but had quietly ceased to believe in the divinity of Christ, the Incarnation and Resurrection. He was clear that a heresy hunt could only harm the Church. It followed that the ritualists, whose fundamental orthodoxy was not in doubt, should not be pursued either. They, too, were a growing minority, not easily separable from the main body of the Church. This was also Salisbury's attitude to demands for a law to curb ritualism more effectively than bishops and ecclesiastical courts had managed to do. His often quoted speech in the Lords on the Public Worship Regulation Bill in May 1874 is a landmark in the Establishment's history. The Church, he stated without qualification, was now too deeply divided for doctrinal unity. He identified the High, the Low and the Broad Church as "the Sacramental, the Emotional and the Philosophical", thus betraying his poor opinion of the dominant Evangelical Protestantism that cut across church and chapel. "Truth . . . refracted through the different *media* of different minds" must enjoy "frank and loyal tolerance". The alternative was the disintegration of the Church of England.[17]

It was a defeatist policy, the only way in which the Church could be saved from herself, and one that the state had to impose upon the factions. A firm though moderate adherent of the "Sacramental" school of Anglicanism, Salisbury wanted to safeguard its influence within the Establishment. Less of a partisan than Liddon, he thought with him that but for the intellectual ability of the Tractarians the Church would have succumbed to "the philosophy of the present century". This did not imply any sympathy with Rome: Salisbury considered that "ultramontanism and infidelity were playing into each other's hands".[18] The gravest threat to the High Church and the Establishment came from the ritualists, whose fondness for the externals of Catholicism went beyond rescuing sixteenth-century rubrics in the Prayer Book from oblivion. Moderate High Churchmen held that it was superfluous and provocative to emphasize their central doctrine of the Real Presence by ceremonial borrowed from Rome. The entire Catholic revival in Anglicanism was jeopardized by a minority which courted prosecution. A royal commission appointed by the Derby government in 1867 was defeated by the inherent difficulty of suppressing ritualist excesses. A comprehensive prohibition of liturgical developments since the Oxford Movement began was out of the question. Partial prohibition involved deciding exactly what was, and was not, permissible, the task that proved too much for the commission. By the mid-1870s Protestant feeling against ritualism had risen to the point where the primate, Archbishop Tait was preparing legislation to counter it, with the backing of his episcopal brethren. Many High Churchmen might say, like Salisbury, that they had "no fancy for the idiots themselves", but they could not leave the ritualists to their fate. It was impossible to crush them without striking at the doctrinal heart of Tractarianism.[19]

The "ritualist absurdities", as he termed them, affected everything that Salisbury was trying to do for the Church.[20] He fought the Archbishop and his bill on three fronts: inside the government, within the Church, and in the Lords. In his view, which was certainly not exaggerated, Tait's radical proposals threatened the Establishment with "civil war". They provided for an advisory board in each diocese made up of an archdeacon, an ecclesiastical lawyer, the chancellor of the diocese, two beneficed clergymen elected by their fellow incumbents, and four laymen chosen by the churchwardens of all the parishes. Acting with these assessors, a bishop was empowered to sequestrate the living of any incumbent failing to comply with an episcopal instruction to discontinue "rash innovations", not further defined. The implications were revolutionary: deprived of the ancient protection furnished by the parson's freehold, beneficed clergy, those pillars of society, would lose much of their status; while the bishops' increased authority was shared with an elective element quite foreign to Anglicanism. Tait – incidentally a Presbyterian by origin – was in fact envisaging a near approach to synodical government of the Church. It is doubtful, however, whether Tait and the bishops who supported him understood the full extent of their radicalism. "Clerical daydreams", commented Salisbury when the proposals were made known to ministers at the end of February 1874, "do not look well when translated into lawyer's language". In correspondence with Disraeli, he demolished a scheme which he called "a perfect curiosity". Even with a right of appeal to the archbishop of the relevant province, it was sure to produce "really disastrous results", setting the laity against the clergy as the "three great schools" struggled for mastery or survival.[21]

From the outset, Salisbury overstated the strength of ritualism to deter the premier from being too much influenced by "the present balance of opinion". This section of the High Church was "numerous enough if it goes against the Establishment to turn the scale . . . earnest to fanaticism . . . and if driven by any act of serious aggression will . . . bring the whole fabric of the Church down about our ears".[22] He used arguments which the premier, "sublimely ignorant" of theology, could appreciate. He invited Disraeli to contemplate the dire political effects of threatening some 12 000 incumbents with the loss of their traditional security and incomes. Broad and Low Churchmen would not be safe from the future appointment of an authoritarian High Church prelate like the recently deceased Wilberforce. The lay patrons of a majority of livings might be expected to take fright at the disregard for rights hitherto protected by law. Elections for the representatives of the laity on the advisory boards could hardly fail to excite ugly emotions; there was reason to fear the intervention of Dissenters in some parts of the country. Legislation was nevertheless imperative: "*something*" had to be done to calm the public mind. He wanted the courts to decide ritual cases: only the judges could be trusted to bring the necessary detachment to those disputes; for that reason he had opposed a final court of appeal for the Church that was composed of ecclesiastics. Furthermore, he stigmatized as "despotic" an episcopal power to deprive or suspend clergy for offences so ill defined as they were in Tait's drafts. Due process of law, incorporating clear guidelines, should apply, with room left for styles of worship congenial to the Church's recognized divisions, and with penalties confined to "individual eccentricities".[23]

In other words, he was prepared to sacrifice the most extravagant of the ritualists if the rest of the High Church were spared. But High Churchmen would have to acknowledge the legitimacy of other schools of Anglicanism as new ideals of consensus and balance gradually imposed themselves in a religious context. Cairns, the Evangelical lord chancellor, with whom Salisbury discussed the situation, also thought Tait's proposals "full of crudities" dangerous to clergy of his way of thinking under bishops who differed from them, and likely to produce ministerial resignations if endorsed by government. A cabinet on 28 March agreed, with the exception of Derby, that the Archbishop's proposals would indeed be "disastrous" but that they had to be supported in some form. "The matter was left for us to meditate on", wrote Carnarvon. "They are all prejudiced", complained Disraeli of his colleagues. Salisbury's moderate and constructive contribution nevertheless earned his gratitude, and showed, he said, the wisdom of prior consultation with the cabinet's principal members. Cairns, with the premier behind him, proceeded to revise the framework of a bill with Tait. The elective element, clerical and lay, in the advisory boards went, replaced by a nominated membership copied from the Church Discipline Act of 1840. A right of appeal to the judicial committee of the privy council was substituted for one to an archbishop. These changes were not enough for Salisbury. Tait was bent on using the altered machinery to suppress all liturgical departures from the Prayer Book rubrics, an aim that far exceeded the putting down of "individual eccentricities". At the cabinet of 25 April, which followed Tait's introduction of his bill in the Lords, Salisbury wished the government to treat the legislation as an open question. Derby professed to see nothing objectionable in a measure "generally popular", even with the clergy.[24]

Disraeli took a middle course for the time being and sought "an understanding among ourselves". It was decided to ask the archbishop to postpone the second reading until the feelings of the clergy assembled in Convocation had been ascertained. Although the response of the lower clergy in both ecclesiastical provinces was unhelpful, Tait did not amend the bill significantly except to drop the advisory board altogether, giving its functions to the diocesan chancellor. On 4 May ministers moved forward, taking Salisbury with them, to a more definite position in favour of the bill when the second reading came on. High Churchmen in Convocation and cabinet were powerless to prevent legislation: "Queen, Lords and Commons are in a state of great apprehension . . . thoroughly sore and irritable", he had advised a prelate who enjoyed his confidence. However, largely through Salisbury's handling of the question within the government, they had removed the institutionalized Protestant democracy from Tait's original plan, and with it much of the pressure on a bishop to take action against his better judgement.[25] It was now that the cabinet witnessed, in Derby's words, "the absence of union and indeed activity of hostile feeling" between High Churchmen and Low: Salisbury, Carnarvon and Gathorne Hardy facing Cairns. Cairns, not Salisbury, was isolated, angry and upset at his colleagues' unwillingness to commit themselves to a still distinctively Protestant posture on the bill he had reshaped. "Disraeli was quite fair and straightforward", commented one of the High Churchmen. Ministers reached a general agreement to support nothing, as the bill went ahead, that did not represent "a *really fair compromise*".[26] Salisbury spoke for the government on the second reading. His appeal, quoted earlier, for mutual tolerance between the warring factions did not please Cairns. At the same time Pusey, Liddon and other leading High Churchmen whom Salisbury had tried to restrain, denounced the bill. The premier was understandably amused to be told by a zealot in the Lords that "the High Church thought nothing of Lord Salisbury".[27]

Disraeli referred to his balancing act in cabinet and parliament as "the greatest thing I have ever done". The second reading passed without a division. At the beginning of the critical committee stage, Salisbury voted in the commanding majority of 137 to 29 when High Church peers brought forward a motion to drop the bill. Cairns then emerged as the government spokesman, to be rewarded by Salisbury's deliberately paradoxical opinion on the third reading that although the amended bill was "harmless, its passing would do more harm than good".[28] They had in fact co-operated to secure what Salisbury identified as the saving features of undesirable legislation: the appointment of a lay judge to hear cases under the Act, and an episcopal power to veto proceedings. Cairns arranged that Lord Shaftesbury, the epitome of Evangelical fervour and resistance to Catholic tendencies in the Church, should move the first of these amendments, which was equally acceptable to those of an Erastian turn of mind. The second also had supporters in opposing camps. The price of the changes was the abandonment of a new clause from Bishop Magee which would have legalized specific liturgical practices, High and Low, inconsistent with the Prayer Book. Salisbury lent himself to a manoeuvre designed to reassure the public about the government's attitude to ritualism. As he explained to MacColl, he could do no more for their brand of churchmanship; ministers were "the last people to whom you should appeal".[29]

The reaction of the Commons to the bill exceeded his worst fears. To avert the substitution of a stronger measure prepared by a Tory backbencher, J.M. Holt, the cabinet were forced to clear their legislative timetable for the one sent down from the Lords. They intimated that, if necessary, the session would be prolonged to ensure its passage. The collective responsibility this implied was not easily accepted by many ministers, and least of all by Salisbury. The premier disliked "Evangelical trash" as heartily as "the Sacerdotal school": but the wider Protestantism of the country, represented by MPs who were neither High Churchmen nor Evangelical Protestants, was arrayed against the ritualists and the moderate High Church compromised by association. Derby found the cabinet of 11 July "the most interesting ... yet". The depth of feeling among his seasoned colleagues on a purely religious matter had previously surprised him: it was now apparent, even to him, that their unity would not survive on a strengthened replacement, should the Commons throw out the Lords' bill. Disraeli treated the problem as strictly political. With the bill they had helped to frame and steer through the Lords, they might hope to retain a controlling influence over the actions of a Commons "passionate" for legislation. Disraeli called for unanimity: Salisbury stood out until he was alone; he did not wish the government to be more closely associated with Tait's clumsy bid to discipline the ritualists. But his tone was conciliatory throughout, and he bowed to what everyone else considered the safest course. The spectre of civil war in the Establishment was abroad. The premier warned the Queen, however, that there might still be resignations, meaning Salisbury's and, evidently, Hardy's.[30]

Resignations would have achieved nothing. The mood of the Commons compelled Gladstone to withdraw the resolutions he had tabled; they envisaged a settlement of the Church's difficulties in terms so broad as to give rise to the suspicion that there was plenty of room for ritualism. Disraeli's language in the House, after the cabinet of 11 July, indulged angry Protestant sentiment, in marked contrast to Hardy's line. More importantly, ministers submitted to an amendment from Holt, which allowed an appeal to the archbishops from an episcopal veto on the commencement of proceedings under the Act. It had been carried against both front benches and presented Tait, in his province, with an unwanted power. As the bill returned to the Lords, Disraeli advised the archbishop that the Commons would insist on maintaining the amendment, seen as a necessary constraint upon prelates sympathetic to the High Church, although it might involve losing the legislation for a year. Salisbury refused to give up a bishop's right to prevent an outbreak of legal warfare in his diocese – even if loss of the bill meant more extensive interference with the Church in the following session. Holt's amendment undermined the position of a bishop, the foundation of ecclesiastical order for High Churchmen of every shade. Salisbury obtained the rejection of this significant change in the Lords, ranging himself against Cairns and speaking defiantly of the Commons. The prelates who swung the vote were responding to a message from Gladstone, threatening to abandon the defence of the Establishment as such if the amendment were not struck out.[31]

This last, dramatic move succeeded beyond its author's expectations. Its effect on the Commons bore witness to the political and religious authority combined in Gladstone's person. It was in his power to translate into legislative action the doubts that many High Churchmen entertained about the value of establishment if it seriously inhibited the freedom to make worship reflect their doctrinal position. Salisbury had apprised the premier of this internal peril menacing the Church when he commented on Tait's early plans. Liddon had kept the prospect of a High Church secession before Salisbury, to whom even the theoretical possibility of disestablishment, a talking point with Gladstone and others, was unwelcome. Disraeli recoiled from endangering the Church, whose unity and security were fundamental to his political creed. The Liberals, however reluctantly, deferred to Gladstone. The Commons accepted the Lords amendment without a division. Disraeli relieved his feelings about Salisbury's independence and outspokenness by calling him in debate "a great master of jibes and flouts and jeers". He went on to speculate that Salisbury had been trying to provoke the Commons into taking up an attitude that would have killed the bill for that session. Colleagues rushed to repair the open breach: within a couple of hours Salisbury received an apology from the premier for his "playful" remarks, and replied similarly, including his regrets for having treated Cairns "somewhat cavalierly". It was not difficult for Disraeli to be magnanimous: he had just forced the strong Churchmen in his cabinet to excise from an endowed schools bill clauses designed to meet Anglican objections to earlier Liberal legislation.[32]

That bill was Salisbury's work: the loss of its substance, to save time in committee that could be allotted to the Public Worship Regulation Bill, angered him. It was not, as he saw at once, a resigning matter; although he rightly interpreted the decision as another concession to the broader Protestantism of moderate men across Church and Chapel.[33] His resentment on this head coloured the Lords speech that elicited Disraeli's intemperate response. From then on the premier and Salisbury achieved a working relationship on Church questions. Its candour and realism appear in Disraeli's request of July 1875 for help with the distribution of ecclesiastical patronage: "Can you suggest a High Church Dean who is not a damned fool, and won't make himself ridiculous?" Salisbury adopted a briskly practical approach to the delicate issues involved in apportioning preferment between schools of churchmanship. For the new bishopric of Truro, where Methodism flourished, "a High Churchman of any kind would be out of place". He recommended a Broad Churchman, not too advanced in his theology, and not someone with a pedagogic background, "schoolmaster bishops are always a doubtful experiment". Disraeli opted for E.W. Benson, formerly Master of Wellington, and a chameleon in ecclesiastical politics. Salisbury urged the claims of High Churchmen like the Oxford contemporary classified in language that a prime minister bored by theological niceties appreciated: "He belongs to the 'Right Centre' in Church matters". It was politically important to keep the High Churchmen in good humour and counteract the "mischievous influence" of Liddon, among others. While Salisbury liked and admired Liddon, he did not think him a safe guide. Temperamentally disinclined to favour those capable of being all things to all men, he nevertheless looked for that useful quality in the ranks of High Churchmen, and found them in W.D. Maclagan, "something of a genius", he drily observed, in enjoying everybody's good opinion. Disraeli made Maclagan bishop of Lichfield, and Salisbury promoted him to be archbishop of York in 1891.[34]

As secretary of state for India Salisbury distributed the Church patronage that went with the portfolio, apportioning bishops and chaplains on the Indian ecclesiastical establishment whose primary responsibility was the spiritual care of the ruling British in the sub-continent. His choice of bishops was carefully balanced, though limited, as he remarked, by the scarcity of promising men ready to sacrifice good English prospects for an Indian see with the attendant risks to life and health. He took pains over a responsibility which other holders of his office regarded as peripheral. With an acute sense of what was possible, he chose a moderate High Churchman, his wife's kinsman Robert Milman, for Calcutta, the metropolitan see, in 1867, and another "very stiff" representative of that school for Bombay: "I hope the sun will thaw him into elasticity", he told Milman. To Lahore he sent Thomas Valpy French, one of the authentic saints of the Victorian Church of England and an Evangelical, as was his selection for Rangoon. Salisbury's letters to Milman, who died in 1876 and was succeeded by a moderate man, are full of practical concern for the Indian church, and hope that it might in time become more of a missionary church if, as widely anticipated, Westernization gradually undermined native religions. Meanwhile a modest expansion of the Establishment in India seemed likely to attract the hostility of political Dissenters at home: "at this moment a bill for increasing the number of Bengal tigers would be received more patiently than a proposal to increase the number of bishops", Salisbury cautioned Milman when they discussed the erection of new dioceses against the background of the excitement over Tait's onslaught upon ritualism. As High Churchmen, Salisbury and Milman could not count on a friendly reception in the Commons if they proceeded by legislation.[35]

Less of a partisan in religious controversy than he had once been, Salisbury was still too much identified with one section of the Church to be able to do for her what was done by his colleague, Richard Cross, Disraeli's home secretary, better known for his interest in the limited social reforms he enacted. No High Churchman, he got through a succession of bills between 1875 and 1878 setting up new sees funded without resort to the taxpayer. Salisbury was glad to see the "apparent worldliness and waste" of episcopal life-styles reduced by the redistribution of ecclesiastical resources involved. Mindful of a warning from Gorst, the party organizer, that too many of the clergy resented the Public Worship Regulation Act, he looked on the creation of bishoprics as a way of restoring confidence in the Church's future among the several factions.[36] His awareness of the clergy's dissatisfaction with their treatment by a Tory government inspired the rearguard action he fought against the burial bills of the later 1870s. The symbolic right of Dissenters to burial with their own graveside services in parish churchyards could not be indefinitely delayed when the Lords had voted to recognize it by 142 to 92 in May 1876. Tait and Disraeli were willing to yield but the "Sacerdotalists" enjoyed wide clerical support on this issue. Hardy's threat of resignation, which might have been ascribed to divisions in the cabinet over the Eastern question, postponed the surrender of another outwork of Anglican privilege. An abandoned outwork, Salisbury pointed out, afforded good cover for the advancing enemy, the Liberationists, whom they were vainly seeking to appease: "If I were pursued by a lion, it would be no use for me to present him with one of my legs and expect him to be satisfied".[37]

The defeatism or indifference of his party mortified Salisbury. He had sought to convince Disraeli that he was too ready to dismiss protests from Churchmen as engineered by the element he particularly disliked. Reminding the premier of their voting power in the Commons was the best way of getting him to listen: Salisbury prevailed upon him to accept the backbench amendment to the 1876 education bill which enabled a qualifying majority of ratepayers to do away with school boards when the Church had made adequate provision for schooling.[38] His standing as Chancellor of Oxford gave him a better position from which to work on Disraeli, who paid more attention to the ancient universities than to elementary schools. Salisbury undertook the further reform of the universities to fit them for the intellectual challenges from within and without to their Christian traditions. As strongly as any secular-minded reformer, he condemned the misuse of endowments to provide dons with comfortable incomes and lives. Collegiate funds, he said bluntly, should be diverted from academic drones to the development of natural sciences, which he advocated with a keenness reinforced by his amateur researches. A command of science was vital to the ability of Christians to hold their own in contemporary debate. In the prevailing atmosphere, however, it was prudent not to put Anglican interests in the foreground. An early sketch of what became his Oxford bill of 1876 aimed at "sufficient security for religious trusts without mentioning the Church of England". If that was scarcely practicable, it indicated his desire to avoid provocation. The instrument of change was a statutory commission modelled on that in the Oxford University Act of the 1850s; he chose its membership, "sufficiently Conservative to be trusted with full powers", thus minimizing parliamentary interference.[39]

This manoeuvre succeeded as well as it did because Salisbury secured the ideal chairman for his purposes in Selborne, a reforming lord chancellor under Gladstone, a devout Tractarian with an old Peelite's respect for institutions that had stood the test of time. A Tory chairman would have raised "incessant storms of cavil and suspicion": Selborne's acceptance of the post as the bill went to parliament improved its chances considerably. Introduced by Salisbury in the Lords, it met with little opposition in the Commons, though his reference to "idle fellowships" was attacked from the Tory side.[40] The low-key presentation of the measure had the disadvantage that the cabinet included it among bills dropped late in the session of 1876 for lack of parliamentary time. The abandonment of his legislation, Salisbury protested, must result in "incalculable" damage to the universities: it would have been better to have left the reform alone than to have shown their enemies how little a Tory government cared about their fate. His unconcealed indignation ensured that the bill, enlarged to make similar provision for Cambridge, was passed in 1877. The Oxford commission did more than he expected: it was his hope that it would be "destructive of nothing" – that mattered. The Anglican character of the university he knew, and of her sister at Cambridge, was unmistakably but gradually modified. Yet without his determination to pre-empt a Liberal administration in the field, that phase of university reform might have been more drastic.[41] As it was, Salisbury enlisted the co-operation of academic conservatives in Oxford by frightening them with the thought that a less friendly government might decide to transfer a sizeable portion of their collective riches to new seats of higher education in the North of England.[42]

His acquisition of political skills that did not come easily to him made this naturally straightforward and outspoken man more formidable. He deployed them in the service of a Church whose weaknesses were all too clear to him. He now realized, if he had not done so before, that the alliance between Church and State in England survived because the question of ultimate authority raised by the Tractarians could only be answered with a reaffirmation of parliament's traditional Erastianism. The story of the Public Worship Regulation Act underlined that truth, so unpalatable to High Churchmen. It was not only the ritualists whose activities threatened the continued existence of the Establishment: those respected leaders of the High Church, Pusey and Liddon, came close, in Salisbury's judgement, to precipitating the final crisis he dreaded. "The bonds which have . . . united the English people to the English Church are being strained with tremendous force", he wrote to Nathaniel Woodard, "and are not far from snapping". In the evident desire of Pusey and Liddon to generalize their practice of confession he saw the fatal step that would introduce into his country the anti-clericalism that beset Continental Catholicism. Nor would the disestablished Church be spared "a number of petty schisms", once freed from the state's restraining hand. The future of Christianity in England was bound up with the perpetuation of the Establishment and the containment of its factional strife. Liddon noted a conversation in which Salisbury was "very much taken up" with Strauss's *Das Leben Jesu*, the pioneering attempt to uncover the essential Christian idea, as the author envisaged it, beneath the historical accretions of two millennia. Salisbury was a more tolerant and sophisticated champion of the Church than either friends or critics generally imagined.[43]

## The India Office

Lady Gwendolen Cecil said of her father's time as secretary of state for India that it was "scarcely . . . remunerative biographically"; a verdict not seriously questioned for half a century.[44] A sight of the private letter-books he kept while at the India Office at once raises doubts about that estimate of his five years there. Unlike most of those who filled that post, he did not merely ensure that the machinery of empire in the sub-continent, reorganized after the Mutiny, ran smoothly and produced policies defensible in notoriously ill-attended debates at Westminster. For the historian of the British in India, the bulky letter-books are full of interest. Faced with complicated problems, discussion of which calls for some specialist knowledge, biographers of the future foreign secretary and prime minister have elected to pass quickly over almost all of them. They have taken a longer look at the relatively familiar topic of Anglo-Russian rivalry in Central Asia and Salisbury's part in shaping Disraelian policy for Britain and India in that region. Salisbury applied to the whole range of Indian administration a mind incapable of accepting conventional wisdom on any important subject without thinking it through. His regular correspondence with viceroys and presidency governors explored the implications of strange land tenures; the immensity of Indian famines, their prevention and the relief of the sufferers; dealings with the semi-independent princely states that covered two-fifths of India's surface; the constitutional relationship between London and the government of India; and, encompassing all these, the pace and consequences of Westernization for India's well-being and for British rule. His impact on these areas of policy naturally varied but was considerably greater than has been assumed. While he left his mark upon the Raj, the experience of overseeing the development of a vast empire of 250 million people, and the impression he made on those who saw him at work, are integral to a portrait of the premier and foreign secretary.[45]

"I believe", runs a striking passage in a memorandum circulated to the Council of India that advised the secretary of state at home, "... all the enduring institutions which human societies have attained have been reached, not of set design and forethought of some group of statesmen, but of that unbidden and uncoerced consequence of many thoughts and wills in succeeding generations, to which, as it obeys no single guiding hand, one may give the name of 'drifting'."[46] This vision of social change is Burkean, and ultimately Providential. On a lower level of explanation, there was room for a "guiding hand", such as his. Intellect and personality made "drifting" a more positive activity where he was concerned than it sounded. It was not in him, any more than it was in Gladstone, to let things go on as before when he had a responsibility for ordering them better. Salisbury did not deceive himself, as others tried to do, about the nature of the British presence in India: it rested on force, which required a moral justification. He was not disposed to repeat his youthful criticism of Britain's imperial morality, characterized, he had asserted in 1855, by "a process of aggression" and the "repression of nationalities" in India and around the world. On the contrary, he thanked Disraeli, twenty years later, for his repudiation of "the growing idea that England ought to pay tribute to India for having conquered her". His Indian policies did allow for a very cautious liberalization of alien rule – and in some important respects were ahead of their time – but his attitude to Indians did not differ from J.S. Mill's. That able servant of the old East India Company, writing after the Mutiny, considered the peoples of

India unfit for more than "a limited and qualified freedom", and fit for that only if it went with "much sterner powers of repression than elsewhere". As he did in discussing other topics, the philosopher-bureaucrat conferred the status of enlightened opinion on the commonplaces of his day.[47]

The memory of the rising in 1857–9 that overthrew British rule across great tracts of Northern India never faded for Salisbury. It strongly influenced his entire policy. He gave priority to agrarian questions; the peasant masses were "depressed enough to be easily made desperate". He explored their condition and the possibilities of rural progress in his correspondence with Sir Richard Temple, who rose through the ranks of the civil service in India to govern, successively, Bengal and Bombay. Before long Salisbury had aligned himself with the school of British administrators whom he termed "the advocates of the ryot". He was perturbed by the incidence of agrarian troubles involving over-taxation of the cultivators, the pressure of usury upon them in the Deccan and Sind, and their oppression by European indigo planters in Bihar and by native landlords in Bengal. "I confess I feel more anxiety about these matters", he told Temple, "than I do concerning . . . the vagaries of Cabul or . . . Ava, or the intrigues of Salar Jung and Dinkar Rao" – the politics of India's frontiers and of her native courts.[48] Salisbury invited his correspondent to suggest ways of tackling "the grave social disease" of which those troubles were symptoms, the poverty and destitution exposed by recurrent famines. Temple could only convey the intractability of the problem and submit palliatives. Salisbury posed two radical alternatives: a strengthening of the tenant-right usual in British India to give the occupier the whole of any increase in the yield from the holding; or large-scale emigration. Without one or the other, he concluded, "obviously the ryots cannot really flourish". Temple would not commit himself to sweeping changes at the expense of native landlords; nor was there anywhere a requirement for Indian immigration of the magnitude Salisbury contemplated.[49]

Salisbury persisted in trying to alleviate peasant indebtedness. "In the whole range of Indian politics there is no question on which greater issues hang", he wrote to the then governor of Bombay, Sir Philip Wodehouse, in whose presidency the Deccan was in 1875 the scene of violent protests against the exactions of money-lenders. Wodehouse demolished Salisbury's proposal, which antedated the disturbances, for land banks lending to the ryots at low rates of interest: it would be unworkable with such poor and irresponsible clients, and politically most unwise. The money-lender was indispensable to rural India, sustaining cultivators who lived close to the margin of existence even while he oppressed them. He might be unpopular, but with the help of native newspapers he could turn the countryside against the government. "Reluctantly", Salisbury dropped the idea of cheap credit to enhance agricultural productivity and deliver the ryots from their bondage to usury. Accepting the money-lender as "an essential ingredient . . . in the country", he contended that it was imperative to control him: and encountered the objections of the viceroy, Lord Lytton, who reinforced Wodehouse's arguments.[50] Eventually, the secretary of state appointed a committee of the Council of India in London to take evidence from expert witnesses on agrarian conditions in the Bombay presidency, and induced Temple, the new governor, to prepare an outline of legislation.

Salisbury wanted "a strong equitable jurisdiction . . . to look behind acknowledge-ments of debt", and cut both principal and interest so as to keep occupiers on their holdings and out of virtual servitude to their creditors. After he had left the India Office, his successor, Lord Cranbrook, the former Gathorne Hardy, overcame the resistance of Lytton and his advisers: the Deccan Agriculturists' Relief Act of 1879 substantially reproduced the objectives and methods which Salisbury had sketched for Temple. The Act helped to set a trend for India, and may fairly be said to have owed much to Salisbury's vision and tenacity.[51]

Three famines – in Orissa (1866), Bengal (1873–4) and South India (1876–8) – impelled him to intervene in the continuous official debate on the treatment and prospects of the ryots. "A population that does not accumulate can make very little fight against famine", he said unanswerably, urging land reform on his cabinet colleague of the 1860s, the Duke of Buckingham and Chandos, who ruled Madras. The taxation extracted from the ryots was the mainstay of Indian finance, and the scope for its reduction very limited. All Salisbury felt able to suggest amounted to a "mite": leniency and regularity of assessment to ensure that these direct taxpayers benefited from good years and rising prices. "It is one of the most painful dis-enchantments of office", he observed wryly, "to find how much of one's discretion has been mortgaged by one's predecessors."[52] Prevented, in one way and another, from doing more to improve the ryots' lot between visitations of famine, he did his utmost to relieve their suffering when it struck. On the day he arrived at the India Office in 1866, he was warned of the approach of a terrible famine in Orissa. "I did nothing for two months", he recalled, "and . . . it is said – a million people died." The warning, from a former governor-general with extensive contacts in India, was not confirmed by official sources until too late. Salisbury never recovered his con-fidence, such as it was, in the British Indian bureaucracy. The enormity of its neg-ligence, like his own sense of guilt, was unforgettable. It excited his indignation by a rigid adherence to classical economic teaching which left the supply of foodstuffs to the operation of market forces in the midst of starvation. He referred bitterly in after years to an administrator, subsequently promoted, whose "sound education in political economy cost half a million lives". He was at first incredulous, then appalled, when he learnt how the officials immediately responsible had behaved. The reigning viceroy, Sir John Lawrence, a veteran Indian civil servant and a national hero for his achievements in the Mutiny, forfeited Salisbury's respect: there was a serious failure of administrative oversight on the part of the government of India.[53]

The tragedy in Orissa, and Salisbury's public reaction to it, inspired calls in the British press for Salisbury to be sent to the India Office when the shadow of mass starvation lay over Bengal. The principle of relief that Salisbury adopted, with Orissa in mind, was simple, and expensive: "waste there must be if there is success". He met some resistance from the viceroy, Lord Northbrook, a former and future Liberal politician, but not from Temple, who was charged with the organization of relief. Salisbury was shocked at the tone of the newspapers in India that catered for the British official and business communities; they described famine as a salutary cure for over-population. "I have never seen in any other organs", he told Temple, "anything so ghastly as the inhumanity which in one or two cases has been talked about the famine." The whole truth was even worse, according to Temple: behind this newspaper criticism of famine relief lurked motives "too sinister to find open expression". Europeans in India resented the heavy expenditure; businessmen's hopes of making still higher profits from the stricken natives were being frustrated.[54] Timely, and more than adequate, aid kept the official mortality down to a negligible figure. Northbrook was not alone in thinking that his government knew better than an unreasonably anxious secretary of state. This experience of famine, or, rather, scarcity, he wrote, should "prove to the good folk at home that their [Indian] governments are to be trusted".[55]

Salisbury was therefore at a disadvantage when famine returned within a few months of Northbrook's departure in 1876 and claimed, perhaps, two million lives in the South. His successor, Lytton, wanted to conserve India's resources for expansion into Afghanistan and beyond. He stepped in to curb what Salisbury admitted was "the enthusiastic prodigality" with which the Duke of Buckingham and his council at Madras were spending on relief. Lytton believed that his action had pre-empted a decision from London, where he asserted that "the power of funk" prevailed, to uphold the Duke's policy. In his letters home to the India Office and to politicians of both parties, he denounced "humanitarian hysterics": let the British public foot the bill for its "cheap sentiment", if it wished to save life at a cost that would bankrupt India.[56] Salisbury knew that on purely financial grounds Lytton was right: and appealed, in vain, to the British Treasury for help. He protested, in vain, at Lytton's insistence that relief must not be so generous as to distort the working of a free market: "In a longer or shorter time demand will attract supply but the longer time may be long enough to starve a population". He had already conceded the restriction of relief to those in imminent danger of death. "Anything short of this we should not shrink from as inhuman."[57] The pressures of the situation drove Salisbury to a tacit change of policy by September 1877, giving up "beyond certain limits" the endeavour to preserve life, which the permanent under-secretary at the India Office, Sir Louis Mallet, thought should not have been left unannounced, although "I doubt whether our public is prepared for this". Salisbury's reply was untypically evasive. He tried to persuade himself that the policy had not really changed; "physical conditions . . . so much against us", and not the lack of money, accounted for the impossibility of adhering to it in full. Lytton, with a singular disregard for old friendship, boasted of his victory over a weak minister and the clamour at home for "cheap vicarious generosity".[58]

This defeat, which Salisbury probably felt as much as any in his career, was not quite the end of the matter. Drawing on the collective experience at his disposal, Salisbury suggested what Lytton called "a famine dictatorship", under which men selected for their tasks would be moved to the affected areas with, in Salisbury's words, "as little doubt and confusion as sailors going into action". He wanted the government of India to recognize in famine a contingency for which it should always be prepared, financially and administratively. The British public's humanitarianism was not to be defied: "sensibility is a strong political force . . . now – just as honour used to be", he advised Lytton in terms that the viceroy understood. From 1877/1878, Indian budgets included an element of famine insurance, while from the commission investigating the repeated calamities that reported in 1880 came a famine code such as Salisbury had envisaged. The scepticism of Lytton and the officials who thought as he did was justified, it has to be said, in that the periodic threat of starvation for millions was not finally removed until Indian independence; a million are believed to have died in the Bengal famine of 1943.[59]

Palmerston when prime minister had looked forward to the gradual absorption of the princely states in directly ruled British India. The policy, to the extent that it was actually pursued, did not survive the Mutiny: by actively helping the British, or by waiting on events, the princes of North and Central India shared their suzerain's position for many critical months. Nevertheless, official India was unwilling to relinquish territory to native rule. In a memorandum for the cabinet in 1867, Salisbury reasserted the political value of the princes in the context of the future of Mysore, a large state administered by the British on behalf of its Hindu ruler since the 1830s. While their existence contributed to the divisions that militated against Indian unity to overthrow "the common enemy", he attached more significance to his other points. Westernization was being enforced through "a gigantic engine of law on a purely European model", unsuited to the East in its rigidity and disregard for custom: but its operation did not extend to native states, and ought not to do so until its effects were clearer. For him, the signal advantage of retaining the rather less than semi-independent princes lay in the careers they offered to "clever and pushing natives . . . energetic spirits . . . [who] will fret under our rule, as not merely an alien domination, but a personal injury to themselves", men from every part of India.[60] Speaking in the Commons, he showed an unusual and sympathetic insight into the minds of those who were even then fit to rule. The good government of a native state "raises . . . self-respect . . . and forms an ideal". The failings of experienced civil servants uncovered by the Orissa famine, he said in the emotion of its recent impact, were more terrible in their inhumanity than the misgovernment of princes and dewans. The latter had a positive role in what he believed, when first at the India Office, was an age of "rapid transition".[61]

He was not, however, prepared for the immediate restoration of Mysore to its maharajahs. He drew a distinction between major states that posed a latent threat, and smaller ones that did not. His attitude to both hardened between his two periods as Indian secretary. He thought the princes' ability to harm the British was steadily declining along with the potential for good that he had seen. The deposition and replacement of the Gaekwar of Baroda, an important state, in 1875 satisfied him that the British might remove a leading ruler with impunity, "unfettered by . . . obligations or customary pledges", such as the princes had relied on since the Mutiny.[62] Northbrook treated the princes with more respect: he and Salisbury differed on the claim of Hyderabad, the biggest native state, under a Muslim dynasty and a formidable minister, Sir Salar Jung, to the extensive territory of Berar leased to the British before the Mutiny. Salisbury dismissed the viceroy's "chancery principles" in the question, and argued in a radical fashion that startled a conservative Whig. The case for not returning Berar, like that for Britain's dominion in the sub-continent, rested on the inhabitants' welfare. "Speaking generally," wrote Salisbury, "I am anxious to push forward the argument for the interests of the people . . . I consider it to be our true role and measure of action: and our observance of it the one justification of our presence." He did not suppose that the British were really popular in Berar, or anywhere else; no doubt Sir Salar Jung could win a plebiscite. The population's wishes, he told Northbrook, were not to be confused with what was best for them.[63] Northbrook quoted Charles James Fox on the pervasive influence of British constitutionalism in India, even on "the most absolute despotism". At the same time, the use of the phrase "the interests of the people" disturbed the viceroy: it advanced a dangerous principle. Salisbury accordingly consented to take the offending words out of his draft despatch on Berar. It was all that he conceded.[64]

Salisbury's historical reputation as a friend of the princes is not borne out by a careful reading of his Indian correspondence. He certainly did not subscribe to Lytton's view of the ryots as "an inert mass", and of relations with India's princes and nobles as "the most important problem now before us". Salisbury allowed Lytton to have his way with the spectacular ceremonial of the Delhi Durbar in 1877, when feudal India was paraded in an orchestrated display of loyalty to the Queen on her proclamation as Empress of India. He had misgivings lest the occasion should attract the same dislike and ridicule at home as Disraeli's imperial gesture in adding to the monarch's titles.[65] On the substance of Lytton's policy, Salisbury was even less encouraging: "it is worth trying", he said. He opined to Disraeli that, if carried through, the policy would, at best, "serve to hide to [sic] the eye of our own people and perhaps of the growing literary class in India, the nakedness of the sword on which we . . . rely". A minute that Salisbury circulated to his council, purporting to approve of the viceroy's initiative, called the princes "glorified Lieutenant-Governors", reduced to that status by the government of India's tightening grip.[66]

The strongest objection that Salisbury had to a set of unreal proposals was to the idea of an Indian privy council chosen from "the biggest natives". The body was to be consultative only, but its creation, which he prevented, raised questions about the constitutional relationship between Britain and India. His concern was with the reaction of the British unofficial community in India: they might seek not equal but preferential treatment in the form of elected membership of the viceroy's legislative council, on which they, like Indians, were represented by appointed members. A native Indian challenge to the supremacy of parliament and British ministers was a distant vision. Few though they were in the sub-continent, the innate desire of the resident British for self-government and their sense of racial superiority made them, Salisbury remarked, "the only enemies who will ever seriously threaten England's power in India".[67] If this conviction of his is minimized or ignored, it becomes hard to understand his disagreements with successive viceroys. Lytton was disparaging of his bureaucracy, "a most unchoice one", and of British businessmen and planters in his empire, "all of the most second-rate kind". They were unwise judgements which Salisbury could not accept, although he condemned, with the viceroy, the brutality that sometimes disfigured the behaviour of Europeans towards helpless natives, especially domestic servants and plantation labour. He was afraid of "a sort of bastard Home Rule cry" uttered by the British in India, the official as well as the unofficial community. Already, he considered, the viceroy's council had succumbed to the illusion that it was a representative assembly defending popular rights against an alien despotism – in London. During his first spell at the India Office, he had overruled the collective experience of his own council on the Mysore question. On his return in 1874, he asserted his authority over Northbrook and his councillors.[68]

One of his first actions on taking up his old post again was to instruct the government of India to send legislative proposals home for approval prior to their introduction into the viceroy's council sitting in its law-making capacity. He explained this move to Northbrook as a refinement of his statutory veto, presently "very clumsy and barbarous", and therefore difficult to employ. The India Councils Bill of the same year created the post of public works member on the viceroy's council against the wishes of Northbrook and his colleagues. An Indian legislation bill, which did not get through parliament for lack of time and because it was known that Northbrook's political friends were going to fight it, would have enabled the secretary of state to veto part of an Indian measure instead of having to sanction or disallow it in its entirety. Northbrook conceded the ultimate responsibility of the secretary of state, with cabinet and parliament behind him, for Indian policy: he resisted what he and his defenders construed as Salisbury's attempt to rule India through private correspondence with the viceroy. Salisbury, on his side, complained that Northbrook told him nothing that he could not discover for himself from the newspapers. The letter of British statutes regulating Indian government favoured Northbrook: the spirit was much less clear. Growing differences came to a head over the question of the Indian cotton duties and their abolition, urged by the industry in Lancashire. The viceroy and his council held that the duties were not protectionist in effect, but merely a means of easing the burden of taxation on the ryot: in their view, abolition meant the exploitation of India by Manchester acting on Westminster and Whitehall. In August 1875, without any reference home, they passed new tariff legislation which preserved the cotton duties, slightly amended.[69]

Salisbury reacted strongly to this assertion of the belief that India was to be governed in India, with little interference from outside. The viceroy and his councillors had plainly put themselves in the wrong by omitting to consult him. Protesting to his friends that Salisbury's public rebuke to the government of India was "highly improper", Northbrook decided, in the next month, to leave India early, ostensibly for family reasons. The Liberal law member of his council, Arthur Hobhouse, who earned Salisbury's lasting dislike, had encouraged Northbrook to consider the secretary of state's conduct since 1874 arbitrary and unconstitutional. He wrote on hearing of the intended departure: "I take it to mean nothing else than that you have been worried and bullied out of office by Lord Salisbury".[70] After the cost of famine relief had imposed a long delay, Lytton used his power to overrule a majority among his councillors inherited from Northbrook and remove most of the duties in 1879. A Liberal ministry at home and a Liberal viceroy rounded off Salisbury's policy. He thus defeated those whom he designated "Anglo-Indian Butts"; an allusion to the founder and current leader of the Irish home rule party.[71]

There was a good economic case for doing away with the cotton duties, as the outcome demonstrated. The number of Indian cotton mills trebled in the decade and a half after they lost such protection as the duties afforded. The emergent industry sprang from British business and investment, the leaders of which Salisbury thought were capable of building on the objections put forward by Northbrook's council, and of stirring up native opinion to demand authentic protectionism. By the removal of currently low duties, Salisbury hoped to make such an agitation harder for British expatriates and Indians faced with going against the orthodoxy of free trade. Europeans, he was afraid, would not long retain control of many millions of Indians, excited by the cry that their interests were being sacrificed to Lancashire's. Such an agitation would probably inflict irreparable damage on liberal Britain's will to hold on to India. The white "home rulers" must tend to legitimise native aspirations in the eyes of the British public. He endeavoured to balance his sincere commitment to "the welfare of the people of India" with the requirements of the industrial democracy at home. To him, as to most of his contemporaries in politics, free trade was indispensable within the empire, because self-evidently in the mother country's interest. He rejected the suggestion that a rich Britain should consent to penalize her trade for the sake of a poor India. "This species of international communism" elicited from him the rejoinder that if poverty were assessed in relative terms, the lowest British working-class taxpayer was "quite as poor as the poorest Indian taxpayer".[72]

To begin with, Salisbury overestimated the speed of economic change in India, and consequently the spread of Westernization. After his brief tenure of the India Office in 1866–7, he declared that "the impression produced on my mind . . . was that I was watching a vast country, as it were, in the act of creation". The growth of the economy in the boom that followed the suppression of the Mutiny gave rise to the sanguine expectations reflected in his letters to the viceroy of those years, Lawrence. He was eager to promote continuing expansion through the major public works wholly or partly undertaken by government in India. Lawrence's financial caution, due largely to anxiety about the weight of taxes upon the ryot, contrasted with the secretary of state's outlook. They were agreed on one urgent exception to the economy favoured by the viceroy: irrigation. There was a perceptible difference between them on the benefits of railway construction. Salisbury imagined, in common with many others, that railways would sustain India's economic development at the rate he believed possible. He greeted as "infallible proof of the . . . rule" Lawrence's report of higher wages wherever the railway penetrated. Yet even before he left his post in March 1867, he was coming to realize that his hopes were pitched too high. Farming much more for subsistence than for profit, the ryots could not generate dramatic expansion simply because the railway had reached them. A line to a thickly populated and intensively cultivated part of Eastern India was, he admitted, "financially indefensible" on the projections. Significantly, it was to have opened Orissa.[73] During his second period at the India Office he paid less attention to economic development as such and more to eroding the massive conservatism of Indian rural society. In doing so, he reckoned that the inevitable political consequences of Westernization would be slow to emerge, and was prepared for judicious action to check their premature appearance.[74]

He thoroughly approved of Temple's interest, as Lieutenant-Governor of Bengal, in trying to foster elementary education: "Nothing will be done either for Christianity or for material progress unless the path can be made a little wider for the advance of new ideas into the Hindoo brain". Salisbury was never optimistic of converting India, but, especially to a Victorian, literacy was the prerequisite for awakening the Oriental masses to modernity in all its forms. In the mean time, there was a displeasing early result of change: the "class of newspaper contributors" writing in the vernacular or in English, and turned out or influenced by the institutions of secondary and higher education which the British had established. Their unorganised literary nationalism was a cause for concern, and its fusion with popular or princely discontent an obvious, though exaggerated, risk. Lytton's Vernacular Press Act of 1878, passed against the background of war in the Near East and its apprehended repercussions in India, had Salisbury's support: the freedom of the press which he thought salutary at home needed to be curbed in the great Eastern dependency. He kept this inchoate nationalist feeling in perspective except in so far as he worried over its exploitation by the Muslim minority strong in Northern India.[75]

The related, and more serious, question of the Indians whose abilities and aspirations qualified them to share in governing their country could not be indefinitely postponed on the assumption that they would enter the service of native princes. Sure that opening more civil appointments held by Europeans to Indians would lower the standard of administration, he yet had no doubt that "the political advantages of gradually effacing the line which separates them from alien conquerors are . . . of great importance". They should, however, be selected without competitive examination, so perpetuating the superiority of Europeans chosen by that method and assured of monopolizing the higher posts. European members of the civil service resented Indians who had successfully competed with British candidates: the morale of expatriate officials was not something that Salisbury could neglect. Nor were successful examinees disproportionately drawn from a tiny minority of Indians, almost all belonging to certain Hindu castes, likely to be satisfactory instruments of British rule; not least because they were susceptible to the sentiments that found expression in the native press. If too many entered by that route, he contemplated its closure, "an indecent and embarrassing necessity". In the event, when this thinking was incorporated in Lytton's reforms of 1879, as modified by Cranbrook at the India Office, there proved to be a shortage of Indian candidates who were educationally inferior and administratively capable.[76]

Salisbury's involvement with India's external relations before he moved to the Foreign Office should be viewed in the context of his place in British foreign policy. There is only room to note his disagreements with successive viceroys over a need to establish a permanent British mission in Afghanistan, the legendary gateway to India. Its presence, Salisbury argued, was indispensable to strengthen British influence over a fiercely Muslim and xenophobic country in its role of a buffer state against Russian expansion in Central Asia. Northbrook adhered to Lawrence's school of thought on frontier policy, which considered the Russian threat to Afghanistan and India to be grossly overstated, and had a healthy respect for the Afghans who in 1842 had wiped out a previous British mission and its supporting garrison. Salisbury neatly summarized his reasons for an alternative approach to Afghanistan. "We cannot conquer it; we cannot leave it alone. We can only spare to it our utmost vigilance." Northbrook was mistaken in believing that he wished to revive the failed policy of the 1840s and reduce the kingdom to a dependency resembling an Indian native state. Lytton, sent out with instructions from Disraeli and Salisbury to take the line which Northbrook had been loath to follow, strove to impose on ministers his own vision of expansion into Afghanistan and beyond. As long as Salisbury was at the India Office, he held in check a viceroy "burning to distinguish himself in a great war." "You are so strong, and I am so weak", confessed Lytton in a rare moment of humility.[77]

"Personal responsibility", said Salisbury in parliament, "is the thing requisite in the government of India". His most persistent critic on the council of India in London, Sir Erskine Perry, fought the trend, as he saw it, to make the viceroy a "puppet". This hostile witness paid tribute to Salisbury's "great pains in administration", while adding that he was "rather a rusher" – by bureaucratic standards, that is. Salisbury reorganized departmental procedures in the India Office to enhance his independence of, and authority over, the permanent under-secretary. The "useful conservative influence" of the council, Perry complained, was circumvented by taking important business in its political committee, which Salisbury tended to dominate. Towards the end of his time, the council grew restive, "getting sore", he observed "at being left outside while all the real work is being done, and . . . only called in to ratify. I may have to give way occasionally in small matters".[78]

He had by 1878 disentangled "the indistinct and confused apportionment of responsibility and power" in the higher direction of an empire. He tried to make his viceroys understand that after the second Reform Act "I am close to the great democracy we all have to obey". His permanent under-secretary spoke of the "contempt for precedent" in a formidable minister, restrained by "humorous cynicism", both features of Salisbury's Indian correspondence. It was not open to any secretary of state to revolutionize British policy in India. Salisbury's thoughts on agrarian reform and their reception show how quickly he came up against the realities behind which official conservatism sheltered. He was indeed an "innovator", handicapped by the weakness of the progressive forces he wanted to stimulate. The servant of Britain as well as of India, he sought to reconcile their interests: imperialism was a fact of his world. The Indian empire was administered with more insight and greater humanity for his stewardship.[79]

# CHAPTER SIX

# The Eastern Question and the Foreign Office

## Diplomatic Realities

From the 1870s to his final departure from the Foreign Office in 1900, Salisbury hardly deviated from his carefully thought out approach to the problem of Britain's future in a changing world. She was part of Europe, but with a difference. A semi-detached policy was both right and possible for her. She must work with the European powers, as the British public expected, but she ought not to sacrifice too much of her freedom of action to their treaty-based alliances. So long as she preserved her essential freedom Salisbury was ready and willing to align Britain with a power, or powers, whose interests coincided with hers in the long or the short run. Bismarck and his methods never appealed to him, nor did he entertain any illusions about the difficulties inherent in negotiating with Russian autocracy. Yet the power he most distrusted was France, not because the Third Republic was a functioning democracy, but because of her deep-seated anglophobia and the volatility of her politicians and people. Moreover, the magnitude of her defeat by Germany in 1870 appeared to preclude a revival of the Anglo-French entente round which Palmerston had built his policy. Militarily weak and disinclined to expend blood and treasure in a trial of strength on Continental battlefields, Britain needed to be on good terms with France's successor as the strongest power on land if she was to count for something in Europe. The Eastern question taught Salisbury to look to Bismarck and Germany for solutions that Britain could not impose. This formative experience did not make a cynic of him in international politics. While he had little patience with the idealism that Gladstone seemed to make his own, and sometimes indulged, Salisbury adopted a humane and prudent pragmatism. It called for skill with limited resources and a lot of nerve; qualities apparent beyond Europe, too, in his handling of the Anglo-American relationship, perhaps the trickiest for any Victorian minister.

Disraeli had looked forward to his first visit to Hatfield since Salisbury's succession with a degree of apprehension rare in a man more than equal to the most embarrassing encounters. By the last years of his government he was a regular guest, on excellent terms with the whole family.[1] The foundation of this transformed relationship was their combination on the Eastern question at the end of months of tension within the cabinet. Salisbury changed sides after his departure in protest at Disraeli's desire for a warlike policy had been imminently expected more than once. He replaced his step-mother's husband, Derby, at the Foreign Office in March 1878. Carnarvon, Salisbury's friend and ally, left two months before Derby. The two resigning ministers were convinced that Salisbury's abandonment of their common resistance to Disraeli was inspired by personal ambition. The most recent historian of the cabinet's divisions can find no explanation of his motives that is quite satisfactory.[2]

The paradoxical answer put forward here is that, in the end, Salisbury could see no way of avoiding a hateful war for the perpetuation of the Ottoman empire except to prepare for one ostentatiously. Britain's historic protection of Turkey, her treaty obligations, anxiety about her own diminished international standing, and her public opinion all ruled out acquiescence in a Russian conquest of Constantinople. Moreover, neither he nor Disraeli believed in the survival of the Ottoman empire in the longer term, and agreed in wanting to begin its disguised and controlled partition. Salisbury always maintained that the Turcophobe Carnarvon's exit from the cabinet was unnecessary: he did not say that of Derby's resignation; their breach was never healed. So far as Europe and the Eurasian empire of Turkey were concerned, Derby was an isolationist. England had little, if anything, to gain and a great deal to lose by being drawn into a clash of empires – Russian, Ottoman and Austrian – on the marches of Europe. Salisbury was, and is still, often represented as an isolationist himself in a European context: wrongly; for him Britain was a European power in need of an ally, or allies, on that continent. In his judgement, which continued to differ from Disraeli's on the point, the country did not want war, only the careful, resolute diplomacy that would save her feelings and her interests. He had assessed her weakness, and Russia's, and built his policy on those calculations when he succeeded Derby.

For many years Salisbury had held that Britain had no option but to make policy reflect her relative weakness among the great powers. After France's defeat in 1870, he contended that there were only three great powers in reality – Russia, Germany and the United States. Britain's standing army, he reminded the Lords, was a hundred thousand strong, Russia's one and a half million, and united Germany's over a million. The United States, with a small regular army, had demonstrated her ability in the Civil War to put two million into the field on the Northern side alone. It was a delusion to suppose that the Royal Navy could compensate for the army. Britain lacked the means to honour commitments in Europe unaided, or, he refrained from adding, to defend Canada in the event of an American invasion. She employed the language of a great power, habitual from the period "when we had a brave spirit", without being able to live up to it. He feared a terrible humiliation at the hands of the genuine powers which would discredit the historic institutions of his country in the eyes of her people. These were not views aired to embarrass the Liberal government of the day; although he criticized its passive reaction to the victorious Germans' treatment of France, seeing in the annexation of Alsace and Lorraine the certain cause of future conflict.[3]

A question to which he always came back was conscription, regarded as politically unacceptable by most of his contemporaries. Discussing it with Carnarvon at this time, he favoured indirect compulsion to obtain recruits for a bigger army. In every town or rural parish that failed to raise its quota by voluntary enlistment, eligible males should draw lots to supply the deficiency, without the Continental possibility of substitutes allowed. The scheme, he pointed out, still permitted the rich to escape because they would ensure that the quota was met by paying men to volunteer; a comment revealing of the practical difficulties involved. That he should have seriously considered anything so certain to be unpopular is an indication of his fears for Britain's safety in a world full of danger for even the greatest powers. He had felt the ignominy of her position in 1864 when she was helpless to rescue Denmark from Austria and Prussia. By the early 1870s Russia, Germany and the United States had all got the better of Britain, or had ignored her, over, respectively, the unilateral abrogation of the Black Sea's neutral status agreed following the Crimean War; the terms of peace with France; and American claims for losses at sea to British-built Confederate raiders during the Civil War. The country, Salisbury told Carnarvon, must decide whether it wanted to be a great power, or not. The pretence that she was one exposed her to international ridicule.[4]

Like Palmerston before him, Salisbury was forced to acknowledge that the libertarianism of all social classes in Britain ruled out conscription. They still expected their government to participate as an equal in the affairs of Europe, and to do so cheaply. Salisbury was one more foreign secretary who had to conduct foreign policy with reference to such unrealistic expectations, making the most of naval strength, national wealth and the social stability envied and respected on the Continent. As far as possible he tried to practise the diplomacy of conviction beside that of weakness. The Eastern question gave him scope for both. He had thought the Ottoman empire ripe for partition since he first entered parliament, and proved to be one of the Turks' most dangerous enemies, as they considered him from the time of the Constantinople Conference in 1876–7. His enmity was at bottom religious: he looked upon Islam as "a false religion", oppressive towards Christians and incapable of assimilating the superior civilisation of the West.[5] His public, however, was used to being told that the continued existence of Turkey in Europe and Asia constituted a vital British interest. Not even the violent outcry in 1876–7 against atrocities perpetrated upon the Sultan's Christian subjects could shake that belief for years to come.

As the British plenipotentiary to the Constantinople conference and later at the Foreign Office, Salisbury was compelled to work for the substantial preservation of Ottoman authority and territory. Germany's interest in preventing the spread of the war between Russia and Turkey which the conference was to have averted, and Russia's exhaustion by her hard won victory, enabled Britain to take the lead in delivering the Turks, at a price. She acquired Cyprus for her own strategic purposes in a limited partition of the Sultan's dominions. Salisbury's insight and nerve carried him through the tricky negotiations that prepared the ground for the Congress of Berlin. The diplomatic triumph there was shared with Disraeli, whose undoubted courage he recognized. But it was Salisbury who managed the business. At home admirers and critics supposed he was determined to prop up the Ottoman empire indefinitely in continuation of the Crimean policy. The Turks, rightly, saw him as intending a stay of execution, nothing more.

The Berlin Congress exhibited Germany under Bismarck as the arbiter of Europe. Palmerston's foreign policy had skilfully exploited an Anglo-French relationship which proved itself in the Crimea and in other places, uneasy though it often was. Salisbury's policy for over twenty years centred on co-operation with Germany. While he shared Derby's distrust of Bismarck, he did not want to distance his country from Europe. Harking back to his pro-Russian stance during the Crimean War, he sometimes regretted that she had not preserved the alliance with Russia to which the first Napoleon finally succumbed. Though the German option was to lose some of its attractions, there was really no alternative from the later 1870s: Germany's interests and those of Britain were convergent; each had her own reasons for wishing to perpetuate peace in the European heartland. They were not yet serious rivals for trade and colonies. Dynastic ties, religious sympathies, memories of Waterloo and earlier campaigns, and to a considerable extent, their political cultures made them natural partners, with the reservations inherent in international relations. "Our foreign affairs go badly", wrote Salisbury when Russia invaded Turkey in 1877. "We adopted the Crimean policy with a great military ally. This ally" – that is, any such ally – "fails us – and the fact is brought home to us that military operations are nowadays impossible to a nation that has no conscription".[6] He stood out against ostentatious preparations for British intervention on land until Russia was in no state to go on fighting, and Austria ventured to challenge her. As that moment approached, he reminded an excited viceroy in India that "Diplomacy which does not rest on force is the most feeble and futile of weapons, and except for bare self-defence, we have not the force".[7] Only Germany possessed the strength necessary to broker a settlement, for the time being, of the Eastern question.

At the end of his first term as foreign secretary Salisbury was satisfied that "Germany is clearly cut out to be our ally". The German conception of an alliance was not his, however. Then and for many years afterwards he resisted entering into a treaty relationship. German complaints of Britain's too independent attitude elicited the dry comment that she had "rather taken a humble part occasionally to emphasize Bismarck's hegemony".[8] The security provided by the entente with Germany was reflected when Britain encountered competition in the course of her global expansion. The rule that Salisbury laid down for an old acquaintance, a governor of Fiji, worried about Germany's appearance in the Pacific, applied to Egypt as much as to some remote archipelago: "The real remedy is to increase your own power there". The Germans in Tonga, the French in Egypt, should be contained by the assertion of real, not hypothetical, British interests which were defensible by the judicious advertisement of force or, if need be, its employment. Such tangible interests ought not to be sacrificed to unreasonable dislike of interference in other countries. The weakest spot in Britannia's armour was North America. From time to time Salisbury mused on a lost opportunity: the British failure to recognize the Confederacy and the consequences that flowed from an irreparable mistake. "America", he remarked in 1872, "would now have been nicely divided into hostile states, and we should have had as little to fear from Washington as . . . from Paris". As it was, the hopeless vulnerability of Canada, for which Britain faced having to fight with the certainty of being defeated, threatened the empire with a potential humiliation of the first magnitude.[9]

## The Return of the Eastern Question

Another phase of the Eastern question opened in 1875 with Turkey's inability to meet in full the interest due on her funded debt and with the revolt of Christian Slavs in Bosnia-Herzegovina. The great powers responded by pressing for internal reforms calculated to improve the position of Christians and diminish the authority of Constantinople in the affected provinces. Turkey displayed unexpected resilience in the face of what was widely assumed to be the final crisis of her empire. She repelled the military intervention in June 1876 of Serbia and Montenegro, her tributary states, despite the Russian officers whom their government allowed to fight with the Serbs. Their presence in the Serbian army was an indication of the Pan-Slav sentiment which reinforced the traditional hostility of Orthodox Russia to the Turk. Another Christian revolt, in Bulgaria, was suppressed between April and June that year with a severity that much European opinion found intolerable. The famous "Bulgarian atrocities" had their greatest impact in Britain. The powers whose earlier initiatives had been rejected either by the Bosnian rebels, or by the Sultan, now increased the pressure on the latter. Neither the Tsarist autocracy nor the British parliamentary state could ignore the feeling that well publicized Turkish excesses had aroused. Austria, Russia's rival for Balkan influence, had reached a supposedly secret understanding with her in July 1876 that outlined a territorial reconstruction of the entire region to follow the anticipated Turkish collapse before her Christian subjects from the Adriatic to the Black Sea. When it was apparent that the Ottoman empire would not be overthrown by rebellion Tsar Alexander II was impelled by the Pan-Slavs, who were represented among his advisers, to envisage other means of realizing the aims discussed with Austria. Germany was concerned to keep the peace between her partners in the Three Emperors' League of 1873, and France was convalescent after defeat. Turkey's only friend, one with nearly fatal reservations, was Britain, or more specifically, Disraeli and some of his cabinet backed by the national unwillingness to lose the fruits of Crimean victory. These events culminated in the unsuccessful Constantinople conference of December 1876 and January 1877, which left Russia and Turkey on the verge of war. Salisbury was present as the British plenipotentiary.[10]

It is necessary to go over what happened in some detail. The British press, Derby advised the editors of *The Times* and the *Daily Telegraph* in August 1875, was making too much of the insurrection in Herzegovina that had spread to Bosnia. Evidence of the Austrian complicity in the revolt and Germany's anxiety about the developing situation, which she communicated to the British government, did not affect this initial assessment. Derby was unmoved by fears of isolation as the powers consulted: "to me it appears that when 'isolated' we have generally been most successful . . .". This did not imply indifference to events in the Ottoman empire. It was an expression of a preference, not of a principle. Before long he was telling Disraeli that they ought not to stand aside from the collective proposals put to Turkey in December 1875 and known as the Andrassy Note: British public opinion, running against Turkey, would find a refusal to take part hard to understand. Disraeli demurred because, he said, "England ought to lead and not to follow". Salisbury also opposed participation, with reasoned argument. The suggested reforms of Ottoman administration should be supported in general terms. The language of the Note, however, pointed to armed intervention and joint Austro-Russian occupation of the rebellious territories, leading to "the gradual reduction of the Porte to the condition of a protected principality under the three Eastern Powers". As a signatory, Britain would have committed herself to a resolution of the Eastern question which "probably . . . we could not stop". Derby was nevertheless able to persuade the premier and cabinet that they must not seem to encourage Turkey to defy the international demand for reform; although he personally did not believe any reforms could reconcile Christian Slavs to their Ottoman rulers.[11]

Only a "temporary delay" was possible, Derby thought, in the Ottoman empire's disintegration. Disraeli and Salisbury doubted whether the respite would be very long. A partition of the crumbling empire, the latter complained in January 1876, was denounced as immoral: there was no other way of averting "the calamities of a gigantic war" as great powers disputed the spoils. Ten years previously, at the India Office, he had marked down the tributary state of Egypt as falling into the British sphere of influence "when the sick man's body comes to be cut up". Then in the autumn of 1875, he was *decidedly* in favour of buying the Khedive's shareholding in the Suez Canal company; approving of the government's action as an announcement to the world that Britain meant to safeguard and extend her Near and Middle Eastern interests. He was also more concerned about Russian expansion in Central Asia than he gave his Indian correspondents to understand. Although, in view of the logistics, it was not sensible to attempt an invasion of India, "the war party at St Petersburg" might discover the "pretext" it needed in incautious language about the Russian advance in the direction of Afghanistan. The resulting conflict would take place on Ottoman territory, not in the Central Asian wilderness, because Russia was exposed in the Black Sea through the Straits controlled by the Sultan: and Britain was vulnerable through her shaky Turkish ally. Britain could best protect India by standing up to Russia in this new phase of the Eastern question and insisting on her strategically placed share if the Ottoman empire was partitioned. At the same time the Salisbury of the 1870s was acutely conscious of the "wretchedly oppressed multitudes" of Christians in the Balkans and Asia Minor whose hopes of throwing off the Muslim yoke centred on Russia. He did not, until many years had passed, agree with Derby that the Muslims and Christians of the Ottoman lands resembled each other in their savagery.[12]

The Bosnian rebels' rejection of the Andrassy Note encouraged Russia and Austria, with the active assistance of German diplomacy, to step up their pressure on the Sultan. The Berlin Memorandum drawn up by the three powers in May 1876 called for a two months' armistice in Bosnia and set out its conditions, unfavourable to the Turks. A final paragraph referred to "efficacious measures" to be taken if the armistice expired without a settlement. The nature of that further action was spelt out in the secret "Treaty" of Reichstadt between Austria and Russia in July: Turkey in Europe distributed between Austria, Russia, Greece, Serbia and Montenegro with autonomy for Bulgaria, Rumelia and Albania, and the status of a free city for Constantinople with its mixed population. Russia contented herself with the strip of Bessarabia lost to her after the Crimean War, and Austria proposed to take Bosnia: but the former's sphere of influence comprised the Eastern, and the latter's the Western, Balkans. Invited to adhere to action under the Berlin agreements, which it had not helped to frame, the British government angrily declined. Warships from all the Christian powers were making for Turkish waters following the murder, by Turks, of the French and German consuls at Salonica, and other signs of the Muslim unrest that led to the deposition of Sultan Abdul Aziz at the end of May. Disraeli "rather startled" the cabinet on 22 May by his talk of seizing the Turkish fleet to prevent it from falling into Russian hands. Ministers consented to strengthen the Royal Navy in the Mediterranean, and added to the reinforcements later in the week. Disraeli acted to force the three emperors to take Britain's wishes into account.[13]

Rebuffed by the Russians, he turned to Germany. Twelve months earlier, he had spoken of "Bismarck . . . being like Napoleon, against whom all Europe had to ally itself". The German chancellor, moreover, had let it be known in January that he would welcome Anglo-German co-operation on the Eastern question. Derby had been suspicious: "what does he want in return? It is not diplomatic custom, and certainly not his, to give much for nothing . . .". The price of the foreign secretary's insularity was clear in the Berlin Memorandum. Disraeli replied to exclusion from collective policy-making by serving notice of Britain's intentions on all the powers whose warships had gathered at Besika Bay near the Southern end of the Dardanelles. He refused "to escape isolation by consenting to play a secondary part". Britain intended to observe the international agreements closing the Straits to foreign navies in peacetime, and invited Europe to echo her. Reflecting on these developments in his diary, Derby conceded that the premier's "policy of determination" had succeeded: "We are more respected and consulted than has been common of late years". Germany, and France too, were approving: Russia, or the Pan-Slavs who influenced a hesitant Tsar, had been reminded of the need to work with others in the East. She did nothing, however, to arrest the spread of war and rebellion in the Balkans. Serbia, her prince urged on by the Pan-Slav Russian consul in Belgrade and her army commanded by a Russian general, attacked her suzerain while the Turks were putting down the rising in Bulgaria. The Ottoman state had effected its change of ruler "with quiet and decision", and its military successes drove the Serbs to seek an armistice in August, which a Russian ultimatum forced on the Turks by October.[14]

A European conference, supported by Disraeli as the best means of defusing a growing crisis, became a matter of urgency to help the defeated Slavs. The Reichstadt agreement of July was quickly overtaken by events. The formidable agitation that sprang up in Britain, calling on the government to restrain and reform what public opinion supposed was a client state rather than an ally, exposed Turkey to renewed danger. Her only friend's ability to come to the rescue was so much affected by the agitation that Disraeli, now in the Lords as Earl of Beaconsfield, and Derby acknowledged, if only to a very few, that "we have changed our policy, and . . . adopted the views of the [Liberal] opposition". Their mediation between Turk and Slav proposed a degree of autonomy for Bosnia-Herzegovina and Bulgaria. In fact, Beaconsfield would have liked to start the process of partition, imagining a division of Turkey in Europe under Britain's leadership. Her portion should be Constantinople, neutralized and a free port, with an "adequate" surrounding area. So long as the city itself, the ultimate goal of Russia's southward expansion, did not fall to the Tsar's lot, the British public might be persuaded that the Crimean War had not been fought in vain, however much of the Ottoman land went to him in one way or another. Beaconsfield's assumption that Turkey could not stave off the break-up of her empire for many more years was almost universal in the West. Queen Victoria, for instance, took up a suggestion from the Coburg King of the Belgians that her second son, who was married to the Tsar's daughter, should be substituted for the Sultan at Constantinople to control the Straits, and given an undetermined but mainly Christian territory. A second deposition in the Turkish capital, of the insane Murad V after a reign of three months, seemed to herald the demise of the dynasty and empire. No one anticipated that his youthful successor, Abdul Hamid II, would rule for more than thirty years and effect the salvation of Turkey by her selective Westernization.[15]

Salisbury saw that Turkey, "a despotism without a despot", was nevertheless "maintaining with success a desperate struggle for national existence". Yet he was, and remained, convinced that the inherent fighting qualities of her Anatolian conscripts could not compensate for irredeemable maladministration and bankruptcy. Not inclined to underestimate the "Russophobia" that Lytton exemplified, he was still tempted to wish that "we could throw ourselves into the arms of Russia and ignore the rest of Europe". The rivalry between Russia and Austria did not permit the adoption of that policy even if British public opinion had been prepared to see Russia take Constantinople, in exchange for recognition of Britain's real interests, as Salisbury defined them, in the rest of the empire. For behind Austria stood Germany: not yet treaty-bound to Austria's survival, but committed to the objectives of European peace and order enshrined in the Three Emperors' League. Salisbury correctly predicted that, in the circumstances, "the form of the Sultanate will have to be kept up longer than the power" to allow new, and existing, Slav states to mature under its nominal overlordship. The victory of Russian Pan-Slavism could be decently disguised to soothe Austria, and his countrymen: "alliance and friendship [with the Turk] is a reproach to us", he told Carnarvon, who was pro-Russian and hostile to the Turks, very largely on religious grounds. He did not say as much to the premier and Derby, but stressed the impact of the domestic agitation that Gladstone headed, and the imperative need to give Ottoman Christians institutional securities against oppression. He urged Beaconsfield not to let Austria – no longer strong enough for her historic role as Britain's Continental ally – prevent an understanding with Russia.[16]

The powers were moving towards a conference that would bring Europe to the aid of the Christian Slavs unable to free themselves from Turkey, and avert direct intervention by Russia. Derby discouraged the premier from seeking a British-led partition: "the risk of war is great . . . the Powers will all want something". He was now fully launched on his prolonged exertions, stretching over eighteen months, to hold back Beaconsfield, who wanted, at least, to stake a British claim if and when Russia struck. At the cabinet on 4 October, the premier obtained its backing, but not the foreign secretary's, for the occupation of Constantinople as "a material guarantee" for Britain's share of the spoils. Against the background of Russian proposals for collective military and naval intervention should Turkey reject the cease-fire to which she had submitted, the War Office embarked on contingency planning. Derby found Salisbury "warlike" in the cabinet discussions: but its members were agreed on resisting Beaconsfield's desire for an Anglo-German pact to uphold the *status quo* across Europe: "It would make us easy about Constantinople", he urged. Salisbury did not subscribe to Derby's jaundiced view of Bismarckian Germany as "a military despotism": but he was wary of the German chancellor: "He may make merely colourable efforts to maintain the *status quo* . . . and . . . claim a promise on our part to take nothing". Yet relying on Germany instead of on Britain's limited capability to mount an amphibious operation at the Golden Horn made sense, unlike Beaconsfield's large talk, from now on, of war and conquests. "He would rather run serious national risks than have his policy called feeble or commonplace", wrote Derby towards the end of October 1876, "to me the first object is to keep England out of trouble". Bismarck, believing that Europe's interests and Germany's were best served by an orderly break-up of the Ottoman empire, along the lines sketched at Reichstadt, supported the British proposal for a conference of the powers, Turkey included.[17]

The German ambassador in London, Count Münster, warned that Russia was bent on war. Derby took this to mean that Germany wanted partition, by negotiation or otherwise. Salisbury was his choice, and Beaconsfield's, as Britain's plenipotentiary. He had shown in cabinet his readiness to confront Russia, if it proved impossible to reach agreement with her. His thinking on the approach to partition was more realistic than the premier's. Partly through the influential High Church network, it was known that his sympathies lay with the Sultan's Christian subjects; Gladstone and like-minded Liberals greeted his nomination with pleasure. That was an important consideration when ministers, and the premier in particular, had been criticized for their hesitancy in condemning Turkish barbarities. Lastly, his ability was plain. Beaconsfield sent him on his way with some superfluous advice: "This is a momentous period in your life and career". Salisbury expected failure: Russia would not be content with any terms which the Turks could be induced to accept, but, he told Derby, "if you continue to think I had better go, I will take my part in the comedy with all solemnity". His instructions, drawn up in the Foreign Office and passed by the cabinet, outlined the autonomy recommended for the Christians who had rebelled, and an ambitious programme of reform. Elected provincial assemblies were to be protected by a collective veto, entrusted to the ambassadors of the powers at Constantinople, on the Sultan's choice of governors.[18]

The admissibility of a foreign occupation of Ottoman territory, not mentioned in the instructions, divided the cabinet. Carnarvon and Cairns, deeply religious men anxious for the endangered Christians, were for allowing the conference to discuss occupation. Disraeli opposed this; while Derby let the Austrian ambassador in London know that he would not regard a Russian advance across the Ottoman frontier as an act of war, though Britain was certain to fight for Constantinople. Salisbury's position, "moderate and sensible", left him nearer to Derby than to the others. His instructions were not modified, but supplementary instructions which followed him to the East sanctioned consideration of a foreign occupation if the conference ended without agreement and the Turks were obdurate. His reception in the European capitals he visited *en route* showed that imperial Turkey's survival was discounted everywhere. Bismarck went into detail about the partition he advocated, pressing Egypt on Britain and leaving the Sultan at Constantinople with an undefined area of the hinterland. "I would sooner we had Asia Minor", observed Beaconsfield. Salisbury concluded that the chancellor wished Russia to assert herself at Turkey's expense, but that, contrary to what Derby suspected, he did not want her to come to blows with Britain. In the German scheme of things, Russia's friendship was indispensable and Britain's useful for the strengths special to her. Bismarck emphasized to Salisbury that a Russian invasion would not pose an immediate threat to Constantinople: if and when it did, Britain might easily occupy the city from the sea. Britain should not, therefore, treat an attack on Turkey as a *casus belli*. In Vienna Count Andrassy looked to acquire Bosnia and had no intention of going to war with Russia. The French also favoured partition, as spectators, and the Italian king sided with Russia in eager expectation of some gains from a general war.[19]

Salisbury travelled with his wife, two of his children, and a staff of Foreign Office clerks, two of whom were to be closely associated with him in later years, Philip Currie and Sir Stafford Northcote's son, Henry. Derby, who did not like her, foresaw that Lady Salisbury, clever and energetic, would complicate her husband's task by the partisanship she usually exhibited. She displayed without reserve the High Church solicitude for the Eastern Orthodox which determined Gladstone's attitude to the Turk. Relations between Salisbury and the resident envoy in Constantinople, Sir Henry Elliot, were strained almost from the start by their differences over policy, compounded by dissatisfaction with his poor information and slowness to comprehend a worsening situation. His offence, in Salisbury's eyes, was to uphold the longstanding British commitment to Turkey without reinterpreting it in a radical fashion. Salisbury required an ambassador who could "manage" the Turks: that was beyond Elliot. The British community in Constantinople took the ambassador's part; as creditors of the Ottoman government, the businessmen among them had an interest in perpetuating, unimpaired, its authority over the Balkan provinces, where much of the Sultan's revenue was raised. They stood to benefit, Salisbury pointed out in his letters home, from Turkish and British expenditure in a war with Russia. The reports of journalists covering the conference for British newspapers reflected the expatriate displeasure with a pro-Russian politician ready to negotiate away Turkey's internationally guaranteed position.[20]

Disraeli was quick to suspect Salisbury of being too much influenced by the High Churchmen conspicuous in the agitation to which his appointment was a concession. "Lyddonism", as the premier called it, ranked high in his political demonology. Salisbury was not, in reality, much impressed by the clerical irruption into foreign policy. Before there was any question of his going to Constantinople, he gave Liddon a lesson in the restraints that statecraft placed upon apparently compelling moral judgements. It was difficult to see, he told him, what could be substituted for the Eurasian power of the Ottoman dynasty, were the righteous indignation of Christendom to sweep it away. Treaties barely twenty years old pledged the signatories to its preservation. Lastly – he was unaware of the understanding reached at Reichstadt – Austria and Russia might be plunged into war over their neighbour's crumbling empire if Britain did not keep them back. Salisbury's High Church friends knew that he was with them in detesting the Turk and hoping for an end to, at least, his rule in Europe. "The time for open speaking has not come yet", he said as he set off for Constantinople to another High Churchman, Lord Bath, one of the few Tories to support Gladstone's crusade. When her husband found the Sultan and his advisers convinced that the government in London neither could nor would abandon them if Russia invaded, Lady Salisbury wrote to Bath from Turkey, asking him to "encourage all peace demonstrations as much as you can . . . but beware of . . . saying whence this counsel comes . . . the country must speak out its will as soon as possible". It is unlikely that Salisbury was ignorant of her letter.[21]

He was not, however, quite the pro-Russian that friends and critics believed him to be. The nature of the Pan-Slavism with which he had to deal in the person of Count N.P. Ignatiev, Russia's ambassador and her representative at the conference, was evident to him, "hatred for the Turks and for the English", for the latter as an embodiment of the liberalism that was corroding the fabric of Holy Russia. But he did not feel for the Russians the "contempt and revulsion" which the Turks inspired in him, and which he did not conceal from the other representatives at the conference. Beaconsfield and Derby were both opposed to the physical coercion of Turkey: and alarmed by reports that Salisbury had adopted a posture so markedly anti-Turkish as to make it hard for Britain to object should Russia resort to force. He had, they feared, got too close to Ignatiev. Even Derby insisted that Constantinople must not fall to Russia; although he thought Britain might very well stand aside in the event of a Russian invasion until it reached the imperial city. In talking to his diplomatic colleagues, Salisbury used language which implied that, in his view, Constantinople had little strategic value for Britain: India's natural line of defence lay along her mountainous border. His countrymen, he remarked, seemed to need a bogy to frighten themselves: once it had been the Pope, now it was Russia.[22]

The plenipotentiaries assembled to negotiate with the Turks and with each other met with determined Turkish resistance to proposals that weakened the Sultan's overriding authority in his threatened European provinces. In preliminary meetings the Christian powers agreed among themselves to reforms in Bulgaria and Bosnia on the lines sketched in Derby's circular invitation to the conference, and to the deployment of several thousand troops from a small Western country – they selected Belgium – in Bulgaria as a gendarmerie during the transition to a new order of things. The latter was a compromise of German origin to keep the Russians out. Beaconsfield had been ready to put 40 000 troops into the province if the Turks invited him to do so.[23] The young Sultan and his grand vizier, Midhat Pasha, were adamant that they would never accept international supervision of reforms to which they assented in principle. As the conference opened, they produced a liberal constitution for the whole empire, with a chamber of deputies elected by secret ballot and equality before the law for all his subjects. This enabled Midhat to argue that the powers' desire to institutionalize external intervention and religious divisions was incompatible with the rights of the nation and its citizens. The plenipotentiaries discounted this surprising development: rightly, for the constitution was shortlived. They were more impressed by the Turks' resolute refusal to give ground on demands intended to undermine the central authority of the Porte.

Bismarck had expressed doubts to Salisbury whether Russia's resources were equal to campaigning through the Balkans to Constantinople. The first dragoman at the Russian embassy described the city as an armed camp; troops and munitions were everywhere on the move. The Turkish newspapers, mouthpieces of government, breathed defiance of Russia. "Je ne vois clair devant nous", he wrote "Je ne vois que du sang et encore du sang en perspective." Salisbury appears to have been a little slow to realise that the Russians, including Ignatiev and other influential Pan-Slavs, did not want war if it could be avoided without loss of face before domestic opinion. He complained that their known reluctance to contemplate actual hostilities had deprived him of his only weapon in dealing with the Turks. The powers were obliged to modify their proposals for close supervision of reforms. The revised version was no more acceptable. At the session of the conference on 8 January 1877, the Ottoman representative rounded on his tormentors and answered a reference from his French antagonist to the Bulgarian massacres with a pointed allusion to atrocities in the history of France. Throughout the Russians relied on co-operation between Ignatiev and Salisbury to overcome Turkish resistance. They were delighted with Salisbury: it had fallen to him, they understood, to carry through a momentous change in British policy and to tell the Turks that if they did not submit to the dictation of the powers, they would be driven from Europe to international applause. The information reaching Beaconsfield from a variety of sources led him to think that Britain's plenipotentiary was "more Russian than Ignatiev" when he had been sent to keep Russia out of Turkey, "not to create an ideal existence for Turkish Christians".[24]

Salisbury was similarly distrustful of the premier, to the extent of sending Carnarvon a cipher for use if the cabinet made decisions "of which neither of us approves". The two friends were afraid of a new Anglo-Turkish alliance as the outcome of Beaconsfield's persistent talk of war to prevent Britain from being relegated to the second rank of European powers. Salisbury sought, and did not obtain, the immediate recall of Elliot, whom he accused of subverting his efforts at getting agreement from the Turks. Elliot, Henry Northcote fairly observed, thought an Englishman who got on so well with Ignatiev, no friend to his country, was "irreclaimable": and left the negotiations to Salisbury. The Turks took this as an indication that the British plenipotentiary did not enjoy the backing of his government. That was not the case, despite the misgivings at home excited by his determination to apply the maximum diplomatic pressure to Turkey. He had, Northcote insisted to his father, "Turkey's true interests" always in view: they did not include ruling over the Christian peoples of the Balkans. Beaconsfield scarcely regretted the failure of the conference: his mind was running on partition. In a letter of 11 January to Carnarvon, written when the failure was clear, Salisbury hoped that his diplomacy and Turkish recalcitrance had turned his compatriots against participation in the inevitable conflict between Russia and Turkey. British statesmen who believed that the road to India lay through the Near and Middle East must find some other means of safeguarding it than the existing Ottoman empire provided. He was also thinking of partition: he and the premier were not as far apart as they seemed.[25]

Before leaving Constantinople, Salisbury reviewed the courses open to the government. He put a choice of three to Derby. Britain might join in the coercion of Turkey by armed force: "but that you will not do". She might let Russia act alone, and intervene diplomatically if the invasion succeeded: "but you may have to content yourself with writing a pathetic despatch". Or she might select "the safest course": agreement with Russia and Austria for their occupation of Bulgaria and Bosnia, respectively, until those regions were judged ready for self-government as tributary states of the Sultan. There was really no alternative: he was – wrongly – sure that the Ottoman administrative machine had almost reached the point of final collapse. He was wrong, again, in supposing that the Russian embassy controlled "a vast network of intrigue" enabling it to accelerate, at will, the Turkish decline into anarchy. Beaconsfield was glad to learn that Salisbury had applied for more assistance to be given to the sapper colonel who had been examining the defences of Constantinople since October 1876, for the extension of this military survey to the harbours of Cyprus and Rhodes, with Batoum on the Black Sea. Like Salisbury, the premier felt that the Treaty of Paris had outlived its usefulness; he wondered how it might be construed to justify the loss of Ottoman territory and "temporary" limitations placed upon the Sultan's freedom of action.[26]

## From the Constantinople Conference to the Russo-Turkish War

Partition was under way before the end of the Constantinople conference. Austria and Russia concluded a secret convention at Budapest in January 1877 which pledged the former to a benevolent neutrality, defined as opposition to further international mediation and to activation of the triple guarantee of Turkey in the Treaty of Paris by herself, Britain and France. In return, Hapsburg Austria, conscious of being "half-encircled" by her Romanov competitor, obtained in this and the second Budapest convention of March a restatement of the broad allocation of territory at Reichstadt, amplified by a promise not to erect a large Slav state in the Eastern Balkans which would be a magnet for Slavs under Austrian rule or influence. The two Budapest conventions led on to the Berlin settlement after the arbitrament of war. Britain's special interests were located in Asiatic Turkey, in the denial of Constantinople itself to Russia, and in access to the Black Sea, where Russia's naval weakness at that date left her Southern ports exposed. There was room for an accommodation with Russia. It was prevented by the beginning of the war between Russia and Turkey: not until the latter had been crushed, after taxing Russian resources to the limit, was it possible for Beaconsfield's government to consent to a substantial measure of partition, veiled, as Salisbury had foreseen, by the fiction of continuing Ottoman sovereignty over regions lost to the Sultan's control. The British public wanted to see Christians protected from misgovernment and massacre: they also wanted the Ottoman empire to endure, a monument to Crimean victories. After the Constantinople conference, Beaconsfield said he would wait on events: but he found it hard to do so, afraid that Britain, and her premier, were being eclipsed by what was passing in the East. It was this restlessness that put an increasing strain on the unity of the cabinet through 1877 and into 1878. Salisbury demonstrated that he knew how to bide his time – one of his great strengths as a foreign minister. It was he, stepping into Derby's shoes, rather than Beaconsfield who gave the public what they wanted.[27]

While Turkish obduracy withstood the pressure applied by the powers, the Constantinople conference enhanced Salisbury's reputation. The Russian diplomat quoted earlier depicted him as looking more like a man of that Eastern world than an Englishman: indeed, with a great black beard turning grey, he reminded this friendly witness of an Eastern Orthodox prelate. Salisbury was "a true Christian" who actually believed in God and in his church, unlike the sophisticates of their diplomatic milieu; a man of feeling and not one to sacrifice everything for political advantage. Nevertheless, the perceptive Russian observer, who advised Ignatiev, did not find Salisbury naïve, summing him up as "a straightforward rival". The British and Russian plenipotentiaries dominated the proceedings. His wife spoke of the personal cost: "The worry and real hopelessness of the whole affair makes it most trying to him". Outwardly there was little sign of strain in his mastery of his brief and the controlled irony of his conversation. He came away with a sense of having "done real work for England, though nothing can be done for Turkey".[28] There were sympathizers with Turkey who supposed from his co-operation with Ignatiev that he had finished by being "devoted bodily and spiritually to the Muscovite". The Queen, though "very Turkish" when Carnarvon saw her in January, was not among them. Salisbury incurred suspicion through his personal and political friendship with Carnarvon, whose letters and telegrams had kept him informed of the cabinet's thinking during his absence. On his return he was invited to transmit a remonstrance from Beaconsfield and Derby about the regular hospitality which Carnarvon extended to Liddon. The cleric continued to criticize both ministers for their inaction and supposed pro-Turkish leanings since the Ottoman Christians first took up arms. Salisbury declined "giving a message of the kind", but he let his friend know that he had been approached.[29]

The agitation against the character and the mere fact of direct Ottoman rule over Balkan Christians angered Beaconsfield, who regarded it as absurdly one-sided. Worse, it restricted Britain's ability to profit from a hard-headed division of the dying empire into client states and spheres of influence, with some judicious annexations. Russian moves, diplomatic and military, for war with Turkey after the conference determined him to flush out those members of his cabinet whose sympathies reputedly lay with the anti-Turkish agitators. At the cabinet of 23 March he announced that there was a clear distinction between "the policy of crusade . . . a nation indulging in sentimental eccentricity" and "the Imperial policy of England". He went on to say that unless the cabinet were united behind him on the Eastern question, he would submit the government's resignation to the Queen. The threat drew, as he intended, a reply from Salisbury. Speaking quietly and with "a becoming seriousness" unexpected in someone who cultivated a light touch, he told Beaconsfield that religious feelings outside and political convictions inside the cabinet could not be ignored. But on "this vast question", the majority of his colleagues stood with Beaconsfield, and he deferred to them. He had quite easily avoided being isolated without relinquishing his opinions or his support; others besides Carnarvon were influenced by him, though less obviously. He had, moreover, struck a different note from Carnarvon, who, having listened with "absolute absorption", showed how uncomfortable he was with Salisbury's assurance that there were no "crusaders" among their number. Two days later, Carnarvon wrote from Windsor in alarm at what he found there. The Queen – "She is ready for war" – believed they were alone in their resistance to Beaconsfield. Carnarvon feared they would be forced into resigning by "the excitement of an European war".[30]

Carnarvon was, and remained, completely opposed to making war as an ally of Islam and Turkey. He believed this to be Salisbury's unshakeable position. Their predicament revived memories of the struggle with Beaconsfield over reform ten years earlier, "the same suspicions, anxieties, intrigues". Salisbury was quite unperturbed: if Beaconsfield had the Queen on his side, he had still to reckon with parliament and the public, "whatever change may come when they see blood, the people are in no humour for war at present". War in the East might be inevitable – "we are rolling down the incline now" – but the attitude of their colleagues did not give immediate cause for concern, and they must not let Beaconsfield pick a quarrel. It was a correct reading of the situation, although Carnarvon felt the strain acutely: "I hate suspense so much that I could almost wish that the fight had come". The divergence between the friends at the cabinet of 23 March and in their letters was to grow as they pursued their common ends by contrasting methods.[31]

The ambassador in London, Count Peter Shuvalov, represented the element in Russia that desired to promote expansion in the Balkans and elsewhere by means short of war, and contested the influence of the Pan-Slavs. His intimacy with Lady Derby gave him privileged access to the foreign secretary, which was to lay husband and wife open to charges that they allowed Shuvalov to know more than he should about the disagreements underlying British policy. The Derbys did not consider that their efforts to keep Britain out of war smacked of disloyalty. The leading Pan-Slavs would also have preferred to gain their ends without having to fight: but through their pressure on him the Tsar's utterances had made it impossible for Russia to acquiesce in Turkey's refusal of ever weaker international demands. Similarly, Beaconsfield's Guildhall speech in November 1876 had committed him to preserving the form, if not the substance, of the Ottoman empire. The London Protocol of the following March was the premier's last attempt to avert a war on which Russia was obliged to embark by the expectations which Alexander II's rhetoric had acknowledged. Ignatiev brought the draft of the protocol to London, where he emphasized how little there was to divide Britain and Russia, and invited himself to Hatfield. The document signed by Derby, Shuvalov and the other resident envoys of the powers urged the Sultan to implement the reforms exhaustively discussed over many months. The cabinet tried, unsuccessfully, to make Britain's participation in this final initiative for peace conditional upon a Russian undertaking to demobilize the forces gathering to attack Turkey.[32]

Derby noted that the ministers most sympathetic to the Christians, Salisbury, Carnarvon, and to some extent Cairns, hoped for "a general change in the East" and gave the impression of being unenthusiastic about the prospect of Turkish agreement to the protocol. Salisbury had welcomed the Russian proposals, telling the premier that if Russia did not satisfy her territorial ambitions in Europe, "She can only find it on the side of Asia". He did not take the threat to India seriously, but it served to check Beaconsfield's hostility to Russia. Modifications which Derby secured in the protocol's wording did not please Salisbury: anything that helped the Turks at this stage was undesirable. In February he had complained to the foreign secretary of the "*insouciance*" that characterized his foreign policy. If a great war engulfed them all, it would be said of him: "'You saw the house was burning . . . asked to help . . . put it out, you replied you had rather wait and see whether the people would come to any conclusion on the subject'". Beaconsfield had been kinder, and more perceptive, in referring to Derby's "salutary apathy", but was now getting restless. Derby's purpose was to keep Britain out of the European conflagration which, he said to a deputation of working men at the Foreign Office in September 1876, would in all probability result from any attempt at partitioning the Ottoman empire. This set him against his oldest friend in politics and against Salisbury, whom he had known since boyhood in what became a family setting. Beaconsfield and Salisbury were ready and eager for partition, though the one professed to be pro-Turkish and the other detested the very idea of an Islamic empire in Christian Europe.[33]

So strong was the contemporary antagonism to Russia that Salisbury trod carefully. The unusually revealing letters he wrote to Lytton in India, a personal friend, exhibited a failing, not yet corrected by experience and the heavier responsibilities of the Foreign Office, which was summed up by the famous soldier who now encountered him: "a clever fellow", observed Sir Garnet Wolseley, ". . . He forms his opinions too quickly, without listening to the views of others, and so is often wrong . . .". Salisbury underestimated both Russia and Turkey. The first "mined by revolution – on the very brink of bankruptcy" could not long sustain military operations at a great distance from her European heartland on Turkey's frontiers, any more than on the Central Asian approaches to India, even against such a foe as

Britain. As for the Sultan, "he has no money – no statesmen – no generals". But the Tsar's army, stretched to breaking-point as it must be by the facts of geography, was "formidable enough for Turkey". British policy could no longer be directed to defending "our impossible . . . client". There was no reason to fear Russia on the Bosphorus, although considerations of prestige would "probably" compel Britain to seek to deny her Constantinople. Russia was too weak at sea to challenge the Royal Navy in the Mediterranean, and her penetration to the regions that really mattered to Britain and India – Egypt with the Suez Canal, and the Persian Gulf. Nothing in the Ottoman lands to the north of them – neither the Balkans, nor Asia Minor – had strategic or purely political value for his country. It was in this context that he threw out a celebrated aphorism: "The commonest error in politics is sticking to the carcasses of dead policies." There was more life in the traditional commitment to Turkey than his ruthless analyses, superficially hard to fault, conceded. The drastic revision of policy which he thought long overdue was not one that most of his colleagues could contemplate. The spell of "dead policies" was proof against his exorcisms in the cabinet room and in discussion with individual ministers.[34]

Yet Salisbury did not look forward to the declaration of war which followed Turkey's swift rejection of the London Protocol. German diplomacy at the Constantinople conference had given him the expected support, but had also appeared to encourage the Turks in their inflexibility. He rightly interpreted these tactics as designed to promote conflict: Bismarck did indeed wish Russia to turn her back on a possible French alliance and slake her appetite for glory and conquest at Turkey's expense instead of Austria's. A Russia weakened by her exertions in the East would be in no state to attack Germany with France, thus dividing the forces of the strongest power in Europe. Salisbury suspected Bismarck of a more sinister design, of planning to keep Russia occupied while Germany launched a pre-emptive strike against France, a nation recovering too quickly from defeat. This time, a German victory might not be beneficial rather than otherwise to Britain: he was worried by indications of a desire to take the Low Countries, or the Dutch kingdom at least, into the German empire. The independence of those countries was a constant of British policy: "it is quite conceivable", he wrote, "that . . . we may be fighting for Holland before two years are out". When Russia invaded Turkey in April 1877, Germany did not move in the West: Bismarck had got his limited war.[35]

"A vassal state to Russia" was Salisbury's vision of the Ottoman empire, shorn of her European provinces and of some Asiatic territory. Constantinople, too, must "infallibly" escape from Britain's control. To retain her influence in the Eastern Mediterranean she required a "*pied-à-terre*" somewhere, not necessarily a large annexation, a base for the fleet and a supporting military presence. In his more realistic moments the premier's ideas were not very different, but intervention on a Crimean scale caught his imagination. Lytton, more Disraelian than Beaconsfield, endeavoured to counter Salisbury's radicalism in his replies. The viceroy represented that abandoning Turkey to her enemies would turn the powerful Muslim minority in India against Britain. As the Caliph, spiritual and temporal head of Islam, the Sultan commanded the loyalty of all true believers. The proclamation of a *jihad*, a holy war, on the infidels invading Turkey and those abetting the aggressor was a disturbing prospect for the British rulers of India.[36] The sub-continent's Muslims had played a leading part in the Mutiny a few years earlier: Salisbury saw in Islam "the only organization and pretty nearly the only ambition hostile to us that is left in India". Lytton had some evidence for his warning, which his correspondent did not altogether ignore, but exaggerated the danger, as he did that from Russia's advance in Central Asia. The viceroy, Salisbury admonished him, should not attempt to dictate foreign policy from and for India. The thought of deferring to the Caliph was not one that a devout Christian cared to entertain. As he remarked to Lytton, "my feelings towards the Sultan in the circumstances resemble those which a secretary of state in Elizabeth's time might have felt towards the Pope". There is no doubt that his wife spoke for him when she said a Russian conquest of Turkey might well have the opposite effect on India's Muslims to that predicted by Lytton, "more likely to frighten them into quietness than anything else".[37]

The professional advice available to Beaconsfield estimated that on the Balkan front the Russian army would take four months to reach Constantinople, and would meet with serious resistance in the Caucasus. As Russia went to war in April, he asked the cabinet to decide, "Were we to act, and if so, how?" The Liberals were divided over coercing Turkey to adopt reforms that gave her Christian subjects in Europe self-government. Lord Hartington, who had led the party in the Commons since Gladstone's retirement in 1875, privately blamed the government and *a fortiori* Gladstone for "our playing the Russian game", which envisaged the destruction of the Ottoman empire rather than exerting Britain's friendly influence to secure "some real improvement" in provincial administration. Beaconsfield was eager to believe that opinion had begun to run strongly against Russia. Called to an interview at Downing Street on 17 April, Salisbury discussed the situation with Carnarvon beforehand. He had thought out his position if the premier's policy was to join Turkey in resisting Russia. Their credentials as supporters of Britain's imperial interests would be established by a proposal from Salisbury to take Crete and its harbours in the expected distribution of Ottoman possessions. Salisbury was also inclined, "on the whole" to keep Russia out of Constantinople. They could then oppose Beaconsfield without being accused of putting their concern for Eastern Christians before Britain.[38] When they met, Beaconsfield was "almost rude" to Salisbury. He wanted to occupy Gallipoli on the European shore of the Dardanelles, with Turkish consent, for the duration of the war; his real intention, Salisbury was certain, being to assist Turkey in the Balkans by safeguarding her capital. Salisbury strenuously objected to what Britain and Europe would see as "in effect an alliance with Turkey", but he left himself room for manoeuvre. It was unnecessary, he went on, to take such a step until Russia was across the Balkan mountain range, and even if she occupied Constantinople, the Royal Navy in the Sea of Marmora "could shell her out of it with ease".[39]

Other prime ministerial interviews preceded the cabinet of 21 April, at which nobody was prepared to second a British defence of Constantinople, with or without direct involvement in the war that was about to start, when Lord John Manners, on whom Beaconsfield could always rely, proposed it. Derby, after temporizing in private, said he was for proceeding "by diplomatic means, not by expeditions". In his diary, he reflected on the incongruity of his siding with "Salisbury & Co.", whose religious hostility to the Turks was distasteful to him. Salisbury, and Carnarvon, with Derby's help, had prevailed; but outsiders – Gladstone for one – supposed from rumours traceable to Beaconsfield and his intimates that "Salisbury is at a discount". The Queen was hinting at abdication if ministers did not stand up to Britain's enemies, internal and external, at a critical juncture. Against this background Gladstone drafted a set of resolutions indicting Turkish misrule and finding the remedy in renewed international pressure. Through Bath, Salisbury sent Gladstone a plea not to table his resolutions, represented as "fatal to peace, and [they] will place the ball at Beaconsfield's feet". These fears – the wording was Bath's – were exaggerated.[40] Although the Liberal divisions forced Gladstone to drop those resolutions which specified action, and the remainder were voted down by a large majority, the premier was held by his colleagues in April and May to an announcement of neutrality in the Eastern conflict, conditional upon Russian abstention from occupying Constantinople or Egypt, from interference with existing access to the Straits and the Suez Canal, and from encroaching upon the *status quo* in the region of the Persian Gulf. The final point seems to have been Salisbury's contribution. Beaconsfield still urged an expedition to the Dardanelles, despite expert advice that it would demand two or three times as many men as he had thought. "He evidently thinks", wrote Derby, "that for England to look on at a war, without interfering, is a humiliating position", regardless of the cost to the Treasury and the economy.[41]

It should be stressed that it was Beaconsfield, and not Salisbury, who had the cabinet against him through the summer of 1877, as the Russians advanced into the Balkans. He solicited the co-operation of Austria, through the foreign secretary and independently of him, but the Emperor Franz Josef was pledged to the Budapest Convention. At home Beaconsfield succeeded over two months in obtaining consent to a vote of credit for the army and navy, which was not put to parliament; to the Mediterranean fleet's move to Besika Bay, ready to enter the Dardanelles; and to reinforcements for British garrisons in the Mediterranean. He believed he could afford to dispense with Salisbury, "who, though a very able man, has no following", and Carnarvon, should they resign on his proposal in mid-July to make an explicit threat of war if Russia entered Constantinople. In the event, only Manners and a recent recruit to the cabinet, Sir Michael Hicks Beach, supported such a move. Obviously shaken by this rejection of his leadership in cabinet, which was a novel experience, Beaconsfield accepted the substitution of a "friendly warning" for a declaration seen as unwise. He turned to Salisbury, whom he had failed to isolate, for help: and to Carnarvon's astonishment, it was forthcoming.[42]

Rumours of Salisbury's departure, with Carnarvon, from the government had been circulating since April. As he told Derby in June, he did not think of resigning: nothing so far had committed the country to fight for Turkey; although public opinion might require Britain to intervene, and that would force him out. He had, he said, been talking to the premier in the same sense. But Beaconsfield's references to him down to the middle of July are almost uniformly hostile: "Salisbury wishes the Russians to take, and indefinitely occupy, Constantinople, acting, as he has done throughout, under the influence . . . of Lyddon [*sic*]"; he had compromised Britain by his attitude and actions at the recent conference. Beaconsfield transmitted the Queen's strictures on his colleague to him: she deplored Salisbury's language in cabinet, reported by the premier; it encouraged "Russia and the Russian party". As for the foreign secretary, his reasoned objections to Beaconsfield's efforts to ensure that Britain cut an impressive figure in the East and Europe filled her with despair: "Another Sovereign must be got to carry out Lord Derby's policy".[43] The quotation from the monarch in Beaconsfield's letter was calculated to appeal to Salisbury. He was as dissatisfied as the Queen and her first minister with Derby's determination to minimize the risks to Britain from a struggle that was not central to her safety and well-being. The unending discussions in cabinet struck Derby as worse than useless: "I do not see what there is to discuss . . . I doubt the wisdom of 'talking over' things when no action is possible. Men only work each other up into a state of agitation, and are then ready to rush into anything rash to relieve it". If the foreign secretary realized the strength of the personal and national ambitions that drove Beaconsfield, they were "to me . . . not very intelligible: as long as our interests are not touched, why should not foreigners settle their own differences in their own way?"[44]

Salisbury recognized that Derby's diplomacy might "prevent evil": but he was impatient for the "positive" measures that could be taken, and should be adopted if Britain's foreign policy was not to be "an emasculate, purposeless vacillation . . . very discreditable: but perhaps . . . what suits the nation best". Both Beaconsfield and Derby ascribed to the middle class a reluctance to see the country drawn into the Eastern war, in contrast to the Court, the aristocracy, the Services and the ill-defined working classes. Salisbury, however, did not conceal his enmity to the Turk in cabinet, saying on one occasion that "Russia at Constantinople would do us no harm". Then he advocated seizing Egypt, which elicited a protest from the foreign secretary. Derby's respect for international law underpinned his view that Britain should not "give the signal for a general scramble" to divide the territories of a friendly state that was not yet a corpse. He was not an aristocratic Cobdenite, but a prudent imperialist whose conception of empire centred on the economic development of India and the settler colonies, where he invested a portion of his enormous wealth.[45] Salisbury, on the other hand, shared the Disraelian vision of Britain's greatness, without the tendency to fantasize. Britain was a European power and could never be indifferent to changes across the Continent that must affect her insular security and the prosperity inseparable from it. There were good reasons for appropriating a "*pied-à-terre*", and something more in the shape of Egypt. Unafraid of Russian expansion, he looked ahead to a renewal of Anglo-French rivalry in the Mediterranean and to the emergence of Germany as a naval power with aspirations that would not be confined to the northern seas. It was not before time to consolidate Britain's position in waters where, five years on, she might not be unchallenged. Moreover, he believed that the extension of British influence over Turkey in Asia, after Europe was lost to Ottoman rule, was not likely to be burdensome: his countrymen's special gift for "governing Orientals *through* Orientals" would counter the Sultan's Russian vassalage.[46]

Carnarvon dated Salisbury's movement towards the premier's thinking from the cabinet of 21 July 1877, when he enlarged upon his support, first expressed a week earlier, for Manners' proposal to send the Mediterranean fleet up to Constantinople. Salisbury, it seemed to his watching friend, was "gathering . . . courage as he proceeded . . . he was ready to send it up at once . . . this . . . turned the balance of parties". If the Russians got to Constantinople, he added, they should not be allowed to hold on to its fortifications.[47] Derby's diary bears out the account that Carnarvon gave of the change in Salisbury. By the end of the month Salisbury was for dispatching the fleet without the Sultan's agreement, and was alone in doing so. The foreign secretary wondered whether he – Derby – was destined to be "the sole seceder on a question of war and peace". At his insistence, taken to the verge of resignation, the Turkish invitation to the fleet which the cabinet decided to solicit was accompanied with assurances of continued neutrality. The Queen, who saw Salisbury at Osborne late in July, was now well satisfied with him: he was prepared, in the last resort, for war, should negotiations prove fruitless. With his aid, Beaconsfield had secured a consensus rather than a definite decision that hostilities must ensue if Russia entered Constantinople, and refused to withdraw; the exception of the city and of the Straits from Russian conquest being the two conditions of British neutrality to which the Tsar's government had not signified its assent. At one end of the cabinet were Beaconsfield, Manners and Hicks Beach, who wanted war with Russia, or a diplomatic triumph over her: at the other were Derby and Carnarvon, agreed in their opposition to war, though for quite different reasons, since Carnarvon was, unlike the foreign secretary, an ardent sympathizer with Eastern Christians. In a couple of weeks Salisbury had travelled much of the way from one side to the other.[48]

He still objected to a Turkish alliance, by that name, apparently envisaging the war in prospect as fought over a prostrate Turkey rather than for her. According to Carnarvon, the change in Salisbury that made his follower "immensely miserable" when it was revealed on 21 July, went deep indeed. When they talked privately, he made a remark which is, superficially, quite out of character and might have come from Beaconsfield: "War was necessary to blow up the whole unsound foreign policy of the country". It is to be explained by his belief that with Derby at the Foreign Office, and before him the Liberal Granville dominated by Gladstone, Britain had become too detached from Europe to be able to take care of herself. The Gladstonian "Concert of Europe" had not worked at the Constantinople conference. Like her peers, Britain should use her undoubted strengths to obtain the co-operation withheld from a power that did not assert herself within the limits set by resources. In the era of Bismarckian statecraft nothing was to be gained by ignoring the realities in which the German chancellor, and Continental statesmen generally, dealt.[49]

The incipient cabinet crisis in July was arrested less by a consensus that was plainly not binding than by the two Turkish victories at Plevna, the fortress that barred the Russians' path through Bulgaria; a third followed in early September. For several months it looked as if Russia would have to settle for a good deal less than her treaty with Austria had given her. In the circumstances, the continuing discussions with the British government shifted to the question of mediation between the combatants. Salisbury regarded as empty an offer of mediation like that under consideration, which was purely diplomatic. He trusted Derby to prevent an under-taking of assistance to Turkey if she accepted terms similar to those in the London Protocol of March. Watching the trend of opinion in the country, he did not think it was sufficiently anti-Russian for the country to submit to war with any enthusi-asm. When parliament met in January or February 1878 after the recess, it would be harder for Beaconsfield to commit Britain to an unwanted war.[50] Lytton in India could not contain himself at the turn of events. In a letter to a member of Salisbury's council at the India Office, also sent to the premier and others at home, he charged unnamed ministers with entertaining the idea of a European combination directed against Germany which was to include Russia. The cause of his imaginings, which amused even the Queen, was Salisbury's remark to him earlier in the year that Germany might absorb Holland, should war between Russia and Turkey give her a free hand in the West. Salisbury excused the viceroy in cabinet, where his con-duct was the subject of comment, as "a little mad", and told Derby "it is not worth taking formal notice of". This strange episode and the general desire to overlook it, were both products of tensions dimly understood beyond the small circle of those involved.[51]

In two of his few speeches outside parliament at the time, delivered the same day to Bradford Tories, Salisbury confidently described Russian power as "very exaggerated". War for Turkey would be as mistaken as the war against her which, he claimed, was the real intention of her British enemies "veiled under useful phraseology". They – the Liberals – did not have "the faintest notion" what to put in the place of the Ottoman empire. He pointedly rebuked his bellicose colleagues; if the government went to fight in person, "to sacrifice . . . their own fortunes and . . . go into the field to be shot", then they might be called "brave and generous". In fact, others would die, and do most of the paying: "I dispute entirely the application of those . . . adjectives, 'brave' and 'generous', to the acts of a government which plunges a nation into war". Derby was still more outspoken, telling a deputation at the Foreign Office that the foreign minister who took France into the war of 1870 "did not come out of it with a light heart – neither he, nor his master, nor his country". The fall of Plevna on 10 December after the fortress of Kars in the Caucasus had been taken in mid-November, dispelled hopes that Britain would not have to choose between peace and war. By now Beaconsfield rightly considered Derby to be for "peace at any price", in the context of the Eastern question, but he counted on Salisbury to support a threat of war if Russia succeeded in taking Constantinople and refused to give it up in a peace treaty.[52]

## The Genesis of a New Foreign Policy

On his return from the Constantinople conference in February 1877, Salisbury invited the peers, and the countrywide audience he was really addressing, to think their way through the Eastern question and the solutions proposed to the hard facts that determined what could and could not be done. He was putting forward principles which were to inform his policy everywhere after he went to the Foreign Office. "Any threat or intimation of a threat . . .", he said, "should never be made by the British Government until it is absolutely prepared to follow up the menace . . . have you picked to pieces in your own mind what you mean by coercion . . . ?" None of the six great powers of Europe were ideally placed to commence operations against the Ottoman empire: "Some . . . like ourselves . . . want a sufficient army . . . others a sufficient navy . . . all probably want sufficient money". But the Crimean War had been fought and the Treaty of Paris signed to maintain "an impossibility": a Turkey capable of significant reform and progress. The conclusion he offered, then, was a *non sequitur*: more advice pressed on an unreceptive ruler and his ministers. A year later, in January 1878, he observed that the Russians poised for victory had been inspired by "strong religious and race feelings . . . they . . . drive all governments, and an autocratic government quicker than others". It was not the duty of Britain to put the suffering humanity of "any populations whatever" first: her government were trustees for the interests of their own country, and their obligations as such overrode all competing claims: "war is righteous or unrighteous according as it is opportune or inopportune".[53]

Self-preservation was the first law of international relations: its cold rationality was indispensable to avert the disasters to individual nations, and to humanity as a whole, that flowed from neglecting its dictates in favour of religious or political imperatives divorced from reality. This was only superficially Machiavellianism. Salisbury was a Christian statesman, but one who did not let himself forget "the motives which actuate most human beings". Calculations of national self-interest made for European peace if, as in the case of the Eastern question, no one stood to benefit from war and its spread.[54] There was no necessary clash between Salisbury's statecraft and the practice of his faith. It is, however, evident why, at this decisive point in his career, some admirers were shocked: his clarity seemed too much like ruthlessness.

As the foreign secretary who negotiated successfully at Berlin, he explained why Britain had waited before intervening and risking "a terrible . . . European war". "We felt it was not our duty", he said, "to take a definite line with respect to the maintenance of the sovereignty of Turkey, until we knew, by the same test of facts, of what the sovereignty of Turkey was made". Her "wretched" system of government and "corrupt" ruling class had been saved, for a while, by the heroism of the Turkish soldiery: "the time of partition . . . had not yet arrived". The treaty made provision within its framework for the aspirations of Balkan Christians; and Britain's separate agreement with Turkey for the occupation of Cyprus was meant to ensure her predominant influence in Asia Minor and the Middle East. The second was the more important achievement; he had repeated within a few days of going to the Foreign Office: "We are trustees for the British empire".[55] He did not openly apologize for the display of *realpolitik* in taking Cyprus in exchange for a guarantee of Turkey in Asia. The treaty of Paris in which the signatories undertook not to do what Russia, Austria and Britain had just done in helping themselves and Balkan protégés to Ottoman territory was an instance of these "misty and shadowy guarantees which bound you to everything in theory and . . . in practice . . . to nothing". With Cyprus for a naval and military base, Britain could be on hand to challenge any attempt by Russia, whose victory over Turkey had exposed the operational limitations of her armies, to dominate the lands through which the Tigris and Euphrates ran. India might be safe from a direct Russian attack, but not from internal unrest encouraged by the spectacle of Britain retreating before Russia in the Middle East: "That was the real danger . . . we had to fear".[56]

In his Lords speech of 18 July 1878, he spoke contemptuously of the discarded policy of "doing nothing" which Derby had defended in and out of the cabinet: had such counsels prevailed in the last two centuries Britain would not have won India and the rest of her empire.[57] He had used similar language in private: its employment in public appeared to vindicate Gladstone. As early as January 1878 the latter was saying that Beaconsfield, "one of the ablest men who ever got into power . . . the greatest bane to . . . political life . . . has fascinated Lord Salisbury . . . [who] would never do what he believed to be wrong: he was overpersuaded". Before long Carnarvon, Bath and Heathcote echoed Gladstone in their perplexity about Salisbury's motives.[58] They overlooked the clue he provided in his parliamentary explanations when he argued, as Palmerston did at the time, that the Crimean War might have been avoided if Britain's will to fight had been made clearer to Russia.[59]

His part in the cabinet struggles that extruded first Carnarvon and then Derby can be better understood in the light of these utterances; so can his subsequent conduct of foreign policy. But he did not draw attention to his debt to the German chancellor in the concluding stages of the Eastern question in the 1870s and afterwards during his initial spell at the Foreign Office. Salisbury had complained that Berlin was "the centre of the great European intrigue and . . . Turkey . . . not of itself of much moment", as the chancellor incited Russia to make war in the East rather than in the West. He made the most of Germany's influence immediately he succeeded Derby. He turned to Bismarck to steer Russia and Austria towards a settlement agreed in substance before the congress of Berlin assembled. "We are the only nation . . . able to look with unmixed satisfaction at the position to which the German empire has attained", he wanted the chancellor to know, articulating a political, not a moral, truth. Britain thus took her place in the Bismarckian scheme of things. She enjoyed Germany's goodwill in Egypt, and to a lesser extent in the attempt to establish a form of indirect rule in Turkey after Berlin.[60]

Salisbury's objection to a Turkish alliance still came between him and the premier when the fall of Plevna in December 1877 compelled the cabinet to decide whether to act on their consensus that the Russians must not have Constantinople. In a succession of meetings from 14 December, Beaconsfield proposed to recall parliament and ask for an increase in defence expenditure first discussed in the summer, while persevering with the attempt to mediate. Salisbury spoke for Derby and Carnarvon in saying that the summons to parliament and the vote of men and money would be seen as "a definitive declaration in favour of the war party". They had enough support from their colleagues for Beaconsfield to tell them, and the Queen, that he was resigning with "half the cabinet at the moment arrayed against him". He did not resign; nor did anyone else. He claimed that the three peers had "surrendered", and that when parliament had met and voted the funds "an army of occupation" would be sent to Turkey.[61] Salisbury had been for coercing Turkey, though happy to leave the operation to Russia. He now told himself, and sought to persuade others, that she could be coerced and helped simultaneously: "I have no objection to a combination of the two [policies]". On the same day, 15 December, and for the same correspondent, he composed a memorandum urging a pause for further consideration before the government launched itself "on the steep slope . . . to war". Otherwise the Turks, having found an ally, would fight on instead of accepting the mediation of the powers, for which they were asking after Plevna: British troops, arriving with instructions to remain in defensive positions around Constantinople, as was still envisaged, would soon have to resist a Russian assault. Derby with "his well known aversion to war" would resign, to the dismay of the party in the country, which saw in him Beaconsfield's political heir. The divided Liberals would be united, like any opposition, by the spectacle of open conflict in the governing party: and, with Derby gone, "any advocate of peace who may have stayed behind" in the cabinet would not be able to hold back the supporters of war.[62]

Salisbury expected Derby to resign: his own resignation was not necessarily going to follow. The hint was taken. He stood his ground at the next cabinet, on 17 December, but that night Cairns, one of the best minds in the cabinet, went to Hatfield in search of an understanding that would keep Salisbury in the government. Observers had felt from the beginning that the government's life would largely depend on the relationship between the premier and Salisbury, without whose talents and reputation it could hardly survive the loss of Derby. Cairns, and through him the premier, agreed to postpone recalling parliament until the second half of January, as Salisbury had previously suggested: "no hot haste – and consequently no implied pledge of immediate action". The lord chancellor and Northcote, who was also trying to bring the premier and Salisbury together, outlined what Salisbury deemed "a good basis" for intervention in the East: Britain to put herself forward as the sole mediator between Turks and Russians; the Mediterranean fleet to be sent up to Constantinople; and Gallipoli, controlling the Dardanelles, to be occupied until Turkey showed herself willing to reach a reasonable settlement with Russia.[63] At the cabinet of 18 December, Beaconsfield did not demand surrender: on the contrary, "his object was peace . . . he had nothing to say to the war party, but wished to be able to mediate with effect". Neither Salisbury nor Derby credited these assurances; while the premier told the Queen and his confidante Lady Bradford that they had submitted, they had gained time and forced him to dissimulate in exchange for an unconvincing display of agreement. His overture to Salisbury a few days later – "we must put an end to all this . . . gossip about war parties and peace parties in the cabinet" – elicited a disappointing reply. Well aware that Lytton had been representing India as ready for war, Salisbury questioned the efficiency of the native army outside its internal security role. The British army had not yet built up the reserves which the Cardwell reforms of the early 1870s had been designed to furnish. Industry, experiencing the onset of the Victorian "great depression" was, he asserted "profoundly averse to war", like the country as a whole, notwithstanding the shift of opinion in the Turks' favour. Austria, Britain's natural ally in the Balkans, was unresponsive to her approaches. If war with Russia did become inevitable it would be "unpopular and unprofitable".[64]

This list of disincentives to fight did not mean that Salisbury had discovered a greater sympathy with Derby's isolationism. He evaded an appeal from the foreign secretary to stand firm against the premier "who believes thoroughly in 'prestige' – as all foreigners do . . . We are in real danger". For prestige was diplomatic capital to Salisbury, as to most politicians. He wished to use it to avoid war. That is clear from the letter he wrote to Carnarvon after his friend had incurred the premier's extreme displeasure by alluding publicly to the madness of war with Russia. Urging Carnarvon not to resign after Beaconsfield had rebuked him with a severity unprecedented in cabinet, he adjured him to remember that "Providence has put in our hands the trust of keeping the country from . . . a wrongful war".[65] They differed, however, over the methods to be employed to that end. As the Russians continued their advance upon Constantinople, brushing aside British and Turkish requests for terms and an armistice, the cabinet debated whether to send the fleet through the Dardanelles. The plan to occupy Gallipoli was dropped after Derby and Carnarvon threatened to resign if it were carried out. At the last moment Salisbury prevented their departure from the government by securing general agreement on sending the fleet to the Straits, but only if the Sultan asked for its protection; a contingency that Carnarvon rightly thought was unlikely. Salisbury, Derby and Cairns had also managed to make the wording of the Queen's speech for the new session rather less pro-Turkish in its tone. But on 23 January Salisbury backed the movement of the fleet to Constantinople without the Sultan's consent, which was not forthcoming. The Ottoman government, he held, was no longer a free agent in view of the collapse of its armies. At this point Carnarvon resigned in protest, followed by Derby. The former, unlike the foreign secretary, persisted in his resignation, when the fleet, having sailed, was ordered back to its anchorage at Besika Bay the next day on the news that Turkey had accepted Russian terms for peace.[66]

"It is the policy of Lord Salisbury that they oppose", wrote Beaconsfield of the two resigning ministers on the 24th. "Until Lord Salisbury was permanently detached from those . . . lords, it was impossible to bring the cabinet to any firm or general decision." Ten ministers combined against two: and the premier saw that it was Salisbury's doing.[67] This is the clearest indication of his influence and importance: his arguments succeeded in uniting the advocates of war with those who wanted to avoid it, but did not identify themselves with Derby's position, or Carnarvon's. Salisbury was for serving notice on Russia that Turkey could not be allowed to become her vassal, though subject to, preferably agreed, losses of territory that would mark the start of a process of partition. Britain's international standing and her public opinion precluded such an outcome to the war that was ending. A show of resolution and of force was necessary to make Russia realize that she had to negotiate with Turkey's traditional ally as well as with the beaten Sultan. In Salisbury's judgement, neither Russia's army nor her finances would stand another war. Britain could only field a small expeditionary corps, but its appearance and Russia's weakness were likely to attract Austrian intervention. Salisbury pressed his colleagues, and a sceptical Derby, to continue trying for the Anglo-Austrian alliance which Vienna was reluctant to conclude. Then and afterwards, he deplored, outside the cabinet, the recall of the fleet as it was entering the Dardanelles. British warships off Constantinople might have deterred Russia from imposing a Carthaginian peace on Turkey. Carnarvon could not, or would not, see that Salisbury was bent on averting war, while punishing Turkey and satisfying the desire of the premier and many Tories for a demonstration of Britain's equality with the great powers.[68]

Carnarvon maintained that the cabinet's agreement on sending the fleet to Constantinople, even though it was recalled, constituted, in effect, a declaration in favour of Turkey which he could not stomach. He was for leaving the Muslim empire to its fate at the hands of a Christian power. While he thought them exaggerated, Salisbury could not be indifferent to Lytton's warnings of pro-Turkish sentiment among Indian Muslims. He was for reducing the Ottoman empire gradually and under cover of protecting her from Russia. "I see", he told Carnarvon, "the difference between the principles on which we were going was too great to be bridged over".[69] Derby withdrew his resignation on 26 January at the premier's request and after receiving an assurance that the Mediterranean fleet would stay out of the Straits. He had previously turned down a suggestion that he should continue in the government but leave the Foreign Office for his choice of several posts. Although he would have been his replacement as foreign secretary, Salisbury was one of those who, in the interests of the party at Westminster and in the country, advised against letting Derby go. Beaconsfield described the withdrawal of the resignation as a "Pyrrhic victory", and with reason. Derby's letter to the intermediary, Northcote, announcing his return, was "purposely stiff and unconciliatory . . . hinting at the probability that I may not return long, and making it clear that I return solely in the hope of preventing mischief as long as I can than from sympathy with the views of my colleagues". He did not expect future cabinets to be pleasant; nor were they. Salisbury, he had noted on the 23rd, was "very warlike . . . his natural . . . pugnacity . . . thoroughly roused".[70]

Reports from St Petersburg seemed to confirm what Salisbury, among others, had foreseen, the Russian intention of establishing "a kind of protectorate" over the Ottoman empire. The extent of Turkey's subjugation was plain from the terms to which she now submitted. The Treaty of San Stefano, signed on 3 March, incorporated Russia's aim of an enlarged autonomous Bulgaria, stretching from the Danube to the Aegean, which Salisbury had resisted at the Constantinople conference. Bosnia was also to be given autonomy: the treaty ignored Austria's interest there, recognized at Reichstadt and Budapest. Serbia got little and Greece nothing. The new Bulgaria, which took almost the whole of Macedonia, included a large Greek population. The remaining directly ruled Turkish possessions in Europe – Thessaly, Epirus, Albania and a slice of Macedonia – were cut off from Constantinople. Russia hoped that, by returning part of her conquests in the Caucasus and leaving the Sultan his capital, she had done enough to placate Britain, without whom Austria was unlikely to risk a confrontation. She withstood the temptation to occupy Constantinople, with all its historic associations for Slavs, though the arrival of a British squadron off the city tested her restraint.[71] The cabinet in London, alarmed at the Russians' continuing advance to within a few miles of Constantinople, had finally ordered their warships into the Sea of Marmora on 15 February over the protests of a frightened Ottoman government. Derby approved of their despatch, seeing no danger of war when Turkey was prostrate and Russia exhausted. Acting on their own responsibility, the British ambassador – now Henry Layard – and the admiral eased the consequent tension by moving the ships away from the immediate vicinity of the city in response to Russian demands. The foreign secretary had already cautioned Count Shuvalov against menacing the squadron's line of retreat by the seizure of Gallipoli. Meanwhile, the government obtained six millions for naval and military preparations from the Commons, where the vote divided the Liberal opposition.[72]

That was the situation when the signature of the peace treaty faced British ministers with the problem of inducing Russia to give up much of what they had been unable to stop her from taking. An international conference was being canvassed, but even a weakened Russia would not negotiate in earnest without an intimation that force lay behind diplomacy. Austria required Britain to finance her mobilization, as she had done in the struggle against Napoleon: Beaconsfield rejected the idea of a subsidy out of hand, but a guaranteed loan was discussed. When excited, the premier talked of a war lasting several years as inevitable and destined to be glorious. At other times he spoke only of a diplomatic rupture if Russian troops entered Constantinople. Derby, who knew him better than anyone, could not decide whether he really wanted war, or was prompted "by the mere fear of seeming weak, also of growing unpopular".[73] Salisbury was ready with a policy that appealed to both sides of the premier. Derby's diary provides the fullest record of the deliberations that culminated in his second resignation at the end of March. Beaconsfield and Salisbury forged a partnership which overcame Derby's "old plan of 'wet-blanketting' every proposal as it is made", postponing action and moderating the language of British diplomacy until the Russians came to believe that they might do what they liked with Turkey in Europe, except occupy Constantinople. Derby's apparent inertia and evasiveness, which infuriated the violently anti-Russian Queen, and, in the end, all his colleagues, masked a stubborn resolve to keep Britain out of dangerous European entanglements. He disagreed, regretfully, with Beaconsfield: Salisbury he never forgave.[74]

On the surface, public opinion, especially in London, was loudly hostile to Russia, even before San Stefano left no doubt that she had overturned the verdict of the Crimean War. The disinclination of Austria's ministers and generals to contemplate a war in which she stood to lose far more than Britain, forced Beaconsfield and his cabinet to call out reservists and bring Indian troops to the Mediterranean, gestures designed to impress in the context of a conference to renegotiate the peace treaty. In reality, as Salisbury had had to remind Lytton, Russia was inaccessible, in the sense that Britain alone could inflict only peripheral damage on the vast extent of her territory. It was not these steps which drove Derby to resign in the last days of March. "They [the cabinet] discussed *corps d'armées*, new Gibraltars, and expeditions from India", reported the premier to the Queen in the middle of the month, ". . . Lord Derby said nothing".[75] It was time, Salisbury urged the cabinet, to acquire from the crumbling Ottoman empire the regional strong-point that would consolidate and extend British influence over Turkey in Asia, the sphere of interest Britain had reserved for herself. Furthermore, appropriation of the selected island or ports would tell Europe, and the British public, that the government had made sure of vital interests, whatever happened at a conference. A "new Gibraltar" would soften the blow to national pride if Russia decided to move into Constantinople, and remain there. The consent of the Sultan, with the Russians at the gates, might be dispensed with. Without his consent, Derby pointed out, Britain would be guilty of "an absolute violation of international law and right" that equated their action with Russian aggression. The Russians would consider themselves free to occupy Constantinople and Gallipoli. Although he did not say so, Derby suspected the premier of wanting to provoke a reaction that would justify war in the eyes of the public. No one supported Derby, but misgivings were voiced in subsequent cabinets.[76]

Salisbury, "by far the most eager for action", echoed Beaconsfield in speaking of national humiliation should Britain fail to assert herself at this juncture. He said in cabinet what he was to repeat in parliament – "truly enough", commented Derby – that scruples like those about the morality of the stroke they were planning would have prevented Britain from building an empire. Derby thought Salisbury saw himself as foreign secretary: a widespread impression among those in the know; not surprisingly, since he had been designated for the post in January. In those March cabinets Salisbury was particularly concerned with the impact of their decisions on the public, whose swelling indignation with Russia was a two-edged weapon, useful to make the Russians pause but dangerous if it got out of hand and propelled the country into a war that few really desired. Beaconsfield was not consistent in wanting war; an intimate, Nathan Rothschild, head of the banking house, told the Liberal leadership in December 1877, that the premier had "no intention or wish for war".[77] Salisbury, like Beaconsfield only more rationally, was bent on recovering lost prestige and the power it conferred. "Prestige is a precious thing to have . . .", he wrote on 15 March, "I trust that when the account comes to be finally drawn up, our balance upon the whole course of events may look a little better than it does now". The recovery of his country's old standing would obviate "the painful process of experiment" – that is, war – to settle "the vital question, which is weaker", Britain or Russia. Advising Temple at Bombay that somewhere between 20 000 and 50 000 men might be needed from India's three presidencies, he believed "the chances are in favour of a peaceful solution . . . [but] matters are far too uncertain yet . . . to say anything more definite".[78]

The cabinet, Beaconsfield told the Queen on 8 March, had taken the detailed management of foreign policy into its own hands. Salisbury and Cairns, who applied his skill as a legal draughtsman to diplomatic communications, assisted the premier. "My chief business", Derby had written some weeks earlier, "is criticism, and I do it conscientiously". On the 27th Beaconsfield proposed the occupation of Cyprus and the Syrian port of Alexandretta, jointly described as "the keys of Asia", by troops from India, and calling out the reserves at home in readiness for an Eastern campaign. In answer to Salisbury, Derby said "no compromise was possible. We had come to the point where two roads diverge, and must choose one or the other". Salisbury felt "especially responsible" for the mistakes of British policy which had to be corrected. Neutrality in the conflict between Turkey and Russia, which once seemed right, was dangerous. Russia refused to listen to Britain, who must make herself heard, "by force if necessary". The peoples of the Middle East and of India would draw their own conclusions unless there was "a visible exertion of our power ... They will look to Russia". It was imperative to act without waiting for the Sultan's permission to take what belonged to him: "If this opportunity is lost, it will not recur". As he anticipated, no one sided with Derby in the face of Salisbury's reasoned but highly charged statement of the case against what Beaconsfield had termed "the terrible acts of weakness committed by us during ... two years".[79] No one, this time, tried to stop Derby from resigning. His successor, naturally Salisbury, was ready with a policy, outlined to the premier on 21 March, that went beyond the measures to safeguard Britain's position in the Middle East and further afield. With or without a conference, by means of "war or negotiations", San Stefano should be revised to confine Russia's Bulgarian satellite to the north of the Balkan range; the territory to the south to be an autonomous Greek province under the Sultan's suzerainty. He also envisaged doing away with international restrictions on the passage of the Straits; they should be treated "as if they were open sea", giving the Royal Navy access to the Black Sea. The bases in the Levant, and a reduction in the Turkish indemnity to Russia under the peace treaty, were the other points in this short letter.[80]

Derby's resistance to the seizure of Cyprus and Alexandretta had its effect. The project was dropped. In his brief resignation speech, he was understood to refer to the only step announced after his last cabinet, the summons to reservists. He hinted at the planned coup in April, and revealed it to the Lords in July after the Berlin congress and treaty when Salisbury denied that ministers had ever taken such a decision, and compared Derby, in respect of his veracity, to Titus Oates. It appears that after 27 March Salisbury and the cabinet very soon realized the importance of working within the law of nations: no orders were issued to the Service departments. The untypical disingenuousness of his attack on Derby reflected the government's embarrassment at the revelations: this put a different complexion upon British policy. Happily for his reputation, Salisbury did not again suggest committing a flagrant breach of international law.[81]

Ministers *had* decided on an expedition to occupy Ottoman territory without its ruler's blessing, Salisbury told Lytton on 29 March. Although the cabinet thought better of their bold initiative, the justification of a new policy was not affected. "'The science of catchwords'" existed to devise slogans for public consumption – "to reconcile the fleeting cry with the enduring judgement".[82] The catchword that he employed was "empire": it satisfied the emotions aroused by the negative character of Derby's policy. An imperial posture at home made it easier for Salisbury to omit any reference to a British share of the Sultan's possessions when he composed the circular despatch of 1 April to the governments of Europe. In it he took his stand on the sanctity of treaties; the Treaty of Paris which Russia had brushed aside at San Stefano must be replaced by a European agreement binding on the signatory powers of 1856. Russia could not be allowed to make conditions, as she was trying to do, about her participation in a conference. However, the circular implied the acceptance of the Bulgaria of San Stefano, if shorn of its extension from the Balkan range to the Aegean. Salisbury stipulated only that Turkey in Europe and Asia should not be "so closely pressed by the political outposts of a greatly superior Power that its independent action, and even existence, is almost impossible". The reasonableness of this proposition intensified the diplomatic pressure on Russia. Austria, fearing "the annihilation of . . . prestige and influence in the Balkan peninsula", responded gratefully to the British lead. The cabinet's willingness to consider hostilities, if all else failed, and the news that Indian troops were being sent to Malta strengthened Britain's hand. So did the involvement of Germany. As soon as he arrived at the Foreign Office, Salisbury sought the intervention of Bismarck, who had reluctantly underwritten Austria's survival in the event of war with Russia, to lessen the risks of an Austro-Russian collision at Constantinople. The danger was exercising the German foreign ministry.[83]

German mediation did not secure a mutual withdrawal of forces: British warships to leave the Sea of Marmora; Russian troops to be pulled back from their positions close to the city. Britain and Russia nevertheless got down to negotiations on the substantial questions between them: "the division of Bulgaria in Europe and the provision of compensation for England in Asia are the two keys of this difficult lock", he advised the ambassador in Berlin. The first was settled by the secret agreement he signed with Shuvalov at the end of May. The Bulgaria of San Stefano was split into three: Bulgaria, so called, between the Danube and the Balkan mountains; "Eastern Rumelia", predominantly Bulgarian and also autonomous; and a Greek province with its Aegean coast under closer Ottoman control. Russia refused to concede Turkey's right to garrison the natural defence line separating the two Bulgarian lands, but Turkish troops were to be excluded from the rest of Eastern Rumelia. She was to recover Southern Bessarabia, lost in 1856, from Rumania, her ally in the war though an Ottoman tributary state, compensated with the Dobrudja region of Bulgaria. Russia agreed, finally, to equal rights for the powers in promoting reform of Ottoman administration in the European provinces left under the Sultan's direct rule; and Britain to most of Russia's gains from Turkey in the Caucasus.[84]

The leaking of these arrangements by a wretchedly paid copyist obliged Salisbury to mislead the peers about its authenticity, for the congress to which all the powers had now agreed did not meet at Berlin until mid-June. "Only one of many things of late which place S[alisbury] in a new light", reflected Carnarvon. Understandably, Derby delighted in the bitter disappointment, vehemently expressed, of those Tories who were labelled "Jingoes" from the music hall song that caught a superficial mood. The Russians had obtained "all they ever wanted and more than they expected". He doubted whether the artificial division between Bulgaria and Eastern Rumelia would last. The silence in the text about Cyprus and Alexandretta was puzzling but he felt sure, as soon as the leak appeared in the *Globe*, that there was no longer any danger to peace. According to Münster, the German ambassador, Salisbury was confident about the conference and these preliminary negotiations, saying "Beaconsfield and I can settle it all", without trouble from their colleagues. Derby could not quite credit this, but it was true.[85] Premier and foreign secretary stood for a combination of policies and should both attend the conference, Salisbury told the cabinet on 1 June. The "philo-Turks" would take from Beaconsfield the "necessary concessions" to Russia which they would not accept from him. To the world outside the cabinet room, the two of them personified the two "different views" of policy in the Near East. If the Jingoes had been able to read Salisbury's letter of 10 April to Odo Russell at Berlin, they might have rebelled, Beaconsfield notwithstanding. He likened Britain in her dealings with Turkey to "a patron whose son is not of age [and who] presents an old and infirm clergyman to the family living", the son being the Greek or Slav population of provinces designed for autonomy, and the aged clergyman their Ottoman suzerain, the days of whose authority were numbered.[86]

The Jingoes' consolation was to be the "compensation for England in Asia" mentioned in Salisbury's subsequent letter to Russell. The report of the staff officer who evaluated the possibilities favoured Cyprus over Alexandretta and Crete. The island was a prerequisite for the treaty-based British ascendancy which Salisbury hoped to establish over Turkey after the conference. He let the Russian ambassador into the "secret" of British intentions. Unsurprised, Shuvalov and his government did not object either to a territorial acquisition, provided that it was not on the Sea of Marmora, or to "some sort of defensive alliance" between Britain and Turkey. The ambassador even suggested that Russia would be "only too glad that we should share with them the burden of *managing this Country* [Turkey]".[87] Salisbury prepared opinion, through *The Times*, for a treaty with Turkey concluded on 24 May, just after the conversation with Shuvalov. *The Times* articles preceded the leaking of the Anglo-Russian agreement, and helped to contain the reaction to its disclosure. The Cyprus Convention, as it became known, was not announced until the closing stages of the congress in Berlin which all the powers mainly interested – Russia, Turkey and Austria – entered after striking bargains with Salisbury. Austria, whose policy was characterized, in his words, by "the insincerity which belongs to weakness", obtained a British understanding to promote her claim to occupy Bosnia-Herzegovina, which, it had been indicated, Russia would not oppose. Bismarck and Salisbury were both anxious to preserve Austria as a great power and the regional counterweight to Russia in the Balkans. She had lost nearly as much by San Stefano as Turkey: they were the two "worst compacted" states in Europe.[88]

Bismarck regarded himself as the "honest broker" of the congress and its vital preliminaries, and, in a real sense, Salisbury acted as his agent. The revelation of the Anglo-Russian agreement in London deprived the proceedings in Berlin during June and July of an atmosphere of crisis. There were theatrical moments, as when Beaconsfield made to leave the congress on Russia's refusal to allow Turkish garrisons along the Balkan range. She gave way: but Turkish troops never took up their positions. The announcement of the Cyprus Convention on 8 July, timed to offset the confirmation of Russia's Asiatic conquests, for the most part, enabled the premier to return home boasting that to peace he had added "peace with honour". It had been plain to Salisbury that Bismarck "meant to have everything his own way": while Beaconsfield, who greatly enjoyed an appearance in the European limelight, showed, his foreign secretary remarked, "such a perfect disregard for facts that it is almost impossible for him to run true". This familiar failing was compounded by deafness and a poor command of French, the common language of the assembled plenipotentiaries. He may have been something of a diplomatic liability: but he protected Salisbury from their domestic critics: "We have no difficulty in carrying out our programme", wrote the latter, "our difficulty is merely the extravagant nonsense talked at home".[89] Yet when Salisbury wanted to capitalize on Britain's resurgence in great power politics and cut free from the continued restrictions on the movement of warships through the Straits, the cabinet in London were unwilling to go so far. He had to content himself with a unilateral declaration that reserved Britain's right to sail ships through when the Sultan was deemed unable to exercise an independent control of the waterway. He and his reluctant government were quite alone in putting their national interest above a succession of treaties negotiated by previous foreign secretaries. At the time Germany and the others did not make an issue of the British action: it raised a hypothetical question. Britain's old Mediterranean rival, France, the second naval power, was not willing to challenge the Straits declaration or the acquisition of Cyprus: "Our relations with Bismarck are particularly good", Salisbury reminded the ambassador at Paris. Like the German chancellor, the British foreign secretary encouraged French colonial expansion, as a distraction for her historical enmities, but away from the Levant. Talking to the French plenipotentiary at Berlin, he pointed him towards North Africa, where the Ottoman tributary state of Tunis was fruit ripe for plucking. In that quarter, he had previously told Lord Lyons in Paris, "we should not have the slightest jealousy or fear" of a French advance.[90]

"The poor Turk is in a bad way", Salisbury had said in April, addressing the Lords. The congress left the sufferer in a worse condition. Rumania, Serbia and Montenegro emerged as independent states; Bulgaria as a tributary state under Russian domination; Eastern Rumelia, without a Turkish military presence and under a Christian governor-general was a good deal more than semi-independent. Austria had acquired Bosnia and Herzegovina, and Britain, Cyprus. Salisbury not only pointed France in the direction of Tunis, he was instrumental in securing the powers' "invitation" to Turkey at the congress, to revise her frontier with Greece in the latter's favour, which in 1881 added Thessaly and part of Epirus to the kingdom.[91] In Egypt, the deposition of the Sultan's hereditary viceroy, the Khedive Ismail, in 1879 underlined an Anglo-French protectorate in all but name, which Salisbury was confident would work to Britain's advantage. Russia in the Eastern, Austria in the Western Balkans, Britain in the Near and Middle East: these three spheres of influence, blurred at the edges, were intended by the powers meeting at Berlin to accommodate conflicting interests and ambitions. The framework held down to 1914, under increasing strain from the Balkan nationalism that neither Russia nor Austria could discipline.

A British hegemony did not materialize, except in Egypt after 1882, to the degree and on the lines envisaged by Salisbury in his correspondence with Layard at Constantinople, an ambassador cast in the proconsular role filled by Stratford de

Redcliffe in Palmerston's day. Starting from the proposition that "Good government in Asia means government by good men", Salisbury's aim was to introduce British advisers into Ottoman provincial administration with much the same role as the residents at Indian princely courts. Aware that the analogy would not please the Turks, he edited references to it in the blue books. Later he thought a few Europeans, and not only British, in senior police and financial appointments might have the desired effect: "They need not be numerous . . . I should have no objection . . . to some Germans, or even . . . Frenchmen", whose inclusion would not harm the predominant influence he sought for Britain; quite the reverse, since international co-operation had decided the new order of things for Turkey. He also tried to obtain from the chancellor of the exchequer a loan tied to the construction by a British company of a strategic railway from the Turkish heartland to Mesopotamia, or to the purchase by another British company of the existing telegraph line through Asia Minor. He described these projects to Northcote as calculated "to promote that pacific invasion of Englishmen which is our principal reliance for . . . getting power over the country". As Salisbury expected, neither a Treasury loan nor a government guarantee of one raised from private investors was forthcoming: politicians and bankers saw Turkey as a bad risk. Without British finance, Salisbury had little hope of saving Turkey from herself: the choice for her ruler and race lay between dependence on Britain and the working out of those self-destructive tendencies which, he believed, they could not master unaided.[92]

Although Bismarck gave an assurance that Germany wished to sustain British influence at Constantinople, he advised caution when it receded. Russia and France inevitably encroached upon Britain's pre-eminence. But that was not the only reason why Salisbury thought it unwise to employ the language of "absolute menace" in dealing with the Ottoman government. It was not Russian and French rivalry that thwarted Salisbury's plans for Turkey so much as her national spirit, reinforced by Islam, and exploited by the new Sultan, Abdul Hamid II: the British minister consistently underrated all three, and especially the last. To that prince belongs the credit for the selective Westernization which extended the life of his empire. Its recovery was under way by the time Salisbury left the Foreign Office in 1880, but Britain's preoccupation with the fate of Christians in Turkish Armenia, the scene of massacre and counter-massacre, obscured the fact. In that region, the reports reaching him suggested, "order and justice seem almost to have disappeared". The secondment of military men to consular posts in Asia Minor was a poor substitute for the planned infiltration of Ottoman government by British advisers and appointees.[93] The correspondence with Layard shows an anxiety, during the last months of the Tory ministry, to minimize British involvement. He no longer wished the press – "a sort of Greek chorus to the political drama" – to suppose that Britain had established "a protectorate, or at least a commanding influence" over the Sultan. Unlike the Egyptian viceroy, Abdul Hamid would be "awkward" to depose.[94]

Salisbury's belief, based on his years at the India Office, that his country excelled in "governing Orientals through Orientals" was, therefore, not borne out by the Turkish experiment. Nor was the flair evident in the Egypt of 1878–80, or in relations with Afghanistan at the same period. Responsibility for the second Afghan war lay not with him, but with his successor at the India Office, Hardy, now ennobled as Viscount Cranbrook. Lytton had escaped from the control of White-hall. Both Afghanistan and Egypt, in so far as they illuminate Salisbury's career and achievement, are better left until later in this study. The extent to which he was disappointed in his hopes of creating a species of protectorate over the Ottoman empire did not register with his countrymen. They remembered and exaggerated his bloodless victory over Russia. No one, perhaps, admired him more than did Beaconsfield, who was nevertheless moved at one point to seek the Queen's help in impressing upon him the need for the "utmost firmness" towards Russia in the aftermath of Berlin.[95] The foreign secretary did not see Russia's slowness to evacu-ate the Balkan territory she had occupied in the same light as the premier. The temptation to Russify Bulgaria and Eastern Rumelia before she went was only to be expected. At that date he anticipated a halt to Russian expansion as internal unrest built up, "such as that of the Nihilists which pays no regard to patriotism". He hoped the disintegration of Turkey's diminished empire, of which he was certain, would not happen before the revolution in Russia. With Russia out of the way, the final partition of the Ottoman lands would be a less bloody business.[96]

"We cannot revive the dead": Salisbury qualified that remark about the Otto-man empire – made to the Lords in May 1879 – by saying that there was time to ascertain whether the reports of its impending demise were true. In that context, he hailed the "secret" Austro-German alliance signed in October 1879 as "glad tidings of great joy" when he spoke at Manchester a few days later. His speech, for which the public were prepared by hints in Tory newspapers, took Britain even nearer to Germany. The German commitment gave Austria the strength she lacked to check further Russian expansion in the Balkans. Whatever later historians have said, the treaty was seen as enhancing the domination of Europe by the German chancellor and his country.[97] Shuvalov, who had worked closely with Salisbury, was "deeply hurt" by his language. Count Münster in London had extracted from the foreign secretary, just before the speech, a "yes" to his question whether Britain would actually fight with Germany and Austria against Russia and a *revanchiste* France; a war in which the British contribution would naturally be naval rather than military. While Salisbury, in line with his future policy, discouraged the Germans, and Beaconsfield, from proceeding with Bismarck's proposal of a formal Anglo-German alliance, his "yes" was not disingenuous. Britain would find it hard to stay out of a general European war: and an indication that she must side with Germany made the conflict less likely. With the Continent at peace, she was free to pursue her economic interests which more and more lay outside Europe.[98]

The severity of the depression that set in from the late 1870s forced the Victor-ians to rethink the comfortable assumptions of their long prosperity since the mid-century. Continental Europe, and the United States, had never been convinced of the advantages of free trade, taken to British lengths. "Everywhere", said Salisbury to the Manchester chamber of commerce, "our business is, if we can, to keep open the avenues of commerce . . . everywhere we see rising round us a thick wall of protection." The defence expenditure of Continental powers was forcing up the tariffs they levied. As the embodiment of free trade, Britain had left her ministers too little with which to bargain for reductions, as the chamber wanted. Her businessmen must look to the "semi-civilized world" where their trade was growing and depended "very much upon the . . . consideration which the power of England retains". Her future, he had told a deputation of Lancashire Tories in August 1878, was to be found in the empire. It was a mistake to suppose that "you can stand still – that there is . . . for nations any stationary point. If you do not grow, you must decay . . . if you grow, you must grow on the same principle of growth as that which animated you from the beginning". Free trading Northern businessmen believed, as firmly as their mercantilist forebears, in the union of profit and power.[99] Alarmed for the security of the two-thirds of their trade that passed through the Mediterranean, Manchester merchants had welcomed the occupation of Cyprus. That was not simply an echo of Beaconsfield's imperial rhetoric: Salisbury offered a cool analysis of Britain's place in a changing world. European peace was a condition of global expansion in which the incidence of little wars, like that in Afghanistan, was a regrettable necessity. He was careful to add that when he talked of expansion he meant the "civilizing influence" of informal empire rather than conquest.[100]

# CHAPTER SEVEN

# A Leader in Waiting

## The Public and the Private Man

As early as June 1878, Count Münster had no doubt that Salisbury would become prime minister and the most influential personality in his country. This was less clear to others. The Queen bestowed the Garter on him after Berlin, and had wanted to give it to him beforehand, in April 1878, so great was her relief and gratitude when he decisively rejected the isolationism of his predecessor at the Foreign Office.[1] Rumour had it that he was ambitious to succeed Beaconsfield; and his wife was certainly ambitious for him, as ever.[2] He had rivals in Cairns, the lord chancellor, a formidable figure in cabinet and the Lords, and Northcote, chancellor of the exchequer and leader of the Commons since Disraeli took his peerage in 1876. Cairns, a deeply evangelical Ulsterman, lacked a following in the lower House despite being a partisan Tory. An old Peelite, Northcote was a competent administrator and parliamentarian whose reliability and experience of the House was held to offset a cross-bench outlook. Although he was the dead man's preferred successor, Salisbury would have been a controversial choice to lead the party in opposition on Beaconsfield's demise in 1881. Estranged from some of his warmest supporters in the past, notably Carnarvon and Bath, who supposed him to have surrendered to Beaconsfield over the Eastern question, Salisbury was regarded with considerable distrust by many peers and MPs. They remembered his rebelliousness, and felt obscurely that his conservatism was not quite what they expected in a leader: too cerebral for Tories by temperament and tradition.[3] Their distrust was compounded by the attitude of some more thoughtful Liberals towards him. The latter perceived that the Cyprus Convention, which their side subjected to intense criticism, concealed Salisbury's determination to maintain peace and his unchanging aversion to the Turk. "I do *not* think", wrote Lord Selborne of Salisbury's conduct in 1878, "his policy was altered by Lord Derby's resignation, so far at least as to the difference between a pacific and a warlike *purpose* was concerned. I believe he had always a pacific settlement and more or less of benefit to the Christian subjects of the Porte in view". He had, surmised this sympathetic opponent, spoken and acted as he did "to bring round . . . his chief, and the noisy section of the party, by humouring them up to the brink of war, in order that they might be satisfied, in the end, by the *display* without the *thing* . . .". [4]

Münster's discernment, and Selborne's, recognized in Salisbury and his handling of foreign affairs political intelligence of a very high order. It was evident in his response to the Tories' defeat in 1880: he read the signs of a greater change than was indicated by a relatively small shift in the distribution of votes, and embraced popular politics so successfully that he was soon a match for Gladstone and for the personification of a new radicalism, Joseph Chamberlain. "Power", he told his heir, "is more and more leaving Parliament and going to the platform". The refashioning and communication of ideas outweighed the admitted importance of machinery to counter the organizational achievements of Birmingham radicalism. Salisbury renewed and enlarged the social dimension of Toryism, outstripping public opinion and being classed with Chamberlain as a "Socialist" by a genuinely alarmed Gladstone. His conservative intent in everything he said appeared from the care he took to identify small with large property in attacking Chamberlain's selective levelling. Speaking all over the country with a frequency unimaginable to any Tory, or Liberal for that matter, before the 1880s, he concentrated on developing the urban Toryism which the party leadership had neglected. Disraeli rarely visited a manufacturing town; in spite of *Sybil* and the celebrated descent on Manchester in 1872, he was remote from industrial Britain. Salisbury showed that he had it in him to emulate Gladstone and establish a community of thought and feeling with mass audiences.[5] Their mutual enemies were secular and Dissenting radicals, the revolutionary Irish well represented among the immigrant minority, and Liberals alleged to have failed in their duty to defend, and to expand, British interests abroad. By 1884 he was sure enough of his ground to adopt something very like the old Chartist demand for equal parliamentary constituencies when household suffrage was extended to the counties.

It was his remarkable success on the platform as much as his boldness in leading the Lords from 1881 that resolved in Salisbury's favour the collective uncertainty which put the Tory leadership into commission between Northcote and himself to await the Queen's choice of a premier if and when the party returned to office. Even then, after Tories in the Lords preferred him to the Duke of Richmond as their leader, "it was generally felt and understood", according to one of his supporters "that the decision gives Salisbury the *united* leadership of the whole party".[6] Northcote, who continued to lead the opposition in the Commons, disagreed, but he did not inspire, then or later. His rival in the Lords was inspiring: if he had too many brains and too much political courage, these, almost everyone was willing to concede when it came to the point in 1885, were faults of the right kind. He had eclipsed Northcote, and Cairns, too.[7] One of his greatest strengths, naturally, was foreign policy. He was not to blame for the Tory government's blunders in Afghanistan and South Africa, exposed as such early in the life of the Gladstone ministry. He had cogent criticisms of Liberal actions in Egypt and the Sudan. The Gladstonian desire to work through the "Concert of Europe" in great power politics

ALLEYN'S SCHOOL LIBRARY

rather than through a good understanding with Germany struck him as unwise and dangerous. Britain's uncomfortable isolation in the Penjdeh crisis of 1885 seemed to prove him right. But it was Ireland, in the grip of a social revolution unwillingly furthered by the Liberals through their land legislation, that elicited some of Salisbury's most powerful strictures on a government whose Irish policy was peculiarly Gladstone's. Salisbury had never had any illusions about the character and vigour of Irish nationality. His unsentimental approach to the Irish question gave him a distinct advantage over those in both British parties who could not, or would not, see Ireland as she really was.

He came to the premiership unusually well equipped for all the problems that crowded in upon him at home and abroad. The respect and liking which the private man enjoyed were no small assets. The great Liberal who was so often one of his targets, had known him since childhood, and was still an occasional visitor to Hatfield after his succession. Writing to his Russian correspondent, Madame Novikov, at the time of Salisbury's mission to Constantinople, Gladstone set his failings, "rough of tongue . . . of unsure judgement" against his virtues in the political arena and outside it, "a great gentleman . . . remarkably clever . . . no Disraelite . . . keeps a conscience, and has plenty of manhood . . .". While this was written with an eye to the lady's contacts in Russia, it fairly represented his opinion of someone with whom he was linked by their common High Churchmanship. When Salisbury did not resign with Carnarvon in January 1878, Gladstone concluded that Beaconsfield had cast a malign spell upon a good man. A little later, as prime minister, he was not so sure of Salisbury's high-mindedness, pained by the realism of an opponent whose "good fame used to be regarded as part of the national estate".[8] Later again, he acquitted Salisbury of personal ambition after seeing his letter to a clerical friend of them both, in which he expressed his distaste for politics and doubted his fitness to lead the Tories for want of "pliancy and optimism . . . I, unfortunately, am very poorly endowed in either respect". Gladstone now thought Salisbury unrealistic in that he did not seem to understand the necessity of whipping up popular feeling to put "some motive power" behind a moderate, but disputed, reform of the electoral system.[9] The Liberal leader was, throughout, more generous to Salisbury than other well informed Liberals: but even radicals were not inclined to demonize him as they did Beaconsfield.

Out of office for five years, Salisbury busied himself, in the intervals of politics, with his estates, hard hit by the long agricultural depression of the late nineteenth century; with the other and varied occupations of a county magnate; and with his amateur scientific experiments. He spent many months on the Continent at his house outside Dieppe, or travelling. In the winter of 1879–80 his health was so poor that reports were circulating of a severe internal complaint and imminent physical breakdown; he was supposed to be taking no exercise and to be sustained by a liberal use of drugs. Always susceptible to minor ailments, and to mild hypochondria, he was soon well enough to undertake the provincial speechmaking in addition to his parliamentary labours. His wife's entertaining furthered her ambitions for him. If he felt, as he did in the early 1880s, out of touch with the party, the remoteness was largely imaginary. His letters, seldom long, show him to have been quite aware of what was happening around him.[10] That is plain from the correspondence he kept up with Lady Janetta Manners, the wife of his cabinet colleague, Lord John. It ranged lightly over politics and any other topics that suggested themselves. In the absence of most of the letters he wrote to his wife, those to Lady Janetta permit one to know a little of Salisbury in his lighter moments – not that his underlying seriousness was ever far below the surface.

Scattered through these letters are comments on his reading – a recommendation of Zola's *L'Assommoir*, on music – "How happy you are to escape Wagner"; and on his cures at Continental spas – "We walk like . . . postmen; drink (salt water) like fishes . . . The terrors of the next walk, or the next drink, fill up the mind". Lady Janetta's mention of one of her good causes, which typically involved restraining somebody, produced sensible advice – "people will always try to defeat a law which interferes too much . . . the police will find it very hard to cope". His light touch deserted him when education came up, and the fate of the half-educated turned out by the schools that existed for the masses – "if no nutriment is provided for the appetites [which] have been sharpened . . . they will find garbage instead, and eat it". At the other end of the social scale, he did not spare Eton – "so bad a school as far as teaching goes, that the boys are at a considerable disadvantage". Though unconvinced of the value of higher education for women, other than governesses, he found it "ridiculous" that educated women should be denied the parliamentary franchise which was about to be extended to agricultural labourers. For one thing, women would be, predominantly, on his side in "the political battle of the future . . . between religion and unbelief". Militant in defence of the Church against her external enemies, he was extraordinarily conciliatory in the practice of his faith: at the London church he often attended the repeated ringing of bells in the communion service irritated him: "They seem to say 'Fight, Fight, Fight' . . . simply . . . to show that the ringer . . . snaps his fingers at the Ultra-Protestants". Such unforced confidences explain why, as prime minister and bishop-maker, he was broadly successful in his efforts to preserve the peace of the Church.[11]

Neither Salisbury nor Lady Janetta could keep off politics for long. She was useful to him as a channel of communication with the old Toryism of which her husband was the most prominent representative left in the Commons. As Northcote's health and his standing declined – "what will the poor people do whom he leaves in the wilderness?" asked Salisbury – the correspondence contained more on the party's shifting fortunes. Earlier, he mused on the questions which the advance of the Left on the Continent compelled every thinking man to reconsider. A letter from France discussed the social malaise that afflicted the bourgeois republic. While he took contributory factors into account, he believed, like other conservatives, that "the decay of religion" was the root cause. In his own country, where the hold of religion was much stronger, socialism was not an immediate but still "a very real danger". It annoyed him that his desire to mitigate the sufferings of the poor by stepping, cautiously, beyond the conventional limits of legislation should be interpreted as "socialist". But, he observed, the epithet did not amount to "a definitely false statement of fact . . . the first of duties is to be pachydermatous". The outward calm was misleading: he might be able to hide his feelings, but he had not grown, and would never grow, a thick skin. Six months away from the premiership and "very despondent" about the course of events at home and abroad, he saw hope in Chamberlain's radicalism, or rather its verbal excesses, as a solvent of the Liberal unity that Gladstone maintained and radicals exploited.[12]

## Popular Politics

The results of the general election of 1880 surprised the Tories, who read into them a fundamental shift away from the old oligarchical politics towards a radicalized democracy.[13] One prominent politician, who had just changed parties, disagreed: Derby, whose estrangement from Beaconsfield and Salisbury over the Eastern question led him to support the Liberals at the election with his name and influence. Always on the watch for a significant political threat to property, this enormously wealthy landowner was glad to note "a singular absence of anything that can be called radicalism" in the campaigning. There was "no trace" of the class feeling he remembered from the Chartist period. He noted, further, that the Established Church had not figured largely in the exchanges between opposing platforms. With very few members "decidedly outside the class . . . conventionally called . . . 'gentlemen'", the new House of Commons was not "democratic". It was afterwards explained to him by John Morley, who was one of them, that radicals and political Dissenters had restrained themselves so as not to divide Liberal forces in the conflict of parties. Morley put the number of genuine radicals at about twenty-five out of over 350 Liberals. Then and later, Derby was not frightened by Chamberlain and his allies, Sir Charles Dilke and Morley.[14] Salisbury thought the scale of the Tories' defeat made it "a perfect catastrophe": the loss of more than a hundred seats in Britain compared with 1874, the worst setback to the party since it was reborn after the First Reform Act, might well lead to its break-up. The "pure 'squire' Conservatism" which, he said a dozen years earlier, had had its day, would be condemned to perpetual opposition by the attractions of Liberalism for the abler and more open-minded without whom no party could flourish. His respect for the power of ideas, eloquently set out, caused him to exaggerate Chamberlain's actual and potential position within the Liberal coalition. "A Jacobin generally finds a revolutionist to help him", wrote this student of the French Revolution. "The only remarkable thing is that so coarse a revolutionist as Chamberlain should have Gladstone for his jackal."[15]

These anxieties determined Salisbury's strategy on and off the platform for five years. His aims were to keep the Tories together, and to present them as a party of government, while educating the public, and moderate Liberals in particular, about the dangers, in which he really believed, from the new model radicalism. Like Northcote, but with greater boldness and more constructively, he worked to create the conditions for a Liberal split. If that perennial Tory hope were realized, the Liberal domination of British politics for half a century would be at an end. Salisbury made the most of Chamberlain's intemperate rhetoric, so much more radical than the proposals he eventually formulated: but it was Gladstone's Irish policy that lent conviction to the Tory's warnings. The Liberal premier, at the head of a cabinet full of large landlords like himself, shared with Ribbonmen and Fenians the responsibility for a social revolution in Ireland.[16]

Salisbury's initial reaction to the defeat of 1880 was to wonder how far it reflected High Church resentment of the Public Worship Regulation Act and of a foreign policy apparently less sympathetic to Ottoman Christians than Gladstone or Carnarvon and at one time Salisbury himself had wanted. In his speeches to mass audiences after the organized militancy of Dissent had gone over to the attack, he replied by identifying Liberationists, and Liberals generally, with the secularism of Bradlaugh and Morley: "Remember what it is for which we struggle . . . first . . . the maintenance of religion . . . there is an old proverb, 'You may know a man by his associates', and infidels are always Liberals". Liberals who were Christians and sincere Dissenters "unknowingly" assisted the enemies of Christianity. His readiness to employ such crude tactics against the political Dissenters he loathed drew some criticism but earned the gratitude of churchmen: it was necessary to take the gloves off when answering Chamberlain's strictures on the Church, or on anything else dear to Conservatives. Salisbury applauded the Tory element among the Wesleyans, the largest of the sects: they were "good patriots and good Christians". The Established Church had many lower-middle- and working-class supporters: the "Christian empire", as he designated it, had even more. The old anti-slavery sentiment retained its hold on public opinion, and on him. He appealed to the collective conscience, on which Gladstone was wont to play, against the Liberal premier's abandonment of the Transvaal's African population to Boer masters. It was evident that he possessed Gladstone's ability to make the exercise of power seem righteous or unrighteous to his hearers.[17]

Religion and empire were socially unifying themes – the second gets fuller treatment later in this chapter. The leitmotiv of Salisbury's speeches, as of Victorian political discourse generally, was class collaboration. That, too, rested on a religious foundation: "my 'Toryism'", he had said long before to someone who knew him unusually well, "[is] very deep distrust of . . . essentially a pagan spirit, discarding the supernatural and worshipping not God but man . . . I cannot put off the conviction that it is dissolving every cement that holds society together". Like their betters, or many of them, plebeian Tories assumed, however inarticulately, a religious sanction behind the existing order. They also understood instinctively the related Burkean concept of change that Salisbury expounded to them without a trace of condescension: "nothing is stable, nothing is permanent in this world . . . but let there be changes worked by the slow process of persuasion, by the natural growth of institutions". Classes should not be left facing revolution "in the attitude of conquerors and conquered". National greatness and prosperity depended on the "profound accord of classes". Some of this had been the stuff of speeches for decades: but in Chamberlain he had an antagonist whose "violent language" was new in a cabinet minister, one not afraid to say in London Society, in front of Salisbury's half-sister, Lady Galloway, "none of us in the upper classes had any idea what was coming . . . a new world, a complete social revolution, the land . . . transferred to the people, all large properties broken up, class distinctions broken down . . .". He advocated an Americanized, not a socialist, Britain: his class warfare was directed against the landed interest, not industrialists, or rentiers such as he had become when he retired from business to enter politics.[18]

As Derby, a cabinet colleague of the Birmingham radical from 1882, commented, Chamberlain's was a vision of the future that did not have a remotely adequate basis in public support. For that reason, Chamberlain was much less specific in his oratory. Salisbury had no need of the proffered reassurance that the working class were "the most conservative section of the community".[19] His counter-attack upon Chamberlain rested on the perception of their conservatism. It was helped by the unease that Gladstone's Irish Land Acts inspired. He linked Chamberlain's assault upon English landlords with the "social revolution", as he rightly called it at the time, in Ireland, which was the work of the premier. Artisans and small shopkeepers might share the indifference on this side of the water to the fate of Irish landlords: they were not indifferent to suggestions that the Gladstonian legislation had jeopardized property in general. "The defence of . . . property", urged Salisbury, "more truly concerns the struggling and industrious classes than those who have . . . secured a certain amount". The Land Acts and the agrarian terrorism that propelled them on to the statute book both expressed "the teaching of Robin Hood". Those at whom he aimed his arguments were not rootless proletarians but men of small property whose bourgeois values permeated the mass of the urban and industrial population. He went on to contend that Liberal policies, Gladstonian and radical, had exacerbated the contemporary recession by the blows which they dealt to confidence. "Confidence and prosperity are convertible terms" he reiterated; both were undermined by politicians who sought to exploit the "discontent of classes" to the detriment of agriculture, business and wages as investment was withheld. Admitting, as he did, that the recession was "much of it . . . beyond human control", the influence he ascribed to political uncertainty was plausible, more especially if his words were taken to refer to a future under Chamberlain rather than Gladstone.[20]

Shortly before he took office in 1885, Salisbury defined his party's evolving creed to add liberty to religion and empire. It was, like so much of what he said, a bid for Liberal votes. The working-class élite disliked, as strongly as he did, "that secular representation of the Inquisition, the modern inspector". The Liberal government, he claimed, favoured the encroachments of this dreaded figure, the greatest danger to personal freedom in an English setting. Yet he was obliged to concede, in the next breath, that the inspector had a legitimate function. For Salisbury was an advocate of social reforms that extended the reach of bureaucracy. He constantly adverted to "the great mission which the next generation has to perform, to make the conditions of life more tolerable to all". There was no question "so overwhelming in its magnitude as . . . relations between the well-to-do and the poor". To an intelligent conservative like his friend Woodard in Manchester, the landed Tories who controlled the party offered little hope: "they have no policy and are too selfish to create one . . . Salisbury will work a miracle if he makes anything of them". Against the odds, he prevailed. The Canon, however, discerned political salvation in the middle-class Toryism to whose substantial presence in Northern towns the Tory leaders had not paid nearly enough attention. Salisbury preferred to encourage the British working class in its characteristic adoption of middle-class values and, at the same time, to hold out the prospect of a society in which "all that is miserable in poverty and struggling shall be abated", carefully chosen words. He acknowledged the religious influence on this growing concern; pointing to "every day . . . a more burning desire" in the Established Church, and Dissent too, to protest at the painful contrast between affluence and deprivation that seemed to threaten Britain's enviable social harmony.[21]

As a young man, Salisbury had reluctantly submitted to the intellectual supremacy of *laissez-faire* economics: it was a political fact, though the weaknesses of a simplistic creed were always plain to him. He had to proceed very cautiously in questioning so powerful an orthodoxy. When he singled out slum housing for detailed, and penetrating analysis, in the newly founded Conservative *National Review*, he gave the impression of having radical intentions which he did not see his way to enacting in an acceptable fashion.[22] Moving for the appointment of a Royal Commission on the housing of the working classes in February 1884, a politically neutral inquiry by arrangement with the government, he disclaimed "any wild schemes of interference". It was "political cowardice" to shrink from investigating the "appalling problem" of overcrowding for fear of the "illegitimate methods" that might be proposed to solve them. Working with Dilke, president of the local government board and chairman of the commission, Salisbury broadened the scope of the inquiry. His "temporary radicalism" impressed Dilke and the trade unionist MP, Henry Broadhurst, when they came to draft a report. However, Salisbury objected to any suggestion of "planting peasant proprietors" in the towns, as he put it; the rights of existing owners must be protected. This solicitude for property reflected the current criticism of ground landlords, like Salisbury himself, easily represented as parasitic upon urban growth. A bill to enfranchise leaseholds on judicially fixed terms had attracted over a hundred votes in the Commons, including those of some Tories, one of them being Lord Randolph Churchill, the rising star on his side of the House.[23]

The fruit of the Commission's labours, a measure that had the almost unanimous support of its members, was introduced by Salisbury as premier in July 1885. As he wished, it concentrated on improving and increasing the housing stock through the amendment and consolidation of previous legislation. His personal contribution to its provisions was the discounted sale of government-owned sites in London for working-class dwellings. Gladstone deemed this proposal "one of the very worst pieces of socialism that has yet come into our view"; and Liberal MPs rendered it inoperable by compelling the Tory minority administration to substitute sale at market value.[24] They were deaf to Salisbury's plea to "come into court with the doctrine of *laissez-faire* when they had clean hands". Yet, his "socialism" apart, the Liberals had developed a healthy respect for his achievements in domestic politics, since going into opposition in 1880; they regarded him, in Gladstone's circle, as "a really good fighting man". Carnarvon summed up a typical Salisbury speech in the 1880s: "singular power – reasoned all through – and spoken from first to last without a single note". The cost of establishing himself as "a man who can rouse people", the equal on the platform of the Liberal giants, was high for someone who was never robust. Half-humorously, he related his experience at Sheffield: "a more filthy atmosphere than ever before it was my lot to breathe – eight thousand very unwashed and enthusiastic persons – only two or three panes in the roof for ventilation." But the labour, "peculiarly difficult and unattractive", was inescapable.[25]

With other men of the Right, then and since, he argued that only the people could resist abuses of power by a democratized legislature. "I do not think it is . . . to be deplored at all", he announced at Liverpool in 1882, as he castigated the Liberal record, ". . . [that] the direct action of the people is superseding the indirect action of its representatives". After he had spoken in Glasgow, defying the Liberals in the conflict between Lords and Commons over the third reform bill, they realized what they were up against. Salisbury had taught his party that "it is only through the masses [that] . . . anything nowadays can be done". Old Tories, in both senses, like Lord John Manners, were relieved and delighted by Salisbury's ability to match the Liberals' populism: "Their clearness and directness will enable them to be 'understanded' of the . . . people", wrote Manners of his colleague's speeches, "and it is to them that an appeal has to be made, for the educated classes are sufficiently with us".[26] Salisbury knew better than to take the latter for granted. In his speeches, "the cool and almost cynical analysis of political facts and tendencies", as *The Times* called it, was intended to reach them as well as the wider public whose outlook was shaped largely by an expanding press. As he told the Tory journalist Alfred Austin in 1882, he was trying to get to "the mass of conservative thought . . . at the bottom of most educated men's minds". He invited his mixed, but of course predominantly half-educated audiences, to think through with him the policies of party and government, which, ultimately, they would determine. The literate newspaper-reading public continued to feel the influence of tradition and deference but inevitably questioned both as the pervasive process of modernization developed.[27]

Salisbury had forecast the public examination of social classes by each other in one of his first speeches in the industrial North. The only defence against social disintegration was education in all its forms, not least the platform oratory of leading politicians reported *in extenso* by a press whose readership found politics absorbing. The North of England was central to Salisbury's strategy. If the Tories could not make headway in that densely populated heartland of industry their prospects nationally were poor. In the years after his party's defeat in 1880 Salisbury gave the North priority over the other regions. He tried to persuade Hicks Beach, now high in the Tory leadership, to leave the West of England for a Manchester seat: to win there would be "a telling triumph . . . and have a decisive effect in other parts of the country". His nephew, A.J. Balfour, took the advice to move to Manchester and "gain perceptibly in force . . . as the representative of a large working-class constituency". At the 1885 election Tory victories in the boroughs across England rewarded Salisbury's courtship of the urban vote. In his recension of Toryism the unforgivable sin was to set class against class. As yet, the principal enemies were Chamberlain with his class politics, and Gladstone accused of appeasement in Ireland and further afield, and of failing to understand the necessities of empire and the economy. Salisbury offered alternatives that transformed perceptions of Toryism. "Conservative policy", said *The Times* in 1883 of his speechmaking, "is no longer a mere string of negations". In common with Chamberlain, he had outrun a public opinion which, Gladstone rightly insisted, was distinctly conservative where property of any kind was concerned. But, like Chamberlain again, he saw, more clearly than most Tories and, perhaps, than Gladstone, that "our absolute sovereign is the people of this country . . . you have a form of government in many points of view purely democratic".[28]

## Empire and the Economy

The Salisbury of the 1880s discovered an admiration for Palmerston which he had not always felt in that statesman's lifetime. With hindsight, he saw in him "the type of an astute and moderate leader", and reproached Gladstone with abandoning the tried and successful policies, at home and abroad, of his old chief. "Nothing but the name", he asserted in November 1880, opening one of the Conservative clubs whose spread was an important factor in the revival of Tory fortunes, "connects the party led by Lord Palmerston with that led by Mr Gladstone".[29] It was not the first time the Tories had sought to appropriate Palmerston's mantle, and the Liberals were not inclined to relinquish it. Gladstone, too, had revised his view of Palmerston, writing in 1876 of "his redeeming qualities . . . a lover of liberty all over the world . . . entirely above flattering", as he accused Disraeli of doing, "the most vulgar appetites and prejudices of the people". Gladstone still considered Palmerston to have had "*something* of a weak side with respect to brag", but was not reluctant to exploit the victorious invasion of Egypt in 1882 for what it was worth in domestic politics. "You have fought the battle of all Christendom, and history acknowledges it", the British consul general in Cairo telegraphed to his political masters on the news of Tel-el-Kebir: "May I also venture to say that it has given the Liberal party a new lease of popularity and power?"[30] For the Gladstone government's withdrawal of the British presence from Afghanistan and the Transvaal, and its concessions to Celtic nationalism, had allowed the Tories to depict it, quite wrongly, as throwing off the responsibilities, and with them the rewards, of empire through a misplaced idealism. Salisbury continued to press this charge in his last, much quoted, article of October 1883 for the *Quarterly Review*, entitled simply "Disintegration", and in his speeches. He was really criticizing the muddled thinking, as it seemed to him, behind Gladstone's policies almost everywhere abroad.[31]

With the partial exception of Cobden, all the leading political figures of the Victorian age were imperialists. But theirs was the imperialism of trade: the liabilities of territorial expansion were well understood. Gladstone might deplore the morality of conquest in Clive's day, but he did not envisage a British retirement from India in the foreseeable future: he had put a son into business in Calcutta. His own considerable investment in Egypt gave him a personal interest in replacing the shortlived nationalist regime of Colonel Arabi Pasha and his associates with one that submitted to its international financial obligations.[32] Salisbury also preferred indirect to direct rule, influence to occupation or annexation: but he too had a son who was to make his career in the East.[33] The formal empire expanded steadily under successive Gladstone ministries to protect tangible British interests from rivals or local complications. He and Salisbury both objected to Jingo expansion for expansion's sake as futile and sometimes dangerous: but Salisbury questioned the wisdom of retreating from Afghanistan and the Transvaal in 1880–81, and from the Sudan in 1885. He had not favoured Lytton's advance into Afghanistan, or Sir Bartle Frere's into the Boer republic; nor did he want to see Britain add the problems of the Sudan to those of Egypt. Once she had established a physical presence in those territories, however, it ought not to be liquidated with the Liberals' improvident haste. Intervention created obligations: to friends and clients among Afghan and Sudanese tribes, and to the helpless African majority in the Transvaal who had believed in assurances of British protection against their enemies.

Loss of face, moreover, involved a loss of power. "I am afraid", he told the peers, "that in Asia allegiance is merely the recognition of superior strength"; withdrawal could but be seen as an admission of weakness. The Afghans would look to Russia, and Britain's diminished reputation must already affect her hold over the Indian peoples. He argued, as he had within the Tory government, for the retention of Kandahar as a sufficient guarantee for British influence inside Afghanistan. Of Britain's retirement from the Transvaal on terms that reflected the Boers' defeat of her troops at Majuba, he said "it is the same wretched story". Afrikaner loyalists in the Cape Colony would draw the obvious conclusion. Again, watching the Liberal cabinet's attempts to avoid taking direct responsibility for the Sudan as the Mahdi's hosts overran the Egyptian garrisons, he found the policy "unintelligible: . . . we know that as it proceeds it is marked by blood".[34] The British expeditionary force dispatched to rescue the last Egyptian governor-general, General Gordon, who was actually the cabinet's selection for the post, arrived too late: and another Christian hero entered the Victorian pantheon. Condemning the futility of so much blood, Sudanese and British, shed with nothing to show for it, Salisbury urged the government not to abandon the whole of the Sudan to the Mahdi: "How can we defend ourselves for having repeated the sad story of Kandahar and the Transvaal . . . our friendship has been a curse to every tribe and nation to whom it has been offered . . . ?" Gladstone discerned a legitimate national feeling in Afghanistan, the Transvaal and the Sudan, to which Liberal Britain had bowed: Salisbury pointed to hundreds of thousands of Africans whose fate in the Transvaal made the London Convention of 1884, consolidating the republic's virtual independence gained three years earlier, an agreement "really in the interest of slavery". In the Sudan slavery triumphed with the Mahdi.[35]

Gladstone and Salisbury emphasized different moral dimensions of British expansion. On another plane Salisbury had the best of the argument. Gladstonian diplomacy was not as ineffectual with the Great Powers as he suggested: it scored a notable success in enforcing the Ottoman cession of Thessaly and part of Epirus to Greece by the threat to occupy the rich port of Smyrna.[36] However, Britain's action separated her from "our natural friends in Europe", as Salisbury called Germany and Austria. He complained that the government was forcing the pace of Turkey's decline. Gladstone had endeavoured to mobilize the "Concert of Europe" against the Sultan, only to see the German powers back away. Salisbury likened the Concert to "an orchestra of which the various members have not the slightest intention of playing the same tune". As an anti-British demonstration, the Three Emperors' Alliance of 1881 between Germany, Austria and Russia reaffirmed the closure of the Straits to foreign warships in peacetime. Bismarck and the Austrians regarded the undoubted influence of Gladstone's liberal idealism in the Balkans as a menace to regional, and indeed European, stability.[37] Salisbury was impatient with the praise which Gladstone bestowed on Russia as the friend of Slav freedom, and with his condemnation of Austria as its enemy. Russia, the Tory reflected, was a despotic state, harshly oppressive in Poland, and Austria a parliamentary monarchy ruling over many loyal Slav subjects. He no more desired to quarrel with Russia than did Bismarck, but he was for a time afraid that the Liberals' "half-romantic and half-literary" enthusiasm for Balkan nationalism might lead them to seek "an exclusive alliance" with Russia.[38]

Salisbury considered the Russian the most untrustworthy of foreign governments, with the republican French a close second. They were the two countries whose relations with Britain were severely strained during this Gladstone ministry. Russia's advance in Central Asia reached the undefined northern border of Afghanistan; and the French resented the position which they had allowed Britain to acquire in Egypt. War with Russia was a real possibility for a few weeks in 1885, while the confrontation with France raised fears of one for some time before that. Salisbury took a very strong line on the Anglo-Russian dispute in his opposition speeches. "Is it possible in common sense to rely on her [Russia's] promises", he asked in April 1885, ". . . say to her, 'There is a point to which you shall not go, and if you go we will spare neither men nor money until you go back'". The government had obtained a vote of credit from parliament against the eventuality of hostilities, and was making its military and naval dispositions: he was trying to prevent ministers from settling, as they did, for arbitration: "it was a fundamental error to attempt to engage in negotiations with Russia for the delimitation of a boundary", he declared in May, when his forthright description of Russia as a "swindler" in her international dealings created a sensation. A shocked Gladstone felt that his language about a great European power "almost" ruled out Salisbury as a future premier.[39]

The future premier was more circumspect in his references to France: war with the second maritime power just across the Channel was altogether more serious than an Anglo-Russian conflict, which would be an affair of naval bombardments and skirmishes in the mountains and deserts of Central Asia inaccessible to large armies far from their bases. As foreign secretary Salisbury had worked to share with France the control of Egypt, which the Khedive Ismail's indebtedness had handed to the two governments on behalf of their financiers and investors.[40] Sharing, he was confident, must be in the interest of the stronger, more enterprising nation, his own: his countrymen would get the better of the French in business and administration, "a result which . . . depends not on any formal acts but on the natural superiority which a good Englishman [is] . . . pretty sure to show". He differed from the French, and from the senior Treasury official, Charles Rivers Wilson, imposed on the Khedive as minister of finance, in his perception of how they should proceed in

Egypt. It was, in Salisbury's view, important to keep European control in the background in order to spare Islamic and national feelings. Not less important was the condition of the fellahin. He summarized what he hoped he had achieved by 1880: "Taxes levied without oppression – perfect agreement with France". The French were pursuing a "bondholder's policy"; but Britain's emphasis was "political": "What we have dreaded is anarchy . . . We don't want another Turkey". The removal of Ismail by the two powers exemplified the salutary firmness that might have saved Turkey from the disasters of the 1870s if the then Sultan had been deposed at the beginning of the decade.[41]

It was Salisbury's contention that the British invasion of Egypt could have been avoided. The resident British representatives had allowed themselves to forget, he wrote, that "nothing would please the Mussulman better than to give both France and England a blow in the face". Ismail's successor, Tewfik, was compelled to accept a ministry dominated by a soldier, Arabi, and others belonging to what the able British controller of finance, Sir Auckland Colvin, warned the Foreign Office was a genuine national movement. The government in London chose to ignore his advice: there was "not the smallest rag or shred of evidence", Gladstone assured the Commons, to suggest that Arabi and his party really aspired to national freedom; theirs was the "rebellion of a military class", supported by a few large landowners and tinged with "a certain . . . religious fanaticism". Egypt was only a Turkish province, not a nation. Alarm for the bondholders, for the safety of Europeans and for the Suez Canal, and a larger concern about the blow that Egyptian independence would deal to the "general fabric" of the Ottoman empire prompted this special pleading.[42] The French, who had pressed for intervention until their public opinion turned against the diversion of strength from the defence of France, left the British to bombard Alexandria and land the force that obtained an easy victory at Tel-el-Kebir in September 1882. Gladstone rejoiced, privately and publicly: "God . . . has prospered us in . . . an honest undertaking. We certainly ought to be in a good humour with our Army, our Navy, our Admirals, our Generals".[43]

The invasion had only become necessary, Salisbury held, because the retreats in Afghanistan and South Africa had so reduced Britain's "military credit" that Arabi felt it was safe to defy her. He was sarcastic about the Liberals' self-congratulation. The shelling of Alexandria; the destruction of the Egyptian army; the treatment of the Khedive, "so ostentatiously" diminished in the eyes of his people as to be impotent without the British; and then the loss of the Sudan constituted a formidable indictment. "Is that", he inquired, "a process . . . likely to leave our name imprinted on . . . [Egyptian] minds . . . with affection and respect?"[44] The religious aspect of the British conquest was one that disturbed him: "nothing", he said before the troops landed, "can be more dangerous than . . . to set Christianity collectively against Islam". He rightly guessed that the cabinet did not know what to do next: "The *status quo* cannot be restored: it never can", he observed. Britain must retain the supremacy in Egypt which she had won on the battlefield: but it was for ministers, and not for the opposition, to devise a means of exercising it that was at once conciliatory and effective.[45] The Liberals realized – some, including Gladstone, more reluctantly than others – that the reconstruction of the Egyptian state required an indefinite military occupation, despite the premier's conviction that it was "madness to suppose . . . we can undertake the government of a Mahometan country in the heart of the Mahometan world, with a population antagonistic to Europeans". While he was similarly convinced that only some form of indirect rule could sensibly be attempted in Egypt, Salisbury did not, at this point, see fit to pretend that the country was anything other than "our luckless puppet".[46]

The problems of empire were related, in Salisbury's speeches, to those of the domestic economy in the grip of recession. The Liberals' Egyptian blunders must have repercussions in the great Indian market: not long before the British invaded, he asked a metropolitan audience to reflect on the paralysis of Egyptian commerce and investment: "if you wish to know whether . . . industry . . . and trade can prosper while glory is tarnished and empire . . . destroyed". He invoked Palmerston, who had "no fear of employing force when force was needed". When the government acted with the requisite firmness, Salisbury urged them not to sacrifice to diplomatic pressures what "the valour of our soldiers has won".[47] As the effect of Gladstone's "Christian war" wore off, Salisbury returned to his theme. The greatness of Britain, he reminded Birmingham Tories in March 1883, derived from war and empire: what would she be without Canada, or India, what would she have been without the defeat of Napoleonic France? The economic foundations of the Victorian empire had not been laid by free trade: and he began, like his party, to flirt with the movement for "fair trade". Professing his active attachment to free trade, he thought it was not "Something so sacred that I may not look at it". Peel and the younger Gladstone had only been able to dismantle protection by persuading contemporary public opinion that other countries would follow suit: but their economic logic had not made the expected converts abroad; tariff barriers were rising instead of falling. On behalf of the Conservatives, he promised an official inquiry into possible action to counter "by diplomacy or otherwise . . . a state of things with . . . [a] fatal effect upon the commerce of this country" – a guarded allusion to selective retaliatory duties.[48]

In the meantime they should condemn the unwise proposal of a Liberal viceroy in India, Lord Ripon, to give native members of the civil service jurisdiction over European offenders. In Turkey and Egypt, China and Japan, the capitulations removed cases involving mainly white British subjects to their own consular courts. The breach of this principle in India had alarmed businessmen and planters. "What would your feelings be", he demanded, "if . . . your life or honour were exposed to the decision . . . of a coloured man?" The resulting insecurity threatened to drive away "English capital, guided by English energy and genius . . . [from] one of your best markets". As a haven for exports shut out from other destinations by rising tariffs, India would be "absolutely destroyed". His message to industrial, and radical, Birmingham was that empire mattered most to them: it was vital to the prosperity that had sustained the good class relations on which domestic confidence and investment depended. "I do not believe . . . England stripped of India . . . of its colonies, humbled before Europe, would be a happy England for the working classes".[49] Thus he linked a hard-headed imperialism to his cautiously progressive Conservatism. His antagonist was "the modern Radical", personified by Chamberlain and bent on politicizing the inevitable tensions between social classes. Even then, Chamberlain was no "little Englander", but he shared the collective responsibility for the setbacks and uncertainties that marked the cabinet's policy overseas, lampooned by Salisbury as "that attempt at the Quakerization of mankind". Their increasing difficulties in Ireland, according to him, owed much to Majuba, "the fatal error . . . the origin of all their failures", which convinced the world that a Liberal government would always yield.[50]

When they appeared on a platform together, *The Times* commented that, in contrast to Northcote's defensiveness, Salisbury was "aggressive all through". The public, he remarked, was interested in great power politics, and empire "almost to the exclusion of everything else". He himself thought those were "undoubtedly the most important" subjects, given the fundamental indifference of the country to radical change. Until they split over Irish home rule, the Liberals were only really vulnerable to charges of mismanaging foreign policy and the empire, and, of course, Ireland in its "imperial aspect", on which Salisbury dwelt. He kept before his mass audiences the danger of a Russian invasion of Afghanistan: the controversy over Ripon's liberalizing policies in India, the unnecessary cause of racial tension; the situation in South Africa – "I decline to look on the whites as the only inhabitants of the country": the unnerving isolation of England in Europe: and the opportunities her isolation gave France to attack the British position in Egypt in complex international negotiations about Egyptian debt and the status of the canal.[51] His speeches during a visit to Manchester, the home of free trade, in April 1884 exploited the anxiety about industry's future outlets in assailing the culpable weakness of Liberal ministries: "the uncivilized outlets . . . more and more precious . . . offer the most profitable business . . . if no foreign power is allowed to . . . introduce its hostile tariffs". Large tracts of Africa and Central Asia were falling into the hands of those who meant to exclude British trade: "Why is our Government powerless to do its duty by the commerce of this country?" Britain's prestige, her "military and political credit", he answered, had declined to the point where other countries had little time for her representations. Working men, to whom political power was passing, had to resist perilous exhortations to conduct foreign policy in "something like the spirit of the Sermon on the Mount".[52]

He was preaching to the converted: Lancashire Tories greeted him with an address that highlighted the integrity of the empire. "It will be our touchstone", he promised. The strain of idealism in Gladstonian Liberalism had survived the Quaker Bright's resignation from the cabinet in protest at the bombardment of Alexandria, and seemed more than ever inappropriate in dealings with European powers, the Boers, or fanatical Muslims. The speeches delivered on his next appearance in the provinces, at Plymouth in June, were derided in Downing Street as "Gunpowder and Glory" for their tone. "Heaven defend the country from his return to . . . power!" exclaimed Gladstone's devoted private secretary. The same source concluded that Salisbury's oratory was "vigorous and effective". It could not be described as merely "Jingo-ish".[53] Like Palmerston at his most responsible, Salisbury spoke of the restraints on Britain's action in the welcome absence of conscription: "God forbid . . . there should be any probability of war with any great European power". He echoed the concern of the mid-1880s for the real strength and preparedness of the navy. Beyond Europe, actual and potential foes were less formidable: and he disputed the virtues which Gladstone attributed to these, when it suited him. To the premier's famous assertion that the Mahdi and his followers represented, in spite of everything, "a people rightly struggling to be free", he retorted, to amused cheers, "My impression . . . is that the Sudanese are struggling for abridging the liberty of other people in the shape of the slave trade". They were both right; as the well informed late Victorian public realized. The Egyptians, too, Salisbury recognized, naturally preferred to be ruled "by those of their own creed . . . race . . . colour": Britain's "atonement" for the damage she had done to their institutions by an invasion that could have been avoided, should take the form of indirect rule on the model of India's princely states. His reiterated insistence on the need for a strong hand in Africa and Asia as the precondition of a liberal imperialism, with a small "l", made sense.[54]

Nevertheless, Derby considered the "able and powerful" Plymouth speeches, in which Salisbury also defended the Established Church and her schools against Dissenting and radical attacks, "singularly injudicious, even for him". There was some force, "historically", in Salisbury's argument, restated on this and many other occasions, that if the empire ceased to grow it must begin to decline. But such language was confirmation of a Tory shift towards becoming "exclusively a military or clerical party". In Derby's view, it was not a development that would enhance the attractions of Toryism for the middle and "probably" the respectable working classes.[55] He was mistaken, perhaps largely because he did not appreciate how Salisbury had safeguarded himself and his party against Jingo extravagance in appealing to imperial aspirations and fears common to Liberals and Tories. In the next few months electoral reform and the position of the Lords moved into the foreground: but he seldom omitted his now familiar perspectives on empire from the fighting speeches in which he dared the Liberals to dissolve. A general election called to overcome the peers' refusal to extend the franchise without a redistribution of seats fair to the Opposition, might well be decided on the government's disappointing record abroad and in Ireland. He left the great towns in no doubt as to where they should find the key to economic recovery and expansion. Working men, he said at Glasgow in October, "will see that a policy which neglects the empire of England does not open to us the markets of the world". The fall in their country's international standing showed in "that heightening of tariffs . . . that closing of markets". This refrain went down so well that he was emboldened to intimate on the eve of taking office in 1885 that enlarging the British internal market to include the colonies was both desirable and compatible with the principle of free trade.[56]

Salisbury had done what Northcote had conspicuously failed to do: he had established in the minds of the mass electorate expanded in 1884 clearer differences between Liberalism and Toryism than in fact existed. In some ways he was closer to Chamberlain: in others to Chamberlain's Whig opponent in the cabinet and on the platform, Lord Hartington: in others again to Gladstone himself. As much a social radical as Chamberlain: a Palmerstonian imperialist like Hartington: as convinced as

Gladstone of the primacy of religion and a religious morality in politics – Salisbury scored when, acknowledging the ability of individual Liberal ministers, he indicted their collective incompetence. The death of Gordon and the Anglo-Russian crisis early in 1885 were the final proofs of an ineptitude and lack of foresight that lowered the cabinet in their own eyes and in those of their adherents in and out of parliament. They contrived to emerge from the Central Asian dispute with some credit: but it was notorious that General Gordon's mission and his attempted rescue were bedevilled by ministerial disagreements. Salisbury believed that Gordon was the wrong man for a task that was an impossible one, given the government's pretence that he was the Khedive's servant, and not theirs. But his fate was their responsibility: no one questioned their Tory critic's sincerity when he condemned the sacrifice of Gordon and of the relief expedition's dead to the divided counsels of their political chiefs.[57]

## A Changing Party and Parliamentary Reform

Salisbury's new Toryism led and shaped a trend, the Tory democracy that Gladstone so much disliked, which had a striking exponent in the son of an old cabinet colleague, Lord Randolph Churchill, whose profound cynicism was not lost on those able to observe him at close quarters. They saw what his latest biographer has decisively exposed, the superficiality and opportunism of his motives.[58] Salisbury, in his speeches, argued for a Toryism that drew on the conservatism of an urban and industrial Britain, middle and working class, without the revolutionary instincts and experience of their Continental counterparts, who had behind them a long tradition of peasant revolt. The English, and Scottish, towns largely reproduced in their political attitudes the deference which governed the countryside, with urban patriciates taking the place of the rural gentry. It was not, therefore, difficult for the Tories to accept that talk of partnership between social classes, which went back to before the Great Reform Bill, must now find expression in policies with a commensurate appeal. It followed that there should be room in Tory cabinets for men from the middle class, who could be identified as such and were not, unlike those who had previously reached it, anxious to forget their origins. The Liberals had advanced further down this road: Cobden could not bring himself to serve under Palmerston, but gave his blessing to the strategy in accordance with which Milner Gibson in 1859, Bright in 1868, and Chamberlain in 1880 entered cabinets full of Whig peers. It was the best way of dealing with politicians who liked to assert that aristocratic leadership was an anachronism, and, in important respects, an actively harmful one.[59]

Salisbury, who had married into the middle class, did not subscribe to Churchill's undiluted snobbery about their presence on Northcote's front bench in the Commons in the persons of W.H. Smith and R.A. Cross. Both had been made cabinet ministers by Churchill's hero, Disraeli, but he did not allow that to detract from his ferocious mockery of the two. As a parliamentary and a platform orator, and as a tactician, he outshone Northcote and those other targets of a born *frondeur*. He and his close associates, Sir Henry Drummond Wolff, J.E. Gorst and Salisbury's nephew A.J. Balfour met a real Tory need when they adopted an independent style of opposition to the large Gladstonian majority, one in refreshing contrast to Northcote's conventional proceedings. They baited Gladstone with amusing impertinence and enough success to ensure that he rose to their taunts, wasting parliamentary time that was in increasingly short supply as Parnell's nationalists fought their own battle against a government whose concessions to them were always inadequate. The "Fourth Party" – as Churchill and his friends were dubbed, to their delight – thought of Salisbury as the Tories' natural leader, possessing the political intelligence and courage in which Northcote was unquestionably deficient. In private conversation, Gladstone, whose secretary Northcote had been in his Peelite days, spoke of his "deplorable want of manhood"; when the Tory leader in the Commons referred to the premier, only half in jest, by his nickname of the "Grand Old Man", he was himself mocked as the "Grand Old Woman". Outwardly loyal to his partner in the headship of the party, Salisbury did not usually demur when Balfour, who enjoyed his uncle's confidence, freely criticised Northcote in their correspondence.[60]

As early as September 1880, Salisbury saw in his partner a fatal handicap to the party's chances of recovering from its electoral reverse: "I see no remedy . . . the efficiency of our party will decay . . . we shall not recover the confidence of the country. For it is the central figure of a party in the Commons to which constituencies are wont to look, if their confidence is asked for that party". The last sentence sheds some light on Salisbury's reluctance to press his claims to an undivided leadership. He defended Northcote against some of Balfour's criticisms: it was sensible for "the leader of . . . a diminished party" to aim at attracting Whigs frightened by the strength of radicalism; even determined opposition in the Commons should be selective, otherwise "the repeated exhibition of large majorities" merely served to underline Tory weakness.[61] Nor was Northcote guilty of neglecting the constituencies: he was a tireless platform speaker; the work, said Balfour, afforded scope for his "peculiar gift for platitudes". Salisbury's contrasting originality reflected his apprehension in 1880 that the decade would mark "the beginning of a serious war of classes". Writing to Woodard after the passage of several years, he was rather less pessimistic, but still expected "a series of quack experiments . . . which will furnish an enormous harvest to dishonest politicians". He was alluding to an excess of the social radicalism which figured in his own speeches. "This", he was afraid, "will be a new element of disintegration". Idealists and working-class electors would have to learn "by hard experience" the limits of state intervention on behalf of those with little or no property.[62]

At the time his mind ran on "Disintegration", the title of his last contribution to the *Quarterly Review* in October 1883; a mordant analysis of developments in Ireland, the empire and party politics at home. The balanced, remarkably harmonious society of the Victorians was endangered by Liberals and radicals who either did not think to ask themselves "whither are they progressing?"; or preferred to conceal their subversive intentions. As on the Continent, the Church and property were the latter's targets. In the circumstances, Salisbury doubted whether it was in the country's true interests to curb the power of a minority in the Commons – exemplified by the Irish nationalists' persistent obstruction of business – to hold up the conduct of ministerial programmes. "Legislative stagnation" might well be better for the nation. Yet he had faith, in the long run, in the collective judgement of the people: "in a modern state the only arbitration possible between classes". After a string of by-election losses in 1880 and 1881, the Liberal government had regained popularity, following the invasion of Egypt.[63] Salisbury told Northcote that they had no alternative but to continue their speaking tours, which they both found physically exhausting: "it is the only weapon we have – and we must go on plugging away". He considered party organization much less important, though more so than his advice suggests.[64] The Tories, like other defeated parties since, were inclined to blame the organizational superiority of the other side, and especially the "caucus", the democratic centralism of the Birmingham radicals. For Salisbury party was, at best, an instrument: what mattered were the ideas it existed to serve.

"The 'machine'", he said on the platform in May 1884, ". . . although it conduces to efficiency, does not conduce to political life." He warned against "the temptation of the wire puller", the assumption that electoral success was everything. Party then became "a mere race, a mere auction", and politics "a mere trade or profession". He maintained that party machines were already too powerful, distancing the Commons from the people they supposedly represented. It was a speech directed at Tories as well as Liberals. Churchill and his friends had taken control of the National Union, set up in 1867 to encourage the spread of constituency associations, in a bid to destroy Northcote politically. Churchill claimed for the Union a place to which it had never aspired since its creation. "All my political actions", he wrote in January 1884, "have been in the direction of endeavouring to get Lord Salisbury recognized as the leader of the Tory party."[65] Salisbury's polite refusal to assist in the destruction of Northcote exposed him to the outspoken attacks that Churchill was making in the name of the National Union, "a popular body", on "the close corporation" of party notables and whips forming the central committee to which the supervision of Tory organization had been entrusted after the 1880 election. Salisbury, advised by Balfour, who sided with his uncle, let the increasing recklessness of Churchill's language take effect: "I see R. C. is doing his best to set the owners of property against him". Bourgeois Tories did not like hostile references to the "aristocratic and privileged classes". His supporters in the National Union realized what others had seen all along, that Churchill was aiming at the leadership for himself. He resigned the chairmanship of the Union in May 1884 when its council overruled him and sought to end the dispute with the central committee.[66]

It was still necessary to conciliate Churchill, who retained a large following and had made himself indispensable in the Commons. He was admitted to the party's inner circle: and the National Union reverted to a subordinate function. It is a measure of Salisbury's authority that he reached a settlement with Churchill and communicated the result to Northcote. The rebel, he reported, offered terms which were "practically a confession . . . that he was indisposed to continue the struggle". Some of Churchill's friends felt badly let down: but his populism was never more than an expedient.[67] Salisbury turned his attention to propaganda, neglected because of "the internecine conflict into which it . . . pleased R.C. to plunge our organization".

He did not favour drawing up a manifesto: "the dual leadership is our difficulty", and the end product, if it avoided giving too many hostages to fortune, must be "a pallid composition, perfectly worthless for the purpose of quotation, placarding and the like". Instead, he wanted a steady flow of speeches and public letters; an old device, the latter, that had not outlived its usefulness. Extracts from these should be circulated for mass consumption. A trial of strength was upon them between the parties and the Houses over the redistribution of seats to accompany an extended franchise. Salisbury's success in ending Churchill's rebellion on terms that restored party unity for the time being prepared him for a duel with Gladstone, on which the future of the Tory party was thought to turn.[68]

The extension of household suffrage to the counties was not something that the Tories liked to oppose directly, despite their misgivings about its effects. It had been under discussion for more than a decade, and was seen as rounding off the reform of 1867 rather than initiating a new era. What had not been attempted in the first two Reform Acts was an allocation of seats that fairly reflected the distribution of the electorate. Interests were represented, as before 1832, in preference to people. Mindful that redistribution had contributed to the undoing of his reform bill in 1866, Gladstone wished to postpone it until the revised franchise had gone through parliament. Otherwise Whigs sitting for small boroughs doomed to extinction and radicals eager for the triumph of democratic principle were likely to fall out, to the Tories' advantage. Salisbury's calculations pointed to the conclusion that an election on the enlarged franchise without redistribution would be disastrous for his party. A premature dissolution of the parliament elected in 1880 was a serious possibility if Gladstone were tempted to review his mandate before a redistribution bill could be passed. It would be a way of resolving, for a while, the Liberals' internal tensions on a wide range of issues. As matters stood, the electoral system was not unfair to the Tories, but the reverse: between two and three thousand votes cast differently would have given them a majority of one in 1880 with a minority of the total vote.[69] The agricultural labourers whom it was now proposed to enfranchise were expected, as the result of radical attacks on landowners, to favour the Liberals on a scale that would, and did, cost the Tories many seats. At the same time, the large minorities of Tory voters in the big towns would continue to be under-represented in the absence of sub-division to create constituencies which they might dominate, given the trend towards residential segregation of the classes. Salisbury was determined to use his rather uncertain control of the Lords to block the extension of the franchise until there was agreement between the parties on redistribution.[70]

On the evidence before them, Salisbury argued that the Tories would benefit from the principle of equality in the size of constituency electorates, the radical demand, though not to the extent of emerging with a majority. The Liberals' confidence of victory, with or without a redistribution acceptable to the opposition, made some of their right wing as anxious as the Tories to limit their party's anticipated gains, assumed to be disproportionately radical. This element in the cabinet and party was also identified with growing criticism of Gladstonian foreign and imperial policies. They suspected him and his devoted foreign secretary, Lord

Granville, of wanting to raise a storm over the postponement of redistribution that would divert attention from their difficulties in Egypt and the Sudan. Salisbury shared their suspicions: the Tory plan was to make a divided government dissolve parliament on its predicament in those regions as the premier tried to escape the consequences of his military victory at Tel-el-Kebir. Gladstone avoided that trap and succeeded in provoking the Tories to a confrontation which he thought must end in their discomfiture, only to find that Salisbury had, in effect, changed the rules of the political game in Disraelian fashion.[71] One of Churchill's most faithful adherents, Gorst, belatedly saw that Salisbury had taken over "Tory democracy", and "will . . . oust us from our legitimate position". Gladstone was similarly discon- certed: when the Lords rejected the franchise bill in July 1884 because the govern- ment declined to show their hand on redistribution, Salisbury was not intimidated by Gladstone's portentous warnings of an irresistible agitation that would drastically reform the Lords. Her husband, Lady Salisbury told the wife of a Liberal cabinet minister, disliked the Upper House and would be glad to return to the Commons if it was swept away. Her supposed indiscretion was one that the premier endeav- oured to turn to account with worried Tory peers and with those on his own side who were equally alarmed.[72]

"It is my opinion", wrote Gladstone in October 1884, after the political tem- perature had been raised by speeches and demonstrations, "that Salisbury (who naturally rules the roost) does not want an accommodation, and does not care if the House of Lords is thrown into the cauldron along with other materials". If Lady Salisbury intended to frighten the premier, she appears to have had an effect, confirming what Gladstone had previously called "the unrestrained character" of her husband's oratory.[73] Gladstone excused his own strictures on the Lords and their leader in language which "*utterly* disgusted" the Queen by claiming that "organic change in the Lords . . . I hate and . . . I am making all this fuss to avoid". But, he informed the Queen's emissary, he still envisaged fighting an election on Lords reform, if the Tory majority in the Upper House proved obdurate. Chamber- lain outdid the premier in his threats, partly to impress their enemies with Gladstone's relative moderation.[74] In fact, the government was always much less assured than it pretended, uncomfortably aware that in the prescient words of Lord Acton, an intimate of the premier, to Mary Gladstone months before the Lords took up their uncompromising position: "The half Reform bill is floated by a half pledge as to redistribution which is personal to himself". As ministers conceded when they sub- stituted an unequivocal pledge to bring in a redistribution bill next year, the Tories had a good case, which was strengthened by the continuing refusal to offer even an outline of the promised measure. Granville was only one of those in the cabinet who doubted an enthusiastic response to a campaign against the Lords: "There is a conservative stratum in the country, and a readiness to react against extreme lan- guage and action", he told Gladstone, as the peers came under sustained fire.[75]

Gladstone disregarded this advice. He was getting the reaction he wanted from apprehensive conservatives in both parties. "For God's sake help to save us from an agitation all summer against our House", wrote the Yorkshire landowner and former Liberal cabinet minister, Lord Halifax, to the Duke of Richmond, before the Lords voted on the franchise bill, ". . . things may be tolerably quiet in some peaceable agricultural county . . . but in our northern counties the radical element will be rampant . . .". Initially resolute, the Duke and others soon began to share the misgivings which Carnarvon had voiced to him ahead of the vote.[76] Salisbury was inflexible: he hoped to secure a dissolution "by hook or by crook", on the existing franchise. He was openly contemptuous of demonstrations organized to coerce the Lords; and quite unmoved when his effigy, wearing a placard that read "Death to Lord Salisbury" was burnt at Leicester on 24 July. To Chamberlain's threat of a march on London by a hundred thousand Midland radicals, Salisbury countered that the Tories would call out their supporters in Lancashire and Middlesex, strongholds of popular Toryism, to defeat those demonstrations against "a good redistribution scheme". Without going into detail, he let it be understood that by "good" he meant democratic.[77] Liberals were taken aback by his boldness: "Salisbury's avowal of numerical principles set me thinking", commented Acton, "I cannot make out whether it is a surrender or a snare". Convinced that "there was nothing like a popular run against the House of Lords", Salisbury was also responding to a shift in Tory thinking signalled by A.B. Forwood at Liverpool, for one, who came out for equal electoral districts; "another sign of dissolution in Toryism", according to Acton. It was, on the contrary, a sign of Tory adaptability and confidence.[78]

Leaving Gladstone "rather puzzled" by the Tories' disinclination to compromise, despite his repeated allusions to "a domestic crisis of the first class", Salisbury took a long Continental holiday. From his watering place he urged colleagues to stand firm as hints were dropped that the government would, after all, produce a redistribution bill that year. Gladstone wanted its introduction without previous negotiation between the parties to be followed by the immediate passage of the rejected franchise bill. Salisbury felt that he could drive a harder bargain.[79]

He returned to undertake a speaking tour in Scotland, in the course of which he was stoned at Dumfries. He had said in March, "Our programme is a very simple one . . . it is 'Appeal to the People'". That is what he now did, "full of fight and invective" before large audiences that were not exclusively drawn from the embattled Tory minority in the industrial West of Scotland. The Lords, he made it clear, were not an effective barrier to a Commons majority led by "an arrogant dictator", unless they had the popular backing which he sought. His ideal of a second chamber was the American Senate: "I wish we could institute it in this country – marvellous in its efficiency and strength". The constitutional dispute, he suggested, had been got up to divert attention from the government's failures at home and abroad: "There is a great temptation to be dishonest". None of its failures was more serious than the plight of industry in the recession, exacerbated by the unsuccessful policies pursued overseas and by doctrinaire objections to a critical re-examination of the comparative merits of free trade and fair trade. It was "mere derision" to talk of reforming parliament to the unemployed, for whom "prosperity or depression makes the difference . . . between a life of hope and a life of despair".[80] The absence of any whiff of compromise from these speeches, and from Salisbury's reception of approaches that were being made to him, disposed one of the shrewdest cabinet Whigs, Lord Kimberley, to think that abolition of the Lords was becoming practical politics, "which will hardly . . . suit the Tory rank and file, however agreeable it might be to their leader".[81]

If Salisbury's tactics had forced Gladstone to appoint a cabinet committee on redistribution as long ago as the beginning of March, he was himself subject to pressures stepped up by Gladstone's efforts. The premier went so far as to alarm the Queen with "a momentous practical inquiry", whether, if the Lords were swept away, "the Monarchy isolated and laid bare", would be secure deprived of its aristocratic context. Victoria and her private secretary, Sir Henry Ponsonby, a Liberal in his political sympathies, worked on Richmond, who was receptive to their urging that the warring parties must compromise to avert the "many disorders" foreseen by Gladstone on his visit to the Court at Balmoral early in September.[82] The Duke, visibly nervous, at once turned to Cairns. Both he and the former lord chancellor had always had reservations about Salisbury's attitude to the periodic disagreements between the Houses when the Liberals were in power. Cairns counselled retreat in statesmanlike language: "in our tempered and balanced constitution a contest resulting in defeat and humiliation of one of the component parties, is a bad thing". The peers' collective will to hold out for a satisfactory redistribution scheme was at best uncertain. Carnarvon recorded in July his "very clear" belief that Salisbury was distrusted by colleagues in the Tory cabinet in waiting and by the rank and file of the party in the Lords. They were afraid of his "supposed rashness" and resented his failure to consult more frankly and widely than he had been doing. Salisbury was adamant that ministers must submit a redistribution bill to the scrutiny of both Houses before the franchise bill became law. His meeting with Cairns and Richmond at the Duke's Highland castle did not produce a change of line: "They will still give trouble in the future – but I hope to pull through", he told his wife.[83]

The Queen was so agitated by the end of October as to say to one of the intermediaries, "if Lord Salisbury won't do what is right, then someone else must take the lead". Gladstone had encouraged Chamberlain to assail Salisbury and the Tories in a speech that elicited a vehement remonstrance from Balmoral. Victoria could not credit the view, to which Salisbury adhered, that the seemingly popular demonstrations against the Lords were "not dangerous . . . but artificial".[84] Yet, as Ponsonby informed Carnarvon, Gladstone was "very uneasy, very anxious . . . would agree to any compromise", faced with the Tories' refusal, for once, to bend rather than break. He, too, was subject to pressures which he could not ignore. Within his cabinet, and outside it, there were Liberals who thought with Hartington since ministers first addressed the topic of reform that "a single-barrelled Reform Bill is a rather lazy electioneering trick". He commented to a sympathetic member of the cabinet: "A Franchise Bill is a very easy and a redistribution Bill is a very difficult job, therefore we are to bring in the first in hopes that we have an opportunity of dissolving upon it without coming to grief on the other". The cabinet's committee on redistribution was an implicit acknowledgment of this conscious weakness in the Liberal arguments.[85] Dilke, to whom the others on the committee left most of the work, wanted to approach Salisbury: although the premier demurred, he was evidently well aware that this radical minister had been in touch with their opponents.

Gladstone himself put it to the Duke of Argyll, another of the monarch's intermediaries, that the Tories might improve their position if the larger boroughs were divided "with a view to severing classes"; there was a similar provision in the Municipal Reform Bill of 1835, added at the instance of a Tory opposition.[86]

It was obvious that the only solution to the impasse lay in a joint redistribution scheme. The suggestion, from more than one quarter, that the whole question should be referred to three or four mediators acceptable to both sides was unrealistic: the responsibility for settling it could not be evaded by such a device.[87] "Party", observed the premier, "is the team that draws the coach". When Salisbury wrote on 9 October that he believed the Tories could reach agreement with Hartington "*alone*", after a speech from the latter calling for an understanding, Gladstone was very glad to let his colleague explore the chances of a settlement. Discussions between Hicks Beach, for the Tories, and Hartington revealed how far the opposition leaders were prepared to go. The universal adoption of single-member constituencies with more or less equal electorates showed that Dilke had been right in warning Gladstone of the "revolutionary criticism" to which far more cautious proposals from the cabinet committee would be exposed from Salisbury. Gladstone hoped to preserve "communities", which the arithmetical approach of the new Toryism did not spare, and even Chamberlain favoured the two-member constituencies that enabled Whiggish and radical Liberals to run in double harness. Hicks Beach's proposals, said a delighted Dilke, were indeed "revolutionary".[88]

Gladstone knew he had been outmanoeuvred. "The Radicals", he explained to the Queen, "had behaved very well in consenting to accept a moderate scheme, but now the concurrence of Conservative views with their own would be irresistible".[89] In those circumstances, he and Salisbury assented to the royal plea to resolve their differences. There must be substantial agreement beforehand, Granville told the Queen, adding, only half in jest, that otherwise "two tails, but no Redistribution Bill, would be left". The cabinet considered their response to "the Salisbury–Beach radical scheme", as Gladstone termed it, while Salisbury restrained the combativeness of Tories excited by a spectacular by-election victory into imagining that they could force the government to dissolve on the existing register.[90] The reintroduced franchise bill completed its Commons stages, unopposed on the third reading. On its unopposed second reading in the Lords on 18 November, a ministerial statement in both Houses made the offer of a conference on redistribution before the bill went any further: Gladstone did not require the opposition to pledge themselves to passing it; a concession which he had withheld only days earlier. For someone who was a conservative at heart, he had been playing a "dangerous game", in the words that Derby used to Granville in August. Salisbury had stood out for the abandonment of Gladstone's original position: but Cairns rightly suspected that he would not have been sorry if "*guerre à outrance*" for the minds and votes of the public had resulted. A radical mood gripped some other leading Tories. Hicks Beach thought "almost any reform of the Lords would be an improvement". Cairns and Richmond, however, were more representative of the party in their desire to avoid the "immense mischief" of an election.[91]

After he and Granville had their first meeting with Salisbury and Northcote, Gladstone noted that they had seen the "Opposition Leaders (or Leader?)". Each "Salisbury conference", as Gladstone designated the meetings that followed, took the participants nearer to the most sweeping change in the country's electoral history. Single-member and equal constituencies became the rule. Salisbury obtained, besides the division of large borough electorates, a strengthening of the distinction between urban and rural seats, the maintenance of which was held to be very much in the Tory interest. The minor issue of university representation, which the Liberals proposed to remove, caused the one sharp disagreement, ended by Lady Salisbury's personal appeal to the premier as a devoted son of Oxford.[92] Dilke, who with Hartington attended all the conferences except the first, wondered whether, when it came to the point, Tory MPs would accept a redistribution bill that broke abruptly with the past. Working closely with the radical baronet at these meetings and in the intervals between them, Salisbury determined their outcome. Chamberlain was amazed at the transformation of a high Tory: "I cannot make head or tail of Salisbury. He appears to be swallowing every word that he has written or spoken". Unlike Gladstone, he had not taken seriously the evolution of Salisbury's politics over the last few years. The latter had resorted to the Disraelian strategy which he had famously condemned. As in his duel of the 1860s with Disraeli, Gladstone might expect to win the election to come, but he had lost the parliamentary battle.[93] So clear was his discomfiture that there were complaints about Salisbury's "dictation" from Liberals in the Commons: it was "perfectly sickening", said Sir Wilfrid Lawson, an influential backbench voice. Their Tory antagonist, whose powers of leadership had been confirmed, asked Alfred Austin of the *Standard*, a recipient of such guidance as he personally gave to the newspapers, not to refer to Gladstone's "'submission' . . . a little too strong".[94]

## Agrarianism and Nationalism in Ireland

One of the first British statesmen to understand that an alien landed class in Ireland was destined to disappear in the near future, Salisbury saw his prediction of 1870 realized over the next thirty years, and contributed significantly to its realization. In opposition in the early 1880s he had to fight for the landlords against the Gladstonian legislation of 1880–82. He did not conceal his belief that he was conducting a rearguard action, in which he was handicapped by the unwillingness of the landlords to help themselves in an economic and political climate that had them clamouring to be bought out by the intervention of the state and its credit. He had supported land purchase in Ireland from its beginnings in Gladstone's Act of 1870, as the long-term solution to an intractable problem which acquired greater urgency with the collapse of the landlords' political authority after 1880. Unlike other statesmen, Salisbury had never thought Irish unrest was fundamentally agrarian. Whilst he attacked Parnell and his nationalists for their involvement with the agrarianism that dismayed liberal opinion in Britain by its methods, he did not exclude some measure of self-government for Ireland, not even home rule. These reflections were not public, but among the politically well informed the impression spread of a growing understanding between Tories and nationalists towards the middle of the decade. There was more to that incipient alliance than the co-ordination of parliamentary tactics to put Gladstone in a minority. The fall of the ministry in June 1885, opposed by the Irish and deserted by some of its own supporters on the budget, brought Salisbury into office when it was evident that the Reform and Redistribution Acts of 1884–5 would give the nationalists a commanding majority in Ireland outside Ulster.

The agricultural depression, which set in from the late 1870s and inspired organized discontent even among substantial English tenant farmers, enabled the Fenian-led Land League to launch an agitation more dangerous, because more controlled, than any yet seen.[95] By the spring of 1880, when the Liberals took over, the League had in many places compelled landowners to reduce rents and suspend evictions, combining in classical Irish style the weapons of popular agitation and intimidation. Lower figures for agrarian crime than had been recorded in the past made the incoming ministry hesitate to pass another in the long succession of coercion bills. Instead they hoped to check the agitation by a temporary restraint on evictions for non-payment of rent. The Lords rejected overwhelmingly, in June 1880, the proposed compensation for disturbance in scheduled districts to tenants unable to pay rent after two bad seasons. Although it was conceived and presented as an exceptional measure limited to occupiers of small holdings valued at £30 a year or less, an Anglo-Irish magnate, Lord Lansdowne, resigned his under-secretaryship in protest, and a number of Liberal peers voted against the government.[96] Salisbury expressed the feeling of his House when he said that the concession would not appease the Irish peasantry in the grip of "a Socialistic anti-rent agitation". But few of those voting against had any illusions about their predicament now that time had confirmed the failure of the Gladstonian policy of conciliation. Early in 1881 Derby found the peers and MPs of a Whig house party at a ducal seat agreed about the temper of the Irish masses, intensely hostile to British rule. The nationalist home rulers, with a majority of Irish MPs since 1874, represented the aspirations of their people. "Under the name and form of popular government", commented Derby, "we are holding Ireland against the will of the Irish". He had thought so for many years; a view not common in Society until home rulers and Land Leaguers forced reality upon its members.[97]

Neither Derby nor his fellow-guests were ready for a momentous change of policy. The pattern of coercion and conciliation was renewed. The 1881 Land Act, which cost Gladstone the resignation of the Duke of Argyll, one of his oldest political friends, from the cabinet, enacted the three Fs, the demand of agrarian agitators since the mid-century. The Act, foreshadowed in the work of a royal commission, was simply "gross confiscation" to Salisbury in respect of "fair rent" as a variation of existing tenancies. Applied to future tenancies, without the element of retrospective legislation, the reference of rent to a tribunal was "not . . . very seriously pernicious". For on the estates of many English landlords it was not the practice to raise the rent during the lifetime of a sitting tenant. "Fair rent" and "fixity of tenure" were, therefore, less objectionable than they seemed, effectively secured as they were by what Salisbury had described as the "embryo tenant-right" of England. "Free sale" of the tenant's occupancy right was the most contentious of the three Fs: it implied co-ownership, which was the essential meaning of tenant-right in Ireland. The landlords had tolerated it, more or less willingly in Protestant Ulster, reluctantly elsewhere, as often as not by turning a blind eye to its existence. There was a causal relationship between the market in tenant-right in this sense and the low rents usual in Ireland; landlords allowed for this significant element in an occupier's costs. Salisbury argued that in theory the tenant should have nothing to sell; the whole of the surplus value left by a less than economic rent belonged to the landlord. This was to ignore facts that could no longer be refused legal recognition. As Gladstone's distinctly conservative lord chancellor, Selborne, said when the 1881 land bill reached the Lords, it continued the process, begun in the 1870 Land Act, of changing the law to reflect the "habits, . . . customs and, therefore, moral rights of the people".[98]

The opposition fought the bill hard in the Commons, while knowing that Gladstone was almost certainly right in telling everyone that "My bill is really a landlord's bill". He genuinely wanted to preserve the Irish landed class within the framework of his legislation, which to Salisbury had only one positive feature – the provision for land purchase on more generous terms than in 1870. There was, he said the following year, no hope of permanently pacifying Ireland except through a large-scale transfer of landed property from owners to occupiers. In the Lords the bill had its second reading without a division. The opposition peers put up what one of them saw as "a sham fight" in committee. Salisbury, at least, was sufficiently plausible to frighten his own side. They, and especially the Irish landlords among them, were "very seriously alarmed" at the momentary prospect that their bill might not pass. The situation in Ireland was deteriorating as agitation and distress combined to paralyse the machinery of justice. At a meeting of Tory peers, Cairns redefined the Lords' constitutional functions to exclude, "in a crisis such as this", the vetoing of controversial legislation not covered by the doctrine, to which Salisbury adhered, that required an electoral mandate for such measures before the Lords gave way. Salisbury took issue with Cairns in language that revealed his "pent up personal feeling", but bowed to the Commons' rejection of amendments that would have altered the character of the bill.[99] While he believed they might have obtained worthwhile changes in the bill, the peers and the party at Westminster were "jubilant" at their deliverance from the threatened collision of the Houses with all its possible consequences. Gladstone was encouraged by this success to talk freely, though not in public, of extending to Britain the central feature of his Act, "free sale", in a bid to capture the farming vote.[100]

That he should have considered such a move, illustrates the erosion of Victorian certainties at that date; nothing had been more certain than property and its rights. One of those Gladstone consulted felt "the bent of his mind was to give everything to the tenant that could be given without too manifest injustice". Letters and diaries tell of the fears which spilled into the conversation at dinner parties: "It reminds me of what one has read of as heralding great revolutions", wrote Carnarvon in

May 1881 after an evening clouded by these anxieties.[101] The assassination of Tsar Alexander II in April by the revolutionary Left and its progress in Western Europe fostered an atmosphere in which the Irish disturbances were viewed as "socialistic" rather than the continuation of a centuries-old struggle. For all his undoubted conservatism, Gladstone was too much of a politician not to read the signs of the times with an eye to party interests. Similarly, Salisbury wanted a dissolution before the reform bill expected from the Liberals in the lifetime of that parliament further weakened the Tories, as seemed likely. He saw his opportunity in the Arrears Bill of 1882 and the failures of government policy leading up to it.

Parnell's arrest in October 1880, his subsequent "no rent" manifesto, and the Land League's efforts to keep tenants from settling with their landlords under the new Land Act intensified a conflict which ended in an uneasy compromise between ministers and the nationalists. The "Kilmainham treaty" in April 1881 freed Parnell, raised the embargo on the land courts, and undertook to bring within the scope of the Act the numerous tenants shut out from its benefits by accumulated arrears of rent. The Irish viceroy and chief secretary resigned, unable to accept a bargain that called in question Britain's will to govern.[102] Within days the chief secretary's replacement, Lord Frederick Cavendish and the permanent under-secretary at Dublin Castle were murdered in broad daylight close to the viceregal residence. Those responsible belonged to a tiny extremist group: but for the time being Gladstone's entire Irish policy appeared to be in ruins. He reacted with a stronger coercion bill and the promised legislation that enabled about 130 000 small tenants out of half a million occupiers to qualify for the protection of the Land Act on payment of a year's rent and proof of inability to pay the rest. The landlord was to receive a further year's rent from the state. Arrears over and above those two years were cancelled by the statute. From a purely legal standpoint, it was a highly questionable piece of legislation: and the peers, emboldened by the government's difficulties, were disposed to throw it out.

Salisbury advised against such provocation, for Gladstone was determined to honour his bargain with Parnell. The Tories in the Lords agreed in July to two amendments: one requiring the landlord's consent to applications for relief from arrears; and the other providing that the value of a tenant's occupancy should be taken into account when his claim was considered. The proposed changes did not render the bill unworkable, given the Irish landlords' financial plight, and they made it more palatable to those distressed by its rough treatment of legal principle. Gladstone could not, however, afford to jeopardize his understanding with the nationalists, the final attempt to reconcile Ireland within the existing constitutional framework of the British Isles. "I admit that all depends on success, and if we fail, we are done for altogether", he had told Derby, who was soon to enter the Liberal cabinet.[103] There were indications that the policy of the Kilmainham treaty, backed by firmness in repressing violence and intimidation, was having some effect. Parnell prepared to capitalize on his defeat of the landlords by relaunching the League with an overtly political goal. It was not only Liberals in Britain who wished the government's Irish policy to succeed. If it did not succeed, Carnarvon put it to Salisbury, the alternatives were "either Irish independence or very stern repression", exceeding anything yet tried in their generation. Gladstone was claiming to have put down a social revolution.[104] The owners of Irish land, well represented in the Upper House, were apprehensive lest the resumed, though diminished flow of rent, should be interrupted. The government's stock had also risen on the bombardment of Alexandria at the beginning of July. "Everything is now Egypt", wrote the premier's secretary. By the time the Tory challenge to the arrears bill in the Lords was mounted in August, the party was afraid of a dissolution in the event of a clash between the Houses.[105]

It was evident to at least one member of the "shadow cabinet" that ministers would never agree to Salisbury's amendments. Nevertheless, the Tory peers appeared to be spoiling for a fight when they first met. On 4 August, before the amendments were voted on, he learnt from his front-bench colleagues that support for them was slipping away. "I will not eat dirt", he was heard to exclaim.[106] He had sadly misjudged his followers. Cairns led the retreat: informing Salisbury that he could not vote for the changes, he brought forward his seasonal departure for the Scottish Highlands. It had been a "great mistake" to take on the government. Salisbury carried the amendments on the 8th. When the Commons rejected them, he polled the peers present at a meeting on the 10th, to discover that sixty out of eighty went with Richmond in refusing to defy the Commons. The party in the Commons, Northcote reported, was unwilling to continue the struggle, and so was he. Cranbrook and Carnarvon stood by Salisbury, but did not conceal their pessimism about the outcome. It was, Salisbury did not hesitate to admit, "a tremendous smash" for him.[107] His leadership and his hopes, such as they were, of reviving the Lords as a power in the constitution had suffered a setback likely to be permanent, it was believed. The short speech Salisbury made in the Lords, drawing attention to the desertion of those beside and behind him, was criticized as an exhibition of temper. "I felt much for Salisbury . . .", wrote Cranbrook, "I saw the iron [had] entered his soul . . . he was badly used by being pressed unanimously to one course and almost as unanimously deserted when the time of trial came."[108]

In fact, that controlled outburst impressed his capacity for leadership on a party that craved it. The Tory peers who had abandoned him experienced, said one of them, the sensations of "whipped hounds". Salisbury's frankness set him apart from more conventional politicians who would not have advertised such a painful reverse. He did so because it was the upper House that had lost face: he had tried to restore its moral courage, drained by its retreats before Gladstone since 1869. On the platform he reiterated that the Lords existed to limit the elective dictatorship of a powerful prime minister and his Commons majority: and envied Americans their possession in the Supreme Court of a greatly superior means of defending democracy against itself: "that gives a stability to the institutions of the country which . . . we look for in vain". His readiness to risk the imposition of a drastic reform on the Lords two years later was influenced by their behaviour over the arrears bill. Their historic privileges and composition were expendable: they could no longer be relied on to discharge their constitutional function.[109]

The Irish landowners whose present and future interests Salisbury was seeking to protect had been the first to retreat. They were not forgiven: "Their notion of self-defence", he remarked scathingly to Northcote, "is that you should fight for them under the condition of not causing them the slightest agitation of mind by your blows". When the fate of landed property in a self-governing Ireland renewed the anxieties of its owners, he was unsympathetic: "I do not pity them", he observed. They might have postponed the day of reckoning with Home Rule for a few years if they had backed him in 1882, but he was not sure that it would have been deferred. As it was, Parnell had gone on to move the national question, as such, into the place formerly held by agrarian demands that had largely been met.[110] Gladstone's hints of devolution for Ireland, which stretched back to 1871, became broader and more frequent, though still so worded as to be capable of being explained away. But in February 1882, looking ahead to the extension of household suffrage to Ireland, Gladstone privately told Derby that, if the nationalists obtained around two-thirds of the Irish representation on the new franchise, their pressure for a Dublin parliament must be "irresistible. They would be strong enough to make their own terms". The Liberal chief whip, Lord Richard Grosvenor, later a Unionist, described the Home Rule majority as a certainty and did not believe nationalists could be satisfied with any arrangement that left Westminster with more than a nominal supremacy. He thought most of the cabinet expected civil war in Ireland "in the end". The ripples from conversations like these spread through the political world, and had a discernible effect on public opinion. After Kilmainham and the assassination of Lord Frederick Cavendish, Derby sensed that a state of mind favourable to the concession of Home Rule was developing in Britain, born of near despair.[111]

Against this background, the Tories, too, began to put out feelers to the nationalists. In the autumn of 1884, Carnarvon met the Irish-Australian politician, Sir Charles Gavan Duffy, a former Young Irelander arrested in the 1848 rebellion, to discuss an elaborate scheme for genuine, though carefully circumscribed autonomy in Ireland. Also present was Carnarvon's cousin, Sir Robert Herbert, the permanent under-secretary at the Colonial Office, whose expert knowledge from the British side of the working of responsible government in the settler colonies complemented Duffy's experience as a premier of Victoria. The ex-premier, who had resettled in his native country, said he was not a Parnellite but "acquiesced" in Parnell's domination of the national movement.[112] Carnarvon's resignation in 1878 was behind him: he attended the "shadow cabinet", and spoke with the authority of someone destined for high office in a Tory administration. In confidence, he was ready to admit that coercion could not be continued indefinitely: a scheme like Duffy's offered the "one chance" of escaping from an intolerable position. Saying that "feeling and judgement" led him to sympathize with Irish aspirations to self-government, he sought reassurance as to the treatment of the Protestant minority. Duffy pointed to his provision for a declaration of fundamental principles in the originating legislation, to the two-thirds majority required for constitutional changes, and to the provincial assemblies that met the special case of Ulster. While the Dublin parliament was to have control of the police and militia, British regulars would still be stationed in Ireland. Although their meeting had to remain a secret, Carnarvon undertook to place an article by Duffy, explaining his proposals, in the Tory *National Review*.

Finally, they considered how to proceed if Carnarvon's colleagues adopted Home Rule in this version.[113]

The meeting between Carnarvon and Duffy, the former's admissions in the course of it, and his approach to the *National Review*, edited by Austin and another well known Tory journalist, W.J. Courthope, signalled a tendency in both British parties to accept Home Rule, in some shape, as inevitable. It was still necessary to proceed with the greatest caution. It was not until February 1885 that Carnarvon apprised Salisbury of his thoughts. The reaction was not one of surprise. Duffy's article had just appeared, arguing that self-government could be accompanied by "securities which satisfy the most timid". Salisbury underlined the difficulties involved in conceding Irish autonomy. He had no objection, in principle, to Home Rule if it contained guaranteed safeguards for the Protestant and propertied minority, to which the nationalists would submit, but was unable to see how his requirements were to be met. Only plenipotentiaries, and not intermediaries such as Duffy, could negotiate an agreement: and they would need the approval of the majority in nationalist Ireland. "The matter is too delicate for discussion on paper", he felt, writing from abroad.[114] He spelt out his reservations some weeks later in a further letter. The exercise of powers transferred to an Irish parliament that could not be trusted to respect the rights and interests of the minority, must be policed by a body "which you *can* trust with sufficient jurisdiction, and sufficiently backed by material force". The American Union had the Supreme Court but its authority had not been able to check the passions that boiled over in the Civil War. Nor could such a body understand the hunger of the Celtic Irish for the land they regarded as rightfully theirs: an expression of the implacable animosity that did not distinguish between alien landlords and the equally alien industrial and farming population in Ulster.[115]

With the clarity natural to him, Salisbury had identified the insoluble problem, in the context of an undivided Ireland, which Carnarvon's licensed explorations of Home Rule raised after he went to Dublin as viceroy in Salisbury's first government, formed soon afterwards. When the Liberals attempted to ignore the problem in 1886, it destroyed the unity of their party.

# CHAPTER EIGHT

# The First Premiership and Ireland, 1885–6

## The First Cabinet: Men and Policies

Gladstone was, and remained, the most popular politician in the country when he resigned in June 1885 following his government's narrow defeat on increased beer and spirits duties in the budget, brought about by Liberal abstentions in the face of a Tory–Irish combination. The cabinet were, however, so deeply divided by disagreements, particularly over Ireland, and by the tension between Hartington and Chamberlain, personifying, respectively, the Whig and radical wings of Liberalism, that resignation came as a relief to some of its members. "An odd situation", Derby had written in May, "... no Parliamentary opposition to fear, the party outside [Westminster] united ... the election prospects ... favourable: yet we have been ... and are, on the verge of disintegration." He doubted whether his old party was in a condition to succeed their rivals. Salisbury, "not much trusted", would have for his leading colleague in the Commons, Churchill, whom Derby summed up as "with all his remarkable cleverness ... thoroughly untrustworthy ... and probably more or less mad". Salisbury's appreciation of the situation hardly differed. He was extremely reluctant to form a minority administration at the mercy of a large Liberal majority, and unable to dissolve until the new and expanded electoral registers were ready in the autumn. There was the added and serious disadvantage of being responsible for Irish policy, instead of waiting to see how it evolved in the hands of Liberal ministers. Hicks Beach, a leading figure in the Tory government that was nevertheless formed, said, years later, that only the Queen's tears had induced Salisbury to change his mind about taking office. Her detestation of Gladstone, and nervous fears of a Liberal drift towards greater radicalism, made her desperate to see the Liberals depart.[1] The more ambitious and partisan Tories were eager to return to government: and a leader could not ignore their mood.[2]

Compelled to take office, Salisbury came to it with clear ideas about the personnel and policies of a ministry formed in unpromising circumstances.[3] Churchill, who had never been a minister, and his friend Hicks Beach, one of the last recruits to Beaconsfield's cabinet, were the only Tories in the Commons capable of holding their own against the formidable parliamentary talents of the Liberal front bench. At his best, the former was a match for Gladstone or Chamberlain, in the House or on the platform: unscrupulous, and amusing, in his debating methods, his brilliantly unfair assaults on the premier had put heart into the demoralized Tory opposition. Churchill believed he could name his own terms for joining a Salisbury administration. In a letter of April 1885 to Salisbury, protesting that Northcote could no longer be left to lead the party in the Commons to defeat, he had compared the despised chief's influence, with characteristic tastelessness, to that of "sewer gas upon the human frame, it sickens, enfeebles . . . and emasculates". He tried then to obtain Salisbury's backing for a singular arrangement that avoided the formal deposition of Northcote in mid-session, which the Liberals would naturally exploit, but transferred the conduct of opposition to Hicks Beach and others of like mind. Churchill and his associates looked to Salisbury for "approval and support". It was not a plan to which the leader in the Lords "bound to Sir S[tafford] N[orthcote] . . . by a tie not of expediency but of honour" could agree; though he did not discourage Churchill and Beach from organizing their forces and so acquiring "considerable political authority".[4] Conscious of the growing threat from Churchill, Northcote had sounded Salisbury the previous year about a strategy aimed at uniting the moderates of both parties, and leaving "Tory Democrats" under Churchill to align themselves with Chamberlain's radicals. He wanted Salisbury's help in keeping "our Tory working men" from going over to that radical coalition. When both Northcote and Churchill appealed for his backing, there was little doubt that the future of the party lay with Salisbury.[5]

On Salisbury's election to the leadership in the Lords in 1881 Richmond told him that the post would not have been his if Lady Salisbury had been the Duchess of Richmond; a remarkable tribute to the efforts of a devoted and highly intelligent wife on her husband's behalf. The Duke, advised by Cairns, remained critical of Salisbury's political style, which made them anxious for their House. After the Arrears Bill had confirmed their divergent attitudes to fighting the Commons, Richmond again deserted his leader over Salisbury's amendments to the government's agricultural holdings bill for England in 1883. Carefully limited by the large landlords in the cabinet to compulsory compensation for a tenant's improvements, it was much more disturbing in principle than in practice. Salisbury commented wryly on his abandonment by peers who were thankful for small mercies; they had dreaded an extension of Irish tenant-right to England.[6] During the recess, Cairns, Cranbrook and Lord Abergavenny, one of the party managers, discussed Salisbury's methods of opposition: the Lords, said Cairns acidly, "must not swagger over amendments as if they were going to stick to them". On the Liberal front bench, Derby recorded his view that Salisbury's utterances, those of "a clever and skilful debater", in the chamber and outside had taken his party so far from the middle ground that "it is impossible for Whigs to join him, as they might join Richmond". But by June 1885 Cairns was dead, Northcote a sick man, and Richmond quite overshadowed by his leader. By his militancy, and his unbroken nerve during the struggle over reform, Salisbury had earned the command of a resurgent Toryism.[7]

His problems in cabinet-making turned on Churchill's desire to deny Northcote the leadership in the Commons under Salisbury, and another senior member of the last Tory cabinet, Cross, a place in the administration. He made acceptance of office conditional upon their demotion. It was, and was seen to be, an outrageous demand: but Hicks Beach and Lord George Hamilton, both stalwarts of Salisbury ministries down to the end, did not think the government would be credible without Churchill, or with him on the backbenches, and were consequently unwilling to serve unless he could be induced to enter the cabinet. The new premier gave Churchill the India Office, marked down for him months earlier. The post had launched his own ministerial career; it recognized Churchill's interest in India, which he had recently visited; and its importance had been enhanced by the Anglo-Russian dispute over Afghanistan's northern border. Churchill failed to exclude Cross, a former home secretary whose parliamentary performances had declined in opposition, but who returned to the Home Office.[8] Northcote, however, went to the Lords, with an earldom to comfort him, the title of first lord of the Treasury, and a share of the first lord's patronage. These consolations did not disguise his fall. Salisbury had to tell him that he should not look on himself as "abandoned or betrayed . . . my conscience is quite clear". Hicks Beach, a friend but not a follower of Churchill, became chancellor of the exchequer and led for the government in the Commons. Outsiders talked of a Salisbury–Churchill ministry, but a majority of the cabinet regarded the latter with dislike and apprehension. Churchill's unquestioned influence with the party in the Commons and the country gave him the power to disrupt a necessarily weak government. He did not determine its policies: his own ideas, for all their lively presentation, lacked the depth and balance of Salisbury's.[9]

The new premier's choice for the Foreign Office, Lytton, did not commend itself to the party. Salisbury put him forward as someone who, unlike Northcote, could not be suspected of Gladstonian leanings abroad. He had been able to restrain Lytton as viceroy and believed they could work together. The ex-viceroy's responsibility for the unwise occupation of Kabul after Salisbury's departure from the India Office, and his identification with the "Beaconsfieldism" denounced by the Liberals, ruled him out. Salisbury therefore substituted himself; an indication of what he thought of his colleagues in that context. The other appointment that helped to set the tone of Toryism with Salisbury in charge was Carnarvon's. He was made viceroy of Ireland, with a seat in the cabinet and an understanding with Salisbury that he was free to explore the possibility of Irish self-government on terms acceptable to British opinion. The implications of Carnarvon's appointment were not lost on politicians and the press, well prepared for a development of this kind, and the cabinet were soon enlightened. While Salisbury gave his first administration a short expectation of life, he did not see it as merely a caretaker government, which was the natural assumption. It was to define a coherent alternative to the dominant Liberalism; a task made easier by the collective self-discipline of a party in government. The cabinet he had chosen was weighted with men temperamentally as well as politically conservative: when they assented to the outline of his thinking, which he gave them in the autumn, it could safely be tried on the public.[10]

His speech at Newport in October was the most important of his years at the head of the party. It may be said to have brought together Gladstonian populism, Disraelian imperialism and the social radicalism of Chamberlain's "Unauthorized Programme". Yet the elements were not borrowed; they had evolved in his thought. Their combination with an older Toryism was at once seen to be a powerful one. He bade farewell to the politics he had known all his life: the House of Commons prorogued in August, not to meet again before the dissolution in November, was the last with a landed majority. In the new era, "all must be professional politicians", he said; democratic politics were inescapable. He presented British democracy with an account of his first months at the Foreign Office, where his sureness of touch had impressed everyone, and with a prospectus of the legislation they might expect from his government if it found favour with the new constituencies. He ranged from hinting at extensive Home Rule for Ireland to the Sunday closing of public houses, one of those questions which, like church rates in his early years in parliament, generated considerable heat at local level. *The Times* remarked that the speech was "for once . . . wanting in brilliance". It was, though unscripted, a manifesto to stand against, and on several issues to outbid, the one Gladstone had just issued.[11]

Salisbury's feelings about the mistakes of Gladstonian foreign policy were not for display. The questions of the hour in that field were Bulgarian union, and Salisbury's continuation of the Liberal attempt to evacuate Egypt without throwing away the tangible gains of Tel-el-Kebir. What he said at Newport had a Gladstonian sound. He and his cabinet were not guilty of the "disloyalty" that breaking with their predecessors' international undertakings, and even with the expectations they had raised, would have involved. He could say with absolute sincerity, "Our object above all things is peace", without adding that his methods differed significantly from those associated with Gladstone. On the subject of Ireland, which he treated as an imperial question profoundly affecting Britain's position in the world, he seemed to be outstripping the Liberals. There was an explicit, encouraging response to Parnell's suggestion in a speech only days before that a mutually acceptable Anglo-Irish relationship might resemble the dual monarchy of Austro-Hungary. As Gladstone was to do, he insisted that he did not mean to risk the integrity of the empire, or minority rights. One result of this passage, on which observers fastened, was to confirm the Liberal leader in his belief that the time had come to establish Irish autonomy within the empire.[12]

The sense that with Salisbury Toryism would undergo a greater change than Disraeli ever contemplated, his rhetoric notwithstanding, was strengthened when he turned to domestic questions. The trend towards more state intervention had come under fire from both wings of the Liberal opposition: Salisbury found it "comical" that they should endeavour to limit the development of their rivals' ideas. It was, he contended, unexceptionally conservative to take up local government reform with a view to combating an imputed desire in some quarters "to imitate Continental plans by drawing all authority back upon the central power". He held, with J.S. Mill, that the localities ought to be allowed to govern themselves at their own level, "not necessarily in the most scientific or . . . accurate fashion, but in a fashion . . . liked by the people over whom they rule". Powers vested in Whitehall should be transferred to the natural unit of local administration, the county. His experience on the royal commission on the housing of the working classes had, however, convinced him that the poor had a genuine grievance in the burden of local rates on occupiers. Rating reform was "indispensable" to the reconstruction of local government, on "this great principle – that all men should pay according to their ability". But he drew the line at permitting the enthusiasts for temperance to impose anything more than Sunday closing, decided locally, on "thirsty souls . . . that seems to me to trench upon the elementary liberties of mankind". As for the role of elective county government in the creation of small holdings and allotments for the agricultural labourers – the most controversial feature of Chamberlain's programme – he did not oppose it, at least not directly. The experiment should be made even if economic forces were very likely to frustrate it. The troubles of clergymen with their glebes in the current agricultural recession illustrated the point: but he was ready to bring in enabling legislation for their sale to meet any real demand for smallholdings or allotments.[13]

All this was to steal the Liberals' clothes with a vengeance. He added insult to injury by dismissing Liberal land reformers as "inventive cockneys", a barbed reference to Chamberlain's London origins. Salisbury went still further in appropriating radical policies when he reached education: the free elementary education for all that Chamberlain advocated was too costly, but the poor ought to receive more help with the fees for schooling their children; they had a moral claim in that attendance was now compulsory. Behind the radicals' liberality with taxes and rates lay the undisguised ambition of driving the financially struggling church schools to the wall, and enforcing more widely what he called "the lifeless, boiled down, mechanical, unreal religious teaching . . . prevalent in Board Schools". The Liberationists were hard at work extracting pledges to disestablishment from a clear majority of Liberal candidates. This danger furnished the matter for Salisbury's peroration: he spoke of a looming disaster, worse than anything known since the inception of parliamentary government. He pictured the Church "stripped and bare", and suffering humanity deprived of its greatest consolation by the abolition of her pastoral organization. Gladstone's election address to his Scottish constituents in September, preparing them for the dissolution foreshadowed in the Queen's speech at the end of the session, had referred to disestablishment as something for those who would come after him. Given his age, that did nothing to reassure the Church's friends: and Salisbury read into Gladstone's words his "last surrender . . . the last of the opinions of his youth . . . sacrificed upon the altar of party". These two Tractarians saw the future of the Church differently. For Salisbury establishment was really "a matter of life and death"; he could not think, as Gladstone did, that the Christian presence in a secular state might even be stronger for its independence. "No compromise" on the Church was the Tories' rallying cry.[14]

The speech had an excellent reception on his own side: the prevailing impression is one of relief that their leader had measured up to the demands upon him. Churchill was lavish in his praise: "never was there . . . a public pronouncement more comprehensive . . . arranged with more consummate skill, and imparted in a manner more likely . . . to impress". It was a model for his own Dartford speech of the following year, when he was preparing to challenge Salisbury. More traditional Tories, in the person of Cranbrook, for one, were equally pleased. Among Whigs worried about their place in politics, Derby remarked how little there was in the speech to offend: "his tone in general is liberal and moderate". Edward Hamilton, in the Gladstonian camp, also found Salisbury "free from Tory prejudice and apprehension", and itemized his positive proposals, concluding, "In short, he picks out of Mr G[ladstone]'s political pudding the best plums".[15] Liberalism, the party of government for over half a century, now had a serious competitor. This change in the nature of the Tory beast had as much to do with Salisbury's domination of British political life for the rest of the century as had the divisive policy on Home Rule which Gladstone was incubating. Hartington, let alone Chamberlain, could not have supported and eventually joined a Tory ministry without the liberal credentials presented at Newport. Far from being revolutionary, Unionism was more progressive than Gladstonian Liberalism; and liberal even in Ireland where coercion and conciliation went hand in hand. In the autumn of 1885, no one supposed that Salisbury, one of the longest serving prime ministers, would relegate the Liberals to almost unbroken opposition well into the 1900s. Few even suspected his full potential. He was seen, and saw himself, as someone qualified to correct the failings of recent foreign policy.

## The Foreign Office

Salisbury had to accommodate Churchill's inconvenient interest in foreign policy. Hicks Beach put forward the suggestion that the Indian secretary should be present when the premier saw the Russian ambassador in the course of continuing negotiations about Afghanistan's disputed northern border. Given the India Office's legitimate concern with the question, the request was not inherently unreasonable. Salisbury deflected it by arguing that the constructive intimacy of his conversations with the Russian ambassador, Baron de Staal, would be impaired. The Russian was bound to introduce someone on his side to balance another British negotiator. More to the point, Churchill's opinions, on any subject, were liable to sudden change. While Churchill did not think an Anglo-Russian war for control of Afghanistan and Persia was imminent, he believed it to be inevitable, saying to Bismarck's son William that a war would be good for Britain, although the desire for it might be lacking in her people. He had exaggerated notions of the damage that the British fleet could inflict on Russia in the Black Sea and on the Pacific coast. As he always had done, Salisbury thought an Asiatic collision with Russia was avoidable. In their almost continuous correspondence, he resisted Churchill's pressure for a stronger line with the Russians.[16] They were agreed on the centrality of an alliance or entente with Germany. On coming into office, Salisbury acted at once to assure the German chancellor of his earnest wish to rebuild the Anglo-German relationship weakened by five years of Bismarck's violent dislike for Gladstonian Liberalism. He met with an encouraging response. The Bismarckian system was designed to isolate

France: Gladstone's ideal of the "Concert of Europe" appeared to subvert the careful arrangements for German hegemony and security. Furthermore, Bismarck loathed and feared the influence of British Liberalism, personified by the outgoing premier, on Germans. He dubbed his German liberal opponents the "Ministerium Gladstone", and attributed to his *bête noire* a master plan to bring Russia and France together, isolating Germany.[17]

Bismarck's imperfect understanding of British politics was fortunate for Salisbury and the Tories: it obscured the similarities between the parties, both liberal by Continental standards. This made it easier for Salisbury, a representative Tory in thinking that his country's liberal institutions were not always suited for export, to attach Britain to the German network of alliances. By doing so, he enlisted Germany's help in the Egyptian imbroglio, and reached the financial agreement with Egypt's other creditors that had eluded the Liberals. He was also better placed than they would have been to exert a limited, but not insignificant, British influence in the Bulgarian crisis that erupted in 1885. Bismarck did not accept his secret proposal of a formal alliance – he was, at that point, anxious not to drive Russia into the arms of France – but a genuine Anglo-German entente came into being. Salisbury's achievement was welcome to the Liberals, who had been worried by Britain's friendlessness in Europe towards the end of their five years. His care not to offend France unnecessarily while making up to Germany was particularly appreciated in Liberal circles. The private letters he wrote to British envoys in the major European capitals show him setting about the construction of a lasting Salisburian system, complementary, rather than subservient, to the Bismarckian. The enterprise was essential for Britain's self-esteem and her safety in an international environment where rumours of war were constantly circulating.[18]

Salisbury kept the making of policy out of the hands of officials; even those closest to him, like Philip Currie, were instruments rather than advisers. Newly appointed at the Foreign Office in the late 1870s, he was nervous of trusting those around him with his secrets – not unnaturally, when a copying clerk sold them to a newspaper – and so made unnecessary work for himself. Later, he learnt to delegate without relaxing his hold on policy. When the Tories went out of office in 1880, he left behind notes of his interviews with the foreign diplomats in London and complained that Dilke, the parliamentary under-secretary in the next government, took unfair advantage of these personal records. From 1885 he did not commit his impressions of those interviews to paper, except in private letters, sometimes to his own envoys abroad or, more often, to the Queen. He carried his country's foreign policy in his head, and explained it more fully and frankly to the ambassadors visiting him at the Foreign Office than to anyone else, including the cabinet. Defending the premier and foreign secretary against Churchill's suspicions that he was being shut out from the exchanges with de Staal because he did not enjoy Salisbury's confidence, Hicks Beach asked him to bear in mind their chief's "peculiar reticence" in transacting business. Of course, Salisbury had little confidence in Churchill: but his secretive methods, well known to Hicks Beach from the last Tory cabinet, were integral to a diplomacy that had succeeded before, and would succeed again.[19]

As his friend emphasized to Churchill, Salisbury was an intensely honourable man. The habitual irony did not indicate, as some have thought and think, an underlying cynicism. Rightly or wrongly, Continental governments were sceptical of Britain's good faith, republican France as much as the conservative empires. In their chancelleries, Gladstone's internationalism was taken to be badly disguised self-interest. The preference for a concert of great powers was calculated to relieve Britain of the anxieties that European alliances inspired. Salisbury believed, with his Continental counterparts, that a concert could never be a substitute for more realistic arrangements. In his talks with the ambassadors of the powers, he sought to persuade them that, subject to the moods of the strongest parliament in Europe, British policy was more constructive and less selfish than their governments supposed. Over the years he came to know the foreign envoys very well: de Staal, the German Count von Hatzfeldt, and the Anglo-Frenchman W.H. Waddington got too close to Salisbury, becoming, as he remarked of Waddington, apologists for a British minister. Partly because of his excellent relations with them, they were left in post for very long periods; the Russian and the German for nearly twenty years each, and the Frenchman for ten. De Staal, who was both charmed and impressed by Salisbury from their first meetings, found negotiating with him *"fort agréable"*: he was a good listener, he discussed controversial questions calmly, and he was quick to take a hint. More importantly, he seemed to be animated by a sincere wish for a better understanding between countries that had been so near to war. Salisbury, he reported after Bulgaria revived Anglo-Russian friction, did not lean to the adventurism of Beaconsfield. Similar perceptions of the new foreign secretary spread through the diplomatic world.[20]

Salisbury was not liked by his own diplomats. They sensed that behind what one chastened Tory called his "formidable politeness", he thought the service "a very inferior instrument" compared with its Continental equivalents. "The large majority of men who enter it", he stated flatly, "are not able men".[21] To follow up his approach to Bismarck, he selected, not the ambassador at Berlin, Sir Edward Malet, but his former private secretary, Philip Currie, assistant under-secretary of state at the Foreign Office. Bismarck informed Currie, who visited him privately at his country house in September 1885, that he was ready to support Britain against France in Egypt. If Anglo-French rivalry threatened to lead to war, "he would not allow the war to take place"; it was not in Germany's interests to let France be strengthened by victory over Britain. On the other hand, neutrality was all he could promise in the event of an Anglo-Russian conflict: Russia must not be turned towards France, leaving Germany to fight the war on two fronts he was determined to avoid. Bismarck's definition of neutrality in this context was distinctly favourable to the Russians: Currie ascertained that he would continue to uphold the treaties that prevented British warships from passing the Straits to attack Russia when Turkey was not a belligerent. What was more, Bismarck continued to argue that a final Russian advance to Constantinople would not harm British and Austrian interests; only Russia herself would lose by extending the territory she had to defend. The weak point in the German chancellor's system, as he conceded, was multi-national Austria: she could neither be absorbed by the German empire, nor left to succumb to Russia. But the ruling circles in Austria were bent on keeping Russia out of Constantinople, and hoped to have Britain with them. Bismarck spoke of his unremitting efforts to erect a dyke against the spread of Russian influence in South Eastern Europe, one that "burst on . . . average once a year, and then he had, like a bricklayer, to patch it up".[22]

The Tsar's empire was, in his view, even less stable than the Third Republic in France, and a perpetual danger to its neighbours. Returning to Britain's problems in Egypt, where he had already been helpful, he promised German backing for Salisbury's planned evacuation of Egypt with a continuing right of re-entry for British forces. It was all Salisbury needed in that quarter. If the chancellor had been less forthcoming elsewhere, his exposition of German policy towards Austria and Russia confirmed Salisbury's analysis, on which, after talking to the ambassador at Vienna, Paget, he based his own policy, not only in South Eastern Europe, but as a whole. Though not noted for his ability, Paget was one of the few Tories in the higher ranks of the diplomatic service. Salisbury saw him at Arlington Street in June 1885, when trying to make up his mind to take office, and satisfied himself about the feasibility of once again lining up Britain and Austria in defence of their mutual concern for the Berlin settlement endangered by Russia. Paget's advice, wrote Salisbury seven years later, weighed heavily with him when he decided to take this opportunity of doing something, if only for a few months, to correct Gladstone's mistakes in foreign policy. Working with Austria, British diplomacy had the benefit of her German protection from Russia. As a result, Salisbury was more active and effective in the Balkans than he would otherwise have been. He also hoped for Austrian assistance in obtaining Germany's goodwill in Egypt. The Currie mission to Bismarck in September, and its outcome, enhanced the value of Anglo-Austrian co-operation. Bismarck's refusal of the full alliance between Britain and Germany that was suggested made Austria an important link with the strongest power in Europe.[23]

The British ambassador at St Petersburg, Sir Robert Morier, was an ardent Liberal; an authority on Germany, and a sympathizer with the German opposition to Bismarck, he was for that reason *persona non grata* with the chancellor. What Salisbury wanted from Morier was not advice but information vital to forming a judgement on the likelihood of peace or war. Who in the Russian government shaped the decisions that affected British interests? The veteran foreign minister, de Giers, had talked to another ambassador of fighting Britain in some months' time, and reports from Berlin and Vienna indicated that he was to be taken seriously. Salisbury divined that Tsar Alexander III was really his own minister, whose foreign policy reflected, at the same time, his position as a real autocrat and his uncertainty. Salisbury agreed with Bismarck in thinking, or rather continuing to think, Russia both unstable and dangerous: militarily strong but without the sound finances that strength required and, as in the 1870s, a prey to political subversion. "We must lead her into all the expense that we can", he explained to Morier, ". . . with her the limit of taxation has been almost reached . . . only a few steps further must push her into the revolution over which she seems to be . . . hanging". The thought of the "terrible calamities" which Russia's internal collapse might inflict upon her people was disturbing. It meant, however, that he was less frightened of an Anglo-Russian war than were some others. Once reasonably sure that Bismarck would not actively support Russia in Central Asia, as he had done in the Penjdeh crisis, Salisbury's diplomatic game took the German powers' attitude into account. The search for agreement with Russia on the Afghans' frontier was slowed down, without provocation, until he judged the time was ripe to conclude it.[24]

The Ottoman Sultan, that unexpected survivor, was justified in his distrust of British governments, whether Liberal or Tory. They wanted his help, as suzerain of Egypt, to regularize Britain's presence there. Sir William White at Constantinople, who had long experience of Europe east of Vienna, was unusual in having worked his way up to that eminence from humble beginnings in the consular service. Salisbury offered the Sultan "a sentimental and not a substantial gain", as suzerain and Caliph of Islam, from lending his authority to the arrangements that Salisbury contemplated. If Abdul Hamid wished for something more, he might provide troops to hold Suakin, at British expense and under British command, against the Mahdists. To do so would strengthen his claims to the overlordship of that coast, disregarded by France, Italy and Britain herself as well as by the new rulers of the Sudan. Salisbury did not approach the Sultan with any humility: "what we cannot do is to dance attendance on his pleasure". He entrusted the negotiation to a special envoy, Sir Henry Drummond Wolff, MP, of the Fourth Party, partly, as Wolff suspected, to get a talented troublemaker away from his close friend Churchill.[25] The Sultan was not tempted to act as the catspaw for a Christian power by sending Ottoman troops to Suakin, and the Egyptian border with the Sudan. He agreed to legitimize the British military presence in Egypt in the sixth article of the Anglo-Turkish convention of 1885, which left the timing of a withdrawal to be decided by London and Constantinople. Ottoman and British commissioners were to reform the Egyptian civil administration and army, jointly with the Khedive. Germany's considerable influence told with Abdul Hamid, whose army was being trained by German officers. Britain's wish to evacuate was not a pretence. Wolseley, her leading general, said openly that stationing fewer than 20 000 men in Egypt imposed too great a strain upon limited resources.[26]

The Wolff convention made the British occupation of Egypt respectable in international law, and appeased its critics at home. The overlapping crisis in the Balkans gave further proof of Salisbury's dexterity. In September 1885 Bulgarian nationalists expelled the Ottoman governor-general from Eastern Rumelia and proclaimed the union of the self-governing province with the principality on the other side of the Balkan range, created by the Berlin congress as an Ottoman tributary state and ruled by Alexander of Battenberg. To begin with, Salisbury was not persuaded that even a big Bulgaria would be strong enough to escape Russian domination. Nor was it possible for him to sanction the unravelling of the Berlin treaty. Greece and Serbia were quick to declare their intention of emulating Bulgaria on expansion. In his regular exchange of ideas on foreign policy with the premier, Churchill stated the "diabolical dilemma" facing the British government. At the India Office he was afraid of the ill effects of leaving the Sultan unsupported against his Christian Slav enemies: "Goodbye to all confidence, assistance or sympathy from the Mussulman

. . . in India, to say nothing of Egypt". If he exaggerated, he had raised an aspect of the question that was not to be ignored.[27]

Churchill knew, as did Salisbury, that the domestic impact of a reviving Eastern question was of more immediate importance than the repercussions of policy in Egypt and the Sudan. The government must not be seen to side with the Sultan against the Bulgarians: Gladstone would certainly be provoked to denounce Abdul Hamid and Tory ministers for going to his aid. The Tories could not afford to present him with a moral issue to exploit in his incomparable fashion. No fonder than Gladstone of the Sultan, Salisbury allowed de Staal and his German and French colleagues to think that he was wrapping himself in the *"drapeau libéral"* for reasons of expediency. It helped to lessen the conservative powers' displeasure with British reluctance to endorse the proposed restoration of the *status quo* in Eastern Rumelia. His alternative, put forward without optimism, was a personal union under Alexander of Battenberg between Congress Bulgaria and the rebellious province; in all other respects they should remain separate entities. This was the solution eventually adopted in April 1886 when the Liberals were, briefly, again in office. Prudently unwilling to occupy a province from which her troops had been excluded since Berlin, Turkey made no move.[28] The dangers crowding in upon all the participants in this Balkan crisis are vividly illustrated by letter from Churchill which no one else in the forefront of British politics then could have written: "It is a pity . . . there is not time before the elections", he observed, "for a revolution at Constantinople, general massacre in European Turkey and a real good set to between Austria and Prussia". If Britain calmly looked on while these catastrophes engulfed half the Continent and menaced the rest, the new electors would surely be grateful.[29]

The suggestion so pleased its author that he would not be put off by Salisbury's omission to refer to it in his next letter. Neither Bulgaria nor her prince were worth the slightest risk to the British empire: "I would like Austria and Russia to fight it out . . . I hate the 'infant liberties' [of Balkan nationalities]". Replying for his uncle, temporarily indisposed, A.J. Balfour, now a cabinet minister, reminded Churchill that the voters were susceptible to concern for those despised liberties, and would not like Russian aggrandizement at the cost of Bulgarian freedom, especially if Turkish troops were deployed in Eastern Rumelia, as the conservative powers wanted. Salisbury worked to win Turkey over to his solution, which left Alexander a vassal of the Sultan. He had an inducement to offer in the protection afforded by the Mediterranean fleet from the locally strong Greek navy. For Bulgarian union had been taken as a signal that the general distribution of territory at Berlin was up for revision. The Greeks were deterred by a mainly British naval demonstration from attempting to liberate more of their country from Turkish rule.[30] The Serbs attacked Bulgaria in November 1885 and were routed: Austria intervened to prevent the victors from overrunning Serbia, which lay within their sphere of influence. The Bulgarians' success, unexpected in view of the Tsar's action in withdrawing its Russian senior officers from their army, led Salisbury to believe that they might be animated by an "independent national feeling". If they were, a big Bulgaria would be a more effective barrier to Russian expansion than had seemed possible.

But Salisbury's sympathy with Balkan Christians was diminishing. Greek irredentism struck him as blind to the "rudimentary laws of morality".[31]

Germany's anxiety to stave off a collision between Austria and Russia, certain if one or the other sent troops into Bulgaria, made this British diplomacy welcome to her. It relieved Bismarck, to some extent, of the embarrassment involved in mediating between rivals for ascendancy in the Balkans, to both of whom he was bound by his web of alliances. Salisbury was in the unusual position of standing well with Bismarck and with Gladstone. The Balkan settlement, important to Germany's undisturbed hegemony and to Britain's prestige, survived with the minimum of alteration that was Salisbury's aim. The Queen, with a daughter and granddaughter married to brothers of Alexander of Battenberg, plied a hard-pressed minister with ardently pro-Bulgarian and anti-Russian sentiments.[32] Salisbury's Balkan policy "delighted" Gladstone; it preserved his cherished Bulgaria from an isolation that would have been fatal to her. The contrast between Churchill's idea of *realpolitik* and Salisbury's responsible statesmanship was complete. It was not open to Britain to cut herself off from Europe and her treaty obligations in the Balkans and the Near East: if she did, "she would be stultifying herself", he said simply. The invasion of Burma in November 1885 was not a Foreign Office war, but one launched by the Government of India under a Liberal viceroy for the usual reasons that governed expansion on the imperial frontiers. It gave Churchill at the India Office a war that he could call his own: and Salisbury indulged him in his interpretation of it: "I quite agree. Burma will pay a very good interest on the expense".[33] When he handed over the Foreign Office to Rosebery in February, he was confident that there would be no change in his overall policy. Morier's valedictory letter to his departing chief was effusive, but bears quotation as coming from a partisan Liberal: Salisbury had "replaced England in her former great position as a European power, and so laid the rails of her international policy that the awkwardest tramcar driver can hardly twist off". The price paid for Bismarck's goodwill, without which Salisbury would probably have had little to show for those, was not high: Salisbury tendered payment by smoothing Germany's colonial path on the East coast of Africa and in the Pacific.[34]

## The Tories and Home Rule

To quote Morier again, Salisbury had in "seven months . . . at the most critical moment of English history recreated a Conservative party that is a living, disciplined organization with living principles". The Newport speech redefined the content of Toryism. As for the personnel of his administration, Salisbury wrote, when the government was forming in June 1885, of a "chaos of rivalries and divisions". When he left office the following February, he had inspired in Churchill as much loyalty as the younger man had it in him to feel. The remainder of his colleagues complained only that he did not give them a strong enough lead in cabinet. On difficult questions, and none was more difficult than Ireland in 1885–6, he preferred to let a collective view develop gradually, with time for private exchanges between cabinets.[35] For both personal and party reasons there was no enthusiasm for replacing him, as he himself suggested the party might, by the Whig Hartington in a coalition with the Liberals opposed to Gladstone and Home Rule. His handling of that question not only held the Tories together: it convinced them and their potential allies that the qualified self-rule for Ireland envisaged by Carnarvon and advocated by Gladstone ought not to be risked in prevailing conditions. By subscribing to the unspoken agreement not to make Ireland an issue in the election at the end of the year, he forced Gladstone to show his hand first on Home Rule. Turned out of office in February, on a vote contrived to patch up the Liberals' crumbling unity, he patiently fostered the emergence of Liberal Unionism, allowing its adherents to move towards him at their own uncertain pace.

The impending expiry of the Crimes Act, the latest instalment of Gladstonian emergency legislation in Ireland, was the public starting point for the incoming cabinet's revision of Irish policy. A wary co-operation with the nationalists at Westminster had furnished the means of defeating the Liberals: the Tory leadership had now to consider how far it was possible to build on those contacts. Churchill's friendly relations with nationalist MPs on a personal level, and the occasional combinations with them in the House to harry the Gladstone ministry, gave rise to loose talk of a compact. Parnell was well aware that Churchill could not answer for the Tories, even if he had wanted to enter into a revolutionary arrangement.[36] Tory concessions to the nationalists dated from February 1885, when the Liberals' troubles were accumulating, and were solicited through Rowland Winn, the chief opposition whip. Winn provided Parnell with assurances on two points in the redistribution of seats bill going through parliament. His party would not seek to reduce the longstanding over-representation of Ireland in the Commons, as Salisbury had urged on his platform speeches. Nor would they try to undo the work of the Irish boundary commissioners. The first was not an insignificant gesture. In his report to the leadership, the chief whip stressed that "no arrangement, compact or agreement" was implied. After the Liberal defeat in June, his nationalist counterpart, Richard Power, approached Winn with what was clearly an invitation to negotiate. Power thought the Irish vote in British constituencies could be organized to influence some fifty seats in favour of one British party or the other. In addition he offered to secure five Ulster seats for the Tories by withdrawing nationalist candidates. At this stage, all he sought in return was the new government's adoption of two small bills: one, of no great importance, on election expenses and another to improve the lot of landless agricultural labourers in Ireland, a very depressed class. The second went through in the remaining weeks of the session.[37]

There is no record of what then took place: but Power's proffered undertaking to "assist you all we can" at the election and beforehand elicited a positive response. Since the Liberals were divided over renewing the Crimes Act, the Tories had little chance but to let it expire.[38] At its first meeting on 26 June the cabinet discussed how to proceed in the light of Salisbury's information that their predecessors had come close to agreeing on an elected council, not to be called a parliament, for the whole of Ireland; Chamberlain's central board scheme was meant. The subject was held over for "more knowledge" of all the factors.[39] As Gladstone and his colleagues had discovered, the liberalization of Irish administration in the name of local government reform pointed inexorably to Home Rule, however it was dressed up. Lord Spencer, the Liberal viceroy of Ireland, said in cabinet that a central board "would be a *Convention* sitting in Dublin". Confronted with the same problem, Tory ministers were ready to leave it with Salisbury and Carnarvon until the outline of a decision was discernible.[40]

In the course of "a very serious talk" with Carnarvon on 6 July, Salisbury was unwilling to go beyond elected provincial councils in Ireland. They would send, he thought for the moment, quite a different message from a central board. But he went on to surmise that many of their party were prepared to go further: and if he was right, "I must stand aside, but you could carry it [Home Rule] out". He was not going to emulate Peel on Catholic emancipation or the Corn Laws, and seemed to be casting his friend for the unenviable role of a statesman who splits his party in the uncomfortable knowledge that virtue must be its own reward. "That, my dear Salisbury", replied Carnarvon, "is not practical. I can do nothing of the sort". Carnarvon certainly was not a credible premier in the very difficult circumstances they were trying to foresee. High-minded, a good speaker and a conscientious administrator, he lacked the nerve for the looming crisis. As is plain from his diary after 1878, he had never really trusted Salisbury since the Eastern question drove them apart, though friendly relations were restored after a while. This entry shows he was uneasy about what was expected of him, and what it would mean for him. The vision of himself as a scapegoat floated before his eyes. He had been chosen for his task in Ireland, Salisbury assured him, "because no one else would have undertaken it in at all the same way". To this Carnarvon recorded himself as saying that Salisbury had pressed him to accept: "we must not have any divergence, and we must be perfectly frank with each other, and have a complete understanding". At this interview he secured his line of retreat: his health was weak, and the Irish viceroyalty too expensive for someone whose English rents had fallen sharply in the current recession; he would not stay in Ireland after the elections were over. Premier and viceroy gave themselves six months in which to come to terms with Parnell.[41]

"I think he was frank", Carnarvon ended his account of their discussion. His statement in the Lords that day, besides confirming that the life of the Crimes Act would not be extended, contained a land purchase bill generous to Irish landlords and tenants at the expense of the British taxpayer. He signalled the government's intention of exploring forms of Home Rule in the words: "The questions of discord must be studied".[42] On the same day, too, he saw Justin McCarthy, a nationalist MP and London journalist, to ask for a meeting with Parnell. He gave McCarthy the impression that he was acting independently of a government which he hoped to convert to his inchoate Home Rule views. The convergence of Tories and nationalists was taken further when on 17 July Churchill, his henchman Gorst, now solicitor-general, and, less clearly, Hicks Beach, dissociated the party from the coercion that Spencer had administered with Tory support. They observed the letter, but not the spirit, of a cabinet decision to refuse an inquiry into a controversial episode of Spencer's viceroyalty, the Maamtrasna murders. There were sharp reactions to the treatment of Spencer from the Queen downwards. Sir Henry James, a future Liberal Unionist minister, called the offending speeches "a disgraceful exhibition", heard in a shocked silence on the Tory benches, followed by indignant protests. Churchill and Hicks Beach had deliberately ignored a warning from the premier before the debate. Salisbury had then to defend them as best he could. They were guilty of an indiscretion: they were not out of step with him.[43] Any doubt on that score is removed by his dismissal of a suggestion that Wolseley should get the Irish command on his return from Africa. To appoint that distinguished Anglo-Irish soldier, whose hostility to Home Rule was well known, "would announce an expectation of insurrection . . . wholly at variance with the policy we are now pursuing".[44]

Carnarvon's interview with Parnell took place on 1 August in the dramatic setting so often described, an empty London house. Only Salisbury and the Irish lord chancellor, Ashbourne, knew of it. Ashbourne, the former Edward Gibson and a Commons frontbencher until the formation of the government, sat in all Salisbury's cabinets, very unusually for a holder of his post. This Dublin lawyer represented the Irish minority who, however, suspected him of being too ready to compromise with the enemy. He agreed with the premier that it would be wise to commit as little as possible to paper in sounding the nationalist leader. Parnell and Carnarvon discussed the central legislature for which, the Irishman emphasized, provincial councils were not an acceptable substitute. The latter came away encouraged to find Parnell "singularly moderate"; prepared, for a time, to leave land legislation with Westminster and to wait for the freedom enjoyed by the settler colonies to protect Irish industries against British competition. After the meeting, Carnarvon and Salisbury talked "long and anxiously" about what lay ahead. Carnarvon was hopeful, pleased with progress made towards an inevitable outcome, as he saw it.[45] Salisbury was not optimistic; he had told the Queen that "the nationalists cannot be trusted . . . any bargain with them would be full of danger". Everything to do with Ireland was "so difficult", Salisbury informed the absent viceroy after the last cabinet meeting of the summer, that ministers made no mention of her problems in the Queen's speech closing the session. The inability of the parliamentary nationalists to control the widespread revival of violence and intimidation after the Crimes Act expired bore out Salisbury's fears. Unless they moved to check the incidence of boycotting, he told Churchill late in September, British opinion would swing against the government and its search for agreement with Parnell.[46]

Churchill, it seems, was the one member of the cabinet steadily opposed to anything that might properly be understood as home rule. His cynicism inclined him to discern a kindred spirit in Parnell. No more coercion; an unarmed civil police instead of "a Gendarmerie"; a system of elective local government similar to that expected for English counties; educational concessions to the Irish Catholic bishops – these were what really interested the nationalists, and would cement their alliance with the Tories. The demand for autonomy, "as old as the hills", was not to be taken literally; Parnell harboured no designs on "classes or institutions". When Carnarvon did not heed his advice, on the main question, Churchill pressed it on

Salisbury: "I trust it will not be . . . necessary to show our hand about local government too much or to allude to Home Rule . . . at all", he wrote from the viceroy's residence in Dublin on 1 October, ". . . The Nationalists . . . do not want us to do so".[47] The Parnellites were saying the opposite to Carnarvon and his able British permanent under-secretary, Sir Robert Hamilton, a convert to Irish self-government. The prominent Fenians in the nationalist ranks were reported to have pledged themselves to Home Rule, "and in no way to use it for going any further in the direction of separation from England". Police intelligence conveyed the gratifying information that the nationalists would accept from Carnarvon what they would not swallow from anyone else, such was his personal prestige. "We have arrived at the point that no half measures will succeed", minuted Hamilton in September, ". . . You must . . . let them govern themselves under efficient safeguards against confiscation and separation".[48]

The cabinet's mind was probably expressed by Iddesleigh, writing on 7 September, who wanted them to arrive at a definite view, one way or the other, before the elections. He was not averse to Home Rule, although not sure what it meant or ought to mean, so long as it did not bring with it "separation from the Empire . . . confiscation . . . and lawlessness". This reflected the mood in political circles for some months past. As the Liberals went out, Dilke commented on the "almost universal feeling . . . in both parties that some form of Home Rule must be tried". Even Wolseley, visiting Dublin in November, suggested after he had met Carnarvon that what he called a "talking Parliament" might be set up to divert the Irish from their aspirations to authentic self-rule.[49] Gladstone was watching the Tories closely, and they him, while he prepared colleagues in his last cabinet for the revelation of December 1885. Parnell, in speeches about which, Churchill said, British newspapers were making "a most foolish fuss", predicted that "with judgement and . . . moderation you will have the two English parties vying with each other in the settlement of the Irish question". Austria-Hungary and Britain's settler colonies were his models for a new Anglo-Irish relationship: either would give Ireland "complete power to rule herself . . . that is practically what we have been asking". It was more, but not much more, than British politicians were considering.[50]

On the day before cabinets resumed in the autumn, Carnarvon let the premier know that, to his mind, the "only solution" to Ireland's worsening problems lay in the concession of a parliament with real, though limited, powers. Salisbury remained opposed to that, in a personal capacity: "I said I had not forgotten", Carnarvon noted, ". . . I desired to avoid all division . . . in the party". At the cabinet of 6 October, very largely devoted to Ireland, he made a brief statement, arguing that the existing structure of Irish government could not withstand "for any length of time" the hostility, outside Protestant Ulster, "of all classes except the landlords": the Land League's successor, the National League, had superseded his administration in the South; the Fenians were poised to intervene directly. An uneasy truce existed between the British authorities and the greater part of the population. On a pattern familiar in recent Irish history, political tensions were fed by rural distress, as agricultural prices fell again, offsetting the reduction of rents under the 1881 Land Act. Carnarvon admitted the risks in granting self-government and spoke of conceding "the shadow without giving the substance or at least the substance of that which would be perilous". These last words exposed the uncertainty fatal to the policy he advocated. Ashbourne seemed to support him but was "not quite clear on the [vital] point". Lord George Hamilton, the younger son of an Ulster magnate, endorsed Carnarvon's presentation of the facts. Carnarvon saw that he had "no real supporters". Hicks Beach commented that they were being advised to side with enemies against friends. Cranbrook and Iddesleigh thought it impossible for Tories to propose an Irish parliament. When Carnarvon sent a memorandum embodying his statement, the premier asked him to include Cranbrook's objection.[51]

Salisbury was caught between his perception of Irish nationality as too strong ever to be reconciled to the Union, and the feelings of his party. Tories were not incapable of appreciating the rational arguments for a subordinate parliament in Dublin, and even those for a legislature as independent of Westminster, in practice, as were the parliaments of self-governing colonies. Reason and sentiment upheld opposing arguments. For Salisbury the decisive one had been, and continued to be, the position of the Irish minority. Yet he did not want to lose an opportunity of removing the Irish question from British politics, where it had worked to the Tories' disadvantage for the best part of a century, and of healing a running sore in Anglo-American relations. Parnell's reference on 5 October to Austria-Hungary gave hope of better provision for defence and the imperial dimension than the loose arrangements linking Britain with virtually independent colonies offered. In spite of the cabinet's reactions to Carnarvon, Salisbury welcomed the nationalists' overture when he spoke at Newport the next day. He felt bound to add that he could not see his way through the obvious difficulties: "we shall be holding out false expectations if we avow a belief which, as yet at all events, we cannot entertain". A guest at Hatfield in November, Lord Lytton found his host's "chief present occupation" was "how to rescue the [loyalist] garrison, and, above all, how to rescue them in time". Otherwise he was "not . . . much alarmed" by any form of Home Rule: Britain would know how to protect herself from a free Ireland. The landlords might be, as they were, bought out over time; the 1885 land purchase bill began the process in earnest. It was not realistic to contemplate the withdrawal of the rest of the minority, at least from its stronghold in the North-East.[52]

Carnarvon's chief secretary, Sir William Hart Dyke, who was not a cabinet minister, inferred from his contacts with the premier that Salisbury was not only opposed to Home Rule himself but believed the party to be averse to "any bold move" towards it. Hart Dyke, a Kentish baronet with little knowledge of Ireland, had embraced the viceroy's policy and lamented "the hopeless indifference, . . . ignorance [and] . . . prejudice" among ministers and backbenchers alike. Carnarvon was not deterred, at the last meeting with Salisbury before the elections, from proposing a joint committee of both Houses on Irish government or, more simply, a viceregal announcement that the goal of policy was "local self-government". Failing either of these initiatives, the storm brewing in Ireland would, he was practically certain, sweep away the landlords' property. Some of them realized the "extreme danger" hanging over their class. They would probably fare rather better if the Tories did not leave their fate to be decided between the Liberals and the nationalists. Salisbury repeated what he had said in July: he was not prepared to make the attempt to carry Home Rule but would give way to someone on the same side who was. The question must go to the full cabinet after the elections. The premier appeared ill and tired: Carnarvon wondered whether Salisbury's "political romance" was nearing its end. He served notice of his intention to give up the viceroyalty if the cabinet's decision went against him; although to minimize the damage to the government he was willing to stay on in another post. With his history of resignations, he recognized "the overwhelming force of the argument that in no circumstances must the party be split".[53]

It was still not clear that the Tories were going to retrace the steps they had taken towards Home Rule. As late as 9 November, Salisbury's speech at the Mansion House, an occasion for stating government policy, laid down only two broad conditions – the preservation of imperial unity and a due regard to the rights of the minority – to limit the search for an Irish settlement; subject to these, he promised to do "all that was possible" to satisfy Ireland. Gladstone interpreted this as an advance upon the "I do not see how" at Newport. But Carnarvon's judgement, and his nerve, were not equal to the situation in which he found himself after exciting hopes and fears all round. He confessed to the Queen, by whom he was received on the day he saw Salisbury in November, that he "felt almost overpowered with the sense of dangers resulting from action in either or any direction". It was Churchill whose stance ensured that the party turned away from Home Rule: the reform of county government, to coincide with its democratization in Britain, was all that the Tories would concede. Persistent rumours to the contrary proved wide of the mark. "Give a conciliatory *non possumus* to Home Rule", he recommended: and if the unrest got out of hand, despatch Wolseley to govern with powers appropriate to the emergency. The Irish American threat he thought unreal. Should there be anxiety on that score, the United States was vulnerable, in the last resort, to naval bombardment of defenceless seaboard towns: he would "diplomatically bully her". "Curious", commented the viceroy on these robust views. They were, however, substantially those of his colleagues, and of the future Unionist alliance.[54] After Carnarvon's November audience of the Queen, Salisbury told her private secretary that the viceroy had not been supported by any other member of the cabinet in his advocacy of Home Rule, although a final decision would be taken when the elections were over.[55]

His present opinion, he went on, was that a "central parliament" would swiftly dispose of accompanying safeguards to the "utter ruin" of loyalists. The policy which Carnarvon urged in good faith was one of complete surrender to Parnell and could only be carried "*now*" at the cost of disrupting both British parties. Hartington had made his opposition to Home Rule plain in a speech as far back as August.[56] Churchill, wanting to preserve the tactical alliance of Tories and nationalists through the elections, reserved his objections for the cabinet. In a long memorandum of December, covering the whole of Conservative policy, he excluded "anything in the nature of an Irish parliament . . . impossible always". "The Disraelian epoch of constant metamorphoses of principle . . . has passed away", he informed one of his Irish friends, the Catholic loyalist Michael Morris. Salisbury, to whom Churchill communicated the letter, professed himself delighted at it. Churchill, that volatile politician, was announcing his intention of appealing to all those Tories who felt instinctively that Home Rule "no matter how you disguise it is the reverse of conservative". Once the elections had taken place, the Irish were no longer useful allies: he warned Salisbury that if Carnarvon "set the signal for concession flying our party will go to pieces"; and referred pointedly to the viceroy's departure from cabinets in 1867 and 1878, "his power to disintegrate, demoralize and shatter". The censure, of course, included Salisbury in the past and the present.[57] At the cabinets of 14 and 15 December Carnarvon argued for his joint committee of both Houses. Most of those who heard him were wholly unsympathetic: their policy, he remarked bitterly, "consists in giving next to nothing and coercing . . . [a] view . . . vigorously . . . expressed". Salisbury conveyed their mood to the Queen: "it was not . . . for the Conservative party to tamper with the question of Home Rule".[58]

Yet Malcolm MacColl, who tried to make himself an intermediary between Salisbury and Gladstone, as someone well known to both, had a rather different impression when in touch with the premier after this cabinet. He reported to Gladstone on 22 December that Salisbury was "prepared to go as far probably as yourself on . . . Home Rule", but seemed "hopeless" of being able to influence the Tories. Gladstone had already approached A.J. Balfour with a suggestion of Liberal backing for the government if they should determine to legislate outside "the lines of party conflict". Salisbury and Balfour looked on this invitation as designed to split the ministerialists instead of Gladstone's own followers; they were contemptuous of the manoeuvre.[59] But Gladstone had correctly understood that Salisbury was not opposed to Home Rule in principle. The essential insight into Salisbury's mind is provided by the "*now*" of his letter to Ponsonby cited above. Gladstone believed that the time had come for a fundamental reconstruction of the Anglo-Irish relationship: after months of careful exploration Salisbury decided that it had not. His estimate of British, and of Irish opinion, was accurate. He did not subscribe to Churchill's notion of what inspired endemic Irish unrest. His colleague was confident that the government could break up the Parnellites by implementing his policies for Ireland. Churchill's hopes were centred upon educational concessions to the Catholic hierarchy, which he expected would decisively undermine Parnellite nationalism. Tories might count on the combination of "priestly influences, and . . . the capricious, unstable and to some extent treacherous character of the Irish nation", historically unable to preserve unity for long against Britain. Superficial, and insulting, though this analysis was, it had the merit of being more realistic, at the time, than a continuing search for agreement on a form of Home Rule. On 15 December, when the cabinet had before them concessions such as Churchill advised, he said afterwards of Carnarvon's university bill framed to please the Catholic bishops: "the bribe should have been larger".[60]

Churchill, supported by Hicks Beach, was not being inconsistent when he contended until the eve of the government's fall in January that more coercion, too, was "impossible". It would rule out a renewal of the Tory–Irish alliance, and furnish the Liberals with a pretext for ejecting a government still in a minority after the electoral gains. The two ministers yielded to Salisbury's argument, calculated to sway men of their temperament, that the Tories must not allow themselves to be branded, in the eyes of the British public, as "the timid party, who let things float because they dare not act". The National League, according to Dublin Castle, was ready to plunge Ireland into revolution.[61] The cabinet also discussed a further, and evidently considerable, land purchase bill, but the restoration of law and order was paramount. Carnarvon continued as viceroy, pending the appointment of a successor, when Cranbrook refused the place, for personal reasons. W.H. Smith, who left the War Office to become chief secretary for the government's last few days, was strong for coercion, and for land purchase, "in a complete manner", without which he did not think Ireland could be pacified. The government announced the forthcoming coercion and land bills in the Queen's Speech on 26 January, going down to defeat later that night on an unrelated question in the ensuing debate.[62] Once Gladstone's conversion to Home Rule was leaked on 17 December, ministers would have liked to be beaten on their opposition to a policy which they had come close to adopting themselves. While Gladstone denied them that advantage, they were henceforth the party of the Union.[63]

Speaking on the Address in January, Salisbury declared, "The disease is not in Ireland. The disease is here – in Westminster". Other countries and governments had overcome the problems that Ireland presented: the British parties had permitted the nationalists to play one against the other, and if they continued to do so, "you are drifting straight to a ruin which will engulf England and Ireland alike". He had turned Gladstone's appeal for a bi-partisan Irish policy on its head by calling for an end to the "instability of purpose" which had characterized Liberals and Tories in their dealings with Parnell. His words were aimed at the future Unionists on the other side. He had resisted as premature Churchill's proposal that these potential rebels should be offered places in a cabinet broadly based on opposition to Gladstone and Home Rule, and support for a range of reasonably advanced policies. Nothing Salisbury said precluded far-reaching measures of conciliation within the framework of the Union. He was not afraid to make the "declaration of war" which, Carnarvon warned the cabinet, a final rejection of Home Rule and the announcement of more coercion entailed.[64] Though far from well, Salisbury did not err in reading the situation in Ireland and in Britain, where many Tories and Liberals were really alarmed by Chamberlain's provocative language. Even at this distance, his calm assurance impresses. "Except Mr Gladstone", he comforted the Queen, "the forces of subversion have no very dangerous champion"; Gladstone, and he alone, not Chamberlain, had the power to radicalize British politics and give the Irish nationalists a parliament which no "paper barricade" could check. Salisbury never underestimated Gladstone's unique personal ability, exercised at every level, to bend men's minds to his political will, "amounting in some cases to infatuation". The elections of 1885 showed how the spell might be broken.[65]

## The General Election of 1885 and the Birth of Unionism

The first general election fought on household suffrage in borough and county produced results that were initially difficult to construe. Significant Tory gains in the boroughs were offset by losses in the counties which Salisbury rightly regarded as transient. In 1880 the Liberals won over two-thirds of English and Welsh borough seats: five years later only half. The counties, Tory by a margin of two to one in 1880, returned a majority of Liberals – and a comfortable one – for the first time since 1832. Scotland, overwhelmingly Liberal in both elections, helped the party to a United Kingdom total of 334 seats against the Tories' 249. The Liberals were eliminated in Ireland, where the nationalists took eighty-five of the 101 seats, with the balance going to the Tories concentrated in Ulster. In England, without Wales, the Liberals' share of the vote fell by a little short of five per cent to 51.4 per cent. Gladstone ascribed this setback to "Fair Trade + Parnell + Church + Chamberlain". On the other hand, the agricultural labourers finally admitted to the political nation responded enthusiastically to Chamberlain's advocacy of compulsory purchase to provide them with smallholdings and allotments. They were also rebelling against the domination of village life by squire and parson, more especially the latter. Urban voters, middle and working class, were attracted by the Tories' apparent willingness to re-examine the orthodoxy of free trade in the contemporary depression. Nor was free elementary education – the item in his programme closest to Chamberlain's heart – a vote-winner among town populations; they complained, as it was, of rising local taxation. His attacks, and those of the Nonconformist militants at his back, on the Church and her schools roused the plebeian Anglicanism of industrial England, a force he badly underestimated. The graduation of income tax, which Chamberlain presented as an avowedly redistributive measure, did not appeal to fellow Liberals brought up to believe with a younger Gladstone that it was anathema. As for the Irish vote in Britain: it was variously thought to have cost the Liberals anything between twenty and sixty-five seats.[66]

Home Rule was not an issue during the election; the party leaderships, undecided about Ireland, saw to that. Gladstone was nevertheless eager to be in power again, for two reasons. Only his party could cope, "(*if* it can)", with the demands of the commanding nationalist majority sure to be returned by the Irish constituencies. Secondly, "the demoralized and dangerous condition of the Tory party" made a change of government imperative. By this he meant that the "Newport programme" bore an uncomfortable resemblance to Chamberlain's agenda. Gladstone equated "Chamberlainism" with "Tory democracy"; both were manifestations of "socialism".[67] Salisbury's speeches after Newport exploited the alarm that Chamberlain excited, but competed with him in addressing the problems of working men. What did they want? "Wages", he answered. "Nothing . . . you can offer is equal in his mind to wages sufficient in amount, and work constantly furnished". One of the Tories' first moves on taking office had been to set up a royal commission on the causes of depression in industry and trade, something he had contemplated in opposition. If he wished the party to avoid involvement with protectionist organizations, then and subsequently, he mocked the Liberals' blind devotion to the "holy and sacred principles of free trade" when he spoke on the hustings. Overseas competition, driving down cereal prices, was responsible for the migration of rural labour to overcrowded towns. He compared retaliatory tariffs to war: "No doubt . . . a bad thing; we would abolish it if we could, but war is the only way of defending ourselves from wrong. Why is it wrong to make it in dealing with our fiscal duties when it is not wrong in other international relations?" Why should imperial preference be deemed "an economical heresy?" He suggested it would be "a happy thing", adding almost as an afterthought, "I do not say it would be possible". The way ahead for their society lay through economic expansion abroad to give British industry the outlets it needed. Radicals talked of dividing the wealth that existed: "the Conservative points the working man forward to . . . wealth . . . as yet uncreated".[68]

This bold vindication of protectionism was hardly less objectionable to Gladstone than Salisbury's proposals for mild state intervention to enlarge the housing stock, which he considered socialist, and it had a far greater impact. Less frightened of Chamberlain than were many Liberals, if he was frightened at all, Salisbury did not argue from conscious weakness: radicals would find the rich man "a very hard nut to crack" in their country. Reginald Brett, beaten at Plymouth, agreed with Gladstone that what his leader called "the imposture . . . the visionary promises of fair trade" had been the Tories' "best card". In Manchester, the historic centre of free trade, the Tories captured all the seats but one, and in London thirty-six to the Liberals' twenty-six. The backward-looking Liberalism of Gladstone's manifesto – the "authorized programme" – failed to inspire; even Hartington described it as "rather a weak production". Chamberlain's "advanced programme", Brett told its author, needed to be "purged *in its details*".[69] The land reform that secured the votes of agricultural labourers was generally condemned as unworkable by more sophisticated judges. Salisbury quoted the shrewder of the intended beneficiaries as saying: "Give me three or four acres? I cannot live upon that". Edward Hamilton believed the Liberals had been damaged more seriously by their mishandling of the Sudan: "war, bungling, bloodshed, heavy expenditure, and nothing to show for it". Salisbury did not spare Gladstone's "marvellous and phenomenal exhibition of vacillation, ineptitude and criminal neglect" in that theatre. It was an effective reply to Derby's accusation that he entertained Disraelian ambitions abroad; which expressed a personal conviction going back to their divergence over the Eastern question in Beaconsfield's cabinet.[70]

Next to "fair trade" Gladstone complained most of "the church power", which hurt Liberals in the boroughs. It was not only Chamberlain and his Nonconformist adherents who brought disestablishment into the election: Derby thought it opportune to say that disestablishment and disendowment could not be indefinitely postponed: "somewhat characteristically", observed Salisbury, ". . . he is anxious to go beforehand and meet defeat".[71] Gladstone had consigned the question to the future in a passage of his manifesto which, however, hinted that its time was coming. Liberal churchmen, headed by three dukes, protested. Salisbury commented drily: "you must not interpret Mr Gladstone's sentiments by the language of ordinary Englishmen. Gladstone must be interpreted by Gladstone". The Tory premier made much of Liberal divisions on an issue which, to him, mattered more than any other: Chamberlain drew attention to the 500 Liberal candidates pledged to disestablishment; Gladstone was ambiguous about it; Derby suggested it should begin with the Church in Wales; G.J. Goschen, a prominent Liberal critic of Gladstone on the right of the party, refused to commit himself one way or the other, saying he would follow his leader. Was he wrong, Salisbury asked, to reject the charge, voiced by Hartington and Granville, that he had recklessly stirred up a dangerous controversy, "a sleeping lion", in Granville's words? The Conservatives would sacrifice "every other consideration that governs us" to the Church, whose fall, on the Continental precedents, must open the floodgates to irreligion. "I do not believe", he declared, ". . . if properly appealed to, the people are against us." It emerged that too many Nonconformists did not like the idea of disestablishment. The results in the boroughs administered a rebuff to their militants which had a lasting effect. So far as England was concerned, the Liberal leadership had good reason to be wary of the Liberationists in future.[72]

There had never been "such a continued rhetorical battle" around the country as Britain witnessed that autumn. Salisbury's performance underlined his pre-eminence on the Tory side. His oratory, universally seen as one of his party's strengths, went with a grasp of electoral management in a democratic age which is a little surprising in the light of his caustic references to "wirepullers", as he liked to designate the servants of the party machine. Aretas Akers-Douglas, the new chief whip and a key figure in the Tory campaign, was asked for his forecast of the result in every contested seat: "It will be a guide as to weak points". Organizations existed to promote ideas, which, for Salisbury, were the stuff of politics. The Primrose League won his approval once its clever, if crude, institutionalization of deference had proved successful. He had been encouraging when the party considered its attitude to trade union candidates standing as Tories: "my impression is that on important questions you will find them straighter than some more cultured persons".[73] That Salisbury was unafraid of being radical in a British setting is apparent from his reception of Churchill's outline of a programme for a ministry broadened to admit anti-Gladstonian Liberals. He did remind his lieutenant of the need to take Conservative feelings into account and to be flexible. If they were to stop short of the "purely popular election" that Churchill urged in their plans for extending elective local government to the counties, it would please metropolitan Tories and public opinion to see the Liberals' promised bill on London government trumped by a "very popular" Tory measure creating eight or nine independent municipalities in the capital. Churchill also wanted to adopt anodyne land reforms such as moderate Liberals favoured: the abolition of primogeniture in cases of intestacy; the enfranchisement of copyholds and land in mortmain as well as of future (not existing) leaseholds. "Except on strategic grounds", said Salisbury of the complete abolition of primogeniture, "it is not worth the trouble of resistance". On leaseholds he had a suggestion worthy of Chamberlain: local authorities might be empowered to advance part of the purchase price to the leaseholder where the ground landlord was willing to sell. There might be a bill to facilitate the sale of all corporate landed property.[74]

The "strategic grounds" to which Salisbury alluded were those that determined his course as a Tory premier and the potential leader of a coalition being widely talked about. Primogeniture, he asked Churchill to remember, was "a bit of a flag" to the Tory rank and file, and should not be given up, even in cases of intestacy, until the Liberals leaving Gladstone needed to be able to show that they had extracted concessions from the Tories they were joining. As Salisbury put it, it was to be "a wedding present . . . whenever the Conservative party leads them to the altar". When the time came "the extra tinge of Liberalism in our policy" would be part of the bargain. He dismissed Churchill's "patriotic offer" to start the process of assimilation, surrendering his cabinet place to Goschen, a leading anti-Gladstonian figure. Whiggish Liberals, wrote Salisbury, might regard Churchill with peculiar aversion but "they hate us as much as they hate you".[75] They certainly distrusted Salisbury, partly for the populism that had demonstrably worked with the urban electorate. As Churchill said respectfully, "the [borough] voters have gone for you so strongly because they believe in the fullness and genuineness of the Newport programme". The election results convinced Churchill that if the Tories were to hold their gains in the towns and win back the lost seats in the counties they must adopt his ideas for strengthening the programme. They should nerve themselves for, "I risk the word, a democratic policy, a casting off and . . . burning of old worn out aristocratic and class garments". He protested at delay in reforming county government, and was now for some "extensive changes in our land system", going well beyond his suggestions a few days before. He took up Chamberlain's argument that rural migration into an overcrowded labour market was attributable to "antiquated" land laws: "This, rightly or wrongly, is the notion in . . . manufacturing minds", he asserted with scant regard for the evidence of the polls.[76]

There was another echo of Chamberlain in Churchill's impatience with Salisbury's wish for a modest church reform bill, prompted by the adverse publicity when the parson's freehold protected an incumbent manifestly unfit for a cure of souls. The premier admitted that anything of the sort required "wary walking". Churchill recalled the disruption of party by the Public Worship Regulation Bill, seeing in ecclesiastical legislation drawn up by a cabinet and whipped through parliament "a monstrosity and possibly a profanity". They were, Salisbury assured him, in broad agreement on the reform of parliamentary procedure, which Churchill decided to treat as urgent in the second half of December. The two of them met with Hicks Beach, more and more in demand to check, and soothe, his friend, to discuss the ministry's presentation of itself in the situation they faced after the election. Churchill got enough to satisfy him personally and politically; the Queen's Speech contained bills for elected county councils in Britain and Ireland; the purchase of glebes by the state to be let to agricultural labourers; simplifying and cheapening the transfer of landownership in the interests of the many; and applying principles derived from the Irish Land Acts to the crofting areas of Scotland, the scenes of a persistent agitation for several years past. An Irish university bill was also prepared, but omitted from the Speech.[77] Salisbury and the cabinet recognized "the necessity of a move in the democratic direction" on local government and other matters: his and their caution reflected the fact that it was not possible to be "a legislating machine" with no more than 249 members in the new Commons. Churchill was not blind to their predicament, and had argued that if the government could not realistically propose what he wanted, they should resign and devote themselves in opposition to restraining "liberal zeal".[78]

Churchill was only superficially a radical and a democrat, but his acute tactical sense told him that "If the Newport programme is not . . . presented to Parliament in a large and generous measure, the Whigs will be justified in their contention that it did not signify real progressive legislation". It was hard to deny the force of this. He had a strong case too, for compelling the cabinet to take seriously his detailed proposals for reforming parliamentary procedure. They went to a cabinet committee after he had threatened resignation. It was a problem exacerbated, but not created, by Irish obstruction from the late 1870s. The legislature of a modern industrial state needed to sit for longer and transact more business than its predecessors. Salisbury was right, however, to single out as "rather perilous – and sure [to] . . . be keenly resisted" a ministerial power to enforce the closure of debate at the end of a sitting.[79] His advice to Churchill not to rush the cabinet on this question and to trust to his chairmanship helps explain how he managed to keep a "strange creature" – Cranbrook's description – in a ministry to which his parliamentary talents – not his demagoguery – were considered indispensable. The younger man's temperament demanded constant reassurance. "You mistook my attitude if you thought it adverse to you", said the premier in the course of these exchanges; something he had to repeat on numerous occasions.[80]

Yet there was little difference – none, Brett told Chamberlain – between Tories and Liberals; both were moving "in a democratic direction". Churchill did not see any difference in foreign or colonial policy, and Chamberlain's radical programme, to the extent that it was radical, had not had the hoped-for impact.[81] It is important not to overestimate the apprehension that Gladstone or Salisbury, Chamberlain or Churchill, might translate their rhetoric into definite ideas for truly radical change. The speculation about a Liberal split when Hartington and Chamberlain disputed the succession to Gladstone did not assume the existence of a great ideological divide in the party. By contrast, Gladstone's resolve to set up a Dublin parliament was deeply divisive, compared at the time and later to Peel's decision to repeal the Corn Laws. Many of those who were to follow him could not share his rediscovered certainty that Anglo-Irish reconciliation was within their grasp. They felt, with Sir William Harcourt, that Ireland was irreconcilable; they were confronting "*race hatred*, which no redress of grievances, however far you may carry concession, will ever cure". Since virtually no one in Britain was willing to contemplate separation of the two countries, the alternatives were the maintenance of the *status quo*, by passing more coercion acts, or a degree of autonomy. Hartington, whose public statements had established him as the leader of a conservative Liberal secession, should there be one, inclined to the second, combined with land purchase on a large scale. He was writing after the Hawarden Kite, and doubted whether British voters would accept "any form of Home Rule, once fully understood".[82] What finally decided him to oppose Gladstone's Home Rule and land purchase bills was not so much British public opinion as the fate of the minority handed over to a parliament dominated by the beneficiaries of Fenianism and Ribbonism. Nothing short of armed intervention could protect them: and that would defeat the purpose of devolution. He was pledged to their defence in "honour and justice" by a speech at Belfast in November 1885.[83]

Unlike Salisbury and Hartington, Gladstone professed himself unable to find out "what protection the Protestants of Ulster want apart from the . . . four provinces".

On this point – whether the nationalists could be trusted not to abuse powers conceded by Westminster – there was no possibility of agreement, either then or after Gladstone revealed his detailed plans. He provided for the landlords but, effectively, left the rest of the minority to the tender mercies of their hereditary enemies. If there was nothing "revolutionary" about the newly elected MPs in Britain, that was not true of the Irish nationalists.[84] Once Gladstone's intentions were known, through his son's calculated indiscretion, there was intense activity behind the scenes, centring on Hartington. It was supposed that a coalition of Tories and seceding Liberals would only be viable under him, or perhaps Goschen, so strong was party feeling among the latter and their prospective partners. Intermediaries of varying status from both these camps, and from the Court, hastened to sound out the two principals. Before Christmas the Tory Duke of Manchester, the complaisant husband of Hartington's mistress, reported, with permission, that the future chief of the Liberal Unionists was firmly against anything like an Irish parliament or a central board in Dublin. Salisbury was right to be cautious and wait for the break with Gladstone: a fortnight later Hartington thought the "best solution" was Home Rule with the landlords bought out. Manchester, a large landowner in Ulster, was on the periphery of Irish politics; he had never before discussed them with Hartington. Disraeli's ennobled private secretary, Lord Rowton, falls into a different category; a link between the monarch, the government and Liberals trying to make up their minds to defy Gladstone.[85]

While she was not informed of Carnarvon's interview with Parnell, the Queen raised no objection to the Tory ministry's exploration of Home Rule. The news of Gladstone's conversion to that policy impelled her to do all she prudently could to frustrate it and him. She had long since come to regard him as dangerously radical and unpatriotic. She begged Goschen and Hartington to distance themselves from their leader: "Out of this might come a coalition, in time", she wrote to the former three days after the Hawarden Kite flew. In mid-January Derby's diary recorded Salisbury's acquiescence in the suggestion that he should serve under Hartington, keeping the Foreign Office for himself. Hartington, like Salisbury, was waiting on events. He had let the premier know, through Manchester, that he could not speak for other Liberals without consulting them. Only Goschen was sure to follow if Hartington broke with Gladstone, Rowton advised the Queen's private secretary, Ponsonby: she should avoid taking a prominent part in the current manoeuvrings. Ponsonby, who did not see eye to eye with his employer on Ireland, was pursuing a policy of his own. He wanted Gladstone and Salisbury to confer; he still expected the premier to bring forward Home Rule: "At least he said so at Newport." This is a good example of the prevailing atmosphere. At the beginning of January Salisbury thought it useless to approach Hartington or Goschen: by the end of the month Churchill believed he would be prepared to lead his colleagues into a Hartington ministry.[86]

Four members of the last Liberal government, including Hartington, the only commoner, declined to rejoin Gladstone when he set about forming a government in February. Chamberlain, and another radical, G.O. Trevelyan, went in on the understanding that the Liberals must, in their turn, try to arrive at a settlement of the Irish question that covered, in Gladstone's summary, "land . . . [and] the other great members of the trilogy, social order, and autonomy".[87] If Parnell was unreasonable and stood out for nothing less than Home Rule on his terms, Chamberlain hoped the Liberal government would resign and let the Tories coerce: "They will be supported for the purpose by a clear majority in the country and probably in the House". Although he had declared against Home Rule before the election, Chamberlain's history as a critic of Irish landlordism and of coercion had not prepared him for outright opposition to the Irish party, whose commitment to undoing the Union he had, like Churchill, never taken seriously enough. His departure from the government in March, unable to accept a full-blown parliament for Ireland, was both a loss and a gain for Gladstonian Liberalism. The defeat of Gladstone's Irish bills in the Commons by the combination of Hartington and Chamberlain with the opposition was a consequence, if the fate of the legislation was not decided until the last minute. He gained, however, by driving Chamberlain out of the party, which became more conservative without him. Chamberlain realized that he had no hope of recasting Liberalism in his image. Gladstone had consolidated his hold on the party so closely identified with him: his challenger's distinctive radicalism was, as he himself foresaw, "smashed".[88]

Salisbury had not foreseen Chamberlain's defection. He anticipated that on the defeat of Home rule, which he expected in the Lower House, Hartington would be the obvious choice to succeed Gladstone, unless the Liberal cabinet opted for the dissolution of a parliament only a few months old. Salisbury did not see how the Tories could govern long dependent on the votes of Hartington and Chamberlain with their respective followers, presumed to be mutually antagonistic. The Tory leader's aim was fusion with the Liberal right; essential, in his judgement, to good, by which he meant stable, parliamentary government in Britain. He was not sanguine about the prospect of fusion in the short term: Hartington and those gathering round him would persist in thinking of themselves as Liberals. The personal rivalry between Hartington and Chamberlain was an added complication. It might not always work in favour of the Tories, as it did when Hartington took the step of voting against the new Liberal government on a non-Irish question with an echo of the "unauthorized programme". "I could not let myself be dragged after Chamberlain", he explained to his mistress.[89] Chamberlain, however, was already modifying the tone and content of his radical politics, disappointed by the programme's reception in the towns. Two days before resigning from the Gladstone cabinet because all his requirements for limiting the action of a Dublin parliament had not been met, the "real Chamberlain" talked without reserve to A.J. Balfour and others. Chamberlain was for strong government, "crushing" Ireland, if necessary, and undertaking "very large" domestic reforms. But, "holding myself quite free in any official capacity to use opposite language", he said he did not want to introduce the statutory tenant-right of the 1881 Irish Land Act into Britain, as he had seemed to imply in recent speeches.[90]

Balfour welcomed Chamberlain as a prospective ally, one whom Tories would not find "lukewarm and slippery", unlike Hartington and his political friends. Salisbury was sceptical, repelled by Chamberlain's cynicism in private: "He has not yet persuaded himself that he has any convictions: and therein lies Gladstone's infinite superiority". He suspected that the rift with Gladstone was caused by personal antagonism rather than differences of principle, but Edward Hamilton, though a devoted Gladstonian, remarked that Chamberlain should be given "credit for honesty of purpose". The sacrifice that he made was real: "The mantle of Mr. Gladstone must have fallen upon him".[91] By the time he resigned, the radical knew that the Liberals were rallying to Gladstone as he maintained that he was only doing what the Tories had it in mind to do when he proposed self-government, with safeguards, and land purchase on a grand scale. Sir Henry James, who went with Hartington, was reported as saying that "Home Rule of some kind must be faced . . . but he cannot bring himself as yet to it". Some supporters of Home Rule were similarly troubled: Spencer, whose conversion was particularly important to Gladstone, did not pretend to be "keen" when Ponsonby spoke to him. "In all great reforms the leaders are always keen", reflected the royal adviser, "But those who talk of Home Rule talk more in the 'What else can you do?' tone".[92]

Gladstone made up for the lack of enthusiasm among his ministers. He turned the tables on Chamberlain by appealing to the masses against the classes; a tactic that perturbed his warmest admirers. The more excitable members of London Society denounced Gladstone to each other, at Liberal and Tory houses, for having raised the spectre of imminent civil war throughout the British state. They frightened themselves with the dire consequences of the developing crisis for financial stability and the economy. Their fears were excusable when the commander-in-chief, the Duke of Cambridge, said openly that if Protestant Ulster rose against Home Rule, the army would refuse to put down the rebellion. Salisbury's speeches, and Churchill's, between February and the rejection of Gladstone's proposals in early June sought an affirmation of the national will to preserve the Union and stand by Irish loyalists.[93] Safeguards to accompany Home Rule must be illusory, said Salisbury in February, "once set up a legislature in Dublin, and that legislature will make an independent nation". It was Parnell's message to the people. For the loyal minority: Home Rule spelt "absolute slavery", and for the empire, as a whole, mortal danger: "I beseech you to think of India". Britain's abandonment of the loyalists would tell the world, and her subject peoples everywhere, that she was retreating from greatness and empire. Privately doubtful, nevertheless, about the popularity of opposition to Home Rule, he strove to encourage it in working-class Tories by linking the struggle with their practical concerns. The party's successes at the polls in London and Lancashire "disposes for ever of the idea that we have any cause to fear the judgement of the working man". He treated as "absolutely false" the reports that he had been poised to give Home Rule. Land purchase, which he continued to support, was not to be rushed through "like a hurricane". The British taxpayer who was to fund its operation under a Dublin parliament would find that the loans were as unsafe in self-governing Ireland as in the Latin American republics proverbial for defaulting.[94]

The speech touched one of the chords of old Toryism in its prophecy of clerical domination in Home Rule Ireland: "The worst government in the world is the government of priests"; though he quickly added, "*corruptio optimi pessima*", the reservation was probably lost on his mass audience. If the Catholic South of Ireland was to have the right of self-determination, so should the Protestant North. He endorsed Churchill's prediction in Belfast on 22 February that Ulster's resistance was unlikely "to remain within the lines of . . . constitutional action".[95] Salisbury scorned the charge of "some great illegality" in the Ulstermen's preparations to defend themselves against enemies bent on suppressing "any independent and free life" in Ireland. To Granville's suggestion that Tories were leaving "the dirty work" of fighting Home Rule in the Commons to their Liberal allies, he replied, "What is clean work . . . in Lord Granville's opinion? I suppose it is turning right round on all your . . . opinions from mere political necessity". The City was reminded that business confidence rested ultimately on national security: Ireland's history of siding with powers hostile to Britain showed what to expect if she obtained self-government; Britain's foes would have a base "at our very doors". The Anglo-Irish connection, he allowed, "has been full of trouble", but the safety of the empire demanded its perpetuation: "I fear there is no remedy . . . It is a chronic disease". This frankness was surpassed when he addressed the National Union on 15 May. His opponents thought he had gone too far. He began by saying there was no objection in principle to extending British local government reforms to Ireland, provided they were not "a step to something very different", and the minority was protected. But the timing and scope of the concession must be carefully judged. While Gladstone was "not . . . dishonest . . . his assurances cannot be trusted". Free institutions were not for everyone, for "Hottentots", Indians and even some Continental nationalities – he mentioned Russians. The Greeks had not made the best use of them. The Irish, "habituated to the use of knives and slugs", were unfit for ordered freedom, really the prerogative of Teutonic races.[96]

"Salisbury's speech!!" exclaimed Gladstone. It had continued with an attack on the Irish Catholic church. The authority and influence of Catholicism had been "grievously misused" in Ireland; history and race were too strong for its undoubted virtues. Landlords, Protestants, the entire loyalist population, which included some Catholics, were the contemporary victims of racial and religious persecution, whatever wrongs the Celtic and Catholic majority had suffered in the past. He dwelt on the savagery of agrarian violence inseparable from nationalist agitation. His alternative policy to Gladstone's, as stated on this occasion, became famous: twenty years of resolute government, and much less than the cost of buying out the landlords spent on resettling a million Irishmen on the Canadian prairie. The declaration was immediately caricatured as "manacles and Manitoba". It was indeed an "extraordinary speech"; astonishing in a politician regarded as a statesman, some Tories did not like it.[97] The speaker seemed not to care whom he offended so long as he reached the British democracy; Gladstone played on class, and Salisbury on national, feeling. The justification of Salisbury's language lay in his insistence that Ireland was not one but "two deeply divided and antagonistic nations". This was the weak point in Gladstone's case, which Salisbury exploited with a genuine passion that deeply impressed even those who disagreed with him. Ireland was not, and could never be, another Canada, all but independent and freely associated with Britain; the restrictions placed on an Irish parliament in Gladstone's bill acknowledged the fact. Hartington and Chamberlain did not then emulate Salisbury's shocking candour. To have done so would have made it very difficult to look forward, as both did, to being reunited before long with the main body of Liberals. But their position was in essence the same as that set out by Salisbury.[98]

Balfour was not alone among the Tories in privately wishing to see Irish MPs removed from Westminster, as the government's bill provided. They were "a solid vote . . . for every Socialistic and subversive proposal . . . likely to be made by the extreme Left". Salisbury's nephew, unlike his uncle, was a reactionary at heart. However, Chamberlain made a continued Irish presence in the House of Commons an absolute requirement, one that Gladstone would not go far enough to meet. Tories had to fight the battle against Home Rule in the Commons, and the ensuing general election, on Chamberlain's terms.[99] He did not intend to cut himself off from Liberalism. After the fateful vote on the night of 7/8 June when ninety-three Liberals voted with the opposition in rejecting the Home Rule bill on its second reading, he explained to Balfour how an understanding might be reached between Tories and anti-Gladstonian Liberals if they were the joint victors in the election which Gladstone proceeded to call. Chamberlain had declined to appear on the same platform with Tories during the fight to defeat the bill and would not join a Tory-dominated administration. Nor did he think that Hartington, who had shared a platform with Tories, could do so. "I do not care about the appearance of power", he said; "what I desire is the reality".[100] He would exact his price for co-operation: and, it transpired, Salisbury was ready to pay it. In the meantime, praising the Liberal Unionists for their patriotism and organizing an electoral pact that ensured their survival, Salisbury fought the election on "one great issue . . . the . . . empire . . . we have inherited . . . the glory of us all". He contrasted the righteous unity of the Unionists, Tory and Liberal, with Gladstone's reckless tactics: "He sets masses against classes". A near-revolutionary situation existed in Ireland – and he capitalized on it. If the Home Rule cause had initially attracted moderate men, especially in Britain, it must end, if it triumphed, in "cruelty, bloodthirstiness, treachery and contempt for every human tie". Unionists responded to this powerful rhetoric: it drove the Gladstonians on to the defensive.[101]

# CHAPTER NINE

# *The New Conservatism in Practice*

## The General Election of 1886 and Virtual Coalition

At the previous election the number of unopposed returns was by far the lowest on record: fourteen in Great Britain, if university seats are excluded; thirteen Liberals and a solitary Conservative. Barely six months later there were no contests in 149 British seats, outside the universities, returning 109 Conservatives and Liberal Unionists against forty Gladstonian Liberals. The resources of both parties were strained by having to fight another election so soon: but Liberal finances and organization suffered badly for the secession of so many MPs. In those British constituencies which saw a contest the Liberal share of the vote dropped by four and a half per cent in England and Wales, rising very slightly in Scotland. As Salisbury had predicted, Home Rule moved the politicians more than the voters. The Tories, with 316 seats all told, up from 249 in 1885, relied on the seventy-seven Liberal Unionists to keep Gladstone out of power when he made way for Salisbury in July, confident that the victory of Home Rule, his last great cause, could not be long delayed. It did not seem probable that the Unionist allies would be able to persuade a democratized electorate to coerce Ireland indefinitely: or that their alliance was strong enough to bear the strain put upon it by the contrasting personalities and opinions of Salisbury, Churchill, Hartington and Chamberlain. Against the odds, Salisbury held the supporters of the Union together by widening the area of agreement to create a Palmerstonian consensus on a range of other issues besides Ireland. Tory policies were steadily subsumed under Unionist policies; a new Conservatism on a Unionist basis replaced the old. The process took time: but, in Salisbury's judgement, there was no alternative. Although neither Hartington nor Chamberlain was yet prepared to take office under the Tories, their co-operation brought a virtual coalition into being on the lines that Chamberlain sketched for Balfour before the election.[1]

In its early years Unionism was sustained by the depth of its convictions about the Irish question, and by the seceding Liberals' distrust and resentment of Gladstone.

Salisbury exploited these feelings in the 1886 election campaign. Speaking at Leeds on 18 June, he opened with an appeal to the working-class fears of Celtic Irish immigration which were a feature of the Victorian scene. Home Rule, if it came, must bring "anarchy and civil war" as the British Protestant minority fought an implacable enemy. The influx of pauperized immigrants fleeing from political and economic collapse would "demoralize the labour market . . . lower . . . wages . . . to that terrible level . . . known in economics as the starvation point . . . every work-man in England . . . will feel the results of our fatal Irish policy". In the prolonged recession, there was already not enough work to go round. The sombre message, delivered with all the authority of a party leader and former prime minister, had an impact which the Liberals strove to minimize. James Kitson, president of the National Liberal Federation, answered Salisbury directly, claiming that Home Rule and its benefits would draw the resident Irish back to their own country. Moreover, argued Kitson, a large employer, a self-governing and peaceful Ireland should be a better market for British industry. Ireland, Salisbury reiterated, was "two nations . . . Our history is a long promise to the loyalist inhabitants". To desert them in the face of such savage foes would be to incur "contempt in every quarter of the globe, and . . . loss in every dependency where your flag floats victorious and unquestioned".[2] It was the lower middle- and working-class voters whom Salisbury addressed with these arguments. The Unionists were very well supported above those social levels. Gladstone's language about class had upset money, whose influence, Hamilton remarked, was pervasive against the offending party, and far more powerful than the displeasure of the aristocracy.[3]

Gladstone's prestige suffered from his compact with the Parnellites and the National League, whose methods he had so recently denounced. Salisbury, too, was compelled to repeat his not very convincing denials that the Tories had contemplated a similar bargain themselves. Chamberlain, who seemed more radical to the public than he really was, carried his Birmingham stronghold for Unionism, but even in the West Midlands his co-operation with Toryism raised suspicions about his motives. The Unionists were helped by the respect felt for a less able and less eloquent politician, Hartington. He, it was said among those closest to Gladstone, "has come best out of the whole business". When John Morley came to write his classic but necessarily circumspect biography of Gladstone, his hero's "machinations" at this period struck him "more and more as the most absolutely indefensible thing in Mr Gladstone's career . . . There were only two honest men . . . Hartington and Parnell". Hartington had been, so far as the world knew, quite consistent in objecting to Irish self-rule; although he had wavered in private. He had led the Liberals in the Commons for five years during Gladstone's semi-retirement after 1875, and was expected to succeed him in the 1880s. If no one ever suspected Hartington of brilliance, his showing in the debates on the Home Rule bill, and on the platform, enhanced his stature. He expressed, less forcefully than Salisbury but with considerable effect, the view that it was morally impossible to entrust the lives and property of the Irish minority to the nationalists.[4] Salisbury thought he was too suggestible, too easily "got at". As he made clear to everyone, Hartington was much less hostile than Chamberlain and some other Liberal rebels to Gladstone. He did not feel inclined to call his former chief "the most conscienciously [sic] unscrupulous leader . . . in the history of English parties", the language of Lord Northbrook, another member of the Liberal cabinet in 1880–85.[5]

Hartington was in an extremely strong position both before and after the 1886 election. His following among the Liberal Unionists heavily outnumbered Chamberlain's. As anticipated, Salisbury offered him the premiership when Gladstone resigned without meeting the new parliament. He declined: the reaction of the Liberal Unionists as a whole, and his own misgivings, precluded acceptance. He did not need reminding that, in Chamberlain's words to Henry James, "it would be a sort of historical catastrophe that the head of the Devonshires should become a Tory official". An unashamed philistine and a devotee of the turf, who gave the misleading impression of being lazy and quickly bored by political life, Hartington was someone in whom Chamberlain, despite their clashes in Gladstone's cabinet, recognized a genuine Liberal.[6] The weight of his family traditions was reinforced by the strenuous objections of Derby, among others. If Hartington were to enter and head a coalition, the rupture with Liberalism would be final; not many Liberal Unionists were disposed to follow him. He would be separated from Chamberlain, "to the injury of both"; the Tories would be his masters and, Derby emphasized, "he could not rely on being treated with good faith: Salisbury might easily find a pretext for breaking up the concern . . . when once the breach between Hartington and the Liberals was complete". While Derby had personal reasons for disliking and distrusting Salisbury, the future premier did not yet inspire the confidence that cemented the Unionist alliance in the 1890s: its adherents, Tory and Liberal, variously found him too radical, or merely too unpredictable, and muttered about a chequered history in Tory politics. Hartington, however, wondered if he was right to reject the Tory offer. Salisbury and his party had exerted themselves to save Liberal Unionists from the electoral disaster which must otherwise have overtaken most of them outside Birmingham. It was also true that the incoming government was, in a real sense, answerable to Liberal Unionists. Without them, the Tories would have resumed their usual role since the Great Reform Bill as the party of opposition.[7]

The Tories, Hartington felt, had "a moral claim upon us". Derby concurred but argued, along with most leading Liberal Unionists, that it did not imply "absolute union". Hartington was not displeased to find Salisbury "desperate" for a coalition at their meeting on 24 July. Salisbury had been troubled by ill health in the form of eczema; possibly a nervous reaction to the strain of the past year. Rumour had it that the doctors did not think he was a good life.[8] Hartington's refusal to be prime minister left Salisbury with the problem of finding a replacement for himself at the Foreign Office to which he did not, for the moment, feel equal if, as in 1885–6, it was combined with the premiership. That there was no obvious candidate for the post of foreign secretary suited Salisbury quite well: he wanted a colleague who would be guided by him. The job was offered to Lord Lyons, ambassador at Paris and a professional diplomat, and to Cranbrook before going to Iddesleigh, not, Salisbury admitted, a "satisfactory" appointment.[9] In the absence of Hartington, Churchill was much the strongest, politically, of Salisbury's colleagues. Derby rightly considered Churchill "too eccentric and crazy to be trusted" but acknowledged that he had in effect "appointed himself" to be chancellor of the exchequer and leader of the House of Commons. He was the second man in the party and the new government, which was, like preceding Tory administrations since the Peelite exodus, short on ability. Salisbury treated him as a partner in power, taking care to keep him fully informed about appointments and policy. Hicks Beach, the previous chancellor and leader in the House, went to Ireland as chief secretary under a viceregal figurehead. Unionism was to be tested almost to its breaking point by an Irish agitation more formidable than ever, in purely political terms, because it could count on Gladstonian Liberal sympathy for a great deal, if not all, of what the nationalists said and did.[10]

The Liberal Unionists called the tune in Irish policy from the beginning: but it was one that Salisbury would have chosen to play. While Ireland could have "no separate existence" from Britain, Salisbury and his Liberal allies were agreed on the necessity of conciliatory measures, starting with a royal commission on the working of the Irish Land Acts which had the extension of land purchase in view. Ireland was so important to the government and Unionism that Churchill thought of the chief secretaryship for himself. His promotion to the Treasury with the leadership of the Commons gave him, at a relatively early age, the power and the opportunity for distinction that he craved. Chamberlain welcomed his rise, seeing in him an ally for change. A protégé of Churchill, Henry Matthews, an English Catholic who as MP for an Irish constituency had flirted with Home Rule in the 1870s, became Home Secretary.[11] Another of his friends, Henry Chaplin, refused the Local Government Board without a seat in the cabinet. It went, outside the cabinet, to C.T. Ritchie, a self-styled representative of plebeian Toryism, who protested furiously to Churchill at the choice of Derby's brother, Frederick Stanley, for the Board of Trade, to which he aspired. To balance the prominence given to Churchill and his associates, Salisbury retained men, and notably Cross, with whom he would have liked to dispense. The weakness of Salisbury's team was palpable.[12] Hartington's proposal to travel abroad for several months in the recess elicited an immediate remonstrance from the premier. Parliament did not meet again until the New Year, but it would be "a very serious misfortune" if the Tory cabinet had to reach decisions on its British and Irish legislation without consulting him: "no one else could take your place. Forgive me for having written with so little circumlocution". The appeal, backed up by the Queen, was irresistible. Apart from anything else he was the Tories' indispensable link with Chamberlain.[13]

A small minority among the Liberal Unionists, the Birmingham radical and his followers exercised an influence out of all proportion to their numbers. When the Gladstonians captured the National Liberal Federation and the Birmingham Liberal Association which he had created, he organized a new "caucus" in the birthplace of the old. Birmingham was henceforth a Unionist city and his secure electoral base. By contrast, Hartington was not sure of re-election in his Lancashire seat if he took office. The newly formed Liberal Unionist Association, the rebels' substitute at national level for the Federation, reflected the division in its ranks: it had two whips, one for the Hartingtonians and one for the radicals. Chamberlain believed in the possibility of Liberal reunion after Gladstone retired or died. In the interval, he told the Association, the Tories should be able to rely on their support, not merely for the session about to begin, but for several years. Churchill, with whom he talked freely for some time, saw that he knew what the government was thinking, and apprised the premier of his views.[14] Salisbury and Chamberlain had said of each other that they could not sit in a cabinet together: it meant "too sharp a curve" for all concerned. The Liberal Unionists, Chamberlain advised Hartington, should stick to a simple rule: "never vote with the Tories unless they are in danger, and . . . vote against them whenever we can safely do so". An independent posture was necessary to maintain their credibility as Liberals, without which they were not much use to the Tories. Churchill's sudden resignation on 20 December obliged them to reconsider their position.[15]

Churchill resigned alone except for a peer in minor office who had been refused promotion and took several weeks to leave. But the departure of their leader in the elected chamber exposed the Tories' crippling lack of confidence in themselves as a party of government, heavily outgunned by the parliamentary strengths of the Gladstonian front bench. Hicks Beach, less of a strong man than his bearing and short temper suggested, was for a collective resignation: he deemed Churchill irreplaceable; the government could not survive without him. The advocate in 1884 of democratizing the distribution of seats was utterly dismayed by Churchill's action in resigning because he could not push to the lengths he desired a policy of economy in public expenditure that emulated Gladstone's thrift with the taxpayer's money. Hicks Beach confessed to Salisbury that he doubted whether "the country *can* be governed, nowadays, by persons holding what you and I should call moderately Conservative opinions". He feared a combination of Churchill and Chamberlain, the subject of unceasing speculation for a couple of years. There were two courses open to the Tories: if they could not succeed in fusing with the Hartingtonians, "I think we can better serve our country . . . in opposition than in office".[16] Salisbury, who expected this from Hicks Beach, had approached Hartington with a renewed offer of coalition and the premiership. The Tories were so weak in the Commons without Churchill that "we run a very great risk of being broken in pieces". Failing a Unionist coalition, there must be a Home Rule ministry: "I do *not* see any alternative". The Queen again seconded Salisbury's appeal.[17] "Shaken and uncertain" about his first refusal in July, Hartington found that his political friends were still opposed to his acceptance. He therefore replied that he would only form a coalition government to avert a dissolution, or on the resignation of the Salisbury ministry construed as an admission of Tory inability to rule unaided. "I said", Salisbury telegraphed Hicks Beach, "I could not make, on behalf of the Conservative party, a confession which would not be true and would be humiliating". Moreover, as Churchill realised almost at once, Salisbury was not going to give in to him, "regardless of what he may bring down in his fall".[18]

The huge resentment of Churchill among more orthodox, and more scrupulous, Tories now came to the surface. W.H. Smith warned the premier on the day Churchill resigned, that he and other members of the cabinet could not put up with Churchill's attempt to impose his will and policies on them. Salisbury had never had any illusions about Churchill as a colleague. After two months' experience of his ways in this government, he thought him "capable of all kinds of monkey tricks".[19] They disagreed on foreign policy, and on the local government bill for England and Wales then under consideration as well as the budget proposals. Churchill chose to progress from hints of resignation to an explicit threat when his demands for bigger reductions in the Army and Navy estimates were resisted by Smith at the War Office and Lord George Hamilton at the Admiralty. In the state of Europe at that time, the Service ministers were right to stand up to the chancellor, who linked his finance with an alternative foreign policy inspired by opportunism in domestic politics and a dangerous misunderstanding of European realities. Salisbury, who recognised that Churchill's undoubted gifts made him a, and perhaps the, potential successor, believed a highly strung man had succumbed to the double pressure of the Treasury and the lead in the Commons, "and when his nerves go, his judgement goes altogether". The party rounded on Churchill: "My position is completely *déclassé*", he wrote despairingly to Chamberlain on 24 December, unable to discern what the future held for him. Oblivious of the exasperation with him that had built up inside the cabinet, he complained that the Tories had thrown him aside, having no further use for a devoted servant of the party.[20] Salisbury had been admonished by Cranbrook, who expressed the general feeling, for his reluctance to assert the premier's authority over his colleagues, and over Churchill in particular.[21]

Salisbury's defence was that he had deferred to Churchill "as much as I possibly could", in the interests of the Union which transcended those of their party. He did not, as Churchill suspected, plan the confrontation between them. Salisbury understood him, perhaps, better than did anyone else in political life. Approached by a supporter who had listened to Churchill's tale of "coldness and indifference", Salisbury responded with a brief analysis of his former colleague's personality: he was "quite untrained: both in impulsiveness and variability, and in a tendency which can only be described by the scholastic word, 'bully', he presents the characteristics of extreme youth". "Whether there is any growth left in him", he added, "I do not know".[22] Aware that his bluff had been called, and conscious of having made an irretrievable blunder, Churchill very soon regretted, bitterly, his separation from Salisbury, that "mighty intellect", who "might have made what he pleased of me". He was wrong, too, in supposing that the premier had given in to the "innate Toryism" of all the rest of the cabinet, so ruling out a junction with the Liberal Unionists. Those allies were bound more tightly to the Tories as a result of the blow he had dealt the ministry. After Hartington's second refusal, they proceeded to discuss reunion with the Gladstonians: but the outcome in March 1887 confirmed that neither side could move without compromising their political integrity. As Harcourt, one of the negotiators in 1887, had observed to Chamberlain during the debates on the Home Rule bill, Salisbury's Irish policy and a government headed by him were the inevitable choice of those who shrank from Gladstone and a self-governing Ireland.[23]

George Goschen, unseated at the last election, was the means by which Salisbury shored up the Unionist alliance at another critical point in its short existence to date. A financial expert, partner in a City bank before he sat in the cabinets of

Russell and Gladstone, Goschen needed a constituency, and the Tories a chancellor of the exchequer. He had become such a conservative Liberal that a Tory seat could be expected to return him. Hartington gave his blessing to the transaction, which he considered left him free to explore Liberal reunion. Although two Liberal Unionist peers who were also invited to join the cabinet, Lansdowne and Northbrook, declined, Goschen's presence in the government gave it new strength.[24] Salisbury consulted him on all important business. The leadership in the Commons passed to W.H. Smith, one of those very respectable, originally middle-class Tories whom Churchill had mocked. The appointment of this poor speaker smacked of desperation: but his palpable honesty and dogged courage endeared him to backbenchers.[25] The fourth member of the cabinet's inner circle over the next five years was Balfour, after he succeeded Hicks Beach, who was temporarily threatened with blindness, as chief secretary for Ireland in March 1887. In the reconstruction of the ministry in January, Salisbury took the Foreign Office. Goschen had urged Iddesleigh's removal on the premier: although the foreign secretary's policy was substantially, if not entirely, that of the premier, worsening health had affected his performance in the cabinet and outside it. Salisbury pressed other posts on him, which were refused. The premier's distress at this unavoidable ruthlessness was compounded when, days later, Iddesleigh collapsed and died before his eyes at Downing Street. Salisbury's habitual reticence about his emotions lifted in reply to a genuinely sympathetic letter from, of all people, Randolph Churchill: "I had . . . for the first time . . . seriously wounded his [Iddesleigh's] feelings. As I looked upon the dead body . . . I felt that politics was a cursed profession".[26]

Both Hartington and the Tories generally objected to making Goschen leader in the Commons as well as chancellor: Hartington because it would identify Liberal Unionists too closely with the governing party, and the Tories because Goschen still called himself a Liberal. Churchill told himself and others that he had been sacrificed to pure Toryism, which Goschen's conservatism would reinforce. He called himself "a moderate progressive politician" who, as such, was regarded by his party with "unrelenting distrust and contempt". It was a grotesque, self-pitying distortion of accepted political fact. His "Dartford programme" of October 1886, billed as radical, inflated the significance of what he, in the course of his speech, said were "matters which ought not to excite party controversy".[27] Cranbrook, whose conservatism was unquestioned, remarked of the speech in his diary: "The Radicals profess to see Radicalism in it . . . I know . . . the progress of democracy involves consequences in all kinds of legislation". Churchill largely reproduced the content of Salisbury's Newport address without the same attention to detail in discussing the impact on private rights. Chamberlain nevertheless saw an opportunity in Churchill's breach with the party, and promised "cordial co-operation . . . you and I are equally adrift from the old organizations". For a couple of years they talked over and canvassed the idea of a new party, born of their joint inspiration. This rather shadowy threat helped Salisbury to enact some far-reaching legislation during the long spell in government that ended in 1892.[28] Writing to Churchill's mother, the widowed Duchess of Marlborough, an old friend who believed her son was sadly misunderstood, Salisbury thought him deficient in the arts of political management:

"as he gains experience he will . . . see that both wings of the [Conservative] party must be considered, those who are most Tory as well as those who are most liberal". The sensitivities of the landed class, their class, had to be taken into account: "without them our party would speedily go to pieces".[29]

Salisbury's rhetoric about change and class seldom made Tories uneasy, while Churchill's displays of cynicism in his social contacts with politicians of all parties naturally sowed distrust. The premier was not only expressing sincerely held views on the need for state intervention to accompany democracy: he was reaching out to Chamberlain, who gave Unionism a radical dimension it could not do without. While Chamberlain's inclusion in the alliance had, and continued to have, the effect of circumscribing his radicalism, he could exert a considerable influence in favour of reforms – the Allotments Act; elected county councils; and, above all, free primary education – which had figured in his "unauthorized programme". In return, he had to refrain from assailing the aristocracy and the Church, the favourite targets of a good radical: but the fundamental conservatism of the country, in which both Salisbury and Gladstone believed, would anyway have been too strong for him. Through Unionism and his emerging partnership with Salisbury, Chamberlain achieved more, as he was to acknowledge, than he could probably have done in a Gladstonian Liberal party unenthusiastic about his social reforms. Hartington and his much larger section of the Liberal Unionists did not always find it easy to keep up with the legislative pace set by Chamberlain and Salisbury. But after the failure of the talks on Liberal reunion at the beginning of 1887, they, and Chamberlain's radical unionists with them, were locked into a virtual coalition with the Tories. Consequently, Hartington, Goschen and like-minded Unionists became more, and not less liberal, for their flight from Gladstone. The extensive Salisbury–Goschen correspondence illustrates the process, one of continuous adjustment to the requirements of a progressive policy.[30]

## The Pacification of Ireland

In one of Salisbury's letters to Goschen there is an arresting reference to "the Irish Republic of the future". He did not believe, and probably never had believed, that the Irish were assimilable by Britain, or, as he almost always referred to her, 'England'. A decade later he commented that while the Boers whom his country were fighting would surely be reconciled to British rule, like the Highlanders after Culloden, the Irish were "exceptionally difficult, owing to their religion", to subdue and absorb into a greater Britain. Religion and race were too powerful a combination for the government of a liberal state to overcome. In his speeches on the Irish question he had sought from the outset of his career to confront British public opinion with unpleasant facts: the implacable enmity of the Celtic Irish for their conquerors, and the enormity of leaving landlords and Protestants to their vengeance. He contrived to drive home these truths, and their implications, from the 1880s. For his time, at any rate, he held Irish separatism in check.[31]

It did not follow that liberalization of British rule in Ireland was excluded, once order had been restored after Gladstone and Parnell had undermined it to the point of breakdown. The Liberal Unionists were keen to see elective county government established on both sides of the Irish Sea, and Salisbury did not disagree with their arguments. Consistently with the views he had first stated on the 1870 Irish land bill, he wanted to extend land purchase, as the permanent solution to agrarian conflict. The uneasiness of British taxpayers and MPs about the repayment of Treasury advances to the tenants might be lessened if local representative institutions could be devised to shoulder, or at least share, the financial responsibility. Two more land purchase acts were passed by Salisbury's second ministry. A local government bill with safeguards against the abuse of power by nationalist majorities that appeared to contradict the principle of the legislation had to be withdrawn. Educational concessions to the Irish Catholic Church, notoriously difficult for any government in the Protestant climate of Britain, were attempted with mixed results. Lastly, the primitive economy on the Western seaboard of Ireland was the subject of unorthodox experiments in state intervention to raise the standard of life. All this was one side of the regime of Arthur Balfour from 1887 to 1892; the other was the restoration of order in the teeth of the nationalists' concerted efforts to impose their agrarian objectives on the landlords and by doing so to demonstrate the impotence of the authorities.[32]

Salisbury's first chief secretary in this government, Hicks Beach, was critical of Irish landlords for not being more "reasonable" in dealing with their tenantry. A typically paternal English squire, without personal experience of Irish landowner- ship and its trials, did not feel comfortable enforcing the letter of the law against small occupiers. They had been rendered liable to eviction by inability to pay judicial rents under the 1881 Land Act, fixed for a fifteen-year term when agricul- tural prices were higher. Salisbury was not indifferent to the plight of these small tenants. He showed himself receptive to Chamberlain's suggestion early in the ministry's life that legislation should distinguish between those who would not pay rent, and those who could not, as the recession worsened. He meant, however, to make that concession and others from a position of strength. Irish landlords, he said, speaking for the newspapers in September 1886, were doubtfully the owners of their properties, "more like mortgagees with a bad security". The combination of the Irish people's inveterate hostility, the curtailment of their rights by successive land acts and the economic situation had deprived landlords of the freedom to discharge the most significant functions of their class: "they can give very little assistance in maintaining social order and in conducting the government of the country". Land purchase to diffuse a peasant proprietary offered the only reason- able hope of "a new anchorage" for Irish society. The beneficiaries might come to identify the property rights they acquired with the law administered in the courts and with the British connection; he did not ever pretend to be sure, or even optimistic, of this outcome. Gladstone's land purchase bill of 1886 had been too ambitious, particularly in its time scale: the transfer of the land to its occupiers was not something that could be accomplished "at once". Meanwhile, the landlords must be defended and the law as it stood upheld.[33]

As democratic nationalism grew stronger in Ireland, the Catholic church was increasingly drawn into the never ending struggle for the land on the popular side. The vindication of Anglo-Saxon notions of right called for a direct assault upon this clerical involvement. Salisbury did not hesitate to stigmatize agrarian agitation and its methods as "systematized fraud . . . recommended by the highest among the religious teachers of the people". He described as "fundamentally wrong" the argument that repression and conciliation should go together: "They must 'take a licking' before conciliation will do them any good". Sir Redvers Buller, the general and Devonshire landlord made permanent under-secretary at Dublin Castle by the Tories to replace an advocate of Home Rule, pressed for the rejected policy, and was himself replaced on Beach's retirement.[34] Salisbury accompanied Balfour's appointment to succeed Beach with a major speech in which he sought to refute the Gladstonian contention that the principle of nationality which Britain had supported elsewhere in Europe should be recognized in Ireland. He compared Irish nationalism unfavourably with its Continental counterparts: they had "never . . . preached doctrines inconsistent with the most rudimentary morality", subversive of order and property. The Irish failed the test of civilized people: awareness that "the great object of society is that wrong should be redressed and . . . crime . . . punished". The victory of nationalism in Ireland through uncontrollable agrarian agitation and violence was not certain if Britain could rouse herself from "an evil dream . . . one of those nightmares where . . . danger or horror presses upon you . . . but something fetters your limbs and paralyses your energies . . . evil is never inevitable if you have the strength to resist it". It was a bid for the moral advantage in a public debate in which he and Unionism could not afford to be beaten. Liberal Unionists were murmuring that Ireland should be left to govern herself because otherwise ungovernable.[35]

"Our national fault", ran a memorable passage in this speech, "is that too much softness has crept into our councils, and we imagine that great national dangers can be conjured away by . . . platitudes and rosewater". The Irish question was a foretaste of other, greater questions on the international and domestic fronts: "vast controversies which shake society to its centre . . . are gathering", a glance at the strides that socialism was making on the Continent. The government's permanent coercion bill, introduced at the end of March 1887, showed that this was not mere rhetoric. While the most serious crimes – murder and wounding – remained triable by jury, intimidation, riot, boycotting, conspiracy to withhold rent, resisting lawful eviction and incitement to commit all these offences were to be dealt with summarily. Care was taken to avoid making martyrs out of those convicted: the bill contained a right of appeal from the court of summary jurisdiction and limited its sentences to a maximum of six months' hard labour. The operation of the law, moreover, was localized and discretionary, enforceable by the authorities in specified, or "proclaimed" districts. The Irish administration was also empowered to designate as dangerous an association whose activities were criminal, and to prosecute its members; a provision drawn to catch the National League.[36] The bill's realism, rather than its details, was unacceptable to the Gladstonian opposition, and unpalatable to Liberal Unionists. Liberals of every hue found it harder than others to swallow a measure that permanently abridged treasured civil liberties in what was supposedly an integral part of the United Kingdom. Smith, the leader of the House, urgently appealed to Hartington and his men for active help in getting the bill through, "as active as if they [had] . . . amalgamated with us". A little later, from the backbenches, Churchill warned Smith that ministers must fight their battles in the Commons and in Ireland with equal determination and discipline: "The loss of one entails the loss of the other".[37]

The Unionist alliance held. When the bill reached the Lords, Salisbury quoted the line, "If England to herself do prove but true", as he reaffirmed his government's belief in its policy. On the platform and at Westminster, commented Hicks Beach, still a member of the cabinet, without office, Unionists had to exploit the British voters' stolid conviction that the Irish were "inferior". "If you can convince him", wrote this usually shrewd politician, "that it isn't only a matter of landlords' rents, but whether we shall continue to govern Ireland – I don't think the Gladstonian agitation will do much harm". The Tories, with Salisbury and Balfour to the fore, prevented the Liberals from capturing public opinion with their protests at the invasion of liberties that were an Englishman's birthright. The purpose of Salisbury's powerful speeches was to make a national audience understand that the Irish were unworthy of enjoying those liberties to the same degree. The Liberal Unionists were particularly unhappy when it came to proclaiming the National League a dangerous association once the bill had passed. Chamberlain went so far as to vote with the Gladstonians on their motion attacking that step. The parliamentary struggle for coercion had nevertheless been won. It remained to be seen whether the battle in Ireland would be lost despite the new legal weapons at the government's disposal.[38]

Hartington had thought that a coercion bill could not be carried against the combined forces of the Liberal opposition and the nationalists. If it were, he told the Duchess of Manchester, popular resistance would defeat the legislation. As the heir to a great estate in the South of Ireland he felt "more and more hopeless . . . but I shall go on fighting as long as it is of any use". Both he and Chamberlain believed the government's Commons majorities hid its real weakness. The return of Churchill and the entry of Hartington into the cabinet were being canvassed. Salisbury was disinclined to heed the suggestions at that apparently critical point. The months spent forcing through the coercion bill and the procedural resolutions that enabled ministers to guillotine debate, had given them a confidence they had not had before.[39] In his correspondence with Balfour, Salisbury gave generally good, and sometimes detailed, advice on working the machinery of law enforcement, not easy when the personnel of the Irish administration were too often as despondent as Hartington and most of the Irish landlords about their prospects. "There is nothing for it but for you to form your own judgement upon every question of procedure, of law, of drafting, &c, &c", he advised Balfour in the autumn of 1887. They discussed tactics: what suited Dublin Castle might very well offend "English prejudice". If that consideration stopped the proclamation of a district, "do not avow a change of policy – even to your pillow: for pillows chatter in Ireland". As an intelligent firmness brought down violence and intimidation, Salisbury pointed out that their success in Ireland was actually making it more difficult to justify coercion to the

British public, "no longer compelled by fear to concede what it naturally dislikes". The Castle had been right to let a nationalist MP in poor health out of prison before the expiry of his sentence; he would have been "far more formidable dead than alive".[40]

The importance of winning what was in many respects a propaganda war led the government to encourage *The Times*, now a fervently Unionist paper, in its attempt to establish a link between Parnell himself and the extremists responsible for the violence of a decade, and specifically with the assassination of Lord Frederick Cavendish and T.H. Burke. Salisbury was eager to see the connection proved before the commission appointed under the special Act to investigate *The Times'* charges. "You say", he wrote in the draft of a letter to his attorney-general, "the government must not expose itself to the suspicion of desiring to fix this guilt upon their opponents. Why not?" He wanted the inquiry to prove Parnell's shared responsibility for a terrible crime "*if it exists* . . . and I have no objection to publish that desire at Charing Cross".[41] The note of doubt was warranted: *The Times'* most serious allegations against Parnell, relating to the murder of Cavendish and Burke, crumbled when shown to rest on the forgeries of a disreputable Dublin journalist, Richard Pigott, who promptly committed suicide. The government sustained a blow to its credibility, which contributed to a depressing succession of by-election defeats. Salisbury fought back: the commission had been set up by "a democratic Parliament . . . elected on a democratic suffrage", and he compared Parnell's idea of truth to that entertained by Baron Munchausen. When the inquiry concluded its protracted labours in February 1890, there was plenty of material in the evidence it had amassed to confirm not only the general relationship between nationalist politics and agrarian unrest but the countenance given to violence and the Fenian involvement with it.[42] If it was argued that the concessions wrung from government and the landlords vindicated the methods employed by agitators and conspirators, Salisbury condemned the moral reasoning without reservation: "You have . . . laid down a doctrine that the end justifies the means, more completely and more recklessly than any school of Jesuits has ever ventured to propose it". He fastened on the racial and the religious dimension of the conflict explored by the commission. He summed up its findings to mean, in practice, "all that is loyal, all that is Protestant" was at risk.[43]

The relevance of Protestantism to the Irish question in all its forms was undisputed a few months later. Parnell's enhanced popularity with British Liberals after the exposure of Pigott's forgeries did not last long. When he entered no defence as co-respondent in the O'Shea divorce, it angered the neo-puritanism in contemporary Britain that was particularly strong in the Liberal party. The Liberal intimation that it was embarrassing to have an adulterer for an ally diminished his leadership. Salisbury mocked the Liberals and savaged the anti-Parnellite nationalists for their self-righteousness: "They have raised one of the most difficult questions in political ethics – how far you are justified in refusing co-operation with a man because, in another field of action, he has done disgraceful things". If this was not quite what his audiences expected, he made the most of the aspect of Parnell's fall that was a gift to the Unionists. When the Irish Catholic bishops declared against Parnell, it could be, and was, taken on both sides of the Irish Sea as showing where power lay in the national movement. "We have seen Home Rule in action", said Salisbury of this clerical intervention, or dictation as he represented it. He dwelt, with relish, on the unedifying spectacle that priestly methods presented in the first of the by-election clashes between Parnell and his nationalist opponents. The Catholic Church's employment of mob violence against the fallen leader told the world what to expect from the ending of Britain's direct rule: "To me at least it is a matter of rejoicing that this . . . has happened". The Protestants of Ulster had every reason to fear "the ruthless hand . . . the sinister domination" of a highly politicized church.[44]

Through the early 1890s, he adverted to this proof, at once comic and shocking, that the Irish were unfit for self-rule. Could they, he asked the Primrose League, imagine Anglican clergymen leading their flocks to vote under threat of physical as well as spiritual punishment? As for nationalist Ireland's divided lay politicians, the ferocity and coarseness of their mutual abuse showed they were unworthy of being compared to the authentic heroes of nationalism – Cavour, Washington, or William Tell. Ireland aspired to independence but, unlike similar movements elsewhere, her national movement had never known "real self-devotion and real oppression". The factionalism that rent the Home Rule party was a fact; so, too, was the mildness of British coercion set against the treatment meted out by the Russians to the Poles, or by the Northern to the vanquished Southern states in America. The nicely calculated restrictions and penalties of the 1887 Criminal Law Amendment Act for Ireland, and the intelligent way in which it was administered, achieved what few people believed could be done without resorting to Draconian measures advocated by soldiers like Wolseley or London clubmen like the Prince of Wales. The thousand agrarian outrages reported in 1886 had been halved by the close of 1889. There were then 150 cases of boycotting against nearly 5000 in the summer of 1887; by January 1891 there were none at all.[45] The very effective weapons of the agrarian and the national struggle had been countered by making good the deficiency which W.H. Smith found at Dublin Castle in 1886 in "fibre and nerve". When the armed Irish constabulary fired on a rioting crowd at Mitchelstown in County Cork, in September 1887, killing two people, nationalists and Gladstonians seized on the incident to discredit "Balfourism", that is, rule with a stronger hand than any government had ventured to use since the advent of the Land League and its successor. Salisbury gave the Irish secretary his full backing, and advised rewriting police standing orders.[46]

His government, he said in November 1887, would not give in to "a policy of worry". "We", he announced to approving Conservatives at the National Union's Oxford conference, "are a Teutonic people. We hold steadily to our opinions". The tactics of nationalist MPs and their Liberal friends would not be allowed to succeed. Ministers faced nightly "the same speakers, the same inanities, the same vituperation expressed in the same brogue". Any one of his ministerial colleagues in the Commons was worth all eighty-six of the Irish tormentors. These robust assaults upon bitter enemies struck some as wanting in the *gravitas* associated with the premiership. They served several purposes: one was to put new heart into the embattled Unionist majority in the Commons, without whose steady support Balfour's talents as a debater and an administrator would have achieved little. To diminish the sympathy in Britain with imprisoned nationalists, Salisbury went further than his nephew when he drew an analogy between the Indian Mutiny, vividly remembered for its atrocities, and Irish unrest; the Indian rebels of the 1850s had not been the object of "any particular delicacy". Salisbury's aim was to toughen the liberal outlook of his compatriots, which was also his own. The harsher tone of Unionism and of imperialism that developed owed much to these pronouncements from some-one more sensitive to the abuse of power exercised by one race over another than were most of his contemporaries.[47]

In Salisbury's policy, repression and conciliation were two faces of the same coin. The fall of agricultural prices since judicial rents were fixed compelled the government to appoint a royal commission and then to act on its report. The recommendations resembled, quite closely, nationalist demands for immediate re-lief to the tenants pending the enlargement of land purchase. Unionists had voted down Parnell's bill of September 1886 which would have cut rents and arrears and brought into the land courts holders of long leases excluded from the benefits of previous legislation, an influential minority. The nationalists replied, as they had threatened, with a fresh offensive against the landlords. Under the "Plan of Campaign" tenants in the targeted estates who were refused reductions specified by the National League paid the reduced rents into a fighting fund for the maintenance of those evicted as a result. It was this initiative, designed to complete the destruction of the landlords' morale, which Balfour managed to contain. On more than a hundred estates, the owners submitted. Where they held out, with the forces of law and order deployed in strength and with, in acute cases, financial help from their wealthier brethren encouraged by government, the cost to the campaign's organizers strained the resources of the national movement as a whole. Both government and nationalists claimed victory when the outcome was more like a draw.[48]

At an early stage of the confrontation ministers framed the 1887 land bill to tide the landlords, tenants and themselves over the political and economic crisis of the moment. Parliament was bound by the 1881 Act to maintain both the judicial rents settled for fifteen years and the exclusion of long leaseholders from the legislation. Salisbury, the cabinet, and the Liberal Unionists outside it had to devise ways of getting round pledges too recent to be ignored without severe embarrassment. The royal commission proposed shortening the fifteen years to five, revising rents in line with prices and bringing leaseholders within an amended Act. Salisbury did not object to the last, although he would have preferred to see it done by a private member's bill. Government ought to distance itself from the innovation to prevent the "contagion" from spreading to Britain. Nor was he opposed to a joint application by landlord and tenant for the variation of the judicial rent. He felt the force of Balfour's view that a general reduction of rent less than halfway through the statutory term would be "fatal" to the landlords. A solution to this, the central problem, was sought in the so-called bankruptcy clauses of the bill as introduced into the Lords while the Commons were occupied with coercion. A tenant in arrears declared bankrupt, on the landlord's petition, or his own, would have his debts scheduled for repayment over a period to be determined by the court, as in the case of other bankrupts. Or, if the tenant were reluctant to be adjudged bankrupt, and wanted greater security he might apply, by way of a new equitable remedy, for a stay of execution, with arrears similarly repaid.[49] Balfour's explanatory memorandum sent to Chamberlain, whose inspiration was acknowledged, stated that those procedures should protect tenants against being driven out by "exorbitant" rents or the pressure of low prices. A large number of Irish evictions had always been initiated to obtain rent rather than to remove a tenant; in the late 1880s Balfour estimated that only a quarter of those served with notice to quit actually went. Under the government's proposals payment of "only an infinitesimal proportion of the arrears", he assured Chamberlain, would keep a tenant on his holding until the most obdurate landlord gave up trying to oust him.[50]

"The origin and defence" of the land bill, Salisbury explained to the Duke of Abercorn, a spokesman for the Irish landlords, was the need to balance the permanent repressive legislation that would "practically disarm" the tenants. There were "impossible rents" in prevailing conditions; both they and the consequent evictions must be curbed: "I have no wish to admit it on the face of an Act of Parliament if I can attain the object without doing so"; hence the face-saving device of bankruptcy proceedings. Conciliation had in fact to accompany repression, instead of preceding it: the coercion and land bills were introduced in the same week.[51] "Somehow or other", he said, "the fabric of social order had to be maintained", after the government were forced to substitute for a three year period the revision of rent that Parnell had demanded for the bill's elaborate provision to that end. Even the landlords criticized what had been devised to spare their legal rights, or what was left of them after the previous land acts. The Liberal Unionists at Westminster and the Protestant tenants of Ulster enforced the surrender to Parnell. There was a serious danger that the Ulstermen might be driven to vote for Gladstonian or even nationalist candidates if the government fell on this question of rent revision and an election ensued. Such a breach in the defences of the Union, Salisbury owned, would be "absolutely fatal to . . . the Empire". Candour, he remarked in the Lords, was the best way to deal with the attacks from all quarters. He viewed this latest bill as no more than an expedient. Irish land law was in "hideous confusion" with property rights divided by Gladstone's legislation between irreconcilable antagonists: those rights should be reunified in the hands of the stronger of the two parties to a hopelessly intractable dispute – the tenants. Freedom of contract could then be restored in Ireland and the government freed from the "morass" of its involvement with rent and other conditions of tenure on hundreds of thousands of holdings.[52]

In the nature of things, Irish land purchase was suspect to the British electorate whose credit as taxpayers was indispensable to the financial operation. The Tories had not hesitated to condemn the risk to the Treasury from the size of Gladstone's scheme in 1886, which entailed the issue of £50 millions in gilt-edged at 3 per cent. Chamberlain joined them in suggesting that a Dublin parliament would be quick to repudiate the interest and principal charged upon the revenue under its control, leaving the British government to meet guaranteed repayments from the general taxation it levied. Gladstone identified the alarm excited by these Unionist predictions as a major cause of his electoral defeat. He nevertheless continued to insist that advances to purchasing tenants should have an Irish security and strongly criticized its omission from Tory land purchase in 1885.[53] The large measure of devolution for Ireland which Chamberlain favoured, after as before his secession, was linked with land purchase. As long as there was not a rival parliament in Dublin, existing Irish representative institutions might be made to assume, and honour, financial obligations in connection with the transfer of land to its occupiers in full ownership. British taxpayers, from whom alone the necessary advances could come, needed a political security for repayment. Salisbury's memorandum on land purchase, composed in October 1887, was sceptical of the Irish tenant's readiness, never mind his ability, to pay instalments of the purchase price exceeding the judicial rent: "All the Constabulary with the British army behind them, will not induce him to pay more". He wished to restrict the call upon the Treasury to a float of five million, plus administrative costs. In the absence of any other elected authority in rural Ireland, the tenant should get his advance from the poor law guardians chosen on a weighted franchise that favoured larger property owners. They were to raise the money by issuing debentures on the security of the land. Since British investors were notoriously unwilling to venture their capital in Ireland, the buyers of the £5 debentures bearing interest at 7.5 per cent to be sold at Post Offices would be the small savers of Ireland, whose thrift provided the country with more branch banks, relative to population, than England or Scotland.[54]

This imaginative scheme was stillborn. The poor law guardians, among whom the nationalists were well represented, could not have borne its weight, regardless of their politics. Nor was it clear that the Irish public would be able, or willing, to find many millions to rescue the landlords from their financial plight. Few of the Irish landed class had any illusions about their position, whether or not Home Rule was indefinitely postponed. In September 1886, Lord Dunraven, who held minor office in the Salisbury ministry, was resigned to seeing the land, including his 15 000 acres in Munster, "practically turned over to the occupiers". To speed up the process he suggested enabling tenants to acquire a half-share in the landlord's property, to be held on perpetual leases at rents 50 per cent below the levels fixed under the 1881 Act.

A Treasury loan for this purpose came to half the sum that Gladstone had proposed to advance earlier the same year. Tenants enjoying such good terms would have the means to buy out the landlords entirely and complete the restoration of Irish land to its Celtic inhabitants.[55] Another and very large landowner in Ireland, the fifth marquess of Lansdowne, governor-general of Canada and a Liberal Unionist, informed Salisbury that "we have to choose between the collapse of the Union and a great agrarian revolution" in the shape of land purchase on the Gladstonian scale. If Ireland were not reconciled by this costly method, British public opinion was likely to concede that Home Rule was the only "*constructive*" alternative. Hard hit by the "Plan of Campaign" on his estates, Lansdowne saw in his urgent proposal a way in which his class in Ireland could recover "something out of the wreck of their fortunes".[56]

Chamberlain, with whom Lansdowne discussed land purchase, believed Home Rule would cease to be "a burning question" once the underlying agrarian discontent had been extinguished. Lansdowne, with a far greater knowledge of Ireland and the Irish, would only say, "We shall never be able to measure the true dimensions of the political problem till the agrarian problem is in a fair way of settlement". As an interim measure, Chamberlain agreed to another five million under a renewal of the 1885 land purchase act before an Irish local government bill was produced.[57] Irish land purchase was understood to be one of the questions on which the Liberal Unionists, and above all Chamberlain, made policy with the Tories from whom, publicly, they liked to keep their distance. Salisbury's suggestions for legislation in his memorandum of October 1887 were on the lines that Chamberlain had sketched in a speech of the previous week: "no others are possible", the premier told W.H. Smith. Naturally, Salisbury had a harder task with land purchase before the audiences he addressed. As in the memorandum for his colleagues, he touched on the possibility of compelling the landlords to sell: and at times appeared to endorse Chamberlain's view that the cry for Home Rule would die down after they had relinquished their precarious hold on the land. He had subsequently to explain that he did not contemplate the extinction of landlords in Ireland: only the erection of a substantial peasant proprietary.[58] When Balfour's bill of 1890 made over thirty million available for land purchase, there was no Tory enthusiasm for it. Hicks Beach wanted it dropped on its reintroduction in the autumn following Liberal and nationalist criticisms of its terms and machinery. Was it wise, he inquired, to say that these millions were being spent, in the words employed in a draft of the Queen's Speech, to bring about "a diminution of political disturbance"? The bill went through, helped by the turmoil prevailing in the nationalist party: but both landlords and tenants found the terms unattractive. The government had been too anxious to convince the British taxpayer that his money and credit were safe in their hands.[59]

The historian Lecky, who was a small Irish landlord, did not think the Union would be strengthened by encouraging, or forcing, landlords to sell. Their peasant successors in ownership, he foresaw, might be more law-abiding for their new status: they would not be better disposed towards Britain. Whatever he said to please Chamberlain, Salisbury thought much the same. He delayed an Irish local government bill, for which Hartington pressed in 1886–7, until order had demonstrably been restored in the countryside and the extension of land purchase was on the statute book. The pressure to include local democracy in the programme of conciliation came from Chamberlain; few other Unionists, even on their Liberal wing, supposed it would weaken the nationalist resolve to extract Home Rule from Westminster. Supporters of the Union were acutely aware, and Gladstonians privately allowed, that the loyalist minority stood in need of protection when county government was democratized in Ireland. Chamberlain, who had resisted minority representation in the debates of the last twenty years on electoral reform, conceded the point in his discussions with Lansdowne.[60]

Another difficulty lay in the widespread belief that elective local government in Ireland must be a halfway house to Home Rule, no matter what ministers said. There were suspicions that policy-makers were moving by stages towards a self-governing Ireland. Sir West Ridgeway, Buller's successor at Dublin Castle, and also a soldier, advocated provincial councils, which Salisbury was known to have considered in 1885. In Ridgeway's outline they were to be indirectly elected with a property qualification for membership, but still signifying something more than the county councils below them. Moreover, Ulster with an electorate "manipulated" to give the Protestants a clear majority in the whole province, where they were nearly outnumbered, could be preserved from nationalist and Catholic domination. "The Home Rulers would thus be dished", unable to speak for a united Ireland, claimed Ridgeway. Ministers took a different view; so did Tories outside the government. Churchill objected to provincial councils as going "too far"; though Carnarvon favoured them, he carried little weight after his viceroyalty.[61] Salisbury gave notice that an Irish local government bill would not contain "the slightest germ of Home Rule", and must have stringent safeguards built into it. Speaking as he did without notes, and prompted by intellectual honesty rather than political expediency, he let it be seen that he could not believe Ireland would ever be reconciled to the Union. In the context of local democracy there, it should be accepted that "the difference between the majority and the minority is permanent"; Unionists would never be safe outside their strongholds in the North East. Balfour's local government bill of 1892 reflected this realism. County and barony, that is, district, councils, were to be elected as in Britain, on a ratepayer franchise but to have such restricted powers that the old instrument of gentry rule in Irish counties, the grand jury, was to co-exist with the new institutions. Balfour could not conceal the absence of any personal conviction that the latter were worth the trouble of setting them up: and the bill was withdrawn.[62]

The government tried and failed where Gladstone had failed in the 1870s to accommodate the Irish Catholic hierarchy's desire for full recognition of their Catholic university. They had a political debt to discharge after the reigning Pope sent an emissary to Ireland in 1887 in an unsuccessful endeavour to restrain clerical sympathy with the resumed agrarian offensive. The reaction in Protestant Britain to the prospect, and difficulties with Pope and bishops, prevented the appearance of a university bill. As a bid to detach prelates like Walsh of Dublin and Croke of Cashel from their commitment to nationalism it was certain to be ineffectual.[63] Its authors did not really think the policy of "killing Home Rule by kindness" would work. Government investment to develop the economy of a very poor region in the West of Ireland by a range of novel initiatives had some success: but the political dividend was disappointing. Even that aid to the "congested districts" needed a warning from Ridgeway of the consequences of letting such measures drop, once they had been announced. The credibility of ministers with nationalists, Irish Unionists and the Irish administration would suffer dangerously. Unionists had to pretend that firmness combined with the succession of reforms was at last succeeding nearly a quarter of a century after Gladstone set out to crush Fenianism and win over the Irish people. Salisbury lent himself to the pretence in a number of his speeches, but it was not one that he could keep up for long. The Irish might be, as he chose to put it on the platform, "a bastard nationality", but they were a distinct nationality for all that.[64]

Before Parnell and the League transformed Irish politics, Salisbury noted that the sentiment of nationality in their country was one of the "truer types of spontaneous popular feeling", with deeper roots than the same sentiment in Italy, or even Hungary, where it enjoyed the approval of most British opinion. In the closing months of this long ministry he made an extraordinary reference to contemporary Ireland as "the Irish republic but I suppose I must call it the Irish province" of Britain, so pervasive was the Celtic nationalism against which he had fought for six years. In another of his speeches he said that he expected the Irish majority, distinguished by race and religion, to return nationalists to Westminster for two generations and more. His hope in Ireland was for the gradual improvement of the native inhabitants to British standards of political behaviour, while retaining their nationalist allegiance, and of economic endeavour, freed from the straitjacket of the Gladstonian land laws.[65] If Britain did not persist in her laudable efforts, "it would mean that the spirit of government has passed from this Imperial land". Repeatedly, he asked his countrymen, so many of whom had voted for Home Rule, to remember that the most powerful states had refused to permit the separation of racial minorities as distinct as the Celtic Irish were and would remain. It was not, thoughtful Unionists realized, a particularly encouraging message: but the impression of courage and sincerity brushing aside the verbal subterfuges habitual to politicians was probably one of the strongest influences working for the maintenance of the Union.[66]

## The Defence of Religion

The anxiety of Churchmen for the future of the Establishment is evident from the diaries of E.W. Benson, Archbishop of Canterbury for the greater part of Salisbury's time as prime minister. Understandably alarmed at the growing influence of political Nonconformity in the Liberal party, he was more troubled by the waning enthusiasm for the Church which he discerned among Tories, at the parliamentary level rather than lower down. The primate did not relish the play of Salisbury's irony, from which prelates were not exempt, and for some years he regarded him as an unworthy and unreliable champion: "I do not believe that S[alisbury] cares for anything but repartee. His friendship to the Church is purely selfish and political". For his part, Salisbury had a poor opinion of Benson's judgement and of the bishops collectively. They had not known, he said in the Lords, how to deal with a "deeply divided" Church, or to prevent the emergence among the laity of a widespread preference for "the elimination of all doctrine upon which anybody disagrees with anybody else". While he thought the maintenance of an established church was indispensable to the hold of Christian belief on the English people, he did not, unlike Benson, confuse institutional privilege and wealth with the cause of Christianity under threat all over Europe.[67] He saw the social function of the revealed truths that institutional religion existed to perpetuate in much the same light as the president of the Trades Union Congress who observed in 1892, "It is due to the religious customs of the country that the avarice of the capitalist has been kept in check". The dictates of economics and the selfish interests of classes had an absolute need of religion to make them morally tolerable and politically safe. The Church of England, to which a large majority of English men and women were more or less faithful, required to be reformed as well as defended. Without reform the perceptible decline of her effectiveness in society and in the salvation of individual souls would continue.[68]

Salisbury was limited in what he could do for the Church by her divisions, by the vested interests entrenched in her structure, and by the indifference or hostility of many MPs. He had to take account of these problems in his distribution of ecclesiastical patronage, in the reforming legislation which the government initiated or to which he gave his blessing, and in his defence of the Establishment from assorted critics. His bishop-making followed the pattern set when he filled Indian sees, and did not differ markedly from Gladstone's practice. The selections for deaneries, canonries and livings to which the Crown presented, had to be made with an eye to the balance between High, Low and Broad Churchmen, and also to party political considerations; but he had a little room for the exercise of a personal preference. There is among his papers at Hatfield a register, which is not comprehensive, of candidates for preferment between 1885 and 1887. In each case the names of their supporters are given: ministers, peers and Conservative MPs feature prominently among them. The candidates' professional strengths, it is clear from the annotations, mattered rather more than their politics, except for the occasional one noted as "Radical".[69] Anglican clergymen were predominantly Tory: their allegiance to one or other of the Church parties was what preoccupied Salisbury. Colleagues hinted, and the interested public complained, that he was too partial to High Churchmen. In fact he was less inclined than Gladstone to favour them. He told Hicks Beach, the cabinet minister most likely to raise the claims of Evangelicals with him, that his choice normally fell on "moderate men – neither ritualist nor ultra-Protestant: because I am convinced that the mass of the English Church are moderate men". Towards the close of the 1886–92 administration, his private secretary stated that in the premier's view of his recent episcopal selections, two, including the historian Mandell Creighton, were definitely Broad Churchmen, and another two, one being an archbishop of York, were Evangelicals, while Westcott of Durham was more Evangelical than Broad.[70]

This indicates the difficulty of identifying an individual's ecclesiastical position when the evolution of Anglican theology made it harder to distinguish between the three great schools in the Church. Nor were moderate men those best able to inspire Christians when the fundamentals of their creed were being questioned by clergy and laity alike. Salisbury, and his wife, strove to persuade Liddon to accept a bishopric in spite of his partisan High Churchmanship and his Gladstonian loyalties. Liddon possessed one of the finest minds in the Church, and ranked among the great preachers. Salisbury valued this frequent visitor to Hatfield as an apologist for the intelligent orthodoxy to which he himself adhered, and enjoyed discussing theology, and other topics, with him. At the same time, he did not want to be too closely associated with a controversial figure in the life of the Church. Long after Liddon's death in 1890, Salisbury, still prime minister, told his ardently High Church heir, Cranborne that the Canon's portrait "would seem strange and out of place hanging at Hatfield".[71] The type of High Churchman that appealed to him was very well represented by his kinsman Edward Talbot. At the instance of Arthur

Balfour and his brother Gerald, a Leeds MP, he took Talbot from Oxford, where he was the first Warden of Keble, to be vicar of Leeds, a post of considerable importance. Then he tried, and failed, to promote him almost at once to the Bench of Bishops; the new vicar was reluctant to leave his provincial capital so soon. Talbot's Anglican Catholicism was altogether more eirenical than Liddon's. Salisbury saw in him someone whose influence on the Bench could help to avert the recurrent nightmare of "civil war" in the national church, "menacing, if not imminent", between the extremes of High and Low. He warned Talbot that when he and Gladstone ceased to lead their respective parties, their successors were unlikely to give preferment even to moderate High Churchmen.[72]

The worst thing about any intensification of the enmity between militants on both wings was that it discredited the Church, especially with "sensitive and conscientious men" whom the bitter disputes of forty years had alienated. Talbot was wanted on the Bench to offset a Gladstonian appointment, Bishop King of Lincoln, whom Benson had successfully prosecuted for ritualism. King was a "firebrand". So, too, was the Evangelical Bishop Ryle of Liverpool, Disraeli's choice. Salisbury did not think the alternative to finding a reasonable High Churchman was promoting a Broad Churchman of the kind that the Queen and the primate liked. Benson, hard to classify, was perhaps more Broad than High.[73] Ecclesiastical patronage was the last, small area of government where the Queen could sometimes insist on her prerogative, particularly with Salisbury. He felt he was at a disadvantage, because his own religious opinions were not popular, when having to select bishops from Broad and Low Churchmen. Consequently, he deferred to the Queen's wishes more often than Gladstone, who was less fastidious, had done. Nevertheless, he entered a strong protest when she proposed Broad Churchmen for two important sees in 1890. The promotions would suggest that his government was "bent on rationalizing the Church". The Queen objected to this "very extraordinary idea", or rather to its expression. It was an allusion to her advanced, though nebulous, theological views; a legacy of the Prince Consort.[74] The "cultivated laity", Salisbury admitted, might find the royal choices congenial: the clergy, by now more High than anything else in their outlook, and the laity, inclined to the Evangelical in theirs, would not. The premier succeeded in diverting Davidson, Dean of Windsor, the Queen's spiritual adviser, from Gloucester to the less prestigious see of Rochester but he had to let Durham go to her candidate, Westcott, a liberal theologian. He did not believe that either Davidson or Westcott would make a good bishop in a major see and said so plainly. The subsequent careers of both, however, showed that he had underestimated them.[75]

Salisbury was not wrong about the inability of theological liberals to check the slow erosion of belief which had set in among the educated and was working down through society. Faced with the Queen's persistent advocacy of Westcott for Durham, he turned to her candidate's writings, and satisfied himself that, though erudite, they revealed "an inferiority of intellectual power". The Court – Victoria and Davidson – also rejected the strongest Evangelical the premier could find for a bishopric, recommended for his eloquence and familiarity with urban conditions: if there was one quality that Salisbury rated more highly than others, doctrine apart, in a potential bishop, it was eloquence.[76] He consulted widely in his search for men to match local circumstances: "Norfolk", he wrote in 1889 when appointing a Dean of Norwich, "is a very Protestant county and could not stand a High Churchman". There was some truth in Benson's remark that the premier feared to offend working-class voters in the North, where Dissent was powerful, by giving Durham a High Church bishop. Salisbury's retrospective identification of Westcott as more a Low than a Broad Churchman underlines his difficulty in discovering Evangelicals whom it would be "decent to appoint"; like Gladstone he thought they were generally out-classed by High and Broad Church candidates. The words quoted are from Benson's diary after the premier sent a cabinet minister to discuss the scarcity with him. A prelate such as John Wordsworth of Salisbury, "learned and holy . . . very High", would, Salisbury needed no telling, plunge Durham into "turmoil".[77] Nor did he need reminding by a Low Church bishop, Bickersteth of Exeter, of "the strength of the Evangelical phalanx . . . far greater than many . . . suppose". It was, Salisbury told an aggressively High Church colleague in 1885, only fair to fill one out of three vacant sees with a Low Churchman. As Bickersteth was to remind him, unneces-sarily, an equitable approach to distributing ecclesiastical patronage had a political dimension. Resentment of the bias against Evangelicals was more significant after the formation of the Unionist alliance: its Nonconformist element sympathized with the complaints of Low Church Tories.[78]

From his days at the India Office Salisbury turned to Talbot for advice about his church appointments: they were kindred spirits, indulging the sense of humour that irritated Benson. Talbot recommended someone for an Indian bishopric as "a fine, vigorous specimen of an *English* High Churchman . . . He is six feet . . . and has a bonhomie and geniality characteristic of the larger animals". Theologically, he and Salisbury were close to one another. Talbot also shrank from "the stronger dogmat-isms about the manner of the Gift in the Eucharist" – that is, from transubstanti-ation as against a real presence – and had the same aversion to "the first beginnings of Mariolatry". His recommendations, usually of other High Churchmen, favoured the "moderate and non-partisan". Putting forward an intimate of Liddon's, he made it clear that he did so because the disciple had come to realize that the master was "limited".[79] Cabinet ministers who took a hand in bishop-making were not so concerned with learning and piety. W.H. Smith, an East Anglian landowner, sought a bishop of Ely who would be "a strong man . . . I care comparatively little as to the section of the Church . . . but he ought to be a painstaking man of business", rather than a preacher or theologian. Cross, the Indian secretary, requested a prelate of the same sort for Carlisle – "as I am much interested in this diocese" – with the injunction that "a High Ritualist or a Low Evangelical would be a disaster". As one of the city's MPs, Hicks Beach wanted a clergyman "fearless . . . and on our side" in Bristol politics to be rewarded with a deanery though "*very* High Church".[80]

The quality of an episcopate chosen primarily to "keep the Church together at a critical time" by their moderation was a handicap in legislating for the Church. The bishops depended on Salisbury to get a tithe bill and a clergy discipline bill through parliament. The first of these badly needed measures took four years to pass; Gladstone's help was decisive in overcoming resistance to the second from a handful of determined Nonconformist radicals who had no desire to see the Establishment purged of abuses. The primate, Benson, who was thought to aspire to "a Canterbury Papacy", learnt that he was politically almost powerless without the Tory party and its leader.[81] Neither his administrative gifts nor his personal Toryism counted for much with a Unionist majority containing a small but influential Nonconformist element, personified by Chamberlain. He suspected Tories of being prepared to appease radicalism at the Church's expense: and interpreted accordingly the suggestion that his country palace at Addington should be sold to raise money for a new diocese to be carved out of his see. "I, of course, am to be largely mulcted", he angrily remarked, criticizing in the privacy of his diary the prominent laymen and Tories concerned. "These blind men do not know . . . they are only guiding on . . . democracy to the House of Lords and [the] revenues of their own order". Salisbury did not always consult, or even inform, him when making bishops. The offer of Rochester to Talbot was made, and accepted, without reference to the primate. "Talbot must sign 'Erastus Roffen'", exclaimed the archbishop. "No appointment has been so Erastian in . . . manner as this". He compared Salisbury's treatment of him with Gladstone's regular consultation, and described himself sadly as a "*quantité négligeable*" in Talbot's eyes.[82]

It took Salisbury's second administration nearly the whole of its life to reform the law relating to tithes. In the depths of the agricultural recession, squires and church-going farmers as well as Nonconformists objected to paying the impost, geared though it was by the Tithes Commutation Act of 1836 to a running average of cereal prices. It is doubtful whether Salisbury could have contrived to pass a tithe bill, at the fifth attempt, without the sense of urgency imparted by the plight of the Welsh clergy. His correspondence testifies to the severe hardship they experienced in a predominantly Nonconformist countryside where tithe was quite widely withheld. The continuing protest, and the accompanying riots, raised the spectre of an Ireland in Wales, "I feel like a Dutchman when he sees a . . . trickle of water running down a dyke", said the premier in discussing the first of the tithe bills. The principle of the legislation, clarified over four years, was to make the owner, instead of the occupier, of land liable for tithes; there was also a provision for their redemption. When the first bill had to be dropped, W.H. Smith, as leader of the Commons, said that many Tories would oppose its reintroduction: he believed landlords could not recover the tithes in higher rents under prevailing conditions. The strain of long hours in the Chamber voting, session after session, for a bill which had few real friends contributed to a crisis of Unionist morale in the later years of this parliament. Benson did not appreciate how hard it was to pass this and other measures in a House unenthusiastic, to say the least, about helping what was still a very wealthy establishment, despite the fall in its agricultural income. He wanted a larger settlement of the question, by way of redemption, than the government could undertake.[83]

The archbishop repeatedly prophesied in his diary a separation between the Church, rejected and offended by her best friends, and property, whose owners "then . . . will . . . find . . . there is no class-right left defensible . . . the aristocracy will go on digging their . . . graves singing like Hamlet's sexton". He tried to persuade Smith that the clergy were "a worse class to discontent than any other". It was, he soon realized, a delusion. The Church needed the Tories, and one Tory in particular, more than they needed her, notwithstanding all that she meant to them, and him. Benson lived in dread lest Gladstone should commit himself to disestablishment, as he did in respect of the Church in Wales from 1887. The Liberals voted in some strength against the tithe bills. A small, chiefly Welsh, band of Nonconformist radicals went further and obstructed Benson's Clergy Discipline Bill. It was not a government measure, but one which he desperately wanted to pass. It limited the protection afforded by the parson's freehold to incumbents whose conduct discredited the Establishment.[84] Benson made little headway with it until in 1891 Salisbury, looking "more mountainous and solid than ever" in conference with the archbishop and the attorney-general, directed the law officer to tell the Liberal Unionist Goschen, acting as leader of the House, to announce the government's intention of seeing the bill through. "You may tell him", the premier instructed Sir Richard Webster, "to say it *very strongly*". Gladstone, whom the Tories had first sounded a couple of years previously, was interested in frustrating the tactics of the Nonconformist militants. Without his support for the use of the closure, Salisbury explained to the primate, the government could not have resorted to a method then reserved for passing the most important bills. As he was obliged to inform another Anglican dignitary in a different ecclesiastical context, the attendance of the Commons majority was not to be relied upon for legislation in the Church's special interests.[85]

The Clergy Discipline Act of 1892 incorporated the main features of a "Church Reform Bill" which Salisbury had contemplated in 1885, to be told by Randolph Churchill that "votes will be lost on every side" as a result. Benson never understood the necessity for an extremely cautious approach to legislating for the Church: Salisbury and the Tories intervened, as a government, only when she could not help herself. The primate's Church patronage bill of the mid-1880s would have ended the sale of presentations to livings and allowed the removal of incumbents unfit for the cure of souls but outside the scope of disciplinary procedures in his other bill. Salisbury in 1885 envisaged dealing with "incompetent" as well as "criminous" clergy: but the archbishop's patronage bill, "thoroughly remodelled" by amendments from the premier himself, was still radical in its invasion of patrons' rights. Though it had Gladstone's support, too, the reform was not given the requisite parliamentary time until two years after Benson's death in 1896.[86] It was overshadowed by a far more pressing question for the Church and for the whole policy of the government and its Liberal Unionist allies.

Education, viewed as inseparable from religion by most people, imposed a growing financial strain on the Established Church, and especially on the working clergy, who contributed heavily from their stipends to the cost of maintaining her schools. The report in 1889 of the royal commission on elementary education approved by Salisbury's first government recommended that denominational schools should be helped out of the rate which provided their Board School rivals with a more generous source of income than the Treasury. This was practically impossible, however, until the turn of the century, when it elicited a reaction very damaging to the Unionists. Nonconformists, who had always grumbled at, if they did not actively oppose, state grants to denominational education, objected violently to its rescue by ratepayers. The school rate, with the poor and general rates, caught the millions otherwise untouched by direct taxation; no politician could offend them with impunity. With some exceptions, the Liberal Unionists, Anglican and Nonconformist, did not like to appear as political friends of the Church, and certainly not in front of the ratepayers. Ironically, Salisbury, her best friend, made matters worse for the Church by one of his boldest strokes. The introduction of free elementary education in 1891, coming on top of pressure from the Education Department to impose standards in elementary schools, without regard to funding, threatened to leave the Church in what Talbot, writing from Leeds, called "a very dark situation".[87] It took vehement protests from Churchmen and sympathetic Tories to secure the withdrawal and revision of new departmental regulations which flowed from the commission's recommendations. The minister responsible, Cranbrook, was, with many of his party, defeatist about the survival of Church schools, and about his ability to control the officials under him. Free education entailed a grant for that purpose to Board and denominational schools over and above their existing grant and rate income. Without rate aid, the Church's position in the educational field was bound to deteriorate. Amendments to the government's bill in their interests merely postponed a financial crisis in her schools.[88]

Salisbury had "the sad conviction that the Church is very weak with the present Conservative party". Cranbrook's handling of the controversial regulations "reduced me to despair", the premier confessed to the same trusted friend; he was deluged with clerical remonstrances. The defence of religion, and not simply of the Establishment, runs through his administrations. From the strict Anglicanism of his parliamentary beginnings, he had moved to the eirenical championship of a Christianity eroded by the secularizing influences that were gaining ground in the last Victorian decades. They were discernible, it seemed to him, in the desire of the Education Department to extend state control over the Church's schools. He warned Cranbrook that the Department's permanent head had united High and Low Churchmen in furious opposition; and they were not the only ones who saw in the regulations "a clever contrivance of Pat Cumin's to swamp the voluntary schools".[89] On the radical Cumin's retirement in 1890, he was glad to learn that a Tory Churchman, G.W. Kekewich, had been chosen to replace him. "The appointment is one of extreme importance", he told Cranbrook. He knew that the successor, an internal promotion, would not find it easy to check the department's leaning towards Board schools and undenominational religion, but "he probably starts . . . with no prepossession against the Church". Within a very short time, Salisbury had turned to a former holder of the post, Sir Francis Sandford, whose churchmanship was stronger than his bureaucratic past, for more helpful advice than Cranbrook and Kekewich supplied in the preparation of his free education bill.[90]

The most effective way of combating the secular spirit of the age, he found, was through his direct appeals to the public. Politicizing religious questions was a regrettable necessity: "it is far too great and sacred a thing to . . . misuse for any lower purpose". But Toryism's links with the Church, and the "considerable assistance" it received from the main Wesleyan connexion, were legitimate; neither the Establishment nor that Methodist body, as such, was identified with a political party.

The Liberals and their Nonconformist allies presented "a totally different picture . . . The chapel is the centre of political organization. The Nonconformist pastor is the leader of the Radical advance". It was not obviously so different from the situation on the Tory side, particularly when he suggested that "hard facts" made a still closer association with organized religion desirable for the Unionists.[91] As for the Church, she could not be reformed without the aid of her political friends: that was the price of establishment, which, however, protected her from the entire dependence on the laity and their politics characteristic of Nonconformity. The tithe bill was urgently needed to deliver the Church from "the farmer's hatred", not too strong a word to describe the feeling in rural Wales. The patronage and discipline bills were required if she was to make good the "terrible arrears", accumulated over many generations, in her pastoral labours. The bishops, and also politicians, were generally loath to emulate his uncomfortable honesty about the state of the Church. Salisbury was rewarded for his courage in taking such unpromising topics to the people. Without the understanding he obtained from his audiences up and down the country, reluctant colleagues and backbenchers would have been harder to move.[92] Salisbury's ability to think ahead and create the climate for legislation, or for resistance to Liberal legislation, was the counterpart in domestic politics of his much studied dispositions in foreign policy. A little later, after hearing Salisbury outline the tactics he had in view on Welsh disestablishment, Benson was filled with admiration for the political skill revealed: "he plays with big questions as a cat with a mouse".[93]

## The New Conservatism and the Old

"It is becoming quite a misnomer to call the . . . government *Conservative*", said that informed spectator, Edward Hamilton, in August 1889, when they had during the last two years passed "really Liberal measures with a smack of radicalism about them".[94] The peers would not have accepted changes on that scale from a Liberal ministry. Hamilton was right: Salisbury gave substance to a new, democratic Toryism talked about since Disraeli. He did this in three ways: by developing the indispensable rhetoric; by his oversight of the machinery of a mass party; and by rhetoric translated into the legislation to which the diarist referred. The most radical instalment of the three was yet to come: the 1891 Education Act, the significance of which contemporaries immediately recognized. It showed that the democratic language was in earnest. Old style Tories expressed their detestation of what he was saying, but they relieved their feelings covertly, like the peer, soon to be in minor office, whose notion of politics was that "he must not put himself into open opposition with [*sic*] the democracy".[95] There were still intractable problems for the Tory–Unionist alliance and its leader in 1892, and one in particular. Salisbury did not discourage the movement for protection in his party, although he emphasized the political obstacles. He let it be seen that, to his mind, the demand made economic sense. Like many Victorians he had remained sceptical about free trade as always and everywhere an unmixed good; pointing out, repeatedly, that Britain's competitors in world markets thought differently. His stance added to the impression which it was his aim to foster, that a Tory government and the Unionist alliance could do more for an industrial nation than the dated Gladstonianism of the Liberals. Yet expositions of Salisbury's policy, at home and abroad, always contained a great deal that did not clash with Gladstone's thinking.[96]

Salisbury could not have developed the rhetoric of the new conservatism without his awareness of what the newspapers were saying, and of what they ought to be saying in the interests of his government.[97] His professed dislike of the social round and contempt for the baser sort of journalism inspired the legend that he deliberately neglected the press, as well as his backbenchers. He needed the papers, like any other politician, using them to project the image of a party and an alliance which preserved the old values while being uniquely capable of reinterpreting them for an industrial democracy. A *Times* man with good connections described Salisbury as the prime minister most accessible to the press: careful about the information he furnished, he gave it freely when he saw fit, and it was valuable. His correspondence with Alfred Austin of the *Standard*, the leading Tory newspaper, was not confined to Foreign Office matters. He discussed his personal prospects, quite frankly, with Austin: "as a peer . . . so helpless politically" that in November 1886 he would almost have welcomed a successful *coup* by Churchill, who, he remarked, would not last long in his place. The *Standard*'s influential leader-writer had put himself "entirely at your disposal in any shape you may deem desirable for the making of public opinion". Acutely conscious of the weakness of Toryism "in intellect, sympathy and *lasting* popular favour", he believed it could not do without both the support of Liberal Unionism, to be assessed in qualitative as much as quantitative terms, and Salisbury's continuing leadership.[98] The latter, Austin told him, was "the country's only safeguard" against other changes besides Irish separatism. Austin was an intermediary between Salisbury and Goschen when the Liberal Unionist stepped into Churchill's shoes, and the possibility of fashioning a single party out of the alliance recurred in the letters exchanged by journalist and premier.[99]

Austin thought, and Salisbury doubted, that specifically working-class issues, agitation for an eight-hour day and higher wages, would dominate the next general election. The journalist urged "frank and frequent manifestations of legitimate sympathy with the deep-rooted determination of those classes to better their lot". A feature of Salisbury's speeches since the early 1880s, displays of feeling for the hopes and anxieties of working men were more marked from the end of the decade. He felt the working class was resistant to "socialist quackeries": but a practical concern for their wants was expedient, and right in itself.[100] It was, Salisbury had written to Austin some years previously, an "absurd delusion" to suppose that the Tories' dislike of democracy implied indifference to the plight of the poor in their society. He soon changed his mind about nascent socialism in Britain, seeing in it by the autumn of 1890 "our great danger". The strength of the Left on the Continent was a factor in his calculations of war and peace at the Foreign Office. His country could not be immune to the infection, though he had little fear that in the long run the opposing social forces would fail to contain it. The correspondence with Austin

corrects some of the misconceptions about Salisbury. It helps to establish his objectives in the speeches that expounded a new conservatism.[101]

The modernizing of Toryism excited the admiration of the Liberal leadership
for an opponent who often seemed to be labouring singlehanded. Harcourt, with
characteristic acerbity, said of the government in 1890, "Bar Lord S[alisbury] they
were like children in difficult times . . . ignorant of what to do and what to say". On
the same occasion, Gladstone hoped "nothing would break down . . . Salisbury,
who was head and shoulders above all his colleagues, and who though he had
committed mistakes was a big-minded and real statesman".[102] Gladstone believed
more strongly than most in the requirement for both parties to perform well in a
two-party system. The premier's physical health appeared uncertain under his official burdens and the strain of platform oratory. By-elections started to go against
the ministry quite early in its life, and the management of the Commons was a
constant struggle.[103] As a peer, Salisbury had to direct his government from outside the arena where its fate hung on shifting votes. His speeches steadied public
opinion and worked a slow transformation in its perception of Toryism. The effect
was visible in Chamberlain's appreciation of the possibilities that opened up for his
constructive radicalism within Unionism.[104]

At the lowest level of debate Salisbury used the platform to refute such allegations, good election material of their kind, as the story which had him saying at the
Hatfield Board of Guardians that a poor man could live on "a herring and a
potato". There was evidently, he observed, "a well organized machinery of lying".
He carried conviction in the farming counties, not always safe for the Tories,
because he made no attempt to hide from himself and a national audience the
severity of the prolonged agricultural depression from which landlords, tenant farmers
and labourers were suffering. They must all realize that his government could help
them only "with the general consent of the community".[105] This was a reference to
pleas for protection voiced with increasing desperation. "We are ruined because
everything is cheaper than it was before", he said wryly. Agricultural interests had
to recognize that "protection was nothing else but civil war"; his estimate of potential opposition in the towns to the reversal of Peel's policy. The government had
no remedy to propose for a stricken countryside, merely palliatives: allotments for
labourers and the creation of a new department under a cabinet minister, the
Board of Agriculture, in the usefulness of which Salisbury scarcely pretended to
believe.[106] Theirs was "a great industrial and political empire" committed to the
urban population of Britain. The two great questions of the immediate future were
the "condition, constitution, [and] defence" of the empire, taking in the fight against
Irish separatism, and, "very closely related" to that first question, "How shall we
maintain our extended commerce, or in other words, how shall we find employment for our teeming millions?" Their international competitors were actively
"envying our empire, occupying our markets".[107]

In that competitive setting, internal divisions – Irish against British, poor against
rich – sapped Britain's strength. With every Victorian premier, he stressed that class
co-operation was the basis of political stability and economic prosperity. No one
could be blind to "the socialist wave rising in every part of the world". He regularly

criticized the Liberals for failing to resist the temptation to exploit "the natural jealousy" of wealth and rank. But even the radical wing of that party, he acknowledged, did not have in mind an orchestrated attack on property. The worst that might be said of them was that their language about Irish landlords, or about Welsh clergymen trying to collect their tithes, played into the hands of a very few socialist agitators.[108] The Trafalgar Square demonstrations of the unemployed in 1886 and 1887, ending in riot, gave a warning that Salisbury heeded. It was not enough to comment, as he did, that "Mr Gladstone approves resistance to authority in Ireland and objects to it in Trafalgar Square". Nor did he react like the alarmed colleague who condemned the socialistic "vile teaching" unreservedly in his diary, and thirsted for their punishment: "Law and order are the privilege of the poor", he said memorably, expressing what was instinctively felt by millions about their wages and savings. The inviolability of property under the law was "the only security . . . we have for our complicated system of commercial activity and progress".[109] The fluctuating recession stretching from the late 1870s to the early 1890s put many out of work, some for long periods: but for those in work real wages were rising; savings banks deposits showed how much the respectable working class had to lose from flirting with revolution.[110]

It was they who listened to Salisbury on the power of capitalism to transform their lives for better, or for worse. The error of capitalism's critics was to think that "governments and parliaments are much more powerful things than they really are", when they existed for purposes which, rightly understood, were limited: "all they can do is to give free play to the living forces of the country". The economy was the greatest of those forces in the sense that when "commerce fails and industry pines, the greatest effort cannot produce satisfactory results for the machinery of government". It did not follow that politicians or the people were helpless to shape their collective destiny. While capitalism left ample scope for peoples, and classes, to better themselves, they must be careful not to disrupt its working.[111] Salisbury did not invoke a selective depression to condemn the strikes that captured attention in the middle years of his administration: "There is a great deal of profit made . . . it is only natural that all who take part in making the profit are as anxious to get as large a share of it for themselves as possible"; but wage claims should not jeopardize employment by deterring investment. This passage on industrial relations is from a speech to the National Union's Nottingham conference in 1889; he had held the same doctrine two years earlier in front of an employers' organization, the Associated Chambers of Commerce: "I do not think it is just to say that the existence . . . of trade unions . . . can be looked upon as a danger" by business. Both sides of industry had to remember that the economic life of an industrial state hinged on "credit and confidence": if these failed "the mighty fabric . . . will crumble into ruin". His aims at home and abroad might be compressed into a single sentence, he said at Nottingham, "if I were asked to define Conservative policy, I should say it was the upholding of confidence".[112]

Salisbury used the speeches he delivered at Nottingham to emphasize and enlarge the social dimension of his Toryism. Some months before the conference, on a day which saw him speaking five times to the Bristol working men's and other

Conservative associations in that city, and again in London, he deplored a "very great" evil, the growing physical separation of classes, as the scale of industry and residential patterns changed, inexorably: "I have no formula to offer you", he said, that would check trends which, in conjunction with current levels of unemployment, posed "a constant peril to the state". The conventional party struggle ought not to distract them from these most serious questions. Part of the best answer he could devise lay in the construction of a political church, similar to that which the socialists had erected in Germany and were trying to found in Britain. His speeches took "popular government" for granted: he appealed for "common sense" in its operation.[113] He sought to show working-class voters only that their practical needs and grievances were not being neglected. The only direct taxation levied upon them – the local rates paid by householders to municipalities, poor law guardians and school boards – had risen much faster than the population to the point where it was onerous for many who paid it.[114] The Salisbury government lightened the burden by increasing the help given from the centre until the structure of local taxation underwent the reconstruction foreshadowed in prime ministerial speeches. Personal as well as real property, Salisbury contended at Nottingham, should be rated. It was too radical a suggestion to be taken up by either side in politics, then or later, although he reverted to it in the years ahead. Too radical, also, was the friendly reference to votes for women in parliamentary elections; already enfranchised for municipal, county and school board elections, they were perceived by Liberal opponents of female suffrage as likely to be a conservative force.[115]

Independently of his colleagues he proceeded to advocate free education. One of his arguments for it was the correlation between the spread of education and the advance of Toryism in the big towns since the 1870 Education Act. He treated the voters he was addressing beyond the conference as quite capable of understanding the motives of their rulers at Westminster. His government's recent Allotments Act, he remarked, was not "wholly disinterested": its authors thought a little property turned people against revolution; he pointed to the salutary influence of an "enormous mass of peasant proprietors" in France. He deliberately assumed that he had a mature democracy before him which could weigh up what it heard. Whether the subject reviewed from the platform was reform of the Lords to admit, as he had long wished, an element of life peers; or the deficiencies of such housing legislation as there was – "you do not solve the question of housing the working classes by turning the dwellers of insanitary dwellings into the streets"; or the weakness of the case for an eight-hour day; or Ireland; or the relevance of his foreign policy to "the industrial classes" – he appealed to reason, much more than to sentiment. The Nottingham conference marked a stage in Salisbury's courtship of the electorate. He sounded less than ever like the unregenerate conservative he was often supposed to be at heart. No one else, Unionist or Liberal, contrived to strike quite the same note. The absence of hyperbole in most of his utterances led observers to use adjectives like "cool" or "cynical", to describe them. He was alive, however, to the part that collective emotion must play in organizing the new conservatism.[116]

His rational, liberal and democratic rhetoric was not at odds with the appeals to religion and patriotism woven into it. The latter themes figured more prominently in the propaganda of the Primrose League; an impressive manifestation of the political church whose growth he fostered without sharing the mentality of its devotees. To begin with, he had been sceptical of the League and its pseudo-medieval trappings. The educated, and not merely Liberals, might laugh at its knights and dames: but the idea of popularizing the ethos of an order of chivalry in the service of a mass party had an astounding success. A membership of less than a thousand in its first year became nearly a quarter of a million in two years, and half a million in three, reaching a million in 1891. If this huge influx was more representative of the lower middle class than of the industrial workers, it was nevertheless a political phenomenon which Salisbury exploited by drawing attention to its underlying significance. The League, in which his wife and other great ladies were active, employed deference to oil the wheels of democracy. He preferred to see something quite new in its rapid diffusion: "We have had political organizations before, but their business has not been to bring the classes together". While the spirit of the League was far less egalitarian than he chose to suggest, its efficacy as an instrument of class co-operation could not be denied. He came back to that, seen as the movement's greatest strength, again and again. The upper, middle and working classes, by their "easy and unfettered intercourse" in a political context had translated Disraeli's imagined Tory democracy into an uncomfortable reality for the Liberals, who had not been able to set up anything like it. Salisbury wanted to think this spontaneity would work against the emergence of "that fatal enemy of . . . progress . . . the professional politician".[117]

Salisbury contrasted the Primrose League with Tory MPs and the party machine. "If I may say so without irreverence", he told the League in May 1886, "you are rather the preaching friars of the message than the regular clergy attached to each district". He is unique among British party leaders in his public distaste for the central machinery that electoral success required with the advent of democracy. The organization under the hand of Captain Middleton, the party's principal agent for the whole of the period spanned by the Salisbury governments, served the Tories well. Full-time agents in half the constituencies by the end of Salisbury's time, supervised by regional agents, and the expansion of centralized propaganda created a modern system of reporting and control. It was qualified by the continuing independence of unsalaried MPs who would only stand so much pressure from the leadership and the whips. Middleton, a former naval officer with no aspirations to make policy and absolutely loyal to Salisbury, was admirably suited to work with him.[118] The inherent tendency of a mass electorate was to create "a mechanical wire-pulled democracy"; a fear widely shared by contemporaries. The outlook of Akers-Douglas, chief whip for a dozen years, did not differ very much from Middleton's: he was a party manager who might raise questions about the viability of policies but who did not otherwise try to shape them. The most important person in the mass party was Salisbury himself. The organizers pestered him for speeches: and he applied a vigorous test to speaking engagements, usually rejecting any which because "non-political . . . would be, in my view, a mere waste of time". The health of the political church, like that of its analogue, exacted unremitting labour. The National Union, representing the constituency associations, had a standing claim on the leader. Its chairman in the early 1890s, Henry Stafford Northcote, knew the premier well enough to be able to joke about its demands: a request for him to appear at a joint Tory and Liberal Unionist demonstration was "only informal – the rattle of the snake before starting with the full venom of the . . . Unionist speech beggars".[119]

The Unionist alliance raised a crop of difficulties at constituency level, as well as at Westminster. The adjustment of relations between the two parties and their respective organizations called for much diplomacy. Outside Chamberlain's strong-hold in the West Midlands the Liberal Unionists depended on the Tories for sur-vival. On the platform Salisbury looked forward to the eventual fusion of the parties, which, he advised the Nottingham conference, could take place only as and when an evolutionary process allowed. "Parties are not like chessmen that you can move this way or that for the interests of the game". But there was, and had to be, movement within the allies' relationship: Tories sensed that it was away from their instinctive conservatism. The partnership removed Toryism's disadvantage before the predominant Liberalism of the country. Salisbury and Chamberlain concurred in putting "big things above party", as the premier declared at Birmingham in November 1891 with Chamberlain sitting beside him.[120] Five years earlier Salisbury had defined the business of government as "the amelioration of the condition of the people . . . by the action of power" on education, and on economic life within the existing framework, with special attention paid to the expansion of trade. "The action of power" in these areas of policy was what interested Chamberlain. Salisbury reminded nervous or disgruntled Tories that the measures his govern-ment enacted stemmed from his Newport programme rather than Chamberlain's "unauthorized programme". He cautioned his radical ally from claiming too much of the credit for allotments, county councils and free education.[121]

The electoral impact in 1885 of Chamberlain's plans for giving agricultural labourers a little land to call their own had a lasting effect. Tories hoped that the 1887 Allotments Act might stave off a demand for something more than plots limited in extent to one acre. There was agitation, especially in the Eastern counties for smallholdings on which a man could live – the "three acres and a cow" of 1885. The strongest supporter of allotments on the Tory benches was Henry Chaplin, a Lincolnshire MP and owner of 12 000 acres in the county. Chancellor of the Duchy of Lancaster, outside the cabinet, in Salisbury's first ministry, he had unsuccessfully sought promotion in July 1886, staying on the backbenches when denied it. A friend, personal and political, of Churchill's, he had maintained before the Unionist victory at the polls that labourers on the large farms common in his part of England cared for nothing – certainly not for resistance to Irish separatism – but "wages – and 'a bit of land'". If the draft bill he had prepared became law, it would only encourage landlords to do what they were already doing, without resort to the compulsion for which he provided. It was compulsion that Salisbury fought to prevent, seeing in it a surrender of principle impossible to excuse by reference to the special circumstances invoked to cover legislation for the Celtic fringe.[122] Balfour, who had drafted proposals of his own some time before, warned his uncle of the price he would pay for refusing to take Chaplin into the cabinet. Chaplin and his following among county members might combine with the Liberals to insert compulsory powers in an allotments bill, leaving Salisbury with no alternative but to include them himself: "It is not a question you can possibly resign on (for you would loose [*sic*] the counties) and . . . it is one on which you are almost sure to be beaten".[123]

Balfour's advice makes clear what was at issue in framing a very modest piece of legislation. Colleagues could not quite understand why Salisbury made so much of principle in this case, when its application was restricted by a careful distinction between allotments and smallholdings. He answered them with a long memorandum detailing his objections. This was compulsory purchase to benefit individuals; quite different, therefore, from taking land for public purposes – building, railways, public health and the like – under Acts of Parliament not regarded as contentious. Henceforth, if he were overruled, expropriation would be decided "solely by the provision of sufficient electoral power to disquiet a certain number of Conservative members". A large landowner might expect to be the target of orders served on him "for the gratification of ill will, arising from local quarrels". The requirement in the proposals before them that the supply of allotments by the local authority should be self-financing must limit their availability, particularly in the vicinity of towns where land values were higher. The resulting disappointment would feed the agitation, such as it was. Quite unconvinced that the existing voluntary arrangements did not suffice, Salisbury argued for public intervention without the element of compulsion – all that was needed where landlords were not doing enough. It was not for Conservatives to introduce legislation "inconsistent with the rights of property as hitherto understood", though they might have to submit to it in the end.[124] Salisbury lost the battle with his cabinet and party. Assurances that otherwise they stood or fell with him seemed absurd to the premier: "It would be more accurate to say that they do not mind using me if in the minutest particulars I will subordinate my views to theirs". He managed to subject the use of compulsion to confirmation by Act of Parliament.[125]

It was because Salisbury had embraced democracy that he was so careful of the rights of property. The Allotments Act imparted "a gentle stimulus" to landowners. The administering authority, usually the poor law guardians, came under the county councils established the following year to replace, in theory, the rule of the landed justices.[126] Salisbury was not isolated when the government carried the Small Holdings Act of 1892. Chaplin, in the cabinet from 1889 as the first president of the new Board of Agriculture, excluded compulsion to begin with, but soon argued for it, citing Middleton's reports on agricultural seats in the Eastern counties. There was also pressure from Chamberlain, to whose proposals for the land, originally conceived in an anti-landlord spirit, a power of compulsory purchase had been integral.[127] By the 1890s, Chamberlain was less interested in land reform, while the social composition of the English county councils elected in 1889 showed that the landed class had little to fear from the rural electorate. It was safe to exclude compulsion from a smallholdings bill, as Balfour insisted, to dissociate Tories and Unionists from continuing radical propaganda for a peasant proprietary. The legislation for county councils had been a long time in the making. Originally, Salisbury would have liked members to sit with co-opted justices who should form a third of the whole council; he also wanted control of the police to remain with the magistrates. Although Churchill, the proponent of ratepayer democracy in the counties, left the government in December 1886, his views prevailed. As he and Chamberlain desired, the well tried urban model of local government was adopted, modified only in respect of the police, jointly controlled by the magistracy and the council.[128] Salisbury's most strongly felt objection had been to transferring the administration of the poor law to the councils. Agricultural labourers, he was afraid, would find it easier to put pressure on their councillors to be generous with relief than on guardians protected against such importunity by the weighted franchise used to select them. On this point, the premier had his way: the poor law was not added to the functions of county councils.[129]

Taking the 1888 Local Government Act in the round, Salisbury could claim that ending the historic role of the justices was a change in form rather than substance. Gentry magistrates had been progressively losing their once comprehensive powers to central government and to competing local authorities since the advent of the new poor law in 1834. Nevertheless, until the first county council elections provided solid reassurance, the outward change appeared a great deal more radical than it really was to some of the affected class. The depth of feeling noted in Carnarvon's diary shows that Salisbury was right to be a little nervous of the possible reaction. He dismissed Carnarvon's criticisms of the local government bill in the Lords as detached from contemporary reality: "He seems to be a person who insists on talking in blank verse on very commonplace topics". The changes they were discussing derived from the last instalment of parliamentary reform. It was not sensible to expect the rural population, "exercising as they do a voting power on all the most important questions of the Empire, to acquiesce in the doctrine that they are not fit to manage their own affairs". Chamberlain could not have put it more bluntly. The only threat to the landed class from the bill lay in the resentment that would be aroused if it did not pass.[130] On the platform, he was sharper; few landed magistrates regularly took part in county administration, and the squires' falling incomes were making it harder for them to do so: "Leisure means incomes obtained without difficulty and trouble". The local government bill also addressed the long-running problem of London's government, on which Gladstone's ministry of 1880–85 had attempted to legislate. There, as in Wales, the measure did harm the Tories. The London county council fell to the self-styled progressives who were Liberals with a radical bent; and the Nonconformist radicalism of the Principality scored notable successes in the Welsh counties. These uncomfortable results were a price worth paying for what was perceived as bold and constructive legislation.[131]

For Salisbury and for Chamberlain free education was the corollary of democracy. Here they encountered disapproval rather than open hostility from many Liberals, including some radicals, and perhaps more Tories. The cost of gratuitous elementary schooling and the implications for the balance of initiative and power between the state and the citizen gave the abstract discussion of government's role an immediacy it had lacked. Cardinal Manning, whose influence extended beyond the Catholic community, protested that "no amount of money can compensate for this surrender of principle". Gladstone disliked this encroachment upon the individualism he prized. So did Cranbrook, in charge of the education department, who reflected on "a great sacrifice of money and of parental duty leading, I fear, to more of both".[132] Salisbury's rationale of free education may not have convinced Cranbrook and other colleagues, but it was hard to attack. Compulsory school attendance from 1876 strained the tiny budgets of the labouring poor, such as those on his estates: he calculated that they were paying fees amounting to sixpence in the pound for a family of three on a wage of £60 a year. They had "a great grievance"; if the state forced the poor to educate their children, it should help them to discharge this obligation. On an electoral level, there were many more labourers than there were clerical objectors alarmed for the future of denominational schools at a financial disadvantage under the new dispensation. As he had first argued in the 1860s, education was the best prophylactic against the spread of radicalism and socialism. It was correctly predicted that few MPs would be prepared to oppose free education: and only a dozen – all Tories – did so on the bill's second reading.[133]

Yet Salisbury distinguished clearly between using public money to facilitate self-help – his central argument for free education – and the extension of governmental authority. He clashed with Cranbrook, who allowed his officials to draw up a plan that reduced the already qualified independence of Church schools as a condition of the increased government funding that made it possible for them to stop charging fees. The premier accused him in cabinet of being unfriendly to denominational education, when he was merely pessimistic about its chances of survival in competition with Board schools publicly funded by rates as well as taxes. It was a sharper repetition of their previous disagreements over departmental regulations governing students in schools, and the Technical Instruction Act of 1889 taking the state into another field. A right to free elementary schooling without a means test was generally taken to be evidence of "a socialist tendency". Salisbury had scouted the propensity to discern in his government's modest social legislation concessions of principle that were subversive of property: "We no more ask what is the derivation or philosophical extraction of a proposal before we adopt it than a wise man would ask the character of a footman's grandfather". He took one definition of socialism to be action by the state to do what private enterprise was capable of doing: in that sense "There is nothing so socialistic as the Mint or the Post Office". The check on that sort of intervention was simply whether the state performed to everyone's satisfaction, as it did in respect of the coinage and the postal service. Another definition of socialism was interference with these private rights, with property, on which the entire economic and social structure rested. The public would be quick to sense where these rights were really endangered: "These fallacies may be trusted to find themselves out".[134]

The Housing of the Working Classes Act of 1890 exemplified Salisbury's idea of the legitimate restriction of private rights. It not only consolidated the powers of compulsory purchase in earlier slum clearance acts but significantly reduced the cost to the ratepayer: valuations of property acquired under this Act discounted the relatively high rents that overcrowding produced, and made deductions for insanitary conditions and disrepair. The Act required local authorities to replace the dwellings they demolished, and empowered them to buy land and build where the supply of working-class housing was inadequate. The local government board's approval was necessary for both slum clearance schemes and the acquisition of land for additional housing. The new London county council made use of the Act to house and rehouse nearly 50 000 people before 1914; but municipal housing accounted for only one half per cent of all new houses in England and Wales over the same period. This modest achievement had to be financed from the rates, and involved resort to the public works loan commissioners, a mid-Victorian entity.[135] In the Lords speech, mentioned above, refuting the accusations of creeping social-ism, Salisbury had spoken of "the great centres of misery" born of the growth of population and industry during the century. He did not hide the difficulty of finding remedies acceptable to the dominant libertarianism and respect for property of all classes. The owners of slum housing in the metropolis and provincial towns were frequently small proprietors, a class well represented on councils and one which keenly resented the steadily increasing burden on ratepayers. The Salisbury minis-try had to proceed carefully and pragmatically "in the long and healthy tradition of English legislation".[136]

Their concern to limit the interventionism of central government while seeking to improve the condition of the urban poor led ministers to perpetuate in the Act the Victorian preference for local initiative in such matters. The legislation was permissive, and the formidable reluctance of vested interests to statutory inter-ference worked against it. Even the unavoidable public health acts elicited angry protests to the premier: C.T. Ritchie, the president of the local government board, needed to assure Salisbury that "It is mere moonshine . . . to talk of armies of inspectors".[137] Nor could the taxpayer be asked, for the time being, to repeat his measured generosity for a budget surplus in the case of free education. Low taxa-tion was an assumed right for contemporaries a generation after Peel's reforming finance had been completed by his disciple Gladstone. If taxes were low for all, the rich had reason to worry about the designs of some radicals on their wealth. These considerations held back the development of a welfare state clearly foreshadowed in the speeches of Salisbury and Chamberlain.

Churchill's budget proposals, on which he resigned, included a sizeable increase in the Gladstonian succession duty, recast as, in Salisbury's words, "a graduated death tax". In 1889 Goschen, pressed for money to pay for the modernization and expansion of the navy, superimposed on the duty, the incidence of which was regulated by consanguinity and not by value, a new estate duty charged at a flat rate of one per cent on realty and personalty where the property passing was worth not less than £10 000. Salisbury had been willing to make this one and a half per cent where the valuation exceeded £50 000.[138] The cabinet would not agree to taxing the sale of leases, treated as income: "To me it seemed a distinct proposal to put income tax on capital", wrote Cranbrook. Higher capital taxation was a temporary expedient to avoid raising the rate of income tax, reduced in Goschen's previous budgets. Gladstone expressed his fears, which were not new, to Hamilton of the Treasury, who shared them: graduating the demands of taxation, of capital or income, might be justifiable "in the abstract . . . but it was attended with much danger, for where was it to stop . . . it might amount to confiscation". Such presentiments seemed to limit the operation of the new estate duty in time, tying it to repayment of the expenditure in connection with the Naval Defence Act of that year. Treasury grants in aid of local spending, under a number of heads, were also rising. For this government's life, these increases and the economy's recovery from the depths of the long depression generated enough revenue to postpone the "indefinite extension" of graduated taxation which Gladstone foresaw. The predicate of low taxation had always been economic growth swelling the receipts from both direct and indirect taxes. The one and a half per cent on large inheritances which Salisbury had envisaged was a sign that more would, sooner rather than later, be exacted from those like himself who could afford to pay.[139]

The rhetoric of both parties, even Gladstone's, looked to more intervention by the state on behalf of the masses, and not just of the weakest in society.[140] C.T. Ritchie at the local government board was the government's specialist in the legislation that this progressive tendency, in both meanings of the adjective, produced. His perception of popular needs embraced an immigration bill to check the largely Jewish influx from the Russian empire: but it was something not covered by the consensus that saw other social measures through parliament.[141] If Ritchie advised him, Salisbury decided what was feasible and conferred greater respectability on the arguments for steps yet to be taken. Anticipating the pressure from below that was visible on the Continent, he encouraged it selectively. Germany's introduction of old age pensions in 1889 moved the national debate on social reform forward. Chamberlain promoted their adoption for his country from 1891: "Nothing . . . was potentially more Radical than this", writes his latest biographer. After an interval for this suggestion, novel from a leading British politician, to sink in, Salisbury discussed it in a lengthy speech devoted to the condition of Britain, as legitimate within the framework of self-help and education: "no nation and no class . . . ever rise . . . except by relying upon their own . . . efforts": but the statesman had "so to shape matters that the greatest possible liberty for the exercise of . . . moral and intellectual qualities should be offered . . . by law". To that end "nothing we can do . . . nothing . . . we did before . . . will equal . . . the measure for free education . . . we passed last year". Old age pensions, funded substantially on insurance principles, "without imposing any serious burden on the rest of the community", should be seen as an expansion of a quintessential Victorian institution, the friendly societies. Government must try to ensure that everybody could provide for what the working class from the labour aristocrats downwards, dreaded, "the days of darkness . . . of helplessness . . . of old age, and . . . the workhouse".[142]

It is surprising how little open criticism there was of Salisbury's new conservatism even when he used such language as this with its implicit condemnation of the capitalist juggernaut. Inevitably, some of his followers viewed his Irish and domestic policies as a series of surrenders. Irish landlords complained of the 1887 Land Act, English landlords of democratic county government and middle-class Tory MPs of the principle and expense of free education. There was, too, aristocratic dislike of ministers who did not belong to landed society, although they were not numerous. Observing Ritchie, recently taken into the cabinet, at a dinner given by a celebrated hostess, Carnarvon thought he "looked very 'middle class'" in those surroundings.

Ritchie, an East India merchant in the City before he entered politics, was "a roughish diamond", Balfour admitted in recommending his elevation. The premier's old Oxford friend, Frederick Lygon, resigned in a huff at being kept out of the cabinet. Salisbury was amused by Beauchamp's complaint that he had not "sufficiently regarded the claims of the hereditary peerage" in his appointments and promotions.[143] This internal opposition came to a head in the Lords on a minor item in the ministerial programme, the Land Transfer Bill. It derived from the Newport programme, which held out the prospect of legislation to simplify and cheapen the registration and transfer of titles to land in the interests of small buyers. Its noble critics chose to interpret it as a damaging intrusion of radicalism into the law of real property that enshrined their class rights. The projected reforms, part of a continuing process, had old radical associations, which was why Salisbury found them politically convenient to adopt. He thought, besides, that the law relating to landownership required further modernization, taking on where the 1882 Settled Estates Act, which he had supported, left off.

He told Halsbury, his very conservative lord chancellor, that the law as it stood was to modern landowners what "armour was to the knights at the close of the middle ages . . . It only prevented them from defending themselves". Halsbury's land transfer bill was nothing more than its title suggested; it did not emancipate proprietors from the residual law of settlement and entail. There was a whiff of radicalism about Salisbury's language when all he had in mind was the economic survival of landlords.[144] The Marquess of Bath, never really reconciled to Salisbury since the latter sided with Beaconsfield in 1878, and Beauchamp led the attack on the bill in July 1889. An unusually large attendance of peers had listened coldly as Salisbury "earnestly" appealed to them not to throw it out. Unmoved by the suggestion that to do so would be publicly unwise, a majority of Tories present voted for the bill's rejection; thanks to the handful of Liberals in the House, it survived narrowly by 113 to 104. A wrecking amendment from Bath to remove property passing by bequest from the scope of compulsory registration was carried against the two front benches.[145] Salisbury withdrew the bill: for behind the peers' resistance lay the powerful professional interest of solicitors, not at all keen on law reform and influential in the Commons. The Lords, commented Derby, had been unintelligently reactionary. Their demonstration seemed only to exhibit the weakness and timidity of their order, when it tried to act independently; a rebellion on such a small piece of government legislation could have no other result.[146]

Salisbury's wish, which had been Palmerston's, to leaven the apathetic lump of the hereditary peerage with a few life peers raised an interesting discussion in cabinet. So good a Tory as W.H. Smith seriously considered the ideas for a fundamental reconstruction of the second chamber for which Lord Rosebery, who was to succeed Gladstone as prime minister in the 1890s, was arguing from the Liberal side. It was not only very rich men who wanted to strengthen the Lords as a defence against "the most revolutionary measures" that might conceivably be sent up to them by a dominant Commons. Smith's fear of disestablishment and disendowment, of sweeping confiscations of property, was soundly based on the precedents of Irish legislation. The opposition of the Lords could not be separated from the question of its powers. As constituted, it was not an effective barrier to destructive change. The cabinet ought to consider all the suggested improvements: the disqualification of manifestly unfit peers from sitting and voting; life peerages; and an elective element drawn from the county councils soon to be established. Ministers settled for not more than fifty life peers and disqualifying the embarrassments; Salisbury had no "great panacea" for a real constitutional problem.[147] These proposals did so little that, without consulting the premier, Smith as leader of the Commons agreed to drop them in return for help from the opposition with getting through the local government bill and the budget in the session of 1888. The Liberals did not like to reinforce, even marginally, a House with a huge Unionist majority, following the flight of Liberal peers from home rule in 1886. Salisbury was caustic at the expense of his colleague. Smith had acted, he informed the Lords, "under the influence of a panic, which, in the face of . . . terrible threats, was not unnatural".[148]

The acknowledged feebleness of the Lords did not diminish the perennial appetite for honours. Their distribution was a prime ministerial activity intensely distasteful to Salisbury but important to his government's health. The peerages, baronetcies and knighthoods he gave out went increasingly to business wealth as the returns from industry and commerce eclipsed those from land.[149] Unionist grumbles, which honours helped to contain, rose in volume when a full legislative programme, by the standards of the time, troubled, or simply wearied, MPs. Their discontent fell off as substantial measures passed into law. On the death of Smith, whose character made up for his limitations as a debater, his place was taken by Arthur Balfour, closer than any other minister to Salisbury. The alternative to Balfour, whose handling of Irish policy and the Irish party in the House and at Dublin Castle, had been one of the successes of the second Salisbury ministry, was Goschen, also a success at the Treasury. Goschen's Unionism had not effaced Tory memories of his Liberal past, and the larger party in the alliance opted for Balfour. Assured of Smith's loyalty and Balfour's, and never forgetting to carry the Liberal Unionists with him, Salisbury had no potential Tory challenger, except, of course, Churchill. An object of greater suspicion than Salisbury ever was to high Tories like the malcontents in the Lords, Churchill did not recover from his miscalculation in December 1886. If there were moments when the power of his oratory was uncomfortable for the government, and occasionally threatening, his lack of consistency and scruple deterred the most faithful supporters. The head of the London Rothschilds, a banker deeply interested in politics, to whom Churchill owed much in every sense, recognized by the beginning of 1889 that his friend was "a hopeless politician".[150]

One reason why Salisbury's democratic and "socialist" tendencies did not count more heavily against him with conventional Tories was his ambivalence towards protectionism, to which many Tories remained attached and which the depression had made an irrepressible topic. From time to time through most of the 1880s he appeared to rule out protection, but, sometimes in the next breath, he adverted to the compelling arguments that he saw for "retaliation". The return of protection in its old form was not practical politics, given the strength of feeling against taxing imported foodstuffs. The plight of British agriculture, especially in the corn growing areas of the Midlands and the South, was such that Salisbury did not exclude some fiscal action in its interest. He raised with Goschen the possibility of reimposing a small duty on imported corn, to balance what he contended was the unfair disadvantage which the level of rates on agricultural land constituted for English producers. Goschen's Gladstonian orthodoxy in finance precluded any such concession. There was a better case, politically, for protecting British industry by "retaliation for the wall of tariffs . . . slowly shutting us out of one market after another". Protection that was selective and penalized imports classified as luxuries would not hurt the consumers noticeably: and if it did, "that evil is only transient . . . and the road to greater advantage" as foreign tariffs were adjusted downwards and Britain had something to bargain with. What he sought from Goschen, and did not get, was some encouragement to develop the line he had been taking in "what was still an academical discussion".[151] "I utterly disbelieve that it is in your power to introduce protection", Salisbury said in the Lords a few weeks afterwards. The attempt must end in strife "which would differ little from civil war". They had to look to the self-correcting machinery of economic laws to bring the country back to its former general prosperity.[152]

It seemed this statement of March 1888 had put paid to the Tory flirtation with protectionism. The "very equivocal language" that Salisbury had hitherto used on the subject could surely not be repeated, although what he had just said was bound to be unpopular with the growing number of Tories eager for protection. Salisbury's renunciation of ambivalence did not last very long. He impressed it upon the directors of the Tory machine, Akers-Douglas and Middleton, that "any movement in favour of protection must come from the people and not from above". They understood that the party should be "carefully dissociated" from organized protectionism, but also that it might be covertly financed. By the early 1890s they were asking "whether you think the . . . moment opportune for an agitation". In 1888, Salisbury reckoned publicly, between a third and a half of Tory MPs and all the Liberals, Unionists and Gladstonians, were firmly opposed to protection.[153] The industrial recovery which set in towards the close of the 1880s eased the protectionist pressure: it did not alter Salisbury's view that free trade's day was over. Tariffs, he said at the Mansion House in November 1890, were "the world's conflict of the future", a substitute for open war. Britain was isolated in her refusal to employ the same means of attack and defence: they would learn "whether that attitude will or will not be sustainable . . . or whether . . . our neighbours will force us to deflect [*sic*] in any degree from the . . . position we adopt". Pending the return of protection, British manufacturers and their workers could find expanding outlets in the empire, and in the additions to empire.

A passage in this speech went to the heart of contemporary imperialism: while the political and religious aspects of empire had their significance, it was driven by economic necessity. The Palmerstonian imperialism of free trade was more important than ever: and Salisbury confirmed its place in his foreign policy. "If there were no hostile tariffs, perhaps we should not be ambitious of dominion", he told the nation, "but we know that every part of the world's surface . . . not under the English flag is a country which . . . probably will be closed to us by a hostile tariff . . . therefore . . . we are anxious above all things to preserve, to unify and strengthen the empire . . . it is to the trade . . . with the empire . . . that we look for the vital force of the commerce of this country". It was his answer to those who questioned his government's acquisition of "large stretches" of Africa. They must realize how intimately "commercial freedom and territorial supremacy" were linked.[154] His Limehouse speech of July 1889 had put these familiar truths starkly in the harsher setting of the East End. "Just conceive what London would be without the empire . . . a collection of multitudes, without employment, without industrial life, sinking down into misery and decay". Common sense and shared interest were the foundations of a bi-partisan imperialism, uniting Gladstone, with his son in a Calcutta merchant house, and Salisbury, one of whose sons left the army for a career in the government of Egypt, Britain's puppet state, as his father had called it. British investors were seeking higher returns than were available at home, where in 1888 Goschen had been able to reduce the interest on the funded debt. That piece of financial engineering, well received by everyone except the holders of Consols, bore witness to the country's stability, and to the reputation for soundness that Salisbury's government enjoyed in the City.[155]

Markets, employment and investment made empire a preoccupation of the new conservatism. It was rather less conservative for that: Salisbury might disapprove of a statutory right to an eight-hour day and the closed shop, but as premier he defended trade unions from the stock criticism that they were bad for business. What was bad for business, he said before the 1892 election, was Britain's helplessness in international trade negotiations unless and until she had some tariffs of her own: "This is very heterodox doctrine, I know, and I should be excommunicated for maintaining it". He regarded trade and imperial expansion, like religion, property or the Union with Ireland as questions which must be rationally discussed before the electorate and submitted to its judgement. The industrial unrest of the late 1880s and 1890s was a symptom, much more than a cause, of the economy's problems and society's. In the same speech, strikes, to the extent that they reflected class tensions, were described as "the last arbitrament of social war".[156] Salisbury's foreign policy commanded the admiration of Gladstone and the Gladstonians because its goals were theirs: peace with the great powers of Europe and with the United States as the precondition of stability and prosperity at home, which were also bound up with the spread of British influence outside Europe by means of trade, investment, emigration and the judicious use of force.

# CHAPTER TEN

# European Security and Imperial Expansion

## The International Situation, 1886–92

Salisbury's foreign policy earned the respect of Liberals because its ends were unexceptionable: peace and security. They were less happy with his methods: Gladstonians and some Liberal Unionists did not like the "German alliance" on which his policy was built.[1] He had their unease in mind when evading German attempts to lock Britain into their close relationship by getting her to accede to the Triple Alliance, the cornerstone of Bismarck's European system. Salisbury's fundamental objection to that step was the unacceptable risk of war with France or Russia, or both. He chose to plead, instead, the unpredictability of the House of Commons and the British electorate as making any such commitment impossible to meet. The excuse was calculated to appeal to the German chancellor's dislike of parliaments and democracy. The surrender of Heligoland, a British possession since 1815, to Germany in 1890 symbolized Britain's desire to stand well with Germany, and was not popular with parliament or the public. The Anglo-German territorial agreement, in which the island's cession was a psychologically important point for the Germans, divided a great tract of East Africa between the two countries. In a speech replete with irony about "partitions of the unknown", given the little they knew of the African interior, Salisbury said that the agreement had "one solid practical merit . . . it has removed possible sources of quarrel" with, he did not need to say, the greatest of the European great powers whose growing colonial ambitions were a worrying source of Anglo-German friction. He invited his critics at home to "read between the lines" of this and his other colonial treaties: they were necessary to damp down the "fire of national self-consciousness" stoked by politicians bent on "self-glorification . . . and . . . by . . . fierce leading articles from one capital to another". Democracy and a popular press were inherently excitable and very dangerous in an era of steadily more destructive and costly armaments.[2]

His speeches, the best guide to what he was trying to do, dwelt on the peril from the arms race: the mounting expectations that strained national budgets might be defensive in intent but they were a potent influence for war. Britain could not refuse to join the race: the Naval Defence Act of 1889 was her response. Nothing is more evocative of the atmosphere among the great powers than Salisbury's open insistence that alliances and treaties afforded little protection against aggression. "Our business", he advised delegates from the self-governing colonies which depended absolutely on the British naval deterrent, "is . . . the tendencies of human nature as we know it in . . . history. Where there is liability to attack, attack will come".[3] To those who grumbled at the expense of modernizing the navy, he forecast that in the conditions of modern warfare defeat must mean "national annihilation". To a trading and investing nation, "a sensitive commercial community like ours", the apprehension of war would not be much less harmful than the fact. He asked the City, which provided his audience, to imagine the "terror and paralysis" resulting from the looming threat of a struggle that engulfed the great powers. His policy was designed to give Britain "not only safety . . . but a sense that safety exists". The real danger of hostilities between Germany and France, or Russia and Austria, or Russia and Turkey, spreading across the Continent, was never far away; its presence is felt throughout Salisbury's correspondence during these years. "Everyone I meet . . . concerned with the City asks me about this", his parliamentary undersecretary at the Foreign Office had written to him in January 1888, ". . . The great number of people who have 'open accounts' know that an outbreak of war would hit them hard".[4]

Salisbury's realism was tempered by diplomatic methods that offset the frankness of the speeches. While Britain must always be strong at sea, and should not neglect her defences on land, she need not be ashamed to further her interests by "showing complaisance and an accommodating spirit to those with whom we have to live". Such a posture was justified if it helped a minister to obtain the result he had in view. "My definition of foreign policy", this public explanation continued, "is that we ought to behave as any gentleman would, . . . who wishes to get on well with his neighbours". The stridency of the Jingoes repelled and alarmed him. No one at this time and afterwards did more to hold them in check, as the Liberals respectfully acknowledged.[5] His candour with the public allowed him to practise secret diplomacy within the structure of the policy he had outlined. The Liberal opposition got wind of the secret Mediterranean agreements of 1887, inspired by Germany, which involved Italy, Austria, Britain and, without her knowledge, Turkey. But they trusted Salisbury not to enter into commitments unacceptable to them, and to him. They refrained from pressing the government for details after repeated assurances that there had been no significant change of policy in Britain's relations with other powers.[6] The agreements were underpinning for the *status quo* on the shores of the Mediterranean and in the Balkans, a declared objective of Salisbury's. The relevant texts did not commit Britain to physical intervention: the other parties liked to think that it was implied, and he did not seek to underline the British interpretation. Even this, as he insisted, purely diplomatic alignment was one that he would have preferred to avoid: "we must join", he remarked when the entente of Britain, Italy and Austria was made more specific on the subject of Ottoman territory, "but I say it with regret . . . we are merely rescuing Bismarck's endangered chestnuts". That is to say, Germany did not want to side openly with Austria against Russia in their differences over Bulgaria; and he wanted the British to protect Italy from the French fleet. Drawing Britain into the provision of security for Germany's partners in the Triple Alliance made it less likely that she would have to fight on two fronts, the German nightmare. Russia and France were also Britain's potential enemies.[7]

As for bringing Turkey within the scope of this mutual support arranged between London, Vienna and Rome, it renewed Salisbury's hopes of breaking up the Ottoman empire, notwithstanding the treaties of Paris and Berlin. The three governments reaffirmed their intention of maintaining the Sultan in his rights: they also contemplated moving into his territory if he acted in a way they deemed "illegal"; a reference to concessions that Russia might extort from him. Where it was a question of standing by Turkey, Salisbury explained to his ambassador in Constantinople, "the understanding . . . uses language much vaguer than those treaties [of Paris and Berlin], and is easier to slip out of". He was inclined to think, because he wanted to, that Germany and Austria, as well as Italy, a country notoriously eager for territorial aggrandizement, were preparing to stake their claims to the possessions of an expiring empire. That was not the case: Turkey's was not the only empire in jeopardy. Germany and her partners, even Italy, were preoccupied with security, which was incompatible with the European consequences of attempting to partition the Ottoman lands.[8]

Germany and Britain were both in search of security: and the Mediterranean agreements constituted, in the eyes of almost everyone concerned, a *de facto* extension of the Triple Alliance to include the British. The Germans considered that Britain was much less grateful than she ought to be. Naturally, Salisbury did not find it necessary or politic to confess the extent of his relief at having mitigated the risks of isolation. Were Britain to be isolated, he advised the Queen, who like most of her subjects overestimated British strength, "it might well happen that adversaries . . . coming against each other on the Continent might treat the English empire as divisible booty by which their differences might be adjusted". In that eventuality, beset by the combined fleets and armies of Europe, Britain could only survive "at fearful cost and risk".[9] He and his colleagues declined to turn the closer relationship with Germany through her partners into a binding one: but the premier promised to go "hand in hand" with Bismarck until British opinion was ready for their cooperation to be reinforced by a treaty. The Germans took the point about public opinion; it was years before they understood that Salisbury meant to evade becoming the fourth member of the Triple Alliance. In the mean time, they expected Britain to give way with a good grace in local conflicts of interest where Germany appeared in remote areas of the world hitherto regarded as falling within Britain's ill-defined "informal empire". Salisbury did not object to German colonial expansion, believing that the openings created, such as they were, would provide modest opportunities for British trade. But where, in an existing market, the British interest was dominant, Germany could not have "a free hand".[10] The tensions arising were largely resolved by handing over Heligoland as part of the settlement of competing Anglo-German claims in East Africa. The significance of relinquishing the island, counter to the wishes of its inhabitants, was not lost on contemporaries. "'Jingoes' would be wild", Cranbrook predicted. Their protests were muted because government and opposition recognized that Heligoland was crucial to the negotiations. Failure to acquiesce in its loss "would force us to change our system of alliances in Europe", wrote Salisbury.[11]

The alternative to Germany as an ally was France: she would exact from Britain the evacuation of Egypt, on her terms. The two nations had outstanding disputes "in every corner of the globe".[12] Her people were a prey to political instability. The republic's politicians indulged an inveterate anglophobia, as being safer than attacks on Germany. Salisbury's patience was tried by the diplomacy that successfully averted collisions with the French, at a price in territory foregone. By 1890 it was clear to him that "we – at least – cannot go on with a policy of exchanges" by which Britain was the loser. He could not have halted British expansion had he wanted. Circumstances forced him to define "informal empire" more precisely than Palmerston needed to do, "i.e. that no other power shall take it".[13] Influence, in this sense, was demonstrated by the chartered companies and mission stations which gave it substance in tropical Africa, and by the appearance of British settlers on the high veldt of Central Africa. Salisbury held that the ancient claims of Portugal, one of the weakest European states, to the latter region were not sustainable. The Portuguese government and people proved slow to grasp facts plain to the British statesman: "if they cannot furnish settlers of their own blood, we can . . . and . . . shall do so whether we – that is, Great Britain – desire it or not". The Portuguese bowed to an imposing show of naval force and Rhodes's pioneer column went up from South Africa to found Fort Salisbury. The whiff of *realpolitik* here is unmistakable, as it is in Salisbury's speech of November 1888 accepting the inevitability of "small wars and rumours of wars" on the imperial frontiers in Africa and Asia. Scarcely worth the attention of the public, they were "merely the surf that marks the edge of the advancing wave of civilization".[14]

The image captivated loyal Gladstonians; it conveyed the liberal idea of empire, which reconciled Salisbury and successive generations to conquests requiring a moral, and not only a political and economic, rationale. In the process of expansion, however moral, the logic of battle was inescapable. Victories created a momentum; he instanced Tel-el-Kebir as the real foundation of the British position in Egypt. Defeats could not be forgotten: Gladstone's retreat from the Transvaal after the British disaster at Majuba was a "terrible blunder", one that "may . . . some day . . . have to be repaired".[15] The failure to save Gordon and withdrawal from the Sudan had to be made good. Even as he thought it prudent to deny that the government intended to reconquer the Sudan from the Mahdists – "We have no wish to be entangled anew in the deserts" – Salisbury referred in confidence to the hope of doing so. The Mahdist regime, at once an institutionalized *jihad* and a state whose economy was based on slavery and slave trading, was the clearest example of an order of things which it would be entirely right to overthrow when the time came. There was enough truth in the belief that British imperialism was everywhere beneficial in its effects to frustrate its domestic opponents. Rival powers, though jealous, could usually be bought off.[16]

The distinctive feature of Britain's empire was the self-governing colony for whom she acted in foreign countries, and where external defence remained with her, by mutual consent. By the 1880s Canada, Australia and New Zealand had between them overtaken the United States in terms of British exports and overseas investment; although America was still the destination of two-thirds of Britain's emigrants. The settler colonies, except for those in South Africa, gave the home government little trouble. Salisbury referred to their economic value on the platform: he was unsure how much they contributed to the empire in other ways. Canada's long-running fisheries dispute with the United States, and Newfoundland's with France, illustrated the disadvantages for Britain of a colonial autonomy that left her responsible before powerful states for the actions of virtually independent governments and legislatures. The political and constitutional relationship of Britain to Canada was, Salisbury warned Chamberlain, his special envoy to Washington in 1887–8, "so unexampled – so anomalous – so eccentric" as to expose her to "wholly unexpected embarrassments".[17] She was caught between American dislike of her imperial role, particularly in North America, and self-interested Canadian loyalty. There was no relief for Britain from those recurring difficulties: in 1890 Salisbury had to show the United States by the naval movements he ordered that London would not be deterred from standing up for Canadian rights to the sealing grounds of the Behring Sea: although he did not think the Canadian attitude to American demands for conservation was sensible. He said what he thought to the Canadian governor-general, a former cabinet colleague: "no obvious English interest is engaged, and where England would suffer economically by [a] rupture, it is quite necessary to be sure we have an unimpeachable case to present to taxpayer and trader". On the other hand, Canada should not be given cause to think that, in default of British protection, she would do well to consider the North American union which many in the United States believed was predestined.[18]

"It is of vital interest to us", Salisbury had no doubt, "that they should not . . . unite". The growth of American population and wealth, and the naval and military potential it represented, was intimidating enough without the addition of Canada who "would not remain separate to please us but only to suit herself".[19] The Australian colonies, not yet federated and in no danger of being absorbed by another power, drove Salisbury to assert British claims in the Pacific, about which he was unenthusiastic. There, too, a risk of war was present: "bloodshed and . . . stupendous cost . . . of which almost the exclusive burden will fall on us for a group of islands . . . to us . . . as valuable as the South Pole". All the disputes involving the settler colonies, including those between Boers and British in South Africa, were defused or successfully compromised in the course of this second administration.[20] If he never lost sight of the limitations of sea power, he made more use of it, according to his first lord of the Admiralty, than any previous foreign secretary had done. The landlocked republican Boers, trying to force their way to the sea through the territory of Britain's Zulu allies, could be checked, he informed the colonial secretary, by the simple expedient of stationing a cruiser off the stretch of coast in question: "I should have no idea of importing an English army to fight the Boers: that is too expensive".[21]

Under Salisbury British foreign policy reflected his unfailing perception of imperial Britain as a singular combination of strength and weakness. He contrived to maximize the former, without undue display, and minimize the latter. It is worth quoting, as *The Times* did, the tribute of the Vienna *Neue Freie Presse* to Salisbury's renewal of British influence in Europe and beyond: "it had got to be almost forgotten that his nation was one of the Great Powers". He conceded that there was force in the criticisms he attracted for holding the premiership and the Foreign Office together. The double burden was exhausting; though he found an intellectual enjoyment in diplomacy not provided by domestic politics. The results were commensurate with the incessant labour. One of his ambassadors whose admiration was not unqualified, Sir Edward Malet, in charge at Berlin of the most important embassy, spoke privately "in high praise" of the unity which Salisbury's unique assumption of both offices gave to the direction of foreign policy.[22]

## The Diplomacy of Security

Developments in Bulgaria worked against the conversion of the Anglo-German entente into the pact that Salisbury had himself solicited in 1885. Tsar Alexander III fiercely resented his Bulgarian namesake's successes in effectively absorbing Eastern Rumelia and defeating Serbia. The client state had acted independently of Russia and seemed likely to escape altogether from her control. The Tsar's drastic response was to order the abduction of Prince Alexander by pro-Russian officers in August 1886. Although the deported ruler was released and made his way back to a hero's welcome from his people, he bowed to the inflexible opposition of Russia and abdicated in September. In a personal message the Tsar had intimated that the "unhappy situation" of Bulgaria would continue unless the prince left the country permanently. Austria, to whom Alexander of Battenberg looked for help, advised him to submit. His subjects, however, rejected Russian dictation in the search for a successor. It ended in "a spectacularly anti-Russian choice": Ferdinand of Saxe-Coburg-Kohary, an Austrian officer and a member of the extended family that had provided Belgium and Portugal with their reigning families and Britain with the Prince Consort.[23] The Austrians were nervous about this Balkan triumph of July 1887 for their influence, and glad of the diplomatic support they received from the Mediterranean agreements in continuing with Britain to resist Russia's demands for Ferdinand's extrusion. To remove him in conformity with international law she needed to act through the Sultan, suzerain of Bulgaria. Austria and Britain persuaded Abdul Hamid II to withhold his co-operation. It was clear to him and his ministers and to everyone else, that the unexpected strength of Bulgarian national sentiment, turned against its Russian mentor, would afford what remained of Turkey in Europe better protection than her treaties with the powers.[24]

Nor should the Tsar be provoked into occupying Bulgaria in order to oust Austria's protégé. That would almost certainly mean war. The Bismarckian network of treaties, enlarged by the Reinsurance Treaty with Russia in June 1887, gave Germany the strongest possible incentive to avert a collision of the Romanov and Hapsburg empires over Bulgaria. Her enemy was France, and her Eastern frontier must not be exposed by having to choose between Austria and Russia. While Bismarck promised support for Russian policy in Bulgaria in the 1887 treaty, he engineered the Mediterranean agreements to shore up Austria's position in Eastern Europe. No one was taken in by these manoeuvres, but no one wanted to plunge the Continent into a war of the Bulgarian succession. The trial of strength between Russia and Austria in the diplomatic arena nevertheless carried the risk of war, if either lost too much face. Russia reacted to her failure with the Sultan by a military build-up on Austria's Galician border. Assuming hostilities to be imminent, the chief of the Prussian general staff, the elder Moltke, proposed a joint pre-emptive strike to the Austrians. The Emperor Franz Josef and his foreign minister, Count Kalnoky, had no illusions about their weakness, and Bismarck was able to defuse the situation created by Russian pique and his generals' preoccupation with military to the exclusion of political considerations.[25]

Initially dismayed by Alexander's removal, which might set the Balkans and Europe aflame, Salisbury believed that "any effective action" on Britain's part was out of the question. Parliament did not, and would not, give him the necessary funds to oil the wheels of Balkan intrigue "where nine out of ten men have their price"; the British army could not spare enough men to take on a minor European power, let alone Russia; and her diplomats had been shown up for what they were, "an ineffective agency". Not only was his a minority administration but cabinet government, "the views of . . . men, usually ignorant . . . and seldom united", did not lend itself to decisive measures in an international crisis.[26] Several members of the cabinet, including both Smith and Churchill, an unusual combination, wanted to leave the Balkans to Russia: Britain's interests lay in the Middle East, where they were served by her occupation of Cyprus and Egypt, and on the North-West frontier of India, where "the real battle" with Russia would be fought. Salisbury, and a majority of their colleagues, dissented from this mistaken realism. The British public, he tried to make Churchill see, was not prepared for a Russian entry into Constantinople.[27] If he accepted that this government could "do no good by an active policy at this moment", the manoeuvres of the great powers might soon present an opportunity for some constructive diplomacy. Britain, Churchill argued, was an Asiatic, not a European power, and should shape her policies accordingly. A withdrawal from Europe formed part of his case for reduced defence spending and lower taxation, which he pressed to the extent of resignation in the last days of December 1886. The failure of Churchill's challenge to the premier and the party's rejection of him relieved Salisbury of the one persistent critic of his foreign policy in the government.[28]

The fate of an independent Bulgaria would be decided between Russia and the two German powers. If Britain attempted to act alone, he explained, "it may make us ultimately ridiculous, as we have no intention of resorting to force by ourselves". He avoided talk of force, employed defensively, until the Mediterranean agreements had attached Britain to the Triple Alliance with the object of underpinning the precarious stability of South-Eastern Europe. The Bulgarian problem continued to be potentially explosive: the powers refrained from recognizing Ferdinand of Coburg until 1896. The risks involved in angering Russia were too great, Salisbury replied when Kalnoky suggested it might be time for recognition in 1889.[29] He encouraged Bulgaria and Turkey to resist Russian pressure to oust Ferdinand, although he preferred the regents who had governed the country since Alexander's abdication to the new prince. Salisbury waited on events and the German powers, using what influence Britain had out of range of the fleet's guns to pursue a "dilatory negative line . . . it is our interest that as little should happen as possible". He sought to impress on the Bulgarians that it was "a matter of life and death" to be patient and keep order in the face of Russian threats and attempts at subversion. Disorder would give the Tsar a pretext for intervention which he could hardly ignore. Salisbury rightly doubted whether Austria would move without German backing: and he did not think, in the year of the Reinsurance Treaty, that Germany was prepared to make an enemy of the Tsar.[30] He welcomed Ferdinand's marriage in 1893 as improving his shaky position with the prospect of an heir. Queen Victoria, who disliked this Coburg cousin as much as she had liked his Battenberg predecessor, was asked, when Ferdinand visited her in 1892, to show him some mark of favour. "It is of the last importance that he should not be murdered or driven from Bulgaria . . .".[31]

The modest British part in helping Bulgaria towards acknowledged independence of her powerful neighbours fitted into a larger design. It was not merely something to gratify mass audiences at home, with their predilection for a liberalism abroad that cost nothing. Salisbury's continuing aim in South-Eastern Europe was to hold off the disintegration of the Ottoman empire, until the time was ripe for a peaceful division of her territory and influence. At Constantinople, always assuming that the Mediterranean fleet could pass the Dardanelles, Britain had the means to coerce the Sultan, or to protect him from the sudden, seaborne Russian descent on his capital that was the subject of persistent rumours, especially in the early 1890s. The young German emperor, Wilhelm II, urged the British to deter the apprehended coup by reinforcing their fleet so as to be able to defend both Turkey from Russia and Italy from France. Salisbury thought the Germans were more interested in the former contingency than the latter. Bismarck's "double game" in trying to assure Russia and Austria of his support for either in Bulgaria was dangerous. It was, moreover, on German advice that the Sultan had strengthened the fortifications of the Dardanelles "to the utmost of his ability"; behaviour consistent with the 1881 declaration by the emperors of Austria, Germany and Russia reaffirming the international closure of the Straits to warships in peacetime. That declaration was directed against Britain, whose right to enter the Straits Salisbury had reserved at the Berlin Congress. He was sceptical of the rumoured attack on Constantinople by sea: the Russian expeditionary force would be at risk from the British fleet in the Sea of Marmora, supposing it to have been forewarned. But he did not exclude the possibility that the Russians "if they are very bold . . . well led, and have luck" might seize the Turkish capital when the fleet was still outside the Strait. Everything therefore depended on getting British warships through the Dardanelles before Russian troops had occupied the city.[32]

Salisbury took precautions well ahead of the German warnings. The fleet in the Mediterranean was reinforced and divided, with its Eastern division under standing orders to remain in the Aegean within forty-eight hours' steaming of the strategic anchorage at Besika Bay. He had also arranged for "watchmen" in the Black Sea to report movements at Russian ports. There were many imponderables; not least the willingness of the Sultan, afraid of Russia and nursing a lively grievance against the British presence in his tributary state of Egypt, to let the fleet through the Dardanelles: "Whether . . . it would be worth our while to force the passage, it is impossible *now* to foresee", wrote Salisbury.[33] He was tempted to leave Turkey to her fate, as Churchill and Smith had advocated in 1886. Just before he left office in 1892, he invited the cabinet to consider a revolution in British foreign and defence policy, prompted by the submission of the directors of naval and military intelligence that the Mediterranean fleet had enough to do in preventing the strong French force at Toulon from joining the squadrons in the Atlantic and the Channel. If the navy really was unable to meet the requirement for a powerful presence in the Eastern Mediterranean, its battleships should definitely be withdrawn from that sea to reinforce the Channel fleet and Britain's first line of defence. Without those battleships, Britain could do nothing to save Constantinople from falling to the Russians. That defeat, said the premier, "appears to be not a speculation but of absolute certainty, according to . . . those two distinguished officers, because we may not stir a finger to prevent it". To soften the blow to the country's international standing, ministers ought to let the world know that Constantinople "is not, in our eyes, worthy of . . . sacrifices and . . . risks".[34]

This was a reversion to the view of the Ottoman empire's *un*importance for Britain which he had avowed at the Constantinople conference fourteen years earlier. It was still not practical politics. His memorandum acknowledged that abandoning Constantinople to Russia must seriously affect Britain's power in the East, and probably India, where it was "so largely dependent on prestige".[35] He did not mention that a naval retreat from the Mediterranean would have deprived the 1887 "secret" agreements with Austria and Italy of their limited value for the powers concerned. Germany, who had inspired the agreements, continued to rely on the Royal Navy to protect Italy's coastline in the event of war between the Triple Alliance and the Franco-Russian combination, strengthened by the entente of 1891 and the plans of their general staffs.[36] If, in the thinking of the French foreign ministry, war with Britain was something to be avoided, despite the friction fermented by their conflicting interests outside Europe, French public opinion was volatile and easily excited against an old enemy. When the eminent general, Lord Wolseley, put his authority behind an invasion scare reminiscent of the more famous one in 1859, Salisbury sharply deprecated his alarmism but explored the nature of the threat in a series of memoranda for his cabinet. It was the period of Boulangism in France: had Boulanger, the general turned nationalist politician, captured the Third Republic, he and his royalist backers might well have channelled the emotions whipped up by his triumph into a war against Britain, less dangerous to France and to the new regime than the hoped-for *revanche*.[37]

Wolseley, adjutant-general at the War Office, had criticized the inadequacy of Britain's defences in a way unusual for a serving officer, even then. Salisbury took immediate steps to allay the concern. He chaired a cabinet committee on the wider problem of national security, and appointed a royal commission on the working of the defence departments, with Hartington at its head and Randolph Churchill, W.H. Smith, and the last Liberal secretary of state for war, Campbell Bannerman, as members. Responsibility was thus shared between the parties. Salisbury put detailed questions to the soldiers, designed to establish that the French would find it impossible to mount an invasion without drawing attention to their preparations. The former chairman of the Great Eastern Railway had a good grasp of the logistics of modern war. He wanted estimates of the rolling stock and sea transport needed to move at least a hundred thousand men to the invasion ports and across the Channel. He also wished to know, since Wolseley was at the War Office, "precisely to what degree of perfection" the department's plans for resisting the invading force, if it got ashore, had been carried.[38] Replying, the director of military intelligence contended that the French would not attempt to invade until the British fleet had lost its control of the Channel. "Our stake is so great", considered the premier, "that full precautions must be taken against even a distant possibility" of a sudden French attack on the south coast, such as the Admiralty, the War Office, and the German general staff, consulted through their London embassy, agreed did exist.[39]

Salisbury was sharply critical of "gaps in the information" when the defence departments had responded to his searching inquiries. He quoted Wolseley against their reliance on naval superiority: "all soldiers who understand the question better than politicians know this to be the greatest of fallacies". He pressed the Admiralty and War Office on their plans, such as they were, in the event of war and invasion. Taking up the German suggestion of a strong "corps of observation" on the coast, he added his own that bridges, railways, tunnels and assorted supplies lying in the invaders' path should be destroyed. The point underlined the seriousness with which he took the threat he played down in public. When, some months later, the Admiralty ruled out a surprise attack, asserting that there was not enough shipping in the French Channel ports for the operation, Salisbury easily proved it wrong. On his instructions, British consuls from Calais to Cherbourg reported a tonnage sufficient to transport 140 000 men, if seized and given, where necessary, French bridge and engine-room crews. The French, he calculated, could move up to 30 000 men a day without exciting suspicion. On these assumptions, the danger was real in the political climate of France at the end of 1888. If the chances of an invasion succeeding were small, they might very well tempt "the kind of soldier who comes to the top in a revolution", that is, Boulanger. Salisbury had a vision of Britain taken unawares one Saturday night after a fifth column of "two or three Irish patriots" had cut the telegraph lines running from the coast. The country would wake up to find the French one day into the estimated four days' march on London.[40]

That summer's mobilization of the reserve fleet in forty-eight hours did not satisfy him: a pre-arranged exercise was not a proper test of the navy's ability to meet such an emergency. His political will informed the Naval Defence Act of 1889 under which eight first-class battleships were built in three years as well as sixty-two other warships, including small, fast vessels for inshore work. It marks the acceleration of Britain's large contribution to the international arms race deplored in Salisbury's speeches from the late 1880s. Britain's annual expenditure on her navy was more than doubled in the course of the 1890s.[41] Her German ally had proposed an exchange of naval intelligence, to which Salisbury agreed: "In the grouping of Europe . . . likely to continue for some years our possible antagonists are the same, viz.: France and Russia". His care to stand well with Germany and her chancellor led him to avoid taking sides in the intermittent friction between the British and German ruling houses, so closely related and so touchy. He discouraged the Queen's liberal-minded daughter, another Victoria and the short-lived Emperor Frederick III's consort, from trying to influence German foreign and domestic policy in "an anti-Bismarckian sense" during her husband's few months on the throne in 1888. She would expose herself, and Britain, to the "most severe risk".[42] Her son, Wilhelm II, whose reactionary and strongly nationalist outlook set him against his parents, might be, in Salisbury's private opinion, "a little off his head", but his British relations must humour him. They were dealing, Salisbury warned Queen Victoria, when Wilhelm's succession was imminent, with a young prince whose moods and actions, "however blameable and unreasonable, will henceforth be political causes of enormous potency".[43]

In that context, he was dismayed by a diplomatic incident arising from the dislike which the new emperor and his uncle, the Prince of Wales, felt for each other. Wilhelm II successfully objected to the Prince's simultaneous presence at the Austrian court when he paid his first state visit to Vienna. Bismarck used the occasion to tell the British premier that nothing of the kind would have happened had "a real defensive alliance" existed between Britain and Germany: and followed up the reminder with a firm proposal for one. Salisbury evaded the offer by pleading, again, the unreliability of a country like his where a democratic legislature dominated the executive: "we leave it on the table without saying yes or no, that is unfortunately all I can do at present". The truth was that he meant from the outset to preserve Britain's "unfettered . . . discretion" in interpreting her political commitment to the Triple Alliance through the Mediterranean agreements and the understanding with Germany that produced them.[44] The guidance he provided for Alfred Austin and his newspaper is instructive. "The service which a paper like the *Standard* can [do] by judicious action on European opinion is very great", he assured Austin. The public and Europe were to be told that Britain "*will* fight" beside Austria and Italy should Russia march into the Balkans but "we can give no specific promises". On the Triple Alliance's other flank, where the Germans really desired British naval help, he left Count Hatzfeldt in no doubt that Britain would not make her fleet available if the adventurism of Italy's king and her politicians drove her to attack France first, on whose metropolitan and colonial territory they harboured designs.[45] Salisbury deeply distrusted the Italian premier in 1887–91, Francesco Crispi, whom he was forced to tolerate by Germany's liking for him, and did not intend to be drawn into war by unwilling involvement in his "trumpery quarrels".[46]

Bismarckian *realpolitik* was as repugnant to Salisbury as it had been when he championed the Danes in the 1860s. The German statesman and his Italian protégé had shown "extreme untrustworthiness" in their relations with Britain, and others, particularly in respect of the colonial questions which loomed larger in great power politics every year. The self-interest of Bismarck's Germany, however, made for

European peace, even if he sometimes threatened it in his anxiety to keep France down and to avoid having to choose between Austria and Russia in the South-East of Europe. When Wilhelm II, determined to assert himself as the real ruler of Germany, dismissed Bismarck in 1890, Salisbury was rewarded for his skill in humouring the emperor. Eager to demonstrate that he was not a reactionary like the fallen minister, Wilhelm let the Russo-German relationship deteriorate and was at moments effusively anglophil. Salisbury saw to it that his British relatives reciprocated, on the surface, the emperor's genuine affection for a grandmother who did not care for him: Wilhelm visited Britain in 1889 and 1891, and did something to slow down the growth of public hostility to Germany, perceived as a commercial and colonial rival.[47] He did not do enough to win Britain over to a closer association with the Continental country outwardly best suited to be her partner in the maintenance of European security. In the advice that Salisbury conveyed to his Liberal successor at the Foreign Office in 1892, Lord Rosebery, he insisted on Britain's freedom from any obligation to furnish "material assistance" under the Mediterranean agreements.[48]

British independence of the European combinations was not so marked as to convince Russia that the Triple Alliance had not, in effect, become quadruple. She felt diminished and menaced: the entente with France was the result.[49] In 1891, on the way back from its historic voyage to the Baltic and Kronstadt, where Alexander III, autocrat of all the Russias, stood bareheaded while the bands played the *Marseillaise*, the French Atlantic fleet was invited to call at Portsmouth. Salisbury wanted to show that Anglo-French colonial rivalry did not exclude mutual goodwill. The occasion, with visiting German royalty kept at a distance by French request, was rightly construed to signal the British premier's regret that Europe should be dividing into two power blocs. It was no more than a gesture: "our interests lie on the side of the Triple Alliance", he said as the French ships lay at Portsmouth.[50] Yet watchers in the capitals of the alliance could have no illusions. The foreign minister at Vienna spoke for them when he remarked on the change of government in Britain. She was not, he told the French ambassador in July 1892, committed to the Triple Alliance, any more than she was to the Franco-Russian entente. What she might do, at the critical moment, would be decided solely by her national interest: "L'Angleterre, celle de Salisbury, comme celle de Gladstone, ne se lie avec personne . . . Personne ne peut compter sur elle". At the German foreign ministry, an expert noted how at the election Gladstone had nothing significant to say against Salisbury's policy abroad but endeavoured to ascribe its strengths to a shared liberal tradition.[51]

## Limiting the Competition of Empires

In the last thirty years of the nineteenth century Britain's empire expanded by some four million square miles, France's by three million, and Germany acquired a million. Most of this expansion took place in Africa. A belief in the continent's potential wealth, spectacularly justified in Southern Africa from the 1880s, was a strong motive for its partition, but not necessarily the strongest. Considerations of prestige, to which the democratic electorates of the three great powers were susceptible, inspired bids for territory and bedevilled negotiations. Humanitarianism and religion were, if nothing else, useful for the reassurance they provided to peoples who liked to see their national policies as instrumental to the spread of civilization. The strategic value of acquisitions, in Africa and elsewhere, was proclaimed, and sometimes real. The seemingly interminable dispute over Samoa, involving Britain, Germany and the United States, showed how difficult it was for great powers to agree on the fate of a small group of islands, without much value for any of them, when their self-esteem was at risk. The British democracies in Australia and New Zealand ensured that London resisted the temptation to let one more Pacific archipelago go to someone, in this case the Germans, who appeared to want it badly.[52] Similarly, the Canadians and Newfoundlanders made Britain stand up for them in their fisheries disputes with America and France. There was no escape for Salisbury from the importunity of his colonial fellow-subjects of the Queen. The settler colonies, so nearly independent, were nevertheless seen, and felt themselves to be, an integral part of Great Britain. It was, finally, an axiom of Victorian foreign policy that Britain could never afford to make an enemy of the United States, given the enormous significance of Anglo-American trade and of British investment there. Salisbury stopped short of outright appeasement: but he took the utmost care to be conciliatory, even, or especially, when he had to resort to a warning naval demonstration. For him compromise was the stuff of imperial diplomacy: and he was a master of the art. He would not allow colonial rivalry to assume really unreasonable proportions.

His counterparts in Europe and America did not dissent from Salisbury's priorities. Everybody wished to avoid the kind of incident in the African wilderness or on the fishing grounds of North America that might lead to war; once blood had been shed, press and public would leave governments little room for manoeuvre. Salisbury might safely joke about the ignorance of the African interior displayed by Europe's negotiators. The irony put their exchanges in perspective: the fate of great nations did not, and ought not to, depend on the outcome. In the 1880s and early 1890s such saving humour was still possible in the state of cartography and of international politics. He was not inclined to make a jest of the British involvement in Egypt. Britain's military presence there, and the degree of political control it underwrote, lacked an adequate basis in international law. Other powers, and notably Germany, exploited French resentment of this dominant position in a country where the influence of the French had recently matched, or exceeded, that of her rival. The internationalization of the Egyptian debt and its shared management by the powers representing their nationals among the state's creditors, imposed a collective check on Britain in Egypt. Salisbury needed German goodwill if the unofficial protectorate was to succeed in its self-appointed task of reconstruction and improvement. With German backing on the commission that administered the debt, Britain could hold her own comfortably enough in the continuing European discussion of the Egyptian question. Salisbury intensely disliked this further limitation on Britain's international freedom of action, and spoke of German blackmail. His ideal, unattainable though he knew it to be, was to be able "to snap our fingers at all the world".[53]

Although he fully supported Evelyn Baring's labours in Egypt, seeing in them the constructive imperialism of which their countrymen were proud, Salisbury regretted the British occupation. The Gladstone government had blundered, he always maintained, in allowing a situation to arise that could only be resolved by that unwise and crude extension of the influence which Britain had already won by peaceful means. The Canal did not require a British force to guard it; nor was it indispensable to imperial communications. Salisbury sought and obtained neutralization of the waterway in the Canal Convention of 1888. In wartime Britain might plead overriding necessity and close it to her enemies. The Convention satisfied the powers who had no objection to letting Britain contain Islamic nationalism in one of its centres. Even the French really wanted no more than the parity of influence they had enjoyed prior to the occupation. The strength of Islam, and its inherent antagonism to a too visible Western presence, added considerably to Salisbury's desire for a military withdrawal from Egypt if it could be arranged without a substantial loss of the authority won at Tel-el-Kebir. The troops were a provocation to Egyptian Muslims and their Turkish suzerain, as well as to the French.[54] Wolff, whose continuing inclination to stir up political mischief through his association with Randolph Churchill made it convenient to keep him abroad, undertook a special mission to Constantinople in 1887. Salisbury envisaged the "neutralization of Egypt", and not only of the Canal, "under English guardianship". This, unsurprisingly, struck the French as a contradiction in terms. There was to be a phased evacuation over five years, subsequently reduced to three, with a right of re-entry, exercisable at Britain's discretion in the event of any perceivable external or internal threat to the Egyptian state as the British left it.[55]

The activities of the international commission administering the debt were to be confined to protecting the interests of creditors. How this might be achieved was not entirely clear. The reconquest of the Sudan, to which Salisbury was not publicly committed, made its appearance in this cabinet memorandum: until it had been effected Britain retained her control over the selection for higher ranks in the Egyptian army she had rebuilt. Salisbury hoped that these arrangements would put an end to the "permanent disagreement with France . . . , which may at any moment take an acute form", and would also be acceptable to the Sultan, as suzerain and Caliph.[56] Moving the troops to Malta or Cyprus, in readiness for a swift return, should enable Britain to "watch over Egypt . . . without offending the Mussulman population by floating the infidel flag among them". In fact, as Salisbury later admitted, Baring's ascendancy, which was partly personal, could not survive an evacuation. So anxious was the premier to liberate himself, as far as possible, from a "disastrous inheritance" in Egypt that he was prepared to risk losing her dominant position there. Some time would have elapsed before the British public, in whom the "national, or acquisitional feeling" grew steadily, realized the extent of the sacrifice made in their name. As it was, the French chose to emphasize the conditional withdrawal of troops from Egypt as an indefinite prolongation of British hegemony, and to ignore a modification of her actual position that might well have been fatal to it. Under the threat of a French occupation of Syria, the Sultan refused to ratify the second Anglo-Turkish Convention signed in 1887, which embodied Salisbury's proposals with little change.[57]

It was the turning point for Salisbury's Egyptian policy. He reverted, intermittently, to the idea of evacuation, but France was implacable, and British public opinion unfavourable. Once more or less resigned to governing Egypt for a long time to come, he looked to the Egyptians, rather than to his diplomacy, to create the conditions for a British retirement. Some years before he had startled Baring by remarking that "The East is decaying for want of revolutions". "A somewhat remarkable statement from a Conservative statesman", mused the proconsul. Baring was always afraid of "a recrudescence of Moslem fanaticism" as the real force behind Arabi's national movement and the signs of its revival; while Salisbury believed Egypt could not be insulated against the current of nationalism running through neighbouring countries. Baring's rule was bearing Western fruit: "If Egypt goes on improving as rapidly as she is . . . now", wrote the premier, "the time will come when she will insist on being free from Turkey, or England, or anybody else".[58] Meanwhile he had to assure Austin and his newspaper that the second Anglo-Turkish Convention was, in intention, "as unGladstonian as anything can be", although Gladstone thoroughly approved of it; British party leaders viewed "the English Chauvinist" with distaste and apprehension. The Sultan's refusal to ratify the convention, therefore, did not harm the government with its own supporters, who welcomed an indefinite extension of Britain's stay in Egypt.[59]

The Islamic world, Salisbury said at Glasgow in May 1891, was resistant to "the modern ideas . . . essential to progress and . . . preservation". It must learn to adapt to Westernization and was doing so. Where it failed to change, it would die. European powers would fight over an expiring Muslim nation. Instancing Morocco, he prophesied that she would be "as great a menace to the peace of Europe as the other Mohammedan countries further to the East used to be". Even Turkey, notwithstanding the endemic strife of Christian and Muslim in Armenia and Crete, was advancing, and Persia too. With their advance "in all that conduces to prosperity or humanity", the danger of the powers falling out over the possessions of the Ottoman Sultan and the Shah receded. There, and in India, it should be remembered that Islamic populations followed "the law of their nature" and would not be converted to Christianity in the near future, but were susceptible to the civilizing influences that ultimately "will lead to truth". This was Salisbury's credo in the Muslim East. As far as the vast Ottoman empire was concerned, his predilection for its Christian subjects had weakened to the point where he acknowledged that "the Christians murder the Mussulmans quite as freely as the Mussulmans murder the Christians". The Greeks were enough to disillusion any man, he let it be known. He had ceased to be the philhellene of the 1870s working for Greece against the Turkish prejudices of Disraeli: a bankrupt and corrupt state, a prey to brigandage, declined to relinquish "magnificent dreams and splendid recollections" of a Greek empire. Greece's policy was to extract territorial concessions from the Turk by threatening to start the Balkan conflagration which the powers were agreed in wanting to prevent. "She is the blackmailer of Europe", he told the British minister in Athens.[60]

The traditional British sympathy for Greece, operating on Salisbury's cabinet and within it, stopped him in the Cretan crisis of 1887 from warning the Greek government of naval action if it proceeded to invade the island: but his diplomatic attitude, and that of the other powers, proved a sufficient deterrent. The "real remedy" for the succession of Balkan crises, he now considered, was a "strong and just" hand at Constantinople. Although he found it expedient to praise Abdul Hamid II in the Glasgow speech, Salisbury persisted in underestimating the Sultan's achievement: Ottoman government was still "feeble, corrupt and vicious", for all that Muslims of the empire "are certainly as good people as the Christians" of a kingdom ruled by near relations of the British Queen.[61] On their side the Sultan and his advisers had long suspected Britain of a grand design to build up a second Indian empire from Egypt and a reconquered Sudan, and to encourage aspirations to independence under her influence in the Arab lands. Britain, they feared, planned to complete the undoing of Ottoman Turkey by throwing her weight behind the erection of a rival Caliphate at Mecca or Cairo as a purely spiritual authority. The extension of British influence over Turkey in Asia had been one of Salisbury's objectives since he first went to the Foreign Office; he was to think seriously of frightening the Turks with his support for a rival Caliphate, and of creating that empire in the Middle East in the form of protected Muslim "statelets". As much as Palmerston and Gladstone, he preferred influence to territory and was acutely aware of liabilities that exceeded the resources at his disposal.[62]

The disadvantages of the Egyptian occupation were offset, increasingly, by Baring's skilful modernization of an Islamic state, and British pride in the process.[63] Persia linked the empire in India with the growing British presence in the Middle East. It was inadvisable, however, for Britain's representatives to invoke her naval might in circumstances that made allusions to it ridiculous. As Salisbury reminded Wolff, sent to the Teheran legation, "Even to the Shah's benighted intelligence, it must be evident that the most magnificent ironclads would not help her greatly" when it was a question of fending off Russia. Besides, the navy could not spare the ships for a sizeable naval demonstration in the Persian Gulf; the nearest were busy protecting Zanzibar and British interests on the East African coast from encroaching powers. Salisbury did not believe Russia could be trusted to honour any agreement with Britain to co-operate in Persia instead of competing for ascendancy. Wolff discussed the possibility in an interview which he obtained with the Tsar in 1889. "The Russians are deceptive in the same way that they are aggressive", commented Salisbury.[64] Nor had he faith in an inflow of British capital to build the railways essential to the country's development. If the Shah, whose financial irresponsibility was notorious, provided guarantees, they would probably be worthless. Premier and cabinet did, however, raise the standing of the British Imperial Bank of Persia, which propped up Persian finances from 1890 with a royal charter. Salisbury was afraid that Persia, reduced to "Russian vassalage", with her resources exploited and railways built by Russian capital, would provide an easier invasion route into Afghanistan and India than the northern approach to which so much attention had been paid. Wolff had considerable success with the bank and other initiatives that strengthened Persia's economy and government.[65]

Salisbury contrasted this constructive influence, working against Russian domination in ways that promoted "the well-being of the Persian people", with diplomatic involvement in the activities of "commercial adventurers . . . very much on the watch" for their chance. "Nothing", he instructed Wolff's successor, "must be pushed merely because it will favour a British speculation unless you are certain that it will do good, or at least, not do harm to Persia itself". The new British minister was also advised to tread warily in seeking to put right misgovernment in an oriental despotism where European motives were naturally suspect, "where we have very few but moral weapons to use, character is of great importance to us". These extracts from his briefing breathe the spirit of Salisbury's policy, combining as it did the practical and the ethical with a nice judgement. The morality of empire was a Victorian preoccupation from which he could not have freed himself if he had wanted. It was much in evidence during the partition of Africa, although other considerations were decisive.[66]

Salisbury always meant to recover the Sudan. Britain upheld Egypt's claim to her lost provinces and Turkey's suzerainty over them. Salisbury contemplated using Turkish troops to garrison Suakin on the Red Sea coast left in Anglo-Egyptian hands, but was not sorry to drop the idea as inconsistent with a compelling reason for Britain's continuing interest in the Sudan. The British public would never believe in the Turkish will to combat the traffic in slaves across the Red Sea to Arabia. The Mahdist state of the Khalifa Abdullahi was based on slavery and holy war, the *jihad*, with its harvest of enslaved captives from the surrounding pagan and Christian Abyssinian peoples. Conscious of the Mahdists' proven fighting qualities, which had tested the British regulars of the Gordon relief expedition, Salisbury did not commit himself publicly to the reconquest of the Sudan. But he depicted the Mahdists as implacable enemies of everything that his contemporaries understood by civilization. The slave trade would not be extirpated, nor would Egypt be safe from attack, until the state that epitomized Islam at its most fanatical and oppressive was defeated. Salisbury's outline of his negotiating position for the abortive Anglo-Turkish convention in 1887 specified, among vital British interests in Egypt, "the pacification of the Sudan"; so long as it was "incomplete" Britain should retain control of appointments to the Egyptian army's senior ranks. That army had already demonstrated its ability, under British leadership, to stand up to Mahdist attacks on the frontier with the Sudan; and at the battle of Toski in August 1889 repelled the *jihad* launched by the Mahdi's successor, the Khalifa, against the infidel and the infidel's Muslim allies, the Khedive and the Ottoman Sultan.[67]

Much as he admired British regimental officers, seen at their best in the selection made for the Egyptian army, Salisbury remembered the failures of British generalship in the attempt to save Gordon. "I do not wish to rub up old sores", he said, speaking on national defence at a City dinner, "but we did wish to relieve a town called Khartoum . . . and the results were not of the most brilliant character". He had assured a provincial audience before the victory at Toski, that the government did not mean to be "entangled anew in the deserts". In fact, he intended to move forward from the existing frontier when the time was ripe, as he had done since he envisaged "a very gradual" recovery of the Sudan in 1885. An advance to Berber, two hundred miles down river from Khartoum, was his "ultimate objective" at the end of the 1880s, he told the London Greek banker and Liberal MP, Pandeli Ralli. Once at Berber, Egypt with her British-led army "becomes master of Khartoum", he had written earlier. The Mahdist state would be securely contained, but he was sceptical when, following the Anglo-Egyptian military successes, Baring and the British commanders wanted to retake the Eastern Sudan from Suakin. He could not credit the optimism that looked ahead to the dissolution of the "fanatical confederacy" – his description – of tribes under the Khalifa's rule. The Eastern Sudan was recovered in 1891, but the casualties suffered by Egyptian troops were heavy and, far from crumbling, the Mahdist state was consolidated, as the Khalifa conciliated political opponents; fostered trade, that with Egypt included; and accumulated grain and munitions. If the Mahdists were now on the defensive, the British and Egyptians had learnt painfully that they continued to be a redoubtable foe. The reconquest of the Sudan was not to be accomplished until Egypt's finances and her army were both stronger.[68]

The strategic value of the Sudan was questionable. General Gordon thought it "a useless possession . . . and ever will be so". There was little material reward to be had from taking the Sudan into the British empire. Salisbury was scathing about the speculative businessmen who pretended that there was: "promoters . . . financiers, contractors . . . who see a prospect of sweeping a shoal of guileless shareholders into the net". The demands of prestige, loudly voiced by Jingoes, were not so easily dismissed. Salisbury held that Gordon, whose memory was soon a cult, had to be avenged: his death in the triumph of militant Islam was not something that Britain, the ruler of Muslim millions, could forget. The Victorian crusade against slavery had still stronger claims on British policy towards the Sudan. So had Egypt: the Egyptian political class had good reason, Salisbury considered, to hold the loss of the Sudanese provinces against Britain. If the plan of evacuating British troops without letting Egypt fall into the hands of nationalists hostile to Western influences, or into those of the French, was to work, the lost territory must be restored to the Khedive. In addition, Riaz Pasha, the veteran Egyptian premier, and Baring were troubled at the thought of letting the Upper Nile pass under the control of another European power – the Italians in Eritrea were nearest – which might proceed to divert some of the flow to irrigation in the Sudan. Egypt's use of Nile water was increasing under Baring's benevolent rule. Salisbury kept this point in view, but he was not inclined to make too much of it.[69]

On the universal assumption that the Mahdist state would succumb to Britain or to a rival power before long, Salisbury's African diplomacy was devoted to keeping the other interested powers at a distance. He regarded Italian ambitions, rightly, as "misplaced and suicidal"; the Mahdist host was more than a match for their badly led and trained, though better armed, forces. Not unaware of their military limitations, the Italians sought British co-operation in the hope of obtaining territory and an equal say in the Sudan's future. The central relationship in Salisbury's foreign policy, with Germany, obliged him to work with her partner in the Triple Alliance: but he gave little away. The Anglo-Italian agreement of 1891 reserved the Khedive's rights if and when Italy entered the Sudan. The treaty of the previous year with Germany shut her out from the Upper Nile in the South. The threat of France remained in the West, notwithstanding the Anglo-French African treaty, also of 1890. As he emphasized to Pandeli Ralli, who had Egyptian interests, there was no question of a swift return to Khartoum: "whether by the diplomatic or the financial road . . . there is no way out . . . except by patience". Egypt, he insisted during this ministry, must pay for the reconquest, and be able to do so without plunging herself back into what he had termed the "international abyss" of rising debt that would leave her, and her British masters, at the mercy of the powers.[70] Normally the British public "in its largest sense" paid little attention to Egypt and the Sudan. He asked Baring to remember that Gladstonian Liberals – or some of them – would probably raise an outcry at the expenditure of British blood and treasure on undoing Sudanese independence. He did not want to stir up the countervailing popular emotions of patriotism and humanity until Egypt was militarily and financially ready to advance. He did, however, mention, in his conversations with ambassadors in London, the indignation his public would feel if Italy or France took the Sudan.[71]

Where Britain had a presence in the rest of Africa, Salisbury acted on a dispassionate judgement of its capacity for expansion. Like Liberal ministers in the first half of the 1880s, he was forced to act by other nations' disregard for the informal empire on African coasts "without being put to inconvenience by protectorates, or anything of that sort". Quite suddenly, her traders, missionaries, a few consuls and fewer warships did not stop the annexation of territory thought, on the spot and at home, to have been "practically under the protection of England". He did not criticize his predecessors for having agreed to the establishment of their authority by other powers in return for the confirmation of British predominance elsewhere: "It was impossible that England should have the right to lock up the whole of Africa". The interior of the continent, largely unexplored, awaited division. Salisbury bought European, and not only German, goodwill by his reasonableness in negotiating the partition of virtually unknown regions. As far as his preoccupations in Europe and Egypt allowed, Salisbury used the doctrine of effective occupation to ensure that Britain got what was worth having. He discouraged hopes of military intervention by government: warfare with savage tribes in those regions would be "the most exhausting, the most terrible, the least remunerative in any sense".[72] He followed the Liberals in proposing to leave expansion in Africa to the chartered companies operating in West, Central and East Africa. He promised to support them along the coasts in the traditional manner, and to provide diplomatic backing. He gave way to the other powers where he discerned "the line of least resistance – neither a [British] company nor a mission station".[73]

In West Africa Salisbury recognized very large claims advanced by the French and based on the questionable doctrine of hinterland. Algeria's hinterland was defined as stretching to the Lower Niger, where the British Royal Niger Company was established. To the embarrassment of the helpful French ambassador in London, Waddington, Salisbury famously described the huge expanses to which Britain waived any claim as "what agriculturalists would call very light land, that is to say, it is the . . . Sahara". By that Anglo-French agreement of August 1890 too, Madagascar was France's to take on the other side of Africa, while she consented to a British protectorate over the Arab sultanate of Zanzibar: each country sacrificed a lesser to a greater interest. East Africa and Zanzibar were rather more important to Britain than her West African possessions. The Sultanate had been the focal point of her drive against the slave trade on the East coast for decades. British influence there was exercised informally, even when force was used in 1859 to defeat a dynastic coup mounted with local French encouragement. Zanzibar's rulers were obliged to renounce the slave trade, but not the institution of slavery, within their dominions. There was no certainty, however, about the extent of their authority on the mainland away from the coast, where their writ was supposed to run from the Somali country to Portuguese Mozambique. Inland, the chief obstacle to and a justification for European penetration were the ravages of a "terrible army of wickedness": Arab slavers trading to the Middle East, despite the treaties that British governments had signed with the Ottoman Sultan and other potentates. Salisbury was no more sentimental about "naked savages" than he was about other victims of evil: but there was nothing cynical in his desire to eradicate the East African slave trade, believed to be growing in the absence of European political control.[74]

Bismarck was as sceptical as Salisbury when it came to the economic prospects of colonies in tropical Africa. The chancellor acquiesced in the clamour of those who wanted Germany to have colonies round the world too, to give her awesome power a new dimension and her rapidly growing industries new markets. Neither Gladstone nor Salisbury opposed the establishment in 1885–6 of German ascendancy along a stretch of the coast north of Mombasa and over the southern half of East Africa, coast and hinterland, divided by a line running from the sea to Lake Victoria. After the Foreign Office's African expert, Sir Percy Anderson, and businessmen had worked on him and his ministers, Salisbury rather reluctantly countenanced the creation in 1888 of Sir William Mackinnon's Imperial British East Africa Company to give substance to the British presence in the northern half of the vast region. He remained unconvinced that it was a good commercial proposition.[75] The rising in 1888 of the coast Arabs against the Germans' "sheer brutality" jeopardized the independence of Zanzibar itself, which Germany had undertaken to respect. She held the Sultan responsible for his former subjects' revolt, and proposed to cow him by naval action. British opinion was sympathetic to the rebels; it had already observed German heavy-handedness in the Pacific islands. "The good-natured Huns of story seem to be as dead as the Dodo", Salisbury admitted. As his colleague W.H. Smith reminded him, Britain had a duty to her missionaries in the affected area and to "her Banias", the British Indian mercantile community in Zanzibar and along the coast, whose interests were suffering. Smith believed in the policy of going "hand in hand" with Germany, which was at risk from her behaviour in East Africa and Samoa. Salisbury assured his leader of the Commons that he had "done nothing but lecture" the German ambassador. He never distinguished between the German government and its agents. "It is in the blood", he said simply of the latter's misdeeds.[76]

The longstanding British connection with Zanzibar compelled her to rescue the Sultan from Germany and also from Italy over her claim to a share of his dwindling possessions on the mainland. Salisbury accepted the suggestion of an international blockade to halt the seaborne slave trade and, what was more significant, prevent arms from reaching the Arab rebels. Britain had warned off the Italians – whose "cynical and arrogant injustice it is impossible to surpass", wrote Salisbury – by intimating that force would be met by force. Although her warships were not a match for the British in those waters, Germany could not be similarly deterred. The German, unlike the Italian, alliance was indispensable. Nor was Bismarck eager for a confrontation; he told the Bundestag that Germany was "in Zanzibar as well as . . . Samoa . . . absolutely at one with the English . . . the old traditional ally"; but he hinted that colonial disagreements might weaken the friendship.[77] The Royal Navy protected Zanzibar and joined in blockading the rebels. In parliament, Salisbury had previously stressed the humanitarianism of the powers: "the most progressive nations of Europe" were fighting slavery in the most effective way by taking and developing a region where it flourished. He did not dissemble with his monarch or his backbenchers: taking part in "this so-called blockade" was a way of containing Germany and Italy as well as of getting at Arab traders that hoisted French colours. With Heligoland as the bait, Germany subsequently agreed to the wider Anglo-German settlement of 1890. Delimitation of boundaries between British and German territory in West, South West and Central Africa was of secondary importance. The completed partition of East Africa reserved Uganda for British expansion, ending German claims there and on the coast north of Mombasa, and recognized a British protectorate over Zanzibar.[78]

The Germans reflected that by being confirmed in possession of the southern half of East Africa they had dispelled the vision of British dominion stretching from the Cape to Cairo entertained by Cecil Rhodes and the Jingoes. Salisbury considered that vision almost ridiculous; it was one "for which it is not very easy to discover any international foundation", and comparable to the Germans' use of the doctrine of hinterland "which they have to a great extent invented". Without fear of contradiction he invited the cabinet to overrule Mackinnon and the explorer H.M. Stanley who were agitating for more than he could, or intended to, deliver. "If you go on confessing that the African topic is a pointless bore", wrote Stanley to *The Times*, alluding to the premier's language in his latest speech, ". . . why grant charters to companies to involve your countrymen in wasteful expenditures of money, labour and life . . . ?" But if Salisbury poured a little cold water on the aspirations which Mackinnon's enterprise and Rhodes's British South Africa Company of 1889 embodied, he went a long way towards satisfying them. By dividing East Africa with Germany, he averted the danger that she would actively sympathize with Portugal further south in the future of Rhodesia and Nyasaland. "The coercion of that power", he advised the cabinet when the Anglo-German agreement was under discussion, "may not be so simple . . . as it will be if only the strength and the obstinacy of Portugal have to be dealt with".[79]

Stanley referred to South Africa as "an El Dorado": from the mid-1880s British immigration and investment rose rapidly as the production of gold and diamonds climbed. The country north of the Limpopo, where they hoped to discover a second Rand, beckoned to the imperial visionaries and the capitalists whose motives were combined in the person of Cecil Rhodes. His company promised to meet the cost of administering the territories it was authorized to occupy. Regarding European expansion as foreordained, Salisbury had marked out Central Africa south of Lake Tanganyika and west of Lake Nyasa for the British. In the Nyasaland protectorate, established in 1890, there were British missionaries to protect and Arab slave traders to drive out, but little else. The Foreign Office took responsibility for its administration, funded by Rhodes's company, after the missionaries objected to being ruled by businessmen. The company acquired all the rest, north and south of the Zambezi, of the region passing under the British flag. Salisbury fought its battles with the Portuguese. They asserted historic claims to "half Africa", which Salisbury traced ultimately to the division of new discoveries between Spain and Portugal by the Borgia pope, Alexander VI, "of saintly memory".[80] A show of force by the navy in the Atlantic and the Indian Ocean brought the government in Lisbon, which announced that it was acting under duress, to recognize a growing British presence in the disputed expanse of Africa. The Portuguese parliament, however, refused to ratify the convention of August 1890. Salisbury withstood pressure from Germany, and Queen Victoria, to spare Portuguese feelings as much as possible for the sake of her none too secure Coburg dynasty: "If the monarchy is so desperately weak that . . . our . . . demands will overthrow it, it is not worth saving", he answered the Germans; an illustration of his unsentimental attitude to royalty generally. The new convention extracted from Portugal gave even more to the Company and the Jingoes, who protested that it still did not give enough. They, like the Portuguese, chose to overlook his reliance on "plain and effective occupation" to inject reality into imperialist dreams. Portugal, he said to those whom he had disappointed, was not the only country where fervent patriots forgot the limitations of national strength, and quoted his favourite Horace: "*Mutato nomine de te fabula narratur*".[81]

Where Britain was well placed to expand, Salisbury safeguarded her prospects. The 1891 Anglo-Portuguese treaty renewed an existing British right to acquire Portugal's territory to the south of the Zambezi if chronic financial embarrassment forced her to sell. But he would not support Rhodes's attempts to buy either the territory or the Portuguese end of the railway to Delagoa Bay, which presented the landlocked Boer republics with an outlet to the sea that was not under British control.[82] Not that he was ever a friend of the Boers: he had condemned the Liberals when in the treaties of 1881 and 1884 they handed over its African populations to their oppressors. It was "a horrible tale of desertion . . . by the British government". He painted a vivid picture of the methods the republics used to subjugate bordering tribes "by the horrible commando system . . . their citizens go out into the wilderness, shoot blacks as if they were game and . . . claim the . . . right to annex". There was plenty of evidence for what he called "the sinister character of the neighbourhood of the Boer". Britain's difficulties in South Africa flowed, he wrote in 1885, from the Liberals' acceptance of defeat in the war of 1880–81 which restored and enlarged the autonomy of the Transvaal. The Boer victory at Majuba could not be final. Derby as colonial secretary had avoided any mention of suzerainty in the 1884 London Convention, reducing the paramountcy that Britain retained to almost nothing.[83]

"For the present", Salisbury believed, ". . . the danger is not acute". The confidence in its destiny that Afrikaner nationalism derived from Majuba encouraged it to hope for supremacy in South Africa. But the Cape was vital to British imperial strategy and could not be relinquished to a Boer-dominated federation. It was assumed that the influx of British immigrants into the Transvaal would before long swamp Afrikanerdom in its heartland, once they were admitted to political equality. For all his dislike of Afrikaners and their ways, Salisbury was in two minds about the future of the Transvaal and South Africa in that event. He thought Sir Henry Loch, the British High Commissioner, must be "a little off his head" in wanting the universal white manhood suffrage that would deliver the republic to "a floating population of mining adventurers . . . not . . . an ideal form of government". Nor would the Transvaal submit to be conquered from within. The republic's rejection in 1890 of a customs union with the self-governing Cape Colony in exchange for Swaziland underlined its determination to resist the imperial embrace. This was not an outcome displeasing to Salisbury, though Knutsford at the Colonial Office had persuaded him to sanction the scheme. He distrusted both President Kruger in the Transvaal and Rhodes, premier of the Cape from that year. In due course, the British would prevail over the Boers by sheer weight of numbers and economic power. Until then, with the Boers' territorial expansion blocked in every direction, the *status quo* was acceptable to Britain.[84]

In Africa Britain faced France and Germany: in India the old fear of Russia on the North-West frontier was strong after the crisis of 1885. Salisbury set out to defuse an exaggerated threat. He had used emotive language in 1885 to warn Russia against seeking a dominant influence over Afghanistan; but on taking office in June he ensured that the border dispute which had occasioned the crisis did not get out of hand. "The quarrel seems very small and unimportant", he informed Churchill at the India Office, who needed to be restrained. The reigning Amir of Afghanistan, to whose independence of Russia Britain was committed, he described as "a diseased barbarian". The subsequent Anglo-Russian negotiations for a general demarcation of Afghanistan's northern frontier were nevertheless difficult. As the Amir's "unpaid attorney", Salisbury could not give too much away in those remote and inhospitable mountains without leading his client to suppose that Britain could not, or would not, stand up for him. Russia's pressure on Afghanistan, like that which she exerted on the Ottoman empire, was a geopolitical phenomenon which could hardly be controlled by the government. "She [Russia] can promise nothing with respect to Affghanistan [*sic*] except that she will eat Constantinople first", he cautioned the ambassador at St Petersburg, Robert Morier. "When it is eaten, she must go forward with all the weight of her augmented mass, in the direction of India". But he did not think that from a strictly military point of view India would be in serious danger if Russia reached Kandahar, the Afghan stronghold from which an invasion would start. As in the past, he considered an attempt to invade was certain to be "a huge disaster – a hot Moscow retreat". Without the support of other powers, Russia could not harm Britain, while the British fleet could do some damage to her ports and trade.[85]

Yet it was unwise to suppose that reason would not yield to emotion. Tsar Alexander III was not immune to a real public opinion worked by the "very flammable chauvinism" of Russian newspapers, and might be swept into an unwanted war by their clamour. The strengthening of the North-West frontier's defences, which Salisbury accepted was necessary, carried a risk of provocation, as he acknowledged in pressing the construction of strategic railways to the frontier on successive viceroys. In the prevailing climate of Russian opinion, a line should not be aimed at Kandahar, suggesting to the potential enemy that a pre-emptive strike was contemplated. For Afghanistan and India were always vulnerable through Persia: largely inaccessible to the British, Persia under Russian occupation or influence posed an effective threat to the western flank of the Amir's unruly tribal kingdom. Although Salisbury did not anticipate that the Russians would launch anything more than a diversionary attack in that quarter while they drove for Constantinople, he was apprehensive of war with Russia at the beginning of the 1890s. If Germany and France fought one another, Russia might seize the chance to realize her Balkan ambitions when the Triple Alliance was fully occupied elsewhere. Persia could not be defended except by "a predatory and partizan warfare" against the invading Russians' lines of communication. A railway running from the north-west corner of Baluchistan, where British, Persian and Afghan territory met in Seistan, to the sea would enable Britain to supply Persia in case of need with "a certain support in troops and . . . more . . . in officers, money and munitions". A railway in those parts, he told Lord Lansdowne, viceroy in 1888, would not pay but its "moral value" would be great.[86]

Without the ability to stiffen Persian resistance by this route, how could Britain hope to keep Afghanistan as a buffer state? The Amir Abdur Rahman must inevitably turn towards Russia: "And what would be the effect upon your Indian populations . . . this is the most serious danger on the North West you have to confront". They would infer that Britain's star was waning in the East. These were arguments which Salisbury had previously put to Cross, his colleague at the India Office: the Seistan railway "would prolong the life of Persia by a great number of years". Lansdowne shrank from the expense, and from the risk that the line would be seen as provocative by Russia. If built, the troops it deployed would have to come from Britain, there were none to spare in India. The attitude of the Indian authorities irritated Salisbury. Their requirements were unreasonable: "if the defence of India depends on . . . a reinforcement of 60 000 British soldiers – India is already lost". Close on half the regular army was currently stationed in the sub-continent.[87]

Sir Frederick Roberts, the celebrated soldier then commander-in-chief in India, was an alarmist who wanted to build railway lines into Afghanistan, and would have liked to make Kandahar and Jalalabad, with the Amir's consent, the first line of defence. With his Afghan laurels, won in 1880, and the response to his ideas in military and political circles, he was someone whom the premier handled carefully in a correspondence about the general's tenure of the Indian command. Salisbury dismissed the "semi-literary programmes" of Roberts' admirers as flawed because they did not take into account the home country's unwillingness to find the money and manpower. "Our people require to have it driven into their heads that if they will not submit to . . . conscription, they must submit to a corresponding limitation of their exploits". Roberts' doubts of the Indian army's loyalty if "any serious external aggression" menaced Britain in India were quite convenient; they held him and his followers back.[88] "In my humble civilian way", Salisbury encouraged them to think of railways to the frontier, not beyond it, and of exploiting with Afghans and Persians Russia's sometimes harsh treatment of Central Asian Muslims: "I look for great assistance from Russian brutality". Roberts' fears might be exaggerated: they were not baseless. Russia's position was strong and would become stronger when her current programme of army reform was complete; when there was a railway to carry her troops to the Afghan border; when death removed Abdur Rahman in Afghanistan; and when the Liberals returned to office in Britain. Without the line to Seistan, or one to the Pishin valley, some seventy miles from Kandahar, "the prospect is not very inspiriting", Salisbury considered. "Providence is generally on the side of the big battalions".[89]

"Two hundred and eighty million people would be ready to rise against us on the first sign of defeat", Roberts assured Lansdowne, reliving the nightmare experience of the Mutiny. In the circumstances, Salisbury did what he could with the weapons of diplomacy and finance to stave off a Russian takeover in Persia, or at least to limit it to the northern half of the country. If Russia eventually concentrated her forces on the Central Asian approaches to India, "nothing can save Persia", he told Morier.[90] Until then, handicapped by the lack of government funds and the preference of British capital for safer investments, he supported Wolff's efforts to underpin British influence with a significant economic presence. Although the practice of decades ruled out a guaranteed Persian loan raised in London, a British businessman, Major Talbot, secured a tobacco monopoly. Wolff failed, however, to obtain Russian agreement to the plan for the two powers to build and run Persia's railways, Russia in the north and Britain in the south. The Shah yielded to Russian pressure to delay all railway construction for ten years; it was an indication of Europe's respect for Britain as a competitor.[91] In briefing Wolff's successor, Sir Frank Lascelles, Salisbury reiterated the value of Persia to India's security and gave Wolff due credit for his achievements. But he warned against exciting suspicion "that we are not labouring for the development but only for the exploitation of Persia". The unpopular tobacco monopoly had that effect. The Legation should not be regarded as "an agency pushing for British speculators".[92]

This note of concern for people who could not escape the domination of Europe, in one form or another, occurs quite often in Salisbury's later correspondence and speeches. His outlook had not changed since he was at the India Office. As a liberal imperialist, he was alive to the reality that the ideas which the dominant Western world exported to the East would be turned against it, sooner rather than later. He also thought, sometimes, that Turkey, Egypt and Persia might be capable of taking what they wanted from the West without losing their Islamic character.[93] In India, where Britain's responsibilities and the problems arising from Westernization were greatest, he questioned the desire of Whig viceroys, Dufferin and Lansdowne, for a small measure of liberalization in Indian government. Their political tradition, which the Unionism of both did not erode outside Ireland and the struggle for

Home Rule, taught them that the Indian National Congress should not be ignored. That organization, moderate and pro-British, asked for elected majorities on the legislative councils at the centre and in the subordinate governments; nominated Indians had sat on them since the reforms following the Mutiny. Dufferin acknowledged that even an indirectly elected minority on the councils below his own – his suggested compromise – was not free from risk: "India is not a country where the machinery of European democratic agitation can be applied with impunity". What was given ought to be accompanied by an announcement that nothing more was to be expected for the next ten or fifteen years. Salisbury, with the cabinet behind him, wanted "a more distinct condemnation of the elective principle" than he got from Dufferin as he departed for the Rome embassy. The lawyers and journalists prominent in the Congress were "in England a very trustworthy class . . . in India they are the class among whom disaffection is strongest".[94]

Cross's bill to amend the legislation of 1861, introduced into the Lords in February 1890, merely increased the nominated membership of the viceroy's and other councils. "Representative government", said Salisbury in the debate, "answers admirably so long as all those . . . represented desire much the same thing". Could Hindu and Muslim, with their ancient enmity, make it work when it had been found unworkable in the Ottoman lands? But he and his ministers accepted an amendment from Northbrook, another Whig Unionist and an ex-viceroy, by which the government of India, subject to the secretary of state's agreement, was to determine the method of selecting non-official councillors. Lansdowne was strongly in favour of conciliating "a minority which, although small, is remarkably intelligent and pertinacious" by some system of indirect election.[95] Sacrificed in that session to domestic and Irish bills in a crowded programme, the bill passed in 1892 with a plea from the premier for British governments, his own included, to think very carefully before they resorted in India to what his 1890 speech had called "the most powerful principle that affects political communities". Within the year, under a Liberal ministry, indirect election on a narrow base had been adopted. Salisbury had yielded to the argument, which Lansdowne employed, that the Liberals would legislate if his cabinet did not. The Tory premier was fearful of the consequences if Gladstone decided to take a closer interest in India and its emergent movement for self-rule. Lansdowne, he complained privately, was still judging the world "from the fireside at Brooks's", the Whig stronghold in clubland. If the viceroy had set a trend, Hindus would in due course establish their ascendancy over Muslims, and "cultured Baboos over . . . traditional families". He was relieved when later in the decade Lord Curzon showed no inclination to emulate Lansdowne.[96]

The colonies of settlement in Australasia and North America provided a complete contrast to India. Attracting more investment and immigration from Britain every year, and by now more important to her than India in purely economic terms, they were not disposed to alter the convenient arrangement that left their external defence and diplomatic representation with Britain. The Australian colonies, Canada and New Zealand all made heavy demands on her. The Australians reacted violently to French or German occupation of island groups thousands of miles from their shores; they looked on the South-West Pacific as a British sea. They commanded, too, considerable sympathy in Britain: their remonstrances addressed to the government in London were quickly taken up at Westminster and in the newspapers. Australians, Canadians and Newfoundlanders complicated Salisbury's diplomacy and gave him some anxious moments. A cabinet discussion in February 1887 moved from the risks of armed conflict with France in the New Hebrides and on the Newfoundland fishing grounds to Britain's lack of preparedness on land and sea. "We live from hand to mouth, and the latter may become a serious question if war were to ensue", wrote Cranbrook. "Who would fill it and could we guard the food ships . . . ?" On the day the cabinet met, Salisbury listed the places round the globe where Anglo-French tension was palpable, and let the ambassador in Paris know that he found himself almost wishing for war between France and Germany "to put a stop to this incessant vexation".[97]

That month saw the first Mediterranean agreement: an insurance policy taken out against war with France. The French envoy in London, Waddington, was understandably "gloomy and rather ill-tempered". The "new democracy" in Britain might be opposed to participation in Continental hostilities: it was not indifferent to the fate of the empire; Churchill had mistaken the public mood a few months earlier when he resigned over the army and navy estimates. Waddington drew his government's attention to the "passionate" debate on an imperial federation that was in progress. If this anglophil Frenchman exaggerated more than a little, with a view to curbing warlike tendencies in France, he was substantially correct.[98] The French foreign ministry was not spoiling for a fight over the New Hebrides or the Newfoundland fisheries. Those cannibal islands became an Anglo-French condominium in 1888. In the North Atlantic dispute the British government was caught between treaty obligations to France dating back to 1713 and the Newfoundlanders' indignation at the impact of French protectionism on their livelihood. Salisbury thought his fellow subjects of the Queen were even more unreasonable than the French: "Oh! Why was Newfoundland created?" he lamented. "Why did the fish not have the good taste to frequent a warmer place?" France was not to be tempted by the suggested exchange of valuable rights in the fisheries for the nearly worthless British West Africa possession of the Gambia. An Anglo-French treaty of 1891 set up arbitration machinery for the recurrent disputes, and a special Act of Parliament confirmed the British government's legal power to enforce its obligations to France on the Newfoundlanders, as the navy had been doing. There was talk of secession in the island legislature. "It is we", answered Salisbury, speaking in the Lords, "who run the whole risk . . . I do not suppose that in the case of a war with France, the French would take the trouble to invade Newfoundland".[99]

Although the premier did not adopt that tone with the much larger and richer Dominion of Canada, Joseph Chamberlain said more than Salisbury saw fit to do. He said it as Salisbury's representative sent in 1887–8 to negotiate with Washington an amicable settlement of the running argument over access to Canadian fisheries and American markets; not to be confused with the separate question of sealing in the Behring Sea. The invitation to Chamberlain was designed to bind an ambitious and restless man to the Unionism that could hardly survive without him. He was willing to be so bound, despite saying in Society that "he doubted the wisdom of joining Lord Salisbury" in office. The Birmingham democrat and businessman was an excellent choice to bargain with republican America and tell home truths to the Canadians. For Salisbury and his ally, fish was overshadowed by the possibility of a customs union between the United States and Canada. Chamberlain declared in a speech before he sailed that such a union and the certain extension of the United States' higher tariffs to the whole of the North American mainland must bring in their wake Canada's "political separation" from Britain. He went further and opined that the existing relationship would not last unless reinforced by "ties of federation". Salisbury observed only that a unified tariff from the Caribbean to the Arctic would indeed be "very serious". In North America Chamberlain pursued the themes of his speech. Imperial federation was "a grand idea", he assured Canadians worried about their country's future and afraid of their giant neighbour.[100]

This public assertion of his intensifying belief in the empire of the future came after a private warning to the Canadian viceroy, the Liberal Unionist and future ruler of India, Lansdowne, that he meant what he had just said at home. The "nominal supremacy" of Britain carried with it such heavy responsibilities that the Canadians ought to be less "stiff" when she negotiated on their behalf. Nor should they be under any illusions as to the reaction of British industry and the British people if they agreed to discounts in favour of American exports: sooner rather than later, they would be on their own politically.[101] The Canadians made little trouble during the negotiations with Washington: and their interest in a customs union rapidly declined. The Chamberlain mission educated both the emissary and his colonial hosts. The latter's dependence on Britain was spelt out when Salisbury and the cabinet resorted to a discreet use of sea power in the dangerous quarrel over sealing grounds in the Behring Sea. The real issue was conservation: the Americans, who were first on the scene, objected to Canadian competition in the exploitation of a dwindling seal population. Colonial obduracy defeated Salisbury's attempts at mediation in the late 1880s, which were followed by American action against Canadian sealers on the high seas. In the course of the continuing tripartite negotiations, the United States laid claim in 1890 to the entire Behring sea as falling within their territorial waters. Salisbury and the cabinet were unanimous in refusing to submit to the "serious loss of reputation and power" involved. They ordered up a cruiser squadron from the China station, before which United States vessels effaced themselves. With this bloodless victory behind him, which he was at pains not to advertise, Salisbury obtained a temporary suspension of sealing while the parties went to arbitration. As a condition of Canada's co-operation, the British Treasury compensated her sealers for the ban: "justifiable if costly" appeasement of angry colonials.[102]

An international tribunal's award disallowed the American claim to sovereignty over the Behring Sea, and restricted sealing: it was a vindication of Salisbury's policy conducted against the background of a sudden deterioration of Anglo-American relations in 1888. The Senate rejected the fisheries agreement that Chamberlain had signed with the Democratic administration which proceeded, in the midst of a presidential election at the end of the year, to expel the British minister, Lord Sackville, in an unsuccessful bid for votes. Salisbury made no protest: Sackville's unguarded comments to reporters on American politics and politicians were "a gross blunder". With the approval of his colleagues, the premier treated the incident as unimportant. Bismarck gave American hostility to Britain as a reason for the binding Anglo-German alliance he proposed shortly afterwards: the convergence of France, and Russia, Britain's other likely enemies, would encourage America to attack if her old antagonist did not get closer to Germany. As the Behring Sea crisis demonstrated, the United States, with her small forces, was not in a position to make war on Britain. No one in Europe, however, doubted her potential for war on land and sea, least of all Salisbury. Like Palmerston, he was prepared to go very far in conciliating the United States, Britain's main trading partner and a nation with, in Gladstone's sober assessment, "a stupendous destiny".[103] As Salisbury emphasized to the next viceroy of Canada, he did not want America to absorb Canada: the blow to Britain's standing would be severe if that were to happen; an unmistakable symptom of imperial decline. Britain had no option but to indulge and champion Canada. Yet he could not share Chamberlain's enthusiasm for imperial federation, telling the Australian statesman, Sir Henry Parkes, that it required "a considerable sacrifice on the part of England of the independence she at present possesses . . . Will it be possible ever for England to consent to this sacrifice?" He did not think so.[104]

Chamberlain's "grand idea" was therefore "so distasteful that all the plans for . . . it . . . would seem in detail impracticable". He added that the "Imperial Council" they were discussing must have room for India and take full account of her interests, not a prospect pleasing to the settler colonies with immigration policies that practically excluded Asiatics.[105] A system of imperial preference was another matter: Salisbury did not conceal from one of its Canadian advocates his personal opinion that "the maintenance of our Empire in its integrity may depend upon fiscal legislation". The obstacle was British popular suspicion of duties on imported food. He hoped the movement away from uncompromising free trade "may be rapid enough to meet the necessities of our time". Prudently conditional in its wording, this letter made it clear enough where Salisbury's sympathies lay. As things were, the balance of interest between Britain and the self-governing colonies had tilted too far against her. Beset by Australians, Newfoundlanders and Canadians, he was "so perturbed [by] . . . what seems to me the unreasonable attitude of the colonies, and their injustice to the mother country" that he refused to meet a colonial delegation in 1890. "I wish to keep out of temptation", he confessed to his colonial secretary, afraid of letting the delegation see what he really felt about them. No good, "but the reverse", could come of being frank. Cabinet ministers might reflect on "the impracticality of dual government" that saddled Britain with a responsibility for the colonies' external affairs that she could not exercise freely. The British public rightly believed the empire's interests were served by trying, as far as possible, to do what the colonies wanted.[106]

"He loves to laugh", said the Russian ambassador, de Staal, of Salisbury. He brought to the Foreign Office a civilized sense of the absurd which he was able to share with the long-serving ambassadors who got to know him extremely well; a great contrast to the prickly colonists. Salisbury spoke to de Staal and the others with unusual candour. He was similarly open when he saw Bismarck's son, Count Herbert – not a favourite with Salisbury, or anyone else – to explain his stance on the control of another island group in the Pacific, Samoa, disputed between Germany, the United States and Britain. He would have been content to see Germany take Samoa, leaving Tonga to Britain and Hawaii to the United States in a fair distribution of Pacific islands: but German hegemony in the shape of an "adviser" should preserve the existing native political structure and commercial access for the traders of other nations. Subject to these conditions, it could not really be of concern to Australia and New Zealand which "nigger chief" ruled in Samoa. Salisbury was ready to back Germany's candidate. America's refusal to let Samoa pass to Germany precluded a settlement on his lines at an international conference at Berlin in 1889.[107] Anglo-German co-operation from Africa to the remote Pacific paid off. Bismarck, publicly sceptical about the value of German expansion beyond Europe, said in the Reichstag that "we have proceeded, and shall ever proceed solely . . . in agreement with the greatest colonial power in the world – England". He ascribed the differences that arose with the British to the behaviour of the men on the spot and disowned, without naming, the Germans responsible.[108]

At the same time, the chancellor threatened Salisbury with the withdrawal of co-operation where it mattered most to Britain, in Egypt, if a British man on the spot, Consul Holmwood, were not removed from his post at Zanzibar. Salisbury objected to the language of menace, but he complied. Bismarck took the opportunity to read the British a lesson in statecraft as he understood it. His guiding principles were national self-interest and strict reciprocity; only in private life could one dispense with payment for services rendered. Herbert Bismarck, more familiar than his father with British thinking, commented that his philosophy might have "a harsh and novel sound" to their ally, unused to Germany's requirements of countries that sought security in her active friendship. "Unimpassioned, unsentimental, and cold as any other business of profit and loss": that was the chancellor's idea of "true diplomacy".[109] Salisbury, and many of his countrymen, found German methods with Africans and Polynesians "atrocious": but, however much they might wish it, there was no escape from what Salisbury bitterly termed, during the Holmwood affair, "this very inconvenient and somewhat humiliating relation" to Germany. Now and again he thought of freeing Britain from her associate, once he had achieved an internationally acceptable settlement of the Egyptian problem. As his letter to the Queen in February 1887, quoted earlier, showed, with the realism that only ever momentarily deserted him, Britain was tied to Germany by more than Egypt.[110] His leader in the Commons, W.H. Smith, who told him that Germany's "cynical brutality" in East Africa and Samoa precluded the full alliance "which might have been", had seen the force of the reasoning behind the Mediterranean agreements: "I should have preferred to stand aside altogether", he said, "It is risky . . . but an utterly selfish policy would probably be disastrous".[111]

If Britain was only a makeweight in the combinations of the Continental powers, she came into her own where naval superiority counted. Under Salisbury, her navy did all that Palmerston had expected of it, and arguably more, as Lord George Hamilton at the Admiralty believed. Zanzibar, where the appearance of British warships averted a German protectorate, Newfoundland and the Behring Sea were major episodes of "gunboat diplomacy", overshadowing its routine, the protection of British subjects and trade, literally from China to Peru, and the extirpation of what was left of the slave trade in the Indian Ocean. Like the army in the protracted pacification of Burma and the containment of Mahdism in the Sudan, the navy was contributing to "the advancing wave of civilization".[112] Not the least of Salisbury's many achievements was his ability to present imperial expansion as an essentially moderate and rational development, and not the prerogative of the Jingoes he so disliked. The strident note that sometimes occurs in his speeches on empire during the years in opposition is not heard again. In his platform speeches the defence and the growth of empire were necessary for economic survival. His vivid word-picture of London without the wealth of empire, a rotting mass of population without hope, summarized his fears if the formal empire declined and did not grow where opportunities presented themselves. Britain's markets in the "informal empire", America and Continental Europe were also under pressure from competitors and tariffs. The rising standard of life that underpinned political stability was no longer secure over the foreseeable future.[113]

Neither Salisbury nor his public, Jingoes excepted, wanted to fight large-scale wars for empire. British businessmen, investors and voters were well pleased, on the whole, with what Salisbury gave them: a share in the co-operative division of territory between imperial powers that was commensurate with Britain's interests and reputation. He explained his diplomacy, prudent but insistent where tangible British interests existed, to foreigners by saying, as he did of Bismarck, "I am afraid . . . he is not aware of what our insular democracy really is". When it suited him to evade a deeper involvement in the affairs of the Continent, he liked to suggest that politicians and electors in Britain lacked any solid convictions. The diplomats were not deceived: his policy was natural to the country which de Staal, the intelligent servant of an autocracy, conceded was the least chauvinist of the powers, notwithstanding her national pride. The British, he asked his government to bear in mind, were "essentially" peaceful and wedded to maintenance of the *status quo*, the rationale of their qualified adherence to the Triple Alliance.[114] Since European governments also wanted to avoid war, though afraid of being isolated and surprised by their enemies, they appreciated Salisbury. Bismarck, and his successor Count Caprivi; Tsar Alexander III; Franz Josef and his ministers in Vienna; the rulers of the Third Republic striving to contain the pressures of Boulangism, all joined Salisbury in a general conspiracy to keep the peace in Europe. The British premier, it may even be said, was a central figure in the unending efforts to control tension. His conception of Britain's relationship to the Triple Alliance was reassuring to the French; hence their subdued comments on that score. As a makeweight in the combinations of Europe, Salisbury's Britain was a force for peace. His successes as an imperialist minister, praised as such by Unionists and Gladstonians alike, should be viewed in that light.

# CHAPTER ELEVEN
## The Politics of Opposition 1892–5

### The 1892 Election and the Integration of Unionism

Salisbury was inclined to believe in the "disease of the pendulum" when too many electors were, in the nature of things, ignorant or indifferent,[1] but the Irish question, which from 1886 appeared to introduce a fundamental difference of opinion between Unionists and Gladstonians, seemed to have lost its immediate menace after the fall of Parnell and the success of coercion, joined to a cautious but unmistakable policy of liberalizing Irish government when the necessary legislation could be got through parliament. The heavy programme of domestic legislation enacted since 1887 had furnished an almost entirely Tory cabinet with impressive credentials as reformers but, given the bi-partisan support which the most important of those measures attracted, it was hard to pretend that they were the political property of the governing alliance. Moreover, their parliamentary labours had wearied the unpaid Unionist backbenchers, driven the exhausted W.H. Smith, leader of the House, into the grave, and tired out his principal colleagues. The intentions of a mildly bored electorate were apparent from the opposition gains at by-elections, totalling twenty-two against the government's two from more than a hundred contests. Ministers, the Russian ambassador remarked, wanted to lose the general election called for July 1892 by an insignificant margin.[2] The desire for rest went with the anticipated satisfaction of watching the Gladstonians struggle in office, as a result of their commitments to Irish home rulers and Welsh Nonconformists and of the expectations they had fostered. Losing some eighty seats, the Unionists retained their English majority and led the Liberals by over forty in the country as a whole. The life of the Liberal ministry hung on the co-operation of the divided Irish nationalists.[3]

Although he welcomed the break from office – "I am beginning to find out how tired I really am", he told his old doctor after the election – Salisbury was not complacent about his defeat. In private, to someone he trusted, he confessed to being really gloomy about the political future. He did not think Gladstone would succeed in passing a Home Rule bill: but he was apprehensive for the House of

Lords as the probable means of its rejection. Once the machinery of the constitution was subject to radical change, "I am afraid it will take to 'evolving' – Heaven knows in what direction". Nor was that all he feared: Gladstone's passionate championship of Irish national freedom might easily be extended to another part of the empire and its embryonic national movement: "I am afraid that if he wins we shall not keep India".[4] That is not to say that he expected sudden and sweeping developments from a Gladstone government: "it takes a long time for a political poison to work", he asserted a little later. The power of Gladstone's emotional politics to set an irreversible trend, as it had in Irish legislation since the late 1860s, might be demonstrated in social questions nearer home. Salisbury may be said to have invited "a revolutionary appeal to the jealousy of the poor"[5] by the thrust of his own campaign oratory: it commenced with one of his most important speeches, at Hastings in May, intended to convince the working class that the alliance he headed had their special interests very much at heart.[6]

Ironically, Gladstone was worried by what a commentator on the Liberalism of the decade described as "a sudden contagion of collectivism" in its ranks. To counteract the subversion of economic orthodoxy, as it appeared to him, he stepped up his recent criticism of "classes and establishments savouring in part of feudal times and principles". An extension of political democracy was needed to carry Home Rule, frustrated by the "leisured . . . educated . . . wealthy . . . titled classes".[7] The Conservative manifesto over Salisbury's signature argued that constitutional change was unnecessary when the working class was strong enough to get, after discussion, whatever "they generally believe will conduce to their welfare. No party will have the power . . . of refusing to listen to their unanimous wish". The manifesto cited free education, elected county councils and state intervention to alleviate chronic distress in the West of Ireland as the most significant reforms for many years, and promised attention to the problems of poverty and to those of industrial relations against a background of strikes and agitation for a statutory eight-hour day.[8] Beforehand, in a loudly cheered passage of the Hastings speech, he mocked the "rabbis" of economic orthodoxy who opposed the return of protection under any circumstances and obscured the flexible doctrine of Adam Smith with the requirements of their secular Mishna and Talmud. Altogether, he and his party had an effective answer to Gladstonian populism, at any rate for English electors. In Scotland and Wales the voting was influenced more by the demand for disestablishment in those two countries than by anything else, particularly in the Principality. But for Salisbury and Gladstone, and for the activists on both sides, Home Rule was the dominant issue: to supporters its advocacy presented British Liberalism at its best; its opponents denounced a cynical and unpatriotic bargain with implacable enemies.[9]

The religious dimension of Home Rule had always been exploited by those bent on resisting the Irish national movement. Gladstone and the Gladstonians replied by condemning the aggressions of Orangeism – a political force on the Clyde and the Mersey, as well as in Ulster. The intervention of the Irish Catholic bishops against Parnell when the nationalists split after 1890 presented Unionism with an opportunity not to be missed. The behaviour of prelates and priests confirmed the fears of Irish Protestants whom, Salisbury never ceased to insist, Britain had an absolute duty to protect. The enhanced political visibility of the Irish Catholic Church raised another point of principle. It was not for the Tories, or the Liberals, to object to clerical participation in politics, given the assistance they received from Church or chapel in the constituencies. But what looked like clerical dictation to a submissive anti-Parnellite majority, and was denounced as such by Unionists and Parnellites, revived the intense British dislike of churchmen who did not know their place, determined as it ought to have been by centuries of progress. Caution and expediency impelled Salisbury to launch a sustained attack on the intolerable presumption, in his eyes, of Irish Catholicism. He explained himself to a reproachful Catholic Tory, the fifteenth Duke of Norfolk, a hereditary spokesman for the small native Catholic element in England; Parnell's adultery could not justify Archbishops Croke and Walsh in assuming overtly political roles: "they have no right to complain if they meet with as little ceremony as if they were really laymen". He sought to define Home Rule as a "purely secular movement", and therefore barred to the clergy, whose political activity should be confined to such matters as education, the marriage laws and the legal aspects of corporate ecclesiastical life where church and state had a common interest. To transgress those narrow limits was to perpetuate "a breach of trust" between institutional religion and the political community.[10]

In the light of Ireland's past, it was vain to expect that the hierarchy should practise the restraint of Anglican bishops who were creatures of prime ministerial patronage. Salisbury was attempting to counteract "the tremendous organized influence" of the Catholic Church, which derived, as he understood very well, from the awe inspired by the sacraments and from the authority enjoyed by those who dispensed them.[11] The theology and history of the Established and Dissenting churches in Britain did not provide a similar basis for acting in default of united national leadership. The British mind excluded the possibility, for a High Churchman like Salisbury as for a Nonconformist. "England is the Protestant nation of the world", he declared in February 1892, looking ahead to an election: "England has resisted more than any other country the domination of the clerical profession". If the Liberals delivered Irish Home Rule, they would create "an ultra-clerical state under the government of Archbishops Croke and Walsh", and make the nationalist majority in Ireland, "which contains all that is unprogressive", absolute master of "all that is enlightened, civilized and progressive". This trenchant expression of the classical British view of Irish Catholic nationalism was designed to embarrass the Gladstonians, and it certainly did so. When he returned to the subject in May, he extricated himself from the charges of anti-Catholicism by saying simply, "I utterly decline to recognize the inhabitants . . . of Ireland as typical members of the Roman Catholic Church".[12] There were, it should be said, English Catholics who privately agreed with him. He struck a grimmer note when he warned Liberals against military coercion of Protestant Ulster, and accused them of virtually inciting "religious civil war".[13]

In Scotland, where the Liberals had increased their customary lead in seats and votes, the conflict between the Kirk's political friends, not all of them Tories by any means, and the advocates of disestablishment worked against the winners at the polls and against Gladstone personally in Midlothian. "The 'church' has pulled down my majority much beyond expectations", he wrote disgustedly.[14] In Wales, disestablishment was the issue that gave the Liberals all but three of the Principality's seats and nearly two-thirds of the vote. Despite the victories of several independent labour candidates – John Burns and Keir Hardie in metropolitan constituencies and Havelock Wilson in Middlesbrough – the election across Britain was fought largely on the priorities which the activists of the National Liberal Federation had indicated at their Newcastle conference in 1891: Home Rule, disestablishment on the Celtic fringe and temperance legislation.[15]

Salisbury did not allow his opposition to the Gladstone and Rosebery ministries to be constrained by their concentration upon those priorities. He made more than he had yet done of the "social questions . . . destined to break up our party", as he sometimes feared; while, for him as for everybody, those questions did not overshadow the implications of Home Rule for the constitution and the empire.[16] He met the Liberal government's commitment to Welsh disestablishment with a defence of the endangered church that seemed to inject new life into old arguments. His wide-ranging speeches over the next three years prepared the ground for the reforms of his final administration, which fell short, in some cases, of the changes he had discussed.

The Liberal Unionist contingent was cut to forty-five in the general election. Their decline was foreshadowed by the loss of Hartington's Lancashire seat in the by-election at the beginning of 1892 that followed his succession as the eighth Duke of Devonshire. Chamberlain and his "Radical Unionists", with a secure electoral base in and around Birmingham for the nucleus of their group, held the fate of the Liberal secession in their hands. The mutual loathing that existed between them and loyal Gladstonians made a move back into the Liberal mainstream extremely difficult to contemplate. Chamberlain's close associate, Sir Henry James, who owed his survival in Bury to the Tories, referred to Gladstone in their correspondence as "this old degraded spider".[17] There were many Tories, and some Liberal Unionists, who deeply distrusted Chamberlain. The Duke of Argyll, the radical's colleague in the Gladstone cabinet of 1880, wished Salisbury to know, in the middle of the election, that "*Chamberlainism* is an unstable element – and an image which may require 'bloody sacrifices'".[18] The Duke was afraid for property and its rights, unnecessarily, because Chamberlain saw his future in Salisbury's new Conservatism, which he naturally preferred to call Unionism with its emphasis shifting from Ireland to empire and social reform. The Tory National Union's Birmingham conference in November 1891 was the occasion for his final rejection of the party he had aspired to lead. He had once spoken of holding property to ransom: before Birmingham he had said that the dread word was spelt "p-e-n-s-i-o-n". The change in him was advertised when two years earlier he turned on the Liberals who had, almost all of them, refused to support Gladstone in endorsing the government's financial provisions for the Queen's grandchildren, carefully limited though it was. He charged his old friends with defeatism about the Crown's role in a democratic age: "let them . . . tell the people . . . that their object . . . is to belittle the monarchy, to make it unpopular, and to prepare the way for destruction".[19]

If the Liberals were "the Nihilists of English politics",[20] Chamberlain looked to Salisbury for the principled leadership he found wanting in Gladstone. Derby interpreted that speech on the Royal grants as "a pledge of fidelity to the Unionist party". The Tories needed him, but he needed them more. On his appearance beside the premier at Birmingham town hall, he was "practically received by Lord Salisbury into the communion of the Conservative faith", as Edward Hamilton put it with partisan irony.[21] He was helped by Salisbury's speeches at Birmingham, which were a full reply to the National Liberal Federation's Newcastle programme of that autumn. Although the Federation's membership was preoccupied with Home Rule, disestablishment and temperance, Salisbury had plenty to say, then and later, about the rest of the programme. It contained reforms – of the Lords, parliamentary franchise, and the law, and taxation relating to land in town and country – which appealed to Chamberlain. They were also broadly compatible with Salisbury's thinking since his "Newport programme" and earlier. He reviewed most of them at Birmingham in his own style, but not less constructively than Chamberlain.[22]

The Lords would go down "like a ninepin" before a Commons majority bent on reforming the upper House; but the shock was likely to spread to other parts of the British constitution: "You cannot have a revolution on limited liability". As it was, the Lords would have the country on their side if they threw out a Liberal Home Rule bill. One man, one vote in parliamentary elections was less urgent than redistribution: Ireland's dwindling population was over-represented. Taking local democracy in the counties down to the level of parish councils seemed to him a waste of legislative power and of country people's energies: "I should rather recommend a circus or something of that kind". Liberals had attacked his government for failing to relieve the rural depression beyond setting up the Board of Agriculture. The self-evident cause of the prolonged depression was the inability of English farmers to grow corn more profitably under free trade: reform of the land laws could have only a marginal effect. He confessed that he could not feel optimistic about the experiment in reviving the "yeomanry", on which his ministers were working in consultation with Chamberlain.[23]

Home Rule was crucial: its passage would signal the loss of Britain's will to rule and dissolution of the empire that was the foundation of economic and political greatness. Without the empire Britain would be reduced to the "direst misery", unable to feed more than a third of her large population. The pressure of foreign competition on agriculture and the social consequences of the rural exodus to the towns was among his topics on the following day when Chamberlain appeared on the same platform. Government and public, he said, to reassure nervous supporters, must be careful not to fall into "economic error" in seeking remedies for these urban evils of overcrowding and unemployment. The policies common to both wings of Unionism were "big things above party". Party was legitimate only in so far as principle sustained it. To illustrate this truth, he essayed a verbal cartoon which delighted the Birmingham audience. Harcourt had once spoken of letting his opponents "stew in their Parnellite juice" when a brief understanding existed between Tories and nationalists: now he was, outwardly, a staunch adherent of Home Rule. Salisbury imagined – "nothing more beautiful" – Gladstone leading the portly Sir William, "his embarrassed, enthusiastic yet hesitating neophyte into a baptismal bath of Parnellite juice". The laughter and cheering told watchers that humour was not the least effective weapon in Salisbury's armoury.[24]

The substantial point that emerged from the proceedings at Birmingham was the Unionists' readiness to keep up with current radicalism and to outpace the Gladstonians. Seen from a Gladstonian angle, there was little, if anything, to choose between Newcastle and Salisbury's answer to it: "one programme is as advanced and certainly as socialistic as the other".[25] "I have nothing to complain of in the Conservative party – very much the contrary", said Chamberlain gratefully, talking to Balfour, after the result of the election was known. The Tories had reason to be grateful to him: in Birmingham and the counties of Staffordshire, Warwickshire and Worcestershire the Unionists carried thirty of the thirty-nine seats. He attributed this triumph to his – and Salisbury's – revision of the "Unauthorized" and Newport programmes. Chamberlain was eager to build on their success: he envisaged a merger of Tories and Liberal Unionists in the "national party" he had long hoped for. Randolph Churchill was to have been his partner in that enterprise; Salisbury had replaced him. "The movement for 'social' legislation is in the air: it is our business to guide it", argued Chamberlain, pressing for a detailed list of measures ranging from employers' liability to old age pensions. They should be announced in the Queen's Speech on the meeting of the new parliament; a good reason for not resigning beforehand. The new Gladstonian and nationalist majority would be put in the position of ousting ministers committed to a policy which their successors could not emulate, since the social items in the Newcastle programme, taken together, went too far for a Gladstone cabinet: "They have no constructive statesmen".[26] He also wanted a share of political honours for his radical Unionists, including a baronetcy for one of his most loyal followers in Birmingham. The appetite of radicals, whether Unionist or Gladstonian, for the lowest hereditary distinction is revealing of their innate moderation.[27]

As Chamberlain took care to emphasize, the impressive Unionist achievement in the West Midlands at the 1892 election posed no sort of threat to traditional Toryism but quite the reverse: his proposals for legislation would be framed on "solid and conservative lines" – and provide Unionism with the social dimension essential to its recovery of power and long-term survival. If Devonshire was alive to the necessity of more state intervention, Chamberlain imputed to him, probably rightly, a lack of enthusiasm for it. The premier used his influence to ease his radical partner's difficulties with Birmingham Tories, describing them as "an unruly body of men who look upon politics as a purely personal matter – and to whom all arguments of a more general kind are addressed in vain". It was, he thought, the cult of Randolph Churchill in Birmingham Toryism that explained their attitude. This is an early example of the frankness that characterized their exchanges. After the public demonstration of their solidarity, Salisbury could ask Chamberlain during the election campaign not to claim too much for his contribution to Unionism: it was upsetting for stiffer and slower Tories. But, while willing to "use phrases which will please Joe", Salisbury was not yet prepared to tie himself down to the programme which Chamberlain had outlined to Balfour. When the Liberals brought in their selection of "social" bills, the Tory leader and the Birmingham chieftain consulted: Chamberlain's views determined Unionist tactics in the Lords to a considerable extent.[28]

The parliamentary handling of the Local Government Bill of 1894 shows how Unionism tempered traditional Conservatism. Salisbury shared the dislike of rural Tories for it: but neither he nor his Tory advisers were indifferent to the hopes of agricultural labourers for some say in local affairs at the level of the parish; the bill went through with amendments to limit its scope for undermining the domination of village life by the labourer's betters.[29] Salisbury believed that without the active help of Liberal Unionists to blunt government attacks on the old-fashioned Toryism of the countryside, he could not safely have deployed his majority in the Lords against those features of the legislation which he most disliked. Devonshire and other Liberal Unionist peers were rather reluctant to be seen championing squires and parsons against a very modest instalment of progress, but the Duke subsequently complained that Salisbury ought to have cut more out of the bill.[30] In Chamberlain's decided view, the employers' liability bill of the same year, altogether more significant than parish councils, offered too little to the industrial working class, though too much for many employers. Salisbury inflicted a slow death upon the measure in the Lords. Their co-operation encouraged Chamberlain to renew his importunity for a Unionist social programme to be unveiled ahead of the next election. He put it to Salisbury that bills embodying its proposals might be introduced into the Lords to dispel the popular impression of that House as a bastion of unthinking conservatism if not of reaction. The Lords had done something that met with popular approval when they rejected Gladstone's Home Rule bill in 1893; they should improve on that success. For they were in some danger: Gladstone in his last Commons speech before retiring had said that their constitutional position must be challenged by the elected chamber.[31]

To Chamberlain's political imagination, one of his strengths, this initiative presented itself as "an antidote to Gladstonian . . . destruction". He was convinced that the "ordinary elector" wanted his reforms and should be led to expect them from the Unionist peers rather than from the hostile majority in the Commons. That was the way to answer the Liberals' election cry against the Lords next time. Like Salisbury, he thought the House needed reforming: but since it was unwilling to be reformed by its friends they had to defend its existing composition and powers: "I think it is courting danger to wait for the enemy's assault". If the Liberals persisted with Home Rule, "political revolution", and Welsh disestablishment, the indulgence of "sectarian prejudices", then the Unionists should confront them with "measures affecting the moral and material well-being of the people", worked out in committees of the Lords. General propositions were not what was required: "We should ask the working-class to choose, with their eyes open". He was untypically submissive in promising not to question Salisbury's judgement – "I . . . shall be quite satisfied" – if he considered the scheme premature and one that asked more of the peers than they were able, or would consent, to deliver. An accompanying memorandum ran through the suggested legislation: bills to control a mainly Jewish problem with immigration, such as Salisbury had already introduced in the Lords during the session of 1894; to shorten the hours of shopworkers, "an excellent item in a social programme"; to set up industrial courts with power to enforce their decisions; to establish "labour bureaux", that is, independent exchanges; to expand the current provision for slum clearance and rebuilding; to help the working class with house purchase – "I attach the greatest importance to this"; to extend the statutory cheap workmen's trains with the aim of enabling people to live further away from factory and mine; and to secure proper compensation for industrial injuries by a reversal of legal principle that made the employers generally liable.[32]

He was cautious about a Unionist alternative to Liberal temperance legislation and timid, unusually, about old age pensions. His limited plans for contributory pensions had not fared well before the royal commission appointed to explore the subject: "I sincerely pity him", wrote Salisbury shortly afterwards; "Chamberlain's emotions" were politically significant. He had no option but to consign his old hostility to the Church and the landed class to the "lumber-room". Before the Tories left office, he had explained, not for the first time, that he would support Welsh disestablishment with his vote only when to do so was not "dangerous". In opposition he had accordingly voted for the Liberals' disestablishment bill: it was not going to pass and he had to think of his Nonconformist followers. He also supported the death duties in Harcourt's budget of 1894. The ill feeling this excited among Tories in the constituencies became serious in 1895: they resented having to give up seats to Liberal Unionist candidates and work for their election. Salisbury admitted to underestimating the resentment, which Chamberlain had overlooked in pressing the claims of his men. The Conservative leader, with little help from Devonshire, contrived to restore harmony between the allies for the general election he called on Rosebery's resignation in June 1895. These were the "less lovely details" of party leadership and organization: Salisbury handled them more skilfully than Gladstone, an equally fastidious man; although, like him, he preferred to leave this side of politics to others if he could.[33] Restrained from upsetting churchmen or squires, Chamberlain's continuing belief in "the Gospel of humanity . . . the extension of state or municipal socialism" made him more than a regional political boss who excelled on the platform. The imperialism with which he is associated was not yet the dominating passion it became after he took the Colonial Office in 1895.[34]

Salisbury's letter in reply to Chamberlain's suggestions for legislation came with a memorandum reviewing his specific proposals. Letter and memorandum are the best indications of the importance that social topics had assumed in contemporary politics. What the two Unionists had to decide was "mainly a question of tactics . . . in the main we agree upon policy". In a passage that ought to be remembered by anyone who doubts his understanding of human nature, he argued that the "unreasonable fear" of too many Conservatives would not be offset by the backing of those "with imagination enough to realize the advantages of our measures". The owners of property were not to be counted on to know that their interests would be best served by Chamberlain's programme. Nor would the masses necessarily credit assertions that such legislation was not to be had from the Liberals. Salisbury doubted whether the role in which Chamberlain cast the Lords was really suitable. The upper House survived as "a checking – not an originating – chamber", nothing more, and because he, in common with most of the political world, could not think how to reform it beyond creating life peers and more *ex officio* members like the law lords added in the 1870s. There were not enough politically active Unionist peers, other than ministers, to man the Lords committees to which Chamberlain wished to entrust the preparation of his bills. The Lords might, however, be used to publicize selected items from the list.[35]

Salisbury considered all but two of those bills "salutary in themselves". The exceptions were early closing of shops and employers' liability. He objected to the first on principle, as potentially harmful to the consumer; and to the second "from the tactical point of view". While a full programme of social legislation was unwise, he wanted to give an airing to the proposals on housing, including house purchase, and industrial arbitration. Chamberlain pressed for rather more; the Tory National Union was moving in the same direction: "Is it not desirable that we should, as a party, make up our minds what we can and will do?" He retained, notwithstanding his rejection of the Grand Old Man, a Gladstonian faith in the power of oratory to change the political weather: "leaders can do almost anything, if they will only give a hint of their intentions early enough". He and Salisbury agreed on giving social problems and the remedies prominence in their speeches. It was Chamberlain's contention that the working classes, more changeable in their allegiance than others, were more inclined to decide on the issues. The experience of increasing the Radical Unionist vote in Birmingham persuaded him that the success could be repeated nationally: "Gladstonianism has been a failure". A sweeping electoral victory lay within the grasp of "Unionism, or Conservatism", if Salisbury was bolder.[36]

Chamberlain's private identification of Unionism with Salisbury's Toryism was not a mental adjustment that Devonshire and his following could easily make. He and his lieutenants did not endow the Liberal Unionist organization outside the West Midlands with the independence and vigour of Chamberlain's creation. The Tory machine was indispensable to the return of Liberal Unionists over most of the country. Yet Devonshire and his friends were as useful to the Tories as Chamberlain and his Radical Unionists. Their Whiggish Liberalism was central to British political history – that undoubted success story – since 1832. When a large majority of Liberal peers went over to Unionism in 1886, it was a real accession of strength for Salisbury and the Tories. Devonshire was a great figure, and popular. He did not attract the personal enmities and suspicion of his motives that surrounded Chamberlain. His conviction that Home Rule must be resisted for the time being was respected by those who thought him mistaken. Salisbury had twice offered him the premiership, and there was speculation, not confined to the Liberal Unionist camp, that he would do so again. As electoral underdogs the Tories stood to benefit from close association with Devonshire's unquestioned liberalism in a way that cannot be measured by guesses at the size of the Liberal Unionist vote in Tory seats. He was a guarantee of the Unionist alliance's inclusion of historic liberalism as Chamberlain was of its openness to social aspirations and working-class radicalism.[37]

Salisbury sometimes grumbled about both Devonshire and Chamberlain. They ought, he felt, to be moving towards a closer relationship with the Tories, short of fusion. What he said about Chamberlain to Akers-Douglas, the Tory chief whip, before the 1895 election applied to the Liberal Unionists generally: "To sit upon the fence for nine years is an unprecedented achievement . . . he can hardly complain because we will not hold his legs to prevent him tumbling upon either side". Salisbury had to work hard disowning unfriendly comments in the *Standard* and intervening to calm the squabbles over the designation of seats as Tory or Liberal Unionist. It was very plainly in the Tory interest to prevent their allies from turning back to the main body of Liberals, if they could, or from standing aside during the election that was in the offing – at one point Chamberlain threatened to go abroad.[38] If Chamberlain was right in thinking that the Tories could not dispense with the Liberal Unionist "crutch", he was also disturbed by signs of a conversion to socialism among organized labour. Resolutions passed by the Trades Union Congress in 1894 "amount to universal confiscation", he announced to Devonshire, "in order to create a collectivist state". Keir Hardie's Independent Labour Party, founded in 1893, was working on the assumption that they should be able to exploit Gladstone's propensity, of which his successor Rosebery was a prisoner, to accommodate pressure groups that had proved themselves worthy of notice: Home Rulers, the temperance lobby and radicals bent on land reform. Fear of that Liberal reaction to the nascent British Left stimulated Chamberlain's proposed social legislation: it was "a popular alternative to wild schemes of . . . revolutionary change" entertained by the ILP. It might be the destiny of Unionism to welcome another secession from the Liberal ranks "of all that remains to them of wealth, intelligence and moderation". If there was never before 1914 any danger that the Liberals would embrace socialism, the idea had obvious uses in the electoral struggle.[39]

## The Tendencies of Liberal Policy Abroad

Lord Rosebery, Gladstone's foreign secretary for the second time, had been very reluctant to take the post again, and not only because he was subject to acute insomnia and depression. He told Sir Philip Currie, the permanent under-secretary at the Foreign Office, that nothing would induce him to serve in the Liberal ministry about to be formed: "he could never get free from them again".[40] As his complaints over the next three years in office testify, he had little sympathy with the legislation to which the incoming government was committed. Yet his ability, eloquence and charm marked him out as a favourite for the succession to Gladstone: he felt the weight of their expectations. What kept him in politics after the death of his wife, a Rothschild heiress, was the belief in himself as the heir to Canning and Palmerston. In practice, this meant that he rarely diverged from the line taken by Salisbury, whom he greatly admired.[41] The esteem was not mutual: Salisbury suspected that the reluctance to join Gladstone stemmed from a fundamental weakness in his character: "I do not feel any confidence in the stability of his decisions. I think he has lost his nerve – and with it his power of deciding." He strongly advised the Queen, who with the Prince of Wales was extremely anxious to see Rosebery at the Foreign Office, against putting pressure on him. Salisbury's choice would have been Lord Kimberley, another of the Whig peers with long experience of office loyal to

Gladstone in 1886: Kimberley could be relied on not to "*do* anything", and would lean on Philip Currie, his cousin, who had been Salisbury's man since accompanying him to Constantinople in 1876. Rosebery was hurt by his predecessor's attitude, and particularly by the refusal to meet him for a review of policy on the change of government.[42]

Rosebery felt the snub was a poor return after years of hard work since 1886 to ensure continuity in foreign policy. Salisbury had, however, written a letter to Currie for Rosebery's eyes. In it he summarized his efforts: "I have gone as far in the direction of pure neutrality as I could safely go". Britain should stay close to the Triple Alliance, and to its weakest member, Italy, without committing herself to fight. An isolated Britain would be, among other things, powerless to stop Russia from taking control of Constantinople. In the light of her popular anglophobia, France was unlikely ever to be a possible ally in that quarter or any other. He counselled judicious encouragement of Bulgaria's emerging nationhood as a first line of defence for Turkey against Russia; and discouragement of Greek designs on outlying portions of the Ottoman empire, especially Crete. Rosebery was in fact both more pro-German and more anti-French than Salisbury: but, quite unlike his predecessor, he let it be seen that he personally resented the language in which Germany expressed her European primacy and her expectations of a semi-detached ally. By the end of his three years in charge of British policy – two as foreign secretary and one as premier – his personality and a certain inability to distinguish between shadow and substance had alienated the Germans, and the French too. He was more susceptible than Salisbury to the emotional appeal of contemporary imperialism, and that much more inclined to the politics of prestige. With Palmerston as his ideal and Salisbury as his model, he lacked the resilience of the first and the judgement of the second. He and the Germans finished by accusing each other of playing "an extremely dangerous game", because neither was able to prevent secondary disagreements from getting out of hand.[43]

There were, Rosebery informed the German ambassador, only two men in Britain who spoke with authority on foreign policy: "Lord Salisbury and I . . . who could contradict us?" This was broadly true, but Rosebery did not command the respect that Salisbury enjoyed. The Germans understood why Salisbury did not advertise his reliance on the Triple Alliance, and tried to keep the diplomacy of the Mediterranean agreements secret. British public opinion would not have taken kindly to more specific acknowledgement of their country's limitations as a great power. Gladstone, according to Rosebery, was conscious of not knowing very much about foreign affairs. He dealt with his aged chief's pro-French leanings by avoiding discussion of them, as far as possible, on the grounds of continuity with Salisbury's policy. The continuity was nevertheless strained by Rosebery's view that Salisbury had given away more than he should have done in the Anglo-German treaty of 1890. While the Germans initially valued Rosebery as, in Hatzfeldt's words, "the only counterweight to the fanciful and more or less francophil tendencies of Gladstone", they wanted him to be more demonstrative of his German sympathies than Salisbury had been of his cool preference of Germany over France or Russia. They expected Rosebery to be at least as co-operative as the statesman he so admired in resolving colonial conflicts of interest. He, on the contrary, demurred even to Wilhelm II's harmless wish to indulge his love of uniforms and his admiration for Britain, which was genuine though always tinged with a politically dangerous jealousy. Granting the imperial request for the colonelcy of a British regiment – Wilhelm was already an admiral in the Royal Navy – would be interpreted as a mark of "either signal gratitude or signal friendship", when neither was justified. The Queen proceeded to bestow the coveted distinction against prime ministerial advice, a tiny and trifling assertion of the monarch's vestigial independence.[44]

Colonial disputes were an irritant in Anglo-German relations, but neither foreign ministry regarded them as anything more. A possible shift in Britain's European alignment away from Germany and towards Russia was serious. Salisbury feared Gladstone's old predilection for Russia, telling Hatzfeldt as he left office that on his return he expected to find Britain allied to Russia. It was an alarming prospect for Germany in the context of the movement of France and Russia towards each other which culminated in the Dual Alliance, the military convention in place by July 1894 and another of contemporary diplomacy's open secrets. The resolution of Anglo-Russian tensions over the delimitation of Afghanistan's northern border in the Pamirs, coincided with the co-operation, superficial though it was, of Britain, France and Russia in the international protest at the treatment of the Armenian minority in Asia Minor. Combined with Rosebery's imperfectly concealed dislike of being seen to defer and compromise, these developments raised the spectre of an Anglo-French-Russian grouping of the powers. Hatzfeldt thought it conceivable that Britain might abandon Turkey to Russia in return for Russian support in the Mediterranean. Although his foreign minister believed that Britain could not make the concessions necessary to satisfy France as well as Russia, he found it worthwhile to discuss the eventuality of a Triple Entente forming to counter the Triple Alliance. The Germans had Rosebery's measure: in the course of an interview with Hatzfeldt in November 1894 his language was not that of someone in a strong position. He promised to do whatever Germany wanted in the long-running Samoa dispute, "but leave us *nominally* the status of participants".[45]

When Hatzfeldt replied that it was time for Britain to side unequivocally with the Triple Alliance, Rosebery readily admitted that if Britain were compelled to fight alone, her fleet could not hold the Mediterranean and defend her shores at the same time. He reminded the ambassador of the link between Britain and Germany through Italy's need for a powerful British presence in the Mediterranean to protect her coasts against France. The German chancellor, Prince Hohenlohe, contrasted Rosebery's conduct of policy with Salisbury's "quiet but effective" style. British policy was in its nature provisional, averse to binding treaties and to blocs, and reflected the personality of the man in charge. Rosebery was far too susceptible to the disappointments and frustrations inherent in statecraft. All the European powers were reassured by Salisbury's continuing influence, hardly diminished, it seemed, by being out of office.[46] The French noted his speech at Cardiff in November 1893 – "one of the most mordant that the ex-prime minister has delivered" – in which he dwelt on the perilous instability of heavily armed Continental states: France and Austria, at that moment, without governments and Italy virtually bankrupt. In the

modern world, great nations in political disarray were "as dangerous as a determined and open enemy can be", given the volatility of public opinion and the logic
that pointed to the use of weaponry when security appeared to be under threat.
The statesman who worried in private about the uncertainties of any future war,
"especially at sea", called for a bigger and better navy: "torpedoes . . . rams . . .
gigantic ironclads . . . new forms of artillery. We do not know how these would
behave; it is to a certain extent a question of speculation what the effect of the first
great naval battle would be . . . Do not imagine . . . this is mere alarmism". At the
beginning of the 1890s the combined naval expenditure of France and Russia was
set to overtake that of Britain.[47]

Britain lay under the shadow of an appalling catastrophe. Yet the Liberal ministry, before Gladstone's retirement in 1894, devoted itself mainly to Home Rule,
Lords reform and other sterile topics. Salisbury's urgent plea for the enlargement
and modernization of the fleet was echoed across the parties. There followed the
naval estimates that drove the aged Gladstone into retirement, forsaken by his
colleagues. Prominent on the Liberal backbenches, the francophil Dilke was equally
concerned about France's strength at sea and her ingrained hostility to this country.
The French chargé d'affaires at the London embassy, in whom Dilke confided,
cautioned his government against letting the British think that peace was in jeopardy. With all her faults, Britain was a force for good in the world: "She lives by
and for peace". The perception of Britain then owed more to Salisbury than to
anyone else; he inspired a degree of trust on the international scene never achieved
by a British minister before or since. His warnings of the dreadful consequences of
war for the state and society were heeded in Europe. A general war, wrote the
Italian foreign minister, Baron Blanc, to the French politician, Léon Say, might end
in a re-enactment of the Paris Commune in the countries involved. While Rosebery
did not, of course, want war, he does not seem to have shared Salisbury's awareness
of universal calamity as a likely outcome.[48]

Under Rosebery's direction, his country's policy in the Far East and Africa was
complicated by the working of the Anglo-German alliance which Salisbury had
shaped to his requirements. German help was only available at a price in 1893
when the British and French navies were reportedly about to clash off the coast of
Siam where the two powers were rivals for influence. The Germans showed what
they could do in the following year: they sided with France in protesting at the
treaty of May 1894 between Britain and the Belgian king as ruler of the Congo Free
State; it was designed to pre-empt a French advance into the Mahdist Sudan.
Leopold II surrendered to the pressure on him not to implement the agreement.[49]
This setback offset Rosebery's earlier success in establishing a British protectorate
over Uganda when the chartered company which had been the instrument of
British expansion in those regions sank under its mounting debt; a piece of unfinished business from the Salisbury government. Gladstone and the Gladstonian
majority in cabinet had been loath to acquire more African territory: Harcourt said
Rosebery had "outjingoed the Jingoes". Salisbury supported Rosebery, stressing
that the consolidation of the British position in Uganda made for free trade with the

promise of new markets, and for the suppression of free trade's negation, the traffic in slaves: "If we wish to grapple with it we must take it by the throat".[50]

Unrelenting critics of Rosebery's imperialism like Harcourt distinguished between his Jingo tone and objectives, and Salisbury's moderation in both respects. Harcourt thought the latter's Anglo-German agreement of 1890 had been "very wise". Colonial disputes "ought not to be allowed to put the European machine out of gear". When Britain possessed so much in every part of the world, "a little give and take" in the Pacific or Africa was only sensible.[51] From a British angle, Rosebery had disrupted the smooth working of the European machine. Although he previously employed the Austrian ambassador as a channel for violent complaints of his German ally – "language . . . which will ricochet through Vienna to Berlin" – he did not seriously frighten them with talk of reconsidering Britain's alignment in Europe. Her isolation among the powers was underlined by the inability of Rosebery and Kimberley to organize collective intervention in the Sino-Japanese war of 1894–5 on behalf of China whose trade was predominantly in British hands.[52] Shortly before the Rosebery ministry fell, Salisbury invited the British people to remember that, alone, "we are practically without power". They must work with others, stronger on land and growing in strength at sea. The "ordinary rules of political science" applied: no matter how deeply public opinion was moved by, in this case, the fate of the Armenians in Turkey; "impotent threats" were counter-productive. No useful purpose was served by the Liberal cabinet's "crusading spirit", which Rosebery did not share. The speech exemplified the Salisbury, "as circumspect as subtle", whom the foreign ministries of the powers admired, sometimes in spite of themselves, and whose resumption of the premiership with the Foreign Office they welcomed.[53]

## 1892–5: The Unifying Themes of Opposition and Victory

During the years in opposition Salisbury portrayed Toryism and Unionism as at once strong and prudent where the world outside was concerned. Resistance to Home Rule was uncompromising and vehement: the Unionist case against giving in to Irish Catholic nationalism was never more forcefully stated than in the speeches he made at the time of the second Home Rule bill. The evocation of British and Protestant feeling had another side to it. A national community should be imbued with an active concern for its weaker members in the life of struggle to which the enormously successful creation of wealth for the whole country condemned them. To these themes he added the defence of the Established Church, which was really in danger from the Liberal commitment to Welsh disestablishment. But he saw a much greater danger to a living Christianity in the difficulties faced by the Church's schools, and in the steady advance of their Board school rivals. He was, publicly, looking to a revision of the 1870 compromise, while trying not to offend the sizeable Nonconformist Unionist vote. Without the aid of the image-makers of late twentieth-century British politics, he outlined the policies of an alliance that was in some respects not conservative at all but full of a radical promise, which the Liberals strove to match. If he kept protectionism in the background, agriculture was not forgotten, as the most conspicuous victim of the doctrinaire liberalism he always questioned and was undermining.

As before, he linked the future of Britain and the empire with victory in the renewed battle to ward off Home Rule. He regretted that the best weapon to counter Irish separatism was not available to him: the fullest use of democracy through that unEnglish device, the referendum, applied to the United Kingdom electorate. Listing the countries with provision for referenda, "almost every other constitutional government", he urged consideration of the only means of defeating unnatural coalitions such as Liberals and Irish nationalists had formed to carry Home Rule, "a majority of fraud and revolution".[54] When Gladstone's bill was before parliament, he visited Ulster to give his sanction to the formidable resistance that was being organized in the half-Protestant province. His language was extraordinary in someone of his standing; nothing like it had been or was to be heard from an ex-premier on the Irish question. He spoke of Archbishop Walsh of Dublin and T.M. Healy, outstanding among the anti-Parnellite nationalist MPs for his invective, as implacable foes perpetuating the racial conflict of centuries: "They represent the enemy against whom England appealed to settlers from Great Britain to come here and help her in her almost impossible task" of bringing order and prosperity to Ireland. At Londonderry, in the west of the province, where the local superiority of the British and Protestant population was less marked, he denounced their opponents as licensed to harry the settler by "the old charter printed in letters of blood in Irish history". He did not spare "a lamentably disciplined corps of Celtic priests, animated not by the spirit of their church but by . . . traditional hatred".[55]

He had already shocked the Liberals by defining "the real Irish question" in the racial and religious terms which the nationalists themselves habitually employed on Irish platforms and in their newspapers. Rosebery said "he would rather cut his arm off than do what Lord Salisbury was going to do". But John Morley, the Irish secretary, and the most ardent supporter of Home Rule in the cabinet after Gladstone himself, saw that Protestant Ulstermen would never submit peacefully to the nationalist majority. He was afraid to outlaw the preparations for rebellion and "perhaps set a match to an explosion".[56] Salisbury tried to make his well meaning countrymen see that there was no possibility of reconciliation under Home Rule between the two nations in Ireland: "That word 'nation' is a powerful word . . . It is mere optimistic folly worthy more of schoolgirls than of men to hide from our eyes the history of the last three centuries . . . There is a dividing line, there are traditions which cannot be reconciled". His outspokenness aroused misgivings in quarters not normally disposed to criticise him. Lady Salisbury defended her husband to the Queen, claiming that his speeches in Belfast and Londonderry, scenes of savage anti-communal rioting since the rise of Home Rule and before, had calmed the fears of the Ulster Protestants. They learnt at firsthand that they did indeed have "powerful friends" in Britain.[57] She was probably right: but it was really British opinion that Salisbury wanted to educate. The Protestant centre of Ulster – the six counties of the present Northern Ireland – was a thriving region, integrated with the economy and society of Britain. At the same time its Protestants were frontiersmen, always conscious of the threat from the nationalists who outnumbered them in five Ulster counties and overwhelmingly in the rest of Ireland. Salisbury's speeches depicted Protestant Ulstermen, not as bigots and oppressors, but as heroic defenders of Britain against her bitterest enemies and against herself. In the pamphlet he wrote for mass circulation through the Unionist organization, he made two points familiar from his attacks on Home Rule over the years. "A crazy and rickety Republic in Ireland", the end result of Gladstone's bill, would furnish hostile powers with a base from which their cruisers could prey on Britain's sea lines, intercepting the food vital to her existence. Giving in to Home Rule must also weaken irredeemably Britain's imperial will: "The taste for surrender spreads like a contagion in the spirit of the community which has once admitted the fatal germ". Subject peoples restrained by awe rather than force would follow where the Celtic Irish had led.[58]

The action of the Lords in throwing out the second Home Rule bill by a margin of ten to one in an exceptionally well attended House handed the Liberals an issue for the next election. In the event they did not succeed in making much of Lords reform because the peers had had *English* public opinion with them in September 1893. It suited Rosebery to advertise that fact in March 1894 when he said Home Rule had to await the conversion of the United Kingdom's "predominant member".[59] Salisbury's relentless exposure of Irish realities discomfited the Gladstonians; he castigated them for their "flabby optimism which disdains history and experience". It was difficult to refute the contention that representative government worked well only in homogeneous communities not fundamentally divided by race and religion, an axiom endorsed by the greatest of Victorian liberal ideologues. It is not easy, perhaps, to realize that by the 1890s the opposition to Home Rule had gained the upper hand intellectually as well as politically. John Morley conceded that in rejecting Gladstone's bill the Lords did not "really resist the will of the British constituencies".[60] That tactical victory in a battle of ideas would not have been possible without Salisbury's contribution. The peasant violence historically inseparable from separatist agitations, the urban riots in industrial Ulster, the internecine warfare on the nationalist side: these seemed to proclaim the unfitness of the Irish for representative government; for them it was likely to prove "the most dangerous curse that can be inflicted".[61]

Yet, as Salisbury implicitly acknowledged, without Ulster Home Rule would have been passed before then. Outside the six counties of the future Northern Ireland there was no popular basis for Unionism. The landed class, though still not displaced from local administration by nationalist county councils, had been deprived of the political authority they once took for granted. In the absence of land purchase on the Gladstonian scale of 1886, their leaders explored the idea of an understanding with the larger of the nationalist parties. St John Brodrick, heir to 6000 acres in County Cork, an English Tory MP and a former minister, put the landlord case to Salisbury and Balfour. Morley was bringing forward a bill to enlarge the tenants' gains from previous legislation: Brodrick, with support from Lansdowne, the Duke of Abercorn and Arthur Smith-Barry argued that if the concessions could be agreed with the anti-Parnellite faction the landlords might obtain not "*absolute finality* . . . [but] a peace of considerable duration". If Morley's bill did not get through, there was the risk of a split in Unionist Ulster where Protestant tenants were naturally tempted by what was on offer. Salisbury did not believe that the anti-Parnellites could be trusted to keep their side of the bargain if one was struck. Even if they were sincerely looking for an accommodation of interests, it was not in their power to deliver a temporary settlement of the land question. He advised the landlords against further weakening their already weak position by entering into a negotiation that was sure to fail.[62] A modern landowner, he told the Lords, and especially one in Ireland, knew how "the Jew of the Middle Ages, or the pariah of India" felt. There might be sympathy for his predicament, but he was "a man . . . who has no rights".[63]

That was to say, the notion of absolute property in land had been killed by Gladstone's Irish land legislation. Nothing had happened since 1870 to change Salisbury's view that the Irish landed class was beyond saving from themselves or from their enemies. Land purchase remained the only solution, when the British public could be persuaded that they were not going to be saddled with a heavy financial liability repudiated by the Irish. Salisbury had passed judgement on the Irish landlords: there was no one to whom they could turn. The best of them – Lansdowne, or Brodrick – understood; the others did not cease to resent his realism. Lansdowne thought better of an approach to the anti-Parnellites but, on the other hand, wanted the Lords to pass Morley's bill if it reached them. Chamberlain, who was consulted, did not think the concessions outlined by Brodrick went far enough; but he too opposed an overture to the nationalists as "a sign of weakness".[64] The Liberal government's fall spared Unionist chiefs and the peers an awkward decision. In discouraging the landlords' contemplated initiative Salisbury was true to his conviction that appeasement of the Celtic Irish was futile. "The manner by which rural public opinion operates [in Ireland]" he said to the Upper House, "is to drag a man out of bed and shoot at his legs" – the probable treatment of tenants who co-operated with their landlords in the future as in the past.[65]

The decline of Ireland, outside the industrial heart of Ulster, was apparently irreversible: the discontent of its diminished Catholic population, barely ten per cent of the United Kingdom total, was containable by a strong government. Working-class Britain presented quite different problems. It was a question of perpetuating the conservatism and patriotism of this huge class, whose respect for law and their betters made possible the smooth transition to democracy. Their growing self-confidence was evident in the increase of trade union membership, tripled in a dozen years after 1888. Trade union leaders were generally Liberals and not drawn to the socialism of the ILP, the Marxist SDF or William Morris's Socialist League. Salisbury addressed himself to unionized labour, still dominated by skilled workers and the miners, but also to those less able to take care of themselves. It was he, not Chamberlain, who made immigration from Eastern Europe, largely Jewish, an issue. The influx into London and several provincial cities undoubtedly had an adverse effect on employment and housing. It threatened, moreover, the homogeneity of a people who had resisted the only previous substantial immigration, from Ireland, that was alien in race and religion, and had confined its permanent legacy to usually well defined districts. The tradition of free entry into the United Kingdom was too strong for Salisbury to get the bill he introduced into the Lords in July 1894 beyond a second reading. The Jewish immigrants were in some sense refugees from institutionalized oppression as well as from dire poverty in Tsarist Russia. Salisbury argued with Devonshire, a guardian of Whiggish liberalism within Unionism, that since the United States, Canada and European countries were erecting barriers against "pauper aliens, it is mathematically evident that they must be turned upon us".[66]

His Aliens Bill was distinctly moderate: the powers it conferred upon government were precautionary, to be used when the need arose. His figures were disputed: he queried the Board of Trade's statistics: "I prefer figures . . . that have not been sweated"; an allusion to the downward pressure of immigrant competition on wage rates. He insisted on the "clear and special right" to exclude both destitute immigrants and the political extremists who used Britain as a base for their assassination plots abroad. The numbers of the former oppressed the ratepayer as well as the wage earner, often the same person: "We have a right to say that our . . . poor rate and our social system is for ourselves". As for the extremists, their admirers were "a real disgrace to this country".[67] He was no more successful in this aim than Palmerston had been with a similar move in the 1850s. A second reading was all he could secure; Devonshire seems to have been dubious about the wisdom of going so far.[68] Salisbury quoted Rosebery on the undesirability of contemporary immigration: but the patrician and middle-class liberalism that pervaded Unionists and Gladstonians alike prevented action until 1905. There was nevertheless a political reward. In the places affected, popular feeling against a significant alien presence was not transient. Salisbury had identified Unionism as the party that cared about the impact of immigration on the most vulnerable members of society. Chamberlain seconded him: the bill of 1894 was "valuable to us for strategic purposes", helping the working class to distinguish their real friends. An aliens bill had in fact been prepared by Ritchie, president of the Local Government Board, in Salisbury's last administration, who sat for a constituency in the East End, where much the biggest concentration of Jewish immigrants was located.[69]

In the autumn of 1894 Howard Vincent, the Tory MP for Sheffield Central, reported that the meetings at which he had spoken in most of the great Northern towns were enthusiastic for Salisbury's Aliens Bill. Working men were aware of the incongruity of encouraging emigration to relieve unemployment and poverty, as the Victorians always had done, while allowing immigration to continue. Want, a Manchester MP reminded Salisbury, was often as severe in industrial Britain as it was in the "congested districts" of the West of Ireland, where the government he headed had concluded that the responsibilities of the state must be widened. The principle of the Irish scheme was applicable to the wretched condition of the urban poor. Nor should the deferential tone of the resolutions carried at Vincent's meetings count against them. The MPs who wrote to Salisbury on these social questions were usually advocates of protection, which their working-class following persisted in regarding as merely common sense.[70] The return of protection was a long-term prospect: "it is outside the dreams of any politician", said Salisbury at Liverpool in February 1893.[71] The extension of state intervention in such fields as housing was much less offensive to the prevailing economic liberalism. It developed a well established trend, and could be rationalized as enhancing individual freedom, and not necessarily circumscribing it by the bureaucratic interference he detested.

Salisbury confronted the "uneasiness and anxiety" about class relations which lay close to the surface. He compared a legitimate "socialism" to the Liberal government's introduction of death duties – the revision of the Gladstonian succession duty of 1853 – in the budget of 1894. The latter, to his mind, was simply a fiscal expedient: it bore harshly on his own class and was to that extent mistaken, but not inherently wrong: "the richer . . . classes are the natural prey of the Chancellor of the Exchequer". Of socialism he said: "That is a word . . . we must carefully analyse. It contains matter that is absolutely poisonous . . . also matter . . . of a less injurious description . . . to use the machinery of the state for . . . objects in which the community generally is agreed . . . in that socialism . . . I can see no harm whatever". The Post Office was obviously better run by government, and state ownership of the railways, although more doubtful, was a subject for discussion. Nor was there any reason to fear socialism in another sense, which he proceeded to commend to the consideration of the National Union at its Edinburgh conference in 1894. The assembled Tories were asked to think hard about more government provision for the deserving poor in old age than the Poor Law permitted, to relieve "terrible individual and social suffering". In examining old age provisions and help with house purchase for the working class, Salisbury was taking forward at an accelerated pace the social Toryism that Gladstone had deplored in the preceding decade. The importance of a "progressive" image to the upper and middle classes was assumed by their best elements. Salisbury and Chamberlain brought the Unionists up to date by broadening their conception of acceptable progress.[72]

Conscious that he was making many of the rank and file nervous, he set out the distinction between taking all the means of production into state ownership – its exponents were "enemies of the human race" – and what they were hearing from him and from Chamberlain, "with whose general objects, I confess, I have the greatest sympathy". They must not cry "wolf, wolf, where there is no wolf". Chamberlain had not got a commitment to the detailed programme he had just submitted: but he was given something more valuable, a restatement of political philosophy that made room for everything he wanted to do by way of social action through the statute-book.[73] Offsetting this shift towards a social radicalism was some sharp criticism from Salisbury of the Liberals' political and religious radicalism. He enjoyed himself mocking the establishment of parish councils, pictured as "emancipating the rural classes from the terrible despotism of the squire and the parson". There was sufficient support for the innovation on his side, and not only among the Liberal Unionists, to hold him back from insisting on all his amendments in the Lords to this part of the 1894 Local Government Bill. Although the powers proposed for parish councils had worried him, the restriction of their expenditure to a penny rate rendered them comparatively harmless in those few places where deference did not maintain the old order in the villages. While he did not welcome, either, the transfer of the Poor Law in the countryside to the new district councils, the councils themselves had been on his government's agenda. He acquiesced in the removal from county magistrates of their Poor Law functions; this vestige of their rule belonged

292

to the past: "There is no advantage in attempting to prolong its existence".[74] In London he was gladdened by the successes of Tories and Liberal Unionists in the triennial elections for the county council which his government had set up in 1888. He censured the ruling Progressives for not doing more to alleviate the dreadful conditions in the East End, "which no one can think about without shuddering sometimes". The Tory creation, he reflected, was too big to be healthy: there should be some delegation of its powers.[75]

What troubled him about local democracy was the tendency of the "leisured classes" to withdraw from its operation, to be replaced by the sort of men who had given municipal politics a bad name across the Atlantic: "I see that, slowly, not very perceptibly, . . . the same malady which has committed such fearful ravages in America has begun to affect us too". Evidence was not lacking. He ascribed Unionist gains in the London county council elections partly to the heartening participation of the upper and middle classes. But in a democracy, national or local, the majority was decisive: he affirmed his confidence that the Liberals were fated to go on "digging deeper and deeper, only to find the stream of Toryism where it dug". The people, he said and to a great extent believed, were conservative in their instincts; the more he saw of them from the platform, the more he thought so. "The stream of Toryism", however, had to be constantly replenished from its source, religion, which in turn depended on the vitality of the Established Church and on the teaching of orthodox Christianity in the schools. Where the Church and her schools were at stake, Salisbury could not rely on Chamberlain, whose outward allegiance to Nonconformity remained an integral part of his political life. The defence of the Welsh Church was conducted mainly by Tories. Salisbury directed a counter-attack which exploited the weak points in the Liberal case: the lost ground recovered by the Church in Wales since the mid-century and the Nonconformists' refusal to agree to a religious census that might not confirm the claim that the Church was heavily outnumbered.[76]

In standing up for the Welsh Church Salisbury used classical Tory arguments clothed in language that made them fresh and lively. Even with the Anglican revival in Wales the Church's position there was exposed: the primate, Archbishop Benson, and his episcopal brethren were apprehensive; the Liberationists still saw Welsh disestablishment as preliminary to a final assault upon the Church in England. "Every cause and every person is stronger for being abused", Salisbury consoled Benson, to whom it had not occurred to see the situation in that light. The united demand of Welsh Liberals, endorsed by their English and Scottish colleagues in the Commons, was not popular in England, where many Nonconformists had little enthusiasm for disestablishment. The verbal violence of militant Nonconformity aided the Church's political champions. Benson's dislike and distrust of Salisbury, lessened by the rescue of the Clergy Discipline Bill in 1892, yielded to admiration of his generalship. Following a council of war on Liberal intentions, his diary acknowledges Salisbury's tactical sense, which he had hitherto failed to appreciate. This nervous prelate, very conscious of his dignity, was able to bear some gentle teasing from his political master. "I wonder at your courage", wrote Salisbury after Benson had been criticized by Gladstonian High Churchmen for openly collaborating with him: "It would be a convenience if Lambeth had a 'Traitor's Gate' on the river through which dangerous politicians might enter secretly".[77] The outline of a campaign to save the Welsh church was settled in meetings at Lambeth and Hatfield between Salisbury and the Archbishop with selected politicians and prelates. It is significant that on these occasions the political figures attending with Salisbury only once included someone else of the first rank, Goschen, from the Unionist leadership. The others were Salisbury's son Cranborne, an ardent Churchman, his son-in-law Wolmer, the Liberal Unionist whip, and Wolmer's aged father Lord Selborne, with Cranbrook and Cross, two veterans of Tory cabinets.[78]

Hicks Beach, who was without question one of the leading Unionists, approved of the formation of a "Church party", or group, on their side of the Commons. It would be, he told the primate kindly, "a very useful body", to which he himself could not adhere. As representing clergy more than the laity, "it . . . must be rather 'Churchy'". Its appearance was, Benson realized, "a dangerous . . . symptom" of the Church's isolation from the mass of the laity. Hicks Beach worked on his fears: the existence of a "party" within a party did not mean, he added, that the Establishment any longer had a choice in national politics; her defenders could only be Conservatives.[79] Salisbury handled Benson and the great issue of disestablishment, for such it was, differently: it would not help the Church to be wholly identified with Toryism. At the Lambeth meetings he pleased Benson, who had no illusions about the Tories, "by his invariably diverting our reliance from Conservatives". He advised the primate and his brethren not to employ Conservative agents and other partisan Tories in organizing their protest: "make much of Liberals. Let Liberal bishops make much of the fact that they *are* Liberals". Although some two-thirds of Liberal MPs were still Anglican, they would vote with the government, whatever their true feelings. The Church's campaign should be aimed at stirring up the electorate: by petitions to the Commons, by "endless letters" to MPs with small majorities, by meetings, leaflets, lectures, magazines – all the well tried methods of political agitation. A failure to organize and sustain a protest would announce a lost cause. The emphasis should be placed on the injustice of disestablishment in legal and social terms. Salisbury was opposed to letting these monitored activities turn into a religious confrontation; he deprecated services of intercession and special prayers.[80]

These tactics served his purpose. The Church and her friends showed they were capable of getting up an agitation that was too widely supported to be dismissed as sectarian or sectional. Gladstone contended that disestablishment met the "national or quasi-national" claims of Wales, which did not enthuse English opinion. As for what the agnostic John Morley had joined other Liberals in calling "religious privilege . . . that great question", the public in England were largely indifferent to assertions that the principle of establishment was wrong and outdated. They might not care for the clericalism of High Churchmen, but Gladstone calculated that three-quarters of them owned to "some kind of membership" of the Church. She satisfied their religious needs with her rites of passage and a substantial minority attended her services with more or less regularity.[81] She was not so closely associated as Nonconformity with the desire to interfere with popular recreation. Salisbury had no hesitation in stigmatizing the "Puritanical hypocrisy" of Nonconformity as the driving force behind the temperance lobby. He was equally scathing in defence of the Welsh Church: "Nothing seems to me more repulsive than that those who stripping a man by the wayside should assure him that they do it from a Christian love of his soul"; the Church's endowments were consecrated to preaching the Gospel among the poor and to the corporal works of mercy. The demand for disestablishment and disendowment was inspired by rancour, above all "the passion of jealousy . . . which can leave nothing behind but . . . perpetual conflict and ever unsatisfied revenge". It was not too highly coloured a description of the bitterness excited by the feud between church and chapel in the Principality. The participation of Morley and other secular radicals in the attack on the Church justified his reference to "those who wish no good . . . to the Christian religion". The Church ought not to be political: but churchmen must resist "spoliation" with all the political influence they could command.[82]

There was a certain unreality about the fighting over the Welsh Church. If disestablishment passed the Commons, the Lords were certain to kill it. Hicks Beach predicted that it would not get beyond the second reading in the house, so little did most ministers and English Liberals care for it. In the event, party discipline held, and the second reading was carried by the surprisingly comfortable majority of forty-four votes: but in committee the majority fell to seven. The bill was lost on the fall of Rosebery's government in June. It had been clear to him that the Church of England stood "like a rock". The attack on her was not good for Liberalism, even in Wales, where it cost the party seats and votes in the 1895 election.[83]

Salisbury, who was "so sharp – and said many amusing things by the way", when discussing the Welsh Church with the primate, was more concerned at the predicament of the Church's schools in England and Wales. By 1895 the children in Board schools – nearly two million – slightly exceeded those being educated by the Church; another half million were in Catholic, Wesleyan and other Voluntary schools. There – and not in Nonconformist attempts to disestablish – lay the real threat to the Church and to orthodox Christian belief. Denied rate aid, and harassed by an unsympathetic bureaucracy, Church schools were losing the battle with their rivals, who taught the "patent compressible religion" characterized by "essential insincerity". Salisbury's remedy, given the hostility of political Nonconformity to rate aid, was to advocate parental freedom to determine a child's religious education in Board schools, thus taking the struggle for faith into the enemy's camp. "It is", he said in a speech of March 1895, "an intolerable idea that the state should come to us, like the censor of the Russian government, and stamp out such parts of our religion as do not suit its secular notions".[84] However, the undenominational religious teaching under the school boards varied quite widely: a sizeable element in the Church was not satisfied with what was being taught locally. Temple, the Broad Church Bishop of London and future primate, did not concur in the principle of parental freedom which, Salisbury told him, was one "so righteous and so important that within the limits of practicability it ought to be pressed at all hazards and on all occasions". The Bishop did not believe that parents with children in Board schools wanted teaching based "on the authority of the Church or of one division of the Church".[85]

The last half-dozen words were a pointed reference to the High Churchmen on the capital's school board who used Anglican control to take the offensive. The moving spirit, Athelstan Riley, had said to Archbishop Benson when first elected, "I go on to the . . . Board to destroy it. Christians ought to destroy it, not save it". Temple was completely opposed to that stance, and content, as were Noncon-formists, to treat the New Testament as "an authoritative text book in itself". This attitude reflected the creeping modernism in Protestant theology. Salisbury had to appeal to him not to divide the Church's forces in the election of 1894 for the school board.[86] After her "in some respects . . . injudicious" supporters had won, he persuaded one of his temporarily unemployed cabinet ministers to fill the chair-manship of the new board. "My Church views are broad", Lord George Hamilton confirmed, accepting out of a sense of duty. "Riley and Co. have put us into a position which is not permanently tenable." In his memoirs Hamilton revealed what he had been sent to do, and did: Salisbury "seemed to think . . . I had an inherent wet blanket element within me to damp down . . . the more violent of the protagonists".[87]

This episode was a warning to Salisbury, if he needed it, of the dangers involved in a revision of the 1870 compromise. He thought of himself as compelled to resist the movement to diffuse in schools a creed from which all fundamental differences had been excised, "this anti-crusade" leading inexorably to "universal unbelief". "You cannot play fast and loose with the deepest . . . convictions of the human mind"; of that he was sure. His awareness of theological developments, and his realization that they were subtly changing the outlook of the educated laity, made him quite explicit about the spiritual peril. In a slowly deteriorating climate for orthodox Christianity, undenominational religion taught to schoolchildren with dog-matic truths left out or played down, "means without teaching the divinity of our Lord. That is the real point on which, in the long run, all . . . will turn". Only the freedom of parents to reject "Board School religion" could preserve the Established Church and its beliefs from becoming, in the not too distant future, irrelevant to national life. The stage was set for the educational battles of his last administration.[88]

The Church, agriculture, death duties and protection were topics that touched one another. The unamended Liberal legislation for parish councils contained pro-visions that struck at the parson's position in relation to parochial trusts and facilit-ies. Salisbury advised Benson that it would be invidious if the necessary amendments were moved by the bishops. The offending clauses had been inserted in response to the anti-clericalism of village radicals, a vocal minority. Some Tories, including two cabinet colleagues, and Liberal Unionists were inclined to indulge the wish for "the deposition of the parson": Salisbury was not.[89] More serious was the mood of tenant farmers, the rural middle class. After lifting a little at the end of the 1880s the long agricultural depression worsened: without the other sources of income that shel-tered many of their landlords from the storm, farmers clamoured for protection against the imports now forcing down livestock and dairy prices while grain prices went lower still. Falling rents – Salisbury gave his tenants a reduction of thirty per cent in December 1894 – were a palliative.[90] As a class, farmers had withstood the temptations that urban demagogues put before them: in desperation they could not but think more urgently than in the earlier part of the depression, of saving themselves at the landlords' expense. Schomberg McDonnell, Salisbury's trusted private secretary when he was in office, summed up for him the debates at the well attended agricultural conference of December 1892, held in London: if the farmers did not get protection in some form, they would "inevitably" demand the Three Fs secured by Irish tenants.[91]

Unable to see how parliament and the town populations could ever be brought to restore protection, McDonnell suggested working up an agitation against the farmers among their landless labourers, who would not benefit, "but the reverse", from a sweeping reform of tenure in the occupier's interest. This was a counsel of despair. Chaplin, who spoke for agriculture in the Tory leadership and addressed the conference, thought the labourers' representatives present, radicals in politics, were likely to side with the farmers. At one moment, he reported, it looked as if an amendment from the floor calling for the Three Fs would be carried by a large majority. There was "great danger" of something of the kind. His solution was the adoption of bi-metallism, then in vogue as a means of stimulating the economy by increasing the money supply and prices with it. Salisbury ruled that out, along with protection and land courts on the Irish model. He was left with the removal of special burdens on agricultural land, that is, of the rates levied upon it. He delayed the announcement of this policy – the "poverty" of which he privately admitted – until hope of some lasting improvement in prices had been dispelled. It was for the Liberals to face the problems of agriculture and incur the unpopularity with rural electors that would punish their failure to discover answers.[92] As Salisbury had foreseen, protection, still politically impossible, was winning friends year by year. When Chaplin uttered the word "protection" in his speech at the conference his audience of farmers drawn from all over the country resembled "people gone mad . . . springing up in their places and cheering frantically". They were not alone in their anxiety to be relieved of the pressure of intense competition. In spite of industry's continuing advance, it was not only struggling sectors and firms that were attracted to protection. There was no longer the old confidence in free trading Britain as the fortunate exception in a protectionist world.[93]

The scenes at the conference made Tory "wire-pullers" think hard about the treatment of protection as an issue for the future. Middleton, the principal agent, registered Salisbury's view that the demand must come from below. But he had the offer of £10 000 from a City figure to finance a campaign and undertook "to raise a cry *from below* with so large a sum". While Akers-Douglas was sceptical, he and Middleton asked for instructions. "Of course", the meeting would be dissociated from the agitation they had instigated. The money furnished an opportunity to test working-class opinion at a safe distance from the next general election. On reflection, it seemed wiser to see how agricultural meetings around the country went in the aftermath of the London conference. The Liberal chancellor of the exchequer, Harcourt, was saying that when his age shortly forced Gladstone to retire, his party would go down to defeat but for the urban fear of protection. He counted on that to bring the Liberal Unionists back into the fold and deny the Tories power for a long time to come. The perception of this inside and outside the London political world was so clear that farmers, who did not really desire a revolution in the tenure of land alien to their traditions, resigned themselves to leaving protection in the background. But the question was not dead: and Salisbury helped to keep it alive.[94]

Eighteen months after this discussion with some of his closest associates, Salisbury showed his hand. Protection, he said at Trowbridge in May, "is dead and cannot be revived"; a categorical statement that shielded him from Liberal criticism. He followed it by dwelling on the harm that free trade had done, and was doing. Two million acres of arable land had gone out of cultivation, sending country people into overcrowded cities: "Just consider . . . the amount of human suffering, the expansion of the terrible problem of the unemployed . . . you will feel . . . the great economical blunder which . . . has deeply tinged with misery the lives of . . . hundreds of thousands of the least powerful, least defended of our population". Hardly the words of a man who regarded free trade as irrevocable. Farmers and their labour force were the victims of an unreasoning application of economic principles. Some of the huge outflow of capital from Britain would be much better invested at home and in agricultural land: "I point out to you the extreme folly of driving this capital away. We want it here." He did not pretend that removing special burdens on land, the policy now revealed, was an adequate remedy for the ills he was thrusting upon the notice of a predominantly urban public. Electors were, in effect, being invited to conclude that only protection could return the stricken corn-growing regions of England to prosperity: and that what was good for agriculture was good for industries fighting to hold markets against foreign competition. No one doubted that Salisbury was friendly to protection.[95]

Salisbury linked the prolonged crisis in agriculture with the introduction of death duties in 1894. This replacement for the succession duty did away with the rule that in the case of property under settlement only the life interest of the deceased was chargeable. The change meant that the duty payable on settled estates rose from as little as one or two per cent to Harcourt's maximum of eight. The money was required to fund the increased naval expenditure almost universally seen as imperative. In the circumstances, Salisbury, unlike his party and the Liberal Unionists, had little to say. The rise in capital taxation, though sharp, was, in Rosebery's careful phrasing, "logically just". Salisbury put it rather differently: he termed the duties "an injustice which may be excused by the serious need". He was opposed to the principle of graduation, which the Victorians had so far tried to avoid, and to the enforced sale of property to meet the Inland Revenue's notional estimates of the value of land or works of art. His alternative was to tax whenever property was sold, or leased, catching "what is called the unearned increment". The state was entitled to a fair share of that element of wealth. He did not make these views public, in contrast to those Unionists who had demanded a bigger fleet and now were loudly condemning the necessary taxation. Devonshire, claiming that the survival of his palace at Chatsworth and its collections was in doubt, headed the protesters.[96] Salisbury spoke on death duties that session: "I am not demurring in the least degree to the extent to which he [Harcourt] wishes to tax rich men", he told the

Primrose League. But, as a matter of fact, landed estates, the most vulnerable form of property, would be the hardest hit. The agriculture and well-being of whole districts would suffer as landowners cut back on their spending.[97]

In the remainder of that speech, he took up protection again. "This tariff war" of their time, in which Britain chose to remain defenceless, was diminishing the chances of work for her people. The message was inescapable: the "social question" probably could not be contained without protection. The human costs of late nineteenth-century capitalism were as shocking to him as they were to any of its critics. Complaining that charities ought not to approach politicians for sermons, he made good use of the obligation: his address on the spiritual needs of the East End in May 1895 was more searching than his previous utterances on the place of religion in a class society. The paternalism of landlords and employers, which had cushioned the impact of an economic transformation, was passing. In the sprawling industrial estates of East London, impersonal limited companies had displaced "the old type of individual, whose conscience can be appealed to, and whose liberality can, therefore, be counted upon". He implored the owners of capital to realize that their comfortable lives rested on the working people in such areas, out of sight and frequently out of mind as a result of the residential segregation that had developed over half a century. He asked them, "as patriots", not to forget that working-class deprivation, and consciousness of neglect, must tell upon the confidence and security of an industrial nation. The worst kind of deprivation was spiritual: in that respect, more important than any other, they were practically destitute. His speech might be cited to illustrate Salisbury's pessimism and detachment from the tasks of social reform awaiting a government with the will to tackle them. Read with other speeches developing the social dimension of his politics, this one was not less constructive in breathing new life into a cliché. The "moral culture" of the masses was the foundation of collective discipline and prosperity: "There is no agency . . . so efficient for this education . . . as the Church of Christ".[98]

# CHAPTER TWELVE

# *Unionist Democracy, 1895–1900*

## The 1895 Election and the First Unionist Government

The election of July 1895 quietened fears that socialism was making headway in Britain. All the Independent Labour Party's candidates and those of the Social Democratic Federation – twenty-eight and four respectively – were defeated. The ILP's share of the votes cast was one per cent. Of the 411 Unionists returned, over a quarter were unopposed; the two per cent rise in the Unionist vote since 1892, when only forty of the seats they won did not see a contest, understated the turn of the political tide. The three Unionist seats in Wales became nine, and in Scotland the allies captured thirty-one out of seventy. Salisbury had formed his administration in June when Rosebery resigned after losing a relatively unimportant division on the army estimates. The new government dissolved parliament: their opponents were demoralized by the mutual hostility existing between Rosebery and Harcourt, rivals for the succession to Gladstone, and by failure to pass the main items in their legislative programme. Denunciations of the House of Lords in the ensuing election left the public unmoved. While the Liberal organization reflected the party's low morale, the Unionist machine maintained the efficiency it had demonstrated since the alliance was born. It put up candidates against almost all of the 447 Liberals, of whom only 177 were successful. Salisbury could confidently refer beforehand to the Liberals' impending defeat.[1] However, the size of the Unionist majority came as a surprise. It was a response to anxieties in industry, and distress in the regions where high farming had flourished. There was also a feeling shared by the outgoing prime minister himself, that the country needed Salisbury to conduct her foreign policy. "I do not complain", he said privately of his reverse, "for I see matter for congratulation in what has occurred to the patriot, though not perhaps to the politician".[2]

For the first time since 1874, the Tories had a majority in the Commons, but it was only ten. The outcome of the election confirmed Salisbury's judgement in forming a coalition; Unionism was now "more homogeneous".[3] If the 71 Liberal Unionists in the Commons were there, most of them, thanks to Tory organization and Tory votes, the Tories could not have done without the difference that Devonshire and Chamberlain had made to their image. Especially in the towns, Unionism helped to free Toryism from reactionary associations going back to the days of Wellington and Lord Eldon. Some of Devonshire's friends thought he should be prime minister: but the offer of the post was not renewed. Instead, Salisbury invited him to take the Foreign Office. Devonshire declined: though apparently genuine, the invitation was not one that he could accept; Britain and Europe were looking forward to Salisbury's return to his old department. The Duke took the post of Lord President, enhanced by the oversight of defence policy through the chairmanship of a standing committee of cabinet. Chamberlain realistically asked for and received the Colonial Office as the instrument of a constructive imperialism tied to economic growth and social improvement at home. Lansdowne went to the War Office; Sir Henry James got a peerage and the Duchy of Lancaster. As Goschen at the Admiralty had previously taken the symbolic step of joining the Carlton and was now considered to be a Conservative, these four made up the Liberal Unionist contingent in the cabinet. Liberal Unionists were well represented, too, at the lower levels of the administration. Salisbury grumbled at the "odious tiresomeness" of having to satisfy the claims of two parties as well as the ambitions of individuals. He had, it transpired, put together a government remarkably free from the tensions that were to be apprehended.[4]

Devonshire's views counted when he chose to express them, but he did not make policy. Lansdowne gave an impression of competence at the War Office which was not borne out by events. Policy was generally made by Salisbury, Chamberlain, Balfour in his former post as leader of the Commons, and Hicks Beach at the Treasury; Goschen's was also a powerful voice. The real meeting of minds was between Salisbury and Chamberlain. "He is literally in love with Chamberlain. I never heard him talk of any colleague as he does of him", wrote his niece by marriage, the clever Lady Frances Balfour, in the autumn of 1895. Although Chamberlain, he complained cheerfully, thought of nothing but imperialism and wanted to fight every power in the world, they had attained a political rapport that seldom failed them. Chamberlain listened to Salisbury, argued with him as no one else did, but never intrigued against him. Their disagreements did not weaken the essential unity of a government that depended upon their mutual understanding and respect. Both were men of ideas, and more so than any of their colleagues. Chamberlain was more urgent and apparently clearer in his hopes for the next few years, Salisbury broader and wiser. Within a very short time the distinction between Tory and Liberal Unionist had all but disappeared. For one thing, the attraction of protectionism now cut across the alliance. To accommodate the Nonconformity strong in Liberal Unionism, religion – that is, legislation in the Church's interest – was to be treated as an open question. But in practice Chamberlain helped forward the educational bills that were the government's most controversial measures; though not even his support could carry the bill of 1896. He and his imperial creed became a cult with younger Tories; unlike him, they felt free to criticize Salisbury for the caution and scepticism with which he regarded their wilder notions of what was desirable or possible.[5]

On the home front Salisbury prepared old Tories, in both senses, for "a new era". "We shall be invited to enter upon a legislative ocean that is unknown to us – and the steering may be difficult", he told the octogenarian Cranbrook.[6] The political conditions, he announced, were ideal for "careful and tentative" advances that eschewed "the predatory principle of legislative benevolence"; that is, they ought not, now, to make property fearful of worse to come. That speech, at Brighton in November 1895, diluted the expectations created when he celebrated the Unionist victory three weeks earlier at Watford. The masses had shown, by rejecting socialism and the radical Irish and Welsh policies of the Liberals, that "they had no sort of notion of destroying what they had been admitted to share in". It was "a turning point in English political history". "Social amelioration" was the question before the country, one that transcended party. "We have . . . as far as we can, to make this country more pleasant to live in for the vast majority . . . we have no panacea, but we can do a great deal"; proceeding by persuasion, and not by decree. A change of party in government was healthy; a retreat from constructive legislation, to which both parties were more or less committed, was not: "I am in favour of the [electoral] pendulum . . . but I do not believe in the pendulum as applied to measures". These two speeches foreshadowed the achievements, compromises and failures of the next five years. He promised not to frighten capitalists "large and small", and he had to keep his word.[7] This aspect of the 1895–1900 administration was, and is, thought to be less significant than his foreign and imperial policies. It did not seem so to that intelligent critic, Edward Hamilton. By the middle of 1897 he began to think Salisbury's was "the most radical government of modern times". The reforming spirit that found expression in the 1897 Workmen's Compensation Act, "to revolutionize the relations between employer and employed", and the 1896 Irish Land Act, "the stiffest . . . ever introduced", did not flourish in spite of Salisbury, but because of him.[8]

## A Reforming Administration: Rhetoric and Substance

Limited as they were by the Unionist members and by public opinion, the partnership of Salisbury and Chamberlain did well to get over the obstacles to two major pieces of legislation in answer to pressing social and economic problems. The Agricultural Land Rating Act passed in 1896 halved the burden of rates on owners and occupiers at the expense of the taxpayer. The Workmen's Compensation Act of the next session effected a legal revolution in shifting the onus of proof in cases of physical injury from employee to employer; many businessmen and lawyers disliked it intensely. Old age pensions encountered strong resistance in parliament and the Treasury: the cost of the war in South Africa forced an indefinite postponement on the ministerial advocates. The Salisbury government also failed to carry its far-reaching education bill in 1896: but interdenominational conflict, not differences of social philosophy, accounted for that serious disappointment. 1896 also saw the passage of a measure providing for official arbitration in industrial disputes. Unlike workmen's compensation and old age pensions, this was not controversial; the mediation of Rosebery, as premier, had settled the bitter coal strike of 1893. Nor was there much objection to other minor instalments of state intervention. If Salisbury doubted whether he could pass another contentious social reform after 1897, he had not changed his mind about the central importance of such initiatives. When he reshuffled the administration after the 1900 election, he explained to the cabinet ministers who were dropped that "social questions . . . likely to attract great attention" made it necessary to introduce new blood.[9]

The Agricultural Land Rating Bill was attacked as indiscriminate; there were numerous local exceptions to the severity of the depression in farming. The Gladstone estates in Flintshire, it was calculated, stood to benefit up to £400 a year on a property where rents were well paid; and a Liberal magnate not far away, Lord Crewe, put his annual gain at £2000.[10] Unionist MPs in urban seats murmured: they were promised an inquiry into the rating system as a whole, the unfairness of which Salisbury had criticized over the years. He emphasized that small proprietors – English peasants – heavily outnumbered the large landowners who were supposed to be the main beneficiaries of the Act. Walter Long, president of the Board of Agriculture, maintained that farmers South of the Tweed were solid for protection. They knew they could not have it: and he argued for helping them generously with government money and credit. Halving the rates on agricultural land for five years in the first instance – twenty-five per cent less than the reduction recommended by the royal commission on agriculture set up in 1894 – and making up the loss to local government from the Treasury was the best that ministers could do for a vocal minority interest.[11] There was widespread sympathy with the Liberal argument that the Act contained a subversive principle. Treasury grants to compensate for lost rates were, in effect, subsidies to landowners and farmers. If their profits were to be subsidized, then why not wages? John Morley conjured up the spectre of "national workshops" from the Paris of 1848. Such protests as this, from a declared radical, exhibited the social conservatism of the Liberals, challenged by politicians who moved with the times. Salisbury did not, on that occasion, take up the point, preferring to deride the opposition for their antagonism to the landed class: "I shall be thought . . . as courageous as the Scotch clergyman who said a word in favour of the 'puir deil'".[12]

He avoided flippancy when he defended the Workmen's Compensation Bill. It was in the tradition of the great Tory Shaftesbury's humanitarian legislation: it did not invade private rights, properly understood. "Mere liberty" must yield, not only to "common humanity", but to social progress: the steady improvement in the condition of the working classes had been assisted by a stream of regulatory Acts in different areas of economic life. It was self-defeating to cry "Socialism" when property was not taken or its value diminished: "you give to every socialist reasoner a basis . . . for pointing to your own extravagances as his proof". Chamberlain's bill had, his Liberal Unionist colleague James opined as it was being drafted, "from the employer's point of view a rather ghastly appearance". Although he had been made colonial secretary, Chamberlain was identified with the bill and took charge of it: he adjured James, a distinguished lawyer, to fight any extensive modification of proposals that were to establish the Unionists' superiority over the Liberals' attempt to legislate in the same field: "it would be fatal . . . if our first social reforms were clearly less favourable to the working classes".[13] If Salisbury's 1891 Education Act was not the beginning of the welfare state, then it was this measure of Chamberlain's. In cabinet and in the Commons he preserved its essential features. Contracting out was permitted only where the employer's obligation to insure against liability could be met by a scheme comparable with that of the Act. With a minimal increase of bureaucracy, Chamberlain had introduced the country to social insurance after years of discussion in the light of the Bismarckian reforms in Germany. Liberals had no doubt that they were witnessing the birth of "socialism, pure and simple". So, too, were Tories; led by the great coalowner of the North East, Lord Londonderry, some of them openly attacked the bill.[14]

It was in reply to Londonderry that Salisbury "in his cleverest of moods", wrote an admiring Liberal, sought to rebut the charge of making a social experiment at the expense of industry. His authority, and his skill with words, quietened the dangerous critics, those on his own side. They were not convinced that in the present climate of opinion, anything more was wanted by way of social reform, and they were not reconciled to the government's stated intentions. There was talk in political circles that another such measure as workmen's compensation from Chamberlain would divide, if it did not upset, the Unionist coalition. The next step, advertised in the speeches of Salisbury and Chamberlain, was old age pensions. If the public finances and economies of Germany and New Zealand were able to support this provision, demonstrably needed, Britain could do so. For every Unionist, or Liberal, frightened of socialism, there was one with no misgivings about extending the frontiers of the state in society. In the first weeks of the new parliament, the Liberals' chief whip, T.E. Ellis, said it was "though nominally . . . Conservative, and has an enormous Unionist majority . . . really the most advanced . . . there has ever been . . . with decided socialist tendencies". Hicks Beach, the Tory chancellor of the exchequer, asked his predecessor Harcourt whether an opposition front bencher was prepared to sit upon an inquiry to devise a scheme for pensions paid through the agency of the friendly societies. The Liberals, Harcourt told him, felt that with income tax at eight pence in the pound, it was out of the question to subject the taxpayer to "such a heavy and indefinite strain". Politically, it was very difficult to see how taxation could be significantly increased in practice when the British working class, unlike its German counterparts, had just evinced almost complete indifference to the Left, Marxist and non-Marxist alike. In that sense, Harcourt was quite right: any appreciable rise in the low tax rates taken for granted could be defined as unacceptable.[15]

After the election, Chamberlain himself doubted whether pensions were practicable. The cabinet nevertheless agreed, before the end of its first year, to appoint a committee of experts, chaired by Lord Rothschild, head of the eponymous banking house, and drawn from the civil service, insurance and the friendly societies. Despite Harcourt's attitude, the idea was to arrive, if possible, at a politically neutral plan, which government and opposition might combine to enact. The "Gladstonian garrison of the Treasury", as Salisbury called its senior officials, worked on Hicks Beach.[16] The experts representing the Treasury's financial orthodoxy, and the vested interests of insurance and the friendly societies, contended that old age pensions and the virtues of self-help were incompatible. The government resorted to a Commons select committee with one of the cabinet, Henry Chaplin, in the chair. Edward Hamilton at the Treasury considered the recommended five shillings a week from taxation, central and local, for the "deserving poor" over sixty-five "ruinous and almost impracticable". He hoped for Hicks Beach's resignation if his colleagues insisted on legislating: and speculated that the ministry might fall on pensions. The cabinet, and his civil servants, knew that the outwardly formidable chancellor would probably give way, as he usually did. The government, with Balfour seconding Chamberlain, had got to the point of a general commitment to pensions. But no one was sure how a pensions bill would be received by Unionist MPs. W.E.H. Lecky, the historian and a member of Chaplin's committee, thought old age pensions "the most dangerous of all forms of state socialism". He feared that many ministers and backbenchers were not deterred by the higher taxes it would bring.[17]

The outbreak of hostilities in South Africa did not put an immediate end to cabinet discussions of pensions: but war taxation, with income tax going up to reach a shilling in the pound, shelved the question. Before that Salisbury was gently urging Hicks Beach towards the realization that the relief of poverty in old age could no longer be left to private charity, the workhouse and the quite inadequate outdoor relief dispensed by some Poor Law unions. Agreeing that they should take care not to commit themselves to heavy expenditure until the size of the problem was clearer, he suggested erring on the side of caution and paying a pension from the age of seventy: "it is very easy to go further afterwards". Naturally anxious not to lose his chancellor, who was threatening to resign over the growth of public spending, the premier fell back on a possible alternative that Chamberlain had mentioned to Hicks Beach much earlier: more generous outdoor relief funded by the Treasury; it would be "both just and wise". Hamilton believed that through its political head his department had killed off a thoroughly undesirable project: "Chamberlain will have to 'whistle' for Old Age Pensions, explaining away the idea as best he can".[18] The archetypal Gladstonian Treasury man was not quite right: during the war and afterwards until the Liberal Act of 1908, pensions were topical. Hicks Beach was practically isolated in the cabinet and the Liberals' imperialist wing was not alone in feeling the attraction of Chamberlain's "socialistic legislation".[19]

In terms of ideas and policy, Unionism and mainstream Liberalism seemed to be converging. Chamberlain, who had seen his vision of a national party take shape in the Unionist coalition, now wished to do away with the party system altogether. Balfour, contemplating the atrophy of Gladstonian Liberalism, asked what was left. Haldane, the future military reformer, had difficulty in distinguishing between his Liberal party and the Unionists, except on one or two social questions. He specified housing the poor, which on the platform Salisbury picked out as desperately in need of further state intervention.[20] A minor act in 1899 to provide loans for house purchase among the respectable and solvent working class was almost an irrelevance. Speaking in the City, where so much wealth was generated, the premier referred to the terrible conditions of slum life nearby: "the scenes . . . are enough to make men sick". Better housing for the millions on or below the poverty line as then defined ought not to be exposed to "class and party attack". Private capital should be involved in any approach to an overwhelming task. Salisbury followed up this speech of May 1900 when he appeared before the National Union in December. He alluded to his Housing of the Working Classes Bill in 1885 which had perturbed Gladstone, and reinforced his social message to Tories and Unionists, victorious in the capital and the country at the 1900 election. The suffering of slum dwellers was "really a scandal to our civilization". "Healthy and adequate accommodation" must be the highest priority for Unionism in the presence of "stern necessities which . . . vast social changes are imposing". They should not be held back, he reiterated, by fear and resentment of those who used acknowledged evils as cover for attacks on property.[21]

Although Salisbury made no attempt to go into detail, his plea for the inhabitants of the slums was not tired rhetoric. He had focused on the most intractable of social problems, complicated by the interests of property owners, small rather than large, and by the constraints upon rates and taxes. It took the revolution of expectations at the end of the 1914–18 war to launch the first large-scale experiment in public housing. Much of the talk about promoting social welfare was indeed empty. Balfour, for instance, was the real cynic in Salisbury's family circle: "All that was really worth reforming had been reformed", he remarked in 1898. One Tory MP resigned his seat in protest at the Salisbury government's measures: elected to refrain from alarming legislation, he averred, it had done the opposite. Like some future historians, such contemporary Tories had not taken the leadership's social rhetoric seriously.[22] If it made an impression on the politically aware minority of the working class, a "morbid footballism" – the young Lloyd George lamented – characterized the masses. While the long rise in real wages was faltering, the times were not nearly hard enough to radicalize a very conservative working class. The great strikes of the 1890s in coal and engineering had little effect on the politics of the labour force. As a component of public opinion, the workers were moved more by the high drama of imperialism than by anything else outside their normal experience. For Salisbury himself, the combination of the Foreign Office, the premiership and the remorseless growth of departmental business did tend to crowd out domestic questions. As Chamberlain became more absorbed in empire-building and diplomacy, his influence for social reform was relaxed. Yet, without the South African war, an old age pensions bill, or a revision of the poor law, would have been included in the government's legislative programme.[23]

The problem of financing social reform was not one that admitted of easy solutions. If a higher income tax in peacetime was effectively ruled out, increased capital and indirect taxes were a possibility. Salisbury, however, loathed the death duties in which he had acquiesced: "this is not an innocent and unquestioned tax", he said in an exchange with Hicks Beach, "It is a law of grievous hardship and oppression . . . abominable injustice" to life tenants of settled estates in changing the basis of taxation. The chancellor, himself a large landowner, objected to leaving open a loophole in Harcourt's legislation discovered by the judges. The death duties were "rather popular than unpopular" with Unionist MPs and candidates. Neither they nor the electors would accept rises in other taxes, direct or indirect, to offset falling receipts from the duties. Their sense of fairness – and Hicks Beach's, too – precluded that course. He found Salisbury's language about the hardships of landed families exaggerated. Since landowners were fiscally vulnerable in a democracy, so few and so conspicuous, it was fortunate for them that the Church and education used up a lot of political energy that was not expended on arguing about Britain's place in the world. Indeed, it sometimes seemed that the politics of religion were more absorbing and emotive than any other kind of political warfare.[24]

## Church and Education

Salisbury gave the Church a sense of direction which her bishops could not supply. After Gladstone no other statesman was capable of that. At the heart of the Establishment's difficulties lay the erosion of orthodox belief, weakening the confidence of the clergy and the attachment of the laity to their teaching. While Salisbury was never tempted to become a Catholic, he acknowledged the strength of the Roman Church derived from her resistance to theological liberalism. He startled Archbishop Benson in 1896 by throwing out the suggestion that "Popery is going to prevail in another generation".[25] Salisbury's address to the British Association in 1893 was a personal contribution to the debate on evolution in which his church was being worsted. At the same time, the value he placed on intellect in candidates for the highest positions in the Church led him to prefer a Broad Churchman and liberal theologian to Canterbury on Benson's death. There were other good reasons for that appointment. As always, the promotion of High Churchmen upset their Evangelical brethren and the Nonconformists. The intensification of the unending conflict over denominational versus undenominational education in elementary schools made it imperative to select a primate acceptable to moderate men on either side. The Unionist coalition's sharpest setback came in its first year when ministers were forced to withdraw the education bill containing, among several controversial changes, Salisbury's prized freedom of parents of children in Board schools to have the religious instruction of their choice. The fate of Church schools continued to trouble a ministry caught in the political and religious crossfire which no government could face without trepidation. Even a small concession remitting the rates on a country parson's tithes was inflammatory: where direct incomes were concerned the Church had few friends anywhere. Feeling ran even higher in the renewed demand for action against the ritualist minority of High Churchmen; many candidates made it an issue at the 1900 election.

An admirer of Darwin's genius, Salisbury began by lauding it in his speech to the assembled scientists, and amateurs of science like himself, at the Oxford meeting of the British Association in 1894. His purpose was to limit the damage that Darwin had done. The sage, and others, had disposed of the "strange idea" that Scripture was a repository of scientific truths. Conversely, it was absurd to suppose that "the laboratory or the microscope could help . . . to penetrate the mysteries which hang over the nature and destiny of the soul of man". That challenging statement provided the theme of his lecture, delivered in the Sheldonian Theatre as chancellor of Oxford in the splendid robes of that office. Natural selection was, as Darwin recognized, no more than speculation if one sought to apply it across the entire world of nature, man included. Scientific advances had explained relatively little: "We live in a small bright oasis of knowledge, surrounded by . . . a vast, unexplained region of impenetrable mystery". He wanted to rehabilitate the argument from design, the believer's standby, and reconcile it with evolution. The "true theory of evolution" remained mysterious and, ultimately, Providential. He concluded with a quotation from the Scottish physicist, William Thomson, whom he raised to the peerage in 1891: "Overwhelmingly strong proofs of intelligent and benevolent design lie around us". This oration is a fundamental text for the understanding of Salisbury: if his utterances were commonly flecked with irony, he found his bearings in supernatural religion.[26]

Bishop-making was not conducted on the rarefied level of the Oxford address, important though it was to choose men capable of defending the Church from doubters and foes. Benson deeply resented it when Salisbury failed to consult him about the choice of new bishops. Rochester went to the premier's High Church cousin, Talbot, in 1895 without reference to the primate, who heard of it, to his intense mortification, from a bishop's wife. Inside the year, he experienced a fresh humiliation in the case of Newcastle: again, neither the premier nor his selection consulted him beforehand or informed him afterwards. The Archbishop saw in the circumstances of these two promotions the deliberate intention of Salisbury and the High Church to ignore him; a Liberal administration, and a newly appointed Evangelical or Broad Church prelate, would not have behaved thus.[27] He was certainly right in considering Erastianism to be more typical of the Tories than of the Liberals in his time. The low opinion that Salisbury had of Benson's judgement rather than dislike of his Broad Churchmanship largely explains their strained relations. Although a convention was developing that bishops should abstain from party politics in their dioceses, cabinet ministers and party managers retained a keen interest in the distribution of ecclesiastical patronage. They usually wished, as in the past, for moderates. Hicks Beach, who had once remonstrated at the neglect of Evangelicals, endorsed an earnest request from the High Church Archdeacon of Bristol for a prelate "wide enough in his sympathies to hold together . . . parties in the Church". Lord Abergavenny, a great figure in the Tory party and a Sussex magnate, approved of the local desire for a "sound moderate" at Chichester: "We don't want a ranting Low Churchman".[28]

Party politics was still a factor, too, at the lower levels of ecclesiastical patronage. Political parsons were indispensable to the struggle for the Church's schools, financially squeezed by what Talbot, as Vicar of Leeds, termed the "killing competition" of the better funded Board schools. Salisbury was conscious that his achievement in carrying free education had made matters worse for the Church: "What we can do we must do quickly, and not despair if it takes time to prepare the sinews of war", he told a big Church deputation in November 1895. The word "despair" oppressed Benson. By the "sinews of war", of course, he meant adequate finance.[29] The education bill of 1896 "will puzzle the Radicals", wrote the Archbishop when he saw it. It was based on three incontestably liberal principles. The first two were decentralization and popular election: there was to be a substantial shift of responsibility from the Education Department in Whitehall to committees of the elected councils in every county and the larger boroughs; entrusted with Church schools to begin with, they were later to replace the school boards. Thirdly, there was freedom of religious instruction for the Church and other denominations, in Board schools where they stipulated for it. On the deputation to Salisbury in 1895 Benson had declared that "the religion of the board schools . . . not ours . . . [is] now a strong dogmatic religion". The existence of that competitor with the state church and Nonconformist unwillingness to see its monopoly breached were the undoing of the government's bill in committee after a deceptively easy passage on second reading. A somewhat larger subvention for Church schools was not an insuperable obstacle, however, as long as Salisbury and the cabinet excluded rate aid for the time being in deference to Chamberlain.[30]

Salisbury had foreseen the real difficulty when shaping his ecclesiastical policy out of office. Too many people – more Tories than had been suspected, the Liberal Unionists in general, and the Liberals and radicals of the opposition – were broadly content with the 1870 compromise. They were not amused by Salisbury's caustic description of "non doctrinal religion . . . the elimination of all doctrines upon which anybody disagrees with anybody else". Benson was justified in saying that the absence of dogma had itself become a dogmatic truth. Moreover, some school boards, where Churchmen were well represented, treated the Establishment schools in a friendly spirit, which stopped short of admitting them to a proportional share of the school rate. When the bill of 1896 had sunk under the weight of amendments in committee, Balfour found that, even in Lancashire, there was no enthusiasm for the revived idea of rate aid for Church schools. The party conference he was attending in that stronghold of popular Toryism opposed it almost unanimously. To some extent, this was due, especially in Lancashire, to a very strong dislike of extending the subvention to Catholic schools. Anxiety not to antagonize the moderate majority of Nonconformists unnecessarily was more influential in lining up most metropolitan Unionist MPs with those from the West Country and the Midlands against rate aid as a partial substitute for the abandoned bill. Ratepayers far outnumbered income tax payers, and Nonconformists were everywhere a force in the constituencies.[31] The Church did obtain extra funding from the Treasury in the Voluntary Schools Act passed in 1897, but that measure was only a stopgap with nearly three-quarters of the money it funded spent on raising teachers' salaries, but not to the Board school level.[32]

The loss of the education bill in 1896 was a severe disappointment for Salisbury. The cabinet compelled him to abandon the legislation by which he set great store. He had hoped to change the settlement of 1870 by introducing the right of parents to denominational religious education in Board schools – a Trojan horse, as it were – and by rescuing Church schools from their financial plight while weakening the hold of an unsympathetic Education Department over them. The plan involved calculated risks: it was obviously uncertain whether county and borough education committees would be more sympathetic than Whitehall to the Church's educational efforts. The existing structure, he continued to feel, must be fatal to the strong denominational education he wanted: "You had much better give no grant at all, and let the money go to build an ironclad", he told Balfour at one point. Friends of the Establishment did not always appreciate the difficulty of coming to its aid without some compromise: Salisbury's eldest son, Cranborne, attacked the bill from the standpoint of the small "church party" in the Commons because it extended secular control over the Church's schools. "No one", said Benson of Cranborne, "is so tremendously fierce towards his friends and so suddenly yielding to his enemies".[33] After the Act of 1897 had given more money, but not nearly enough, to the Church's schools, and another of the same session had provided additional help for the neediest Board schools, further changes in the educational system were inevitable. The prime minister was adamant that reforms must not leave the denominational teaching of religion at a disadvantage. The Church was clamouring for rate aid; while pressure was growing for the public funding of secondary schools, assistance to which from rates and taxes had been encouraged by Tory legislation of 1889–90. Sooner rather than later, the Tories and their Liberal Unionist allies would have to attempt an ever more comprehensive bill than the one which their leaders had signally failed to carry in 1896. Balfour only got the money for Church schools through the Commons in 1897 by the use of tactics that reduced the Unionist majority, and the whole House, to "a mere voting machine".[34]

As the struggle to keep Church schools open forced ministers to go to their rescue, so the falling receipts from tithes obliged them to help country parsons; two-thirds of the livings in England and Wales were worth less than £160 a year. The Tithe Rent Charge Act of 1899 relieved all incumbents, including the better off, of rates on their tithes, reimbursing local authorities from taxes for half the cost. The hostility the measure encountered was quite disproportionate to its very modest scale. "The government has bowled us a good loose ball", exulted Harcourt, "and if we don't score freely off it we shall be very feeble players". Hicks Beach and Chamberlain had opposed any relief for the clergy. The chancellor, conventional Churchman though he was, brushed aside a recommendation in their favour from the current royal commission on local taxation: he saw no reason why parsons should be singled out for such generous treatment when rates were rising inexorably for everyone. "Many of the clergy", he warned the cabinet, "are exceptionally unpopular with our party in the House . . . I can hardly conceive a bill more difficult to pass". It would be denounced by a united opposition as a fresh endowment of the Establishment from public funds. Salisbury was the bill's only real friend in the government, and he got his way. Colleagues recognized what the Church, and clerical morale, meant to him. It was the prime minister who extracted an interim report from the royal commission containing the controversial recommendation. The bill's passage strained the loyalty of backbenchers; one crossed the floor in protest.[35]

On the third reading, the ministerial majority of nearly 150 fell to sixty-five. As when he was last in office, Salisbury had shown himself prepared to use all his authority over the Unionist coalition to enact what was not very important legislation in the eyes of many of his parliamentary supporters. The government paid for his determination at the by-elections in the two-member constituency of Oldham in July 1899: the Unionists' loss of both seats was attributed in part to urban resentment of rating relief for parsons, landowners and farmers.[36] On the other hand,

Benson had spoken for a large body of clerical opinion when he sought to persuade Salisbury's attorney-general that the clergy would change their predominantly Tory politics if an administration dominated by Tories gave "no practical help". One of his concerns was the Benefices Bill which originated as the Church Patronage Bill in the mid-1880s, designed to end the sale of advowsons and make arrangements for the elimination of clergy clearly unfit for their responsibilities whose behaviour did not bring them within the scope of the Clergy Discipline Act of 1892. Salisbury and Gladstone promised Benson their support in 1887, but after nearly ten years the premier pleaded shortage of parliamentary time in reply to a collective approach from the bishops. In his letter to the attorney-general Benson depicted the Benefices Bill as a test of the Church's ability to reform herself while remaining established. He accused ministers of letting themselves be misled by "simoniacal clergy". Yet he had been uncomfortable about the radicalism of his bill in curbing patrons' rights: "I can't feel that as a bishop it is my place to . . . set an example of confiscation". To laymen, he conceded, the bill might have a narrowly clerical aspect, at odds with the historic involvement of the laity in the workings of Church patronage and suggesting, even, a naked "'desire for power' . . . too absurd, except that it *is* said".[37]

What drove the primate on was the fear of a movement for disestablishment from within the Church, born of the frustrations of younger High Church clergy, able and articulate men. He imagined them saying, "Patronage is the grossest case for reform . . . Church principle cannot live in association with the modern English state. We work henceforth for its dissociation. It is now the only freedom". The High Church sympathies of Salisbury's family circle were engaged. His son-in-law, the second earl of Selborne, a junior minister, used the same arguments as Benson with Balfour: a clerical revolt against the government and the Church's subordination to the state was conceivable. Failure to enact the Benefices Bill would give the internal advocates of disestablishment "an immense accretion of strength". Cranborne and his brother, Lord Hugh Cecil, deplored the attitude of their father's government towards the Church. "My indignation is cooling into contempt and even pity", said the latter at the close of 1896. The bill's omission from the legislative programme was "an astonishing blunder". He talked of members' "total contempt" of the Church and her political influence.[38] Such language held by the prime minister's nearest relatives shows how ardent churchmen wilfully misunderstood an ecclesiastical policy which, in the end, produced the results they desired, or something not far short of them. Answering for his uncle, Balfour told the primate and Selborne that the Tory party's loyalty to the Establishment was deeper than that of the Church to Toryism. Would the Liberal party of Harcourt and Morley, a thoroughgoing Erastian and an agnostic radical, be a credible alternative in politics for good churchmen? He thought they might be placated by "some measure of Presbyterian liberty" in Church government, that is, greater freedom for the Convocations of Canterbury and York.[39]

Nothing of the kind was possible: High Churchmen were making the Establishment unpopular with politicians and the public. In that climate Salisbury did well to get a modified Benefices Bill through in 1898. The debates brought together Nonconformist militants opposed to anything that fortified the Church, Tories uneasy about the invasion of hallowed private rights, and Low Churchmen reluctant to enlarge the powers of bishops. Under the Act advowsons might still be sold, with safeguards, but the sale of next presentations, in which a regular market existed, was abolished without compensation. Lecky compared the legislation unfavourably with Gladstone's Irish Church Act, which had compensated patrons for their lost rights. The Benefices Act also empowered bishops to refuse institution to prospective incumbents for reasons of moral, mental or physical incapacity, debt or neglect of duty in a previous benefice. Salisbury had by this measure and the Clergy Discipline Act of 1892 eventually realized his stated aim, when first prime minister, of dealing with "criminous . . . and perhaps also . . . incompetent clergy". If he was himself an Erastian, as Benson believed, it was because only the state could prevent the Establishment from being torn to pieces by its divisions.[40]

A substantial minority of Anglican clergymen had now adopted more or less of the ritualist practices which the Public Worship Regulation Act was intended to check. The extremists among them were also more numerous, protected by the episcopal veto on ritual prosecutions. The perception that the Church's Protestant hue was fading gave rise to a serious agitation at the turn of the century. Salisbury was wrong to term it "very superficial" in February 1899. Mandell Creighton, the Broad Church Bishop of London, was taken aback by the intensity of the desire to persecute "still as great . . . in this nineteenth century as hundreds of years ago". He blamed the Low Churchmen and Nonconformists rather than their opponents for an ugly confrontation. While Salisbury detested the "pure Ultra-Protestantism" of Harcourt who enjoyed himself "beating away at the Protestant big drum", he too held the ritualists responsible for "the crisis in the church" as it was designated. Harcourt's participation – "too foolish not to be sincere", commented Salisbury – made the outcry against ritualism distinctly awkward for a coalition sharply divided on its merits. In reality, Harcourt was content with the government's promise that ecclesiastical preferment would be denied to anyone whose use of ritual broke the existing law.[41] A Commons motion to that effect in April 1899 was strengthened on the insistence of the House. Its wording, which Salisbury took a hand in drafting, did not suffice for those who, without being Protestant zealots, were genuinely worried by the activities of extreme High Churchmen. Backbenchers introduced a succession of bills to remove the bishop's veto in ritual cases. "Abolishing the . . . veto means giving the Church over to civil war", replied Salisbury when Devonshire raised the question with him.[42]

The issues contested in 1874 came up again. Without the protection of the veto, Salisbury explained to the duke, who was not *au fait* with such matters, churchmen of all schools might be caught by a prosecution, so out of date were the liturgical rubrics possessing the force of law. The Bench of Bishops, led by the two archbishops, was putting the Church's house in order: only a handful of "hot-headed idiots" would stand out against the selective prohibitions of incense and of candles when carried in processions. That left many innovations which had been accepted under a very broad "*modus vivendi*" worked out since the 1870s. If bishops lost the power to stop prosecutions aimed at those now established practices, Low Churchmen were vulnerable, too, in their disregard of ritual enjoined by the rubrics. The hard core of ritualists, "as combative as any set of men I have ever seen", would certainly retaliate. Salisbury reminded Devonshire how in 1874 he had fought for the veto against Disraeli and Cairns. Its abolition must remain an open question in accordance with the understanding between Tory and Liberal Unionist leaders when the government was formed. Salisbury and Balfour held to this line. But in repelling the bid to do away with the veto which was supported by a clear majority of the Liberals and a significant minority of Unionists in May 1899, they undertook to legislate if the bishops failed to curb ritualism. The voting seemed to bear out a gloomy prediction from Lord Rothschild that the upsurge of religious strife spelt "*the end* of the government . . . anti-Popery . . . will drown all other cries".[43] The church discipline bills, reintroduced year after year until 1911 and centred on abolition of the veto, were a factor in electoral calculations, though one that affected fewer seats than expected.[44]

After Salisbury's retirement Balfour, as his successor, resorted to another royal commission on ritual, whose recommendations the Liberal administration of Campbell Bannerman prudently relegated to the Convocations for two decades of neglect. The high-water mark of anti-ritualist agitation had been reached in 1899–1900 when Salisbury's skilful defence of the *status quo* contained the "anarchy" with which High Church extremists were menacing the Establishment and the Protestant reaction that gave warning of open warfare.[45] He was more robust with the temperance lobby: no mean antagonist, it enlisted Churchmen and Tories as well as the Nonconformist Liberals who were its backbone. A delegation headed by Bishops Westcott of Durham and Creighton of London, two Broad Churchmen, was sent away with some incisive remarks about the value of freedom on which they proposed to encroach further: "I confess to the Bishop of Durham that in many cases I do make an idol of individual liberty, and dealing only with secular considerations I consider it the noblest idol before which any human being can bow down . . . these feelings exist very strongly . . . you have not the power even if you have the right to contend against them".[46] It was this – very English – ability to combine a principled libertarianism with his flexible attachment to the institutional inheritance that helped to make Salisbury such a formidable politician. He confronted, when he did not disarm, doctrinaire Liberals and radicals. The Established Church, and the Christianity to which he thought her indispensable in his time, had in him a champion who advanced and took the moral high ground which a John Morley imagined was safe from capture by Conservatives. But the unfinished business of the Church and religion in the 1895 parliament – education – presented problems that were likely to be insuperable.

## The Irish Future

Unionist policy in Ireland evolved to such an extent between 1895 and 1900 that its loyal adherents began to doubt the Salisbury government's good faith. The 1896 Irish Land Act upset the landlords who wanted better terms for the state-assisted purchase of their property and, pending its liquidation, more income from their tenants and less interference with their property rights. Their resentment found an outlet in co-operation with the nationalists in protests at the unequal treatment of Britain and Ireland revealed by an inquiry into their financial relationship. The 1898 Irish Local Government Act might have been unavoidable, but it excluded landowning magistrates from county government, handed over to elected county councils under nationalist control everywhere outside the Protestant North East. It struck level-headed observers as "a Home Rule Bill in disguise". There were those who persuaded themselves that the accumulation of conciliatory and constructive measures under Unionist governments was slowly effecting change for the better in Irish attitudes.[47] Salisbury never subscribed to the transient optimism. It did not surprise him that in December 1899 the Dublin crowds should cheer the announcement of British defeats in the South African war. In the aftermath of the Jameson Raid, he held up the Transvaal and its disputed British suzerainty as "an extreme case of Home Rule . . . that throws a lurid light on what might have happened in Ireland". The nationalists in a Dublin parliament would emulate the Boers of the Transvaal and seek the help of foreign powers when their interests clashed with Britain's. As the subsequent war with the Boer republics drew to a close, he told the party there was no solution in sight to the perennial Irish question: "Ireland is a responsibility . . . you cannot escape . . . Do the Irish love you better than they did? . . . They do not". A self-governing Ireland able, like the republics, to import munitions would, he said prophetically, prove "a threat to your empire much more serious than that . . . experienced from the Boers".[48]

The Irish Land Bill of 1896 was the work of Balfour's brother Gerald, chief secretary for Ireland without a place in the cabinet, where Lords Cadogan, the viceroy, and Ashbourne, the lord chancellor of Ireland, sat. It was Gerald Balfour, on what Salisbury, and others, now called "the left wing of the party" and an abler man than Cadogan, who made policy and shaped legislation. "I cannot doubt the signs of a real change of feeling", he confidently informed the prime minister within three months of arriving in Ireland.[49] His land bill, to which the cabinet agreed, was intended to capitalize on the supposed improvement in Irish sentiment. He tried to please both landlords and tenants in further defining the dual ownership created by the 1881 Land Act so as to diminish the antagonism it had institutionalized. Lansdowne, one of the largest Irish landlords, was as such the cabinet minister most interested in the attempt to introduce a degree of harmony into a system of tenure regarded as unsatisfactory by all concerned. He doubted whether "a kind of ill assorted partnership", in which both parties were suffering from the fall in agricultural prices, would work better for the proposed definitions of rival interests: "We are only putting a patch upon rotten cloth". Salisbury ventured to hope that the bill avoided treading "on any of the special corns of . . . Irish landlords". They disliked it intensely, and were infuriated by additional concessions to the tenants made at the committee stage in the House of Commons. Neither Gerald Balfour's family nor Cadogan owned land in Ireland: Salisbury entrusted the bill to Lansdowne in the Lords, where such strength as Irish landlords possessed was concentrated. The Marquess was someone "who can show the scars of wounds received in the great land war".[50]

Lansdowne steered the bill through his House to the accompaniment that Salisbury predicted of "curses not loud but deep from the landlords behind us". In private, some of the angry Irish peers asserted that they were being driven into the arms of the Home Rulers. They carried amendments against their front bench which, after the Commons had dealt with them, made little difference to the bill in its final form. Nevertheless, the landlords' revolt was on an impressive scale: twenty-nine, headed by the Duke of Abercorn and Lord Ardilaun, of the Guinness brewing dynasty, opposed the government in all six divisions between 6 and 13 August; and another twenty-seven did so in four or five of the six votes without ever supporting ministers.[51] Remarkably, Salisbury left the argument to Lansdowne and other colleagues. Irish landlords, he commented afterwards, had "the privilege" of having taken up more of parliament's time than any other interest. They redoubled their protests when judicial rents fixed in the 1880s came up for statutory revision in 1897 and were generally reduced in the prevailing depression. Salisbury advised a deputation from the Irish Landowners' Convention to raise the volume of their complaints: "unless an injured class comes out and shows fight, it inevitably goes to the wall". The government conceded an inquiry into the fairness of the revised rents, whose findings were inconclusive.[52] As Dufferin, one of the most intelligent of his class in Ireland, recognized after an initial remonstrance, the Land Commission's awards did broadly reflect the pressure of prices upon the tenants. The inquiry was only a device to give landlords, and their English sympathizers in both Houses, time to grasp how little the Unionists could do for them beyond bringing in another and more attractive scheme of land purchase. Salisbury exhorted them to be realistic: dual ownership was "entirely disastrous" and unjust to owners as a class, but it was impossible to undo the legislation without undermining confidence, "the greatest economical error".[53]

The way out of this nearly hopeless situation lay through land purchase, which had been checked by the disappointing terms of the 1891 Act. The Act of 1896 revived sales by the fresh incentives it provided for owners to sell and occupiers to buy. Coupled with reduced rents, this encouraged landlords to seek funding for the massive operation their leaders had discussed since Gladstone completed his agrarian revolution. Abercorn approached Salisbury in October 1900 at the start of the tripartite process of bargaining – between landlords, tenants and government – that was to culminate in the Act of 1903; a landmark in Irish history. "The land position in this country", he wrote, ". . . is getting desperate", for the owners, that is. George Wyndham, Gerald Balfour's successor as Irish secretary, thought both sides in Ireland were poised to agree, if the price was right.[54] Salisbury's ability to play a waiting game in diplomacy has often been admired: the same qualities were apparent in his Irish policy. The people of Celtic Ireland would resist assimilation by Britain indefinitely: but he could, with some justification, refer to "the defeated Home Rulers". The land question was close to the solution he had envisaged for so long. Arthur Balfour, who advised and defended his brother, judged that the time was ripe for the long promised democratization of local government outside the towns, once the 1896 land bill was through. If their estates were soon to disappear under land purchase – "How can you quicken the pace?", asked Gerald Balfour in the Commons – the landed class would lose what political influence they still had with or without the establishment of nationalist county councils.[55] Harcourt taunted Lecky, "the modern Gibbon", with the passing of his order, the English "Garrison" in Ireland. Glumly contemplating the local government bill, Lecky hoped it would not do "*much* harm, that is all I can say".[56]

Sore at their treatment in the session of 1896, the more vocal of the landlords embarrassed the government by supporting the nationalists who sought compensation for Ireland's over-taxation, as estimated by the Liberal royal commission. Salisbury disputed the commissioners' interpretation of the facts, though the government found more money for the Irish. He had, he told Cadogan, been a party, "unwittingly", to a "disastrous" land bill in the tradition of Gladstone's legislation. As a consequence, he was "almost disabled" from championing the rights of property in Ireland. The years 1895–6 had been a particularly exacting period at the Foreign Office, and it is difficult not to suspect that he was rather surprised by the vigour of the landlords' reaction. He wanted them to bear in mind that the task of British Conservatives at home would have been a good deal easier had they acquiesced in Home Rule and freed themselves from the "dead weight" of the continuing nationalist presence in parliament. If the offending landlords persisted in making trouble for a Unionist ministry, they would "try our patience severely . . . great issues may in the end be turned by it". The hint of menace did its work.[57]

Gerald Balfour and his Irish Unionist collaborator, Horace Plunkett, clung to their perception of the Irish question as "fundamentally economic rather than political". The national delight at British reverses in South Africa proved them wrong. The younger Balfour's promotion to the Board of Trade and the cabinet in October 1900 may have averted another outbreak on the part of the Unionists. A resurgence of agrarian violence underlined the failure of his hopes. Lecky's assessment of the Irish mood in 1902 sums up what Salisbury was trying to achieve over almost twenty years. Despite the recent setbacks there was "a growing weariness of agitation . . . a gradual dropping away from it of large classes". Land purchase would help the change, but nothing dramatic was to be expected.[58] Salisbury was incapable even of such qualified optimism. He regarded a slow shift of this kind as vulnerable to swings of fortune in the battle of British parties. The Liberals were still committed to Home Rule if they secured a parliamentary majority by enough to overawe the Lords. "Do not", he cautioned friends of the Union, "look . . . to the supposed assistance from weak-kneed imperialists on the other side". Unionism and imperialism were inseparable: he traced the birth of the latter as the greatest political force in their country's life to Gladstone's adoption of Home Rule. The events of 1886 fired the imperial spirit: "That it was which Mr Gladstone stumbled against and aroused and challenged its wrath". Ironically, the more hot-headed Unionists classed him among the "weak-kneed" for the careful moderation of his policies at the Foreign Office.[59]

# CHAPTER THIRTEEN

# *The System under Strain: Diplomacy and War, 1895–1900*

## Britain, Germany and the Kruger Telegram

"I believe Salisbury to be by nature . . . a man of peace . . . I at least will be no party to vex him on that account", Harcourt told John Morley in January 1898. His unavowed aim in politics, he said in December, after the premier's triumph in the Fashoda crisis, was to support Salisbury personally and keep the Unionist government in power. Harcourt saw Salisbury, as he had done from the late 1880s, as the only "real check . . . on Imperialism". Though he professed "the most sovereign disbelief" in the value of the African empire which Salisbury had just extended by reconquering the Sudan, he trusted him to preserve the long Victorian peace with other powers.[1] Salisbury had made ready for war over Fashoda: but he was enforcing the ministerial declaration of Sir Edward Grey in the Rosebery administration that the Nile Valley was barred to Britain's rivals. While responsible Frenchmen did not want to fight a maritime and colonial war, in which they were certain to be the losers, over the swamps of the Southern Sudan, they were further constrained by the thought of an unfriendly Germany on their Eastern frontier. As Salisbury drew a large dividend on his investment in the relationship with Germany and the Triple Alliance, the French failed to interest Russia, their European ally, in an African quarrel. He prevented rising Anglo-German tensions from derailing his diplomacy by treaties of 1898, 1899 and 1900 which partitioned territory and influence with her in Africa, the Pacific and China, without giving very much away. Consequently, Britain accommodated the German abandonment of Bismarck's comparative restraint for *Weltpolitik* and naval expansion, a change of course signalled by Germany's display of sympathy with the Transvaal following the Jameson Raid. The uneasy co-operation of the two empires was maintained by the correct attitude of the German government during the South African war of 1899–1902, when German public opinion, and Continental opinion generally, sided with the Boer republics.[2]

Germany's new ambitions induced feelings of insecurity in Britain as she faced challenges from France in Africa, the United States in South America, and Russia in the Far East. Salisbury's colleagues questioned a semi-detached position in Europe and the world: and looked to full partnership with another great power, Germany or – as Chamberlain suggested at times – the United States. Salisbury sanctioned Chamberlain's conversations with the Germans from 1898, and himself glanced back to the Anglo-Russian alliance against the first Napoleon. With Continental Europe dominated by two armed camps and America the possessor of a navy that enabled her to seize the Spanish American colonies in the Caribbean and the Pacific, the cabinet no longer deferred to Salisbury as they had done when great issues of foreign policy came up. They could not forget the miscarriage in 1895–6 of his designs on Turkey, which he wrongly thought were close to being realized. It was the worst setback of his time at the Foreign Office; ending the hope of a final, comprehensive partition to make "satisfied powers" of all those who had expectations from the dying Ottoman empire. Unwilling, as ever, to let his country be committed to fighting with, and for, a Continental power, he improved on the Gladstonian ideal he had once derided as quite unrealistic and spoke of an "inchoate federation of Europe".[3]

The Germans welcomed Salisbury's resumption of his burden in 1895. He confirmed that his policy had not changed: "we wish to lean to the Triple Alliance without belonging to it".[4] The Germans had accepted this stance since he first went to the Foreign Office: now they felt they had waited long enough for it to change. What they desired was a return to the policy of the Younger Pitt when that minister put all his strength behind the defence of national interest jointly with those of other powers. Baron von Holstein, the grey eminence of the Wilhelmstrasse, contrasted this European spirit with Salisbury's evasion of his obligations. The British premier used Germany, and other powers, to pick Britain's chestnuts out of the fire. In 1901 when Britain and Germany had been trying to find an acceptable basis for the closer alignment that both wanted, Holstein described British policy in his time as inspired by the "theory of chestnuts": and Salisbury as having acted on it more openly than any of his predecessors. It was a sufficient explanation of the "general hatred" of Britain on the Continent. German irritation with Salisbury was increased by the apparently limitless growth of the British empire. The German chancellor, Prince Hohenlohe, saw in the Jameson raid, and international reaction to it, a chance to impress the dangers of isolation on the British without seeming to menace their position in the areas of greatest concern to them, India, Egypt and the Far East. A common front of European powers on the Transvaal would serve notice that they were not prepared for Britain's "progressive confiscation" of the globe. She might learn her lesson and join the grouping of the powers – the Triple Alliance – that best served her interests.[5]

Any hope that this diplomatic blackmail would have the intended effect was blighted by Wilhelm II's notorious telegram to President Kruger of the Transvaal congratulating him on having successfully defended the republic's independence, which, of course, Britain did not recognize. The public outrage in Britain surprised practically everyone. Count Münster at Paris, drawing on his twelve years' experience of the London embassy, told Holstein that the telegram and its wording were "a match to set fire to an accumulation of . . . hatred". In Münster's unpalatable view, the British had "tolerated a great deal" from the advocates of colonial expansion whom Bismarck and his successor had encouraged. The language and actions of those imperialists, coupled with anxiety about Germany's penetration of world markets, had created an anti-German party in Britain.[6] Neither Hatzfeldt nor the emperor had perceived the latent feeling there. The many Germans in the City found it almost impossible to do business for several days, and the atmosphere in clubland was extraordinarily hostile. The Queen entreated Salisbury to see that "innocent and good German residents" did not suffer. The press in the two countries, he replied, was doing "infinite harm". The Kruger telegram was a turning-point in Anglo-German relations. Münster's perception of "the most tragic . . . mistrust and hatred" was correct: neither British nor German ministers could suppress the antagonism that had been dramatically exposed; but they did their best to check it as damaging to common interests.[7]

The rapid arrival of a powerful British squadron off the East African coast, within striking distance of the Transvaal's outlet to the sea in Portuguese territory at Delagoa Bay, reminded the Germans of their limitations outside Europe if they were tempted to translate words into action. Salisbury uttered no threats. "The Germans' only idea of diplomacy is to stamp heavily on your toes", he observed; his style was very different.[8] The German emperor and his advisers lost little time in drawing the obvious conclusion. His country's expanding mercantile marine, Wilhelm complained, had only four cruisers to protect it from Britain's 130. The First Navy Law of April 1898 called for the construction of fifty cruisers in addition to nineteen battleships; the Second Navy Law of June 1900 doubled the size of his fleet. Its creator, Admiral von Tirpitz, his sovereign, and German ministers did not like to state publicly what was self-evident: that "England's world domination" was their target. Wilhelm spoke of making the navy the equal of his army, but the German generals were sceptical. For them *Weltpolitik* took second place to security in Europe. Their thinking goes far to explain the durability of Anglo-German co-operation after the Kruger telegram and while Salisbury was prime minister. The emperor, his foreign secretary, von Bülow, later his chancellor, and Tirpitz accepted that there must be a lengthy transition before Germany could match Britain's "enormous fleet".[9] Wilhelm's naval brother, Henry of Prussia, "with tears in his eyes" deplored the Kruger telegram, and regretted speeches made by the emperor and himself. He considered Germany's position between Russia and France to be "most precarious". While anxiety not to strain Russo-German relations further worked against a formal and binding British alliance, the existing co-operation with Britain, however uneasy, was indispensable for the time being.[10]

Germany's well documented working relationship with Britain rested on the complementary nature of their armed forces. Salisbury's appraisal of British resources written for the newly established "committee of defence" in October 1895 outlined the strategic considerations that continued to guide him at the Foreign Office. A major Continental campaign, as distinct from amphibious operations, lay outside the committee's remit until the day – "I hope a distant one" – when Britain would be compelled to adopt conscription. As before, he criticized the Admiralty's dispositions: they reflected the unco-ordinated demands of several departments, including his own, instead of some "large scheme of imperial defence". The committee should review the size and type of warships allotted to the Mediterranean fleet in the light of its tasks: what were they? Was the fleet essential to prevent the junction of the Toulon squadron with the rest of France's battle fleet? Or was it primarily an instrument of British diplomacy from Turkey to Morocco? Similarly, he wanted to know whether the ships on the China station were supposed to take on the French and Russian navies in those seas, or were they there to impress the Chinese authorities? Or for both purposes? On the coasts of Latin America and Africa, in the Indian Ocean and along the great rivers of China, "English policy . . . largely turns on the amount of assistance that can be counted on from the fleet". Gunboat diplomacy required an adequate number of gunboats capable of operating in shallow water, "a matter of the first consideration". As acutely as Palmerston in the 1850s and 1860s, he felt the dangers inseparable from Britain's peculiar combination of strength and weakness. His memorandum stressed the needs of home defence, naval and military, bearing in mind the latest developments in the technology of war.[11]

Germany's value as an ally was, therefore, undiminished. When he famously referred to "splendid isolation", Salisbury was being ironical at the expense of those who believed in the possibility. "I still think . . . the German powers are our natural allies", he advised the ambassador in Paris after the Kruger telegram had revealed the potential for Anglo-German conflict. But he wished to edge a little closer to France, if he could. The French and the Russians had not shown any enthusiasm for German suggestions that they might all come forward to give Kruger's republic diplomatic support. On the other hand, the Triple Alliance did not wish to alienate Britain: her defection to the other camp, or her withdrawal from the politics of European combinations, would be a blow to collective stability in Europe, Germany's overriding interest. Her government was glad to receive Hatzfeldt's assurance that Salisbury was "no supporter of 'splendid isolation'", and open to the idea of a stronger commitment to Germany and her allies.[12] For one thing, his plans for the Ottoman empire were wholly incompatible with isolationism. On coming into office in 1895, he at once revived the periodic discussion of a partition of Turkey in Europe and Asia. The moment was propitious.

## From Constantinople to Fashoda and after

Salisbury's great disappointment in the East showed what he could not do without Germany, or perhaps with her. The compensating success of his insistence that the Sudan was a British preserve owed something to the Germans. Salisbury made sure of their refusal to help France even with some gesture of Continental solidarity such as they had sought at the time of the Jameson Raid, by a painless transaction. Shortly before the African crisis broke, Britain and Germany agreed to divide Portugal's empire between them in the event of her bankruptcy, which did not occur. Fashoda was not a victory for "splendid isolation": it was the French who were isolated, for earlier in 1898 Salisbury had given way to the Russians in the Far East with Africa and the Nile Valley in mind. Almost certainly, he would have challenged France even if Europe had come to her aid by staging a diplomatic demonstration; there was no danger of anything else on the part of Germany and Russia. British public opinion, and his own firm belief that ultimately diplomacy rested on willingness to fight, left him no choice. But careful planning left Britain with the upper hand in all respects. It was never part of Salisbury's policy to have the Continental powers ranged against Britain.[13]

The Turks' terrible vengeance upon the troublesome Armenian minority in the mid-1890s aroused international concern and a storm of indignation in Britain. The Rosebery ministry sent strongly worded protests and moved the Mediterranean fleet nearer the Straits. Salisbury, then in opposition, interpreted the disturbances as conclusive evidence that Abdul Hamid II's empire was beyond recovery. In a letter to Philip Currie, now ambassador to Turkey, he sketched the distribution of the Ottoman lands among the powers: Russia might have Asia Minor; Britain, Syria and Mesopotamia; Austria the port of Salonica to take her Balkan sphere of influence to the Aegean; Italy, Albania; and France, Tripoli, with a slice of Morocco, which was not, of course, part of the Sultan's dominions. Arabia he seems to have seen as the appanage of an Arab Caliph under British patronage. The Straits were to be open to all the powers, giving Britain the access to the Black Sea for her warships that Salisbury had claimed at the Berlin congress. Perhaps to balance her very substantial gains, he envisaged "some kind of autonomy" for Egypt, which he continued to think of evacuating. "Alas! these are mere dreams – nobody agrees with me", he wrote: but in July and August 1895 he shared his dream with the French and German ambassadors.[14] The Germans' initial response, through Hatzfeldt, was encouraging, although agreement to divide up the Sultan's inheritance clearly implied a fundamental revision of existing great power relationships. The Dual and Triple Alliances would be deprived of their rationale in a Europe of powers reconciled by their digestion of the Ottoman empire. "There are too many alliances", said Salisbury a little later.[15] The Germans were probably right in reflecting that partition on a grand scale would set the powers against each other. They were right, too, in suspecting that Salisbury hoped to lessen Britain's dependence on the Triple Alliance by renewing the old friendship with Russia, who was to realize historic aims in his "dreams". Wilhelm informed Salisbury, when they met on board his yacht at Cowes in August 1895, that in the German view Turkey was neither moribund nor beyond redemption. Salisbury had come forward with his "incendiary project" that would plunge the Balkans and Continental Europe into a general war with Britain as a spectator, and the beneficiary of her rivals' exhaustion.[16]

Hatzfeldt defended Salisbury, whose purpose in wanting to partition Turkey was not to set the Continent alight but to prevent a conflagration by ensuring that everyone was "more or less satisfied". If France was implacably anti-German, she would find herself isolated from her Russian partner. The Germans were, however, justified in their assessment of Turkey's prospects. Impatient to see the end of "the detestable Turks", Salisbury ignored the findings of Schomberg McDonnell, who had visited Constantinople in 1894. Abdul Hamid II might be an unregenerate Oriental despot, but the defences of the Dardanelles – coastal batteries and minefields directed against the Royal Navy – were in good order, "strong enough to stop anything coming up".[17] Although he had publicly acknowledged the tenacity of the Sultan's political will, half-concealed by unending tergiversation, Salisbury did not remember the warnings of Currie, who thought Britain had seriously underestimated Abdul Hamid, "an extraordinarily strong ruler". After savage rioting against the Armenians of the Turkish capital, he decided to act independently of the other powers in the autumn of 1895. Russia had vetoed an Austrian proposal to send the fleets of all six Christian powers up to Constantinople, and take control of the city through the standing conference of their ambassadors set up earlier in this latest crisis of the Sultan's regime.[18] The premier asked the cabinet for authority to send British warships through the Dardanelles and was refused it, when the first naval lord, Admiral Richards, appeared before them and insisted that his ships could not be risked in the Dardanelles. Salisbury did not hide his displeasure with the navy, on which his administrations had spent so much and which he now found wanting in the Nelson touch.[19]

Unable to coerce the Sultan in his capital or to prevent a Russian attack through the less well guarded Bosphorus, Britain was in a far weaker position to help the Armenians or to keep Russia from taking Constantinople without the international agreement that Salisbury contemplated. The cabinet's support of Richards and his political chief, Goschen, in November 1895 was peculiarly mortifying for Salisbury: "I am administering a policy in which I entirely disbelieve, and which I fear may lead to much disgrace", he wrote with, for him, unusual heat in a ministerial exchange. Without a plausible threat of force, there was no stopping the butchery at which the Ottoman authorities had connived. Everyone who spoke in cabinet backed Balfour and Chamberlain in opposing the bold stroke with the fleet which might have been the signal for international negotiations to dismember the empire. He had menaced the Sultan with partition in a speech of the previous August, but Britain's weapon had now broken in his hands.[20] He still hoped to persuade Russia, in particular, that internationally agreed intervention was desirable, but the talks with Tsar Nicholas II at Balmoral in September 1896 were fruitless. Nicholas, more interested in the Far East, was not tempted by Constantinople. All he wanted from Turkey was control of the Straits, "the door to the room in which he lived", but not at the price of disturbing the *status quo*. "He seems to me", said Salisbury perceptively of the Tsar, "to stick in a sort of despair. If Turkey falls, there will be [European] war, which he hates: if nothing is done, it [the Ottoman empire] will fall: but he does not see that anything can be done".[21] In the short term, at any rate, the Tsar's timidity was prudent: no one except Salisbury wished to bring forward the day when the powers would have to try for agreement on the fate of an empire on which they had conflicting designs.

Very soon Salisbury had to join in shoring up Turkey. The restless Christian majority in Crete had risen against her rule in 1895, and the philhellenes in the cabinet, where Chamberlain and James were true to their Liberal origins, sympathized. Salisbury had a struggle to maintain Britain's leading part in the international naval presence that tried to keep Greek aid from reaching the rebels. The cabinet objected to an extension of the blockade to the Greek mainland then, and again when Greece mobilized for war with Turkey. Salisbury's illusions about Greece were long gone: "The Greeks", he said flatly, "are a contemptible race". Their invasion of Turkey in April 1897 rapidly ended in disaster; the German-trained Ottoman army drove deep into Greek territory. The powers, with Britain's full co-operation, secured a Turkish withdrawal and a large indemnity from Greece. It was thanks to Greece, Salisbury complained, that "the Sultan has been raised on . . . a pinnacle", and his empire given a new lease of life. He was the loser in a long duel with Abdul Hamid, whose downfall he had predicted for so many years.[22] The collective judgement of the powers whom he had vainly tried to interest in partition could not be trusted "with even the slenderest portion of executive authority". Britain's best course was to reduce her traditional responsibilities in Turkey and concentrate on building up her position in Egypt as a basis for a rather less ambitious policy in the Near and Middle East.[23]

This succinct exposition, for Currie's benefit, of a reluctant change in his thinking was an acknowledgement of defeat. The agitators on behalf of Armenians and Greeks looked on him as a friend whose hand was being strengthened by their demands for action. When he disappointed them, he explained why. He felt obliged to ask his old acquaintance Malcolm MacColl, a pamphleteer for the Armenians, not to visit Hatfield: "You carry a flag", and the foreign press suggested that the premier was behind an agitation to weaken Turkey for selfish British purposes. Salisbury had let MacColl know how much he regretted agreement between Austria and Russia to keep the Ottoman empire intact for as far ahead as their governments could see. "Yet there are things which the most powerful combination cannot do", he ended that letter; unmistakable encouragement to continue the public pressure. His Gladstonian cousin Edward Talbot, Bishop of Rochester, was favoured with a fuller account of the hopes he could not relinquish after his defeat in cabinet. Forcing the Dardanelles was permanently excluded, since the Admiralty estimated that it would cost "several ironclads", and Britain did not have the troops for large-scale operations on land. Blockading the rich port of Smyrna, the threat which worked for Gladstone in 1880, was ruled out by the concern of British and Continental bondholders for interest payments secured upon the Turkish customs. "A policy of bluff . . . hard to defend" would not deceive Abdul Hamid. But, against the evidence, Salisbury clung to the belief that the Ottoman state must crumble from within: "Every symptom of decay is showing". He comforted the bishop, and himself, with Blake's line about the mills of God. Though wary, and a little contemptuous of "clerical fire-eaters", he saw Turkey through their eyes.[24]

The old assumption that the defence of Turkey was a vital British interest had lost its hold on the Tory party and the patriotic electors. They were ready to see the Ottoman empire break up "for the sake of the pickings" – when Britain was virtually helpless to act. In the cabinet, Balfour, Hicks Beach and Goschen were affected by the pro-Greek clamour which Harcourt exploited as war between Greece and Turkey approached. It was not long since Salisbury himself had described the Turks to Nonconformists as "of the race of Genghiz and Tamerlane . . . they belong to a religion . . . capable of the most atrocious perversion and corruption of any religion on the face of the earth". He then had to remind the public that their navy could not, in fact, "go anywhere and do anything".[25] Briefly afraid for the coalition's survival if the feeling against Turkey got out of hand, he was able to satisfy it, and his own inclinations, when the powers, Britain included, compelled Turkey to give up her Greek conquests. The premier rediscovered a solution to Europe's present and future problems that had failed him when he wanted the representatives to take control of Constantinople. "The federated action . . . the federation of Europe is the only hope we have", he told the Lords on the eve of war. The settlement afterwards imposed on the combatants demonstrated what "the concert, or as I prefer to call it, the inchoate federation of Europe" could do when it achieved unanimity.[26]

When Salisbury's colleagues stopped him from sending the fleet through the Dardanelles and thwarted a policy very personal to him, they questioned his considerable independence of the cabinet in making policy. In a letter to Balfour after the event, Lord George Hamilton asked him to remember that his uncle was "a strong and proud man". Salisbury might be moved to resign by the indictment of his mistakes since he took the Foreign Office. "Our past folly" must not be discussed in front of the entire cabinet. Hamilton thought "the German alliance" had merely served to drive France and Russia together, and "brought us kicks from Germany and insults from other nations". They could not afford to lose the premier, who should be talked round in private, "not put . . . in the dock before his own cabinet", but ministers differed on an alternative structure for foreign policy. Balfour and Devonshire, much more important figures than George Hamilton, were to favour closer relations with Germany. Hicks Beach said, "We cannot buck the Concert of Europe". Chamberlain disagreed: "What use was the Concert?", he asked the Russian ambassador, quite unmoved by Salisbury's declaration in November 1897 that it alone stood between a Europe trapped in the arms race and catastrophe. The only sound policy for Britain, according to Chamberlain, was an Anglo-Russian entente leading to one with France. While he soon changed his mind, he and other leading members of the government were informally engaged in reviewing their options.[27]

At the same time Salisbury's wish to distance Britain from Turkey was too radical for the cabinet. "What our huge fleet is doing or expected to do in the Mediterranean is one of the mysteries of official strategy", he told Devonshire as chairman of the defence committee. The route to India was only five days shorter through the Canal than round the Cape; Egypt might be reinforced from the Red Sea. The Admiralty's conservatism prevailed. As for opening the Straits, Devonshire was glad to agree that the navy's excessive respect for their defences and the opposition of Germany, Austria and Russia made it an academic question.[28] The German press noted with pleasure the premier's admission in November 1896 that Britain was unable to "bend the councils and the forces of gigantic powers to whatever . . . policy . . . seems to us . . . desirable". "The Saul of 1895 has become the Paul of 1896", observed the Berlin *National Zeitung* of his pleas for international co-operation. The Germans had no intention of letting Britain slip away from them. Even before Admiral Richards' "decree" that the Royal Navy could not do what Salisbury took for granted, von Bülow said what very many Germans thought: "We cannot", he wrote "leave John Bull in any doubt that we will not jump into the sea . . . to salvage the pearl of his world status . . . But neither should we allow him to fear that once he had made up his mind to swim, we will not come to his aid when others were trying to . . . push him under". The letter expresses memorably the mingled disdain and insecurity with which Germany's ruling circles regarded rival powers.[29]

In all the circumstances Chamberlain found Salisbury receptive when he argued for strengthening Britain's position in Africa and Asia by giving Germany what she had long wanted: a defensive alliance in Europe which might be accompanied by co-operation elsewhere: "very desirable", Salisbury told him, "but can we get it?" The colonial secretary tried, negotiating with the premier's knowledge and approval.[30] Ironically, it was now the Germans who felt that their interests were probably best served by a semi-detached relationship. Nevertheless, a colonial treaty cemented the renewed Anglo-German understanding, as in 1890. It was agreed to divide Portugal's large empire between them if that minor power, close to bankruptcy, accepted and defaulted upon a loan from Britain and Germany with her colonial possessions as security. In the event, Portugal evaded the proffered loan, but the operation of the treaty would have given Britain Delagoa Bay, and Germany most of the rest of the Portuguese empire. The cabinet backed Chamberlain when Salisbury opposed admitting Germany to talks already going on with Portugal about control of a port vital to an independent Transvaal.[31] Although the details of the agreement, signed in August 1898, were negotiated by Balfour in the prime minister's absence on the Riviera convalescing from the effects of winter and overwork, the gist had been settled between Salisbury and the German ambassador. The treaty exhibited the Emperor Wilhelm as "arbiter of the world", so von Bülow assured him. Salisbury confessed to his dislike of agreeing to a prospective distribution of other people's property, and untypically blamed Balfour for consenting to it: Hatzfeldt had to remind him of his personal involvement. Chamberlain spoke of Germany's "blackmail" driving a hard and distasteful bargain, but it served its purpose. She was, at least outwardly, helpful during the Fashoda crisis of the next few weeks, and refrained from making difficulties for Britain in the South African war.[32]

Salisbury had predicted the blackmail, but considered the terms of the treaty "quite satisfactory", though he hoped it would not become operative for many years, if ever. Chamberlain's education in international politics had some way to go: he was not prepared for appeasement of France as well as Germany, and needed a good deal of persuasion to moderate his demands during the Anglo-French negotiations to reconcile the two countries' claims in uncharted areas of West Africa. Salisbury suspected that the German emperor actually hoped for war between Britain and France, which must be to Germany's advantage, and Chamberlain was ready, even eager, to fight for what he imagined was a great new market in West Africa. Fortunately the French government was well aware that Salisbury did not subscribe to the colonial secretary's quite unreal expectations. This supposedly hard-headed Midland businessman credited the promises of Sir George Goldie, and compared the prospects of his Royal Niger Company in the Muslim chiefdoms of Sokoto and Gando to those of Clive and the East India

Company in eighteenth-century Bengal. "There is no loot to get except in Goldie's dreams", commented Salisbury with his painful memories of the City and its promises.[33] His correspondence with Chamberlain shows how he countered the pressure for a confrontation with France, if only at the conference table in Paris. Despite the angry noises from Jingoes and their French equivalents, Chamberlain was made to see that neither government thought the disputed tracts were worth a war. He made the most of the agreement signed in June 1898: it secured Northern Nigeria for Britain, but France already had the lion's share of West Africa after the treaties earlier in the 1890s.[34]

While Salisbury also had the possibility of war in view, he did not mean to fight over West Africa. Goldie was simply "a great nuisance – his knowledge of foreign relations must have been acquired in a music hall". But he sought to protect the colonial secretary from the sharper criticisms of their colleagues by insisting that where Britain's claims were credible, she should defend them "in earnest" as the necessary condition of getting the French to "behave decently".[35] He sent Chamberlain detailed advice on the places to be given up "to enable the French to recede from untenable positions without discredit". For the British likewise had claimed too much: "a case common in diplomacy". A combination of great firmness – "lose no time in collecting Hausas [native infantry] and gunboats" – and flexibility in negotiation did its work.[36] The naval preparations reported by the French embassy in February 1898 were in part a precaution against a war started by a clash in the West African bush after Chamberlain's language had raised the temperature alarmingly. Salisbury did not allow him to indulge for long in a dangerous display of obstinacy: "if we will not negotiate, and they will not retreat, exasperation will increase . . . without bringing any solution". He saw no pretext for war that would convince a public not exclusively composed of Jingoes. On the contrary, claims exposed as "shady" would hurt the government at home and abroad.[37]

Chamberlain's victory over the French, proclaimed as such, was really due to Salisbury. The treaty resembled the outcome of negotiations foreshadowed in the premier's letter of the previous October to the ambassador in Paris. Salisbury instructed Sir Edmund Monson to tell the French foreign minister that "we have a democracy quite as unreasonable [as theirs], and . . . our newspapers can use very bad language if they try". The two governments understood each other and the problem represented on the British side by Chamberlain.[38] Both were reserving their strength, political and diplomatic, for the challenge to Britain at Fashoda. The arrival of Commandant Marchand and his small party on the White Nile in July 1898 was the expected intrusion of France into the Sudan, which Kitchener and his Anglo-Egyptian army were reconquering. The enforced departure of the French expedition in November eclipsed Chamberlain's supposed success in West Africa. Colleagues who had urged him to restrain Chamberlain in West Africa, had no choice but to demand a French withdrawal from the Sudan. The public's "undoubted aversion" from war with a great power vanished momentarily when they thought they, as victors in a popular campaign, might be forced to share the Sudan with France. It was a reaction that Salisbury had foreseen: the Grey declaration of 1895 left him very little room for manoeuvre.[39]

Unlike the French, Salisbury was ready to fight for the Nile Valley. The government in Paris played out a game of bluff. Delcassé, the French foreign minister, told his Russian counterpart in October that he did not believe the stand off on the Nile would lead to "a serious misunderstanding". The London embassy had noted Salisbury's remarks in May to a private meeting of the Bankers' Association: it was opportune, the premier said, to increase defence spending and cultivate friendly relations with other powers. The City promptly raised marine insurance rates by fifteen per cent in anticipation of war within six months. The Royal Navy maintained a high state of readiness: the far smaller French navy did not. No less important were his diplomatic preparations. In his family circle, where his son-in-law Selborne, Chamberlain's under-secretary, was an ardent imperialist, he was driven to spell out what was implicit in his deference to Germany and Russia. For the time being, everything turned on the Nile Valley: "If you want to understand my policy at this moment in any part of the world – in Europe, Asia, Africa or the South Seas – you have constantly to remember that".[40] As the French bowed to the inevitable, Salisbury endeavoured to make the retreat from Fashoda as little of a humiliation as possible. In bringing the French round, he relied on Monson and, quite as much, on the French ambassador, de Courcel, who knew the premier's mind better than did most of his cabinet. As directed, Monson "kept nothing back" in his conversations with Delcassé. De Courcel was impressed by Salisbury's "unquestionable goodwill" and his concern for French feelings. He stressed the extreme difficulty of the premier's position: Chamberlain, Hicks Beach and Devonshire had public opinion behind them, in opposing anything like concession to France. The national mood frightened the ambassador: he warned Delcassé, who was holding out for negotiated access to the Nile as the price of evacuating Fashoda, that the British public would not tolerate a French presence either on the Nile, except for purely commercial access, or in the Bahr-al-Ghazal. The mobilization of the British fleet underlined the representations of the two ambassadors; the country, on the whole, was readier for war than at any time since the Crimea.[41]

It appears that Salisbury hinted to de Courcel at a personal inclination to offer some territorial concession in the Bahr-al-Ghazal. Chamberlain got wind of this and, urged on by G.E. Buckle of *The Times*, objected to what he considered the continuation of a deplorable trend.[42] He had previously complained of concessions to the French in Madagascar, Siam and Tunis, inciting them to ask for more "until we shall finally be driven into war". Salisbury provided a full explanation of his aims and methods in each case. On the insistence of the ambassador in Paris, he had refrained from publicizing the check to French encroachment upon Siam in the treaty of 1896. Acquiescence in a French protectorate over Madagascar went with France's recognition of the change in Zanzibar's status. In Tunis, it was hoped to conclude a new commercial treaty that ran for a shorter period in return for a lower tariff.[43] With rare humility Chamberlain apologized, alluding to the general belief, "which I ignorantly shared", that the French had had the best of these bargains. Yet the dissatisfaction with Salisbury was palpable among anxious imperialists across the parties. In June 1898 *Punch* published a cartoon which depicted Chamberlain showing the premier through a door marked "Exit from Office". There was talk, reproduced by some historians, of Salisbury's failing powers, even of senility. The Prince of Wales, who echoed the gossip in Society, denounced him to his sister, the Empress Frederick, as Britain absorbed the news that Marchand was on the Nile: "He seems to have completely lost his energy, if not his head! All he does [is] to give way . . .". Wiser men shared the Prince's sense of declining national prestige; relieved at France's submission at Fashoda, they were not reassured about Britain's international standing.[44]

Immediately after Fashoda, Chamberlain was reported to have said that he and other ministers, Balfour included, thought Salisbury did not possess the nerve "to provoke the necessary crisis" with France, that is, a war. It was not humbug to congratulate Salisbury a few weeks later on "a real triumph" in his handling of foreign policy since the beginning of 1898, and not only in Africa. He realized how much had been gained by the consummate diplomacy that had made him restive: "Germany . . . comparatively friendly and Russia . . . on her best behaviour". From then on the differences between the two lay in their public attitudes rather than in their ideas about policy. In one of his best known speeches, to the Primrose League in May 1898, Salisbury had made a pragmatic division of the nations into "the living and the dying", who would succumb to their healthy competitors "from the necessities of politics or under the pretence of philanthropy". This was the bleakest realism: with Chamberlain, he believed that Britain's will to greatness was destined to be tried "to the utmost" in the years ahead. Her empire and "growing enormous trade" would not protect her from jealous rivals; she must be prepared to defend what she had amassed "against all comers" while playing her rightful part in any territorial "rearrangement".[45] The jealousy was acute; Hatzfeldt said the size of Britain's empire was "excessive" when he and Salisbury were discussing how to share out the Portuguese colonies. On that occasion, Salisbury rejected the suggestion that German friendship might be bought by some modest cession of British territory, but he had to purchase it at Portugal's expense, prospectively, and in the autumn of 1899 he was constrained to surrender the British share of control in Samoa to Germany and the United States. Chamberlain advised Salisbury to submit, once again, to "undisguised blackmail": the South African war was on the point of breaking out and official German encouragement of the Boers was a complication to be avoided. The colonial secretary's education in the conduct of foreign policy made further progress.[46]

The Germans used a settlement, on their terms, of the long-running Samoan dispute – an otherwise "not very important matter", said Salisbury – to test Britain's spirit of partnership. He and his ministers, he explained, were glad to have pleased Germany "without in the least diminishing the . . . advantages of England", for the naval anchorage in German Samoa was inferior to the harbours available to America in those islands and to Britain in neighbouring Tonga. He had to think of antipodean objections to seeing Britain leave Samoa, but also wanted to indicate by his posture that she had not lost her freedom of action in more important questions. Valuable as Anglo-German understanding was to the two nations and to Europe, he refused to admit that it had "a special value for England separately" in the

Samoan or any other context.[47] When war in South Africa increased fears of isolation, he neither minimized the perils nor prepared the public for some diminution of Britain's semi-independence of Europe and its alliances. Speaking in May 1900 Salisbury laid more emphasis than ever before on the danger of invasion: "armies become large, navies are founded" – a reference to the German Navy Laws – ". . . all may, by one of those . . . currents which sweep across the ocean of international politics, be united in one great wave to dash on our shores". His audience was aware of Continental sympathy with the Boers, and he knew of moves among the powers to get up a diplomatic combination that would impose a South African peace on Britain. She had "no security except in . . . our own right arm". If conscription was an impossibility, as he thought, he suggested supplementing the militia, yeomanry and volunteers with another force raised by local initiative: "it is not a thing which can come from the centre". Soldiers and amateurs of war found the proposal risible: part-time warriors were no match for professional armies.[48]

Foreign and domestic opinion was surprised by the speech's "intentionally sensational and . . . macabre pessimism"; a comment from *Le Temps* of Paris, quoted by *The Times*. Chamberlain had sounded a more positive note at Leicester in November 1899, but the German answer was brutally discouraging. He pleaded for "a new Triple Alliance" of Britain, Germany and the United States: von Bülow spoke in the Reichstag of building a German fleet strong enough to resist a British attack, a contingency taken seriously.[49] For there were those arguing for a preventive war on Germany. One of them was the military attaché in Berlin, who wrote "*we must go for the Germans* and that right soon, or they will go for us later". The German fear was of another Copenhagen, the destruction of a growing fleet in its harbours. Not tempted to violate international law, Salisbury had come to think by 1900 that a policy constructed round the "alliance" with Germany had outlived its usefulness for European security and the controlled expansion of empires. "I have no wish to quarrel with her", he told the viceroy of India, "but my faith in her is infinitesimal".[50] His principal colleagues, no fonder of Germany, lacked his clear-sightedness, and his nerve. The insubstantial Anglo-German agreement on China in October 1900 was some consolation to them. As Salisbury handed over the Foreign Office to his successor that month, Philip Currie, ambassador to Italy, ventured to tell him that the diplomatic history of the last few years illustrated the risks of isolation: "It would seem worthwhile to make some sacrifices to get out of it".[51] The Germans doubted whether he could be induced to give up the relatively free hand he had hitherto possessed. His weakened authority in cabinet after he left the Foreign Office still left him with the final say in its policies.[52]

The burden of armaments drove Nicholas II and his advisers to organize the conference at the Hague in 1899 which attempted to find a substitute for force and the costly preparations for its use. Nicholas' well meaning initiative was "not serious", in Salisbury's private opinion. Sceptical about the chances of moving international relations on to a higher plane, he nevertheless exerted himself to secure, against German opposition, a tribunal to which states could, if they desired, refer their disagreements. Goschen at the Admiralty deprecated the innovation, pointing out that a resort to arbitration over Fashoda would have allowed the French time to make their fleet ready for war.[53] Salisbury had seen permanent arbitration machinery as a valuable means of defusing recurrent problems with the United States. Neither international arbitration nor a good relationship with democratic America figured in German *Weltpolitik*: she was a potential enemy. Suspected in Germany of pro-American leanings in the Samoan negotiations and the Spanish American war of 1898, Salisbury did not see America through Chamberlain's eyes, as the ideal partner of his global imaginings. But she had an importance for Britain that could only grow.

## America, China and India

Salisbury wished the Germans to understand that Britain was "particularly poly-gamous" in her foreign relations, not "monogamous", as they thought she ought to be.[54] Germany might be central to his policy: but he, and even the ministers inclined to draw closer to their ally, had no intention of being turned against the United States by the requirements of *Weltpolitik* at its most ambitious. The British had so much to lose by making an enemy of America that they would always endure considerable provocation from that quarter. Wilhelm II and his advisers realized this; so did the Americans.[55] China, where British business had by far the largest share of external trade, was a part of the world where Britain would have liked to enlist American co-operation in maintaining the 'open door' to commerce as Russia and Germany expanded their interests in the largest and richest of the "dying nations". America's unwillingness to commit herself obliged Salisbury to fall back on Germany as the counterweight to Russia, whose eventual domination of China could not be averted but should be delayed. His pessimism and doubts about the Anglo-German agreement on China concluded in 1900 were exasperating for those in his cabinet who badly wanted Britain to be more assertive in the Far East, with Germany firmly beside her. These criticisms grew sharper as the Boxer rebellion further weakened the Chinese empire. Less cautious and less perceptive politicians than Salisbury complained to each other of his timidity and inertia. No one was more of a Jingo in his correspondence than George Curzon, the parliamentary under-secretary at the Foreign Office whom the premier had chosen to be viceroy of India when still in his thirties. Like Lord Ellenborough half a century earlier, Curzon dreamed of extending British influence in the Middle East from India. He fretted over Salisbury's unshakeable refusal to be indignant with the other powers interested in Persia and the Gulf. But they agreed about the internal situation in India. Salisbury believed that it called for an energetic but not a liberalizing ruler.

The awakening of the United States to the opportunities and temptations of a great power accompanied the rebirth of her navy, neglected since the Civil War. The means of implementing the Monroe doctrine of 1823 that sought to exclude Europe from the American hemisphere would soon be available. As a new mood took hold of American politicians, and to some extent of her people, the administration of President Cleveland decided to exploit an old boundary dispute between Britain and Venezuela, in which the United States had previously offered to mediate. In

August 1895 the secretary of state, Richard Olney, published a dispatch that invited the parties to go to arbitration, and in doing so found the existence of the colony of British Guiana "unnatural and inexpedient". Asked, very unusually, to reply before the President's annual message to Congress, Salisbury did not answer within the specified time. Then in two dispatches he rejected this interpretation of the Monroe doctrine and, after detailed examination, the Venezuelan claim. He declined to contemplate the transfer of a large slice of the colony with the inhabitants, at the behest of arbitrators, "however eminent", to a state that had its full share of the failings characteristic of Latin American republics. Cleveland met the British rebuff by summoning Congress to hear him call in December 1895 for America to adjudicate upon the Anglo-Venezuelan dispute and enforce her findings. His language seemed to suggest that war was in the offing, and the American press spelt out the implied menace.[56]

The good sense of the Salisbury government and their people was demonstrated in the ensuing crisis, which followed hard on the failure to coerce Turkey in the latest phase of the Eastern question and was concurrent with the storm raised by the Jameson Raid and the Kruger telegram. The young American battle fleet would not even be second to Britain's until 1908. Sharply falling share prices in New York, protests from the American electors and the unfavourable international reaction told the President and Olney that they had miscalculated. Salisbury's tactics, endorsed by the cabinet, were simply to wait "until the . . . excitement had cooled somewhat". The London newspapers took their cue from Downing Street: they regretted, they deplored, and they hoped for American restraint. Salisbury wanted to know more about the division of American opinions. Hostility to Britain was reputed to be stronger inland, away from the Eastern Seaboard at risk from the Royal Navy. Did this mean that only British sea power held America back from war? "Then it is bound to come in a few years . . . the question arises – have we any interest in delaying it?"[57] Admiral Richards, the first naval lord, and Dufferin, the ambassador in Paris, who had governed Canada, expected their country to be attacked when the American navy was of a size to take on the British fleet divided between the Atlantic and the Mediterranean. Salisbury himself doubted whether anti-British feeling was general: but a war with America was, for him, "something more than a possibility and . . . much more of a reality" than one with France or Russia. He and his often parsimonious chancellor of the exchequer were united in increasing the navy estimates.[58]

Yet nothing like war fever could be discerned in Britain. Balfour said an Anglo-American conflict must involve "some of the unnatural horror of a civil war". Businessmen urged acceptance of arbitration in a form agreed by Britain and not imposed upon her: "it would lift a great cloud from our commerce", wrote the Liverpool shipowner, Sir William Forwood. Salisbury anticipated these pleas not to fight over "a swamp where a man cannot live".[59] In mid-January he advised Devonshire on the line to take: the Americans evidently had not studied Britain's case for her colonial border with Venezuela, and she had "never had any intention of adopting any policy at variance with the doctrines laid down by President Monroe", which had their origin in Canning's proposal for a joint declaration aimed at the other powers of Europe. On 31 January Salisbury made these points in a speech that also contained a celebration of the imperial unity which was apparent in Canada's reaction to the crisis: "something mightier than formulas or statutes is driving the empire together".[60] In fact, he was prepared to go back on his refusal of arbitration in December. A worsening of Anglo-American relations was so clearly not in Britain's interests that he decided to sacrifice the area of British Guiana claimed by Venezuela where there was no settlement worth the name. After some argument, the American and British governments adopted this principle, which subsequent arbitration confirmed. The award was, in reality, predetermined by "negotiation and compromise", as Salisbury intended. "Neither of us", he warned Chamberlain, "could ever hold [up] our heads again" if the "settled districts" were handed to Venezuela by the arbitrators. The faces of both governments were saved. It had been plain to the British, all along, that Cleveland and his party were trying to make political capital out of a contrived dispute ahead of the 1896 presidential election.[61]

The importance of good relations with the United States outweighed Salisbury's distrust of international tribunals. He was always afraid of arbitrators' hidden prejudices. "Who would have guessed", he said in this context, "at the intense hatred of England" uncovered by German reactions to the Kruger telegram? Britain – "we are at present unpopular in many countries" – must have difficulty in getting an impartial hearing. He therefore ruled out unrestricted arbitration under the general arbitration treaty between Britain and the United States which he proposed in February 1896. His proposal sprang directly from the current quarrel with America, and the danger of future quarrels: "a great deal of troublesome dispute might be pushed out of the way, without great risk". The distinctive feature of Salisbury's scheme was the exclusion of a third country from the process of arbitration. A standing tribunal had jurisdiction over matters not deemed by either state to involve "honour . . . or territorial integrity". Awards were subject to review by five judges from the supreme court of the *protesting* nation, who might refer it for further negotiation. This "tentative treatment" of problems that arose between the two states was meant to build confidence in the working of the new institutions. For some time, and perhaps indefinitely, Salisbury wished to leave "a hole of escape" from unwelcome judgements. The modified version of the scheme accepted by the American administration contained a neutral umpire at the first stage, and at the second substituted three judges from each country. Salisbury successfully insisted, however, that five of the six judges reviewing an award would have to agree if a disputed award were to be upheld.[62]

When he announced the signing of this treaty in the Lords, Salisbury described it, to laughter, as "an invaluable bulwark to defend the Minister from the Jingoes". An American administration, he suggested, would have even more reason to be grateful for such protection against the volatility inherent in democracy. If no system of arbitration could halt the arms race – a characteristic allusion to unpleasant facts – the Anglo-American treaty was a step towards the peaceful resolution of dangerous disputes. Salisbury's demeanour exhibited his relief and satisfaction at having successfully completed a negotiation by which he set great store. It was a sharp disappointment when the United States senate withheld approval of the treaty. His labours had not been wasted: fewer Americans were disposed to see an enemy in Britain; a tendency reinforced by her attitude during the Spanish American war next year. British opinion was generally sympathetic to America; and Salisbury had identified Spain as "possibly" another of the dying nations, in whose remaining colonial possessions Britain had no sort of interest. Germany and the other European powers evinced a contrasting solicitude for Spain.[63] The British had their reward when the ambassador in Washington reported that the "comical efforts" of his German colleague to form a common front with the United States in Samoa had met with "nothing but snubs". Though unwilling to tie themselves to any power, the Americans were closer to the British than at any time in their independent history. But their detachment, maintained until 1917, compelled Salisbury to yield in Samoa and turn to Germany in China.[64]

A patriot and an imperialist, Salisbury detested those who unwittingly caricatured patriotism and empire. He sometimes teased the Jingoes a little in his speeches: "they exist in all countries . . . very excitable . . . critics". In confidence, he occasionally expressed his disgust: "The Jingoes will lie egregiously, as is their habit", he remarked when they accused him of incurring national humiliation by his too patient diplomacy before the difficult year of 1898 reached its triumphant conclusion.[65] The Jingoes were usually quiet where America was concerned: Chamberlain's desire to make a friend of her ensured that. They could not be keener than Salisbury to dismember Turkey. Africa excited them but not as much as China, where there was more to defend and to gain. The shift of Russian expansion to the Far East naturally made the British fear for their commanding share of China trade, and for the prospects of its growth. From the mid-1890s Salisbury tried to secure the backing of America, Germany and Japan, the newest of the powers, for a policy of the "open door" in China. Keeping the door open was obviously a British rather than a collective interest: all three refused their support. Japan "politely", Germany "rudely", and the United States "with a contemptuous snub". If she had Russia behind her, China could not be made to continue the treaty arrangements forced upon her after the Anglo-Chinese wars of forty years ago: a British expeditionary corps of some 40 000 men – all there was to spare for that distant theatre – would be pitted against a Russian army backed by a Chinese population of 400 million. Such an attempt at coercion unaided by any other power, would be "simple lunacy". China was not Egypt or the Sudan: Britain had no alternative to military co-operation with other powers, failing which Russia must be predominant when she was ready.[66]

This appreciation of an uncomfortable position, written early in 1890, went to Henry Northcote, a loyal and influential backbencher and an old friend, prominent in the National Union. It was not only Jingoes who were disturbed by British acquiescence in Russia's occupation of Port Arthur in March 1898, which completed her penetration of Manchuria. In Salisbury's absence, five cabinets discussed Britain's response. Curzon, who attended to help Balfour represent the Foreign Office, reported a "bloodcurdling speech" from Chamberlain in favour of going to war. By quoting the premier's opinion, a rather hesitant Balfour carried the decision to leave Port Arthur and Manchuria to the Russians, and to placate domestic critics by the enforced lease of another harbour for the Royal Navy's China squadron at Wei-Hai-Wei, nearly opposite Port Arthur on the approaches to the Bay of Pechili. The acquisition – one more example of how Western sea power could be used to extract concessions from the Chinese – was presented as safeguarding British interests in Northern China. As such, it was of little use: but it satisfied the backbenches. Resignations from the "Pig Tail Committee" of Jingoes who had taken up China came "as thick as autumnal leaves in Vallombrosa" – Curzon's simile from Milton. *The Times*, previously hostile, threw its weight behind ministers, attacking the dissidents fiercely. Once Chamberlain decided that he would rather fight France over West Africa than Russia, he reproduced Salisbury's arguments in the Commons with a frankness that appalled Curzon, whose conception of statecraft excluded the honesty that was integral to Salisbury's diplomatic method. "We suffered agonies on the front bench", the future foreign secretary complained, "as he proceeded to explain *seriatim* how we were not strong enough – without an ally – to stand up against Russia in the Far East, to preserve the independence of China, to exercise a controlling influence there, and even to maintain the 'open door' . . .". Differing much less from the premier than was, and is, supposed, Chamberlain generally ended by agreeing with him, though seldom unreservedly as in this speech.[67]

The seizure of Port Arthur was doubly galling for the British in that it took place a couple of weeks after Russia abruptly terminated the exchanges following Salisbury's overture for an Anglo-Russian "partition of preponderance" in China. Chamberlain, who talked to de Staal of an alliance with Russia in December 1897, was against this initiative in January 1898, one which Goschen and Hicks Beach approved. The last named unwisely sought to raise the stakes in a speech at Swansea on 17 January: Britain would keep the door open in China "at whatever cost . . . even if necessary the cost of war". Unmoved, Salisbury was thinking of the European dimension of an agreement. Remembering their recent dissent from his policy towards Greece, he was careful to take the cabinet with him: "I don't want to be trampled upon again". He allowed himself to hope that Anglo-Russian co-operation in the Far East might lead to "some change" in the alignment of the great powers in Europe. Although the Russian autocrat was an incongruous ally for a government answering to the mother of parliaments, as he was for the French republic, he would provide an escape from the growing discomfort of the Anglo-German entente. The thought stayed with him in the late 1890s. But, he told Balfour, "the real crux is Port Arthur". Russia, whose main rival in Manchuria and Korea was Japan, wanted "an assurance of our indifference" to her occupation of that strategic place. While Britain's inability to cut loose from Germany, in China as in the rest of the world, prevented agreement with Russia, Salisbury did, in effect, trade Port Arthur for Russian indifference to France's appeal for help in the Fashoda crisis. Since Fashoda lay in the future, the initial reaction of the Jingoes, and of many Unionists who did not like to be so designated, appeared to spell the end of Salisbury's personal ascendancy in the making of foreign policy by his successive governments.[68]

According to *The Times*'s local correspondents, Lancashire, where the cotton industry feared for the great Chinese market of its dreams, would vote "solid" against the government if given the chance. Moberly Bell, assistant editor on the paper, deplored Curzon's failure to resign in protest at Russia's advance into the Chinese empire. Resignation would have secured the Foreign Office for him in a Balfour administration in a year or two. Salisbury foresaw a political storm. Even a sympathetic observer like Edward Hamilton shared the feeling that despite Wei-Hai-Wei, Far Eastern policy was a "fiasco". The premier defended himself to Alfred Austin. It was impossible to say whether Russia would have fought if Britain had sent her ships into Port Arthur. In such circumstances war often resulted from "passing paroxysms of passion". Once Britain was at war with Russia – not an alarming prospect if the combatants were left to themselves – Germany and France would levy their blackmail in Africa: "And fighting them all would be a great strain". Then he made his familiar point: without an army "on the modern scale", Britain's use of force in China was strictly limited. He had never supposed that the British electorate had the stomach for a European conflict. His analysis of the demand for war echoed Gladstone twenty years earlier: it was loud in "the London papers, clubland and Society". The noise they made was deceptive. Experience seemed to show that however much the mass of voters might enjoy the idea of a belligerent policy, they objected to it in practice. They rewarded Palmerston with a majority of eighty at the 1865 election for having abandoned Denmark to her enemies: and punished Beaconsfield in 1880 for his "forward" policy in two continents. "How will the third investigation of the problem work out?", he asked. "No one can tell, but I think it will have the effect of splitting the party".[69]

The party did not split because, in China as elsewhere, Salisbury used every means short of war with her rivals, to perpetuate the British hold on Chinese trade. Railways were the key to the future of a huge country. With Port Arthur Russia obtained the concession for a railway linking it to lines under previous concessions that were to run through Manchuria and down into Siberia and the port of Vladivostock. The integration of these lines, and of the Trans-Siberian railway under construction, with an expanding network in the heart of China was an imperial design which the British had to counter. In the competition for railway concessions, Russia had a financial advantage in the indebtedness of the Peking government to their Russo-Chinese bank. Loans and railways went together around the globe. The real war in China would be fought with capital, which ought to suit the British, so long as their objections to concessions for Russia – and Germany – were backed by readiness to furnish the money themselves. "I see no other mode of fighting", he replied to his eager under-secretary, ". . . [but] I see no sign of that passionate desire to invest in Chinese railways, either in this country, or in any other". The shortage of available funds induced the "patriotic capitalists" of the Hong Kong and Shanghai and Deutsche Asiatische Banks to unite in a Chinese loan. The Russians took that as evidence that the British were not seriously interested in the partition of influence proposed by Salisbury. But the good sense of reducing international tension by a division of the Chinese empire into spheres of interest prevailed by the following year: an agreement of April 1899 restricted

Russian and British railway concessions to China north and south of the Great Wall, respectively.[70]

Salisbury expected the breathing space thus gained to last little longer than the time needed to complete the Trans-Siberian railway and build a line from Southern Manchuria to Peking. He speculated on the possibility of getting the empire's capital moved nearly a thousand miles further south to Nanking on the Yangtse-Kiang: British gunboats on the great waterway might, with Chinese help, cripple the communications of a Russian army advancing deep into the interior. Salisbury's sympathy with a legitimate nationalism almost everywhere made him aware of its potential strength in China. Coercion was necessary in the interests both of the Chinese and the British, if Russia was to be held off. "Our business . . . is to use every occasion . . . for frightening the Chinese government", he minuted.[71] He was explicit in his personal guidance to Lord Charles Beresford, the naval officer and former Tory MP, sent out in 1898 to report on the prospects for Britain in China: "We shall not get on long with China without having to apply the whip in some form . . . how many of our present gunboats could destroy or threaten how many of their important towns?" The presence of gunboats on the main rivers should roughly balance that of Russian troops on the frontier with Siberia. Britain's secret service expenditure did not run to bribing China ministers and officials: hers "must be a heavy sword . . . to outweigh the golden motives . . . in the opposite scale". The surprising brutality of these extracts has to be set against his view that Beresford might do "a great deal of good", if, as Lord Charles himself suggested, he advised the Chinese on their defences.[72]

Beresford was quickly convinced that only an alliance with one or more of the industrial great powers could prevent Russia from shutting the "open door" on Britain: the policy Salisbury had tried and failed to implement. His speeches to British businessmen in Shanghai embarrassed the government at home; and elicited a warning from Salisbury that if he persisted in criticizing them, he would be treated as a political enemy. Shortly afterwards, the Boxer rising, a fierce popular protest against the slow subjugation of China by the foreigner, had the anticipated result of bringing about an international involvement with the stricken empire which checked Russian ambitions. A "dying nation" proved to have life in it; even the corrupt regime of the Dowager Empress Tzu Hsi covertly encouraged the movement that progressed from rioting to open warfare. From June 1900 the Western legations in Peking, defended by their own military guards as was customary at diplomatic posts in the East, were under siege. Believing them to have succumbed, Salisbury resisted the pressure on him to "boss the show" in an international operation to recover northern China from the rebels.[73] In his coolest and "most wicked mood", he objected to inviting the Russians and Japanese to take part. There would be a price to pay in terms of territory and influence in China. For the same reason, he was reluctant to work with the Russians and the Germans. In a joint operation, the Russians, given their military superiority, "would have our policy in their hands . . . we should find they had occupied all the best positions". The crisis, in his judgement, was local, that is, confined to northern China, and should not be inflated to Britain's disadvantage.[74]

The letters written to Curzon in India by his successor as parliamentary under-secretary at the Foreign Office, St John Brodrick, show Salisbury giving ground before proposals for a unified command in China and for the participation of the Japanese in particular. Brodrick was an enthusiastic imperialist; but his account can be confirmed from other sources, including the correspondence of the Indian secretary, Lord George Hamilton, with Curzon. "He seems disposed to let things settle themselves", wrote Hamilton of the premier in July 1900, "which may mean the massacre of every Christian in China". Yet by then Salisbury had consented to approach the Japanese, and the Americans, telling the former that without a large contingent from them, Peking would go to Russia. "Lord S[alisbury] played him magnificently", said Brodrick, who was present at the Japanese diplomat's interview. Salisbury preferred what he called "a Waterloo arrangement" for the forces converging on Peking: independent commanders co-operating as Wellington and Blücher had done.[75] If Brodrick is to be believed, Balfour and Goschen hinted at displacing the prime minister, "which none of us will do". Salisbury yielded to argument, not to pressure: "he is more powerful than ever", Brodrick concluded. The combined representatives of the powers and the cabinet were needed to overcome his opposition to the appointment of the German field-marshal, von Waldersee, to command the growing international army of reconquest. The taking of Peking where the legations held out, by Russian and British troops in August, before von Waldersee left Germany, proved his point as far as the campaign was concerned.[76]

Russia also saw the internationalization of the war in China as a threat. After the capture of Peking she announced the withdrawal of her troops. The German emperor and his ministers interpreted this as a snub to their crusading zeal on behalf of Western civilization. Those in the British government who wanted closer relations with Germany were glad to join her in the declared intention to maintain the integrity of the Chinese empire and its openness to trade. As the wording of the mutual pledge indicated, neither power was committed to anything more than the exercise of their influence to preserve the order of things restored by the Boxers' defeat. Salisbury did not conceal his dislike of the treaty signed in October 1900 from his colleagues or the public: "not . . . necessary . . . it seemed consistent with the policy of pleasing Germany to which so many of our [Unionist] friends are attached". In his speech at the Mansion House in November he deliberately belittled a diplomatic achievement widely understood to signal a deepening Anglo-German collaboration and the partition of China. He referred to "an agreement of no great eccentricity or peculiarity". The "stupendous task of governing China" was best left to the Chinese.[77] His tone reflected disappointment at the German refusal to identify Russia as the enemy in the treaty. All Salisbury could get was the excision of the 38th parallel from the text as limiting the pact's operation to the south of that line. Although he looked on Peking as "predestined to Russia", he did not wish to accelerate the passing of the capital and north China with it, into Russian control. Cabinet ministers friendly to Germany, and especially Devonshire, were indignant at the German attitude. For the Germans the diplomacy of the 1900 treaty steered a middle course between Britain and Russia, teaching both to reckon with her as an equal in China.[78]

Some months after the treaty was signed, a unilateral statement from von Bülow removed Manchuria from its scope. This did not make for trust between Britain and Germany, but was not otherwise of much significance. Manchuria was really lost to the British, whose influence in China was to be measured by trade and, at that moment, by the potential investment in railways. "The politics of China are the politics of railways": that was true, Salisbury held, wherever Western nations competed to develop the unappropriated regions of the world. His sense of proportion did not desert him: he teased far-flung consuls, "and men more lofty than consuls", for whom every railway concession that went to a foreign power was a setback likely to be fatal to their country. A railway was not "a portable rolled-up thing you carry in your pocket": it required large amounts of finance from European syndicates and, added the sometime chairman of the Great Eastern Railway to an audience of railway directors, prudent examination whether "the right, on paper, to cover the Chinese empire with railways" was remunerative. From the mid-1890s the Chinese were alive to the importance, economic and political, of railways: they kept some of the new lines out of the concession hunters' grasp, if they had to be funded by loans raised abroad. However, Britain retained an overwhelming share of the foreign trade stimulated by an expanding network. China's imports from Britain and her possessions rose by nearly half to £33 million between 1895 and 1908, when those from Russia stood at £422 000. British business had nothing to fear provided the door to its market remained open. Salisbury's refusal to be pushed into over-reacting to Russia was demonstrably the right policy.[79]

In the war of 1894–5 with China and again in the Boxer rebellion, Japan had established herself as a regional power, the first Asian nation to modernize successfully.[80] The German foreign ministry, among others, saw in her a natural ally for Britain. Salisbury thought Japan was as likely to side with Russia as against her, if the latter took the trouble to find "some bribe" in the shape of a further slice of Chinese territory to go with what Russia, Germany and France had allowed her to keep in 1895. "Platonic assurances of affection" from the Japanese were to be discounted. What mattered to Salisbury in the 1890s was Anglo-Japanese trade: it was of "the highest importance" to stop valuable contracts from going to Germany. He told a new envoy in Tokyo to be more active in promoting British firms than had been usual in his time at the Foreign Office; German competition everywhere was forcing a change in the practice. The Far East was still what it had been for Palmerston, a problem of "informal empire", that is, of commercial expansion; though it now involved a dangerous rivalry between the great powers.[81]

India was a problem of a different kind. In Curzon she had from 1898 a ruler with little of Lansdowne's mild liberalism, and even less of the caution that most viceroys displayed in the conduct of India's external relations.[82] Curzon pressed his claims to the viceroyalty on Salisbury: if they were strong, George Hamilton, who was to be his secretary of state, had reservations about Curzon's political views and his judgement. The India Office, where he had served as parliamentary under-secretary in 1891–2, pronounced him "a regular Jingo with Russia on the brain". Hamilton recommended tying him down to a statement of policy approved by the cabinet so as to prevent a repetition of the home government's experiences with Lytton. Curzon, like Lytton, aspired to put India at the centre of British foreign policy: Salisbury had been able to control Lytton while he was at the India Office, and he restrained Curzon, who never dared challenge him directly. Premier and viceroy broadly agreed on internal policy: no extension of the India Councils Act but efficient and just administration sensitive to the rights of Indians.[83]

In the previous viceroy's time Salisbury had been "very hot" for commissioning a few selected Indian princes and nobles in the British army. The successful resistance to this symbolic step, which enjoyed royal backing, revealed the intensity of official and military prejudice – of the "damned nigger element", as he termed it – in India and at home. His cabinet colleagues shrank from placing British officers and men under an Indian – "Tommy Atkins will be incurably prejudiced". Salisbury looked ahead to the not very distant future as the political consciousness of India's millions matured. In Russia subject races were eligible for the highest ranks of the army: the British were not much better than the Turks, who excluded Christians from military service altogether. Salisbury could not suppose that Indians would indefinitely submit to the "mark of contempt" inflicted by exclusion from the British army, and restriction to the lowest commissioned ranks in the Indian army. "It is painful", he confided to Henry Northcote, who was governing Bombay, "to see the dominant race deliberately going over into the abyss". If trouble on the North West frontier could not be strictly contained, "a spasm of sedition will shoot from one end of India to the other". It was the fear that haunted a veteran of Indian service such as Roberts with his memories of the Mutiny; but in Salisbury's case it derived from his clearer perception that the old India which had risen in 1857 would be incited to rise again and led by the new India born of Westernization.[84]

Salisbury had not changed his mind about the improbability of a full-scale Russian assault upon India through Afghanistan. As in his India Office days, he was afraid of disturbances on the frontier, inspired or exploited by Russia, spreading to the plains: "She won't try to conquer . . . It will be enough for her if she can shatter our government and reduce India to anarchy". Russian policy-makers had their eyes fixed on China: but Salisbury assumed that they counted on compelling Britain to give way there, when the time arrived, by a diversionary attack upon India from Afghanistan. It was the same tactic with a different object, that he had faced when the Near East had a higher priority for Russia. A combination of Russia, the Amir and restless frontier tribes would impose an "enormous" strain on the British ability to hold the mountain passes and maintain order behind them. Agreement with Russia and the Amir in 1894–6 brought a precarious stability to disputed borderlands: Salisbury did not think any of the three states could make it last; each was subject to strong pressures.[85] The best means of defence for Britain in India was an attack on Afghanistan. On the perennial question of how and where to meet the threat of invasion, his views had undergone a significant change since he kept Lytton back. "It is quite right to avoid a forward policy if you can", he remarked to Curzon, then at the Foreign Office, in 1897, "but you cannot". The tribesmen obliged the British to mount punitive expeditions up against a natural frontier. Policy, complicated by changes of government at home, was "Jingo and penitence in alternate doses". Campaigns like that of 1897 to curb the tribes in one stretch or another of the long border region settled nothing. Salisbury would have liked to "strike a heavy blow and have done with it": but he did not let Curzon have his head as viceroy. The Sudan, South Africa and China, and the necessity of conciliating Russia, checked a forward movement.[86]

So did a shortage of money for the strategic railway to Seistan which the premier had been urging for many years. It was just as well: for Curzon, whose extensive travels a few years earlier had made him an authority on Persia, was eager to confront Russia in the unending battle for influence at the court of the Shah, notwithstanding Salisbury's admonition to remember how hard it was to control "these spoilt children" – Oriental rulers.[87] He disagreed with the prime minister's assessment of Russian intentions in Asia, believing St Petersburg was bent on driving through Persia to the Gulf. He was also inclined to make much of French and German interest in those waters. Salisbury's secret agreements in 1891 and 1899 with the Sultan of Muscat and Oman and the Sheikh of Kuwait confirmed Britain's local ascendancy, which his actions enforced more discreetly than Curzon wished. The "regular Jingo" vehemently criticized the premier, to others, for "throwing bones to keep the various dogs quiet (Madagascar, Tunis, Heligoland, Samoa, Siam) . . . *I would be as strong in small things as in big*". Salisbury had gently pointed out that the French possessed treaty rights in Muscat and Oman which must be taken into account and that "Paris is as much worth considering as Muscat". He declined to believe that the Dual Alliance was working to a plan in the Gulf and Persia, if operative there at all. France and Russia had little in common besides fear of Germany. The Anglo-French dispute over coaling facilities for the French navy at Muscat was defused. Seen by Turkey and Germany as a possible terminus for the planned railway from Asia Minor to Mesopotamia, Kuwait ceased to be a potential source of friction once the Germans learnt of Britain's agreement with the Sheikh. Salisbury had no objection to the eventual appearance of the Bagdadbahn on the Turkish shore of the Gulf: it would help to counter Russia's influence in those parts.[88]

In complete contrast to Curzon, he did not seek to retain "exclusive" control of what had been "a British lake". The "key for deciphering . . . modern politics", Salisbury explained at some length to the viceroy, was not to be found in Russian designs on the British empire. His aim, avowed in this and subsequent exercises in persuasion addressed to Curzon, was to foster "a mutual temper of apathetic tolerance" between the powers, in which they might attempt to adjust their interests without animosity.[89] The row at Muscat proceeded from the zeal displayed by the local agents of Britain and France, from the *morbus consularis*, as he liked to call it, and from the old antagonism between the two nations. Delivering an implied rebuke, he dwelt on the consequences "if we are arrogant and force treaties to mean what suits us", in the Sultanate, or anywhere else. Should the British interpretation of the relevant treaty be "obviously" strained, French chauvinism, deeply wounded by Fashoda, was almost certain to boil over, leaving Salisbury's government with no choice but to climb down: their public opinion would not be prepared to fight over coaling facilities for French warships in a remote principality. Curzon and Brodrick lamented the premier's principled inertia, as it seemed to them, in their correspondence. The viceroy, with his literary gifts, imagined Salisbury "at the bar of history which does not forgive apathy, because it rests upon experience, or cynicism because it is backed by character".[90]

Experience and character, backed by the reconquest of the Sudan and Fashoda, meant that Salisbury was not to be moved when Russia, Germany and France were all making "at various rates" for the Gulf ports. The expansion of the West was not to be halted by signs of revival in the Ottoman empire, and there were few such signs in the Persia of 1900. Salisbury kept in view the partition of Persia into zones of influence: but he did not see how to arrest Russia's progress. Britain could not bribe the Shah and his ministers for want of the secret funds at the Russian legation's disposal; nor could she rescue the insolvent state with a loan. The Russian loan of 1900, accompanied by a stipulation that Persia should not borrow from any other country, was a blow to Britain's hopes of maintaining something like parity with her rival. Give him half an hour with the Shah, Curzon declared, and he would transform the situation: but with Salisbury in charge "we shall go paltering on to ultimate humiliation if not disaster". This, of course, was not for the premier's ears. Salisbury was discriminating in his use of threats; they were a last resort in the East as in the West. He refused to countenance the maritime blockade with which the British minister in Teheran, Sir Mortimer Durand, menaced the Persians in 1898, if a promotion to which he took exception was not revoked. There was no precedent since Palmerston's time for the employment of force in relation to a question of that kind.[91]

A talented official from the Indian Civil Service, Durand was a man after Curzon's heart – one of those, moreover, who expected to have to fight great powers in the inexorable course of imperial expansion. Britain had lost the battle for influence before the 1900 loan: and Salisbury blamed the minister and his staff. "Why has Russia won?", he invited Durand to reflect. The Teheran legation had a distinctive outlook traceable to its history as an outpost of the government of India. Persia was not under British protection – and Britain lacked the military resources to protect her. Yet the legation interfered more in the internal affairs of the state to which it was accredited than the missions in China, Siam and Turkey, much more than those in South America. Durand's language, in the tradition of a British resident at an Indian prince's court, had handed the diplomatic contest to Russia. "Orientals are no doubt mainly accessible to fear", he wrote, "but are they not also accessible to resentment, especially if the fear is hollow?"[92] Curzon claimed that the policy he advocated and Durand practised was simply a continuation of the past: the maintenance of British hegemony in Persia and the Gulf without annexation or occupation. Without the Seistan railway on Persia's border with Baluchistan, Salisbury reiterated, Britain had only her naval strength to deploy. The navy could deny Germany Kuwait and Russia Bandar Abbas at the mouth of the Gulf, places where "we have the power of resistance if we care to use it . . . but . . . the day of free, individual, coercive action is almost passed by". Germany, France and Russia were supposedly friendly powers with whom Britain had to share influence and territory on a global scale. Russia had outbid the British in Persia, helped by their blunders, and was close to establishing "a virtual protectorate".[93]

341

Persia was not at the centre of British policy but a "mainly Indian interest". Since Curzon did not have the money for a strategic railway to the Persian border, Salisbury's analysis of what was and was not feasible could not be refuted. Lansdowne, who succeeded him at the Foreign Office in October 1900, was prompted by the viceroy's "rather querulous language" to examine the Persian question for himself, and upheld the premier. The war in South Africa brought everyone to recognize the truth of what Salisbury had always preached: Britain was far less independent and secure than many politicians and the public had realized, despite recurrent scares and the navy's preparedness. He made Brodrick see in January 1900 that with only one division left at home and talk of a Continental league against Britain, they could not risk uniting the powers by holding the language he desired to Germany over Kuwait.[94] Salisbury's cautious methods, minimizing international publicity, were effective in strengthening Britain's position at Kuwait. It could not be said she had lost very much anywhere by his imperviousness to the arguments of those who confused relative with absolute decline. The reconquest of the Sudan in 1896–9, rounded off by his diplomatic victory over Fashoda, exemplified qualities wanting in so many of his critics: forethought, patience and timing.

## The Reconquest of the Sudan in Salisbury's Policy

Recovering the Sudan from its fanatical rulers pleased Jingoes, Christians of every kind, public opinion generally and members of the Triple Alliance; and displeased nobody except the French. It was a victory for Western civilization as well as for the British empire. It seemed to further Salisbury's hopes for Egypt and it was a setback for militant Islam everywhere. The diplomatic and military operations went according to plan but Islam proved resilient in defeat. Until the final push to Khartoum in 1898 there was no firm decision to occupy the whole country in the government's lifetime. Salisbury had always considered the destruction of the Mahdia a long-term aim which might not be realised in his day. He was no more inclined than he had been to underestimate Sudanese resistance; indeed, he may be said to have overestimated the military problems. The diplomacy was less anxious work until Fashoda. Yet there was a sense of anti-climax about his Sudanese achievement: he found himself having to deprecate the religious enthusiasm which had made the reconquest a much less controversial enterprise than had once seemed likely. The British gift for governing Muslim peoples, in which Salisbury put a qualified trust, could not be exercised to Christianize the Sudan. Islam was too deeply rooted for its foreign overlords in Egypt and the Sudan to impose their civilization.[95]

Salisbury was adept at employing the sort of arguments that Jingoes professed to relish. No one thought the valley of the Nile was richer than the plains of China, "the only question was, which were we able to rule". China was too big, populous and civilized, and the competition from other powers too strong, for Britain to take.[96] His motives for reconquering the Sudan were complex. The religious dimension of the undertaking meant as much to this sophisticated believer as it did to simpler men. He viewed the Mahdia's impending downfall as a defeat for the "false religion" of Islam. He had watched its contemporary resurgence with unaffected concern. As British and Egyptian troops advanced in the Sudan, he spoke of the impact that Turkey's defeat of Christian Greece in 1897 had on Muslims wherever they confronted the West: "A slight . . . an exaggerated victory, has recalled the past of a thousand years ago, when they were victorious in every part of the world . . . they cannot but believe that that glorious period of their history is to be repeated".[97] The battle of Omdurman in September 1898 dispelled fears that Salisbury had entertained since the Liberals decided to abandon the Sudan in 1884. Kitchener's army made good the Gladstonian retreat before Islam at its most aggressive and avenged the death of Gordon, the "Christian hero". The overthrow of a state built on slavery and the *jihad* presented advocates of reconquest with the clearest moral imperative. Slaves made up an estimated twenty to thirty per cent of the population, and there was a substantial, though unquantifiable, slave trade to Arabia and beyond, as the *jihad* brought in a steady supply of captives from the pagan tribes of the region and border warfare with Christian Abyssinia.[98]

In the later years of the Khalifa Abdullahi, the Mahdia was, if anything, more formidable than ever, notwithstanding its extrusion from much of the Eastern Sudan. Its warriors were more than a match for the Italians on that frontier. The vulnerability of demoralized Italian forces to a Mahdist onslaught after General Baratieri had been routed by the Abyssinians at Adowa in 1896 decided the timing of the first British advance. A regime that was the embodiment of the *jihad* menaced Egypt, Britain in Egypt and the other European states whose expansion in Africa brought them within range. It is doubtful whether Egypt, divorced from the Sudan, was as important to Salisbury as is usually claimed. An indefinite British occupation of Egypt was the diplomatic liability it had always been: Salisbury continued to speculate down to the late 1890s on the prospects for evacuation. But the occupation could not be safely ended without recovering the Sudan. Sir Redvers Buller, a distinguished soldier and someone of more liberal opinions than most generals, spelt this out to a French diplomat: the reconquest of the Sudan was a precondition of Britain's withdrawal; afterwards she would be free to leave, proud of her achievements and only too glad to be out of Egypt.[99]

A military demonstration on the Egyptian frontier would have sufficed to help the Italians in 1896, banishing any thoughts the Mahdists may have had of concentrating their armies in the East. Salisbury substituted an occupation of the Sudan as far as Dongola. The total collapse in Africa of Italy's pretensions to be a great power would weaken the Triple Alliance in the European war on two fronts which the Germans feared, and they called on Britain to contain her enemy. Salisbury could not well refuse; nor did he wish to. Cromer's reaction showed that Egypt and the Sudan were inseparable for British policy-makers. Giving his reasons against evacuating Egypt, he stated that to the best of his belief the Khalifa had an army on the frontier "only waiting for us to go". The danger he saw to Britain and the West from resurgent Islam took several forms, which might combine if Egypt fell to the Mahdia. The internal situation in Egypt had been significantly affected, if outwardly little was changed, by the crisis of 1893–4 when the young Khedive Abbas II tried to free himself from Cromer's tutelage. The Egyptian officers of the

British-led and trained army, the compliant premier Riaz and the tame legislature all revealed their true, anti-British sentiments. The real ruler of the country for ten years came close to losing his nerve. Rosebery at the Foreign Office sustained him: Cromer's personal system of indirect rule was rescued by overt threats of force if the Khedive did not submit. Cromer believed the desire for national independence reflected the "nature of a Mahometan population" inspired by "ignorant fanaticism".[100]

It would be nearer the truth to say that a Muslim people, or its leading elements, had divined his profound dislike of their faith, "a religion", he had written, "which clashes with public and private morality". It was his hope that in time the pervasive influence of Westernization would turn the Islamic nationalism to which he was implacably opposed into something more acceptable to his Whiggish liberalism. But after 1893–4 he had few illusions about the popularity of his rule. The fanatical host on the frontier and the Egyptians with their partly Westernized leadership were two manifestations of Islam. Another was Pan-Islam, the idea of an alliance of Muslim peoples against the West, which had been taken up by the Sultan and Caliph Abdul Hamid II, to enhance his political and religious influence. Cromer's misgivings about advancing into the Sudan reflected his anxieties. While he wanted to conserve his budgetary savings for other and peaceful purposes, the question that worried him, and Salisbury, was far more serious: how would the Egyptian army behave when asked, not to defend their country, but to invade a devoutly Muslim state at the behest of infidels? The organization and technology of modern war – a railway bypassing the Nile cataracts and river gunboats above that point – and the British units fighting beside the Egyptians were not enough to ensure success. Kitchener, in command, and Cromer agreed on the necessity of an early action on the march to Dongola. "I wanted to know whether the Egyptian troops would fight", the latter reported to Salisbury. "On this everything depended".[101] The battle of Firket in June 1896 was reassuring. What he wanted, Salisbury explained to the French ambassador, was an Egypt capable of standing by herself, and the showing of her army at Firket gave grounds for optimism.[102]

Cromer, however, was unsure, and opposed going on to Khartoum from Dongola: "no sufficiently important English interest is involved to justify the loss of life and money". What was the Sudan worth? Salisbury thought it wise to allude in parliament to expectations of proft from the reconquest: "countless treasures of industry and commerce which that fertile valley of the Nile is . . . to carry down as of old". For Cromer, it did not matter if the French forestalled Britain in the rest of the Sudan, "large tracts of useless territory". What trade there was would flow south to Uganda, or north to the British occupied areas. His arguments might have been put forward by a latter-day disciple of Cobden. But Cromer was no Cobdenite. He not only feared for Egypt if her army could not rise to its supreme test in the Mahdist heartland: he wondered whether it could hold the territory just regained. News of the Khalifa's preparations to resist a push to Khartoum alarmed him.[103] Salisbury himself was clearly in two minds about the risks they were running. Even before Firket he was tempted to regard the Khalifa, in purely military terms, as a "bogie [sic]". Yet when he sanctioned the advance to Dongola after consulting his colleagues, he had suggested elaborate precautions prompted by "the inferiority of your fellaheen troops". The move forward, never outstripping supplies, should be marked by an extraordinary caution: "there is no reason why your fellaheen should ever fight except behind entrenchments". Admittedly, this would be "an inglorious mode of warfare" but it was one to which Kitchener might be driven. Kitchener's progress to Dongola or to Khartoum, though reasoned, was rather bolder than that outlined in a letter presuming, unusually for Salisbury, to tell the soldiers how to fight this campaign. The premier was preaching to the converted when he dwelt on the vital requirement for an invasion of the Sudan: the proximity of rail and river. They were expensive operations: the British Treasury had to find the money for the advance from Dongola.[104]

The case for going on grew stronger in the eighteen months between the fall of Dongola and the cabinet's decision to proceed. "Pan-Islam has to a certain extent been grafted on to Anglophobia", wrote Cromer late in 1896. He hoped something would happen to diminish the Ottoman Sultan's prestige: "It would produce an excellent effect here". Instead, Muslims took heart from the defeat of Greece. If the danger from Pan-Islam was exaggerated and Abdul Hamid's exploitation of it largely bluff, the British were impressed by its spread. Salisbury had criticized Gladstone in 1882 for the spirit in which he had launched his invasion of Egypt. Now it was his turn to invade a country more fiercely Muslim than Egypt: a year before the final move on Khartoum, he spoke of "our desire to extirpate from the earth one of the vilest despotisms . . . ever seen . . . compared with which the worst performances of the worst minion of the Palace at Constantinople are bright and saintly deeds".[105] Cromer, who had demanded and received large British reinforcements for the Sudan, remained anxious, but the renewed campaign went forward with the precision that distinguished Kitchener's generalship. As Salisbury drily commented, the slaughter at Omdurman in September, where 11 000 of the Khalifa's men fell and fewer than fifty British and Egyptians, was on a scale to satisfy the appetite of excited patriots for bloodshed and glory. He was quick to point out to Kitchener that the conquered land could not be ruled in a spirit of righteous vengeance.[106]

Marchand and his tiny expedition would undoubtedly have been killed or captured by the Mahdists but for their overthrow as the Frenchmen reached the Sudan. Kitchener's victory gave substance to declarations that the Nile Valley was a British sphere. The Salisbury government fortified its claim by the condominium in the Sudan imposed on Egypt in January 1899. Britain's half-share was justified by the right of conquest. But between Dongola and Khartoum the Turkish victory over Greece compelled Salisbury to rethink his tentative plans, well known to diplomats, for a second Indian empire in the Middle East on the demise of imperial Turkey, and for evacuating a grateful Egypt. Without a British military presence, Cromer's Westernizing reforms would not survive a combination of reinvigorated Turkish suzerainty and the Khedive. If the Ottoman empire was reviving, Salisbury observed in 1897, "it follows that Egypt must be given back to the Moslems – which no one except the Moslems would approve". Ultimately, Britain's position in Egypt rested, as it had from the beginning, on the arbitrament of war, and should be consolidated by extending the authority conferred by conquest up the Nile "to its source". In this letter to Currie at Constantinople, he reduced a Middle Eastern empire to one on the Nile.[107] Even then, it would not be simple to hold Egypt and the Sudan, as Islam felt its strength returning. "I always feel", Cromer confessed before the war between Turkey and Greece, "that I am skating on the thinnest possible ice . . . it is a constant subject of astonishment to me that it bears at all". Only the timidity of the Khedive, "our best guarantee", preserved Cromer's ascendancy.[108]

Egyptian nationalists had mixed feelings about the recovery of the Sudan: Kitchener's triumph was plainly a defeat for Islam. Some of them had hoped that the Egyptian army would be beaten, and talked of welcome Mahdist counter-attack reaching Cairo. Politically minded Egyptians regretted the discomfiture of the French over Fashoda, and resented the condominium agreement: their soldiers had fought, it transpired, to hand over half the Sudan to Britain. The belief was widespread, and not only in Egypt, that the British intended to use their enhanced authority and prestige to convert an informal into a formal protectorate. Salisbury was forced to deny the report, while affirming that nothing would be allowed to change the verdict of Tel-el-Kebir, "the beginning of our modern Anglo-Egyptian history".[109] He supported Cromer's protest at the Church of England's desire to erect a bishopric covering Egypt and the Sudan. The new see, wrote Cromer, would be understood as "the first outward visible sign of our supremacy in the Sudan", and corroboration of frightening rumours: "From that to the idea that a general policy of proselytism is to be adopted is a mere step". The language of the Church's representative in the Middle East, the bishop in Jerusalem, horrified Cromer: it fed Egyptian fears of a formal protectorate, or annexation. Salisbury pressed Cromer's objections, which were also his own, on the primate, Archbishop Temple: he solicited and obtained discouragement of this missionary enterprise. Given the political situation in Egypt and the Sudan, it carried "a serious risk . . . of bloodshed" and was certain to cause "dangerous resentment" for a very small spiritual return, since Muslims were notoriously hard to convert. Though Temple was helpful, Salisbury had to issue a public warning to the churches in June 1900. Addressing the Society for the Propagation of the Gospel, whose proceedings opened with the national anthem, he said that the risk of a Muslim explosion was real, and intimated that their efforts in Islamic countries were misplaced: "remember . . . you are dealing with a force which a pure, though mistaken, theism gives to a vast population. You will not convert them." It was an eloquent defence of the policy which Cromer had already established in the Sudan, of restricting missionary activity to the pagans of the South.[110]

Salisbury's speech to the Society for the Propagation of the Gospel followed the mutiny of two Egyptian battalions at Khartoum in January 1900, emboldened by humiliating British reverses in South Africa. Cromer had little doubt that the Egyptian officers were participating in a wider conspiracy enjoying the Khedive's tacit support. The ensuing reduction of the Egyptian army was undertaken to meet "a danger of considerable gravity": a general uprising against the Christian power. "Moslems and Arabs", said Salisbury in another context, ". . . hate us . . . our religion and our special notions with a particular hatred". As a general principle, he was for governing "half-civilized peoples" through protectorates that left native institutions in place as "more acceptable . . . and more suitable for them than direct dominion".[111] That option was excluded in the Sudan by the nature of the conquest and by the existence of the condominium, nominal though it was. Its administration was for some years in the hands of soldiers. Salisbury impressed it on Kitchener, as the first governor-general, that reconciling the peoples of the Nile Valley to Western rule was "a task of the extremest difficulty". Western education was the one way of effecting that reconciliation. It was not very practical advice, except as a warning to Kitchener, whose attitude to the conquered was suspect. The speech of June 1900 showed what Salisbury really thought, and reflected Indian experience. The British ruled the Sudan by reconstructing the machinery of orthodox Islam and presenting themselves as its protector. The *qadi*, the judge applying the *Shari'a*, Islamic law, was an integral part of their administration. Slavery and the slave trade were slowly extinguished, but the *mores* of Sudanese society were not transformed, as Salisbury assumed they would eventually be, by a Westernized élite. The pattern of the future, and its irony, was clear to Wilfrid Scawen Blunt, an old opponent of Salisbury's policies in the Near East and Ireland. Salisbury had let "the Exeter Hall people and the bishops and the clergy" anticipate a Christian triumph, knowing that a "strictly Mohammedan" regime administered by the British must be the outcome.[112]

## Britain and the Boers

The slow extinction of slavery in the Sudan under the British represented a settled policy. Salisbury had been insistent during the rapid growth of British Africa that abolition should be gradual to avoid disrupting the traditional institutions of society. Giving offence to "powerful classes" in the Oil Rivers protectorate recently established in the Niger delta, he told a prominent humanitarian in 1890, risked making enemies of the slave trading Muslim chiefs to the north, as yet hardly touched by Britain's expansion. With or without prompting from him, the Germans and French in neighbouring territories would probably do their best to "kindle the spark into a flame". The explanation was necessary because the Liberal *Daily News* had reported the premier as telling a deputation from the Aborigines' Protection Society that slavery was "needful in that part of the world".[113] On the other side of the continent, Zanzibar presented the same problem: ministers argued among themselves about the continuance of slavery in a protectorate. "Our very modern doctrines upon slavery", wrote Salisbury, should not be enforced without compensation for a broken British promise to respect the legal ownership of slaves. A rising of the Arab clove-planters would be costly to suppress.[114] He disliked the "philanthropic pack" whose moral absolutes took no account of time and place. They were much less vocal about the black majority in the Boer republics who, although not legally enslaved, had few rights.[115] Salisbury had condemned their abandonment by Britain after Majuba. He did not, before the close of the 1890s, think that either they or the British immigrants in the Transvaal who protested at their exclusion from citizenship were so badly treated as to justify the imperial power in going to war. For the status of both would improve when the white newcomers and the wealth they created came to dominate the Boer state, as would happen in view of their numerical superiority over its citizens. The Jameson Raid in December 1895 was not an unexpected development. Salisbury did not underestimate the impatience of Rhodes and Milner to bring forward that day; nor did he fail to appreciate the strength of the Afrikaner nationalists' belief in their destiny.

The conspiracy between Rhodes, prime minister of the Cape Colony, and the leaders of the Uitlander majority of the Transvaal's white population was a natural consequence of the Boers' equally natural refusal to extend political rights to the immigrants. As Salisbury commented, the success of the operation led by Dr Jameson would have effectively answered the objections to it in international law. It was too late to stop Jameson when the British premier let Chamberlain know on 30 December that "it would be better if the revolution which transfers the Transvaal to British rulers were entirely the result of the action of internal forces, and not of Cecil Rhodes' intervention, or of ours". The preparations for a rising in Johannesburg were an open secret: in October Chamberlain leased to Rhodes' Chartered Company the strip of Bechuanaland from which the expedition started. Jameson was the company's administrator in Rhodesia, an imperial territory; his men were white troopers in the company's service. Several of the officers held commissions in the British army or reserve forces. The Uitlanders in Johannesburg prudently called off the rising, but Jameson went ahead on his own responsibility, believing that they would rally to him. Cut off and taken prisoner by Boer commandos on 2 January 1896, he and his followers had involved Britain in their defeat. Chamberlain's prompt repudiation of them and his subsequent denials of complicity before a Commons select committee were hardly convincing. It did not matter at home, except superficially. Public opinion was sympathetic to the raiders; and their political friends in Britain, on both sides, were greatly helped by the fury at Germany's condemnation of the attack on the Transvaal.[116]

The self-governing Cape Colony and the British South Africa Company were powers in their own right. When they were combined in the person of Rhodes, it was difficult for a British government to control the course of events. He had made himself the focus of resistance to Afrikaner nationalism, strong in the Cape Colony as well as in the republics to the north: but Salisbury was far from taking for granted the loyalty of British South Africans to the mother country and her interests. They could not be sure, he cautioned Chamberlain, what the relationship of a new Transvaal would be to the Crown and the Cape. Rhodes' imperial vision was not generally shared by the capitalists of the Rand, who might prefer to maintain the ruling Boers' virtual separation from the empire. Salisbury's first reaction to the news that Jameson had ridden across the Transvaal frontier to certain failure was to say that no harm seemed likely to be done, "except to Rhodes' reputation", which did not displease him. But the swift resignation of Rhodes as premier of the Cape, where he forfeited the Afrikaner support necessary to keep him in office, marked the deepening of the division between Boer and Briton that led inexorably to war in 1899. To Afrikaners Jameson's defeat was another Majuba. Chamberlain expressed his disgust for those Jingoes who persisted in imagining that the Boers could easily be overcome:

"It makes me sick", he minuted to Lansdowne at the War Office in March 1896, "to hear our braggarts depreciate the Boers . . . they have beaten Englishmen". Reinforcements were later sent to guard against the danger that the Transvaal Boers might overcome the relatively small garrison of British regulars in South Africa.[117]

In the slowly worsening situation, Salisbury's influence was exerted against the drift to war. Time, he believed, was on the side of the British. Given their growing numbers in South Africa, he counted on their ability, over a couple of generations, to assimilate the Boers. It was not, however, possible to leave the Uitlanders' legitimate grievances without redress for an indefinite period. The Transvaal's veteran president, Paul Kruger, was alarmed by a speech from Salisbury at the end of 1896 which appeared to menace the republic. Salisbury described the Transvaal as an illustration of the dangers of Home Rule which he opposed in Ireland. Though a majority, Uitlanders were as helpless as Protestant Ulstermen would be under a Dublin government. The treaty arrangements in force precluded British intervention in the internal affairs of the Transvaal. They also very seriously limited imperial control of foreign relations, leaving room for the involvement of other powers in the republic's disputes with Britain. While he said that he had yet to investigate the Uitlander problem for himself, "I know it tells what would have been the complaint and sorrow of our Ulster people if we had handed them over to the tender mercies of Home Rule". In answer to the protest that this elicited, he disavowed any intention of subverting the independence of Kruger's state: "I was insisting on that independence as an example of the position to which Ireland would come . . . I never spoke of the Transvaal as being now a colony". But he declined to take back the substance of remarks depicting the Transvaal as the oppressor of her unwelcome immigrant majority: "Make of the above such a case as you think will satisfy the old gentleman", he instructed Chamberlain.[118]

For Salisbury kept in view those dimensions of war in South Africa which he feared his colonial secretary would overlook. They must carry public opinion with them. The reinforcements sent in 1897 might look provocative to the government's critics in Britain, although Kruger was investing in armaments that seemed excessive to her potential foe. The additional British troops should be found defensive positions. The other point he raised with Chamberlain was the opportunity with which the feeling of the Dutch for their kinsmen in South Africa – "the one sentimental spot in the Dutch heart" – would present Germany. The Emperor Wilhelm's desire for a strong navy would be brought nearer realization if Germany and maritime Holland were to be united in a full-blown defence union. Then Britain might have to protect her eastern as well as her southern coast from attack. The reasons for Salisbury's anxiety to avoid war were, as he said, "wholly unconnected with Africa". He did not delude himself about the mood of Afrikanerdom: "The Boer will hate us for another half century", he wrote when hostilities were imminent in 1899.[119] A mutual reduction of forces in South Africa, discussed in the last months before the war, was unrealistic. The Transvaal would not adhere to the undertaking, and was certain to use it against Britain.

The republic's leaders wrongly supposed that in the end and perhaps all along the divergent views of Salisbury and Chamberlain would work in their favour. It is true that in July 1899 Salisbury told the Queen that the cabinet, "excepting, perhaps, Mr Chamberlain", and the country were reluctant to go to war in South Africa. But there was no deep disagreement between the two colleagues, only a difference of emphasis. The grievances of the Uitlanders and the ambitions of Afrikaner nationalism were inescapable. So, too, was the continuing influence of Rhodes and the British Jingoes who identified with him. Both Salisbury and Chamberlain disliked and distrusted Rhodes, but their high commissioner at the Cape from 1897, the ardent imperialist Alfred Milner, was as eager as Rhodes to see the erection of a British South Africa. Milner's belief that, sooner rather than later, war was the alternative to enfranchisement of the Uitlanders in the Transvaal quickened the pace of events. "It looks", said Salisbury disapprovingly in August 1899, "as if he had been spoiling for a fight with some glee".[120] Two years of negotiation from 1897 increased tension to the point where by the summer of 1899 Chamberlain was calling on the Australian and Canadian colonies for their aid in an approaching conflict. More than once the Transvaal made concessions in response to the announcement of reinforcements for South Africa; its offers on the franchise were being improved under steady pressure. It was not unreasonable to suppose that Kruger would bow to an ultimatum accompanying the final British demands. As Salisbury explained to one of his MPs in September, his government did not mean to be bound by legal niceties: "all that we have done" he went on, "would have been done if the word suzerainty had never been uttered. 'Neighbourhood' is quite enough", to justify intervention, that is. Britain was not willing to tolerate "a permanent establishment of racial and social war because the Boers are . . . deaf to the most elementary claims of justice".[121]

The use of the concept of "neighbourhood" was debatable in international law, to say the least. It is one more instance of the realism of Salisbury's judgements, sometimes concealed by diplomatic language. He did not allow Chamberlain or Milner to make up his mind for him. "In political life", he replied to a worried Liberal Unionist, Leonard Courtney, a few days afterwards, "you have to guess at the facts with such indications as you can get". He, and his cabinet, understood the objections of the Transvaal Boers to being swamped by alien immigrants, and Chamberlain envisaged phasing in the change. Salisbury had been ready to consider the issue of the franchise on its merits, but in the course of the negotiations he came to two firm conclusions. Kruger was using the question to obtain an effective renunciation of suzerainty. What was more serious, the Transvaal president had an "understanding" with his counterpart in the Orange Free State and with the leaders of the Cape Dutch: they aspired to a Dutch South Africa.[122] When the war began in October, Salisbury did not need to justify a British ultimatum. For the Transvaal acted first, to take advantage of the slowness with which the War Office was shipping troops to South Africa.[123]

Pre-empting a British advance or the rejection of a demand for a reversal of the empire's military build-up was a calculated gamble. The history of the Transvaal's successful revolt against Britain in 1880–81 suggested that ministers in London would not stand their ground after a sharp initial setback had again exposed the limitations of their army and the determination of the Boers to secure their full independence. Yet before their ultimatum the Transvaal put out a feeler to Salisbury, seeking to bypass Milner and the colonial secretary. They may have been encouraged by the tone rather than the substance of Salisbury's remarks in the Lords at the end of July, when he said he could make allowances for the Boer fear of being swamped by alien whites, and regretted the failure to devise a scheme that "would have given sufficient protection to the Uitlanders . . . without entirely annihilating the Dutch". An interview, authorized by Salisbury, took place between one of his secretaries, Eric Barrington of the Foreign Office, and the Transvaal's English agent, Montagu White, at which the latter represented that the republic "would jump at any chance of a pacific solution". The Transvaal proposed sending a delegation to confer in the British capital with a committee of the cabinet, "not Mr Chamberlain only". When Barrington sought to persuade him that Chamberlain's despatches to Pretoria represented the mind of the cabinet, White alluded to Salisbury's personal success in defusing the Venezuelan crisis: "You have been so clever in averting . . . war . . . you could do so now". At the same time White passed on the information that it was "very probable" the Transvaal would strike before Britain had got her forces into position.[124]

The overture was not one to which Salisbury could have responded positively. He and Chamberlain did not disagree on the evolution of their policy over two years. But if Salisbury had no alternative policy, he would dearly have liked to avoid a war for which he could feel no enthusiasm whatever. Strategy, prestige and the settled British population committed Britain in South Africa. Her rapidly growing investment there was not so large as to determine policy independently of other factors. While no one in Britain foresaw the duration and the cost of the coming war, or the damage it would do to her reputation, Salisbury did not anticipate that it would add to the strength of the empire. "I see . . . the necessity for considerable military effort", he told Lansdowne in August 1899, ". . . all for people whom we despise and territory which will bring no power or profit to England". His priorities were not those of Rhodes and the British in South Africa. In September he sent a memorandum round the cabinet insisting that he had not, as Chamberlain declared, contemplated stiffening the terms to be put to the Transvaal: "It would widely extend the impression of our bad faith . . . which unfortunately prevails in many quarters" – with good reason after the colonial secretary's part in the Jameson Raid. The passage in the Queen's speech on 17 October – six days after the Boer ultimatum expired – was deliberately low key, as, too, was the gloss upon it in the ensuing debate.[125]

"The only time when swagger may be of some use", he gently instructed a colleague, "is when the facts on which it is founded are contested". He left the verbal assault on Kruger to others. The essence of the policy that had led to war was the obligation to white South Africans. Suzerainty, though it had assumed greater importance than it originally possessed, was secondary. Britain's duty was to ensure that the warring white races were equal, and that there was "kindly and improving treatment of those . . . indigenous races of whose destiny, I fear, we have been too forgetful".[126] Salisbury's concentration on these themes, combined with the Boers' appearance as the aggressors, made for an unforced national unity. As in the case of the Sudan, the Nonconformist conscience was quiet to begin with: the Boers had not been forgiven for their hostility to the missionary champions of black Africans. What undermined the consensus was the startling success of the Boers in the field for some months, and their dogged resistance thereafter. Not altogether unfairly, Salisbury attracted some of the blame for the record of military and administrative incompetence. His standing with the Unionist parties suffered. His foreign policy, more admired than criticized for so long, was questioned at every level within the coalition and by its supporting newspapers. Age, health and bereavement help to account for the change, but the war on the veldt was instrumental.

# CHAPTER FOURTEEN

# *Anti-climax*

## An Aura of Failure

"The English here are like things with their tails cut off", wrote Lloyd George, in Welsh, of the parliamentary reaction to the news that as late as March 1902 Boer guerrillas were capable of defeating a sizeable British column and capturing the general in command after some of his men had run away.[1] The extravagant expectations of victory in 1900, when President Kruger went into European exile, had lost their savour. Although the Boer leaders submitted not long after the mortifying reverse of Tweebosch, the war had undeniably lowered Britain's prestige and heightened the anxiety, always present, about her future. But Salisbury remained a great figure to the public. He had behind him, somewhat to his surprise, the very slightly decreased Unionist majority in the election his government called for October 1900. He rightly interpreted it as a vote of confidence in the bi-partisan policy of overcoming the Boers and integrating them with the empire rather than in the governing coalition. The similarity between the policies of government and opposition on many of the issues before the electorate made him think that the British party system might be breaking up.[2] Inside the government, those who wanted him to move from the Foreign Office while continuing as prime minister saw their wish granted after his victory. If their concern for his health was genuine, they were also anxious for some change in the foreign policy he had pursued with the approval of their opponents. Without being able to define their aim clearly, they looked for more security and much the same freedom of action. Lansdowne, whom Salisbury selected to follow him at the Foreign Office, tried and failed to conclude the formal alliance with Germany that Chamberlain had explored fruitlessly in 1898. Prime minister still, Salisbury advised against the terms available but acquiesced in the Anglo-Japanese treaty of 1902, which entailed a departure from his international practice. The decline of his authority over the cabinet, exaggerated by some of its members, was apparent in other matters besides Foreign Office business.

The death of his wife in November 1899 after a long illness was more than a grievous personal loss. Her activity as a political hostess – an intelligent and vigorous champion of her husband – had done a great deal to offset the complaints of Salisbury's remoteness from ministers outside the cabinet and MPs. Hit hard on a personal level by her decline and disappearance from his life – his unmarried daughter Gwendolen replaced her, to some extent – he did not allow it to distract him from incessant toil. Rest had to be forced on a tiring man by sickness and convalescence; even then he was only momentarily out of touch. Naturally, the disasters in South Africa swelled the murmurs, heard from time to time since the 1880s, that the premiership and the Foreign Office ought not to be held by one man. It had been obvious from the press attacks on him before Fashoda that the real objection was to his policy; solicitude for his weakening health in 1899–1900 masked discontent with the "as it seems steady declension in power and grip of the Prime Minister". This picture of Salisbury simply reflected Lord George Hamilton's desire for a different response to events in China. There, as elsewhere, he and others found Salisbury wanting in his treatment of Germany: the concessions made to her over the years were "so clumsy in . . . methods and manner as to cause more offence than good feeling". This echoed some German criticism, especially from the Emperor. More disturbing to a conventional and generally loyal colleague was Salisbury's speech on the war in South Africa at the opening of the new session in February 1900: "the worst . . . I have ever seen attached to his name: cynical, satirical . . . wholly devoid of sound argument [as] an appreciation of the great crisis through which we are passing". In fact, Salisbury had analysed the failure of the British in the campaign to date, at several levels and as if he were in opposition. His ministers had reason to feel aggrieved. They, or a number of them, wished for a greater say in making foreign policy, and "unity of purpose" in making war.[3]

The concerted move to persuade Salisbury to relinquish his department can be observed in the letters of George Hamilton, those of St John Brodrick and Balfour's correspondence. The last exerted a decisive influence. Brodrick related how in the summer of 1900 Arthur Balfour fumed over his uncle's "apathy". The Queen held the key to his departure from the Foreign Office: as her minister, Salisbury might tell the monarch much less than he once did, but he retained a very strong sense of duty to the throne and to Victoria personally. If she pressed him to lay down that part of his double burden, he would probably do so at his age after five years that had taxed his strength. Even Balfour was not sure what his uncle would decide to do.[4] He resorted to an intermediary, the former chief whip, Akers-Douglas, taken into the cabinet in 1895, who up to the last moment saw "great difficulty" in getting Salisbury away from the Foreign Office. The Queen hesitated to ask him to give it up. One of the Liberal Unionists in the cabinet, James, had been assuring her that both the British public and the diplomatic world would regard him as "the only foreign minister", whose going would have a disastrous effect. "This has sunk in", reported Akers-Douglas from Balmoral. Victoria said she would press him to stay, not go, unless Salisbury himself and his doctors were "*really*" sure that the load he was carrying must be reduced. There was no question, Balfour replied, of letting his uncle continue at the Foreign Office: his health did not permit it, and Lansdowne, the replacement envisaged by Salisbury and the few he consulted, "will not alarm the public". The Queen in the Highlands proposed to send Akers-Douglas to Hatfield: "She shrinks from the task of telling him *she* thinks he ought to go".[5]

She had received a letter from the prime minister confirming that the doctors recommended lightening his burden, but adding that he felt strong enough to shoulder undiminished responsibilities. Salisbury knew that his health was a pretext: "outside opinion", he informed the Queen, "rather favoured a separation of the duties of Prime Minister and Foreign Office". He left the decision about his future to her: but she dispatched a reluctant Akers-Douglas southwards to represent, successfully, that opinion inside as well as outside the government wanted the change. Salisbury thought the position of a prime minister in the Lords was inherently weak and regretted his peerage. Rosebery's difficulties with the Liberal cabinet in 1894–5 were a case in point. "I could only leave the Foreign Office and remain Prime Minister by taking another office", he argued to a privileged critic, George Curzon, in 1898. The premiership had "no staff, no pay, no legal powers". The office of first lord of the Treasury, which he had held briefly in 1886–7, carried a salary, but without a prime ministerial presence in the Commons it did not give Salisbury what he sought. The head of a government, if he was in the Lords, needed the political weight of a great department of state. That was the lesson of his second administration, when he faced Churchill. He could not defer to the contrary view, however plausible the arguments: "To accept it now would be to accept a vote of censure".[6] Two and a half years later, he did take a salaried sinecure, the privy seal; no other course was open to him on the grounds of age and health that justified his retirement as foreign secretary.

The wider reconstruction of the ministry only increased the unrest among Unionist MPs. They freely criticized the promotion of three of Salisbury's family circle, too many not to be resented: his son-in-law the Liberal Unionist Selborne, an able minister, fully in sympathy with Chamberlain's imperialism, succeeded Goschen at the Admiralty; Gerald Balfour at the Board of Trade and Cranborne as undersecretary at the Foreign Office were less obviously qualified for their posts. Ridley, Chaplin and Cross were asked to give up the Home Office, the Local Government Board and the Privy Seal respectively. Goschen was glad to leave active politics, although he had hoped for an earldom instead of a viscountcy to gild his retirement. James survived narrowly, by virtue of his past services to Liberal Unionism. St John Brodrick followed Lansdowne at the War Office; C.T. Ritchie took the Home Office and Walter Long the Local Government Board. These were the main changes at cabinet level and they disappointed all round. Devonshire, who like Chamberlain was consulted, said that they had made "a great mess" of the reshuffle.[7] In evicting Chaplin and Ridley, Salisbury told them that fresh blood was imperative to tackle the "social questions" which he expected to occupy the new parliament. The premier did not try very hard to move Hicks Beach, who disliked the prospect of old age pensions quite as much as the Jingo mood in the government ranks, and decided that he would stay on at the Treasury for the time being to fight rising expenditure. "He seemed . . . anxious to establish that if he left us it would not be his fault", Salisbury recorded. Chamberlain had suggested offering him the Admiralty: but the chancellor was too big a man politically to be sent where he did not want to go.[8]

If St John Brodrick is to be believed, Salisbury without the Foreign Office was scarcely more than a figurehead. When illness did not keep him away, he was "epigrammatic and demoralizing to the last degree"; that is to say, apt to disconcert younger and less reflective members of the cabinet. It was not possible to ignore him in his own field, as Brodrick said he was ignored in other areas.[9] When he handed over the day to day running of his department to Lansdowne, it was to someone who did not see himself as breaking with the policy he inherited. If he was less independent of the cabinet, the new minister listened to his predecessor. Installed in a room at the Foreign Office, Salisbury was there, according to George Hamilton, more often than he had ever been. No one, apparently, thought of replacing him as prime minister until he determined on going. In October 1900 the government could not have spared him. On the evidence of his most persistent critic in the cabinet – though Brodrick did not attack him to his face – Salisbury remained capable of interventions for which his colleagues were grateful. There was a general unwillingness to let "the extreme Jingo party" dictate to them. Even in the last months before his resignation in July 1902, when he felt himself to be failing physically, he could display the brilliance that captivated everyone who worked with him.[10]

Down to the end, the party called on Salisbury for the oratory that had inspired Tories and Unionists since he emerged as Gladstone's rival on the platform. These final speeches were forward-looking and their message unchanged. He was, if anything, more urgent in his references to the moral demands of poverty on the state and property. Unionist MPs were, however, more interested in such questions as ritualism and temperance.[11] On the war, *Le Temps* of Paris wondered at his "invincible optimism" as the politically debilitating conflict dragged on, but conceded that he was not out of touch with his people. The French military attaché in London summed up the difference between Chamberlain's imperialism and Salisbury's neatly: with his ability to take the long view and his preference for it, the elder of the two old men was not in a hurry; Chamberlain, at sixty-six, was impatient to begin laying at least the economic foundations of imperial federation.[12] Whether they favoured a cautious start with protection, or shrank from it, the cabinet could no longer share the premier's confidence in a strong navy and the avoidance of a firm commitment to fight beside an ally, or allies, on the Continent. Balfour was oppressed by the realization, forced upon him by the war, that his country was militarily a third-rate power in a world more frightening than he had supposed. "I owe everything to Lord Salisbury", wrote George Hamilton, ". . . but he is not the man to tackle this critical situation". Salisbury's reputation stood higher with the Liberals, who correctly predicted that after him the Unionists would fall out among themselves. Despite his now large Tory following, Chamberlain had the aspect of a "political bogy", and not only to the opposition.[13] Balfour was, therefore, the unquestioned successor, under whose leadership the Liberal prophecy was fulfilled. Salisbury closed his career and died a year later with nothing like the volume of tributes that had marked Gladstone's retirement and passing. Had he gone after Fashoda, contemporaries, and historians, would have been kinder. In retrospect, his last years in office were not wasted.

## Leadership in War

"All wars are horrible", Salisbury told the Primrose League in May 1902, shortly before the Boer surrender. "It is frightful to reflect on the human misery . . . they involve". It was, he insisted all along, a just war. He countered the protests of the "pro-Boers", initially a very small minority of Liberals who came out against what they saw as territorial expansion regardless of right and driven by the exigency of the Stock Exchange. John Morley's denunciation of the imminent conflict as morally wrong was scathing about anticipations of profit in the City: "You may send the price of Mr Rhodes' Chartereds up to a point beyond the dreams of avarice. Yes, even then it will be wrong". Salisbury rejected that view of the war, so eloquently stated by Morley in September 1899, when he defended the government in November: "The cabinet has not had one farthing . . . from the Transvaal or . . . any other gold field"; a rash assertion when South African mining shares featured in a great many portfolios, if not in his own. The war was not being fought to acquire gold-fields and territory but solely to ensure "equal rights for . . . all races, and security for . . . the Empire".[14] The second of those war aims overshadowed the first after the "Black Week" of Boer victories in December. "We have been living in a fool's paradise", wrote Edward Hamilton in his diary. ". . . I never remember to have seen London more depressed". The conflict in South Africa now formed part of the larger concern for Britain's fate in a new century, which it seemed she was beginning with few friends abroad. "The elements and causes of menace and peril" that Salisbury went over in his speeches compelled his country to demonstrate her vitality in answer to Boer aggression, and prove the world mistaken in "the impression that we should never fight again".[15]

Consequently, Britain was safer for having resisted the Boers, provided she did not neglect the defences strengthened during the crisis, and particularly the army. The extended guerrilla phase of "this lamentable war" undeniably increased the political strain on the Unionist government. The Liberal leader, Campbell Banner-man, was moved to condemn the "methods of barbarism" involved in relocating Boer farming families to concentration camps, so called. The prime minister repeated that there could be no compromise with the guerrillas: the rest of the world was watching; give way in South Africa and "you will soon find you have no territory to defend" – anywhere. It was a trial that Britain had experienced before, and one that other countries had known.[16] In the Indian Mutiny the rebels had been beaten after similar operations over many months. France had crushed the Vendeans, Russia the Caucasians, Austria the Bosnians in guerrilla wars: was Britain to fail where they had succeeded? He used these arguments in his reply to the Tsar's plea on behalf of "a small people desperately defending their country". Would Nicholas II have complied with an ultimatum from Sweden to halt the movement of troops into his partly Swedish grand duchy of Finland – a case analogous to the Boer demand in 1899 that Britain should countermand her reinforcements for the Cape Colony? As for the duration of the fighting, which gave it the aspect of a "war of extermination", Russia's subjugation of the Caucasus had taken a quarter of a century.[17]

It was necessary, however, to offer the Boers inducements to lay down their arms, even though over half the Boer population of the two republics were either prisoners of war or had been removed to concentration camps. Salisbury had declared that "real independent government" in the Transvaal and the Orange Free State must be ended to prevent a recurrence of hostilities. "Perhaps", he added, "I should not be wrong in supposing that the first responsibility is that we must protect . . . native races". Eighteen months later, in November 1901, he promised the Boers self-government after the war, in due course, but "their independence is not consistent with our security".[18] The promise was written into the peace treaty signed in May 1902 between the British and the guerrillas' wandering leaders. In the preceding negotiations the Boers expressed their anxiety about the British attitude towards the African majority which, they complained, was being incited to turn on them. The settlement did nothing for the Africans: a tacit condition of its acceptance was its silence on their position under the new order. This was only one way in which Salisbury and his ministers felt that the moral advantage they had enjoyed at the start of the war had been eroded. They shared the unease at the spectacle presented by operations after the fall of Pretoria in June 1900. The prime minister's favourite general, Kitchener, compelled the enemy to come to terms by steadily depriving them of food, shelter and freedom of movement. This efficient ruthlessness, when directed against white men, was an uncomfortable novelty. Salisbury tried to keep it within bounds: they had to remember not only British opinion but the impact of "unwise measures" on the collective memory of the Boers whom they meant to integrate within the British empire. "Some degree of proof" was requisite before saboteurs of railways and telegraphs were shot; mere proximity ought not to establish guilt. Nor was it sensible to burn the house of a Boer commander just because he had refused to admit defeat.[19]

Salisbury was reasonably confident that the Boers could be absorbed by the dominant white race. If he was too optimistic in this respect, he did not deceive himself about the professional failings of the British army which the campaign had revealed, again and again, until the foe submitted to the sheer weight of numbers. The Boers fielded 60 000 men at most while the imperial forces built up to some 450 000. Surprised and out-manoeuvred, the British were slow to realize their inferiority, not in equipment, but in tactics and also morale. The government was naturally blamed for military incompetence. Foreign criticism, the moral discomfort of rounding up Boer civilians and national embarrassment at the soldiers' ineptitude sapped enthusiasm over nearly two years of guerrilla warfare following the apparently conclusive battles of 1900. "We have to push it through", said Salisbury of the war as it stretched on, calling for "dogged determination".[20] Acutely conscious of the absurd figure that Britain had cut before other nations since the war began, he quickly saw that only the methods that Kitchener employed would overcome the Boers' continuing resistance. Salisbury wanted, and got, the system of internal blockade that wore down the guerrillas: "You will not conquer these people until you have starved them out", he advised a hesitant Brodrick. Depriving the Boer commandos of practically unlimited mobility and supplies was legitimate and politically defensible, unlike the excessive severity to which he subsequently objected. Within the diminishing but still huge areas left to him, the elusive enemy should be hunted by flying columns that emulated the commandos' boldness, tactical sense and speed.[21]

Kitchener, who held the supreme command in South Africa from the end of 1900, had a very powerful friend in Salisbury. That was underlined when the prime minister ruled out London as the venue for peace talks between British and Boer delegations: Milner and Kitchener must be free to settle at a distance from the pressures that would be brought to bear on the British negotiators in London. The soldier's personality, standing at home and purposefulness made him the effective leader on the British side, at the conference table as in war.[22] Both he and Salisbury had been exasperated by the poor showing of subordinate commanders in pursuit of the formidable guerrillas, who even succeeded in getting a few more of the Cape and Natal Boers to join them when they invaded those colonies in 1901. Salisbury was dismayed, in private, by the performance of all ranks in what he, as much as anyone, felt was an "interminable" struggle, ". . . are our officers very inferior to what they used to be?" he asked. They seemed unable, or unwilling, to learn from the ambushes into which they fell with "very disheartening" regularity. "If we had had an army of Red Indians", he observed, "we should have been in many respects better off". British defeats in the opening phases of the war, when large formations attacked the Boers in strong defensive positions, had taught the generals a painful lesson: modern weapons had enormously strengthened an intelligent and resolute defence. Before the arrival of Roberts and Kitchener after "Black Week" in December 1899, Buller and other generals were outclassed by the citizen soldiers who led the Boers.[23]

The army's weaknesses were well known to politicians. Salisbury had avoided the part-time soldiering common in his class – he fended off his father's attempt to make him a militia colonel by pleading that the thought gave him stomach-ache – but he took an informed interest in the service. At the time of Cardwell's reforms in the 1870s he had argued against the abolition of purchase, seeing in it a mitigation of seniority's worst effects. In 1896 he raised the subject with his war minister, Lansdowne, after Cromer, himself once a regular soldier, had offered some "plain spoken" comments on the existing system. Modifications to promotion by seniority had not gone far enough: but he characteristically remarked on the difficulty of working the reformed machinery. Lansdowne's extremely complacent reply assured him that a new professionalism was discernible among younger officers, "and I am convinced that incompetency among the seniors will become rarer". Both Salisbury and Lansdowne deferred to "the Trades Union spirit which animates our army", to quote the first during the South African war. The social influence of the army – so strongly represented in Society and parliament – deterred governments from army reform between Cardwell and Haldane.[24] Salisbury thought of sending Kitchener from a pacified South Africa to the War Office as adjutant general, but concluded that without longer experience of high command he would "knock his head against a wall". The consequences of this political caution were serious: after a campaign against the tribes on the North West frontier in 1897 Lansdowne noted that the training and discipline of several battalions of British infantry had failed them in a theatre of war familiar to the army. Following the disasters of December 1899 Hicks Beach was one of those who drew attention to the deficiencies of regular cavalry: "If it is useless on the open veldt, *a fortiori* it would be useless in an enclosed country like this". Its drill and tactics were obsolete.[25]

If Salisbury and the government were criticized for their comparative neglect of the army, they and their public worked on the assumption that the navy and its continuous modernization came first. The prime minister was to blame, perhaps, for not making it clear to the cabinet that, in his opinion, they underrated the Boers, politically and militarily. Devonshire, as chairman of the defence committee, admitted to thinking that the Boers would never have the "audacity" to invade British territory: "we thought we could choose our own time". Looking ahead to the awkward questions that were going to be asked in parliament, the duke was anxious to shift some of the responsibility for "committing ourselves to a warlike policy with quite inadequate preparation" to the soldiers in the War Office.[26] Salisbury was braver: he indicted the organization of the state, dangerously outdated, in a Europe where the study of war and its requirements was deemed to be of primary importance. "In this matter we enjoy splendid isolation", he said sardonically. The Transvaal was supposed to have spent £800 000 in one year on intelligence compared with the "ridiculously small" amount of secret service money available to the British government. The first lesson of the war was that intelligence had to be paid for. There was no room for "spiritual complacency" about Britain's clean hands in that respect. Essential features of the British constitution must not be exempt from the broad review of national security he considered urgent: "there is something in your machinery that is wrong".[27]

The defects were many. He listed conscription, promotion by seniority, the relationship between parliament and the military, and Treasury control of public expenditure as questions that would have to be faced. He opposed the reintroduction of the old militia ballot, a form of selective conscription. It would have the appearance of a panic measure, causing "sinister pleasure and anticipation . . . [to] our enemies abroad". Promotion by seniority, he believed, did not prevail to the same extent in Continental armies. Parliament's authority over the War Office and the army was severely limited by the action of the Treasury. The Treasury's detailed control of departmental budgets in the spirit of Gladstonian economy had not been exercised "for the public benefit". These were all criticisms he had voiced previously: in the context of a succession of humiliating defeats they were taken to be special pleading. He was forced to make "a sort of apology" for his strictures on the Treasury: but his other points were valid. The reforming Liberal governments of 1905–14 tackled structural change in the army in time for an infinitely greater conflict. Salisbury's perception of what needed to be done could not be faulted: but his bid for support over the heads of colleagues implicitly censured for lacking his insight offended by its disregard for the conventions and for his own responsibility.[28]

Salisbury's political leadership in war reassured and restrained his countrymen. Enthusiasm for empire reached its peak in these years. The volunteer contingents from the settler colonies serving in South Africa were a striking manifestation of imperial sentiment. People forgot the well developed independence and the centrifugal tendencies of the self-governing empire. It was devoid, Salisbury reminded them, of "any coercing or retaining force" such as held its Continental counterparts together. His success at home in repelling the pro-Boers and the milder attacks of the opposition front bench was recognized. Lord Spencer, the most respected of the Liberal elder statesmen, could see no difference between the "New Liberalism" of his party's rhetoric for the twentieth century and the Unionism of the Salisbury ministry.[29] As a "great national asset" in himself – Edward Hamilton's description of him in 1902 – Salisbury had the moral stature to acknowledge and deplore the deaths of Boer women and children in the insanitary and overcrowded concentration camps while continuing the policy. "War is a terrible thing", he answered Malcolm MacColl, and the Boers should have remembered that. Burning farms and "the horrors of the . . . camps" resulted from military necessity, of which generals were the judges. Salisbury thought MacColl was probably right in arguing that the harshness of these measures would lose the Unionists many votes at the next election. If they did not do so, the compensation of £3 million for the destruction of their property given to the Boers under the terms of peace had done its work in Britain and South Africa. The rights and wrongs of the war were not an issue when the Unionists suffered their crushing defeat at the polls in 1906.[30]

"The generals thought it necessary". It was Salisbury's practice to back the man on the spot so long as he acted within instructions that set out their objectives clearly. He had distrusted the judgement of Sir Redvers Buller, sent to South Africa as commander-in-chief in 1899 when that officer was under-secretary for Ireland in 1886–7. The "note of instability" in his telegrams from the front was disturbing. His disastrous assault on the Boer positions at Colenso in December showed that he, like the other generals in the first few months of the campaign, was completely mistaken in his estimate of the enemy. After Colenso he went to the other extreme: his pessimism impelled Lord Roberts to tell Lansdowne that they were in serious danger of losing the war, and to propose himself as commander-in-chief in South Africa. The situation, and his standing, made Roberts' offer difficult to refuse. Salisbury had reservations about him, apart from his age. In his correspondence about the internal and external threats to India, this veteran of the Mutiny and Afghanistan had tended to be alarmist. Salisbury accepted him for South Africa, but with Kitchener as his chief of staff, and in fact deputy.[31] The prime minister had believed in Kitchener since the advance to Dongola in 1896: "a very remarkable performance", Salisbury wrote at the time, ". . . by the secrecy and swiftness of his movements, he has been able to do his work almost without any loss of life on his side". He wanted Kitchener in South Africa as soon as possible: "Time is everything, and his presence would be a stiffener". Although Kitchener disappointed at the battle of Paardeberg in February 1900, when it was Roberts' cautious tactics that made good his errors, the Egyptian general's ruthlessness with subordinates and understanding of irregular warfare on the veldt undoubtedly shortened the hunt for the Boer commandos. Salisbury's polite contempt for more conventional warriors emerged in his suggestion that Buller, who had many friends at Court and in Society, ought to go to India as commander-in-chief: "he is not a bad soldier *in peace*".[32]

Amid the gloom and humiliation of December 1899, Salisbury was sharply criticized even by those nearest to him. Selborne, then still an under-secretary, pressed for "a committee of public safety", on French revolutionary lines, to consist of Balfour, Lansdowne and Goschen, the other service minister. When parliament was not sitting, and often when it was, Salisbury worked from Hatfield, while Chamberlain retired to Birmingham in the recess: "it is a wise thing", said Selborne unanswerably, "to stamp a war with the spirit of direction". Salisbury and his whole cabinet gave a strong impression of having failed to do so. The defence committee that Devonshire chaired kept no minutes and took few decisions. A bigger war committee, on which Salisbury of course sat, existed beside it after the reshuffle of October 1900. The damaging impression that no one was really in charge persisted. It was not entirely unfair: in his conduct of the war Salisbury bore little resemblance to Palmerston during the Crimean conflict with his long experience of military administration and his very different temperament. On the other hand, the record shows that the prime minister, following the campaign as closely as he did, was fully involved in the most important questions and decisions relating to command and strategy after the War Office, Buller and the other generals in the field had comprehensively demonstrated their incapacity. Kitchener was his choice, and he endorsed Kitchener's methods. He did not pretend to enjoy the war, as Palmerston had enjoyed the shorter struggle with Russia. Salisbury imparted a sense of direction to government and people by his vindication of British motives, and also by his care to prevent the war from spreading.[33]

Seizure of Delagoa Bay, the Boers' outlet to the sea in Portuguese territory, was a standing temptation until Pretoria fell, especially at the lowest point of Britain's fortunes. Balfour, for one, hoped for Germany's acquiescence in a temporary occupation of the place, for which Portugal would be very expensively compensated at the rate of £100 000 a week. Salisbury asked the cabinet to remember that under her recent treaty with Britain, Germany had an interest in seeing Portugal descend into bankruptcy, which was to bring the recent partition agreement into force. As for France, she had every incentive to oppose a step to which Portugal would never willingly consent. Nor would Europe credit British assurances that the occupation was limited in time: "They cannot forget Egypt". He concluded by quoting a friendly warning from Belgium that occupying Delagoa Bay might very well unite the Continent in arms against Britain. Later, when the military wanted to pursue the fugitive Kruger into Portuguese territory and strip him of the documents and bullion he was taking into exile, the prime minister condemned the suggestion – "I think Roberts must have lost his head". It would be "mere brigandage". Salisbury's good sense, his regard for international law, and the facts of British sea power averted the formation of a Continental League to impose peace on his country; an idea canvassed more than once during the war. To say that Britain fought the Boer war "in splendid isolation" is misleading. Salisbury was adamant that even a blockade of Delagoa bay was impossible: neither Germany nor France would submit to it; as matters stood, they objected to searches for contraband of war.[34] In March 1900 he turned to the defence committee for a review of military resources on the premise that war with France within the next few months posed a threat of invasion when Britain was almost denuded of regular troops. By September he judged that the immediate danger had passed with Kruger's flight from the Transvaal. At any moment, France was dangerous only in so far as Germany withdrew her friendship from Britain. As always, Salisbury tried to prevent that consideration from tying Britain too closely to the greatest Continental power.[35]

## The Fear of Isolation

Unlike the public, politicians and diplomats were acutely conscious of the decline of Britain's prestige resulting from the army's failures in South Africa. The French ambassador in London, Cambon, thought it ridiculous to give Roberts a Roman triumph on his return from the war. Prince Münster, the German envoy in Paris and a former ambassador to Britain, who was no anglophobe, told the French foreign minister that the British demonstrably lacked an army worthy of the name. Even in London Society, predominantly Unionist, there were those informed critics who maintained that "our army system is rotten . . . (excepting a few regiments) . . . we should be no good against a European power".[36] Count von Wolff-Metternich, Hatzfeldt's successor at the London embassy in 1901, described the troops he had seen in the British capital as a "*rabble*". The Russian representative in Berlin, Count Osten-Sacken, went further and assured Wilhelm II that, in the opinion of one of Russia's best admirals, the Royal Navy, too, was worth little: three small European navies would be a match for it. The German emperor laughed, and suggested the ambassador should try telling that to the Greeks, Danes and Portuguese. Nevertheless, in October 1899 and again early in 1900, Wilhelm and his latest chancellor, von Bülow, sounded other powers about the formation of a Continental league to intimidate Britain into settling with the Boers. These, however, were ploys to step up pressure on her to accelerate the Samoan negotiations and then to indicate displeasure with the searches of German merchantmen for contraband of war. Wilhelm let the British know, simultaneously, that "sundry people are preparing to take liberties and foster intrigues" at their expense. So long as their navy was unchallengeable, "I do not care a fiddlestick for a few lost fights in Africa". France, Cambon ventured to point out to his government, had been the emperor's dupe, to the extent that she had responded to Germany's advances.[37]

As the British who had dealings with him understood, ambivalence rather than duplicity characterized Wilhelm's attitude to their country. He resented the independence that she displayed under Salisbury. It was not enough for him that Salisbury believed in a strong Germany as a necessity for both Britain and Europe. The emperor looked forward to the day when Germany had a battle fleet nearer in size to Britain's. Then she might be "chosen by the Lord as the instrument of His wrath". Writing to the Dutch queen, who had appealed for German diplomatic intervention in South Africa, he imagined their combined fleets dominating the seas, an aspiration that Salisbury had foreseen. The powers were not going to unite against Britain. He cited their reaction to the Jameson raid. "France has only one enemy in the world, and that is Germany", the French ambassador in London had said at the time, while the current foreign minister of Russia had remarked in 1898 that South Africa "leaves us absolutely cold". Through the Dutch, the emperor had recommended American mediation to Kruger: in global politics Britain took more notice of the United States than of European powers. For Britain's position in Europe was stronger than it seemed. The possibility that she might withdraw from the most onerous of her few firm commitments to the Continent alarmed the Germans. It would destroy the European balance if Salisbury and Chamberlain, deciding to concentrate on British interests in Africa and China, practically invited Russia to help herself to the Straits and much else. The British premier encouraged these fears by remarking that the world had turned its attention from the Balkans to the Far East and other regions.[38] Wolff-Metternich criticized the conclusions freely drawn from the setbacks in South Africa. Germany had not had to equip and supply a single army corps for service outside Europe. The British had by the middle of 1900 sent 200 000 men to a far off war; no other people, said one German general, could have done as much.[39]

If Britain was not to be underestimated, even on land, the Continental powers were satisfied that her "splendid isolation", as they insisted on terming Salisbury's policy, was a thing of the past. According to Friedrich von Holstein, the *éminence grise* of the German foreign ministry, an Anglo-German alliance was dictated by the evolution of super-powers: America, Russia and perhaps Japan. This was also Chamberlain's reasoning; although he had none of the German hostility to the United States, and ideally wanted a pact between Britain and Germany to embrace America. In another of his candid interviews with German representatives in London, Salisbury regretted the talk of a closer relationship when it revived in the darkest period of the South African war.[40] As the Anglo-German exchanges begun again by Chamberlain, with prime ministerial sanction, petered out nearly two years afterwards, Wolff-Metternich found the prime minister untroubled by the prospect of isolation while Britain believed in herself and in her fleet. Von Bülow acknowledged a great man in Salisbury; Chamberlain he mistakenly summed up as "a modern businessman . . . quite unscrupulous" in his ways. The conservative German aristocrats who served Wilhelm II had a certain affinity with Salisbury, however much they disagreed with his policies. They hoped to work on him through Balfour and Chamberlain. When premier and ambassador met in June 1900, Hatzfeldt emphasized the debt to Germany who had ensured at moments of tension that France could not attack Britain without fearing for her own safety. Von Bülow noted on his report the need to frighten the British with the continuing possibility of a combination between Germany, France and Russia aimed at them.[41]

These tactics made a considerable impression on Salisbury's colleagues. Britain's nicely judged distance from the Triple Alliance did not prevent defence expenditure from rising indefinitely, with at best a doubtful prospect of greater security. Hicks Beach, who registered his strong objections to this financial trend, owned that he had never seriously resisted spending more on the navy and did not wish to oppose anything that was really necessary to strengthen it further. Salisbury was withering about "the hallucinations of . . . admirals" and dismissed the scare that the French navy might fall on British shipping around the globe without a formal declaration of war. "The utmost they could do would be to confiscate a couple of P & O steamers". "Even if the French are pirates", he observed, "they are not idiotic pirates". The fears that inspired the scare were, however, real. It was not long since the interception of British supplies of imported food in wartime had been the subject of a cabinet memorandum from Ritchie at the Board of Trade.[42] "I realized", Salisbury confessed to the chancellor of the exchequer in 1901, "that we were in [the] face of a Jingo hurricane, . . . driving before it under bare poles". He dared not risk breaking up the cabinet until South Africa was pacified. Larger Service estimates than the country had been accustomed to seeing could be turned to account in defence of his foreign policy. The spending on armaments reassured those worried by British isolation.[43]

Salisbury's critics were not united. That ardent believer in imperial expansion, Curzon, sided with the prime minister in criticizing the proponents of integrating Britain with one or other of the European alliances. His secretary of state, George Hamilton, argued persuasively that if the governments of the German emperor, the Tsar and the Third Republic were less unfriendly than their peoples, there was no certainty that any of them could withstand popular pressure: "We are, I am afraid, universally detested". The disadvantages of a permanent commitment to another great power were generally overstated. The Germans probably would attempt to call the tune in such an arrangement, but reinforcement of their camp ought to make for lasting peace in Europe, and a reduction in everyone's bills for armaments. The Indian secretary was a prey to "very great anxiety" for an essentially commercial empire on whose trade her rivals had designs. The strain of the war in South Africa, "physically and financially", influenced his desire for the additional security that a treaty-bound ally would provide. Hamilton's letters to the viceroy exhibit the loss of confidence which turned the cabinet towards Germany. "All statesmen of imperialist instinct", Hamilton felt, were oppressed by the thought of Britain "isolated and alone", as the international situation deteriorated.[44] He, like Hicks Beach, considered that at a shilling in the pound, the rate imposed by the war, income tax had reached its ceiling, and even then he was not sure it would pay for an army capable of defending the empire at all points against the hostile combination of the powers recently foreshadowed. Lansdowne at the Foreign Office circulated his personal misgivings about future survival to the cabinet. It is unlikely, moreover, that Hamilton was the only minister to feel what no one put into a minute: that there were other parts of the world besides the Boer republics where Britain had "not [a] very strong legal or moral claim" to ascendancy, and lacked the means to enforce it without a struggle.[45]

Balfour might speak of Britain as a third-rate power, but his "conviction" of overall weakness was not shared by Salisbury and Chamberlain. The latter wished to make a powerful nation stronger in close association with a worthy partner: Salisbury did not think in terms of global domination. Nor was he more concerned for the future, once the critical period of the war had passed, than he had previously been. He was, if anything, inclined to take a slightly more cheerful view. His belief in German goodwill was "infinitesimal"; the French chamber of deputies was "full of Krugers"; Russian policy was "unscrupulous"; and he had never doubted that "Austria's disintegration is preparing". But, rightly, he did not consider that they could succeed in forming, let alone sustaining, a common front against Britain.[46] Though politely expressed, his attitude infuriated Holstein. The German recognized the "systematic anglophobia" of his countrymen, waxing through the 1890s, but attributed its intensity to Salisbury's "insufferable personality". The prime minister's policy was that of "a confidence trickster": he leant on Germany but evaded his European responsibilities. With Britain as its fourth member the Triple Alliance would be impregnable and peace assured. The Younger Pitt's coalitions against Revolutionary and Napoleonic France represented the insular power's true policy of pursuing her interests "*in concert with*" her peers on the Continent. For good measure Holstein accused Salisbury of being pro-French over the decade that included Fashoda. The British statesman would continue to act on the "theory of chestnuts", getting Germany to underwrite her security in Europe and enter a partnership of sorts in China.[47]

Holstein spoke of the "general hatred" which Salisbury's selfishness and opportunism incurred. If this vision of the prime minister was distorted by an unprofessional animus, the description of Europe's resentment was not too highly coloured. Many of the British cabinet were shaken by the realization of their country's unpopularity. It did not surprise Salisbury: "our character for *hubris* all over the Continent is a very bad one". Yet Von Bülow and the ambassadors in London did not find the Salisbury they knew "intolerable", although their imperial master reacted sharply to the coolness with which he received Germany's intimations of her wishes in the era of *Weltpolitik*. The Germans were not pressed to enlarge the Triple Alliance. As Salisbury noted, the rival alliance of France and Russia had lost much of its value for both participants at the turn of the century. Russia's adherence to the letter rather than to the assumed spirit of their agreement during the Fashoda crisis had exposed France's weakness. The Tsar and his ministers were increasingly taken up with expansion in the Far East, where Germany did not intend to confront her for Britain's sake. In that context, the Germans set a high price on "some form of alliance" with Britain to replace the looser relationship that satisfied Salisbury.[48] Approached by Britain for a defensive alliance, they offered her inclusion in their system of security, which would commit the new entrant to fighting for Austria and Italy as well as Germany if they were attacked by the other camp. The British also proposed to extend the two governments' co-operation outside Europe to Morocco, where Germans were keenly interested in becoming the dominant power as the native ruler's authority crumbled. Lansdowne conveyed Salisbury's unease in the Anglo-German talks. As Chamberlain had told von Bülow earlier, Salisbury did not want such an alliance with Germany any more than he did with France or Russia; the prime minister was a very shrewd statesman who believed it was always best to keep one's hands free.[49]

Renewed discussion of a formal alliance with Germany, for the last time in Salisbury's long official life, was not cut short by his statement of the case against it, circulated to the cabinet in May 1901. But the arguments he used deprived the British initiative of the indispensable momentum among his ministers. He was unimpressed by Wilhelm's repeated insistence that Britain could no longer distance herself from Europe and its combinations: "Count Hatzfeldt speaks of our 'isolation' as . . . a serious danger. *Have we ever felt that danger practically?*" The answer, of course, was yes, as his platform speeches attested. He was no more convincing when he claimed, as he had done before, that the dependence of a British government on Westminster's shifting moods was an insuperable obstacle to a binding commitment. He had himself solicited just such a pact in 1885. He was on much firmer ground in arguing that even the emperor's government, more independent of the Reichstag than he was of the House of Commons, would find it difficult to ignore "*bitter murmurs in every rank of German society*" at a promise to defend Britain, although it would be reciprocated. Von Bülow admitted that anti-British feeling in Germany exceeded the growing dislike and apprehension with which moderate British opinion looked on his country. One might talk, as both sides did in the course of the negotiation, of a natural kinship between branches of the "great Teutonic Race". There was no disputing Salisbury's most telling point: the liability of having to defend Germany and Austria from Russia in the heart of Europe was far heavier than the present burden of securing the British Isles from a French invasion.[50]

Salisbury's nerve held when he contemplated the Continental threat, whether seen as coming from Germany, from France and Russia, or from all three. One of his private secretaries, Eric Barrington, was reported as saying in July 1901 that over the last few months the prime minister had more than once been disposed to accept Germany's terms, but had decided that there was no "external necessity" driving him to take the fateful step. Lansdowne, Balfour and Hamilton could not be easy about their chief's estimate of the dangers they faced, which his analysis had cut down to size. But they saw that the terms were too stiff: "too big a fence to ride at", said Lansdowne to Wolff-Metternich in December after he and Salisbury had finally arrived at their decision. The documents, German and British, show that Lansdowne kept Salisbury fully informed and deferred to him, bringing his name and his views into discussions with the emperor and the diplomats. The British, "and above all Lord Salisbury", wrote Wilhelm in August, should open their eyes to the slow but steady decline in their international standing.[51] Well aware of the change, Salisbury was thinking, like the emperor and his admirals, of a global rather than a European balance of power. "It is very sad", he commented on the accumulating evidence of the United States' economic power with its potential for war, "but I am afraid America is bound to forge ahead and nothing can restore the equality between us". British intervention in the Civil War, perpetuating the split between North and South, might have restricted the future strength of a divided America to "manageable proportions". "*Two* such chances", he said bleakly, "are not given to a nation in the course of its career". The emperor told Lansdowne that if Britain turned towards America or Russia, she would surely be "pulverized" between them.[52] It was not the conclusion that Salisbury drew from the rise of America and another unnerving development, the rapid modernization of Russia.

He did not expect to have to fight the United States. Germany had enough to do watching her enemies on both flanks; the considered view of her generals. But he did not try to disguise the seriousness of relative decline. Britain, he warned the Associated Chambers of Commerce in March 1901, must be ready "to meet adversaries of whom it is undoubtedly true that as every decade passes, they become more powerful and dangerous".[53]

Yet the feelers that his government was putting out to Germany at the time did not stop him from implicitly contrasting the pessimism of his colleagues with the determination of businessmen facing German competition in their markets at home and abroad: "The spectre of Germany does not . . . induce them to despair of their country". The German menace to their trade had been exaggerated by journalists under "the necessity . . . of producing adequate copy". Britain's recovery from her early defeats in South Africa, he said later, had shown rivals that she could hold her own. They deceived themselves in imputing to her a collective failure of the will to survive and grow in a hostile environment.[54] Salisbury's last major speech as prime minister in May 1902 celebrated the quickening development of the settler colonies, on whose "irresistible power . . . the majestic fabric of the future empire" would be erected. Their growth, however, could not be forced without regard to the complex problems of every kind that imperial federation raised. "There is nothing more dangerous than to force a decision before a decision is ready"; a succinct expression of his constructive caution.[55]

The Anglo-German search for a better understanding, von Bülow complained, had always been frustrated by Salisbury's systematic evasion of closer ties. "You ask too much for your friendship", he had replied ironically, since 1898 and before then. Holstein, whose influence was such that even the emperor was afraid of him, still discerned a sinister motive in Salisbury's resistance to absorption into the Triple Alliance, and did not care who knew it. In a letter to Chirol of *The Times* he declared that "in all probability" the prime minister was counting on the great European war "which would perhaps have come already if all parties concerned were not by this time aware that Lord Salisbury is waiting for it". He was nearer the truth when he said "strict isolation" constituted Salisbury's defence against what his German critic revealingly called "the war epidemic" that all the powers were anxious to prevent while advancing their national interests by other means at their disposal. To say it yet again, "strict isolation", quite impracticable for a great power with an empire so widely spread, had never been Salisbury's aim: but his assessment of British interests, which it is hard to fault, required that the European powers should be kept at a safe distance, and it had provided for co-operation with the strongest of them.[56]

Lansdowne did not agree: he feared for Britain in Europe and the world. In the speech of May 1902 Salisbury reaffirmed his faith in the navy's ability to protect the empire which the natural barriers of sea, desert and mountain placed beyond the reach of Europe's conscript armies. But the navy alone could not stop Russia if and when she decided to exploit the huge advantage that proximity gave her in China. The Germans, it was clear to prime minister and foreign secretary, had no intention of standing up to Russia for the "open door", if to do so was inconvenient.[57]

The alternative to Germany in the East was Japan, who made the first move for a regional alliance with Britain. Their squadrons at sea, combined with Japanese land forces, were a credible deterrent to Russia and France if they aspired to a bloodless victory. The draft Anglo-Japanese treaty bound the signatories to mutual defence in the event of attack by two other powers in the area covered by the Chinese empire including the nominally subject Korean peninsula, where Japan and Russia disputed control of an ancient monarchy. The proposals met the demand on the Unionist benches that the government should be seen to be taking some effective action to stave off the predicted Russian domination of China, after the disappointment of the 1900 agreement with Germany. Alive to the predicament of British ministers, the Japanese drove a hard bargain. "There is no limit: and no escape", Salisbury protested. The British were committed to fight without any provision for a review of the circumstances leading to war. The Japanese offer to announce a policy of non-aggression was unsatisfactory: "It is a sentiment, not a stipulation". He remained absolutely opposed to "surrendering without reserve . . . the right of deciding whether we shall or shall not stake the resources of Empire on the issue of a mighty conflict".[58]

Balfour would have preferred Germany to Japan as an ally: but he accepted Salisbury's argument that ill-feeling between the German and British peoples was too strong. The agreement with Japan, Lansdowne argued, had the merit of re-stricting the "areas of entanglement": but only for Japan if it came into operation; Britain would have to take on Russia and France all over the world. Salisbury did not persist in opposing the treaty, which was signed at the end of January 1902. He chose not to kill it in cabinet, as he could have done. Hicks Beach and Ritchie were among those "very unhappy" with its one-sided obligations.[59] A minute from Salis-bury in the following March was wholly unrepentant in reasserting his dislike for treaties all too likely to outlive the wishes of states bound to their observance. "Our treaty obligations will follow our national inclinations and not precede them": as proof of that he cited the indifference of Austria, France and Britain to the post-Crimean guarantee of the Ottoman empire when Russia invaded in 1877. He doubted whether the invasion of Belgium would necessarily oblige Britain to fight the aggressor. Everything depended on public opinion and the attitude taken by the government of the day. His acquiescence in the Anglo-Japanese treaty is to be explained in the light of that doctrine which he had long held. It did not mark the end of isolation, as is often thought. The "area of entanglement" was remote; and the Japanese turned down the British suggestion of including India.[60] Balfour did not expect the Japanese leadership to be more trustworthy than that of the Triple Alliance. The Austrian chargé d'affaires in London, Count Albert Mensdorff, who was popular at Court and in Society, maintained that the English, at the highest level, were not Germanophobes, "and even Lord Salisbury is not an adversary of Germany". The "old gentleman" was, still, a political heavyweight and a thorough-bred Englishman. The English were not Continentals: what looked like malice and treachery, from the angle of Berlin, was really only their inherent "superficiality and confusion".[61]

If kindly meant, this was absurd; Holstein was more complimentary. Real-ism, tempered by humanity, distinguished Salisbury's policy, which his successors continued until August 1914. His sense of personal responsibility, under Providence, never deserted him. The trends of that age were clearer to him than they were to many, perhaps most, of his educated contemporaries; but he was immune to the crude determinism of good minds in his time. The abilities and reputations of individuals might make a difference on which the fate of peoples, and of Europe, hung. He instanced Pope Leo XIII, his old foe Abdul Hamid II and Franz Josef as men who had "by the simple process of dying, the power to throw the world into confusion". When he slipped quietly into retirement in July 1902, little changed outwardly. He had overcome the fear of isolation that gripped some of his ministers in 1900 and 1901. The continuity of his methods in foreign policy was assured, for as long as governments and the public remembered that the purpose of national security was peace with the powers, and America, as the precondition of the empire's prosperity and stability. If they did not lose their nerve, they might escape the Armageddon which general and naval staffs were preparing. Lansdowne, and Grey until the eve of the Great War, did not depart from Salisbury's policy in moving away from Germany and towards France and Russia: he had the possibility in mind, and the semi-detached position of Britain in Europe was preserved. It was, however, the resigning minister's singular achievement in domestic politics which *The Times*, critical of his actions or inaction abroad for years, saluted: the Conservative had enjoyed "a longer term of office as the favourite minister of democracy than . . . Mr Gladstone".[62]

## Old Policies and New

The preoccupation of premier and cabinet with the war in South Africa and its cost postponed old age pensions indefinitely. The weakness of the British Left, patently no threat to property in any shape, deprived Unionism of a powerful incentive to give more substance to the social rhetoric of Salisbury and Chamberlain. Keeping the government together until the war was over precluded experiments that would close off the return to a peacetime level of income tax. It was personally an uncomfortable position for Salisbury with his long public record as a critic of admitted deprivation and suffering; but it does not seem to have been one that greatly troubled his colleagues. Even Chamberlain, now the old man in a hurry that Gladstone had been, was much more interested in trying to build on the community of sentiment between the mother country and the settler colonies impressively demonstrated during the war. Both he and Salisbury were pushed by Balfour and a majority of their colleagues into endorsing a momentous piece of domestic legislation to which they had principled objections. While the Education Act of 1902 was by any standards a major social reform, it went through, from beginning to end, as the financial rescue of Church schools. The political price which the Church and her friends had to pay was an extension of secular control over her huge investment in education. The Erastian Devonshire saw nothing wrong in this enlargement of his department's responsibilities. Politically, it was a disaster for Unionists. Liberal Unionism never recovered from the widespread indignation of its adherents at what

ALLEYN'S SCHOOL LIBRARY

they considered a betrayal of moderate Nonconformity. In return for supporting Unionism, they assumed a right of veto over any significant change to the structure of the 1870 Education Act, and had indeed exercised it in 1896. They refused to see the new measure for what it really was, a large instalment of the policy of comprehension they had always wanted. The misunderstanding that surrounded the legislation lent credence to the mistaken view that Salisbury had lost interest in social reforms to rank with those which he and Chamberlain had carried in the 1890s.

Salisbury had learnt the lesson administered by the Commons in 1896, by Tories as well as Liberal Unionists. His government and their majority could not legislate for the Church on her terms, if they could legislate at all. The notion that he headed a very strong ministry was "one of the most foolish . . . that ever obtained currency". Resistance to Home Rule and support for the South African war obscured a "congenital division" in the cabinet, evident on most other matters but especially on those touching the relationship between Church and Dissent. He did not count on winning any Commons vote that involved religious loyalties and enmities; where they and "all internal questions" were concerned, the Liberal Unionists among his cabinet ministers were Liberals still. Writing in December 1901, Salisbury could not see his way to a solution of the Church's acute problems with the financing of her schools. He and Chamberlain would have preferred to avoid a reform of the dimensions which the bill of 1902 was to take. It is hard to understand why, after initial hesitation, the cabinet chose to run the risks plainly visible to the prime minister and his ablest colleague.[63]

But ministers did not divide along the lines he predicted. Salisbury and Chamberlain, the spokesman for Nonconformist Unionists, were on the same side, outnumbered by those who went with Balfour and Devonshire. In his memorandum of December 1901 to the cabinet, Salisbury recommended postponing radical change if more money could be found for Church schools without it. Chamberlain looked ahead to the alienation of Nonconformist electors from Unionism that resulted on a large scale. Balfour saw in the Church's crisis the chance, and the duty, to modernize the entire school system. Britain's relative decline in the world was being attributed to the limitations of a free and compulsory schooling that did little more than teach the three Rs. In recent years, Balfour had been showing signs of impatience with his uncle's caution, though it was usually justified by events. An ambitious education bill, taking forward the work of 1870, would be a good start for him as Salisbury's successor, and it would renew the government's vigour, drained by the war. The impression of a prime minister physically and mentally tired was fostered by confidences from Balfour's trusted private secretary, J.S. Sandars, for one. He spoke of Salisbury "now . . . the great difficulty – he cannot be induced to put his back into anything . . . his wonderful fluency is deserting him". Balfour asserted his authority, in effect, over a tiring chief, and over a formidable rival for the succession in Chamberlain, when the cabinet proceeded to frame what a genuine radical, Lloyd George, hailed as "a most revolutionary . . . bill".[64]

It replaced the school boards with the county council, and its urban equivalents, charged with administering the public sector in elementary education, and developing it gradually in secondary education. The Church's elementary schools were put on the same financial footing as their rivals and given rate aid, but only if both the managers of a denominational school and the local council agreed. In that case, the council was to have control of a school's secular teaching and minority representation among its managers. However, on the eve of Salisbury's resignation in July 1902 Balfour accepted an amendment in committee that compelled councils to extend rate aid to all church schools. The Nonconformist revolt of which Chamberlain had warned took place immediately, commencing with the next by-election. The Anglican majority on the Unionist side felt that they were driven to compulsory rate aid by the pressure on the Church's resources, including their own pockets.[65] Even moderate Nonconformists had always resented the taxpayer's contribution to denominational education: putting Church schools on the rates was more than many of them could stand. How far Balfour and Devonshire had underestimated the strength of religious convictions emerged again when another amendment aimed at ritualist parsons, but politically wider in its scope, gave councils a say in determining religious instruction in the schools they were now obliged to support. Salisbury, by then in retirement, let it be known that he disapproved of a "gratuitous affront" to the clergy. He had made it clear to Devonshire in 1900 that he would never consent to any encroachment by central or local government on the teaching of religion in schools belonging to the Church. The Duke regarded the claims of belief with indifference, when they were not a nuisance. Balfour's theological liberalism – he took Communion impartially in the Scottish and the English church – had been less obvious while he lived in his uncle's shadow.[66]

It was Salisbury's very detestation of evangelical Protestantism, which surfaced in a parliamentary reference to "the pitiless Puritan yoke" in 1901, that made him wary of its latent power. In domestic as in foreign policy, his inaction was considered. Though he erred in thinking the cabinet too divided to legislate on education as it had, the electorate was more religiously minded than Unionist politicians had become. He was not alone in foreseeing the adverse reaction to the education bill. George Hamilton said that Balfour and the Duke had not "gauged the full extent and intensity of the numerous and contradictory influences . . . to be either consulted or overcome".[67] The prime minister was not out of touch with the public. His sensitivity to issues that spelt disaster for Unionists was apparent on the question that tore them apart under Balfour's leadership. Worries about foreign competition and the arms race were moving protection into the forefront of politics. In respect of greater imperial unity, the topic bound up with protection, Salisbury adhered to his practice of discussing some broadly desirable change and reminding his mass audience of the inherent drawbacks. The rising tide of emigration to the settler colonies, the expanding markets for British industry, the returns on investment there, their democratic credentials, and colonial participation in the war – all these created a near-universal disposition to favour continuing, and if possible closer, relations with the self-governing empire. The infant Labour party was no exception. It could be argued that flourishing trade with the settler colonies made preferential tariffs superfluous as a reinforcement of very strong ties. Salisbury was inclined to "let sleeping dogs lie". "I am afraid the dog is awake", replied Schomberg McDonnell. Chamberlain hoped to exploit Hicks Beach's imposition of a small revenue duty on imported corn and flour in the budget of 1902, but the idea that it might be varied for colonial imports attracted sharp criticism in the Commons.[68]

Edward Hamilton, with whom the chancellor conferred at the Treasury, had no fears for free trade from the new tax: consumers were too much for politicians and producers. It was the point that Salisbury had repeated in his utterances on protection down the years. Democracy was King, and also stood in the path of the "socialism" which Gladstone detested in him. He had to tone down his speech of December 1900 on housing when he defended it in the Lords. It had not been his intention to pledge the government to more interference in the housing market than current legislation sanctioned: "I fear that, to the end, in some form or other, private enterprise must be our main reliance"; an allusion to the exaggerated hopes placed in housing trusts. Ratepayers' burdens prevented any substantial expansion of local government expenditure in that field. He reproached "some of the best friends of the poor", clerical and lay, with deterring capital investment in working-class housing by their attacks on its providers as "slum landlords". He came back to the subject of state intervention only days afterwards in a speech to businessmen: adding to the responsibilities and powers of government might be morally attractive but it must tend to discourage investment. Yet he could not hide from himself and the public "something of a contradiction between our obvious prosperity on some sides, and the great dread and apprehension which exist on others". His social conscience had not atrophied; nor was failing health the reason for this untypical defeatism. The active sympathy which he and Chamberlain displayed for the insecurity and hardship familiar to the masses had helped Unionism to put down deep roots in the population. Their language, and the important measures they had enacted, were viewed sceptically by Unionist peers and MPs without much political imagination. The government's electoral successes, 1900 following on 1895, suggested to them that further legislation of the same magnitude was not warranted by popular demand.[69]

Lightly taxed, except by local government in the big towns, respectable working men were not anxious to pay towards new provision for the welfare of the under-class, as they would have to do. This fact, and the derisory vote for Labour, removed any sense of urgency from consideration of social reform for several years. Chamberlain's concentration upon empire and protection was an acknowledgement of working-class priorities: employment and wages before social welfare. To his party, Salisbury's eloquent concern for those condemned to poverty and the fear of it, did not appear to be relevant to the political present. Some Unionists were eager for temperance legislation, an old-fashioned remedy for society's ills which Salisbury consistently opposed as an infringement of personal freedom. It was another, if relatively minor, cause of complaint against him. The Salisbury of the early 1900s did not strike Unionists as too conservative in the party sense or in principle. He was not conservative enough for partisan churchmen; too near the Liberal position on free trade *versus* tariffs; and still ahead of Unionism, on the whole, in the greater importance he attached to the social dimension of politics.

Salisbury and Chamberlain held Unionism together after it was born of Gladstone's determination to force Home Rule on the divided Liberals. The new party that grew out of the Tories, Hartington's conservative Liberals and Chamberlain's handful of radicals resembled Gladstonian Liberalism in being a broad church. Salisbury's reconciliation of these conflicting tendencies did not seem likely to outlive him. Rosebery was only one well qualified observer who thought so. The split between tariff reformers and free traders from 1903 owed a lot to Salisbury's previous encouragement of a return to protection if and when public opinion was ready. Without him to restrain both it and Chamberlain the protectionist tendency launched its destructive bid to capture Unionism. If he had tamed Chamberlain, as Gladstone did not succeed in doing, he had also given him full scope for his talents and assisted in his transformation into the idol of the younger and bolder Tories. Nevertheless, the combined protests of Salisbury and Chamberlain could not avert the cardinal error of the education bill, compounded by the fatal amendment making rate aid mandatory. It may be that the Unionists did not deserve to be led by two such men, lifelong rebels against the conventional wisdom that normally governs political parties. For all his cleverness and courage, Balfour was incapable of inspiring devotion, and he lacked the intuition which very seldom deserted his uncle in later years, the secret of his extraordinary achievements.

# The Balance Sheet

"The archaeology of opinion" was how Salisbury described the activity of those contemporaries who scrutinized his record for inconsistencies with a supposedly rigid Toryism.[1] His face was set firmly towards the future: he had little patience with nostalgia. With his talent for popularizing the fundamental truths of political philosophy, he had no difficulty in persuading naturally conservative audiences that the future must grow out of the past if they were to be spared the terrible experiences of America in the Civil War or the French in 1848 and 1871. Whether the topic was Ireland, or something less fraught, they could not wish the past away: "No one is to blame for the history they have inherited. But the history is there".[2] The level of intelligent discussion assumed in his speeches reflected social realities: the Victorian advance of literacy and prosperity, and the nature of class in Britain. His first party leader, the fourteenth Earl of Derby, had pointed out that the country was blessed with a complicated but flexible class structure in which competing interests tended to converge rather than diverge: for every man whose social status was clear, there were hundreds about whom "two people would probably not agree whether they belonged to the higher, or higher-middle, to the lower-middle, or to the lower class".[3] Although this was a politic exaggeration, it did not seriously misrepresent the situation that frustrated Marx's hopes and made the popular politics of Palmerston, Gladstone and Salisbury possible. Of those three, Salisbury had the hardest task: to educate "the stupidest party"[4] in the management of a democracy under conditions arguably more favourable to property and privilege than those prevailing on the Continent.

The popular character of Disraeli's Toryism never carried conviction in the narrow arena of Westminster. When Salisbury's leadership took shape, it was easier to move the party forward after the loss of a sense of direction following its defeat in 1886 and its poor showing in opposition. The "Tory democracy" of Randolph Churchill was Disraelian in its lack of substance. Salisbury made good the deficiency when he went to the people in the early 1880s at the same time as he sought to reanimate the Lords after fifty years of constitutional decline. He used the Upper

House to force a democratic redistribution of constituencies on Gladstone, who was not a radical on the content, as distinct from the language, of electoral reform. Many of Salisbury's fellow peers and some of his colleagues in the shadow cabinet were apprehensive in 1884, but his rhetoric had fostered the emergence of a body of Tory opinion in the Commons and the country that was unafraid of confronting Gladstone and his radical allies with their own populism. As this study has emphasized, he frightened Liberals, and especially Gladstone, by his readiness to encourage social reforms considered incompatible with Victorian freedoms. While Gladstone's decision to adopt Home Rule split his party, it was the change in Toryism wrought by Salisbury that gave the Unionist alliance its staying power. Their differences, personal and political, ruled out a successful partnership between Gladstone and Chamberlain: one between Salisbury and Chamberlain seemed less incongruous with every year that passed after 1886.

There was no "crisis of Conservatism" while Salisbury led the Tories. For the first time since the Great Reform Bill, they established themselves as the party of government, and effectively absorbed the Liberal Unionists. So little was left of their old Conservatism that, as Salisbury himself felt, party was near to losing its usefulness as the organizing principle of British political life.[5] The Salisbury governments, combining stability with the cautious progress in social legislation for which the prime minister argued, preserved Britain's singular immunity to the rise of the Left across later nineteenth-century Europe. After the fashion of Palmerston and Gladstone, but more boldly, the language he employed was designed to associate the literate and respectable working class of the towns with the rule of those above them. His speeches are the clearest illustration of an inevitable development. Undertaken willingly, it helped to perpetuate the obstinate belief of the British masses, then, that they were not oppressed. Salisbury's Toryism and Unionism treated as axiomatic the traditional freedom of the individual in Britain, including the more recent freedom of labour to organize, and the exemption of the great majority from direct taxation as well as from burdensome indirect taxes. Rising real wages took much of the pain out of the long contemporary recessions, while Salisbury kept economic policy before the public. By constantly recurring to the case for a moderate protectionism that would bring Britain into line with other nations, he gave voters the choice, which they did not take, to express their dissatisfaction with free trade.

Even Ireland was only a partial exception to this process of democratization. If Salisbury did not share Gerald Balfour's illusions about the superficiality of Irish national feeling, a firm hand – that is, repression – was relaxed, once agrarian agitation had been fought to a standstill. The 1898 Local Government Act, which ended the rule of the landlords in the Irish countryside, was seen for what it proved to be, a halfway house to Home Rule, or something more. The disarray of the nationalists after Parnell and the continuing decline of the Irish population outside the industrial corner of the North East, made Home Rule seem less threatening, if not more acceptable. No one put the case against it more powerfully than Salisbury: the streak of ruthlessness in him was apparent when he exploited the violence and intimidation that were held to disqualify the Celtic Irish from ruling themselves and the British and Protestant minority among them. His strictures upon the Irish national character were not easily forgotten, and served their purpose in succeeding elections. He and his Unionist public saw the Irish question in its international and imperial context: Britain simply could not afford to indulge the separatism rejected by the United States and by the multi-national Continental empires.

The looser framework of a liberal empire was vulnerable to a failure of political will at the centre, commencing with surrender to the Home Rulers. Salisbury, however, did not favour federation with the self-governing empire as he undoubtedly favoured protection; and a preference for indirect rule characterized him in India and elsewhere in the dependent empire. The demands of the settler colonies upon the imperial power were certainly irritating and sometimes a cause of real anxiety: but they, rather than India, demonstrated the spirit and the rewards of British expansion. Another manifestation of that spirit, the African territories acquired very largely while Salisbury was at the Foreign Office, justified his doubts of their economic value, except, of course, in Southern Africa. He had not wanted Britain to maintain a physical presence in Egypt after the Sudan was recovered and Gordon avenged. The acquisitions in East and West Africa formed part of the diplomatic bargaining primarily intended to underpin Britain's position in Europe, though he had also to accommodate traders, missionaries and, not least, Jingoes. He was reluctant to embark on the new war with Afrikaner nationalism in South Africa which he had nevertheless foreseen: Majuba, like the death of Gordon at Khartoum, was living history. One way or another, by British immigration or by British arms, Boer domination of South Africa had to be averted. In his calculations, strategic and political factors, not omitting the welfare of black Africans, outweighed the investments on the Rand.

The South African war confirmed the soundness of Salisbury's foreign policy, if the army let him down badly in the field. He had always taught his countrymen that "where there is liability to attack, attack will come":[6] Britain and her possessions provided a tempting target for her rivals. An ever stronger navy – his contribution to the international arms race – was not enough in itself. In addition to the threat of invasion across the Channel, Britain's global network of trade, investment and colonies required the confidence derived from power and security if it was to continue to flourish. The fear that the great powers of the Continent might combine on land and sea to "treat the English empire as divisible booty" inspired his policy.[7] He guarded against the latent peril by attaching Britain to the greatest of them, but not as closely as Germany wished. Salisbury offered, and delivered, co-operation that took much of the risk out of British expansion beyond Europe. The partition of East Africa in 1890 and the proposed partition of the Portuguese empire in 1898 bought Germany's official goodwill, well worth having at the time of Fashoda and in the South African conflict. As he admitted, the Anglo-German relationship was not ideal, and occasionally humiliating: but it made a dangerous world relatively safe for his country. On the other hand, he resisted integration with the Triple Alliance: it would leave Britain with no escape from the Armageddon which he saw must sooner or later engulf a Europe divided into armed camps.

Salisbury believed a peaceful division of the Ottoman empire might have reduced tension all round among the European powers. The failure to obtain their agreement was his worst disappointment at the Foreign Office. It did not affect the admiration of Liberals for his policy as a whole: his aims of peace, prosperity and national security without a binding commitment to a Continental alliance, differed from theirs only in laying more emphasis on security and empire. Where the morality of war is concerned, Salisbury stands with Gladstone rather than with Disraeli or Chamberlain. If Salisbury thought less of Gladstone than the Liberal statesman did of him, they had a great deal in common as men profoundly influenced by their religious formation in the Oxford Movement. The evolutionary politics they both adopted was pragmatic: their Tractarian vision of human nature and history remained intact. "Nothing is stable, nothing is permanent in this world", said Salisbury on the platform:[8] and it might have been Gladstone. Their passionate loyalty to the idea of a Christian society, dated though it seemed to many minds, still had a compelling appeal. The familiar depiction of Salisbury as someone whose statecraft reflected a "settled and sardonic belief that things are as they are in the most ironic of possible worlds" is quite misleading.[9] Man's fallen nature did not relieve him of the obligation to make the same world a better place than he found it, for his time at least. Robert Cecil's intellect and his faith, it was remarked, had the quality that one discerns in Pascal.[10]

# Manuscript Sources

| | |
|---|---|
| Acland P. | Acland papers, Bodleian Library |
| Austin P. | Austin papers, Bristol University Library |
| Avebury P. | Avebury papers, British Library, London (Department of Manuscripts) |
| Benson D. | Archbishop Benson diaries and papers, Trinity College, Cambridge |
| Benson P. | Archbishop Benson papers, Lambeth Palace Library, London |
| Balfour P. | Balfour papers, British Library, London (Department of Manuscripts) |
| Bertie P. | Bertie papers, British Library, London (Department of Manuscripts) |
| Cabinet P. | Cabinet papers (microfilm), Cambridge University Library |
| Cadogan P. | Cadogan papers, House of Lords Record Office |
| Cairns P. | Cairns papers, Public Record Office |
| Carlingford P. | Carlingford diaries, British Library, London (Department of Manuscripts) |
| Carnarvon P. | Carnarvon diaries and papers, British Library, London (Department of Manuscripts) |
| Carnarvon P. (P.R.O.) | Carnarvon papers, Public Record Office |
| Chamberlain P. | Chamberlain papers, Birmingham University Library |
| Chilston P. | Chilston papers (1st Viscount), Kent Record Office, Maidstone |
| Churchill P. | Lord Randolph Churchill papers, Cambridge University Library |
| Council of India P. | Council of India papers, British Library, London (Oriental and India Office) |
| Cranbrook P. | Cranbrook papers, East Suffolk Record Office, Ipswich |
| Cromer P. | Cromer papers, Public Record Office |

Cross P.  Cross papers, British Library, London (Department of Manuscripts)

Curzon P.  Curzon papers, British Library, London (Oriental and India Office)

Derby P.  Derby diaries and papers (14th and 15th Earls) Liverpool Record Office

Devonshire P.  Devonshire papers (8th Duke), Chatsworth House, Derbyshire

Dilke P.  Dilke papers, British Library, London (Department of Manuscripts)

Dufferin P.  Dufferin and Ava papers, British Library, London (Oriental and India Office)

Durand P.  Durand papers, School of Oriental and African Studies, London

Gladstone P.  Gladstone papers, British Library, London (Department of Manuscripts)

Goodwood P.  Goodwood papers (6th Duke of Richmond and Gordon), West Sussex Record Office

Granville P.  Granville papers, Public Record Office

Halsbury P.  Halsbury papers, British Library, London (Department of Manuscripts)

Hambleden P.  Hambleden papers, W.H. Smith Ltd

Hamilton P.  Sir E.W. Hamilton diaries and papers, British Library, London (Department of Manuscripts)

Hobbs P.  Hobbs papers (16th Earl of Derby), Corpus Christi College, Cambridge

Hughenden P.  Hughenden papers (microfilm), Cambridge University Library

Iddesleigh P.  Iddesleigh diaries and papers, British Library, London (Department of Manuscripts)

Jomini-Onou P.  Jomini-Onou papers, British Library, London (Department of Manuscripts)

Lansdowne P.  Lansdowne papers (5th Marquess), British Library, London (Department of Manuscripts); and Lansdowne papers (5th Marquess), British Library, London (Oriental and India Office)

Lascelles P.  Lascelles papers, Public Record Office

Lawrence P.  Lawrence papers, British Library (Oriental and India Office)

Layard P.  Layard papers, British Library, London (Department of Manuscripts)

Liddon D.  Liddon diaries, Liddon House, London

Long P.  Long papers, Wiltshire Record Office

Lytton P.  Lytton papers (1st Earl and Countess), British Library, London (Department of Manuscripts); and Lytton papers, British Library, London (Oriental and India Office)

| | |
|---|---|
| Malet P. | Malet papers, Public Record Office |
| Midleton P. | Midleton papers, British Library, London (Department of Manuscripts) |
| Midleton P. (P.R.O.) | Midleton papers, Public Record Office |
| Monson P. | Monson papers, Bodleian Library |
| Morier P. | Morier papers, Balliol College, Oxford |
| Northbrook P. | Northbrook papers, British Library, London (Oriental and India Office) |
| Paget P. | Paget papers, British Library, London (Department of Manuscripts) |
| Royal Archives | Queen Victoria's correspondence and journal; papers of Edward VII, Windsor |
| Ripon P. | Ripon papers (1st Marquess), British Library, London (Department of Manuscripts) |
| Roberts P. | Roberts papers, National Army Museum, London |
| St Aldwyn P. | St Aldwyn papers (1st Earl), Gloucestershire Record Office, Gloucester |
| Salisbury P. | Salisbury papers (3rd and 4th Marquesses), Hatfield House, Hertfordshire |
| Satow P. | Satow papers, Public Record Office |
| Scott P. | Sir Charles Scott papers, British Library, London (Department of Manuscripts) |
| Selborne P. (Bodleian) | Selborne papers (2nd Earl), Bodleian Library, Oxford |
| Selborne P. (Lambeth) | Selborne papers (1st Earl), Lambeth Palace Library, London |
| Simmons P. | Simmons papers, Public Record Office |
| Stanmore P. | Stanmore papers, British Library, London (Department of Manuscripts) |
| Tait P. | Archbishop Tait papers, Lambeth Palace Library |
| Temple P. | Archbishop Temple papers, Lambeth Palace Library, London |
| White P. | White papers, Public Record Office |

# *Notes*

## Abbreviations

| | |
|---|---|
| **Benson/D.** | Diaries of Archbishop Benson, at Trinity College, Cambridge. |
| **B.Q.R.** | *Bentley's Quarterly Review* |
| **Carlingford/D.** | Unpublished diaries of Chichester Fortescue, Baron Carlingford, in the Department of Manuscripts, British Library |
| **Carnarvon/D.** | Unpublished diaries of the 4th Earl of Carnarvon, in the Department of Manuscripts, British Library |
| **Cranbrook/D.** | N.E. Johnson (ed.), *The Diary of Gathorne Hardy, later Lord Cranbrook, 1866–1872. Political Selections* (Oxford, 1981) |
| **D.D.** | J.R. Vincent (ed.), *A Selection from the Diaries of Edward Henry Stanley, 15th Earl of Derby between September 1869 and March 1878*, Camden 5th series (London, 1994) |
| **D.D.C.P.** | J.R. Vincent (ed.), *Disraeli, Derby and the Conservative Party. Journals and Memoirs of Edward Henry, Lord Stanley, 1849–1869* (Hassocks, Sussex, 1978) |
| **D.D.F.** | Ministère des Affaires Etrangères, *Documents Diplomatiques Français, 1871–1914*, série 1 and 2, 32 vols (Paris, 1929–62) |
| **D.D., L.R.O.** | Unpublished diaries of the 15th Earl of Derby in the Liverpool Record Office |
| **EWH/D.** | Unpublished diaries of Sir Edward Hamilton, in the Department of Manuscripts, British Library |
| **Gladstone Diaries.** | H.C.G. Matthew (ed.), *The Gladstone Diaries, and Cabinet Minutes and Prime Ministerial Correspondence*, 14 vols (Oxford, 1968–94) |
| **Gladstone–Granville Correspondence 1868–1876 and 1876–1886.** | A. Ramm (ed.), *The Political Correspondence of Mr Gladstone and Lord Granville, 1868–1876*, 2 vols (London, 1952) and *1876–1886*, 2 vols (London, 1962) |
| **3H, 4H.** | *Hansard's Parliamentary Debates*, 3rd and 4th series |
| **HHM/3M (or 4M).** | Papers of the 3rd and 4th Marquesses of Salisbury, at Hatfield House, Hertfordshire |

| | |
|---|---|
| **J.C.P.** | Papers of Joseph Chamberlain at the University of Birmingham. |
| **Liddon/D.** | Unpublished diaries of Canon H.P. Liddon, at Liddon House, London |
| **M. & B., Disraeli.** | W.F. Monypenny and G.E. Buckle, *The Life of Benjamin Disraeli, Earl of Beaconsfield*, new edn, 2 vols (London, 1929) |
| **P. and L.** | E.D. Steele, *Palmerston and Liberalism, 1855–1865* (Cambridge, 1991) |
| **P.E.A.** | *Politique Extérieure de l'Allemagne, 1870–1914*, 32 vols (Paris, 1927–1939), the French translation of the published German diplomatic documents, *Die Grosse Politik der europäischen Kabinette*, 40 vols in 54 (Berlin, 1922–6) |
| **Q.V.L. (2) or (3)** | G.E. Buckle (ed.), *The Letters of Queen Victoria, . . . Second Series . . . between . . . 1862 and 1878*, 2 vols (London, 1926) and *Third Series . . . between . . . 1886 and 1901*, 3 vols (London, 1930–32) |
| **Q.R.** | *Quarterly Review* |
| **R.A.** | Royal Archives, Windsor Castle |
| **Salisbury, I to V.** | Lady Gwendolen Cecil, *Life of Robert, Marquess of Salisbury*, 4 vols (London, 1929–32); vol. V is the unpublished and incomplete MS made available to me by Hugh Cecil. |
| **S.M.P.** | Lord Blake and Hugh Cecil (eds), *Salisbury: The Man and his Policies* (London, 1987) |
| **S.R.** | *Saturday Review* |
| **T.T.** | *The Times* |

# Introduction

1. G.R. Elton, *Modern Historians on British History, 1485–1945* (London, 1970), pp. 111–12.

2. A.L. Kennedy, *Salisbury, 1830–1903: Portrait of a Statesman* (London, 1953); Robert Taylor, *Lord Salisbury* (London, 1975).

3. Jeremy Bentham, *The Theory of Legislation*, ed. C.K. Ogden (London, 1931), pp. 109–26.

4. HHM/3M/DD, Salisbury to G.M.W. Sandford, MP, 25/11/65. The marriage in question was that of Princess Helena to Christian of Schleswig-Holstein-Sonderburg-Augustenburg.

5. Hugh Cecil, "Lady Gwendolen Cecil: Salisbury's Biographer", in *S.M.P.*, pp. 60–89, on this remarkable woman.

6. Sir T. Erskine May, *The Constitutional History of England since the Accession of George the Third, 1760–1860* (3 vols) (London, 1871), p. 165.

   Among living historians, Lord Blake considers Salisbury "a great foreign minister, [but] essentially negative, indeed reactionary in home affairs", *The Conservative Party from Peel to Churchill* (London, 1970), p. 132. While Professor P.T. Marsh's estimate is more generous, he still sees Salisbury as someone who "held back the popular tide for twenty years", *The Discipline of Popular Government: Lord Salisbury's Domestic Statecraft, 1881–1902* (Hassocks, Sussex, 1978), p. 326. Professor Paul Smith is clear that "into the 'progressive' strain of modern Conservatism he simply will not fit", *Lord Salisbury on Politics. A Selection from his Articles in the Quarterly Review, 1860–1883* (Cambridge, 1972), p. 1. Professor H.C.G. Matthew is sharper about "the narrow cynicism of Salisbury", *Gladstone Diaries*, X, pp. cxxxix–cxl. Even the short biography by Mr Robert Taylor – a sympathetic portrait – concludes that its subject was generally "on the defensive", *Lord Salisbury*, p. 191. Though an admirer of Salisbury, Maurice Cowling does not differ very much

from these and other critics: the party leader and prime minister found the democracy born of the 1867 and 1884 Reform Acts as "perhaps less objectionable than he
had expected – succeeding, through his public *persona*, in mitigating some part of its
nastiness", *Religion and Public Doctrine in Modern England* (2 vols) (Cambridge, 1980–85), I,
p. 387.

7.  HHM/3M/C, Salisbury to Lord Lytton, 2/11/77.
8.  *Gladstone Diaries*, XI, pp. 417–18, Gladstone to Lord Southesk, 27/10/85.
9.  *Q.V.L.* (3), I, pp. 613–14, Salisbury to the Queen, 10/6/90; *T.T.*, 10/11/97, at the
    Mansion House.
10. *Ibid.*, 6/5/85, Hackney, and 10/11/97.
11. *Ibid.*, 30/6/98, at the United Club; *P.E.A.*, X, pp. 123–4, Count von Hatzfeldt, ambas-
    sador in London, to the German foreign ministry, 16/5/98.
12. The years spanned by Salisbury's governments, 1885–1902, have been seen as part of
    an extended "crisis of Conservatism" in E.H.H. Green, *The Crisis of Conservatism* (Lon-
    don, 1995). Since the Unionist alliance won three out of four general elections between
    1886 and 1900, the Liberals had more reason, then, to worry about their identity and
    their future.
13. HHM/3M/E, Salisbury to Goschen, 5/10/90; A. Ponsonby, *Henry Ponsonby: Queen
    Victoria's Private Secretary* (London, 1942), pp. 199–200, Salisbury to Ponsonby, 29/11/
    85; *T.T.*, 8/7/93, at the Junior Constitutional Club.
14. Hughenden P. (B/XX/Ce), Salisbury's memorandum of 2/3/74 on legislation upon
    ritualism; HHM/3M/D, Salisbury to his cousin, the Rev. E.S. Talbot, 5/3/90; Devon-
    shire P. (340. 2833), Salisbury to his cabinet colleague, the 8th Duke of Devonshire,
    24/9/1900 – three examples of his use of the words "civil war" to describe the threat
    of disruption hanging over the Establishment.
15. J.M. Hughes, *Emotion and High Politics: Personal Relations at the Summit in Later Nineteenth-
    Century Britain and Germany* (Berkeley and Los Angeles, 1983), ch. 4; A. Meyendorff,
    *Correspondance Diplomatique de M. de Staal (1889–1900)* (2 vols) (Paris, 1929), II, p. 70, de
    Staal to Giers, 5/11/90; E.W. Hamilton P. (48618), John Morley to Sir E.W. Hamilton,
    31/7/02.
16. *Psalms*, 116: 11; HHM/3M/E, the 8th Duke of Argyll to Salisbury, 16/7/92.
17. *T.T.*, 24/5/86 and 22/5/89, 20/4/94 to the Primrose League; H. Pelling, "The Work-
    ing Class and the Origins of the Welfare State", in H. Pelling, *Popular Politics and Society
    in Late Victorian Britain* (London, 1968); and R. McKibbin, "Why was there no Marxism
    in Britain?", in R. McKibbin, *The Ideologies of Class: Social Relations in Britain, 1880–1950*
    (Oxford, 1990).
18. HHM/3M/D, Salisbury to Lady Janetta Manners, 25/6/84.
19. *T.T.*, 20/6/1900; *Q.R.*, October 1871, "The Commune and the Internationale", p. 560;
    and see the excellent dissertation by S.T. Wang, "Lord Salisbury and Nationality in the
    East" (Ph.D thesis, University of Leeds, 1994).
20. *T.T.*, 19/5/92, at Hastings; 22/5/89, to the Primrose League.

## Chapter 1: Formative Influences

1.  EWH/D (48652), 19/4/90; Lady Longford, *Wellington: Pillar of State* (London, 1972),
    pp. 297–8, for Lady Salisbury's close friendship with the "Iron Duke".
2.  J. Morley, *The Life of Richard Cobden* (2 vols) (London, 1896), p. 220, Cobden to W.S.
    Lindsay, MP, 23/3/58.

3. *Hertford Mercury*, 12/4/68. The main sources for the young Robert Cecil's family and upbringing are: *Salisbury*, I, ch. i; Lord David Cecil, *The Cecils of Hatfield House* (London, 1973); and Kenneth Rose, *The Later Cecils* (London, 1975).

4. *Salisbury*, I, pp. 8–16; Cecil, *The Cecils of Hatfield House*, pp. 219–21. The trials and rewards of an Etonian schooling in the first half of the nineteenth century are described in S.G. Checkland, *The Gladstones: A Family Biography 1764–1851* (Cambridge, 1971), pp. 131–9, 201–16.

5. *Salisbury*, I, pp. 13–16, Robert to his father, 13 and 14/5/44.

6. *S.R.*, 8/12/60, "Private and Public Schools", pp. 727–8.

7. J. Otter, *Nathaniel Woodard. A Memoir of his Life* (London, 1925); *S.R.*, 8/12/1860, pp. 727–8.

8. *Ibid.*

9. Cecil's time at Oxford is described in *Salisbury*, I, pp. 20–25; Cecil, *The Cecils of Hatfield House*, pp. 222–4; F. Meyrick, *Memories of Life at Oxford* (London, 1905), pp. 84–5; and J.F.A. Mason, "Lord Salisbury: A Librarian's View", in *S.M.P.*, pp. 10–12. The best introduction to Tractarian Oxford is by P.B. Nockles in M.G. Brock and M.C. Curthoys, *The History of the University of Oxford*, vol. VI, pt i (Oxford, 1997), ch. 7.

10. HHM/3M/Diary, 12/7/51.

11. H.A. Morrah, *The Oxford Union, 1823–1923* (London, 1923), pp. 137–9; Meyrick, *Memories of Life at Oxford*, p. 85; *Salisbury*, I, pp. 20–25.

12. HHM/3M/Misc., Palmer to A.D. Godley, 17/5/51.

13. HHM/3M/Diary, 3/12/51, 7/2/52.

14. *Salisbury*, I, ch. iv, devoted to Cecil's religious beliefs; Cecil, *The Cecils of Hatfield House*, pp. 222–3; Carnarvon P. (60758), Salisbury to Carnarvon, 22/2/70.

15. HHM/3M/Diary, 17/4/52; *Salisbury*, I, p. 28, letter of 5/12/51.

16. *Ibid.*, pp. 25, 49.

17. Cecil, *The Cecils of Hatfield House*, p. 213, for a sketch of Cecil's stepmother; *P. and L.*, pp. 349–56 for the colonies of settlement at this period.

18. HHM/3M/Diary, 3/12/51, 7/2/52.

19. *Ibid.*, E. Scott (ed.), *Lord Robert Cecil's Gold Fields Diary* (Melbourne, 1945), p. 19; *Salisbury*, I, pp. 29–34, letters to several correspondents.

20. *Ibid.*, p. 29; G. Rowell, *Themes and Personalities of the Catholic Revival in Anglicanism* (Oxford, 1983), pp. 166–71, for a portrait of the Tractarian Bishop Gray.

21. J.E.T. Rogers (ed.), *Speeches on Public Policy by the Rt Hon. John Bright* (London, 1878), p. 300.

22. Quoted in *P. and L.*, p. 178.

23. *Salisbury*, I, pp. 22, 32–4, letters to Conybeare and Salisbury.

24. Quoted in C.C. O'Brien, *The Great Melody: A Thematic Biography of Edmund Burke* (London, 1992), p. xxxii.

25. *Salisbury*, I, pp. 35–8, Cecil to Salisbury, 2/9/52.

26. *Ibid.*, pp. 38–40, Cecil to Lady Mary Salisbury; pp. 50–1, Cecil to Lord Salisbury, April 1855.

27. *Ibid.*, pp. 65–9; quotation from p. 67, Salisbury to Disraeli, 23/12/58.

# Chapter 2: The Rising Politician

1. *Salisbury*, I, pp. 49, 52–65; Cecil, *The Cecils of Hatfield House*, pp. 251–3.

2. Lady Gwendolen Cecil, "Lord Salisbury in Private Life", in *S.M.P.*, esp. pp. 52–3.

3. *Salisbury*, I, pp. 58–62, Cecil to Salisbury, 27/11/56, 1/5/57; HHM/3M/E, statement by Mary, Lady Salisbury, 18/7/56.

4. *D.D.C.P.*, p. 222 (21/7/64); *Salisbury*, I, pp. 63–9; 1st Earl of Selborne, *Memorials, Pt II: Personal and Political, 1865–1895* (2 vols) (London, 1898), I, p. 8; F.M.L. Thompson, "Private Property and Public Policy", in *S.M.P.*, p. 258.

5. 3rd Earl of Malmesbury, *Memoirs of an Ex-Minister* (London, 1885), p. 350, diary, 9/2/55.

6. The word "progressive" is May's in his influential *Constitutional History of England since the Accession of George the Third, 1760–1866*, I, p. 165.

7. The Toryism of these years has been studied in R.M. Stewart, *The Foundations of the Conservative Party 1830–1867* (London, 1978) and his "'The Conservative Reaction': Lord Robert Cecil and Party Politics", in *S.M.P.*, pp. 90–115; Blake, *The Conservative Party from Peel to Churchill*, chs 3–4 and his *Disraeli* (London, 1966); and also in *P. and L.*, ch. 6, in the context of the dominant Liberalism.

8. *D.D.C.P.*, pp. 200, 208 (28/7/63, 21/7/64).

9. *Salisbury*, I, p. 66.

10. *D.D.C.P.*, pp. 206, 211 (30/1/64, 11/3/64). For the attacks on Disraeli, see pp. 28–42 below.

11. *P. and L.*, p. 62; *3H*, cxxxvii, 185–6 (27/3/55).

12. *P. and L.*, p. 50.

13. J.B. Conacher, *Britain and the Crimea: Problems of War and Peace* (London, 1987), p. 70; M. & B., *Disraeli*, I, p. 1443 (2/2/56).

14. *3H*, cxliv, 1538–41 (27/2/57); *P. and L.*, chs 10, 11 and 13 for foreign policy and empire under the Palmerston governments.

15. *S.R.*, 7/1/60, "The Story of New Zealand", pp. 19–20.

16. *Salisbury*, I, p. 87, Cecil to his wife, 14/2/59.

17. *3H*, clxix, 1151–8 (6/3/63); clviii, 1833–6 (31/5/60); cxli, 1413–15 (5/3/61). T.A. Jenkins (ed.), *The Parliamentary Diaries of Sir John Trelawny* (London, 1990), p. 311 (10/3/65), for Cecil's pointed defence of Maori rights.

18. *3H*, clxix, 1157 (6/3/63); clxv, 1229 (7/3/62); *P. and L.*, pp. 153, 40.

19. Iddesleigh P. (50063A–pt i), diary, 22/2/66.

20. *3H*, clxvi, 842–53 (5/7/64); quotation from 851.

21. *D.D.C.P.*, pp. 207, 215 (3/2/64, 6/5/64).

22. D.D., L.R.O., 5/7/64; Austin P. (DM 668), Salisbury to Alfred Austin, 17/8/98; *Q.R.*, July 1864, "The House of Commons", p. 276.

23. *Ibid.*, April 1864, "Foreign Policy of England", pp. 483–4.

24. G.W.E. Russell (ed.), *Malcolm MacColl. Memoirs and Correspondence* (London, 1914), p. 110.

25. *P. and L.*, p. 367.

26. *Q.R.*, July 1864, pp. 281, 275.

27. *T.T.*, 23/9/59.

28. *Ibid.*, 23/10/62; *Q.R.*, July 1865, "The Elections", p. 282; *D.D.C.P.*, p. 262 (30/8/66).

29. J.S. Mill, *Utilitarianism: Liberty: Representative Government* (London, 1954), pp. 185–202 (ch. ii of "Considerations on Representative Government").

30. *T.T.*, 23/9/59.

31. *B.Q.R.*, March 1859, "English Politics and Parties", pp. 4–6.

32. *Salisbury*, I, pp. 85–6, Cecil to Salisbury, 25/7/59; *ibid.*, pp. 94–6, Cecil to Exeter, 5/6/60, to Salisbury, 24/7/60.

33. Malmesbury, *Memoirs*, p. 379, diary, 26/4/56; R.A.J. Walling, *The Diaries of John Bright* (London, 1936), pp. 185–6 (20/2/55); *D.D.C.P.*, 21/2/58.

34. *P. and L.*, pp. 143–4.
35. *3H*, clxix, 512–15 (22/3/58).
36. Gladstone P. (44211), Herbert to Gladstone, 12/5/59.
37. *Salisbury*, I, p. 94, Cecil to Exeter, 5/6/60; *3H*, cxlix, 42 (1/3/58), Derby's ministerial statement; *ibid.*, cliii, 476–81 (21/3/59).
38. *Ibid.*, 479.
39. *P. and L.*, p. 173, 224; Shee P. (60341), Palmerston to Sir George Shee, Bt, 11/5/37; Beauvale P. (60464), Palmerston to Sir F. Lamb, 6/4/33.
40. *3H*, cliii, 478–9 (21/3/59); *T.T.*, 23/10/62.
41. *Economist*, 22/7/65; *Churchman*, 27/4/55.
42. *P. and L.*, ch. 7; J.P. Parry, *Democracy and Religion: Gladstone and the Liberal Party, 1867–1875* (Cambridge, 1986), pp. 80–102.
43. *Salisbury*, I, p. 98, Cecil to Carnarvon, 31/3/61.
44. Malmesbury, *Memoirs*, p. 537, Disraeli to Malmesbury, 22/2/61; *Guardian*, 19/7/65; *Q.R.*, July 1865, "The Church in her Relations to Political Parties", pp. 204–5; *3H*, clxxi, 640 (9/6/63); *Q.R.*, July 1862, "The Bicentenary", p. 267.
45. *3H*, clxi, 1509–11 (6/3/61); *Q.R.*, July 1862, p. 260.
46. *3H*, clxx, 928 (29/4/63); HHM/Family Papers, vol. xv, Bishop John Jackson of Lincoln to Cecil, 18/6/55, Cecil to the Rev. Thomas Shaw of Stamford, 20/6/55.
47. *Leeds Mercury*, 1/7/65.
48. Otter, *Woodard*, pp. 101–2, Salisbury to Adderley, 14/11/55; *ibid.*, p. 110, Cecil at Brighton, 2/12/56; *ibid.*, pp. 117–18, Salisbury to Woodard, 19/11/57.
49. *T.T.*, 24/12/59.
50. B. Connell (ed.), *Regina v. Palmerston. The Correspondence between Queen Victoria and her Foreign and Prime Minister* (London, 1962), p. 229, Palmerston to the Queen, 18/10/57.
51. *T.T.*, 10/11/56, 17/4/57; Marx in *Karl Marx and Frederick Engels in Britain* (Moscow, 1953), p. 459, "A London Workers' Meeting", 28/1/62.
52. *T.T.*, 18/11/64; Otter, *Woodard*, p. 141, Cecil to Woodard, 1861.
53. *3H*, clxxv, 1030 (1/6/64).
54. *Salisbury*, I, pp. 50–51, Cecil to Salisbury, 2/4/55.
55. D.D., L.R.O., 28/7/61; *Q.V.L.* (2), I, p. 171, Palmerston to the Queen, 18/4/64.
56. *3H*, clvii, 2214–15 (23/4/60); clviii, 1974–7 (4/6/60).
57. *3H*, clvii, 392–3 (12/3/60).
58. *P. and L.*, pp. 33–4, 209; *Q.R.*, April 1860, "The Budget and the Reform Bill", reprinted in Smith, *Lord Salisbury on Politics*, pp. 125–6.
59. *T.T.*, 23/10/62.
60. Iddesleigh P. (50053A–pt i), diary, 28/2/66.
61. J.F.A. Mason, "Lord Salisbury: A Librarian's View", in *S.M.P.*, pp. 17–18; Otter, *Woodard*, p. 137, Cecil to Woodard, 1861.
62. Mason in *S.M.P.*, p. 18; *Salisbury*, I, p. 71; M. Pinto-Duschinsky, *The Political Thought of Lord Salisbury, 1854–1868* (London, 1967), pp. 31–8; Thompson, "Private Property and Public Policy", in *S.M.P.*, p. 275, for an example of Escott's lack of scruple.
63. Pinto-Duschinsky, *The Political Thought of Lord Salisbury*, pp. 157–88, lists Cecil's contributions to these publications.
64. *Oxford Essays*, IV (London, 1858), pp. 63, 70, 57, 66; Edmund Burke, *Reflections on the French Revolution* (London, 1953), pp. 56–7.
65. *B.Q.R.*, March 1859, pp. 3, 6, 12; W.E. Gladstone, "The Declining Efficiency of Parliament", *Q.R.*, September 1856, pp. 521 ff.
66. *B.Q.R.*, March 1859, p. 27; *P. and L.*, pp. 70–71; *B.Q.R.*, July 1859, pp. 360–61.

67. *Salisbury*, I, p. 86, Cecil to Salisbury, 25/7/59.
68. *P. and L.*, p. 160.
69. *B.Q.R.*, January 1860, "The Coming Political Campaign", p. 329; *Q.R.*, April 1860, "The Budget and the Reform Bill", in Smith, *Lord Salisbury on Politics*, pp. 123, 133, 137; Morley, *Cobden*, II, pp. 229–33, Cobden to Sale, 4/7/59, for the verbal agreement between Palmerston and Cobden, quotation from p. 232; *3H*, clviii, 1991 (4/6/60), for Russell's complaint.
70. *Salisbury*, I, p. 96, Cecil to Salisbury, 24/7/60.
71. *Q.R.*, April 1860, in Smith, *Lord Salisbury on Politics*, p. 158.
72. *Q.R.*, July 1860, "The Conservative Reaction", pp. 291, 296, 300.
73. Quotations from *Q.R.*, January 1861, "The Income Tax and its Rivals", p. 244; *ibid.*, October 1861, "Church Rates", pp. 548–9; *ibid.*, July 1862, "The Bicentenary", p. 262.
74. Meyrick, *Memories of Life at Oxford*, pp. 88–9, Cecil to Meyrick, 1865.
75. *Ibid.*
76. *Salisbury*, I, p. 170.
77. *Q.R.*, July 1861, pp. 249, 283.
78. *Ibid.*, p. 285; *ibid.*, October 1862, "The Confederate Struggle and Recognition", pp. 542, 553, 555.
79. *P. and L.*, pp. 298–9; *Q.R.*, October 1862, p. 570.
80. *Ibid.*, pp. 556, 562.
81. *Ibid.*, July 1864, "The House of Commons", in Smith, *Lord Salisbury on Politics*, p. 178; *Q.R.*, July 1865, "The Elections", p. 290; *3H*, clxxv, 324 (11/5/64) for Gladstone's words.
82. C.K. Webster, *The Foreign Policy of Castlereagh, 1815–22* (2 vols) (London 1925).
83. *Q.R.*, January 1862, "Lord Castlereagh", pp. 201–38, esp. pp. 234, 214.
84. *Ibid.*, April 1861, "Lord Stanhope's Life of Pitt", pp. 559, 537, 562, 565.
85. *Ibid.*, p. 559.
86. *Ibid.*, April 1863, "Poland", pp. 448–81.
87. *Ibid.*, April 1864, "The Foreign Policy of England", pp. 481–529, quotation from p. 484; *B.Q.R.*, July 1859, p. 372.
88. M.M. Bevington, *The Saturday Review (1855–1868)* (New York, 1941); *Salisbury*, I, pp. 82–3.
89. *S.R.*, 11/6/59, "The Artless Dodger", pp. 709–10; *ibid.*, 18/6/59, "And is Old Double dead?", p. 744; *ibid.*, 9/4/59, "Constitutional Illusions", pp. 429–30.
90. *Ibid.*, 7/1/63, "Ministerial Speeches", pp. 7–8.
91. *Ibid.*, 19/1/61, "German Literature", pp. 78–80.
92. *Ibid.*, 5/3/64, "The New Test", pp. 274–5; *ibid.*, 2/4/64, "The New Religious Movements", pp. 406–7; *ibid.*, 14/1/60, "The Late Bishop Wilson", pp. 52–3; *ibid.*, 23/2/61, "The Turnbull Deputation", pp. 193–4.
93. *Ibid.*, 30/1/64, "Poverty", pp. 129–30; *ibid.*, 23/1/64, "An Overriding Providence", pp. 101–2.
94. Thompson, "Private Property and Public Policy", in *S.M.P.*, pp. 257–8.
95. Mason, "Lord Salisbury: A Librarian's View", in *S.M.P.*, p. 17; HHM/3M/E, Cranborne to Salisbury, 14/5, 17/5, 12/6/66.
96. *Ibid.*, Cranborne to Salisbury, 29/10/66. See Chapter 4, pp. 62–3 for his time at the Great Eastern Railway.
97. HHM/3M/E, the 9th Earl Waldegrave, a family friend and trustee, to Salisbury, 28/11/83, on Salisbury's proposed investments. R. Harcourt Williams, *The Salisbury–Balfour Correspondence 1861–1892* (Hertfordshire Record Society, 1988), p. 395, note by Salisbury's private secretary on Balfour to Salisbury, 29/2/92.
98. *Q.R.*, October 1867, in Smith, *Lord Salisbury on Politics*, pp. 264–5.

## Chapter 3: The Second Reform Act

1. *D.D.C.P.*, p. 204, 18/12/63; Iddesleigh P. (50063A), diary, 20/2, 8/3 and 29/6/66.
2. The literature on parliamentary reform in the mid-1860s is large: M.J. Cowling, *1867: Disraeli, Gladstone and Revolution: The Passing of the Second Reform Bill* (London, 1967) is outstanding. Blake, *The Conservative Party from Peel to Churchill*, ch. 4 is the best introduction, supplemented by F.B. Smith, *The Making of the Second Reform Bill* (Cambridge, 1966).
3. *P. and L.*, pp. 223, 413 n52; *D.D.C.P.*, p. 261 (24/7/66); *Cranbrook/D.*, pp. 20–21 (29/7/66).
4. *T.T.*, 7/4/66.
5. *3H*, clxxxii, 875 (23/3/66); *D.D.C.P.*, p. 248 (23/3/66); *Q.R.*, January 1866, "The Coming Session", pp. 250–80; *3H*, clxxxii, 233 (13/3/66).
6. *3H*, clxxxiii, 1520–3 (30/5/66); *Q.R.*, April 1866, in Smith, *Lord Salisbury on Politics*, pp. 195–225, quotations from pp. 207–8.
7. Selborne, *Memorials, Pt II*, vol. I, pp. 65–6, quoting his Commons speech on 30/5/66.
8. Cited by F.W. Hirst, "Mr Gladstone as Leader of the House and Reformer, 1865–1868", in Wemyss Reid (ed.), *The Life of William Ewart Gladstone* (London, 1899), p. 490.
9. *3H*, clxxxiii, 6–24 (27/4/66), quotations from 8, 9, 16.
10. *Ibid.*, 10.
11. *Q.R.*, July 1866, "The Change of Ministry", in Smith, *Lord Salisbury on Politics*, p. 234; *P. and L.*, p. 23, Gladstone to his wife, 25/5/61: "It is true that I seem to be both at the Conservative and at the Radical ends of the Cabinet. I do not know how it has come about, but it was not my desire."
12. Smith, *Lord Salisbury on Politics*, p. 197 n3; the lines are from *Henry IV, Pt I*; *ibid.*, Cecil in *Q.R.*, July 1866, pp. 251, 241, 246–7.
13. *Ibid.*, pp. 247, 252.
14. Carnarvon/D. (60898), 22 and 27/10/66.
15. *Salisbury*, I, p. 218. There is an extract from this letter, dated 4/12/66, among Cranborne's letters to and from his father in HHM/3M/E; the correspondent is not identified.
16. Carnarvon/D. (60899), 28/2 and 1/4/67; *Salisbury*, I, p. 214, Disraeli to Cranborne, 26/12/66; *ibid.*, pp. 212–13, Cranborne to Salisbury, 9/1/67; Carnarvon/D. (60898), 27/10/66.
17. *Ibid.*, 31/10/66; *D.D.C.P.*, p. 272 (1/11/66); A. Hardinge, *The Life of the 4th Earl of Carnarvon* (3 vols) (London, 1925), I, p. 335.
18. Carnarvon/D. (60898), 8/11/66.
19. *D.D.C.P.*, pp. 272, 274 (1 and 8/11/66).
20. *Salisbury*, I, pp. 212–13, Cranborne to Salisbury, 9/1/67; *D.D.C.P.*, p. 277 (4/12/66); *Q.V.L.* (2), I, p. 388, Derby to the Queen, 10/1/67, sets out the premier's approach to legislating on reform.
21. Carnarvon/D. (60898), 31/10/66, 25/12/66; *D.D.C.P.*, p. 283 (5/1/67); *Salisbury*, I, pp. 214–15, 225, Cranborne to Disraeli, 2/1 and 1/2/67.
22. *Salisbury*, I, p. 226; Cowling, *1867: Disraeli, Gladstone and Revolution*, pp. 138, 141; *D.D.C.P.*, pp. 288–90 (11 to 19/2/67). The additional votes were for holders of professional qualifications, depositors in savings banks and direct taxpayers.
23. Carnarvon/D. (60899), 21/2/67.
24. *Ibid.*, 23/2/67.
25. *Ibid.*, 24/2/67; *Cranbrook/D.*, pp. 31–32 (26/2/67).

26. Carnarvon/D. (60899), 25/2/67; *Salisbury*, I, p. 234.
27. *Ibid.*, pp. 233–4, Cranborne to Derby, 24/2/67; *Cranbrook/D.*, pp. 31–32 (26/2/67).
28. Carnarvon/D. (60899), 25/2/67; *Q.V.L.* (2), I, pp. 399–401, Derby to the Queen, 25/2/67; *D.D.C.P.*, pp. 290–91 (25/2/67).
29. *Ibid.* and *Cranbrook/D.*, pp. 31–32 (26/2/67); H.C.G. Matthew, *Gladstone, 1809–1874* (Oxford, 1986), pp. 141–42: in this context, as in others, "Gladstone's political ferocity had been a ferocity of constant moderation". *Q.V.L.* (2), I, Disraeli to the Queen, 26 and 28/2/67.
30. Carnarvon/D. (60899), 26, 27 and 28/2/67.
31. *D.D.C.P.*, pp. 288, 290–92 (11/2 and 19 to 28/2/67); *Cranbrook/D.*, p. 27 (4/12/66).
32. *Ibid.*, p. 32 (2/3/67).
33. *D.D.C.P.*, p. 293 (5/3/67).
34. *Q.V.L.* (2) I, pp. 407–9, Disraeli to General Charles Grey, private secretary to the Queen, 15/3/67.
35. *3H*, clxxxvi, 83–9 (18/3/67), quotations from 88–9; *ibid.*, 93, for Disraeli's reply.
36. *D.D.C.P.*, p. 294 (9/3/97); Carnarvon/D. (60899), 21/3/67; *3H*, clxxxvi, 88 (18/3/67).
37. *P. and L.*, p. 69, Palmerston to Sir William Temple, 24/12/55.
38. HHM/3M/DD, Cranborne to G.M.W. Sandford, MP, 1/5/68.
39. *Q.V.L.* (2), I, p. 408, Disraeli to General Grey, 15/3/67.
40. *Ibid.*, p. 413, Disraeli to the Queen, 21/3/67; *Cranbrook/D.*, p. 37 (13/4/67).
41. *Salisbury*, I, pp. 254–5, Cranborne to Carnarvon, 1/4/67; Carnarvon/D. (60899), 20 and 21/3/67; *Gladstone Diaries*, VI, p. 513 (12/4/67).
42. J. Morley, *The Life of William Ewart Gladstone* (2 vols) (London, 1905), I, pp. 867–9; esp. the extract from Robert Phillimore's diary, 10 and 24/5/67; *3H*, clxxxviii, 1527–8 (15/7/67).
43. *Q.V.L.* (2), I, p. 451, the Queen's journal, 24/7/67.
44. *3H*, clxxxviii, 1109–15 (5/7/67).
45. Carnarvon/D. (60899), 15/5/67.
46. *D.D.C.P.*, p. 300 (9/4/67).
47. *3H*, clxxxviii, 1115 (5/7/67).
48. *3H*, clxxxvi, 1572 (11/4/67); *ibid.*, clxxxviii, 192 (20/6/67); *ibid.*, 639 (27/6/67); *ibid.*, 1098 (5/7/67); *ibid.*, 515 (25/6/67).
49. *Cranbrook/D.*, p. 45 (16/7/67).
50. *Gladstone Diaries*, VI, p. 536 (15/3/67).
51. *3H*, clxxxviii, 1528–9 (15/7/67).
52. *Ibid.*, 1530–1 (15/7/67) and 1099–1100 (5/7/67).
53. *Ibid.*, 1533–9 (15/7/67); *Q.V.L.* (2), I, p. 445, Disraeli to the Queen, 15/7/67.
54. *3H*, clxxxviii, 1536 (15/7/67); HHM/3M/H, Milman to Cranborne, 16/5/67; *Salisbury*, I, pp. 261–2, J.A. Shaw-Stewart to Cranborne, 15/4/67.
55. *Ibid.*, pp. 262–4, Cranborne to Shaw-Stewart, 17/4/67.
56. *Q.R.*, October 1867, in Smith, *Lord Salisbury on Politics*, pp. 261–2, 264–5.
57. Carnarvon/D. (60899), 27/10/67.
58. *Ibid.*, 29/10/67.
59. Carnarvon P. (60758), Cranborne to Carnarvon, 24/2/68; *3H*, cxc, 968–70 (19/2/68).
60. Carnarvon P. (60758), Cranborne to Carnarvon, 27/2/68; partly printed in *Salisbury*, I, p. 291.
61. *3H*, cxci, 532–41 (30/3/68), quotations from 533, 540; *D.D.C.P.*, p. 331 (2/3/68). For the Irish church question in its last phase see P.M.H. Bell, *Disestablishment in Ireland and Wales* (London, 1969) and Parry, *Democracy and Religion*, ch. 5.

62. *Cranbrook/D.*, pp. 68–9 (1 and 4/4/68).
63. *Ibid.*, 4/4/68; *D.D.C.P.*, pp. 331–2 (15 and 30/3/68); Carnarvon/D. (60900), 26/6/68.
64. *P. and L.*, p. 226.
65. *Salisbury*, I, pp. 293–4, Salisbury to J.D. Coleridge, MP, 18/4/68; HHM/3M/E, Salisbury to R.W.G. Gaussen, 11/5/68.
66. *Ibid.*
67. *Ibid.*, 11 and 18/5/68.
68. *Salisbury*, I, p. 211, Cranborne to H.W.D. Acland, 4/12/67.
69. *3H*, clxxxix, 952 (6/8/67); *Q.V.L.* (2), I, p. 518, Disraeli to the Queen, 23/3/68.
70. Carnarvon/D. (60899), 2/7/67; Acland P. (d. 74), Salisbury to Acland, 14/12/68.
71. *T.T.*, 18/4/68.
72. HHM/3M/D, Bath to Salisbury, 8/2/69, Salisbury to Bath, 15/11/68.
73. *T.T.*, 28/10/68, first speech on 27/10/68.
74. *Ibid.*, second speech.
75. *Ibid.*, 30/10/68.
76. *Ibid.*
77. Morley, *Cobden*, II, p. 350, Cobden to Bright, 29/12/59.

## Chapter 4: The Conscience of the Party

1. *D.D.*, p. 147 (29/10/73). The incomplete evidence for Salisbury's wealth and its management has been carefully examined by F.M.L. Thompson, "Private Property and Public Policy", in *S.M.P.*, pp. 252–89; HHM/3M/E, Waldegrave to Salisbury, 28/11/83 on a choice of investments.
2. HHM/3M/E, Salisbury to Rear Admiral F.A. Maxse, 29/3/94; *D.D.*, p. 109 (19/6/72).
3. Thompson, *S.M.P.*, pp. 258–9; Mason, "Lord Salisbury", in *S.M.P.*, pp. 19–20; T.C. Barker, "Lord Salisbury: Chairman of the Great Eastern Railway, 1868–72", in Sheila Marriner (ed.), *Business and Businessmen* (Liverpool, 1978).
4. Carnarvon/D. (60903), 8/6/71.
5. HHM/3M/C [India], Salisbury to Sir Richard Temple, 27/9/76; Thompson, *S.M.P.*, p. 265. Reluctance to borrow for improvement limited his expenditure under that head, but he exaggerated when he told a friend "I am obliged to invest in foreign stocks and leave the property unimproved", HHM/3M/D, Salisbury to Bath, 22/4/73.
6. Thompson, *S.M.P.*; quotation from p. 273.
7. *Ibid.*, pp. 281–2.
8. *3H*, clxxvi, 2048–9 (25/7/64), on Poor Relief (Metropolis) Bill; *Q.R.*, October 1872, in Smith, *Lord Salisbury on Politics*, p. 300.
9. Thompson, *S.M.P.*, pp. 280–81.
10. *Salisbury*, II, pp. 1–18 and Lady Gwendolen's "Lord Salisbury in Private Life", *S.M.P.*, pp. 30–59; HHM/3M/C, memorandum by Salisbury, 13/1/73, on the responsibilities of county magistrates.
11. HHM/3M/E, Salisbury to the Countess of Galloway (draft), 1/6/86; *ibid.*, Salisbury to Maxse, 29/3/94. Some light is shed on Salisbury's relations with his stepmother, his half-brothers and half-sister and her second husband in the introduction to J.R. Vincent (ed.), *The Later Derby Diaries, Home Rule, Liberal Unionism, and Aristocratic Life in Late Victorian England*, privately printed (Bristol, 1981). He expressed "a strong view – coming perhaps, from personal experience" that younger sons should be treated as generously as possible, HHM/3M/D, Salisbury to Bath, 22/4/73.

12. *Salisbury*, II, p. 5.
13. *Gladstone–Granville Correspondence, 1868–1876*, I, p. 29, Gladstone to Granville, 21/6/69.
14. E.J. Feuchtwanger, *Disraeli, Democracy and the Tory Party* (Oxford, 1968), pp. 4–8; C.C. Weston, "Salisbury and the Lords", *Historical Journal* (1982), pp. 103–29.
15. N. Gash, *Reaction and Reconstruction in English politics, 1832–52* (Oxford, 1965), ch. 2; E.A. Smith, *The House of Lords in British Politics and Society, 1832–1911* (London, 1992).
16. *S.R.*, 3/8/61, "The House of Lords", pp. 113–14; *D.D.C.P.*, pp. 176–7 (6/10/61); *P. and L.*, pp. 225–6.
17. *3H*, cxcv, 463 (9/4/69).
18. *Ibid.*, cxciii, 89 (26/6/68); *ibid.*, cxcvii, 81–96 (17/6/69), quotations from 84–5.
19. Carnarvon/D. (60901), 17/6/69; Carnarvon P. (61071), Carnarvon to Sir William Heathcote, MP, 3/10/67.
20. Carnarvon/D. (60900), 24/4/68, the views of the two dukes on "getting rid of Disraeli"; Malmesbury, *Memoirs*, p. 644, diary, 19/12/69.
21. *Cranbrook/D.*, p. 89 (19/12/68); *D.D.C.P.*, p. 240 (3/3/69); Carnarvon/D. (60901), 11/6/69; D.D., L.R.O., 6/6/69.
22. Morley, *Gladstone*, I, p. 902, Gladstone to General Grey, 5/6/69; *Q.V.L.* (2), I, p. 611, Granville to the Queen, 17/6/69.
23. *Gladstone–Granville Correspondence, 1868–1876*, I, pp. 29, 40–42, Gladstone to Granville, 21/6/69 and Granville's memorandum, 4/8/69, on recent ministerial contacts with Salisbury and Cairns; Carnarvon/D. (60902), 16 and 19/7/69; *Q.V.L.* (2), I, p. 617, Gladstone to the Queen, 13/7/69.
24. *Ibid.*, pp. 619–20, Gladstone to the Queen, 20–21/7/69; Carnarvon/D. (60901), 22/7/69.
25. *Ibid.*, and *Q.V.L.* (2), I, pp. 621–2, Granville to the Queen, 22/7/69.
26. Malmesbury, *Memoirs*, pp. 660–61, Cairns' circular, 24/7/69; Feuchtwanger, *Disraeli, Democracy and the Tory Party*, pp. 5–7; Carnarvon/D. (60902), 4 and 19/2/70.
27. *D.D.*, p. 51 (20/2/70); Carnarvon/D. (60902), 19/2/70.
28. *Ibid.*, 6, 12, 21 and 22/2/70; Carnarvon P. (60758), Salisbury to Carnarvon, 22/2/70.
29. *Ibid.*; *D.D.C.P.*, p. 345 (15/11/69).
30. *Q.R.*, October 1869, pp. 538–61, quotations from pp. 550–51; E.D. Steele, *Irish Land and British Politics: Tenant-Right and Nationality, 1865–1870* (Cambridge, 1974), pp. 308–10; *Salisbury*, II, pp. 25–7.
31. *D.D.*, p. 111 (7/7/72); Carnarvon/D. (60902), 7 and 28/7/70; *Salisbury*, II, p. 25, Salisbury to Carnarvon, 20/6/70.
32. Carnarvon/D. (60903), 1/5 and 3/7/71; HHM/3M/D, Salisbury to Cairns, 14/2/69.
33. *Salisbury*, I, p. 211, Cranborne to Acland, 4/2/67; Goodwood P. (864), Salisbury to Richmond, 1/8/72; Lord Colonsay and Oronsay was a Tory peer.
34. *Cranbrook/D.*, p. 117 (30/6/70); *D.D.*, p. 79 (6/5/71).
35. Quoted in Steele, *Irish Land and British Politics*, pp. 307, 312.
36. *S.R.*, 7/2/61, "The Bull and the Frog", p. 585; *ibid.*, 8/4/64, "Tenant Right", pp. 522–3.
37. Steele, *Irish Land and British Politics*, p. 309.
38. *3H*, ccii, 888, Richmond; 863–4, Halifax; 864–5, Salisbury (24/6/70).
39. Steele, *Irish Land and British Politics*, p. 310; *3H*, ccii, 1437–8 (5/7/69).
40. Carnarvon/D. (60902), 22/7/70; *Salisbury*, II, pp. 25–6, Salisbury to Carnarvon, 20/2/72, on the ballot.
41. *Ibid.*, p. 27; D.D., L.R.O., 17/7/71.

42. Parry, *Democracy and Religion* is an authoritative study of the churches and politics at the time. See also W.O. Chadwick, *The Victorian Church* (2 vols) (London, 1966–70) and G.I.T. Machin, *Politics and the Churches in Great Britain, 1832–1868* and *1869–1921* (Oxford, 1977, 1987).

43. J.O. Johnston, *Life and Letters of Henry Parry Liddon* (London, 1904).

44. Otter, *Woodard*, p. 257, Salisbury to Woodard, October 1873; *3H*, ccxvii, 283 (14/7/73).

45. P. Gordon (ed.), *The Red Earl: The Papers of the Fifth Earl Spencer, 1835–1910*, vol. I (Northampton, 1981), p. 124, Spencer to Horace Seymour, 17/7/74; Liddon/D. 8/7/71.

46. HHM/3M/H, Liddon to Salisbury, 10/3/71; *ibid.*, 4M /387, Salisbury to Cranborne, 9/1/83.

47. HHM/3M/H, Liddon to Salisbury, 6 and 10/3/71.

48. Russell, *MacColl*, pp. 273–5, Salisbury to MacColl, 29/10, 8, 13 and 25/12/72.

49. *Cranbrook/D.*, p. 166 (23/11/72); *T.T.*, 1/2/73 (col. 12c).

50. *Ibid.*, leading article and (col. 12a) report.

51. Carnarvon P. (60758), Salisbury to Carnarvon, 13/10/72; *T.T.*, 11/10/72. The Duke of Alba, Spanish viceroy in the sixteenth-century Netherlands personified religious persecution, and the first-century Jewish sage Gamaliel its antithesis.

52. P. Marsh, *The Victorian Church in Decline: Archbishop Tait and the Church of England, 1868–1882* (London, 1969), p. 141; *Q.V.L.* (2), II, p. 306, Gladstone to the Queen, 22/1/74, deploring the advance of theological liberalism in the universities and elsewhere.

53. *3H*, cciii, 206 (14/7/70). While he negotiated behind the scenes, he preferred to defend the Establishment and religion in the open; doing so had "a great effect upon . . . willingness and capacity to fight future battles: and Churchmen and Oxford have so many . . . still to fight", Selborne P. (Lambeth MS, 1864), Salisbury to Sir R. Palmer, attorney general, 31/7/70.

54. E.g. HHM/3M/H, Liddon to Salisbury, 28/2/71; *3H*, ccvi, 344, 347–8 (8/5/71).

55. Parry, *Democracy and Religion*, p. 308.

56. *T.T.*, 12/10/72, at Leeds; Liddon/D, 5/1/72.

57. *T.T.*, 12/10/72, Leeds; *3H*, ccvi, 1772–3 (9/6/71).

58. HHM/3M/H, Bishop Magee to Salisbury, 23/7/73; Parry, *Democracy and Religion*, pp. 374–6.

59. Mill, *Utilitarianism: Liberty: Representative Government*, pp. 160–61 (ch. v of *On Liberty*); *T.T.*, 30/1/72, at Manchester.

60. *Salisbury*, I, pp. 135–7; *3H*, clxxiii, 1677–82 (8/3/64), resolution on education.

61. Otter, *Woodard*, p. 264, Salisbury to Woodard, 1876.

62. Ripon P. (43519), Salisbury to Earl de Grey and Ripon, 7/7/72, lord president with responsibility for the Education Department.

63. Otter, *Woodard*, pp. 241–2, Fraser to Woodard, 23/6/71; HHM/3M/E, Gorst to Salisbury, 30/12/75.

64. Otter, *Woodard*, pp. 244, 232, Salisbury to Woodard, 1871, 1870; Parry, *Democracy and Religion*, p. 310.

65. *3H*, ccvii, 862–9 (30/6/71), quotation from 868.

66. Otter, *Woodard*, p. 232, Salisbury to Woodard, 1870; *Cranbrook/D.*, p. 127 (21/2/71).

67. *D.D.*, pp. 79–80 (6/5/71).

68. *Q.R.*, October 1871, "The Commune and the Internationale", pp. 549–80.

69. *Ibid.*, pp. 560, 557.

70. *D.D.*, p. 82 (16/6/71); *Q.R.*, October 1871, pp. 554, 580, 575.

71. *Ibid.*, p. 575; *Gladstone–Granville Correspondence, 1868–1876*, II, p. 274, Gladstone to Granville, 15/10/71; Feuchtwanger, *Disraeli, Democracy and the Tory Party*, pp. 91–4; *T.T.*, 16/10/71.

72. *D.D.*, pp. 85–6, 26/7/71; *Gladstone–Granville Correspondence*, II, p. 275, Gladstone to Granville, 17/10/71.

73. *T.T.*, 16/10/71, "A New Social Movement" reprints the *Daily News* letter.

74. *Ibid.*, leading article; *Q.R.*, October 1872, "The Position of Parties", pp. 558–93; quotations from p. 583.

75. *T.T.*, 31/1/72: a leading article elicited by Salisbury's Manchester speech on education; *T.T.*, 30/1/72 and pp. 77–8 above.

76. *T.T.*, 29/11/72.

77. *Q.R.*, October 1873, "The Programme of the Radicals", in Smith, *Lord Salisbury on Politics*, p. 331; *T.T.*, 18/10/73.

78. *Ibid.*; Ripon P. (43519), Salisbury to de Grey, 1/8/70; HHM/3M/D, Salisbury to Bath, 24/9/73.

79. *D.D.*, p. 86 (26/7/71); P. Smith, *Disraelian Conservatism and Social Reform* (London, 1967) on rhetoric and substance in the Tory leader's social policy; Carnarvon P. (60758), Salisbury to Carnarvon, 4/3/73.

## Chapter 5: The Making of a Statesman

1. *Cranbrook/D.*, pp. 148–9 (1 and 2/2/72); Iddesleigh P. (50063A–pt ii), diary, 12/7/80.

2. *D.D.*, pp. 74, 98 (2/2/71, 8/2/72).

3. Cross P. (51263), Salisbury to R.A. Cross, home secretary, 31/10/74.

4. *Gladstone Diaries*, VII, p. 310, Gladstone to E. Hawkins, provost of Oriel, 17/6/70.

5. *D.D.*, pp. 161–2 (8/2/74).

6. Carnarvon/D. (60906), 6/12/74; *D.D.*, pp. 163–4 (14/2/74), 161–2 (8/2/74); *Salisbury*, II, pp. 43–4, Salisbury to his wife, 8/2/74.

7. Carnarvon/D. (60906), 6 and 8/2/74; Salisbury's account of this is in the letter to his wife on the same day, *Salisbury*, II, pp. 43–4.

8. Carnarvon/D. (60906), 8/2/74, 13/7, 1 and 10/10/73.

9. *Ibid.*, 8/2/74; HHM/3M/MCD, Lady Derby to Salisbury, 9, 12 and 15/2/74, quotation from 12/2; *Salisbury*, II, pp. 46–7, Salisbury to his wife, 15/2/74.

10. Carnarvon/D. (60906), 8/2/74; *Salisbury*, II, pp. 44–7, Salisbury to his wife, 10 and 15/2/74; Carnarvon P. (61073), Heathcote to Carnarvon, 14/2/74.

11. *Salisbury*, II, pp. 46–7, Salisbury to his wife, 15/2/74.

12. *D.D.*, pp. 163–4 (14/2/74); Carnarvon P. (60758), Salisbury to Carnarvon, 15/2/74.

13. *Ibid.*, Salisbury to Carnarvon, 18/2/74; *Q.V.L.* (2), II, pp. 390–91, memorandum by the Queen, 18/2/74; *Salisbury*, II, pp. 49–51, Salisbury to his wife, 18 and 22/2/74.

14. *T.T.*, 19/2/74; *Salisbury*, II, pp. 50–51, Salisbury to his wife, 22/2/74.

15. *Ibid.*, p. 63, Salisbury to Carnarvon, 24/7/74.

16. Carnarvon P. (60758), Salisbury to Carnarvon, 10/2/74.

17. *Q.V.L.* (2), II, p. 309, Gladstone to the Queen, 22/1/74; *Salisbury*, II, pp. 57–8.

18. Carnarvon/D. (60906), 4/9/74; Liddon/D., 12/10/75.

19. *Salisbury*, II, p. 47, Salisbury to his wife, 15/2/74. Marsh, *The Victorian Church in Decline*, ch. 7, and J. Bentley, *Ritualism and Politics* (Oxford, 1978) are standard accounts of the ritualist crisis.

20. HHM/3M/Lady Salisbury's papers, Salisbury to Bishop Robert Milman of Calcutta, 27/3/74.

21. Hughenden P. (B/XX/Ce), "Proposal to give more power to Bishops: Note on Archbishop's Memorandum", by Salisbury, 2/3/74, and Salisbury to Disraeli, undated (Ce/180); *ibid.*, Salisbury to Disraeli, two undated letters (Ce/174 and 176), and undated memorandum (Ce/174a), on "The Archbishop's Proposed Bill".

22. *Ibid.*, memorandum by Salisbury, 2/3/74, and Salisbury to Disraeli, 22/2/74.

23. *Salisbury*, II, p. 50, Salisbury to his wife, 18/2/74; Hughenden P. (B/XX/Ce), undated memorandum (Ce/174a) by Salisbury on "The Archbishop's Proposed Bill" and Salisbury to Disraeli, undated (Ce/176).

24. M. & B., *Disraeli*, II, pp. 659–60, Cairns to Disraeli, 25/3/74 and Disraeli to Lady Bradford, 26/3/74; *Q.V.L.* (2), II, pp. 332–3 and 334–5, Disraeli to the Queen, 28/3 and 25/4/74; Carnarvon/D. (60906), 25/4/74.

25. *Ibid.*; HHM/3M/Lady Salisbury's papers, Salisbury to Bishop Milman, 27/3/74.

26. *D.D.*, p. 173 (9/5/74); Carnarvon/D. (60906), 9/5/74.

27. M. & B., *Disraeli*, II, pp. 661–2, Cairns to Disraeli, n.d., Disraeli to Lady Bradford, 5/6/74.

28. *Ibid.*; *3H*, ccxx, 408 (25/6/74).

29. HHM/3M/D, Salisbury to MacColl, 9/6/74.

30. *Q.V.L.* (2), II, pp. 433, 342–3, Disraeli to the Queen, 8/12/75, 11, 12 and 13/7/74; *D.D.*, pp. 174–5 (11/7/74); Carnarvon/D. (60906), 11/7/74.

31. Parry, *Democracy and Religion*, pp. 416–17; *3H*, ccxxi, 1251–4 (4/8/74), for Salisbury's defiance.

32. Disraeli in *3H*, ccxxi, 1358–9 (5/8/74); *Cranbrook/D.*, p. 217 (6/8/74); *Salisbury*, II, pp. 61–2, Disraeli to Salisbury, Salisbury to Disraeli, both 5/8/74.

33. *Salisbury*, II, pp. 62–3, Salisbury to Carnarvon, 23 and 24/7/74; *D.D.*, p. 176 (24/7/74); D.D., L.R.O., 25/7/74.

34. HHM/3M/D, Disraeli to Salisbury, 28/10/75; Salisbury to Disraeli, 29/8/76, 20/12/78.

35. HHM/3M/Lady Salisbury's papers, Salisbury to Bishop Milman, 15/2/76, 27/3/74. He described Milman himself as "at first sight . . . rough and eccentric", but was confident that he would make a good bishop, as he did, Lawrence P. (MSS. Eur. F.90/28), Cranborne to Lawrence, 18/1/67.

36. Cross P. (51263), Salisbury to Cross, 31/10/74, 1/7/75; HHM/3M/E, J.E. Gorst to Salisbury, 5/10/74.

37. M. & B., *Disraeli*, II, pp. 1033–4, Disraeli to the Queen, 20/2/77; *Cranbrook/D.*, p. 321, 325–6 (13/5 and 17/6/77); Salisbury in *3H*, ccxxix, 652 (15/5/76) and ccxxxiii, 1890 (26/4/77).

38. HHM/3M/D, Salisbury to Disraeli, 22/7/76.

39. W.R. Ward, *Victorian Oxford* (London, 1965), ch. 13; *Salisbury*, II, pp. 64–5; Salisbury in *3H*, ccxxvii, 791–805 (24/2/76); HHM/3M/D, Salisbury to Disraeli, 13/10/74; and Salisbury to Gathorne Hardy, secretary of state for war and MP for Oxford University, 12/2/75.

40. Selborne P. (Lambeth MS, 1866), Salisbury to Selborne, 8/3/76, printed in Selborne, *Memorials, Pt II*, vol. I, pp. 373–4; *Cranbrook/D.*, p. 280 (7/7/76).

41. HHM/3M/D, Salisbury to Disraeli, 24/6/76; Selborne, *Memorials, Pt II*, vol. I, pp. 373–7.

42. HHM/3M/D, Salisbury to Disraeli, 2/2/75.

43. Otter, *Woodard*, pp. 284–5, Salisbury to Woodard, 21/10/77, 28/1/78; Liddon/D., 5/1/72. The influence of the German theologian, D.F. Strauss' *Das Leben Jesu* (1835; translated by George Eliot in 1846) was inescapable.

44. *Salisbury*, II, p. 65.

45. This section is a recension of the author's essay "Salisbury at the India Office", in *S.M.P.*, pp. 116–47. S. Gopal, *British Policy in India 1858–1905* (Cambridge, 1965) depicts Salisbury as a less than liberal imperialist; so, too, does E.C. Moulton in *Lord Northbrook's Indian Administration, 1872–1876* (New York, 1965). Salisbury's parliament-ary and permanent under-secretaries at the India Office recorded their impressions of the able minister they served: Lord George Hamilton, *Parliamentary Reminiscences and Reflections, 1886–1906* (London, 1922), pp. 73–4, with his comments to Lady Gwendolen Cecil in *S.M.P.*, p. 79, and Sir Louis Mallet in his memoir of Northbrook, *Thomas George, Earl of Northbrook, G.C.S.I.* (London, 1908), esp. pp. 90–91, quoting Northbrook's kinsman and private secretary, the future Lord Cromer. There is a substantial and as yet unpublished study by P.R. Brumpton, "Salisbury at the India Office, 1866–67 and 1874–78" (Ph.D thesis, University of Leeds, 1994).

46. Council of India: Memoranda and Papers, C/138, Salisbury's minute on survey settle-ment in Madras 20/4/75.

47. *3H*, cxxxvii, 1185–6 (26/7/55); HHM/3M/D, Salisbury to Disraeli, 16/7/75; Mill, *Utilitarianism: Liberty: Representative Government*, p. 179 (ch. i of "Considerations on Repres-entative Government").

48. HHM/3M/C [India], Salisbury to Temple, 1/9/75; Council of India: Memoranda and Papers, C/138, Salisbury's minute on survey settlement in Madras, 20/4/75. For Sir Salar Jung and Sir Dinkar Rao, see their entries in the index to this book.

49. HHM/3M/C [India], Salisbury to Temple, 26/2/75, 19/4/75; Temple's side of the correspondence is in HHM/3M/E. M.H. Baden-Powell, *The Land Systems of British India* (3 vols) (Oxford, 1892) remains authoritative in its complex field.

50. HHM/3M/C [India], Salisbury to Wodehouse, 3/2/76, 21/6/75, 18/2/76, and for Wodehouse's replies, *ibid.*, class E; Lytton held that government interference with the money-lenders would "shake to its foundations the entire credit system of our empire", HHM/3M/E, Lytton to Salisbury, 17/11/77.

51. HHM/3M/C [India], Salisbury to Temple, 18/5/77; T.R. Metcalf, "The British and the Moneylender in Nineteenth-century India", *Journal of Modern History* (1962); I.J. Catanach, *Rural Credit in Western India, 1875–1930* (Berkeley and Los Angeles, 1970), ch. 1.

52. HHM/3M/C [India], Salisbury to Buckingham, 8/2/78; Council of India: Memor-anda and Papers, Salisbury's minute on survey settlement in Madras, 20/4/75; HHM/3M/C [India], Salisbury to Lord Hobart, Buckingham's predecessor at Madras, 26/2/75. B.M. Bhatia, *Famines in India, 1860–1965*, 2nd edn (London, 1967) is a standard work on a huge subject.

53. HHM/3M/C [India], Salisbury to Northbrook, viceroy of India, 30/4/75; *ibid.*, Salis-bury to Lytton, 11/1/78; Lawrence P. (MSS Eur. F.90/27), Cranborne to Lawrence, 16/9 and 2/10/66.

54. HHM/3M/C [India], Salisbury to Temple, 3/7 and 19/6/74; Moulton, *Lord Northbrook's Indian Administration*, pp. 101–3; HHM/3M/E, Temple to Salisbury, 14/7 and 2/8/74.

55. Northbrook P. (MSS Eur. C144/22), Northbrook to Sir Louis Mallet, permanent under-secretary at the India Office, 31/8/74.

56. HHM/3M/C [India], Salisbury to Lytton, 4/5/77; Lytton P. (MSS. Eur. E 218/19, pt iii), Lytton to Sir John Strachey, 24/10/77 and Charles Villiers, MP, 22/10/77; *ibid.*

(E 218/19, pt i), Lytton to Mallet, 11/1/77 and (E 218/18), M. Grant Duff, MP, 10/12/76.

57.  Iddesleigh P. (50019), Salisbury to Sir Stafford Northcote, chancellor of the exchequer, 29/8, 15 and 26/9/77; HHM/3M/C [India], Salisbury to Lytton, 10/8/77, 23/2/77.

58.  HHM/3M/E, Mallet to Salisbury, 3/9/77; *ibid.*, class D, Salisbury to Mallet, 6/9/77; Lytton P. (MSS Eur. E 218/19, pt iii), Lytton to Villiers, 22/10/77.

59.  HHM/3M/C [India], Salisbury to Sir John Strachey, finance member of the viceroy's council, 27/8/77; *ibid.*, class E, Lytton to Salisbury, 29/2/77; *ibid.*, class C [India], Salisbury to Lytton, 16/2/77.

60.  HHM/3M/B, Salisbury's memorandum on the Mysore question [January 1867].

61.  *3H*, clxxxv, 839–46 (22/2/67); *ibid.*, clxxvii (24/5/67).

62.  HHM/3M/C [India], Salisbury to Northbrook, 30/7/75.

63.  Moulton, *Lord Northbrook's Indian Administration*, pp. 126–7; HHM/3M/C [India], Salisbury to Northbrook, 19/11/75 (first letter of this date) and 25/8/75.

64.  HHM/3M/E, Northbrook to Salisbury, 30/9/75; *ibid.*, class C [India], Salisbury to Northbrook (first letter of this date), 19/11/75.

65.  HHM/3M/E, Lytton to Salisbury, 11/5/76; *ibid.*, class D, Salisbury to Mallet, 11/1/77.

66.  HHM/3M/C [India], Salisbury to Lytton, 9/5/76; Hughenden P. (B/XX/Ce), Salisbury to Disraeli, 7/6/76; Council of India: Memoranda and Papers, C/139, Salisbury's minute, 2/11/76, on secret letter from India no. 47.

67.  HHM/3M/E, Lytton to Salisbury, 30/7/76; *ibid.*, class C [India], Salisbury to Lytton, 30/8/76.

68.  *Ibid.*, class E, Lytton to Salisbury, 5/8/76; *Salisbury*, II, p. 67; HHM/3M/C [India], Salisbury to Lytton, 1/2/78 and 31/3/76. For the policy-making machinery, see n78 below.

69.  Steele, "Salisbury at the India Office", *S.M.P.*, pp. 136–41; quotation from HHM/3M/C [India], Salisbury to Northbrook, 6/3/74.

70.  Northbrook P. (MSS Eur. C144/23), Northbrook to Lord George Hamilton, MP, parliamentary under-secretary for India, 7/4/76; *ibid.* (C144/18), Hobhouse to Northbrook, 5/1/76. There are a number of hostile references to the influence of Hobhouse in Salisbury's letters.

71.  HHM/3M/C [India], Salisbury to Lytton, 20/4/77.

72.  Steele, in *S.M.P.*, pp. 134–5; quotations from *3H*, clxxxv, 840 (22/2/67) and HHM/3M/C [India], Salisbury to Sir B. Frere, member of the Council of India, 10/12/75.

73.  *3H*, clxxxvii, 1025 (24/5/67); Lawrence P. (MSS Eur. F.90/27), Cranborne to Lawrence, 3/1/66, and (F.90/28), 18/2/67.

74.  B.B. Misra, *The Indian Middle Classes* (London, 1965), ch. 12, and A. Seal, *The Emergence of Indian Nationalism: Competition and Collaboration in the Late Nineteenth Century* (Cambridge, 1968) are landmarks in the historiography of Westernization.

75.  HHM/3M/C [India], Salisbury to Temple, 5/2/75; *ibid.*, Salisbury to Northbrook, 21/5/75 and Gopal, *British Policy in India*, pp. 118–20.

76.  *Ibid.*, pp. 116–18; HHM/3M/C [India], Salisbury to Lytton, 2/11 and 13/4/77.

77.  D. Gillard, *The Struggle for Asia: A Study in British and Russian Imperialism, 1828–1914* (London, 1977) is a good introduction to a topic popular with historians. Quotations from HHM/3M/C [India], Salisbury to Northbrook, 5/3/75; *ibid.*, class D, Salisbury to Derby, foreign secretary, 21/6/77, and class E, Lytton to Salisbury, 18/5/76.

78.  *3H*, clxxxix, 1382 (2/8/67); Northbrook P. (MSS Eur. C144/23), Perry to Northbrook, 9/7/75 and (C144/22), 20/3/74; HHM/3M/C [India], Salisbury to Lytton, 25/5/77.

On the policy-making machinery: A.B. Keith, *A Constitutional History of India, 1600–1935* (London, 1936) and S.N. Singh, *The Secretary of State for India and his Council* (Delhi, 1962). "Don't let yourself be guided by anyone in the Office, for there is no one competent to guide you" he told his successor as secretary of state in 1867, referring to officials and councillors alike, Iddesleigh P. (50019), Cranborne to Northcote, 22/3/67. More tolerant and better prepared in his second term at the India Office, he was essentially unchanged.

79. HHM/3M/E, Cranborne to R.D. Mangles, member of the Council of India, 5/6/67; *ibid.*, class C [India], Salisbury to Lytton, 2/11/77; Mallet, *Northbrook*, pp. 90, 92 – Mallet's own views.

## Chapter 6: The Eastern Question and the Foreign Office

1. M. & B., *Disraeli*, II, pp. 795, 1261, Disraeli to Lady Bradford, 17/12/75, 4/1/78.
2. Carnarvon D. (60911), 13/2/78; *D.D.*, p. 523 (8/3/78); R. Millman, *Britain and the Eastern Question 1875–1878* (Oxford, 1979), pp. 356, 456–61.

   D. Gillard, "Salisbury", in K.M. Wilson (ed.), *British Foreign Secretaries and Foreign Policy from Crimean War to World War* (London, 1987) for an overview of Salisbury at the Foreign Office, to be read with L.M. Penson's *Foreign Affairs under the Third Marquis of Salisbury* (London, 1962) and C.H.D. Howard, *Britain and the Casus Belli, 1822–1902: A Study of Britain's International Position from Canning to Salisbury* (London, 1974). P. Kennedy, *The Rise of the Anglo-German Antagonism, 1860–1914* (London, 1980) and his *The Realities behind Diplomacy: Background Influences on British External Policy, 1865–1980* (London, 1981) are central to the study of foreign policy in Salisbury's day.
3. *3H*, cciv, 1360–68 (14/7/70).
4. Carnarvon P. (60758), Salisbury to Carnarvon, 30/1/71, 6/1/72.
5. *T.T.*, 30/1/98. Fear of an Islamic revival was always present to him: "Many . . . symptoms appear to me to indicate a great ferment in the Mahommedan world"; to Beaconsfield, 13/9/?1878 in Hughenden P. (B/XX/Ce).
6. HHM/3M/C [India], Salisbury to Buckingham, 20/7/77.
7. *Ibid.*, Salisbury to Lytton, 8/3/77.
8. HHM/3M/A, Salisbury to Lord Odo Russell, ambassador at Berlin, 14/1 and 25/2/80. For the circumstances of Salisbury's brief departure from his policy of evading a formal Anglo-German alliance, see Chapter 8, pp. 177–83.
9. Stanmore P. (49209), Salisbury to Sir A. Gordon, 13/1/79; HHM/3M/DD, to G.M.W. Sandford, 3/5/72.
10. The Eastern question and this critical phase in its history have been extensively studied. Millman, *Britain and the Eastern Question*, stands out as a detailed examination of the great power diplomacy seen mainly from London; R.W. Seton Watson, *Disraeli, Gladstone and the Eastern Question* (London, 1935) remains well worth reading. R.T. Shannon, *Gladstone and the Bulgarian Agitation* (London, 1963) is essential for the British domestic context. For Russia and Austria in this Eastern crisis there are B.H. Sumner, *Russia and the Balkans, 1870–1880* (Oxford, 1937) and F.R. Bridge, *The Habsburg Monarchy among the Great Powers, 1815–1918* (New York and Oxford, 1990); for Turkey, F.A.K. Yasamee, *Ottoman Diplomacy: Abdülhamid II and the Great Powers, 1878–1880* (Istanbul, 1996), chs 1–4, is invaluable. The role of Germany, or rather Bismarck, is best approached through the published German diplomatic documents used here in the French translation, cited as *P[olitique] E[xtérieure de l']A[llemagne]*.

11. *D.D.*, pp. 240–41 (29/8 and 6/9/75), 243 (16/9/75), 265–6, 269–70 (7, 15 and 18/1/76); Derby P. (DER 16/2/7), Salisbury to Derby, 7/1/76.

12. *D.D.*, pp. 247–8 (3/11/75), 266 (9/1/76); *Salisbury*, II, p. 80, Salisbury to Sir Louis Mallet, 14/1/76; HHM/3M/D, Cranborne to Stanley, 17/10/66 and to Mallet, 2/7 and 5/9/75; Carnarvon P. (61074), Carnarvon to Heathcote, 18/9/76; *Q.V.L.* (2), II, pp. 428, 471, the Queen's journal, 24/11/75, and Derby to General H.F. Ponsonby, private secretary to the Queen, 10/7/76.

13. Millman, *Britain and the Eastern Question*, p. 88; Carnarvon/D. (60908) and *D.D.*, p. 298, both 22/5/76.

14. *Q.V.L.* (2), II, p. 391, the Queen's journal, 6/5/75, p. 457, Disraeli to the Queen, 7/6/76; *D.D.*, pp. 276 (9/2/76), 300–31 (9/6/76); D.D., L.R.O., 9/6/76 for a passage omitted from the published diaries.

15. HHM/3M/D, Beaconsfield (Disraeli) to Derby, 4/9/76; *Q.V.L.* (2), II, pp. 475–6, Leopold II to the Queen, 27/8/76, pp. 496–8, Beaconsfield to the Queen, 11/11/76; Yasamee, *Ottoman Diplomacy*, ch. 2.

16. Millman, *Britain and the Eastern Question*, p. 172, Salisbury to Lytton, 5/9/76; HHM/3M/D, Salisbury to Mallet, 3/8/76; *Salisbury*, II, pp. 84–7, Salisbury to Mallet, and Beaconsfield, both 23/9/76, to Carnarvon, 13/9/76.

17. Millman, *Britain and the Eastern Question*, p. 518 n9, Derby to Beaconsfield, 5/9/76; *D.D.*, pp. 240 (1/9/75), 331–2 (4/10/76), 335–7 (19 and 24/10/76); *Cranbrook/D.*, p. 292 (1/10/76); M. & B., *Disraeli*, II, p. 953, Beaconsfield to Derby, 17/10/76; HHM/3M/D, Beaconsfield to Salisbury, 17/10/76, Salisbury to Beaconsfield, 17 and 18/10/76.

18. *D.D.*, p. 340 (2 and 3/11/76); D.D., L.R.O., 8/11/76: the announcement of Salisbury's mission was well received on all sides: "his church connections will do something to conciliate the Christian fanatics . . ."; *Salisbury*, II, p. 95, Beaconsfield to Salisbury, 10/11/76, p. 90, Salisbury to Derby, 3/11/76; Millman, *Britain and the Eastern Question*, pp. 205–6.

19. *D.D.*, pp. 344–5 (16 and 18/11/76); *Salisbury*, II, pp. 95–107, Salisbury to Derby, 21 to 30/11/76; M. & B., *Disraeli*, II, pp. 975–6, Beaconsfield to Salisbury, 29/11/76.

20. *D.D.*, p. 345 (19/11/76); Millman, *Britain and the Eastern Question*, p. 196, Salisbury to Derby, 23/10/76; *Salisbury*, II, pp. 117–18, 123, Salisbury to Derby, 26/12/76, to Carnarvon, 19/1/77.

21. M. & B., *Disraeli*, II, pp. 966–7, Beaconsfield to Salisbury, 17/10/76, to Derby, 1/11/76; Liddon/D., 10/8/76; HHM/3M/D, Salisbury to Bath, 10/11/76 and Lady Salisbury to Bath, 25/1/77.

22. Derby P. (DER 16/2/7), Salisbury to Derby, 4/1/77; *P.E.A.*, II, pp. 83–5, von Werther, ambassador at Constantinople, to von Bülow, secretary of state, 14/1/77.

23. M. & B., *Disraeli*, II, pp. 975–8 (29/11 and 1/12/76); Yasamee, *Ottoman Diplomacy*, pp. 16–17.

24. *Salisbury*, II, pp. 96–7, Salisbury to Derby, 23/11/76, pp. 122–3, to Mallet, 11/1/77; Jomini-Onou P. (3187 and 3227/3228), M.K. Onou to an unnamed correspondent, 24/11 and to his wife, 15/12/76; D.D., L.R.O., 9/1/77; M. & B., *Disraeli*, II, pp. 983–4, Beaconsfield to Derby, 30/12/76.

25. Carnarvon P. (60758), Salisbury to Carnarvon, 14/12/76 and *ibid.* (60761), Carnarvon to Salisbury, 25/12/76; Iddesleigh P. (50032), Henry to Sir Stafford Northcote, 16/1/77; HHM/3M/D, Beaconsfield to Salisbury, 6/2/77; *Salisbury*, II, pp. 121–2, Salisbury to Carnarvon, 11/1/77.

26. *Ibid.*, p. 124, Salisbury to Derby, 19/1/77; M. & B., *Disraeli*, II, pp. 988–9, Beaconsfield to Derby, 30/12/76.

27. Bridge, *Habsburg Monarchy*, p. 118, memorandum for the Emperor Franz Josef, November 1876; *Salisbury*, II, pp. 86–7, Salisbury to Mallet, 23/11/76; *Q.V.L.* (2), II, pp. 519–20, General Ponsonby to the Queen, 19/1/77, reporting Beaconsfield's views.

28. Jomini-Onou P. (3227/3228), Onou to his wife, 1 and 15/12/76; Carnarvon P. (60759), Lady Salisbury to Carnarvon [January 1877].

29. Layard P. (38955), Lord Hammond, formerly permanent under-secretary at the Foreign Office, to A.H. Layard, 12/3/77; Carnarvon/D. (60909), 17/1, 22/2/77.

30. *Q.V.L.* (2), II, pp. 524–6, Beaconsfield to the Queen, 23/1/77; Carnarvon P. (60761), Carnarvon to Salisbury, 25/3/77.

31. *Ibid.*; and *Salisbury*, II, pp. 138–9, Salisbury to Carnarvon, 26/3/77.

32. Millman, *Britain and the Eastern Question*, p. 211; Carnarvon/D. (60909), 18/3/77; *Salisbury*, II, pp. 132–3.

33. *D.D.*, p. 383 (17/3/77); *Salisbury*, II, p. 131, Salisbury to Beaconsfield, 12/3/77; Derby P. (DER 16/2/7), Salisbury to Derby, 15/2/77; M. & B., *Disraeli*, II, pp. 902–3, 934–5, Disraeli to Lady Bradford, 6/6/76; and Derby's response to the deputation, 11/9/76.

34. Millman, *Britain and the Eastern Question*, p. 540 n77, Wolseley to R. Wolseley, 15/1/77; *Salisbury*, II, pp. 129, 142–3, 145, 154–5, Salisbury to Lytton, 16/2, 27/4, 25/5, 6/7/77; HHM/3M/C [India], Salisbury to Lytton, 9/2/77.

35. *Salisbury*, II, pp. 128–9, Salisbury to Lytton, 16/2 and 2/3/77.

36. *Ibid.*, pp. 130, 144–6, Salisbury to Lytton, 9/3, 21/5 and 15/6/77.

37. HHM/3M/C [India], Salisbury to Buckingham, 24/3/76 and Lytton, 25/6/77; *ibid.*, class D, Lady Salisbury to Bath [29/11/77].

38. *Q.V.L.* (2), II, pp. 529–30, Beaconsfield, secret memorandum for the Queen, 23/4/77; Gordon, *The Red Earl*, I, p. 128, Hartington to Spencer, 16/11/76; Carnarvon/D. (60909), 16/4/77.

39. Carnarvon P. (60759), Salisbury to Carnarvon, 18/4/77; *Q.V.L.* (2), II, pp. 530–31, Beaconsfield's secret memorandum no. 2, 23/4/77, refers to his conversation with Salisbury on 17 April.

40. *D.D.*, pp. 391–2 (21/4/77); *Gladstone–Granville Correspondence, 1876–1886*, I, pp. 35–6, Gladstone to Granville, 23/4/77, Granville to Gladstone, 27/4/77; *Cranbrook/D.*, p. 317 (22/4/77).

41. *D.D.*, pp. 393–4, 396–8 (25/4 and 1/5/77).

42. Millman, *Britain and the Eastern Question*, p. 308, Beaconsfield to the Queen, 12/7/77; *D.D.*, pp. 419–20 (14/7/77); Hardinge, *Carnarvon*, II, p. 359, Carnarvon's retrospective memorandum, 1879, on the cabinet and the Eastern question, 1876–8.

43. *Cranbrook/D.*, p. 320 (6/5/77); *D.D.*, p. 410 (18/6/77); M. & B., *Disraeli*, II, pp. 1016–18, Beaconsfield to Salisbury, 14/6/77, and to Derby, 17/6/77.

44. *Ibid.*, pp. 1013–14, Derby to Beaconsfield, ? 26/5/77; *D.D.*, p. 427 (2/8/77).

45. *Salisbury*, II, p. 141, Salisbury to Carnarvon, 27/5/77; *D.D.*, pp. 392, 410, 413 (21/4, 16/6, 30/6/77); D.D., L.R.O., 1889, summary of his wealth at the start of the year.

46. *Salisbury*, II, p. 130, Salisbury to Lytton, 9/3/77; HHM/3M/A, Salisbury to Wolseley, 9/8/78.

47. Hardinge, *Carnarvon*, II, pp. 358–9; M. & B., *Disraeli*, II, pp. 1073–4, Beaconsfield to the Queen, 16/7/77; *D.D.*, p. 422 (21/7/77).

48. *Ibid.*, pp. 423–6 (28, 30 and 31/7/77); *Q.V.L.* (2), II, p. 554, the Queen to Beaconsfield, 25/7/77.

49. *D.D.*, pp. 422–3 (21/7/77); Hardinge, *Carnarvon*, II, p. 360.
50. Carnarvon P. (60759), Salisbury to Carnarvon, 14/10/77.
51. Lytton P. (MSS Eur. E 218/19 pt ii), Lytton to Sir Henry Rawlinson, 28/7/77; *Cranbrook/D.*, p. 338 (5/9/77); Derby P. (DER 16/2/7), Salisbury to Derby, 8/10/77 and *D.D.*, pp. 442–3 (7 and 9/10/77).
52. *T.T.*, 12/10/77; *D.D.*, p. 445 (12/10/77), Derby found Salisbury's views "in general very fair and sound"; M. & B., *Disraeli*, II, p. 1068, Derby's remarks to the deputation on 28/11/77; *ibid.*, pp. 1065–7, Beaconsfield to the Queen, 3/11/77.
53. *3H*, ccxxxii, 54–6 (8/2/77); *ibid.*, 689–98 (20/2/77); *ibid.*, ccxxxvii, 54, 56 (17/1/78).
54. *Ibid.*, 56.
55. *Ibid.*, ccxli, 1804–5 (18/7/78); *ibid.*, ccxxxix, 837 (8/4/78).
56. *Ibid.*, ccxlii, 509 (29/7/78) and cclxi, 1814 (18/7/78).
57. *Ibid.*, 1811–12.
58. *D.D.*, p. 523 (8/3/78); Liddon/D., 31/1/78; Carnarvon/D. (60911), 17/6/78 and (60913), 17/4/79, copy of Carnarvon to Bath of the same date. Carnarvon P. (60771), Bath to Carnarvon, 15/9/78 and (61074), Heathcote to Carnarvon, 18/6/78, Carnarvon to Heathcote, 19/6/78.
59. *3H*, ccxli, 1814 (18/7/78).
60. HHM/3M/C [India], Salisbury to Lytton, 16/3/77; *Salisbury*, II, p. 242, Salisbury to Russell (Berlin), 10/4/78.
61. *D.D.*, p. 465 (17/12/77); M. & B., *Disraeli*, II, p. 1077, Beaconsfield to the Queen 17/12/77; and in *Q.V.L.* (2), II, pp. 577–8, 582 (18/12, 29/12/77).
62. *Salisbury*, II, pp. 163–4, Salisbury to Northcote, 15/12/77, and memorandum.
63. M. & B., *Disraeli*, II, pp. 1076–9, Beaconsfield to the Queen, 17/12/77 (two letters) and 18/12/77, memorandum of the day's cabinet. Selborne, *Memorials, Pt II*, vol. I, p. 333, Selborne to Sir A. Gordon, 6/9/74; *D.D.*, pp. 464–6 (17 and 18/12/77); Iddesleigh P. (50019), Salisbury to Northcote, 16 and 18/12/77.
64. *D.D.*, pp. 465–6 (18/12/77); *Salisbury*, II, pp. 166–70, Salisbury to Bath, 19/12, Beaconsfield to Salisbury, 24/12 and Salisbury to Beaconsfield, 26/12/77; M. & B., *Disraeli*, II, pp. 1078–9, Beaconsfield to the Queen, 18/12/77, memorandum of the day's cabinet, and Lady Bradford, 19/12/77: "I have triumphed . . . the recusants fell upon their knees".
65. *Salisbury*, II, pp. 170–71, Derby to Salisbury, 23/12/77, 175–6, Salisbury to Carnarvon, 8/1/78; Hardinge, *Carnarvon*, II, pp. 368–9.
66. *D.D.*, pp. 481–3, and n26, 489–90 (8/1 to 14/1 and 23/1/78); M. & B., *Disraeli*, II, pp. 1091–2, 1101–2, Beaconsfield to the Queen, 12 and 24/1/78; Hardinge, *Carnarvon*, II, pp. 372–6, memorandum of 1879: "had I known that this counter-order would be given, I do not think it would have altered my decision".
67. M. & B., *Disraeli*, II, p. 1101, Beaconsfield to the Queen, 24/1/78.
68. *D.D.*, pp. 488–9 (21/1/78); *Salisbury*, II, pp. 193–4.
69. *Ibid.*, p. 192, Salisbury to Carnarvon, 27/1/77.
70. M. & B., *Disraeli*, II, pp. 1108–9, Beaconsfield to Salisbury, 27/1/78; *D.D.*, pp. 490, 493 (23 and 26/1/78).
71. *Ibid.*, p. 500 (4/2/78).
72. Millman, *Britain and the Eastern Question*, p. 394.
73. *D.D.*, pp. 505, 511, 515 (11/2, 18 and 24/2/78).
74. Carnarvon/D. (60911), 13/3/78, a conversation with Lady Derby; Millman, *Britain and the Eastern Question*, p. 456.

75. Bridge, *Habsburg Monarchy*, p. 123; HHM/3M/C [India], Salisbury to Lytton, 13/7/77; M. & B., *Disraeli*, II, p. 1131, Beaconsfield to the Queen, 16/3/78.
76. *D.D.*, pp. 517–19 (27/2 and 2/3/78).
77. *Ibid.*, pp. 522–3 (7 and 8/3/78); Selborne P. (Lambeth MS. 1866), Granville to Selborne, 27/12/77.
78. HHM/3M/C [India], Salisbury to Lytton and Temple, both 15/3/78.
79. M. & B., *Disraeli*, II, pp. 1126–8, Beaconsfield to the Queen, 8/3/78; *ibid.*, pp. 1137–8, Derby's notes of the discussion in cabinet, 27/3/78: the source of the quotations here from Salisbury; *D.D.*, pp. 509, 552–3 (15/2 and 27/3/78).
80. *Salisbury*, II, p. 213, Salisbury to Beaconsfield, 21/3/78.
81. *3H*, ccxxxix, 100–103 (28/3/78), 789 (8/4/78), Derby; *ibid.*, cclxi, 1808–11 (18/7/78), Salisbury; *Cranbrook/D.*, 19/7/78.
    In response to protests, Salisbury substituted "not correct" for "not true". His letter to Northcote on 19 July (*Salisbury*, II, p. 222), drew a distinction between cabinet "conversation" about taking something from Turkey and "any definite proposal for seizure without the consent of the Sultan".
82. HHM/3M/C [India], Salisbury to Lytton, 29/3/78.
83. *Salisbury*, II, pp. 228–9; the full text is in H. Temperley and L.M. Penson, *Foundations of British Foreign Policy from Pitt (1792) to Salisbury (1902)* (London, 1966), pp. 372–80; Bridge, *Habsburg Monarchy*, pp. 123, 125; Millman, *Britain and the Eastern Question*, p. 419.
84. *Ibid.*, pp. 421–5 and 441–2; *Salisbury*, II, pp. 244–5, Salisbury to Russell (Berlin), 17/4/78.
85. *Ibid.*, pp. 262–3, Salisbury in the Lords, 3/6/78; Carnarvon/D. (60911), 17/6/78; *D.D.*, *L.R.O.*, 3/5, 5 and 17/6/78.
86. C.H.D. Howard and P. Gordon (eds), "The Cabinet Journal of Dudley Ryder, Viscount Sandon", *Bulletin of the Institute of Historical Research* (1974), special supplement no. 10, pp. 16–17 (1/6/78); *Salisbury*, II, p. 243.
87. *Ibid.*, pp. 244–5, Salisbury to Russell, 17/10/78; *ibid.*, p. 215, Salisbury to Col. R. Home, R.E., 5/8/78; Howard and Gordon, "The Cabinet Journal of . . . Viscount Sandon", pp. 9–10 (24/5/78).
88. *Ibid.*, p. 13, 27/5/78; *Salisbury*, II, pp. 244–6, Salisbury to Sir Henry Elliot, ambassador at Vienna, 10/4 and Russell, 17/10/78.
89. *Ibid.*, pp. 280, 286–7, Salisbury to his wife, 13 and 23/6/78. W.N. Medlicott, *The Congress of Berlin and After*, 2nd edn (London, 1963) and D.E. Lee, *Great Britain and the Cyprus Convention Policy of 1878* (Cambridge, 1934) for detailed histories of the conference and the acquisition of Cyprus.
90. Medlicott, *The Congress of Berlin and After*, pp. 112–13; Howard and Gordon, "The Cabinet Journal of . . . Viscount Sandon", p. 32 (25/6/78); Lee, *Cyprus Convention*, p. 196, for the text of the British declaration; HHM/3M/A, Salisbury to Lord Lyons, 11/5 and 5/6/78.
91. *3H*, cccxxxix, 829 (8/4/78); Monson P. (MSS Eng. hist. c.593), Salisbury to Sir Edmund Monson, minister at Athens, 4/11/89.
92. Layard P. (39138), Salisbury to Layard, 17/7 and 7/8/78; *ibid.* (39139), 23/1, 8/5 and 30/10/79, 8/1/80; *Salisbury*, II, pp. 306–10, Salisbury to Northcote, 5 and 22/8/78.
93. Layard P. (39139), Salisbury to Layard, 8/1/80; Yasamee, *Ottoman Diplomacy*, ch. 2.
94. Layard P. (39139), Salisbury to Layard, 20/8/79.
95. M. & B., *Disraeli*, II, p. 1267, Beaconsfield to the Queen, 27/11/78.

96. Layard P. (39138), Salisbury to Layard, 29/10/78 and (39139), 19/2/80.
97. *3H*, ccxlvi, 564 (16/5/79) on the future of Turkey: "We cannot revive the dead . . . we can at least give time for ascertaining whether these gloomy anticipations are correct"; *T.T.*, 18/10/79, second speech at the Free Trade Hall.
98. D.D., L.R.O., 2/11/79; *P.E.A.*, III, pp. 129–50, Münster to Bismarck, 17/10/79; *Salisbury*, II, pp. 364–9, Salisbury to Beaconsfield, 29/9, 13 and 15/10/79.
99. *T.T.*, 18/10/79, first speech at the Free Trade Hall; *ibid.*, 2/8/78.
100. HHM/3M/H, Nathaniel Woodard, now a canon of Manchester, to Salisbury, 8/11/76; *T.T.*, 2/8/78.

# Chapter 7: A Leader in Waiting

1. *P.E.A.*, II, pp. 301–3, Münster to Bismarck, 10/6/78; M. & B., *Disraeli*, II, pp. 1157–8, Beaconsfield to the Queen, 12/4/78.
2. *Cranbrook/D.*, p. 476, 10/5/81; Carnarvon P. (60913), 17/4/79, copy of Carnarvon to Bath of the same date.
3. *Ibid.*; D.D., L.R.O., 24/2/79; HHM/3M/E, Lady Janetta Manners to Salisbury, 19/4/81.
4. Selborne P. (Lambeth MS. 1873), Selborne to Sir A. Gordon, 12/9/78.
5. HHM/4M/387, Salisbury to Cranborne, 22/2/81; *Salisbury*, III, p. 34.
6. Lytton P. (59611), Lytton to his wife [10/5/81].
7. D.W.R. Bahlman, *The Diary of Sir Edward Hamilton* (2 vols) (Oxford, 1972), I, p. 291 (25/6/82). Cairns died in April 1885.
8. W.T. Stead, *The M.P. for Russia* (2 vols) (London, 1909), I, p. 272, Gladstone to Mme Novikov, 22/11/76; Liddon/D., 31/1/78; Bahlman, *Hamilton*, I, p. 131 (19/4/81).
9. *Ibid.*, II, pp. 652–3 (12 and 14/7/84); Russell, *MacColl*, pp. 92–3, Salisbury to MacColl, 11/7/84.
10. D.D., L.R.O., 7/2/80; HHM/3M/D, Salisbury to H.J.B. Manners, 8/7/82.
11. *Ibid.*, Salisbury to Lady Janetta Manners, 1/2, 12/7/81, 1/5, 14 and 25/6/84, 19/1 and 11/3/85; also *Salisbury*, III, pp. 36–7 (8/7/80).
12. HHM/3M/D, Salisbury to Lady Janetta Manners, 14/11/82, 21/9/83, 16/3/84, 19/1/85.
13. T.O. Lloyd, *The General Election of 1880* (Oxford, 1968) for analysis of the contest. H.J. Hanham, *Elections and Party Management: Politics in the Time of Disraeli and Gladstone* (London, 1964) for a broader study of the electoral system of the time.
14. D.D., L.R.O., 30/3, 3/4, 7/4/80.
15. HHM/3M/D, Salisbury to Lady Janetta Manners, 18/4/80; *Salisbury*, I, pp. 293–4, Salisbury to Carnarvon, 24/4/68; Otter, *Woodard*, p. 313, Salisbury to Woodard, 13/8/83.
16. Marsh, *Discipline of Popular Government*, ch. 1, "Defiance", for one view of Salisbury's political posture in the early 1880s.
17. HHM/3M/D, Salisbury to Lady Janetta Manners, 18/4/80; *T.T.*, 23/4/85, Welshpool, 5/6/84, Plymouth, 17 and 18/4/84, Manchester.
18. Acland P. (MS. Acland d. 74), Salisbury to H.W. Acland, 22/11/69; *T.T.*, 14/4/82, Liverpool, 17 and 18/4/84, Manchester; D.D., L.R.O., 2/6/85, Derby added that Lady Galloway was a reliable witness; P. Marsh, *Joseph Chamberlain: Entrepreneur in Politics*

(New Haven and London, 1994), ch. 7 for Salisbury's antagonist and future partner in the mid-1880s.

19.  *Ibid.*, and HHM/3M/E, Lord George Hamilton, MP to Salisbury, 5/12/86.

20.  *T.T.*, 13 and 14/4/82, Liverpool; 17/4/84, 23/4/85.

21.  *Ibid.*, 23/4/85; 31/10/83, Derby; 14/4/84; Otter, *Woodard*, p. 302, Woodard to Canon E.C. Lowe, 1881.

22.  *National Review*, November 1883; Marsh, *Discipline of Popular Government*, pp. 51–2; Gladstone's private secretary wrote that Salisbury's article embodied "the very essence of Socialist principles", Bahlman, *Hamilton*, II, p. 499 (5/11/83).

23.  *3H*, cclxxxiv, 1689–90 (22/2/84); D. Nicholls, *The Lost Prime Minister: A Life of Sir Charles Dilke* (London, 1995), 131–2; Dilke P. (43876), Salisbury to Dilke, 7/2/85; D.D., L.R.O., 19/3/84.

24.  *3H*, ccxcix, 889–97 (16/7/85); *Gladstone Diaries*, XI, p. 380, Gladstone to E.L. Stanley, MP, 4/8/85; *Salisbury*, III, pp. 80–81.

25.  *3H*, ccxcix, 1174 (29/7/85); Bahlman, *Hamilton*, II, pp. 416–17 (3/4/83); Carnarvon/ D. (60921), 30/10/83; HHM/3M/D, Salisbury to Lady Janetta Manners, 27/7/84; HHM/4M/387, Salisbury to Cranborne, 22/2/84.

26.  *T.T.*, 14/4/82; Bahlman, *Hamilton*, II, p. 697 (3/4/83); HHM/3M/D, Lord John Manners to Salisbury, 27/11/82.

27.  *T.T.*, 24/11/87, leading article; Austin P. (DM 668), Salisbury to Alfred Austin, 20/ 10/82.

28.  E.D. Steele, "Lord Salisbury and his Northern Audiences", *Northern History* (1995), pp. 223–40; *T.T.*, 30/10/68, 31/3/83; St Aldwyn P. (D2455/PCC/69), Salisbury to Hicks Beach, 9/8/85; Harcourt Williams, *Salisbury–Balfour Correspondence*, p. 101, Salisbury to Balfour, 16/12/83; D.D., L.R.O., 2/11/83, Gladstone in conversation with Derby; *3H*, ccxcviii, 318 (12/5/85).

29.  Russell, *MacColl*, p. 110; *T.T.*, 20/11/80, at Henley.

30.  Cowling, *1867: Disraeli, Gladstone and Revolution*, ch. 9, "Palmerston's Mantle"; *Gladstone–Granville Correspondence, 1876–1886*, I, p. 1, Gladstone to Granville, 20/8/76; Sir Edward Malet, quoted in E.D. Steele, "Britain and Egypt, 1882–1914", in K.M. Wilson (ed.), *Imperialism and Nationalism in the Middle East: The Anglo-Egyptian Experience, 1882–1982* (London, 1983), p. 2.

31.  Reprinted in Smith, *Lord Salisbury on Politics*, pp. 338–76.

32.  Bahlman, *Hamilton*, II, p. 602 (26/4/84); *Gladstone Diaries*, X, pp. lxxi–lxxii. R. Robinson and J. Gallagher, *Africa and the Victorians: The Official Mind of Imperialism* (London, 1961), ch. 1, "The Spirit of Victorian Expansion" remains the best discussion of the motives for empire and its enlargement.

33.  Lord Edward Cecil, author of *The Leisure of an Egyptian Official* (London, 1921).

34.  *3H*, cclix, 123 (3/3/81); cclx, 318 (31/3/81); and cclxxxv, 630–31 (6/3/84).

35.  *Ibid.*, ccxcvii, 1279 (1/5/85), cclxxxvi, 10 (17/3/84).

36.  Morley, *Gladstone*, II, pp. 248–9; Montenegro was also a beneficiary of the British action.

37.  *T.T.*, 27/10/80, second speech at Taunton; *3H*, cclv, 176 (21/5/80); Bridge, *Habsburg Monarchy*, pp. 140–44.

38.  Harcourt Williams, *Salisbury–Balfour Correspondence*, pp. 35–7, Salisbury to Balfour, 18/ 3/80, with his memorandum of the same date; *T.T.*, 27/10/80, second speech at Taunton.

39.  *Salisbury*, III, pp. 129–30, Salisbury to Lord Cairns, 3/2/85; *T.T.*, 22/4/85, Wrexham; *ibid.*, 6/5/85, Hackney; Bahlman, *Hamilton*, II, p. 857 (5/5/85).

40. *Salisbury*, II, pp. 329–35, 348–59; Lord Newton, *Lord Lyons* (2 vols) (London, 1913), I, ch. xiii.

41. HHM/3M/A, Salisbury to Lyons, 10/8/78; Iddesleigh P. (50019), Salisbury to Northcote, 14/4, 10/8/79; to F.C. Lascelles, 28/3/79 in *Salisbury*, III, pp. 349–50.

42. Iddesleigh P. (50020), Salisbury to Northcote, 16/9/81; Lord Cromer, *Modern Egypt* (2 vols) (London, 1908), I, p. 219; *3H*, cclxxii, 1578 (24/7/82); *ibid.*, cclxxiii, 1947 (16/8/82); *Gladstone–Granville Correspondence, 1876–1886*, I, pp. 447–8, Gladstone to Granville, 17/10/82; Steele, "Britain and Egypt, 1882–1914", in Wilson, *Imperialism and Nationalism in the Middle East*, pp. 3–4.

43. Quoted in A.J.P. Taylor, *The Trouble Makers: Dissent over Foreign Policy, 1792–1939* (London, 1957), p. 89.

44. Iddesleigh P. (50020), Salisbury to Northcote, 29/9/82; *3H*, clxxxiv, 576–7 (12/2/84).

45. *Ibid.*, cclxxii, 1504 (24/7/82); Iddesleigh P. (50020), Salisbury to Northcote, 29/9/82.

46. Steele, "Britain and Egypt, 1882–1914" in Wilson, *Imperialism and Nationalism in the Middle East*, p. 7; *T.T.*, 6/8/85.

47. *Ibid.*, 30/6, 24/11/82, London and Edinburgh.

48. Gladstone P. (44545), Gladstone to Shaftesbury, 18/9/82; *T.T.*, 29/3, 30/3/83, Birmingham, second speech on 30/3.

49. M. Bennett, *The Ilberts in India, 1882–1886: An Imperial Miniature* (London, 1995) for the intentions of C.P. Ilbert, Ripon's law member, and the reactions to his Jurisdiction Bill; and Gopal, *British Policy in India*, 148–9. Salisbury in *T.T.*, 30/3/83, second speech.

50. *Ibid.*, 31/5, 10/5/83, Bermondsey and Knightsbridge.

51. *Ibid.*, 10/3/83, leading article; 21/5/85; 31/10/83, third speech at Reading; 31/1/84, Hertford.

52. *Ibid.*, 17/4/84.

53. *Ibid.*, 18/4/84; Bahlman, *Hamilton*, II, p. 630 (5/6/84).

54. *T.T.*, 5/4/85; Morley, *Gladstone*, II, p. 384.

55. D.D., L.R.O., 6/6/84.

56. *T.T.*, 2/10, first speech, 4/10/84, 23/4/85, Welshpool. B.H. Brown, *The Tariff Reform Movement in Great Britain, 1881–95* (New York, 1941), for this phase of the revival of protectionism.

57. *T.T.*, 17/4/84, 23/4/85.

58. R.F. Foster, *Lord Randolph Churchill: A Political Life* (Oxford, 1988); R.T. Shannon, *The Age of Salisbury, 1882–1902: Unionism and Empire* (London, 1996) is a history of the changing party.

59. D.D., L.R.O., p. 82 (1/12/82): the diarist's social classification of his colleagues in the second Gladstone ministry concluded that "It would be difficult to find a cabinet with less admixture of anything that in France would be called democracy in its composition"; the two members from "the middle and trading class", the radicals Dilke and Chamberlain, were, respectively, a baronet and "they say not far from a millionaire".

60. Foster, *Churchill*, p. 63; Bahlman, *Hamilton*, pp. 192 (1/12/81), 291 (25/6/82).

61. Harcourt Williams, *Salisbury–Balfour Correspondence*, pp. 51, 53, Salisbury to Balfour, 29/9 and 5/10/80; Austin P. (DM 668), Salisbury to Austin, 11/6/84.

62. Harcourt Williams, *Salisbury–Balfour Correspondence*, p. 82, Balfour to Salisbury, 19/9/80; *ibid.*, p. 40, Salisbury to Balfour, 10/4/80. Otter, *Woodard*, pp. 308–9, Salisbury to Woodard, 1/1/83.

63. Smith, *Lord Salisbury on Politics*; quotations from pp. 355, 359, 346.

64. Iddesleigh P. (50020), Salisbury to Northcote, 17/10/82.
65. *T.T.*, 15/5/84, London, at a Tory working men's dinner; Foster, *Churchill*, chs 3 and 4; Churchill P. (RCHL 1/2/274a), Churchill to Markham Spofforth, 27/1/84.
66. *Ibid.* (1/2/222), Salisbury to Churchill, 11/12/83; (1/2/306a), Churchill to Salisbury, 6/3/84; H.E. Gorst, *The Fourth Party* (London, 1906), p. 277, Churchill to Salisbury, 3/4/84; Foster, *Churchill*, pp. 158–9.
67. Carnarvon/D. (60923), 10/7/84; Iddesleigh P. (50020), Salisbury to Northcote, 26/7/84.
68. Austin P. (DM 668), Salisbury to Austin, 24/7/84.
69. Carnarvon P. (60759), Salisbury to Carnarvon, 25/3/82.
70. Andrew Jones, *The Politics of Reform, 1884* (Cambridge, 1972), for the Liberal and Tory contributions to the last of the great nineteenth-century Reform Acts.
71. Salisbury made his calculations public in the *National Review* for October 1884, pp. 145–62, "The Value of Redistribution: A Note on Electoral Statistics"; *Gladstone Diaries*, XI, p. 180, Gladstone to Argyll, 30/7/84; P. Jackson, *The Last of the Whigs: A Political Biography of Lord Hartington, later 8th Duke of Devonshire* (London and Toronto, 1994), p. 162; Carlingford/D. (63692), 4/7/84; Harcourt Williams, *Salisbury–Balfour Correspondence*, p. 109, Salisbury to Balfour, 15/6/84.
72. Gorst, *The Fourth Party*, 294, Gorst to Wolff, 4/6/84; *Gladstone Diaries*, XI, pp. 225–6, Gladstone to Lord Hartington, 13/10/84, to Lord Winmarleigh, 13/10/84.
73. *Ibid.*, and p. 201, Gladstone to Argyll, 31/8/84.
74. *Q.V.L.* (2), III, p. 539, the Queen to Ponsonby, 16/9/84; Morley, *Gladstone*, II, p. 370, in conversation with Ponsonby, September 1884; *Gladstone Diaries*, XI, 15/9/84; Carlingford/D. (63692), 22/10/84.
75. H. Paul (ed.), *Letters of Lord Acton* (London, 1904), p. 174, Acton to Mary Gladstone, 17/3/84; *Gladstone–Granville Correspondence, 1876–1886*, II, p. 226, Granville to Gladstone, 15/8/84.
76. Goodwood P. (872), Halifax to Richmond, 13/7/84; Carnarvon/D. (60923), 10/7/84.
77. Goodwood P. (872), Salisbury to Richmond, 14/6/84; Carlingford/D. (63692), 8/7/84; *T.T.*, 25/7/84, and Salisbury at Manchester, 11/8/84.
78. Paul, *Letters of Lord Acton*, pp. 190, 192, Acton to Mary Gladstone, 15 and 29/8/84.
79. Bahlman, *Hamilton*, II, p. 673 (20/8/84); *Gladstone–Granville Correspondence, 1876–1886*, II, pp. 221, 231, Gladstone to Granville, 1 and 18/8/84; HHM/3M/D, Salisbury to Lady Janetta Manners, 2/9/84.
80. *T.T.*, 13/3, 2 and 22/10/84.
81. Ripon P. (43526), Kimberley to Ripon, 31/10/84.
82. *Gladstone Diaries*, XI, pp. 186, 198–9, Gladstone to Dilke, 8/8 and cabinet minutes, 9/8, to Ponsonby, with memorandum, 25/8/84; *Q.V.L.* (2), II, pp. 537–8, the Queen's journal, 8 and 14/9/84.
83. Goodwood P. (872), Cairns to Richmond, 19/9/84; Carnarvon/D. (60923), 18/7/84; *Salisbury*, III, p. 116, Salisbury to his wife, 12/10/84.
84. *Q.V.L.* (2), III, p. 561, the Queen's journal, 29/10/84; *Gladstone Diaries*, XI, p. 220, Gladstone to Chamberlain, 6/10/81: "You may safely denounce him to your heart's content"; *Q.V.L.* (2), III, pp. 548–9, the Queen's journal, 9 and 10/10/84.
85. Carnarvon/D. (60923), 22/10/84; Gordon, *The Red Earl*, I, pp. 252–3, Hartington to Lord Spencer, viceroy of Ireland, 18/10/83.
86. Bahlman, *Hamilton*, II, p. 690 (26/9/84); Nicholls, *The Lost Prime Minister*, p. 168; *Gladstone Diaries*, XI, p. 214, Gladstone to Argyll, 28/9/84.

87. Carnarvon/D. (60923), 22/10/84.

88. *Gladstone Diaries*, XI, pp. 215 and n1, 217, Dilke's cabinet memorandum of 20/9, Gladstone to Dilke, 29/9, to Hartington, 1/10/84; *Q.V.L.* (2), III, pp. 548–9, 551–3, the Queen's journal, 10/10, Salisbury to Ponsonby, 20/10/84; Nicholls, *The Lost Prime Minister*, pp. 147–8.

89. Carlingford/D. (63692), 6/11/84, summarizing Gladstone to the Queen.

90. *Q.V.L.* (2), III, p. 567, Granville to the Queen, 7/11/84; *Gladstone Diaries*, p. 236, Gladstone to Derby, 7/11/84.

91. Carlingford/D. (63692), 18/11/84; D.D., L.R.O., 18/8/84; Goodwood P. (872), Cairns to Richmond, 5/11/84; Carnarvon/D. (60923), 24/10/84.

92. *Gladstone Diaries*, XI, pp. 244–5, 251–2 (19/11 and memorandum of 28/11/84); *Salisbury*, III, pp. 123–4.

93. Nicholls, *The Lost Prime Minister*, pp. 147–51; Jackson, *The Last of the Whigs*, pp. 177–8; Dilke P. (43938), Chamberlain to Dilke, recorded in the latter's "Memoir" [22/11/84].

94. Carlingford/D. (63692), 19/11/84; Marsh, *Discipline of Popular Government*, p. 46, Dilke to Sir M. Grant Duff, 15/8/84; Austin P. (DM 668), Salisbury to Austin, 24/11/84.

95. P. Bew, *Land and the National Question in Ireland, 1858–82* (Atlantic Highlands, NJ, 1979); S. Clark, *Social Origins of the Irish Land War* (Princeton, NJ, 1979), and B.L. Solow, *The Land Question and the Irish Economy, 1870–1903* (Cambridge, Mass., 1971). C.C. O'Brien, *Parnell and his Party, 1880–1890* (Oxford, 1957) on the organization that combined agrarianism and nationalism with unprecedented success.

96. Ripon P. (43570), Northbrook, first lord of the Admiralty, to Ripon, 6/8/80: "We had a terrible thrashing in the Lords. All London was in a panic about the little bill, and our old friends ran away faster than the Tories"; Bew, *Land and the National Question in Ireland*, pp. 119–20.

97. *3H*, ccliv, 1929–30 (2/8/80); D.D., L.R.O., 19/2/81.

98. Harcourt Williams, *Salisbury–Balfour Correspondence*, p. 63, Salisbury to Balfour, 31/1/81; HHM/3M/C [India], Salisbury to Temple, 27/9/76; *3H*, cclxiv, 516 (2/8/81).

99. *Gladstone Diaries*, X, p. 91 n3; *3H*, cclxvi, 1514–15 (24/2/82); Carnarvon/D. (60917), 1, 3, 15 and 16/8/81.

100. *Gladstone Diaries*, XI, p. 656, printing the Derby diary for 28/10/81.

101. *Ibid.*, and Carnarvon/D. (60916), 11/5/81.

102. Bew, *Land and the National Question in Ireland*, ch. 9; the resignations were those of Earl Cowper and W.E. Forster.

103. HHM/3M/D, Salisbury to Lady Janetta Manners, 24/7/82; D.D., L.R.O., 2/5/82.

104. Carnarvon/D. (60918), 7/5/82; *ibid.*, 16/6/82. Gladstone was reported as saying to his Tory brother, Sir Thomas: "I have at least done this – I have . . . put down a social revolution in Ireland".

105. Bahlman, *Hamilton*, I, p. 312 (27/7/82).

106. *Cranbrook/D.*, p. 499 (19 and 22/7/82); Carnarvon/D. (60919), 4/8/82.

107. Goodwood P. (871), Cairns to Richmond, 4, 6 and 17/8/82; *Cranbrook/D.*, p. 501 (11/8/82); Carnarvon/D. (60919), 10/8/82; *Salisbury*, III, p. 54, Salisbury to his wife, 10/8/82.

108. D.D., L.R.O., 12/8/82; *3H*, cclxxiii, 1330–35 (10/8/82); *Cranbrook/D.*, p. 501 (11/8/82).

109. *Salisbury*, III, p. 56; *T.T.*, 24/11/82, Edinburgh.

110. Iddesleigh P. (50020), Salisbury to Northcote, 10/8, 21/12/84.

111. E.D. Steele, "Gladstone and Ireland", *Irish Historical Studies* (1970), pp. 58–88; D.D., L.R.O., 10, 12 and 28/2, 13/3, 9/6/82.

112. Carnarvon/D. (60919), 18/10/84, partly printed in Hardinge, *Carnarvon*, III, pp. 148–50.

113. *Ibid.*

114. *National Review*, February 1885, pp. 723–33; Carnarvon P. (60760), Salisbury to Carnarvon, 10/2/85.

115. *Ibid.*, Salisbury to Carnarvon, 21/3/85.

## Chapter 8: The First Premiership and Ireland, 1885–6

1. A.B. Cooke and J.R. Vincent, *Lord Carlingford's Journal: Reflections of a Cabinet Minister, 1885* (Oxford, 1971), pp. 73–4, 113–14 (28/2, 9/6/85); D.D., L.R.O., 19/5/85; EWH/D. (48672), 6/1/98.

2. A.B. Cooke and J.R. Vincent, *The Governing Passion: Cabinet Government and Party Politics in Britain, 1885–86* (Brighton, 1974) is a reconstruction, day by day, of political activity at the highest level on both sides.

3. Bahlman, *Hamilton*, II, pp. 887–96; *Q.V.L.* (2), III, pp. 663–78 *passim*; Cooke and Vincent, *The Governing Passion*, pp. 266–9, for Salisbury's hard bargaining with Gladstone to ensure that his minority administration survived the remaining weeks of the session.

4. HHM/3M/E, Churchill to Salisbury, 28/4/85; Churchill P. (RCHL 1/5/597d), Salisbury to Churchill, 28/4/85.

5. HHM/3M/E, Northcote to Salisbury, 3/6/84.

6. *Cranbrook/D.*, p. 476 (10/5/81); D.D., L.R.O., 21/2, 21/4/81; HHM/3M/D, Salisbury to H.J.B. Manners, 23/8/83.

7. Goodwood P. (871), Cairns to Richmond, 29/10/83; Marsh, *Discipline of Popular Government*, pp. 29–30; D.D., L.R.O., 26/8/83.

8. *Q.V.L.* (2), III, pp. 663–4, 667–8, the Queen's journal, 12/6/85 and Salisbury to the Queen, 15/6/85; HHM/3M/D, Hicks Beach to Salisbury, 10/6/85, and (class E), Hamilton to Salisbury, 15/6/85; Carnarvon/D. (60922), 17/5/84, Lady Salisbury to the diarist.

9. *Salisbury*, III, p. 139, Salisbury to Northcote, 16/6/85.

10. Cooke and Vincent, *The Governing Passion*, p. 263, Salisbury to Northcote, 14/6/85; Hardinge, *Carnarvon*, II, pp. 156–9, Carnarvon's note of his views, 15/6/85, and his letter to Salisbury, 16/6/85.

11. *T.T.*, 8/10/85, quotations from Salisbury's introductory remarks to the National Union at Newport, and *The Times* leading article. His main speech is reprinted in H.W. Lucy (ed.), *Speeches of the Marquis of Salisbury* (London, 1885); *Gladstone Diaries*, X, p. cxxxviii.

12. Lucy, *Speeches*, pp. 176–82.

13. *Ibid.*, pp. 188–97.

14. *Ibid.*, pp. 198–204.

15. HHM/3M/E, Churchill to Salisbury, 8/10/85; *Cranbrook/D.*, p. 577 (8/10/85); D.D., L.R.O., 8/10/85; EWH/D. (48641), 8/10/85.

16. St Aldwyn P. (D2455/PC/69), Salisbury to Hicks Beach, 19/8/85; *P.E.A.*, IV, pp. 191–3, Count William Bismarck to his father, 19/8/85.

17. *Ibid.*, pp. 228–31, Bismarck to Hatzfeldt (London), 9/12/85; F. Stern, *Gold and Iron: Bismarck, Bleichröder, and the Building of the German Empire* (London, 1980), p. 527.

18. R.L. Greaves, *Persia and the Defence of India, 1884–1892* (London, 1959), ch. vi for the offer to Bismarck, esp. pp. 93–4, copy of paper shown to Bismarck's son Count Herbert by Philip Currie, acting for Salisbury, 3/8/85.

19. A. Ramm, "Lord Salisbury at the Foreign Office", in R. Bullen (ed.), *The Foreign Office, 1782–1982* (Frederick, Maryland, 1984), pp. 46–65; D.D., L.R.O., 14/6/78; Curzon P. (MSS Eur. F. 112/1(a)), Salisbury to Curzon, 23/3/96; Churchill P. (RCHL 1/7/809), Hicks Beach to Churchill, 17/8/85.

20. HHM/3M/D, Salisbury to the Queen, 8/11/87; Meyendorff, *Correspondance Diplomatique de M. de Staal*, I, pp. 237 n1, 278–80, de Staal to N.K. Giers, foreign minister, 10/7, 12/12/85.

21. 4th Earl of Dunraven, *Past Times and Pastimes* (2 vols) (London, 1922), I, p. 188; *Q.V.L.* (2), I, p. 104, Salisbury to the Queen, 29/8/85; C.H.D. Howard (ed.), *The Diary of Edward Goschen* (London, 1980), p. 9, undated draft from Edward to G.J. Goschen, his brother in the cabinet [1896]: "if he [Salisbury] hates the service as he is said to do, the service perfectly loathes him".

22. HHM/3M/E, Currie's memorandum of his talks with Bismarck, 28–30/9/85; summarized in *Salisbury*, III, pp. 257–61.

23. *Ibid.*; and Paget P. (51228), Salisbury to Paget, 14/12/82 and (51229), 16/8/92.

24. A. Ramm, *Sir Robert Morier* (Oxford 1973); Morier P. (box 21), Salisbury to Morier, 16/9/85; HHM/3M/E, W.H. Smith, secretary of state for war, to Salisbury, 9/8/85. The Russians were not disposed to force the pace, D. Geyer, *Russian Imperialism* (Leamington Spa, 1987), p. 114.

25. C.L. Smith, *The Embassy of Sir William White at Constantinople, 1886–91* (London, 1957); Yasamee, *Ottoman Diplomacy*, ch. 11; Churchill P. (RCHL 1/8/907), Wolff to Churchill, 21/9/85.

26. HHM/3M/A, Salisbury to Wolff, 8/9/85; *D.D.F.*, vol. 6, pp. 173–4, de Courcel (Berlin) to Freycinet, foreign minister, 5/1/86.

27. Paget P. (51228), Salisbury to Paget, 24/9/85; HHM/3M/E, Churchill to Salisbury, 20/9/85.

28. *Ibid.*; and Meyendorff, *Correspondance Diplomatique de M. de Staal*, I, pp. 278–80, de Staal to Giers, 12/12/85; G. Martel, *Imperial Diplomacy: Rosebery and the Failure of Foreign Policy* (London and Montreal, 1986), ch. 1.

29. HHM/3M/E, Churchill to Salisbury, 11/10/85.

30. *Ibid.*, Churchill to Salisbury, 28/10/85 and (class D), Balfour to Churchill, 29/10/85; Morier P. (box 21), Salisbury to Morier, 20/1/86.

31. *Ibid.*, Salisbury to Morier, 2/12/85 and 20/1/86.

32. *Ibid.*, Salisbury to Morier, 2/12/85; R.A., H29/12, Salisbury to the Queen, 17/1/86; *Q.V.L.* (2), III, pp. 693–5, the Queen to Salisbury, 25/9, Salisbury to the Queen, 28/9/85.

33. *Gladstone Diaries*, XI, pp. 438–9, Gladstone to Rosebery, 1/12/85 and Bryce, 2/12/85; *Q.V.L.* (2), III, p. 692, Salisbury to the Queen, 24/9/85; HHM/3M/D, Salisbury to Churchill, 16/10/85.

34. Paget P. (51228), Salisbury to Paget, 5/2/86; HHM/3M/E, Morier to Salisbury, 29/2/85; Iddesleigh P. (50020), Salisbury to Iddesleigh, 24/8/85.

35. HHM/3M/E, Morier to Salisbury, 29/2/86; *Salisbury*, III, pp. 139, 169–70, Salisbury to Northcote, 16/6/85, and Hicks Beach's recollections.

36. Foster, *Churchill*, pp. 225–9; Cooke and Vincent, *The Governing Passion*, pp. 68–70.

37. HHM/3M/E, Winn to Salisbury, 28/2/85 and Winn's note of the approach from Power, 20/6/85.

38. *Ibid.*, and Cooke and Vincent, *The Governing Passion*, pp. 266–7.

39. Iddesleigh P. (50063A–pt ii), diary, 26/6/85; *Cranbrook/D.*, p. 565 (27/6/85).

40. Cooke and Vincent, *Lord Carlingford's Journal*, p. 100 (9/5/85).

41. Carnarvon/D. (60925), 6/7/85.
42. *Ibid.*, and Carnarvon in the Lords, quoted in Viscount (Herbert) Gladstone, *After Thirty Years* (London, 1928), p. 391.
43. Cooke and Vincent, *The Governing Passion*, pp. 272–3; *Q.V.L.* (2), III, pp. 687–8, the Queen to Salisbury, 18/7/85; Gordon, *The Red Earl*, I, p. 312, James to Spencer, 18/7/85; *Salisbury*, III, pp. 145–6, Salisbury to Hicks Beach, 16/7 and the Queen, 20/7/85.
44. HHM/3M/D, Salisbury to W.H. Smith, 21/7/85.
45. Hardinge, *Carnarvon*, III, pp. 174, 180; Carnarvon/D. (60925), 1/8/85.
46. *Salisbury*, III, p. 146, Salisbury to the Queen, 20/7/85; Carnarvon P. (P.R.O. 30/6/55), Salisbury to Carnarvon, 12/8/85; Churchill P. (RCHL 1/8/927a), Salisbury to Churchill, 29/8/85.
47. HHM/3M/E, Churchill to Salisbury, 1/10/85; Churchill P. (RCHL 1/8/978), Churchill to Lord Justice Fitzgibbon (Dublin), 14/10/85; Carnarvon P. (P.R.O. 30/6/55), Churchill to Carnarvon, 29/8/85.
48. *Ibid.* (P.R.O. 30/6/67), Hamilton to Carnarvon, 1/8/85, and Hamilton's minute of 23/9/85.
49. Hardinge, *Carnarvon*, III, pp. 191–2, Iddesleigh to Carnarvon, 7/9/85; Dilke P. (43894), Dilke to Grant Duff, 16/6/85; Carnarvon/D. (60925), 29/11/85.
50. Carnarvon P. (P.R.O. 30/6/55), Churchill to Carnarvon, 27/8/85; P.S. O'Hegarty, *A History of Ireland under the Union, 1801–1922* (London, 1952), pp. 534–5, 539–40.
51. Carnarvon/D. (60925), 5, 6 and 9/10/85; Hardinge, *Carnarvon*, III, pp. 192–5; Iddesleigh P. (50063A–pt ii), diary, 6/10/85.
52. Lucy, *Speeches*, pp. 183–5; Dufferin and Ava P. (MSS Eur. F. 130/20–21). Lytton to Lord Dufferin, viceroy of India, November 1885.
53. Hardinge, *Carnarvon*, III, pp. 196–9; Carnarvon/D. (60925), 20/11/85.
54. Lucy, *Speeches*, p. 251; *Gladstone Diaries*, XI, pp. 427–8, Gladstone to Hartington. 10/11/85; Hardinge, *Carnarvon*, III, p. 200, Carnarvon to Salisbury, 25/11/85; Carnarvon P. (P.R.O. 30/6/67), Carnarvon's undated note on Churchill's views.
55. A. Ponsonby, *Henry Ponsonby* (London, 1942), pp. 199–200, Salisbury to Ponsonby, 29/11/85.
56. *Ibid.*; and Jackson, *The Last of the Whigs*, p. 194.
57. Churchill P. (RCHL 1/10/1126), Churchill's undated memorandum on the political situation [December 1885]; *ibid.* (1/110/1145), Churchill to Morris, 7/12/85; HHM/3M/E, Churchill to Salisbury, 16/12/85.
58. Hardinge, *Carnarvon*, III, p. 206; Carnarvon/D. (60925), 14/12/85; *Q.V.L.* (2), III, p. 711, Salisbury to the Queen, 14/12/85.
59. Russell, *MacColl*, pp. 122–4, MacColl to Gladstone, 22/12/85; *Gladstone Diaries*, XI, pp. 447–8, 455, diary for 15/12/85, and Gladstone to Balfour, 20/12/85; Harcourt Williams, *Salisbury–Balfour Correspondence*, pp. 127–8, Balfour to Salisbury, 23 and 24/12/85; HHM/3M/D, Salisbury to Churchill, 24/12/85: "His [Gladstone's] hypocrisy makes me sick".
60. Churchill P. (RCHL 1/10/1126), Churchill's undated memorandum [December 1885]; Cooke and Vincent, *The Governing Passion*, p. 293.
61. Churchill P. (RCHL 1/10/1126), Churchill's undated memorandum [December 1885]; *ibid.* (1/11/1362b), Salisbury to Churchill, 16/1/86.
62. HHM/3M/D, W.H. Smith to Salisbury, 25/1/86 and (telegram) Salisbury to Smith, 26/1/86; *Cranbrook/D.*, pp. 589–90 (16/1/86).

63. Churchill P. (RCHL 1/10/1186), Churchill to General Sir Frederick Roberts, 13/12/85; Hambleden P. (P S 9/96), Iddesleigh to W.H. Smith, 22/12/85.

64. *3H*, cccii, 68–9 (21/1/86); Churchill P. (RCHL 1/10/1126), Churchill's undated memorandum [December 1885], and Salisbury to Churchill (RCHL 1/10/1157a), 9/12/85; Carnarvon/D. (60925), 18/1/86.

65. *Q.V.L.* (3), I, p. 34, Salisbury to the Queen, 31/1/86; *T.T.*, 8/2/86, to Hertfordshire MPs meeting in London.

66. *Gladstone Diaries*, XI, p. 436, Gladstone to Lord Richard Grosvenor, Liberal chief whip, 27/11/85; A. Offer, *Property and Politics, 1870–1914* (Cambridge, 1981) on the political implications of local rates; B. Kinnear, *The British Voter* (1968), p. 13, put the number of Liberal constituencies lost by the Irish vote at between twenty-five and twenty-seven. W.C. Lubenow, *Parliamentary Politics and the Home Rule Crisis: The British House of Commons in 1886* (Oxford, 1988), p. 63, sums up the Commons after the 1884 Reform Act as, still, "highly landed, highly bourgeois, and even more highly professional".

67. *Gladstone Diaries*, XI, pp. 394, 417–8, Gladstone to Chamberlain, 9/9/85 and Lord Southesk, 27/10/85; *Gladstone–Granville Correspondence, 1876–1886*, II, p. 393, Gladstone to Granville, 9/9/85.

68. *T.T.*, 16/10, 5/11/85; Cooke and Vincent, *The Governing Passion*, p. 274; HHM/3M/D, Salisbury to Winn, 4/9/84.

69. *T.T.*, 5/11/85; J.C.P. (JC 5/6/3), Brett (later the 2nd Viscount Esher) to Chamberlain, 9/12/85; *Gladstone Diaries*, XI, p. 440, Gladstone's address of thanks to the electors of Midlothian, 4/12/85; Jackson, *The Last of the Whigs*, p. 201.

70. D.D., L.R.O., 16/10/85; *T.T.*, 16/10, 24/11/85; EWH/D. (48642), 3/12/85.

71. *Gladstone Diaries*, XI, p. 440, Gladstone's address of thanks at Midlothian, 4/12/85; *T.T.*, 16/10/85.

72. Selborne, *Memorials, Pt II*, vol. II, p. 181 and n1; *T.T.*, 16/10 and 5/11/85; EWH/D. (48642), 8/12/85: "it appears that among Nonconformists even the idea of Disestablishment is by no means liked".

73. D.D., L.R.O., 16/10/85; Chilston P. (U564/C18), Salisbury to Akers-Douglas, 3/4 and 27/11/85; M. Pugh, *The Tories and the People, 1880–1935* (Oxford, 1985) for the Primrose League.

74. Churchill P. (RCHL 1/10/1126), Churchill's undated memorandum on the political situation [December 1885] and (RCHL 1/10/1157a), Salisbury to Churchill, 9/12/85.

75. *Ibid.*, and Salisbury to Churchill (1118b), 30/11/85.

76. HHM/3M/E, Churchill to Salisbury, 9/12/85.

77. *Ibid.*, and Churchill P. (RCHL 1/10/1157a and 1177b), Salisbury to Churchill, 9 and 16/12/85; Cooke and Vincent, *The Governing Passion*, p. 298.

78. *Cranbrook/D.*, p. 589 (10/1/86); HHM/3M/E, Churchill to Salisbury, 9/12/85.

79. *Ibid.*, and Churchill P. (RCHL 1/10/1180b), Salisbury to Churchill, 21/12/85.

80. *Cranbrook/D.*, p. 585 (6/12/85); Churchill P. (RCHL 1/10/1177b), Salisbury to Churchill, 16/12/85.

81. J.C.P. (JC 5/6/3), Brett to Chamberlain, 9/12/85; Churchill P. (RCHL 1/10/1126), Churchill's undated memorandum [December 1885].

82. *Salisbury*, III, p. 281, Salisbury to Bath, 27/12/85; Jackson, *The Last of the Whigs*, p. 210, Harcourt to Hartington, 8/12/85; Devonshire P. (340.1884), Hartington to Lord Lansdowne, governor-general of Canada, 4/1/86.

83. Jackson, *The Last of the Whigs*, p. 203, Hartington at Belfast, 5/11/85.

84. *Gladstone Diaries*, XI, pp. 432–3, Gladstone to Hartington, 18/11/85; D.D., L.R.O., 2/1/86: "I except the Irishmen, whose object is revolution".

85. HHM/3M/D, Manchester to H.J.B. Manners, Salisbury's private secretary, 23/12/85; Devonshire P. (340.1884), Hartington to Lansdowne, 4/1/86.

86. *Q.V.L.* (2), III, pp. 712–13, 717–18, the Queen to Goschen, 20/12 and 29/12/85; D.D., L.R.O., 14/1/86; Ponsonby, *Henry Ponsonby*, pp. 203–6, Ponsonby to his wife, 3, 5 and 7/1/86; Cooke and Vincent, *The Governing Passion*, pp. 45, 308.

87. The other three who refused to serve were Derby, Northbrook and Selborne; *Gladstone Diaries*, XI, p. 488, Gladstone to John Morley, MP, 2/2/86.

88. J.C.P. (JC 5/50/68), Chamberlain to Henry Labouchere, MP, 15/2/86 with following letters, and (JC 5/50/60), 3/1/86.

89. Churchill P. (RCHL 1/12/1438a), Salisbury to Churchill, 29/3/86; Devonshire P. (uncatalogued), Hartington to the Duchess of Manchester, 26/2/86.

90. J.C.P. (JC 5/50/41), Chamberlain to Labouchere, 4/12/85; Harcourt Williams, *Salisbury–Balfour Correspondence*, pp. 133–8, Balfour to Salisbury, 24/3/86; the others present were both Liberals, Albert Grey, MP, and the newly ennobled Lord Rothschild.

91. *Ibid.*, pp. 158–9, Salisbury to Balfour, 29/3/86; EWH/D. (48644), 31/5/86.

92. *Gladstone Diaries*, XI, p. 537 and n2, Sir R.E. Welby, secretary to the Treasury, to Gladstone, 21/4/86 and Gladstone to Welby, 22/4/86; EWH/D. (48644), 6/6/86; Ponsonby, *Henry Ponsonby*, p. 209, Ponsonby to his wife, 8/3/86.

93. EWH/D. (48643), 3/5/86: Gladstone's latest missive to his Scottish constituents (*T.T.*, 4/5/86) was "an appeal . . . to the masses . . . much better left unsaid"; *ibid.*, 7/3 and 16/4/86 for London Society and the Duke of Cambridge.

94. *T.T.*, 18/2, 4/3/86.

95. *Ibid.*, and Foster, *Churchill*, p. 256.

96. *T.T.*, 11/5 and 17/5/86.

97. *Gladstone Diaries*, XI, pp. 555–6, 16/5 and 17/5/86, memorandum of Gladstone's conversations with Ponsonby; *T.T.*, 17/5/86; Churchill P. (RCHL 1/13/1504), Henry Chaplin, MP, to Churchill, 18/5/86.

98. *T.T.*, 17/5/86.

99. Harcourt Williams, *Salisbury–Balfour Correspondence*, pp. 139–40, memorandum from Balfour: "Note of a conversation before debate on Govt. of Ireland Bill, 1886", between Balfour, Brett and Chamberlain; *ibid.*, p. 140, Balfour to Salisbury, 10/5/86.

100. *Ibid.*, pp. 143–5, memorandum from Balfour: "Conversation held . . . June 13th with Chamberlain".

101. *T.T.*, 19 and 30/6/86.

# Chapter 9: The New Conservatism in Practice

1. Churchill P. (RCHL 1/12/1440b), Salisbury to Churchill, 31/3/86; Lubenow, *Parliamentary Politics and the Home Rule Crisis*, ch. 7, p. 319, concluded that "The Home Rule crisis . . . created a polarization of the political nation along ideological, rather than social, lines".

2. *T.T.*, 19/6 and 30/6/86, London; *Leeds Mercury*, 22 and 28/6, 2/7/86, Kitson, and Herbert Gladstone, a Leeds MP, 2/7/86.

3. EWH/D. (48644), 12/7/86.

4. Marsh, *Chamberlain*, pp. 250–54; EWH/D. (48644), 1/6/86; Edward Hamilton P. (48618), Morley to Hamilton, 31/7/02.

5. Churchill P. (RCHL 1/12/1416a and 1576a), Salisbury to Churchill, 16/2 and 25/7/86; Cooke and Vincent, *The Governing Passion*, p. 488 n162, Northbrook to Dufferin, 30/7/86.

6. Jackson, *The Last of the Whigs*, p. 244.

7. D.D., L.R.O., 12/7/86.

8. *Ibid.*, 21 and 22/7/86; Jackson, *The Last of the Whigs*, p. 242.

9. Churchill P. (RCHL 1/13/1580a), Salisbury to Churchill, 27/7/86; *Cranbrook/D.*, pp. 614–16, (28/7/86).

10. D.D., L.R.O., 23 and 29/7/86; Foster, *Churchill*, pp. 272–3.

11. *Salisbury*, III, pp. 311–12, Salisbury to Carnarvon, 25/7/86; Marsh, *Chamberlain*, p. 261; D. Thornley, *Isaac Butt and Home Rule* (London, 1964), p. 59.

12. Churchill P. (RCHL 1/13/1591c and 1/14/1698), Salisbury to Churchill, 30/7/86, and Ritchie to Churchill, 1/8/86.

13. Devonshire P. (340. 2053 and 2053A), Salisbury and the Queen to Hartington, both 19/10/86; D.D., L.R.O., 24/7/86.

14. Cooke and Vincent, *The Governing Passion*, pp. 444–5.

15. Jackson, *The Last of the Whigs*, p. 246; Devonshire P. (340. 2043), Chamberlain to Hartington, 9/9/86.

16. HHM/3M/D, Hicks Beach to Salisbury, 25/12/86. The peer who eventually left the ministry was Lord Dunraven.

17. Devonshire P. (340. 2070 and 2072A), Salisbury and the Queen to Hartington, 24 and 25/12/86.

18. D.D., L.R.O., 24/7/86; Devonshire P. (340. 2068 and 2073), Brett and Derby to Hartington, 24 and 26/12/86; HHM/3M/D, Salisbury to Hicks Beach (telegram), n.d. [December 1886]; *Q.V.L.* (3), I, p. 240, Salisbury to the Queen, 31/12/86.

19. HHM/3M/D, Smith to Salisbury, 20/12/86; *Salisbury*, III, p. 318, Salisbury to his wife, 17/9/86.

20. Chilston P. (U564/C18), Salisbury to Akers-Douglas, 26/12/86; J.C.P. (JC 5/14/27), Churchill to Chamberlain, 24/12/86. See Chapter 10 p. 249 below for the disagreement over foreign policy.

21. *Salisbury*, III, pp. 326–7, Cranbrook to Salisbury, 23/11, and Salisbury to Cranbrook, 25/11/86; *Cranbrook/D.*, p. 636 (23/11/86).

22. *Salisbury*, III, p. 322, Salisbury to Lord George Hamilton, 25/12/86; HHM/3M/D, Salisbury to Sir J.F. Stephen, 30/12/86, passage not printed in *Salisbury*, III, pp. 336–7.

23. *Salisbury*, III, quotations from p. 336; J.C.P. (JC 5/14/37 and 38/52), Churchill and Harcourt to Chamberlain, 24/12, 30/5/86.

24. T.J. Spinner, *George Joachim Goschen: The Transformation of a Victorian Liberal* (Cambridge, 1973); HHM/3M/D, Salisbury to Cranbrook, 1 and 7/1/87.

25. 3rd Viscount Chilston, *W. H. Smith* (London, 1965).

26. *Salisbury*, III, pp. 340–45, Salisbury to Hicks Beach and Churchill, 6 and 14/1/87; Hambleden P. (P S 12/24), unsigned memorandum in Salisbury's hand, 10/1/87.

27. Churchill P. (RCHL 1/19/2332), Churchill to Lord Dunraven, 12/1/87; Foster, *Churchill*, p. 294.

28. *Cranbrook/D.*, p. 633 (5/10/86); Churchill P. (RCHL 1/18/2210), Chamberlain to Churchill, 23/12/86.

29. *Ibid.* (RCHL 1/19/2314), Salisbury to Frances Anne, Duchess of Marlborough, 11/1/87; cf. A. Adonis, *Making Aristocracy Work* (Oxford, 1993).

30. Marsh, *Discipline of Popular Government*, pp. 125–6.

31. HHM/3M/D, Salisbury to Goschen, 5/10/90; C. Whibley, *Lord John Manners and his Friends* (2 vols) (Edinburgh, 1925), II, Salisbury to the 7th Duke of Rutland (Lord John Manners), January 1900.

32. L.P. Curtis, *Coercion and Conciliation in Ireland, 1880–1892: A Study in Conservative Unionism* (Princeton, NJ, 1963).

33. Lady Victoria Hicks Beach, *Life of Sir Michael Hicks Beach, Earl St Aldwyn* (2 vols) (London, 1932); Churchill P. (RCHL 1/14/1637), Churchill to Hicks Beach, 5/8/86; *T.T.*, 23/9/86, St Albans.

34. *T.T.*, 22/2/87; St Aldwyn P. (D2455/PCC/69), Salisbury to Hicks Beach, 23/2/87; *Q.V.L.* (3), I, pp. 278–9, the Queen's journal, 2/3/87.

35. *T.T.*, 7/3/87, National Conservative Club; EWH/D. (48645), 3/3/87.

36. *T.T.*, 7/3/87; Curtis, *Coercion and Conciliation in Ireland*, pp. 180 ff.

37. Devonshire P. (340. 2116), Smith to Hartington, 30/3/87; Hambleden P. (P S 12/58), Churchill to Smith, 16/4/87.

38. *3H*, cccxvii, 1141–6 (18/7/87); Churchill P. (RCHL 1/19/2439), Hicks Beach to Churchill, 9/4/87; Marsh, *Discipline of Popular Government*, p. 123.

39. Jackson, *The Last of the Whigs*, p. 270, Hartington to the Duchess of Manchester, 11/2/87; Churchill P. (RCHL 20/2472, 2593), Chamberlain to Churchill, 13/7/87, Churchill to Sir F. Roberts, 10/5/87 and (RCHL 20/2614, 2617, 2624a) the Duchess of Marlborough, 3, 8 and 17/8/87; *Cranbrook/D.*, p. 681 (17/8/87).

40. Harcourt Williams, *Salisbury–Balfour Correspondence*, pp. 212, 228–9, 234, 257, Salisbury to Balfour, 14/10 and 24/12/87, 18/1 and 20/9/88.

41. HHM/3M/DD, Salisbury to Sir Richard Webster (draft), 13/9/88.

42. *T.T.*, 20/3/98, Watford; *Cranbrook/D.*, pp. 727, 757 (28/2 and 1/3/88, 15/2/98).

43. *3H*, ccxlii, 1367–8 (21/3/90).

44. F.S.L. Lyons, *The Fall of Parnell* (London, 1960) and F. Callanan, *The Parnell Split* (Cork, 1992); *T.T.*, 4/12/90, Rossendale, 22/1/91, Cambridge.

45. *Ibid.*, 22/4/91; EWH/D. (48645), 13/3/87, for the Prince's views; Curtis, *Coercion and Conciliation in Ireland*, pp. 264–5.

46. HHM/3M/E, Smith to Salisbury, 3/2/86; Harcourt Williams, *Salisbury–Balfour Correspondence*, p. 205 (15/9/87).

47. *T.T.*, 24/11/87, Oxford, 1/12/88, Edinburgh, fourth speech of the day.

48. Curtis, *Coercion and Conciliation in Ireland*, ch. xii; J.S. Donnelly, *The Land and People of Nineteenth Century Cork* (London, 1975), ch. vii for a local study.

49. Harcourt Williams, *Salisbury–Balfour Correspondence*, pp. 178–80, Salisbury to Balfour, 8/3/87, Balfour to Salisbury, 9/3/87; Curtis, *Coercion and Conciliation in Ireland*, pp. 337–8.

50. *Ibid.* and J.C.P. (JC 5/5/1/and 1A), Balfour to Chamberlain, 31/3/87, with memorandum on the Irish land bill.

51. HHM/3M/D, Salisbury to the 2nd Duke of Abercorn, 26 and 30/5/87.

52. *3H*, cccxix, 12–15 (11/8/87), cccxvi, 1450–58, 1575–7 (1 and 4/7/87); HHM/3M/C, Salisbury to Sir James Caird, 22/11/87.

53. H.C.G. Matthew in *Gladstone Diaries*, X, pp. cli–cliii, Gladstone had more than halved the size of the final operation in the course of its preparation. Reid, *The Life of William Ewart Gladstone*, p. 704.

54. HHM/3M/B, "Suggestions for a Bill to enable tenants to purchase the holdings they occupy in Ireland", October 1887; Harcourt Williams, *Salisbury–Balfour Correspondence*, p. 210, Salisbury to Balfour, 3/10/87.

55. HHM/3M/E, Dunraven to Salisbury, September 1887; all land purchase schemes included the minority of Protestant tenants.

56. *Ibid.*, Lansdowne to Salisbury, 7/12/87.

57. J.C.P. (JC 5/23/121), Chamberlain to Hartington, 1/8/86, and (JC 5/51/1), Lansdowne to Chamberlain, 17/7/88; HHM/3M/E, Lansdowne to Salisbury 15/1/88 on his conversation with Chamberlain in Canada.

58. HHM/3M/D, Salisbury to Smith, 16/10/87; *T.T.*, 24/11/87, Oxford, 24/4/89, Bristol, fifth speech of the day.

59. HHM/3M/E, Hicks Beach to Salisbury, 6 and 16/11/90; *ibid.*, class F, the Queen to Salisbury, 18/2/90, for the monarch's uneasiness about "the increase of peasant proprietorship in Ireland. Isn't that rather dangerous?" Curtis, *Coercion and Conciliation in Ireland*, pp. 350–51, for the details of this legislation.

60. D.D., L.R.O., 22/12/89; EWH/D. (48650), 14/1/89 and (48654), 14/10/90, conversation with John Morley, who thought "it would be disgraceful to leave landlords to the tender mercies of the Irish"; HHM/3M/E, Lansdowne to Salisbury, 15/1/88. In 1888 the premier alluded to "the impossibility of a compulsory scheme, at least at present", Harcourt Williams, *Salisbury–Balfour Correspondence*, p. 257, Salisbury to Balfour, 20/9/88.

61. Balfour P. (48910), Ridgeway to Balfour, 8/10/89 with his memorandum on "Local Government in Ireland", 6/10/89 and (48911), 19/10/91; J.C.P. (JC 9/2/2/6), Ridgeway to Chamberlain, 17/10/97; Carnarvon/D. (60933), 24/7/89; D.D., L.R.O., 30/3/87 for Lord Kimberley's view that the English would be reconciled to Irish Home Rule "provided it came gradually".

62. *T.T.*, 24/4/89, fifth speech of the day at Bristol; Harcourt Williams, *Salisbury–Balfour Correspondence*, p. 370, Balfour to Salisbury, 2/11/91; *Cranbrook/D.*, p. 818 (20/2/92).

63. Harcourt Williams, *Salisbury–Balfour Correspondence*, pp. 221–2, 293–4, 296, Balfour's memorandum on higher education for Irish Catholics, October 1887, Balfour to Salisbury, 17/9/89 and Salisbury to Balfour, 23/10/89.

64. Balfour P. (49810), Ridgeway to Balfour, 10/7/89; *T.T.*, 11/4/88, Carnarvon, 20/3/89, Watford, 16/7/91, United Club, 20/12/87, at Derby.

65. HHM/3M/A, Salisbury to Wolff, 5/11/78; *T.T.*, 3/2/92, 23/5/90, London.

66. *Ibid.*, 20/12/87, Derby, 24/4/89, fifth speech of the day at Bristol, 4/12/90, Rossendale, 25/11/91, Birmingham.

67. Benson/D., 21/7/87; *4H*, xii, 37–8 (4/5/93), Salisbury and the Tories also championed the Church of Scotland against the threat of disestablishment, which figured prominently in Scottish elections, H. Pelling, *Social Geography of British Elections, 1885–1910* (London, 1967), pp. 372–5.

68. J. Harris, *Private Lives, Public Spirit: Britain 1870–1914* (London, 1994), pp. 158–9.

69. HHM/3M, "Bishoprics and other high church appointments, 1885 & 1886 & 1887".

70. HHM/3M/D, Salisbury to Hicks Beach, 24/10/89 and the Hon. Schomberg McDonnell to F. Perrott, 13/6/91.

71. Johnson, *Liddon*, p. 378, diary, 26/4/90; *Q.V.L.* (3), I, pp. 427–8, 595, R.T. Davidson, Dean of Windsor, to the Queen, 7/7/88, Salisbury to the Queen, 13/4/90; HHM/4M/387, Salisbury to Cranborne, 22/3/01.

72. Harcourt Williams, *Salisbury–Balfour Correspondence*, pp. 256–7, Balfour to Salisbury, 17/9/88, Salisbury to Balfour, 20/9/88; HHM/3M/D, Salisbury to Talbot, 5/3 and, class H, Talbot to Salisbury, 11/3/90.

73. *Ibid.*, class C, Salisbury to J.H. Bailey, 30/7/90; *Q.V.L.* (3), I, pp. 558–60, Salisbury to Ponsonby, 26/1/90.

74. R.A., D10/173, Salisbury to the Queen, 30/8/90; *Q.V.L.* (3), I, pp. 634–5, the Queen to Archbishop Benson, 1/9/90; *Cranbrook/D.*, pp. 715–16 (10/9/88), a Tractarian minister on the Queen's religious opinions.

75. R.A., D10/173, Salisbury to the Queen, 30/8/90; *Q.V.L.* (3), I, pp. 558–60, 644–5, Salisbury to Ponsonby, 26/1/90, and to the Queen, 3/10/90.

76. R.A., D13/A/110, Salisbury to Ponsonby, 2/2/90; *Q.V.L.* (3), I, pp. 560–62, Dean Davidson to Ponsonby, 29/1/90.

77. R.A., D10/90, Salisbury to the Queen, 27/4/89 and, D13/A/100, to Ponsonby, 2/1/90; Benson/D., 22/2/90, 2/12/89.

78. HHM/3M/H, E.H. Bickersteth to Salisbury, 17/3/90 and, class D, Salisbury to the 6th Earl Beauchamp, 17/12/85.

79. *Ibid.*, class H, Talbot to Salisbury, 1/6/76, 29/7/01, 29/10/91, 13/12/90.

80. *Ibid.*, class E, Smith, Viscount Cross, Hicks Beach, to Salisbury, 5/11/85, 27/11/91, 7/10/91.

81. R.A., D13/A/110, Salisbury to Ponsonby, 2/2/90; Rowell, *The Vision Glorious*, p. 154.

82. There is a substantial biography of the primate by his son A.C. Benson, *The Life of Edward White Benson* (2 vols) (London, 1899). Benson/D., 9/9/87, 15/8/95.

83. Machin, *Politics and the Churches in Great Britain, 1869–1921*, p. 186; Benson/D., 31/1/87, 14/12/87.

84. *Ibid.*, 9/9, 12/9, 14/12/87; Benson P. (TCC: letters, 1889–92), Benson to George Cubitt, MP, 2/4/91, a confession of his helplessness in secular politics: "I know so little of how any of these things are done".

85. Benson/D., 25 and 30/7/91, 16/5/92; Benson P. (LPL: vol. 110), Salisbury to Benson, 6/6/92; HHM/3M/C, Salisbury to Robert Gregory, Dean of St Paul's, 2/6/92.

86. Churchill P. (RCHL 1/10/1157a), Salisbury to Churchill, 9/12/85; HHM/3M/E, Churchill to Salisbury, 9/12/85; *Cranbrook/D.*, p. 659 (16/3/87); Benson/D., 12/4, 18/7/87.

87. G. Sutherland, *Policy-making in Elementary Education, 1870–1895* (Oxford, 1981); HHM/3M/H, Talbot to Salisbury, 19/7/91.

88. *Cranbrook/D.*, pp. 677–8, 805 (27/7/87, 16/7/91): "Salisbury provoked me to some display of temper. He charged me with being Anti Voluntary Schools."

89. HHM/3M/D, Salisbury to Lady Janetta Manners, 16/7/91, 12/5/89, to Cranbrook, 24/4/89.

90. *Ibid.*, Salisbury to Cranbrook, 17/1/90; *Cranbrook/D.*, pp. 755, 805 (17/1/90, 16/7/91).

91. *T.T.*, 23/5/87, at the Constitutional Club, London.

92. *Ibid.*, 25/11/91, Birmingham, 24/11/87, Oxford, 21/12/88, Scarborough, third speech of the day.

93. Benson/D., 4/3/93.

94. EWH/D. (48651), 1/8/89.

95. Carnarvon/D. (60930), 25/6/88, the 7th Earl of Jersey.

96. Salisbury's awareness of the difficulties facing British industry in an increasingly competitive world antedated the concern discussed by E.H.H. Green in *The Crisis of Conservatism*, ch. 9.

97. S. Koss, *The Rise and Fall of the Political Press in Britain* (2 vols) (London, 1981–4), I, for instances of Salisbury's contacts with the press.

98. EWH/D. (48645), 5/2/87; A. Austin, *The Autobiography of Alfred Austin* (2 vols) (London, 1911), II, p. 248, Salisbury to Austin, 30/11/86; HHM/3M/E, Austin to Salisbury, 9 and 10/7/85. Salisbury rewarded Austin, an indifferent versifier, with the appointment of Poet Laureate in 1896.

99. *Ibid.*, Austin to Salisbury, 29/11/86, 1/1/87 and class E, Salisbury to Austin, 26/6 and 3/8/87.

100. *Salisbury*, IV, pp. 206–7, Salisbury to Austin, 2/12/89; HHM/3M/E, Austin to Salisbury, 30/11/89.

101. Austin P. (DM 668), Salisbury to Austin, 25/11/83, 20/10/90; Morier P. (box 23), Salisbury to Morier, 22/10/90.

102. EWH/D. (48653), 10/7/90.

103. The Unionists suffered a net loss of twenty seats at by-elections 1886–92.

104. Marsh, *Chamberlain*, pp. 302–3.

105. *T.T.*, 29/7/87, Norwich, 24/11/87, Oxford; C.S. Orwin and E.H. Whetham, *History of British Agriculture, 1845–1914* (London, 1964), pp. 258–61.

106. *T.T.*, 20/12/87, Derby, third speech of the day, and 20/11/87, Oxford, first speech; HHM/3M/E, Salisbury to Lytton, 17/1/88, seeking information about the French department of agriculture: "Have they any power? What, if any, proceedings require authorization at their hands?"; *3H*, cccxxxviii, 80–83 (11/7/83), Salisbury on the Board of Agriculture Bill.

107. *T.T.*, 11/4/88, Carnarvon, 1/12/88, Edinburgh, fourth speech.

108. *Ibid.*, 23/5/90, 16/7/91, London.

109. *Ibid.*, 24/11/87, Oxford, first speech; *Cranbrook/D.*, p. 597 (10/2/87).

110. D.D., L.R.O., 29/6/84, on mounting deposits in savings banks: "This does not look like distress in the working class". While it has been suggested that over half the deposits may have come from the lower ranks of the middle class, average income per capita is estimated to have risen from 25 to 150 per cent above subsistence between 1870 and 1914, Harris, *Private Lives, Public Spirit: Britain, 1870–1914*, pp. 33, 111.

111. *T.T.*, 25/8/89, to the London Chamber of Commerce.

112. *Ibid.*, 27/11/89, Nottingham; 5/3/91; 10/11/87, Lord Mayor's banquet.

113. *Ibid.*, 24/4/89, Bristol, fourth and fifth speeches.

114. *Ibid.*, 27 and 28/11/89, at the Nottingham conference; A.L. Lowell, *The Government of England* (2 vols) (New York, 1908), II, pp. 192–3.

115. In assigning the proceeds of specified taxes to local authorities, the Local Government Act of 1888, and subsequent legislation in 1890 and 1894, provided them with an expanding source of income to replace exchequer grants tied to a variety of services. Rising subventions to school boards and voluntary schools were not included. Lowell, *The Government of England*, II, pp. 189–90; *T.T.*, 1/12/88 and 20/3/89 for references to women's suffrage. Gladstone continued to feel that "the country is not really ripe for the change", Bahlman, *Hamilton*, II, p. 634 (10/3/84).

116. *T.T.*, 27/11/89 and, on allotments, 28/11/89; *ibid.*, leading article, 24/11/87.

117. Pugh, *The Tories and the People*, pp. 27, 42: "No other party approached so closely to a party of social integration before 1900"; *T.T.*, 22/5/89.

118. *Ibid.*, 20/5/86; Marsh, *Discipline of Popular Government*, ch. 6, "The Middleton machine".

119. *T.T.*, 22/5/89; Chilston P. (U564/C18), Salisbury to Akers-Douglas, 16/9/94; HHM/3M/E, H.S. Northcote to Salisbury, 18/2/93.

120. M.C. Hurst, *Joseph Chamberlain and West Midland Politics*, Dugdale Society Occasional Papers, no. 15 (1962); *T.T.*, 27/11/89 and 26/11/91.

121. *Ibid.*, 20/5/86; J.C.P. (JC 5/67/17), Salisbury to Chamberlain, 22/6/92.

122. HHM/3M/E, Chaplin to Salisbury, 20/4, 4/5/86.

123. Harcourt Williams, *Salisbury–Balfour Correspondence*, pp. 155–6, 1/8/86.

124. HHM/3M/E, Edward Stanhope, secretary of state for war, to Salisbury, 30/1/87; *ibid.*, class B, "Allotments Bill. Note of Objections", December 1886.

125. HHM/3M/D, Salisbury to W.H. Smith, undated [1887]; F. Pollock, *The Land Laws* (London, 1896), p. 162; and see Long P. (947/6), the 4th Earl of Onslow's memorandum, 31/1/87, criticizing Salisbury's resistance to compulsion; Long was parliamentary secretary to C.T. Ritchie at the Local Government Board.

126. Pollock, *Land Laws*, p. 162.

127. Harcourt Williams, *Salisbury–Balfour Correspondence*, pp. 381–3, memorandum by Balfour, 29/12/91; HHM/3M/E, Chaplin to Salisbury, 9/8/89, 25/12/91.

128. Harcourt Williams, *Salisbury–Balfour Correspondence*, pp. 381–3, memorandum by Balfour, 29/12/91; J.P.D. Dunbabin, "The politics of the establishment of county councils", *Historical Journal* (1963), pp. 226–52; Churchill P. (RCHL 1/17/2081), Salisbury to Churchill, 28/11/86.

129. Cranbrook P. (T501/263), Salisbury to Cranbrook, 28/11/86, reporting Hartington's support for "my ideas and apprehensions as to the Poor Law"; HHM/3M/D, Salisbury to Hicks Beach, 1/12/86.

130. *3H*, cccxxix, 928–33 (31/7/88); Carnarvon/D. (60930), 25/6/88, the misgivings of Sir Matthew White Ridley, MP, a future cabinet minister; *ibid.* (60931), 6/8/88, the committee stage of the legislation in the Lords, "The bill is simply odious to them".

131. *T.T.*, 11/4/88, at Carnarvon; Harcourt Williams, *Salisbury–Balfour Correspondence*, p. 284, Salisbury to Balfour, 6/2/89; EWH/D. (48647), 20 and 22/3/88.

132. Harcourt Williams, *Salisbury–Balfour Correspondence*, pp. 342–3, H.E. Manning, Cardinal Archbishop of Westminster, to the Rev. J. Nunn, 22/6/91, with Balfour to private secretary, 20/6/91; *Cranbrook/D.,*, p. 781 (28/11/90).

133. *Salisbury*, IV, pp. 157, 159–60, Salisbury to Cranbrook, 10/12/89, to W.H. Smith, 27/10/91, and Lord Harrowby, 9/7/91; EWH/D. (48656), 26/6/91.

134. Marsh, *Discipline of Popular Government*, pp. 169–71; *Cranbrook/D.*, p. 805 (16/7/91); EWH/D. (48655), 24/4/91; *3H*, cccxliv, 1239–44 (19/5/90), Salisbury in the Lords.

135. Lowell, *The Government of England*, II, pp. 221–2; M.J. Daunton, *House and Home in the Victorian City: Working-Class Housing, 1850–1914* (London, 1983), pp. 30–31; B.J. Barber, "Aspects of Municipal Government, 1835–1914", the 1890 Act in the case of Leeds, in D. Fraser (ed.), *A History of Modern Leeds* (Manchester, 1980), pp. 311–15.

136. *3H*, ccxliv, 1239–44 (19/5/90).

137. HHM/3M/E, G.C.T. Bartley, MP, an urban Tory and former party organizer, to Salisbury, 1/6/91, C.T. Ritchie to Salisbury, 2/6/91.

138. Harcourt Williams, *Salisbury–Balfour Correspondence*, pp. 166–7, Salisbury to Balfour, 18/12/86; Foster, *Churchill*, pp. 300–301; HHM/3M/D (Goschen), undated memorandum by Salisbury, "Defence Loan Bill" [1889]; A.N. Porter, "Lord Salisbury, Foreign Policy and Domestic Finance", in *S.M.P.*, pp. 166–9.

139. *Cranbrook/D.*, p. 733 (14/4/89); *Salisbury*, IV, pp. 191–2, Salisbury to Goschen, 3/3/89; EWH/D. (48650), 2/5/89.

140. For this development in Liberalism, D.A. Hamer, *Liberal Politics in the Age of Gladstone and Rosebery* (Oxford, 1972), and M. Barker, *Gladstone and Radicalism. The Reconstruction of the Liberal Party in Britain, 1885–94* (New York, 1975).

141. HHM/3M/E, Ritchie to Salisbury, 9/11/87, 21/1/90.

142. Marsh, *Chamberlain*, p. 330; *T.T.*, 3/2/92.

143. Carnarvon/D. (60931), 6/7/88; Harcourt Williams, *Salisbury–Balfour Correspondence*, pp. 155–6, Balfour to Salisbury, 1/8/86; HHM/3M/D, Salisbury to Smith, 13/3/87.

144. Halsbury P. (56371), Salisbury to Halsbury, 29/10/86.

145. D.D., L.R.O., 25/6 and 5/7/89; *Cranbrook/D.*, p. 741 and n1 (6/7/89).

146. D.D., L.R.O., 5/7/89. The letters of Lord Limerick, the Tory whip in the Lords, contain an analysis of the voting on this measure, HHM/3M/E, Limerick to Salisbury, 22/6/89, 'Monday night', and 8/7/89.

147. HHM/3M/E, memorandum by W.H. Smith, 23/1/88; *3H*, cccxxvii, 387–96 (18/6/88).

148. *Ibid.*, cccxxviii, 871 (10/7/88); HHM/3M/D, Salisbury to Smith, 11/7/88.

149. F.M.L. Thompson, *English Landed Society in the Nineteenth Century* (London, 1963), pp. 292–9; Mason "A Librarian's View", in *S.M.P.* and Green, *The Crisis of Conservatism*, pp. 107–8 for the administration of the honours system under Salisbury.

150. *Salisbury*, IV, pp. 217–21; Harcourt Williams, *Salisbury–Balfour Correspondence*, p. 361, Balfour to Salisbury [15/10/91]; EWH/D. (48650), 2/1/89.

151. HHM/3M/D, Salisbury to Goschen, 21/1/87.

152. *3H*, cccxxiii, 829–32 (12/3/88).

153. D.D., L.R.O., 13/3/88; HHM/3M/E, McDonnell to Salisbury, 17/12/92; *T.T.*, 20/6/91, Salisbury to a deputation from the Empire Trade League, at the Foreign Office: "Your duty is plain. You have to . . . spare no opportunity and no effort of impressing it [the protectionist case] upon your fellow electors"; *ibid.*, 3/5/88, to an agricultural deputation. Green, *The Crisis of Conservatism*, p. 334, lists forty-seven Tory MPs as supporters of fair trade in the 1880s; the hard core of protectionists in politics.

154. *T.T.*, 11/11/90.

155. *Ibid.*, 17/7/89; *Salisbury*, IV, p. 204, Salisbury to the Duchess of Rutland (Lady Janetta Manners), 1/4/88: the premier wryly wished he were the holder of "an ideal Consols, never liable to be converted".

156. *T.T.*, 5/3/91, Associated Chambers of Commerce, 19/5/92, Hastings.

# Chapter 10: European Security and Imperial Expansion

1. *Q.V.L.* (3), I, pp. 613–14, Salisbury to the Queen, 10/6/90; EWH/D. (48651), 17/10/89; *D.D.F.*, vol. 7, pp. 5–7, Waddington to Flourens, foreign minister, 3/1/88, on Derby and Liberal Unionist opposition to an Anglo-German pact.

2. *T.T.*, 7/8/90, at the Mansion House.

3. *Ibid.*, 5/4/88, at the Colonial Conference, London.

4. *Ibid.*, 10/11/88, at the Lord Mayor's banquet; HHM/3M/E, Sir James Fergusson, Bt, to Salisbury, 14/1/88.

5. *T.T.*, 28/2/89, at the London Chamber of Commerce; EWH/D. (48653), 20/6/90, Rosebery.

6. The very independent and well informed radical, Henry Labouchere, was answered by his own leader when he challenged ministers to reveal what had been agreed: unwilling "to fetter the free discretion and free agency of this country in contingencies which have not yet developed themselves", Gladstone praised Salisbury's "sound principles in foreign policy", *3H*, cccxii, 1187–92 (22/2/88); J.N. Figgis and R.V. Laurence (eds), *Selections from the Correspondence of the First Lord Acton* (London, 1917), p. 186, Gladstone to Acton, 24/2/88.

7. C.J. Lowe, *Salisbury and the Mediterranean, 1886–1896* (London, 1965) for a discussion of the agreements in their wider context; White P. (F.O. 364/1), Salisbury to Sir William White (Constantinople), 2/11/87.

8. A.J.P. Taylor, *The Struggle for Mastery in Europe, 1848–1918* (London, 1957), p. 321; White P. (F.O. 364/8 pt 2), Salisbury to White, 14/12/87.

9. *Q.V.L.* (3), I, pp. 272–3.

10. *P.E.A.*, VI, pp. 331–3, Count Herbert Bismarck, from London, to Prince Bismarck, 22/3/89; HHM/3M/A, Salisbury to Malet (Berlin), 12/2/89, 18/9/88.

11. *Q.V.L.* (3), I, pp. 612–14, the Queen to Salisbury, 9/6, Salisbury to the Queen, 10/6/90; *Cranbrook/D.*, pp. 768–9 (8/6/90).

12. Morier P. (box 22), Salisbury to Morier, 27/4/87.

13. HHM/3M/C, Salisbury to J. Crowe (Paris), 21/1/87; *ibid.*, class E, to Lytton, 19/9, 29/12/87 and, class D, to Goschen, 29/9/91.

14. P.R. Warhurst, *Anglo-Portuguese Relations in South Central Africa, 1890–1900* (London, 1962); Morier P. (box 22), Salisbury to Morier, 11/2/91; *T.T.*, 10/11/88, at the Mansion House.

15. EWH/D. (48649), 10/11/88; *T.T.*, 23/11/82; HHM/3M/C, Salisbury to Sir Richard Fowler, MP, Lord Mayor of London, 10/9/85.

16. *T.T.*, 21/12/88; HHM/3M/D, Salisbury to the Queen, 25/12/88; P.M. Holt, *The Mahdist State in the Sudan, 1881–1898* (Oxford, 1958).

17. *T.T.*, 1/12/88; HHM/3M/A, Salisbury to Chamberlain, 31/12/87; Marsh, *Chamberlain*, pp. 280–99 for the mission to the United States and Canada.

18. H.C. Allen, *Great Britain and the United States: A History of Anglo-American Relations (1783–1952)* (London, 1954); *Salisbury*, IV, pp. 345–54; Hobbs P. (20/5), Salisbury to Lord Stanley of Preston, 23/7/90.

19. *Ibid.* (20/7), Salisbury to Stanley, 7/7/91.

20. HHM/3M/D, Salisbury to Sir Henry Holland, colonial secretary, 27/4/87.

21. HHM/3M/E, Lord George Hamilton to Salisbury, 1889; Hobbs P. (4/5), Salisbury to Stanley, 18/12/85. Salisbury never lost sight of the actual and political cost of his policies, Porter, "Lord Salisbury, Foreign Policy and Domestic Finance, 1860–1900" in *S.M.P.*

22. *T.T.*, 9/3/88; HHM/3M/D, Salisbury to H.J.B. Manners, 16/7/86, written when he was conducting the search for a foreign secretary that ended with Iddesleigh; D.D., L.R.O., 10/9/90.

23. S. Constant, *Foxy Ferdinand, 1861–1948, Tsar of Bulgaria* (London, 1979), p. 33; Bridge, *Habsburg Monarchy*, p. 179.

24. Yasamee, *Ottoman Diplomacy*, ch. 17.

25. Taylor, *The Struggle for Mastery in Europe*, pp. 319–23; Bridge, *Habsburg Monarchy*, pp. 181–2.

26. *Q.V.L.* (3), I, pp. 182–3, 193–5, Salisbury to the Queen, 23 and 29/8/86; HHM/3M/D, Salisbury to the Queen, 24/8/86 on the news of the coup against Alexander in Bulgaria: "It is disastrous to have lost the bulwark against Russian aggression . . . built with so much care".

27. *Q.V.L.* (3), I, pp. 201–3, Salisbury to the Queen, 7/9/86; Wilson, *British Foreign Secretaries and Foreign Policy*, pp. 202–3, Salisbury to Churchill, 28/9, 1/10/86.

28. *Q.V.L.* (3), I, p. 202, Salisbury to the Queen, 7/9/86; *P.E.A.*, IV, pp. 284–5, Hatzfeldt (London) to Prince Bismarck, 20/9/86, reporting Churchill's talk; Foster, *Churchill*, 306.

29. *Q.V.L.* (3), I, p. 220, Salisbury to the Queen, 29/10/86; Constant, *Foxy Ferdinand*, p. 121.

30. White P. (F.O. 364/1), Salisbury to White, 23/8/87; HHM/3M/C, Salisbury to N.R. O'Conor, consul-general at Sofia, 23/8/87.

31. *Q.V.L.* (3), II, pp. 122–3, Salisbury to the Queen, 3/6/92.

32. Harcourt Williams, *Salisbury–Balfour Correspondence*, pp. 399–40, Colonel L.V. Swaine, military attaché, Berlin, to Sir E.B. Malet, ambassador, 2/3/92; HHM/3M/A,

Salisbury to HRH the Duke of Edinburgh, commanding the Mediterranean squadron, 27/3/88; Simmons P. (F.O. 358/6), Salisbury to Field Marshal Sir Lintorn Simmons, 26 and 30/9/91, a former inspector-general of fortifications at the War Office, and as such involved in consultations about the defence of the Straits in 1876–8.

33.   *Ibid.*, Salisbury to Simmons, 30/9/91.

34.   Cabinet P. (CAB /37/31/10), memorandum by Salisbury, 4/6/92.

35.   *Ibid.*, and K.M. Wilson, "Constantinople or Cairo: Lord Salisbury and the partition of the Ottoman empire, 1886–1897", in Wilson, *Imperialism and Nationalism in the Middle East: The Anglo-Egyptian Experience 1882–1982*, pp. 26–55.

36.   HHM/3M/A, Salisbury to Edinburgh, 27/3/88; Taylor, *The Struggle for Mastery in Europe*, pp. 338–9.

37.   *3H*, cccxxvii, 1704–10 (29/6/88); *Cranbrook/D.*, pp. 704, 710 (12/5, 30/6/88); T. Zeldin, *France, 1848–1945* (2 vols) (Oxford, 1973), I, pp. 641–5 for the phenomenon of Boulangism.

38.   *Salisbury*, IV, pp. 183–7; Jackson, *The Last of the Whigs*, pp. 282–3; Cabinet P. (CAB 37/21/14), memorandum on defence by Salisbury, 6/6/88.

39.   *Ibid.* (CAB 37/21/15), memorandum on "A French invasion" by Maj.-Gen. H. Brackenbury, 8/6/88 and (CAB 37/21/18), "French invasion" by Salisbury, 29/6/88.

40.   *Ibid.*, and a further memorandum by Salisbury on "French invasion", 6/11/88.

41.   *Ibid.*, and A. J. Marder, *British Naval Policy, 1880–1905* (London, 1941).

42.   HHM/3M/D, Salisbury to Lord George Hamilton, 24/12/87; *Salisbury*, IV, pp. 96–7, Salisbury to Malet (Berlin), 14/3/88.

43.   *Ibid.*, pp. 111–13, Salisbury to Sir A. Paget, 16/10/88; *Q.V.L.* (3), I, p. 398, Salisbury to the Queen, 21/4/88; A. Ramm (ed.), *Beloved and Darling Child: Last Letters between Queen Victoria and Her Eldest Daughter, 1886–1901* (Stroud, 1990) conveys the atmosphere between Coburg and Hohenzollern.

44.   *Salisbury*, IV, pp. 111–12, Salisbury to Paget, 16/10/88; *P.E.A.*, VI, pp. 324–7, Prince Bismarck to Hatzfeldt, 11/1/89; *ibid.*, pp. 331–3, Count Herbert Bismarck, from London, to Prince Bismarck, 22/3/89, with Salisbury's explanation, furnished after consulting the cabinet and Hartington for the Liberal Unionists; *Cranbrook/D.*, 725 (8/2/89), for a comment on the "impossible" conditions of a defence alliance directed against France but not Russia; *Q.V.L.* (3), I, pp. 272–3, Salisbury to the Queen, 10/2/87.

45.   HHM/3M/D, Salisbury to Austin, 8/3/87, partly printed in *Salisbury*, IV, pp. 24–5; *Q.V.L.* (3), I, pp. 268–70, Salisbury to the Queen.

46.   *Salisbury*, IV, p. 105, Salisbury to Lord Dufferin, ambassador at Rome, 28/12/88; D. Mack Smith, *Italy and its Monarchy* (New Haven and London, 1989), pp. 89–93.

47.   *Q.V.L.* (3), I, pp. 459–60, Salisbury to the Queen, 25/12/88; D.D., L.R.O., 23/7/89; Ramm, *Beloved and Darling Child*, the Queen to the Empress Frederick, 14/8/89; *Salisbury*, IV, pp. 366–8; Malet P. (F.O. 343/2), Salisbury to Malet, 16/8/92.

48.   *Salisbury*, IV, p. 405, Salisbury to Sir Philip Currie, 18/8/92.

49.   H. Seton Watson, *The Russian Empire, 1801–1917* (Oxford, 1967), pp. 572–3 and S.F. Kennan, *The Fateful Alliance: France, Russia and the Coming of the First World War* (London, 1984), p. 22.

50.   *Q.V.L.* (3), II, pp. 61–2, 64–5, Salisbury to the Queen, 18 and 22/8/91.

51.   *D.D.F.*, vol. 9, pp. 577–8, Decrais, ambassador at Vienna, to Ribot, foreign minister, 10/7/97; *P.E.A.*, VII, pp. 213–16, memorandum by Raschdau, counsellor, 20/7/92.

52. P.M. Kennedy, *The Samoan Tangle: A Study in Anglo-German Relations* (Dublin, 1974).

53. *Salisbury*, IV, pp. 41–2, Salisbury to Wolff, 23/2/87.

54. 1st Earl of Cromer, *Modern Egypt* (2 vols) (London, 1908); A. Lutfi al-Sayyid, *Egypt and Cromer: A Study in Anglo-Egyptian Relations* (London, 1968); D.A. Farnie, *East and West of Suez: The Suez Canal in History* (Oxford, 1969), esp. pp. 292, 337–42; Steele, "Britain and Egypt, 1882–1914", in Wilson, *Imperialism and Nationalism in the Middle East: The Anglo-Egyptian Experience, 1882–1982*.

55. *Cranbrook/D.*, pp. 654–6 (21/1/87); HHM/3M/B, "Suggestions for the neutralization of Egypt under English guardianship", 8/2/87, MS of Salisbury's memorandum for the cabinet; Yasamee, *Ottoman Diplomacy*, pp. 211–12 and ch. 16 *passim*.

56. HHM/3M/B, Salisbury's Egyptian memorandum, 8/2/87; *Q.V.L.* (3), I, pp. 272–3, Salisbury to the Queen, 10/2/87.

57. HHM/3M/A, Salisbury to Baring, 21/1/87, and Sir Clare Ford, ambassador at Constantinople, 2/3/92; *Salisbury*, IV, pp. 40–42, Salisbury to Malet (Berlin) and Wolff at Constantinople, both 23/1/87.

58. Cromer P. (F.O. 633/6), Baring to Lord Granville, 2/11/83; Lord Zetland, *Lord Cromer* (London, 1932), p. 199, Cromer to Salisbury, 1890; HHM/3M/A, Salisbury to Ford (Constantinople), 2/3/92, partly printed in *Salisbury*, IV, pp. 391–2.

59. HHM/3M/D, Salisbury to Austin, 5/6/87 and Wolff, 23/2/87.

60. *T.T.*, 21/5/91, first speech at Glasgow; R.A., H45/205, Salisbury to the Queen, 17/9/91; Monson P. (MSS Eng. hist. c.593), Salisbury to Monson, 4/11/89.

61. *Salisbury*, IV, pp. 133–4; R.A., H45/205, Salisbury to the Queen, 17/9/91.

62. Yasamee, *Ottoman Diplomacy*, pp. 89–90; Wilson, "Constantinople or Cairo", in *Imperialism and Nationalism in the Middle East: The Anglo-Egyptian Experience, 1882–1982*, esp. pp. 42–3.

63. Marsh, *Chamberlain*, pp. 318–9.

64. HHM/3M/A, Salisbury to Wolff, 18/9/88 and 27/5/90; F. Kazemzadeh, *Russia and Britain in Persia 1864–1914* (New Haven and London, 1968) for the context. The Shah was Nasr-ul-Din, who ruled from 1843 to 1896.

65. HHM/3M/A, Salisbury to Lascelles, 6/10/91.

66. *Ibid.*

67. *Ibid.*, Salisbury to Baring, 28/12/88; Holt, *The Mahdist State in the Sudan, 1881–1898*; E.D. Steele, "Lord Salisbury, the 'False Religion' of Islam and the Reconquest of the Sudan", in E.M. Spiers (ed.), *Sudan: The Reconquest Reassessed* (London, 1998) for developments in the Sudan. HHM/3M/B, Salisbury's Egyptian memorandum, 8/2/87.

68. *T.T.*, 23/5/90, 21/12/88; HHM/3M/A, Salisbury to H.M. Egerton, acting consul-general at Cairo, 14/8/85, and to Baring, 21/11/90; *ibid.*, class D, Salisbury to Ralli, 11/7/89.

69. Cromer, *Modern Egypt*, II, p. 390; HHM/3M/A, Salisbury to Baring, 28/12/88; *3H*, cclxxxiv, 576 (12/2/84), for Salisbury's early recognition of Egyptian national feeling about the Sudan; Robinson and Gallagher, *Africa and the Victorians*, pp. 283–4.

70. *Salisbury*, IV, p. 326, 15/11/89; G.N. Sanderson, *England, Europe and the Upper Nile, 1882–1899* (Edinburgh, 1965) for the diplomacy of the reconquest; HHM/3M/D, Salisbury to Ralli, 11/7/89 and, class A, to Wolff, 30/11/85.

71. HHM/3M/A, Salisbury to Baring, 28/12/88; *D.D.F.*, vol. 8, p. 71, Waddington to Ribot, foreign minister, 29/4/90.

72. *3H*, cccxlvi, 1265–6 (10/7/90); *ibid.*, cccxxviii, 550 (6/7/88); Robinson and Gallagher, *Africa and the Victorians*, for the politicians and the chartered companies.

73. *Ibid.* and HHM/3M/D, Salisbury to Knutsford, 22/1/90.

74. Robinson and Gallagher, *Africa and the Victorians*, pp. 300–304; *Salisbury*, IV, p. 324; *3H*, cccxxviii, 550 (6/7/88).

75. Taylor, *The Struggle for Mastery in Europe*, pp. 293–4; Anderson enjoyed a position of "relative independence" in the department under Salisbury, Ramm, "Lord Salisbury and the Foreign Office", in Bullen, *The Foreign Office, 1782–1982*, p. 49, and W.R. Louis, "Sir Percy Anderson's Grand African Strategy, 1883–1896", *English Historical Review* (1966), pp. 292–314; Robinson and Gallagher, *Africa and the Victorians*, pp. 200–202.

76. HHM/3M/D, Salisbury to W.H. Smith, 29/10/88, Smith to Salisbury, 29/1/89; Hambleden P. (P S 14/10), Salisbury to Smith, 31/1/89.

77. *Salisbury*, IV, p. 236, Salisbury to Goschen, 14/10/88; *T.T.*, 23/1/89 in HHM/3M/D, Smith to Salisbury, 29/1/89.

78. *3H*, cccxxviii, 546 (6/7/88); HHM/3M/D, Salisbury to Sir J. Kennaway, MP, 4/11/88, passage not printed in *Salisbury*, IV, pp. 237–8; *Q.V.L.* (3), I, pp. 443–4, 613–14, Salisbury to the Queen, 29/10/88, 10/6/90; for German irredentism Heligoland was the "equivalent" of the African claims that were renounced, Taylor, *The Struggle for Mastery in Europe*, pp. 329–30 n3.

79. Cabinet P. (CAB/37/28/38), memorandum by Salisbury, 2/6/90; *T.T.*, 28/5/90.

80. *Salisbury*, IV, pp. 241–5; *Q.V.L.* (3), I, p. 543, Ponsonby to the Queen, 27/2/89; *3H*, cccxxviii, 548 (6/7/88).

81. *Salisbury*, IV, pp. 272–3, Salisbury to Hatzfeldt, 31/3/91; Robinson and Gallagher, *Africa and the Victorians*, p. 247; *3H*, cccliv, 137–40 (11/6/91) and, cccxliv, 1102–4 (16/5/90), where the Latin translates, "Change the name, and it's about you, that story". The pressures on him were not allowed to "obscure the fact that there was a code of international morality which Salisbury was not going to offend", Warhurst, *Anglo-Portuguese Relations in South Central Africa*, p. 46.

82. Robinson and Gallagher, *Africa and the Victorians*, pp. 220–21.

83. *T.T.*, 4/10/84, Glasgow; HHM/3M/C, Salisbury to Sir Robert Fowler, MP, Lord Mayor of London, 10/9/85.

84. *Ibid.*, and class E, Salisbury to Knutsford, 14/9/91.

85. *T.T.*, 23/4/85, Welshpool, 6/5/85, Hackney; Gopal, *British Policy in India*, pp. 137–9, 215–16; HHM/3M/D, Salisbury to Churchill, 25/6/85; Morier P. (box 22), Salisbury to Morier, 11/5/87; Ramm, *Sir Robert Morier*, pp. 235–8, Salisbury to Morier, 2/10/86.

86. Dufferin P. (MSS Eur. F.130/2713), Salisbury to Dufferin, 14/9/87; Cross P. (51264), Salisbury to Cross, 31/12/88; HHM/3M/E, Salisbury to Lansdowne, 21/10/91.

87. *Ibid.*; and Cross P. (51264), Salisbury to Cross, 31/12/88, 17/3/91.

88. Roberts P. (7101/23/80), Salisbury to Roberts, 6/7/85; HHM/3M/E, memorandum by Roberts, 22/8/88.

89. Roberts P. (7101/23/80), Salisbury to Roberts, 11/10/88, 1/10/89, 29/9/90.

90. *Ibid.* (7101/23/99), Roberts to Lansdowne, 24/4/91; Morier P. (box 24), Salisbury to Morier, 10/5/91.

91. Greaves, *Persia and the Defence of India*, pp. 174–5; Kazemzadeh, *Russia and Britain in Persia, 1864–1914*, chs. 3–5; Gopal, *British Policy in India*, pp. 220–21.

92. HHM/3M/A, Salisbury to Lascelles, 6/10/91.

93. *Salisbury*, IV, pp. 391–2, Salisbury to Ford (Constantinople), 2/3/92; *T.T.*, 21/5/91.

94. B. Martin, *New India, 1885: British Official Policy and the Emergence of the Indian National Congress* (Berkeley and Los Angeles, 1961); Sir A. Lyall, *The Life of the Marquis of Dufferin and Ava* (2 vols) (London, 1905), II, pp. 151–2, memorandum by Dufferin, 1886; Cross

P. (51264), Salisbury to Cross, 14/2/89; *Salisbury*, IV, pp. 194–6, "The Indian Reform Bill", memorandum by Salisbury, 31/12/88.

95. *3H*, cccxlii, 98–100 (6/3/90); *Salisbury*, IV, pp. 196–7; Lansdowne P. (I.O.L., MSS Eur. D. 558/12b), Lansdowne to Salisbury, 3/5/90.

96. *Salisbury*, IV, pp. 200–202; Cross P. (51264), 21/7/92, 18/7/02.

97. *Cranbrook/D.*, p. 650 (6/2/87); HHM/3M/A, Salisbury to Lord Lyons, 5/2/87.

98. *Ibid.*, Salisbury to Lyons, 19/2/87; *D.D.F.*, vol. 6 (bis), pp. 64–5, Waddington to Flourens, foreign minister, 22/2/87.

99. *Salisbury*, IV, pp. 354–63; HHM/3M/D, Salisbury to Knutsford, 10/12/89, passage not printed in *Salisbury*, IV, p. 356; *3H*, ccclii, 36 (4/5/91).

100. Marsh, *Chamberlain*, pp. 281–2, 284–5, 294–5; EWH/D. (48646), 22/7/87; HHM/3M/D, Salisbury to Chamberlain, 18/11/87.

101. Lansdowne P. (L (5)110), Chamberlain to Lansdowne, 11/11/87.

102. *Salisbury*, IV, pp. 345–54; *ibid.*, p. 351, Salisbury to the Queen, 24/5/90; *Cranbrook/D.*, p. 79 (29/5/91).

103. *Ibid.*, p. 717 (1/11/88); *P.E.A.*, VI, pp. 324–7, Prince Bismarck to Hatzfeldt, 11/1/89; Bahlman, *Hamilton*, I, p. 197 (12/12/81).

104. Hobbs P. (20/7), Salisbury to Lord Stanley of Preston, 7/7/91; HHM/3M/C, Salisbury to Sir Henry Parkes, 23/12/89.

105. *Ibid.*

106. *Ibid.*, Salisbury to Col. Denison, Toronto, 21/3/91, and, class D, Salisbury to Knutsford, 26/6/90, passage not printed in *Salisbury*, IV, p. 352; *Cranbrook/D.*, p. 767 (19/5/90).

107. Meyendorff, *Correspondance Diplomatique de M. de Staal*, II, p. 70, de Staal to Giers, 5/11/90; *P.E.A.*, VI, pp. 17–22, memorandum by Count Herbert Bismarck, from London, 24/8/87; Kennedy, *The Samoan Tangle*, for a detailed account of the triangular dispute.

108. *Salisbury*, IV, pp. 125–6.

109. *P.E.A.*, VI, pp. 288–9, 291, von Plessen, chargé d'affaires, London, to the foreign ministry, 28/4, 2/5/87, Bismarck to von Plessen, 27 and 29/4/87; HHM/3M/E, C.S. Scott, chargé d'affaires, Berlin, to Salisbury, 24/4/87.

110. Malet P. (F.O. 343/2), Salisbury to Malet, 13/4/87; *Salisbury*, IV, pp. 40–41, Salisbury to Malet, 23/2/87.

111. HHM/3M/E, Smith to Salisbury, 9/1/89 and 17/11/87.

112. HHM/3M/E, memorandum by Lord George Hamilton, 1889.

113. *T.T.*, 17/7/89, Limehouse.

114. *P.E.A.*, VI, pp. 17–22, memorandum by Count Herbert Bismarck, 24/8/87; Meyendorff, *Correspondance Diplomatique de M. de Staal*, II, pp. 16–17, 137–8, de Staal to Giers, 29/1/89, 16/6/91.

## Chapter 11: The Politics of Opposition 1892–5

1. *T.T.*, 20/4/93, to the Primrose League.

2. Meyendorff, *Correspondance diplomatique de M. de Staal*, II, pp. 170–71, de Staal to Giers, 31/5/92.

3. *T.T.*, 20/4/93; Salisbury pointed out that 800 votes in English and Scottish marginal constituencies accounted for the Home Rule majority: "a victory of that kind carries very little moral prestige".

4. Acland P. (MS. Acland d.74), Salisbury to Acland, 24/8/92.

5. *4H*, xxi, 364–7 (13/2/94); *Q.V.L.* (3), II, pp. 126–7, Salisbury to the Queen, 2/7/92.

6. Meyendorff, *Correspondance diplomatique de M. de Staal*, II, pp. 170–1 de Staal to Giers, 31/5/92: on the marked expression of Salisbury's concern for the working class at Hastings.

7. F.W. Hirst, "Mr Gladstone's Fourth Premiership and Final Retirement, 1892–1897", in Wemyss Reid, *The Life of William Ewart Gladstone*, p. 721; *ibid.*, p. 722, Gladstone at Edinburgh, 30/6/92; *Gladstone Diaries*, XII, p. xlvii, quoting Gladstone in *Lloyd's Weekly Newspaper*, 4/5/90.

8. *T.T.*, 28/6/92.

9. *Ibid.*, 19 and 21/5/92, the speech and comment by *Le Temps* of Paris.

10. *T.T.*, 4/7/92; HHM/3M/E, Salisbury to Norfolk, 20/11/91.

11. *Ibid.*

12. *T.T.*, 3/2/92, Exeter, 7/5/92, to the Primrose League.

13. *Cranbrook/D.*, p. 673 (1/7/87), the opinion of J.L. Patterson, Bishop of Emmaus *in partibus*; *T.T.*, 7/5/92.

14. *Gladstone Diaries*, XII, p. xlix.

15. *T.T.*, 2 and 3/10/91, for the proceedings of the conference.

16. Harcourt Williams, *Salisbury–Balfour Correspondence*, p. 430.

17. *Cranbrook/D.*, p. 816 (25/1/92); J.C.P. (JC 5/46/24), James to Chamberlain, 8/7/92.

18. HHM/3M/E, Argyll to Salisbury, 16/7/92.

19. Marsh, *Chamberlain*, p. 335; EWH/D. (48651 and 6), 30/7/89, 27/11/91; C.W. Boyd, *Mr Chamberlain's Speeches* (2 vols) (London, 1914), I, pp. 318 ff.

20. *Ibid.*

21. D.D., L.R.O., 30/7/09, EWH/D. (48656), 27/11/91.

22. *T.T.*, 25 and 26/11/91.

23. *Ibid.*, 25/11/91.

24. *Ibid.*, 25 and 26/11/91.

25. EWH/D. (48656), 25/11/91.

26. Harcourt Williams, *Salisbury–Balfour Correspondence*, pp. 427–30, Balfour to Salisbury, 24/7/92.

27. *Ibid.*, and HHM/3M/E, Chamberlain to Salisbury, 23/7/92.

28. Harcourt Williams, *Salisbury–Balfour Correspondence*, pp. 427–30, Balfour to Salisbury, 24/7, Salisbury to Balfour, 26/7/92; J.C.P. (JC 5/67/15, 17, 18), Salisbury to Chamberlain, 18/11/91, 22/6/92, Lord Wolmer, Liberal Unionist chief whip, to Chamberlain, 19/6/92.

29. *Ibid.* (JC 5/67/20), Salisbury to Chamberlain, 21/1/94; Selborne P. (Bodleian MS. Selborne 5/17–18), Salisbury to Wolmer, 29/1/94.

30. *Ibid.*

31. Marsh, *Discipline of Popular Government*, pp. 230–31; Selborne P. (Bodleian MS. Selborne 8/40–41), Chamberlain to Wolmer, 12/10/94; J.C.P. (JC 5/67/21), Chamberlain to Salisbury, 29/10/94.

32. *Ibid.*, and memorandum dated October 1894.

33. Marsh, *Chamberlain*, pp. 349–52; Selborne P. (Bodleian MS. Selborne 5/21–28), Salisbury to Selborne, 13 and 20/4/95; Harcourt Williams, *Salisbury–Balfour Correspondence*, pp. 427–30, Balfour to Salisbury, 24/7/92.

34. Austin P. (DM 668), Chamberlain to Austin, 16/2/91.

35. J.C.P. (JC 5/67/22), Salisbury to Chamberlain, 9/11/94.

36. *Ibid.*, memorandum by Salisbury, 9/11/94 on Chamberlain's proposals for legislation, and (JC 5/67/24), Chamberlain to Salisbury, 15/11/94.

37. Jackson, *The Last of the Whigs*, p. 291.
38. Chilston P. (U564/C18), Salisbury to Akers-Douglas, 16/4/95; Selborne P. (Bodleian MS. Selborne 5/25–28), Salisbury to Wolmer, 30/4/95; Jackson, *The Last of the Whigs*, pp. 293–4.
39. Devonshire P. (340. 2587–8 and 2608), Chamberlain to Devonshire, and memorandum, 13/11/94, 19/4/95.
40. *Q.V.L.* (3), II, pp. 140–41, memorandum by the Queen, 12/8/92.
41. Martel, *Imperial Diplomacy*, p. 13; R.R. James, *Rosebery* (London, 1963), for a portrait.
42. HHM/4M/387, Salisbury to Cranborne, 12/8/92; *Q.V.L.* (3), II, pp. 140–41, memorandum by the Queen, 12/8/92; Ponsonby, *Henry Ponsonby*, p. 276, Rosebery to Ponsonby, 21/8/92.
43. Two paragraphs of his letter to Currie, 18/8/92 are in *Salisbury*, IV, pp. 404–5, and the full version is in HHM/3M/D; *Q.V.L.* (3), II, pp. 404–5, Rosebery to the Queen, 13/6/94.
44. *P.E.A.*, IX, pp. 20–23, 118–22, Hatzfeldt to Count Caprivi, German chancellor, 6/12/93, 1/6/94, and VIII, pp. 247–54 (24/11/92) (both letters of that date); EWH/D. (48653), 20/6/90; *Q.V.L.* (3), II, pp. 391–2, Rosebery to the Queen, 11/4/94.
45. *P.E.A.*, VIII, pp. 247–50, Hatzfeldt to Caprivi, 24/11/92 (first letter); *ibid.*, IX, pp. 210–20, Hatzfeldt to Hohenlohe, Caprivi's successor, 11/11/94, and von Marschall, foreign minister, 16/11/94.
46. *Ibid.*, pp. 118–22, 257–9, Hatzfeldt to Caprivi, 1/6/94, Hohenlohe to von Eulenburg (Vienna), 13/12/94.
47. *D.D.F.*, vol. 10, pp. 668–72, D'Estournelles de Constant, chargé d'affaires, London, to Develle, foreign minister, 2/12/93; *T.T.*, 29/11/93; Liddon/D., 6/1/89, a conversation at Hatfield.
48. *D.D.F.*, vol. 10, pp. 668–72, D'Estournelles de Constant to Develle, foreign minister, 2/12/93 and, vol. 11, pp. 14–15, Blanc to Say, 12/1/94.
49. Taylor, *The Struggle for Mastery in Europe*, pp. 349–53; Martel, *Imperial Diplomacy*, pp. 203–15.
50. A.G. Gardiner, *The Life of Sir William Harcourt* (2 vols) (London, 1923), II, p. 227, Harcourt to Lord Spencer, 4/1/93; *4H*, xxv, 146–52 (1/6/94); *ibid.*, viii, 16–26 (31/1/93).
51. Gardiner, *Harcourt*, II, p. 326, Harcourt to Lord Kimberley, 8/12/94.
52. *Q.V.L.* (3), II, pp. 404–5, Rosebery to the Queen, 14/6/94; Taylor, *The Struggle for Mastery in Europe*, pp. 343, 355–7; Martel, *Imperial Diplomacy*, pp. 126–36, 216–20, 242–6: two conflicting interpretations of Rosebery's diplomacy.
53. *T.T.*, 24/5/95, Bradford; *D.D.F.*, vol. 11, pp. 71–6 Cambon (Constantinople) to Casimir Perier, foreign minister, 20/2/94; *P.E.A.*, VIII, pp. 250–54, Hatzfeldt to Caprivi, 24/11/92 (second letter).
54. *T.T.*, 8/7/93, at the Junior Carlton Club.
55. *Ibid.*, 25 and 27/5/93, Belfast and Londonderry.
56. *4H*, viii, 20–24 (31/1/93); H.G. Hutchinson (ed.), *Private Diaries of Sir Algernon West* (London, 1922), pp. 147, 149–50, 10 and 23/3/93; P. Buckland, *Irish Unionism 2: The Ulster Experience* (Dublin, 1972), chs 1 and 2 for the situation in the north of Ireland.
57. *T.T.*, 27/5/93; *Q.V.L.* (3), II, p. 258, Lady Salisbury to the Queen, 3/6/93.
58. *Salisbury*, V, ch. i, pp. 4–8, a pamphlet entitled *The Case Against Home Rule from an International Point of View* (London, 1893); *T.T.*, 19/10/93, Preston.
59. *4H*, xxii, 32 (12/3/94).
60. *T.T.*, 8/7/93; Mill, *Utilitarianism: Liberty: Representative Government*, p. 361 (ch. xvi of "Considerations on Representative Government"); Hamer, *Morley*, p. 283.

61. *4H*, v, 632 (8/9/93).

62. Balfour P. (49720), Brodrick to Balfour, 26/10/94; Midleton P. (P.R.O. 30/67/27), Salisbury to Brodrick, 20/10/94, with memorandum; M. Davitt, *The Fall of Feudalism in Ireland* (Shannon, Ireland, 1970), pp. 669–72.

63. *4H*, xxviii, 960 (14/8/94).

64. J.C.P. (JC 5/51/3) Lansdowne to Chamberlain, 21/11/94; *ibid.* (JC 8/5/1/18), Chamberlain's memorandum on the Evicted Tenants Bill, 24/11/94; Balfour P. (49720), Brodrick to Balfour, 25/12/94.

65. *4H*, xxviii, 960 (14/8/94).

66. H. Pelling, *Origins of the Labour Party, 1880–1900* (Oxford, 1954); McKibbin, "Why was there no Marxism in Britain?", in McKibbin, *The Ideologies of Class*; J. Buckman, *Immigrants and the Class Struggle: The Jewish Immigrant in Leeds, 1880–1914* (Manchester, 1983), a case study of this controversial immigration and its social consequences; Devonshire P. (340. 2564), Salisbury to Devonshire, 6/7/94.

67. *4H*, xxvii, 132, 143 (17/7/94), xxvi, 1049–50 (6/7/94).

68. Devonshire P. (340. 2564), Salisbury to Devonshire, 6/7/94.

69. J.C.P. (JC 5/67/21), memorandum, October 1894, with Chamberlain to Salisbury, 29/10/94; HHM/3M/E, Ritchie to Salisbury, 21/1/90.

70. *Ibid.*, Vincent to Salisbury, 23/11/94, Fergusson to Salisbury, 7/11/90.

71. *T.T.*, 6/2/93, Liverpool.

72. *Ibid.*, 9/6/94, to Conservative Unionist parliamentary candidates, and 31/10/94, Edinburgh.

73. *Ibid.*, 31/10/94; J.C.P. (JC 5/67/21), Chamberlain to Salisbury, 29/10/94.

74. *T.T.*, 30/11/97, in South Wales; Orwin and Whetham, *History of British Agriculture*, p. 294; Devonshire P. (340. 2532), Salisbury to Devonshire, 3/1/94; Harcourt Williams, *Salisbury–Balfour Correspondence*, p. 384, Salisbury to Balfour, 2/1/92; *4H*, xxi, 68–70 (5/2/94).

75. *T.T.*, 26/3/95, at the Constitutional Club; Cadogan P. (CAD/514), Salisbury to Cadogan, 13/1/92; P. Waller, *Town, City and Nation: England 1850–1914* (Oxford, 1983), ch. 2 for the problems of London's government.

76. *4H*, xxi, 68–70 (5/2/94); *T.T.*, 20/4 and 15/6/94, to the Primrose League and the Church Defence Institution; Bell, *Disestablishment in Ireland and Wales*, for the background.

77. Benson/D., 5/5/93; Benson P. (LPL: vol. 122), Salisbury to Benson, 30/4/94.

78. Benson/D., 4/3/93, 5 and 25/5/94.

79. Benson P. (TCC: vol. for 1892–6), Benson to Bishop E.S. Talbot of Rochester, 8/3/94; Benson/D., 8/3/94.

80. Benson/D., 4/3/94; S. Koss, *Nonconformity in Modern British Politics* (London, 1975), p. 227, for the religious affiliations of Liberal MPs in 1900.

81. *Q.V.L.* (3), II, pp. 233–5, Gladstone to the Queen, 26/2/93; *T.T.*, 2/10/91.

82. *4H*, xix, 1707–8 (1/2/94); *T.T.*, 15/6/94; K.O. Morgan, *Wales in British Politics* (Cardiff, 1970), pp. 133–60.

83. Benson P. (TCC: vol. for 1892–6), Benson to Talbot, 8/3/94; *Q.V.L.* (3), II, pp. 380–81, the Queen's journal, 10/3/94.

84. Benson/D., 4/3/93; *T.T.*, 18/10/93, Preston, 22/3/95, at a meeting in aid of Church schools.

85. HHM/3M/H, Salisbury to Frederick Temple, 19/7/94, Temple to Salisbury, 25/7/94.

86. Benson/D., 23/11/94; HHM/3M/H, Temple to Salisbury, 25/11/94, Salisbury to Temple, 19/7/94.

87. HHM/3M/E, Hamilton to Salisbury, 26/11/94; Lord George Hamilton, *Parliamentary Reminiscences and Reflections, 1880–1906* (London, 1922), p. 233.
88. *4H*, xvi, 1849–51 (4/9/93); *T.T.*, 23/9/95.
89. Benson/D., 24/1/94; HHM/3M/E, Cadogan to Salisbury, 7/1/92, Chaplin to Salisbury, 31/1/92.
90. Orwin and Whetham, *History of British Agriculture*, pp. 258–61; *T.T.*, 15/12/94.
91. HHM/3M/E, McDonnell to Salisbury, 9/12/92.
92. *Ibid.*, and Chaplin to Salisbury, 9/12/92; Green, *The Crisis of Conservatism*, pp. 114–16; Harcourt Williams, *Salisbury–Balfour Correspondence*, pp. 441–2, Salisbury to Balfour, 31/12/92.
93. HHM/3M/E, Chaplin to Salisbury, 9/12/92.
94. *Ibid.*, McDonnell to Salisbury, 17 and 28/12/92, 6/1/93.
95. *T.T.*, 4/5/94, Trowbridge.
96. *Salisbury*, V, pp. 11–17, quotation from a memorandum by Salisbury, 17/5/94; *Q.V.L.* (3), II, pp. 415–16, Rosebery to the Queen, 13/7/94; Jackson, *The Last of the Whigs*, pp. 289–90; Thompson, *English Landed Society in the Nineteenth Century*, p. 325, for the relatively modest effect of Harcourt's duties.
97. *T.T.*, 9/6/94.
98. *Ibid.*, and 11/5/95, at the Bishop of St Albans' fund for spiritual provision in East London; Acland P. (MS. Acland d.74), Salisbury to Acland, 25/2/93.

## Chapter 12: Unionist Democracy, 1895–1900

1. *Q.V.L.* (3), II, pp. 521–3, memorandum by the Queen, 22/6/95; Chilston P. (U564/C18), Salisbury to Akers-Douglas, 27/7/95.
2. *Q.V.L.* (3), II, pp. 521–3, memorandum by the Queen, 22/6/95: Rosebery on tendering his government's resignation; Avebury P. (49661), Rosebery to Sir J. Lubbock, MP, 23/8/95.
3. *Salisbury*, V, ch. ii, pp. 37–8, Salisbury to Cranbrook, 22/7/95.
4. Marsh, *Chamberlain*, pp. 367–8; Jackson, *The Last of the Whigs*, pp. 291–4; HHM/3M/A, Salisbury to Currie (Constantinople), 1/7/95: "How much simpler [is] the Sultan's method of substituting one party for the other".
5. Lady Frances Balfour (A.J. Balfour's sister-in-law and the Duke of Argyll's daughter), *Ne Obliviscaris: Dinna Forget* (2 vols) (London, 1930), II, pp. 270–71 (26/11/95); Jackson, *The Last of the Whigs*, pp. 296–9, argues that Devonshire was more assertive than has been suggested.
6. *Salisbury*, V, ch. ii, pp. 37–8, Salisbury to Cranbrook, 22/7/95.
7. *T.T.*, 31/10, Watford, 20/11/95, Brighton.
8. EWH/D. (48671), 19/5/97.
9. Marsh, *Discipline of Popular Government*, p. 269, Salisbury to Balfour, 22/8/95; HHM/3M/E, Salisbury to Chaplin, 20/10/1900.
10. EWH/D. (48669), 30/4, 21/7/96.
11. *4H*, xlii, 1071–6 (9/7/96); Long P. (Wilts. R.O.: 947/40), Long's memorandum on government loans for agriculture [1895].
12. Hamer, *Morley*, p. 308; *4H*, xlii, 1073 (9/7/96).
13. *Ibid.*, li, 1435–8 (29/7/97); J.C.P. (JC 5/46/88 and 132), James to Chamberlain, 20/1/96, Chamberlain to James, 27/1/96.

14. Marsh, *Chamberlain*, p. 398; E.P. Hennock, *British Social Reform and German Precedents* (Oxford, 1986); EWH/D. (48671), 19/5/97, quoting Frank Lockwood, MP; Londonderry took his opposition from parliament to the constituencies, publicizing the shift in his party's outlook with bitter complaints of its "almost socialistic" policies, Londonderry to Alfred Appleby, secretary, Newcastle Conservative Association, *Daily News*, 6/8/97.

15. EWH/D. (48669 and 71–2), 21/7, 21/12/97, 18/3, 4/6/96.

16. Marsh, *Chamberlain*, p. 358; Long P. (Wilts. R.O.: 947/56/4), "Old age pensions", memorandum by Hicks Beach, 18/6/96; J.C.P. (JC 5/67/56), Salisbury to Chamberlain, 13/12/96.

17. EWH/D. (48675), 27/7, 1/8/99; Marsh, *Discipline of Popular Government*, p. 268; F. Lecky, *A Memoir of the Rt Hon. W.E.H. Lecky* (London, 1909), pp. 328–9, Lecky to A. Booth, 1899.

18. St Aldwyn P. (D2455/PCC/69), Salisbury to Hicks Beach, 30/8, 18/10/99; EWH/D. (48675), 8 and 26/11/99.

19. The *Fortnightly Review*, in an article headed "Palmerston – with Pensions" was calling for "a strong foreign policy and socialistic legislation"; EWH/D. (48675), 30/7/99; M. Freeden, *The New Liberalism and the Ideology of Social Reform* (Oxford, 1978), for the Liberal trend.

20. EWH/D. (48669, 48672 and 76), 19/5/96, 13/2/98, 8/4/1900.

21. Marsh, *Chamberlain*, p. 459; *T.T.*, 30/5, 19/12/1900.

22. EWH/D. (48672–3), 13/2, 13/5/98.

23. K.O. Morgan (ed.), *Lloyd George. Family Letters, 1885–1936* (Cardiff and London, 1973), p. 91, Lloyd George to his wife, 19/11/95; Marsh, *Discipline of Popular Government*, p. 268, believes the government might have foundered on pensions: "The war finally saved them".

24. HHM/3M/E, Salisbury to Hicks Beach, 7/5/98, Hicks Beach to Salisbury, 8/5/98.

25. Benson P. (TCC: vol. for 1892–6), Benson to Bishop Davidson of Winchester, June 1896.

26. Lord Salisbury, *Evolution: A Retrospect*, revised edn (London, 1896), pp. 13–15, 57.

27. Benson/D., 15/8, 22/11/95.

28. HHM/3M/E, Hicks Beach to Salisbury, 27/1/97, Abergavenny to McDonnell, 27/10/95.

29. HHM/3M/H, Talbot to Salisbury, 7/12/94; Benson/D., 20/11/95.

30. *Ibid.*, 8/4/96, 20/11/95; Marsh, *Discipline of Popular Government*, p. 252.

31. *4H*, xii, 38 (4/5/93); HHM/3M/E, Balfour to Salisbury, 18/11/96.

32. HHM/3M/H, Archbishop W.D. Maclagan of York to Salisbury, 18/12/01.

33. Balfour P. (49690), Salisbury to Balfour, 20/11/96; Benson/D., 7/6/96.

34. Devonshire P. (340. 2818), Salisbury to Devonshire, 21/1/1900; A.S.T. Griffith Boscawen, *Fourteen Years in Parliament* (London, 1907), p. 116.

35. EWH/D. (48674–5), 21/3, 23/6/99; HHM/3M/B, memorandum by Hicks Beach, 16/3/99; Griffith Boscawen, *Fourteen Years in Parliament*, p. 155.

36. EWH/D. (48675), 7/7/99; R. Churchill, *Winston S. Churchill: Youth, 1874–1900* (London, 1966), pp. 445–6.

37. Benson P. (TCC: vol. for 1892–6), Benson to Sir Richard Webster, 15/9/96 (draft), the letter as sent is in the Balfour P. (49851); Benson/D., 23/7/92.

38. *Ibid.*, 16/7/96; Balfour P. (49707, 49831), Selborne to Balfour, 24/6/96, Lord Hugh Cecil to Lady Frances Balfour, 15/12/96: "I rejoice . . . when I read in the newspapers that Lord Cranborne and his brother are embarrassing the Government".

39. *Ibid.* (49707), Selborne to Balfour, 26/6/96, quoting Balfour, and (49851), Balfour to Webster, 6/10/96, replying to the primate's letter of 15/9/96 to the attorney-general.

40. W.E.H. Lecky, *Democracy and Liberty*, new edn (2 vols) (London, 1908), I, p. xix; HHM/ 3M/D, Salisbury to Churchill, 9/12/85.

41. Russell, *MacColl*, p. 219, Salisbury to MacColl, 1/8/98, 9/2/99; R.A., the Queen's journal, 8/2/99; EWH/D. (48674), 4/12/98.

42. Balfour P. (49691), Salisbury's draft [11/4/99] and (49757), Salisbury to Cranborne, 2/4/99; HHM/3M/E, Devonshire to Salisbury, 22 and 24/9/1900, relaying the views of the 6th Earl of Portsmouth, a Liberal Unionist; Devonshire P. (340. 2833), Salisbury to Devonshire, 24/9/1900.

43. *Ibid.*; and EWH/D. (48674), 2/4/99.

44. HHM/3M/E, Chamberlain to Salisbury, 31/8/1900; *ibid.* (Balfour), memorandum by Sir W.H. Walrond, chief whip [July 1900].

45. Machin, *Politics and the Churches in Great Britain, 1869 to 1921*, p. 249; Russell, *MacColl*, p. 219, Salisbury to MacColl, 1/8/98.

46. *T.T.*, 8/2/96.

47. EWH/D. (48673), 13/5/98; J.R. Vincent (ed.), *The Crawford Papers* (Manchester, 1984), pp. 42–3 (29/8/97), for the hopes of Lord Balcarres, MP (later 27th Earl of Crawford).

48. *T.T.*, 1/2/96, 6/2/02, to the Nonconformist Unionist Association, and the Junior Carlton Club.

49. Cadogan P. (CAD/756), Salisbury to Cadogan, 22/11/95; HHM/3M/E, G.W. Balfour to Salisbury, 25/9/95; A. Gailey, *Ireland and the Death of Kindness: The Experience of Constructive Unionism 1890–1905* (Cork, 1987), on Gerald Balfour's policy as chief secretary, 1895–1900.

50. EWH/D. (48669), 15/7/96; Lansdowne P. (L (5)162), memorandum on "Irish Land Bill", with Lansdowne to G.W. Balfour, 6/4/96; Cadogan P. (CAD/756), Salisbury to Cadogan, 22/11/95, 25/2/96.

51. *Ibid.*; EWH/D. (48669), 17/7/96, the reaction of the Earl of Arran, owner of some 35 000 acres in Mayo and Donegal; HHM/3M/E (McDonnell), analysis of voting in the Lords on 6, 7 and 13/8/96; counting owners of Irish land only.

52. EWH/D. (48669), 8/8/96; *T.T.*, 15/8/96; Gailey, *Ireland and the Death of Kindness*, p. 117.

53. HHM/3M/E, Dufferin to Salisbury, 11/12/96, 8/2/97; and Schomberg McDonnell, the younger son of an Irish landowning family, the earls of Antrim, to Salisbury, October 1899, laying the blame for the sub-commissioners' downward revision of rents at the door of the chief secretary himself: "They got the 'mot d'ordre' from Mr G. Balfour that rents were too high". "But what evidence have we got?", minuted the premier in reply; *4H*, li, 861–5 (23/7/97).

54. HHM/3M/E, Abercorn to Salisbury, 3/10/1900; Balfour P. (49803), Wyndham to Balfour, 26/11/1900.

55. Cadogan P. (CAD/971), Salisbury to Cadogan, 22/12/96; J.E. Pomfret, *The Struggle for the Land in Ireland* (Princeton, N.J., 1930), p. 272.

56. *4H*, xliii, 970–1 (27/7/96); Lecky, *W.E.H. Lecky*, pp. 323–4, Lecky to Judge Gowan.

57. Cadogan P. (CAD/971), Salisbury to Cadogan, 22/12/96.

58. Balfour P. (49292), Plunkett to A.J. Balfour, 9/2/1900, and see his "Memorandum on the Irish policy of the Government", 12/5/97, Long P. (Wilts. R.O.: 947/74); EWH/ D. (48677), 28/10/1900, "The Irish Unionist party would revolt under any further term of his [G.W. Balfour's] Chief Secretaryship"; R.A., W74/6, memorandum by Lecky [1902].

59. *T.T.*, 6/2/02, 19/5/99, to a party dinner at the Hotel Cecil.

# Chapter 13: The System under Strain:
## Diplomacy and War, 1895–1900

1. Gardiner, *Harcourt*, II, p. 449, Harcourt to Morley, 6/1/98; EWH/D. (48674), 4/12/98.

2. *4H*, xxxii, 405–6 (28/3/95), Grey's statement.
   J.A.S. Grenville, *Lord Salisbury and Foreign Policy: The Close of the Nineteenth Century* (London, 1976); Kennedy, *The Rise of the Anglo-German Antagonism, 1860–1914*; Z. Steiner, *The Foreign Office and Foreign Policy, 1898–1914* (Cambridge, 1969); and C.H.D. Howard, *Splendid Isolation: A Study of Ideas Concerning Britain's International Position and Foreign Policy during the Later Years of the Third Marquess of Salisbury* (London, 1967) are pre-eminent in the literature on Salisbury's final period at the Foreign Office.

3. G.P. Gooch and H.W.V. Temperley (eds), *British Documents on the Origins of the War, 1898–1914* (London, 1926–38), VI, p. 780, Salisbury to E.B. Iwan-Muller, 31/8/96, then of the *Daily Telegraph*; *T.T.*, 10/11/97.

4. *Q.V.L.* (3), II, pp. 535–6, Wilhelm II to the Queen, 12/7/95; Lascelles P. (F.O. 800/9), Salisbury to Sir F.C. Lascelles (Berlin), 10/3/96.

5. *P.E.A.*, XX, pp. 251–4, memorandum by Baron von Holstein, 14/6/10; XI, pp. 52–3, 61–2, Hohenlohe to Münster (Paris), 1/1/96, and memorandum by Holstein, 30/12/95.

6. N. Rich and M.H. Fisher, *The Holstein Papers* (4 vols) (Cambridge, 1955–63), III, pp. 584–5, Münster to Holstein, 13/1/96.

7. HHM/3M/F, the Queen to Salisbury, Salisbury to the Queen, both 9/1/96; Rich and Fisher, *Holstein Papers*, III, pp. 584–5, Münster to Holstein, 13/1/96.

8. *Salisbury*, V, ch. vii, p. 16.

9. *P.E.A.*, XII, pp. 194–5, 296–9, Wilhelm II to Hohenlohe, 25/10/96, Hatzfeldt to Hohenlohe, 20/1/97; H.H. Herwig, *The German Naval Officer Corps. A Social and Political History* (Oxford, 1973), pp. 8, 14, 15 n3; H.W. Koch (ed.), *The Origins of the First World War. Great Power Rivalry and German War Aims* (London, 1972), p. 41, the views in 1896 of the future Admiral von Müller, chief of the Imperial Naval Cabinet, 1906–18.

10. HHM/3M/A (89/50), "Memorandum of interview between Lord Charles Beresford and Prince Henry, November 18, 1898", a cabinet print.

11. HHM/3M/E (Lansdowne), "Committee of Defence", memorandum by Salisbury, October 1895.

12. *T.T.*, 10/11/96, an instance of the expression in a major speech; *Salisbury*, V, ch. vii, p. 20, Salisbury to Dufferin, 14/1/96; Rich and Fisher, *Holstein Papers*, III, p. 596.

13. Taylor, *The Struggle for Mastery in Europe*, p. 382, saw in Fashoda "a triumph for 'splendid isolation'"; *Salisbury*, V, ch. x, pp. 16–17.

14. *Ibid.*, ch. iii, p. 15, Salisbury to Currie, 14/2/94; Wilson, "Constantinople or Cairo", in *Imperialism and Nationalism in the Middle East: The Anglo-Egyptian Experience*, esp. pp. 42–3, is to be compared with Grenville, *Lord Salisbury and Foreign Policy*, ch. ii, esp. p. 43.

15. *P.E.A.*, X, pp. 87–9, 92–5, Hatzfeldt to Holstein, 31/7/95, to foreign ministry, 3/8/95; *ibid.*, pp. 147–8, Hatzfeldt to Hohenlohe, 31/8/95, with the French ambassador's comments on his exchanges with Salisbury; *D.D.F.*, vol. 12, pp. 114–17, 195–6, 484–9, de Courcel (London) to Hanotaux, foreign minister, 12/7, 29/8/95, to Berthelot, foreign minister, 13/3/96.

16. *P.E.A.*, X, pp. 106, 96–7, 90–91, 120–21, Hatzfeldt to foreign ministry, 7/8/95, Holstein to von Kiderlen, counsellor in attendance on the Emperor, 3/8/95, von Rotenhan, under-secretary of state, to Hatzfeldt, 1/8/95, Holstein to Hatzfeldt, 14/8/95.

17. *P.E.A.*, X, pp. 123–4, Hatzfeldt to foreign ministry, 16/8/95; Balfour, *Ne Obliviscaris*, II, pp. 270–71 (26/11/95); HHM/3M/E, McDonnell to Salisbury, 17/5/94.
18. *T.T.*, 21/5/91, Glasgow; HHM/3M/E, Currie to Salisbury, 21/10/94; Taylor, *The Struggle for Mastery in Europe*, pp. 359–61.
19. Marder, *British Naval Policy*, pp. 244–5.
20. Wilson, "Drawing the Line at Constantinople", in Wilson, *British Foreign Secretaries and Foreign Policy*, pp. 205–6, 212, Salisbury to Goschen, 28/11, 23/12/95; *4H*, xxxvi, 47–50 (15/8/95).
21. Cabinet P. (CAB 37/42/35), memorandum by Salisbury on conversations with the Tsar, 22/9/96; HHM/3M/A, Salisbury to Currie, 5/10/96.
22. *Salisbury*, V, ch. viii; *Q.V.L.* (3), III, p. 155, Salisbury to Sir A. Bigge, private secretary to the Queen, 27/4/97; R.A., the Queen's journal, 10/5/97.
23. HHM/3M/E, Salisbury to Currie, 19/10/97.
24. Russell, *MacColl*, pp. 160, 150–51, Salisbury to MacColl, 21/9, 9/9/96; G. Stephenson, *Edward Stuart Talbot, 1844–1934* (London, 1936), pp. 126–7, Salisbury to Talbot, 24/10/96; HHM/3M/A, Salisbury to Currie, 5/10/96.
25. HHM/3M/A, Salisbury to Currie, 16/1/97; *Salisbury*, V, ch. viii, pp. 6–7, Salisbury to the Queen, 17/2/97; R.A., the Queen's journal, 1/4/97; *T.T.*, 1/2/96, 10/11/96, at the Mansion House.
26. *Salisbury*, V, ch. viii, p. 7, Salisbury to Goschen, 18/2/97; *4H*, xlvii, 1009–14 (19/3/97); *T.T.*, 10/11/97, at the Mansion House.
27. Balfour P. (49778 and 49695), Hamilton and Hicks Beach to Balfour, 12/1/96, 16/12/95; Meyendorff, *Correspondance Diplomatique de M. de Staal*, II, pp. 355–8, de Staal to Muraviev, foreign minister, 22/12/97; *T.T.*, 10/11/97.
28. Devonshire P. (340. 2697 and 2695), Salisbury to Devonshire, 7/10/96, and to Goschen, 16/9/96; HHM/3M/E, Devonshire to Salisbury, 13/9, 8/10/96.
29. *T.T.*, 10, 11 and 12/11/96; Devonshire P. (340. 2697), Salisbury to Devonshire, 7/10/96; Rich and Fisher, *Holstein Papers*, III, p. 550, von Bülow to Holstein, 24/10/95.
30. J.C.P. (JC 5/67/91), Salisbury to Chamberlain, 2/5/98; Marsh, *Chamberlain*, p. 436, believes Chamberlain "found himself caught in a web of deceit" through his inexperience of diplomacy.
31. *P.E.A.*, XIV, pp. 127–30, von Bülow to Hatzfeldt, 3/4/98; Robinson and Gallagher, *Africa and the Victorians*, pp. 446–8; Marsh, *Chamberlain*, pp. 440–41.
32. *P.E.A.*, XIV, pp. 228–9, 351–3, Hatzfeldt to foreign ministry, 14/6/98, and von Bülow to Wilhelm II, 24/8/98; Rich and Fisher, *Holstein Papers*, IV, p. 140, Hatzfeldt to Holstein, 8/7/98; Robinson and Gallagher, *Africa and the Victorians*, pp. 447–8.
33. Balfour P. (49691), Salisbury to Balfour, 9/4, 31/8/98; Robinson and Gallagher, *Africa and the Victorians*, pp. 405–8, quoting Salisbury to Chamberlain, 3/6/98; Marsh, *Chamberlain*, 426–32.
34. J.C.P. (JC 5/67/96), Chamberlain to Salisbury, 2/6/98, complained of the difficulties he had encountered in Africa and at the negotiating table because the French were "risking a war which they rightly believe we are anxious to avoid". His memorandum of 3/6/98 (JC 5/67/98), acceding to Salisbury's wishes for a last concession, stated that the other side "profit greatly by their bluff and their misdeeds".
35. Selborne P. (Bodleian: MS. Selborne 5/49–50), Salisbury to Selborne, 26/8/97; St Aldwyn P. (D2455/PCC/69), Salisbury to Hicks Beach, 3/10/97.
36. Quotations from a long letter at the outset, J.C.P. (JC 5/67/82), Salisbury to Chamberlain, 17/9/97.

37. *Ibid.*, and *D.D.F.*, vol. 14, pp. 104–5, naval attaché, London, to minister of marine, 20/2/98.

38. HHM/3M/A, Salisbury to Monson, 19 and 26/10/97. Compare Marsh, *Chamberlain*, p. 432, and Robinson and Gallagher, *Africa and the Victorians*, p. 408, on what Chamberlain had achieved.

39. *Ibid.*, p. 406, and HHM/3M/A, Salisbury to Monson, 19/10/97.

40. *P.E.A.*, XV, p. 84, Tsar Nicholas II to Wilhelm II, 3/11/98; *D.D.F.*, vol. 14, pp. 288–93, Geoffroy, chargé d'affaires, London, to Hanotaux, foreign minister, 17/5/98; *Salisbury*, V, ch. x, pp. 16–17.

41. *D.D.F.*, vol. 14, pp. 708–10, 719–22, 727–32, de Courcel to Hanotaux, foreign minister, 26, 28 and 29/10/98; Monson P. (MS. Eng. hist. c 1214), Sir T.H. Sanderson, permanent under-secretary at the Foreign Office, to Monson, 27/9/98.

42. Marsh, *Chamberlain*, p. 432, Chamberlain to Lansdowne, 27/10/98; J.C.P. (JC 6/42/10), Buckle to Chamberlain, 26/10/98.

43. HHM/3M/E, Chamberlain to Salisbury, 6/6/97; J.C.P. (JC 5/67/78), Salisbury to Chamberlain, 7/6/97. On Tunis, see Cross P. (51264), undated memorandum by Salisbury with his letter to Cross, 30/12/97, and A. Marsden, *British Diplomacy and Tunis, 1875–1902: A Case Study in Salisbury's Mediterranean Policy* (Edinburgh, 1971).

44. HHM/3M/E, Chamberlain to Salisbury, 8/6/97; Sanderson, *England, Europe and the Upper Nile*, p. 400; R.A., Add. MS. A4/76, Wales to the Empress Frederick, 13/9/98.

45. *P.E.A.*, XV, pp. 88–90, Count Wolff-Metternich, later ambassador in London, to von Richthofen at the foreign ministry, 6/11/98; J.C.P. (JC 11/30/139), Chamberlain to Salisbury, 23/12/98; *T.T.*, 5/5/98.

46. G.S. Papadopoulos, "Lord Salisbury and the Projected Anglo-German Alliance of 1898", *Bulletin of the Institute of Historical Research* (1953), pp. 214–18, Salisbury to Lascelles, 11/5/98; HHM/3M/E, Chamberlain to Salisbury, 18/9/99; J.C.P. (JC 11/30/179, 182), Salisbury to Chamberlain, 18 and 19/9/99.

47. *T.T.*, 10/11/99, at the Lord Mayor's banquet; Kennedy, *The Samoan Tangle*, chs 4 and 5; HHM/3M/A, Salisbury to Hatzfeldt, 15/9/99.

48. *T.T.*, 10/5/1900, to the Primrose League.

49. *Ibid.*, 11/5/1900; Marsh, *Chamberlain*, p. 479; Rich and Fisher, *Holstein Papers*, IV, p. 173 n5.

50. D.S. MacDiarmid, *The Life of Lieutenant-General Sir James Moncrieff Grierson* (London, 1923), p. 133, Grierson to an unnamed correspondent in the Intelligence Department of the War Office, November/December 1897; S. Gwynn (ed.), *The Letters and Friendships of Sir Cecil Spring-Rice: A Record* (London, 1929), pp. 242–4, Spring-Rice of the Berlin embassy to Francis Villiers at the Foreign Office, 26/12/97, on the imperative need to arm against Germany; Curzon P. (MSS Eur. F.111/159), Salisbury to Curzon, 17/10/1900.

51. HHM/3M/A, Currie to Salisbury, 24/10/1900; *Q.V.L.* (3), III, p. 22, the Queen to Salisbury, 14/1/96, with her feeling, then, that "our *isolation* is dangerous".

52. Rich and Fisher, *Holstein Papers*, IV, pp. 71–3, Hatzfeldt to von Bülow, 20/4/98; *P.E.A.*, XVII, pp. 140–45, memorandum by von Bülow, at Windsor, 24/11/99.

53. *Ibid.*, XV, p. 226, XVI, pp. 260–61, Hatzfeldt to Hohenlohe, 26/1 and 30/6/99; M. Tate, *The Disarmament Illusion: The Movement for a Limitation of Armaments to 1907* (London, 1971), ch. xv for the first Hague conference and Salisbury's part in it.

54. *The Times* Archives: Saunders Papers, George Saunders, *The Times* correspondent in Berlin to Valentine Chirol, head of *The Times* foreign department, 21/4/99. I owe this reference to the kindness of Dr K.M. Wilson.

55. *P.E.A.*, XVIII, pp. 150–56, Wolff-Metternich to von Bülow, 24/6/98, and, XIV, pp. 164–5, minute by Wilhelm II on von Holleben (Washington) to Hohenlohe, 22/4/98.

56. *Salisbury*, V, ch. vi, quotations from p. 5. The Venezuelan crisis and its implications for Anglo-American relations are studied in Grenville, *Lord Salisbury and Foreign Policy*, ch. iii, and A.E. Campbell, *Great Britain and the United States, 1895–1903* (London, 1960).

57. K. Bourne, *Britain and the Balance of Power in North America, 1815–1903* (London, 1967), p. 338; J.C.P. (JC 5/67/36), Salisbury to Chamberlain, 30/12/95; HHM/3M/E, Salisbury to Buckle of *The Times*, 28/1/96, resisting superficial changes in the American position; Devonshire P. (340. 2680), Salisbury to Devonshire, 16/1/96.

58. Bourne, *Britain and the Balance of Power in North America*, p. 338; *P.E.A.*, XI, pp. 47–9, Münster (Paris) to Hohenlohe, 25/12/95; St Aldwyn P. (D 2455/PCC/69), Salisbury to Hicks Beach, 2/1/96.

59. Bourne, *Britain and the Balance of Power in North America*, p. 411; HHM/3M/E, Sir William Forwood to Curzon, 21/1/96, with Curzon to Salisbury, 23/1/96.

60. Devonshire P. (340. 2679), Salisbury to Devonshire, 14/1/96; *T.T.*, 1/2/96, to the Nonconformist Unionist Association.

61. *Salisbury*, V, ch. vi, p. 10, Salisbury to Chamberlain, 31/1/96; Devonshire P. (340. 2683), Salisbury to Devonshire, 22/2/96; J.C.P. (JC 5/67/54), Salisbury to Chamberlain, 12/8/96; HHM/3M/Misc., Salisbury to H.S. Northcote, 1/7/96.

62. J.C.P. (JC 5/67/54), Salisbury to Chamberlain, 12/8/96; Devonshire P. (340. 2683), 22/2/96; HHM/3M/A, Salisbury to Sir J. Pauncefote, ambassador at Washington, 7 and 21/2/96.

63. *4H*, xlv, 32–3 (19/1/97); *Salisbury*, V, ch. vi, pp. 17–19; HHM/3M/A, Salisbury to Wolff, now ambassador at Madrid, 24/6/96; *P.E.A.*, XIV, pp. 164–5, minute by Wilhelm II on von Holleben (Washington) to Hohenlohe, 22/4/98.

64. HHM/3M/A, Pauncefote to Salisbury, 17/3/99.

65. *4H*, xlv, 32–3 (19/1/97); Curzon P. (MSS Eur. F.112/1(b)), Salisbury to Curzon, 2/8/98. Grenville, *Lord Salisbury and Foreign Policy*, chs vi, xiii, xiv; and L.K. Young, *British Policy in China, 1895–1902* (Oxford, 1970) for Britain and the Chinese empire at this period.

66. HHM/3M/Misc., Salisbury to H.S. Northcote, 26/2/96.

67. HHM/3M/E, Curzon to Salisbury, 11 and 19/4, 12/6/98; EWH/D. (48673), 31/3/98; *4H*, lviii, 1423–38 for Chamberlain's speech (10/6/98).

68. Taylor, *The Struggle for Mastery in Europe*, p. 375; Meyendorff, *Correspondance Diplomatique de M. de Staal*, II, pp. 355–8, de Staal to Muraviev, 22/12/97; Balfour P. (S.R.O. G.D. 433/2/69/15), Salisbury to Balfour, 6/1/98: I owe this and other references to the Balfour Papers at the Scottish Record Office to the kindness of Mr Robin Harcourt Williams. V.A. Hicks Beach, *Life of Sir Michael Hicks Beach (Earl St Aldwyn)* (2 vols) (London, 1932), II, p. 59, speech at Swansea, 17/1/98.

69. EWH/D. (48673), 31/3, 5/5/98; Austin P. (DM668), Salisbury to Austin, 17/8/98.

70. Curzon P. (MSS Eur. F.112/1(b)), Salisbury to Curzon, 15/4, 20/5 and 4/6/98; Young, *British Policy in China*, pp. 93–5.

71. Bertie P. (63013), minute by Salisbury, 20/5 on Bertie's minute of 19/5/99.

72. G.M. Bennett, *Charlie B: A Biography of Admiral Lord Beresford of Metemmah and Curraghmore* (London, 1968), pp. 215–16, Salisbury to Beresford, 18/8/98; HHM/3M/Misc., Salisbury to H.S. Northcote, 24/7/98.

73. *Ibid.*, Salisbury to H.S. Northcote, 26/2/99; Curzon P. (MSS Eur. F.111/146 and 10A), Lord George Hamilton to Curzon, 3/8/1900, St John Brodrick to Curzon, 15/6/1900.

74. *Ibid.*, Brodrick to Curzon, 22/6/1900; Midleton P. (P.R.O. 30/67/5), Salisbury to Brodrick,15/6/1900.

75. Curzon P. (MSS Eur. F.111/146 and 10A), Lord George Hamilton to Curzon, 20/7/1900, Brodrick to Curzon, 22 and 29/6/1900.

76. *Ibid.*, 29/6/1900.

77. Midleton P. (P.R.O. 30/67/5), Salisbury to Brodrick, 8/10/1900; *T.T.*, 10/11/1900.

78. *P.E.A.*, XIX, pp. 91–2, Hatzfeldt to foreign ministry, 8 and 9/10/96, von Eckardstein, first secretary in London, to foreign ministry, 22/10/96; Curzon P. (MSS Eur. F.111/10B), Brodrick to Curzon, 6/7/1900.

79. Taylor, *The Struggle for Mastery in Europe*, p. 395; *T.T.*, 17/5/99; Young, *British Policy in China, 1895–1902*, ch. iv.

80. I.H. Nish, *The Anglo-Japanese Alliance: The Diplomacy of Two Island Empires, 1894–1907* (London, 1966).

81. *P.E.A.*, XIV, pp. 262–5, von Richthofen, acting foreign secretary, to Hatzfeldt, 6/7/98; HHM/3M/E, Chamberlain to Salisbury, 31/12/97, for his interest in an "unwritten alliance" with Japan; Satow P. (P.R.O. 30/33/5/2), Salisbury to Sir E.M. Satow, minister to Japan, 3/10/95.

82. D. Dilks, *Curzon in India* (2 vols) (London, 1969), and D. Gilmour, *Curzon* (London, 1994).

83. HHM/3M/E, Curzon to Salisbury, 18/4/97, and Hamilton to Salisbury, 4/6/98.

84. Lansdowne P. (L (5) 27), Lord George Hamilton to Lansdowne, 30/12/97, Lansdowne, at the War Office, to Hamilton, January 1898; Long P. (Wilts. R.O.; 947/56/12), "Commissions in the British Army for Native Indians", memorandum by Lord George Hamilton, 15/1/98, with extracts from correspondence and minutes relating to the question; HHM/3M/Misc., Salisbury to Lord (H.S.) Northcote, now governor of Bombay, 8/6/1900.

85. HHM/3M/Misc., Salisbury to Northcote, 8/6/1900; Gopal, *British Policy in India*, p. 218.

86. HHM/3M/Misc., Salisbury to Northcote, 8/6/1900; Curzon P. (MSS Eur. F.112/1(b)), Salisbury to Curzon, 2/9/97.

87. HHM/3M/Misc., Salisbury to Northcote, 8/6/1900; Curzon P. (MSS Eur. F.111/1(b)), Salisbury to Curzon, 14/10/97.

88. Dilks, *Curzon in India*, I, p. 153, Curzon to Lord Selborne, 9/4/1900; Curzon P. (MSS Eur. F.111/158), Salisbury to Curzon, 21/4/99; *P.E.A.*, XVII, pp. 236–8, von Eckardstein, London, to von Bülow, 22/1/1900.

89. *Ibid.*, and Midleton P. (50074), Curzon to Brodrick, 19/7/1900; Curzon P. (MSS Eur. F.111/158), Salisbury to Curzon, 21/4/1900.

90. *Ibid.* (MSS Eur. F.111/159), Salisbury to Curzon, August 1900; Midleton P. (50074), Curzon to Brodrick, 19/1/1900.

91. Curzon P. (MSS Eur. F.111/159), Salisbury to Curzon, 17/10/1900, Curzon to Lord George Hamilton, 5/4/1900; HHM/3M/A, Salisbury to Durand, 7/9/98.

92. Durand P. (MS. 257247(15)), Durand to his wife, 2/2/96; HHM/3M/A, Salisbury to Durand, 8/8/99.

93. Curzon P. (MSS Eur. F.111/159), Curzon to Salisbury, 12/7/1900, and (F.111/223–225), Salisbury to Curzon, 23/9/01.

94.  *Ibid.*, and (F.111/10A), Brodrick to Curzon, 9/2/1900; HHM/3M/E, Lansdowne to Salisbury, 22/9/01.

95.  HHM/3M/A, Salisbury to Cromer, 2/3/1900: "the peculiar power of establishing a dominion over the wilder races is not found by any means in *every* British officer . . .". This section is a shortened version of E.D. Steele, "Lord Salisbury, the 'False Religion' of Islam, and the Reconquest of the Sudan", in Spiers, *Sudan: The Reconquest Reassessed.*

96.  Midleton P. (P.R.O. 30/67/4), Salisbury to Brodrick, 23/8/99.

97.  *T.T.*, 30/6/98, at the United Club; *4H*, liii, 42–7 (8/2/98).

98.  Salisbury in *T.T.*, 21/5/85 and 10/5/1900 on Gordon; Holt, *The Mahdist State in the Sudan 1881–1898*, for the structure and working of a fiercely Islamic regime.

99.  HHM/3M/A, Salisbury to Cromer, 13/3/96; J. Gooch, *Army, State and Society in Italy, 1870–1915* (London, 1989), ch. 5 "African Adventure"; *D.D.F.*, vol. 11, pp. 463–4, D'Estournelles de Constant, chargé d'affaires, London, to Hanotaux, foreign minister, 19/12/94.

100. HHM/3M/A, Cromer to Salisbury, 27/2/96; Steele, "Britain and Egypt, 1882–1914", in Wilson, *Imperialism and Nationalism in the Middle East: The Anglo-Egyptian Experience*, pp. 16–17; Gladstone P. (44203), Harcourt to Gladstone, 9/2/93, quoting a draft despatch from Rosebery inspired by Cromer.

101. Cromer P. (P.R.O., F.O. 633/6), Baring (Cromer) to Lord Granville, 2/11/83; J.M. Landau, *The Politics of Pan-Islam: Ideology and Organization* (Oxford, 1990), ch. i; HHM/3M/A, Cromer to Salisbury, 13/6/96.

102. *D.D.F.*, vol. 12, pp. 638–9, de Courcel to Hanotaux, foreign minister, 12/6/96.

103. HHM/3M/A, Cromer to Salisbury, 22/10, 25/12/97, and Cromer's memorandum on "The Sudan question", 5/11/97; Salisbury in *4H*, xlv, 32 (19/1/97).

104. HHM/3M/A, Salisbury to Cromer, 5/6 and 20/3/96; P. Magnus, *Kitchener: Portrait of an Imperialist* (London, 1961), p. 99: "Kitchener appreciated that their [the Mahdists'] morale was higher than that of the Egyptian army"; Cromer, *Modern Egypt*, II, pp. 91–2.

105. HHM/3M/A, Cromer to Salisbury, 31/10/96; *Salisbury*, IV, pp. 391–2, Salisbury to Sir C. Ford, 2/3/92; *4H*, xlv, 32 (19/1/97).

106. A.E. Gathorne Hardy, *Gathorne Hardy, First Earl of Cranbrook* (2 vols) (London, 1910), II, pp. 368–9, quoting Salisbury to Cranbrook after Omdurman; HHM/3M/A, Salisbury to Kitchener, 21/11/98.

107. Sanderson, *England, Europe and the Upper Nile*, for the moves to consolidate the reconquest by giving the Sudan a new status in international law and the empire; *D.D.F.*, vol. 9, pp. 210–11, Cambon (Constantinople) to Ribot, foreign minister, 14/6/92 and, vol. 13, pp. 116–20, 163–4, de Courcel (London) and de Noailles (Berlin), to Hanotaux, 18/1 and 3/2/97; HHM/3M/A, Salisbury to Currie, 19/10/97.

108. Cromer P. (P.R.O., F.O. 633/6), Cromer to Salisbury, 6/2/97.

109. *Ibid.*, Cromer to Salisbury, 3/11/99; M. Al-Rahim, *Imperialism and Nationalism in the Sudan: A Study in Constitutional and Political Development, 1899–1956* (Oxford, 1967), p. 26; *T.T.*, 10/11/98.

110. Cromer P. (P.R.O., F.O. 633/6), Cromer to Salisbury, 2/2/99, 22/2/1900, enclosing an extract from the *Daily News*, 16/2/1900; Temple P. (vol. 33), Salisbury to Temple, 14/3/1900, Temple to Salisbury, 27/3/1900; *T.T.*, 20/6/1900; M.W. Daly, *Empire on the Nile: The Anglo-Egyptian Sudan, 1898–1934* (Cambridge, 1986), p. 251.

111. Daly, *Empire on the Nile*, pp. 33–7; Cromer P. (P.R.O., F.O. 633/6), Cromer to Salisbury, 27/4, 9/11/1900; St Aldwyn P. (D2455/PCC/69), Salisbury to Hicks Beach, 2/9/96.

112. HHM/3M/A, Salisbury to Kitchener, 21/11/98; Daly, *Empire on the Nile*, pp. 166, 278–87; W.S. Blunt, *My Diaries, 1888–1914* (2 vols) (London, 1921), I, p. 311 (13/1/99). Exeter Hall in the Strand was synonymous with the missionary lobby.

113. HHM/3M/C, Salisbury to the Rev. John Mackenzie, 26/7/90; *ibid.*, class E, draft of a letter to the *Daily News*, 14/7/[90] in Salisbury's hand, wrongly filed under Buckle of *The Times*, with a covering note to his private secretary, Eric Barrington, 23/7/90.

114. St Aldwyn P. (D2455/PCC/69), Salisbury to Hicks Beach, 31/12/96, 2/3/97.

115. Curzon P. (MSS Eur. F.112/1(b)), minute by Salisbury, 25/6/97 on the maltreatment of labour in the Congo Free State. G.N. Uzoigwe, *Britain and the Conquest of Africa: The Age of Slavery* (Ann Arbor, 1974) for an African historian's view of British policy at the time.

116. J.C.P. (JC 5/67/5/35, 37), Salisbury to Chamberlain, 30 and 31/12/95; and see J. van der Poel, *The Jameson Raid* (London, 1951); Marsh, *Chamberlain*, ch. 13, with A.N. Porter, *The Origins of the South African War: Joseph Chamberlain and the Diplomacy of Imperialism, 1895–9* (Manchester, 1980); and J.S. Marais, *The Fall of Kruger's Republic* (Oxford, 1961).

117. J.C.P. (JC 5/67/35, 37), Salisbury to Chamberlain, 30 and 31/12/95; Lansdowne P. (L (5) 110), Chamberlain to Lansdowne, 9/3/96; J.G. Lockhart and C.M. Woodhouse, *Rhodes: The Colossus of Southern Africa* (London, 1963) is a good study of this central figure in late Victorian imperialism.

118. *T.T.*, 1/2/96; J.C.P. (JC 5/67/46), Salisbury to Chamberlain, 12/2/96.

119. *Ibid.* (JC 5/67/77, 117), Salisbury to Chamberlain, 16/4/97, 29/8/99.

120. R.A., the Queen's journal, 18/7/99; Porter, *Origins of the South African War*, p. 249: "The differences between the Colonial Secretary and the Prime Minister . . . were . . . essentially tactical ones, not ones of principle"; Marsh, *Chamberlain*, pp. 373, 462–9; J.C.P. (JC 11/30/166), Salisbury to Chamberlain, 17/8/99.

121. Marsh, *Chamberlain*, pp. 400, 465; HHM/3M/Correspondence relating to the 3rd Marquess' letters to others: Salisbury to J.M. Maclean, MP, 25/9/99 (transcript).

122. G.P. Gooch, *Life of Lord Courtney* (London, 1920), pp. 377–8, Salisbury to L.H. Courtney, MP, 5/10/99; J.C.P. (JC 5/5/39), Balfour to Chamberlain, 6/5/99; HHM/3M/B, memorandum on South Africa by Balfour, 1/5/99; Marsh, *Chamberlain*, p. 474.

123. HHM/3M/E, W. Long, president of the Board of Agriculture, to Salisbury, 25/9/99, said what others thought: "No doubt politically it would simplify matters if we were to be attacked".

124. *4H*, lxxv, 661–4 (28/7/99); HHM/3M/B, Eric Barrington, private secretary to Salisbury, 26 and 28/9/99, and Foreign Office to Salisbury, 23 and 25/9/99.

125. Quoted in Taylor, *The Struggle for Mastery in Europe*, p. 387, Salisbury to Lansdowne, 30/8/99; HHM/3M/B, "Memorandum respecting Transvaal negotiations", by Salisbury, 7/9/99; *4H*, lxxvii, 16–22 (17/10/99).

126. Lansdowne P. (L (5) 49), Salisbury to Lansdowne, 26/10/99; *4H*, lxxv, 16–22 (17/10/99).

# Chapter 14: Anti-climax

1. Morgan, *Lloyd George: Family Letters*, p. 129, Lloyd George to his wife, 11 and 12/3/02, on the news of Lord Methuen's defeat at Tweebosch, March 1902.

2. Curzon P. (MSS Eur. F.111/159), Salisbury to Curzon, 17/10/1900. The Labour vote at this election rose to 1.3 per cent of the total, with two members returned.

3. *T.T.*, leading articles, 28/3 and 5/5/98; Curzon P. (MSS Eur. F.111/221–222, 145 and 147), Hamilton to Curzon, 27/7, 27/4, 1/2 and 22/8/1900; *4H*, lxxviii, 26–35 (30/1/1900), Salisbury's speech; Balfour P. (49707), Selborne to Balfour, 14/2/99.

4. Curzon P. (MSS Eur. F.111/10B), Brodrick to Curzon, 6/7 and 14/9/1900; Balfour P. (49720), Brodrick to Balfour, 26/9/1900.

5. *Ibid.* (49772), Akers-Douglas to Balfour, [17/10/1900], Balfour to Akers-Douglas, 18/10/1900, Akers-Douglas to Balfour, 19/10/1900.

6. *Ibid.*, Akers-Douglas to Balfour, 20/10/1900, quoting Salisbury to Bigge, 13/10/1900; HHM/3M/E, Salisbury to Lord Northcote, 9/8/02; Curzon P. (MSS Eur. F.112/1(b)), Salisbury to Curzon, 15/4/98.

7. Balfour P. (49691), Salisbury to Balfour, 21/10 and 9/12/1900; J.P. Cornford, "The Parliamentary Foundations of the Hotel Cecil", in R. Robson, *Ideas and Institutions of Victorian Britain* (London, 1967), pp. 268, 308–9; Howard, *The Diary of Edward Goschen*, pp. 64 (17/10/1900), Goschen's desire for an earldom instead of the viscountcy he received; EWH/D. (48677), 24/12/1900.

8. HHM/3M/E, Salisbury to Chaplin, 20/10/1900, referred to Ridley as acquiescing in a similarly worded request to step down; Balfour P. (S.R.O., GD433/2/73/4), Salisbury to Balfour, 16 and 19/10/1900.

9. Curzon P. (MSS Eur. F.111.10B), Brodrick to Curzon, 26/4, 15/2/01.

10. *Ibid.* (MSS. Eur. F.111/147 and 10B), Hamilton to Curzon, 20/12/01, Brodrick to Curzon, 22/11/01, 25/7/02; Balfour P. (S.R.O., GD433/2/73/4), Salisbury to Balfour, 19/10/1900; EWH/D. (48679), 22/1/02.

11. *T.T.*, 19/12/1900, to the National Union; Curzon P. (MSS Eur. F.111/10B and 160), Brodrick to Curzon, 26/4/01, Hamilton to Curzon, 14/2/01.

12. *T.T.*, 15/2/01, quoting *Le Temps* of Paris; *D.D.F.*, 2e série, II, pp. 304–6, military attaché, London, to war minister, 14/5/02.

13. *T.T.*, 8/5/02, Salisbury to the Primrose League; Curzon P. (MSS Eur. F.111/160), Hamilton to Curzon, 4/7 and 28/6/01; EWH/D. (48678), Rosebery, 17/3/01; Balfour P. (49772), Balfour to Akers-Douglas, 18/10/1900.

14. *T.T.*, 8/5/02, Primrose League, 10/11/99, Lord Mayor's banquet; A.J.P. Taylor, *Essays in English History* (Harmondsworth, Middlesex, 1976), pp. 185–6; Marsh, *Chamberlain*, 694 n10, Chamberlain did not dispose of his South African gold shares until the war began.

15. EWH/D. (48675), 16/12/99; *T.T.*, 10/5/1900, Primrose League, 14/5/01, National Union; T. Pakenham, *The Boer War* (London, 1979) is a recent history of the war.

16. *T.T.*, 14/5/01, 11/11/01, Mansion House, 27/6/01, United Club.

17. HHM/3M/F, memorandum by Salisbury, 16/6/01.

18. Magnus, *Kitchener*, 183; *T.T.*, 30/5/1900, City of London Conservative Association, 11/11/01.

19. Midleton P. (P.R.O. 30/67/8), Salisbury to Brodrick, 22/11/01.

20. *T.T.*, 11/11/01 and 19/12/1900.

21. Lansdowne P. (L (5) 49), Salisbury to Lansdowne, 15/12/99; Midleton P. (P.R.O. 30/67/6), Salisbury to Brodrick, 19/2/1900.

22. HHM/3M/E, Salisbury to Lansdowne, 28/1/02 (draft), and, class B, minute by Salisbury, 11/4/02, insisting that Kitchener must have a witness to his talks with the Boer leaders but "it does not matter who"; Magnus, *Kitchener*, pp. 185–7.

23. Curzon P. (MSS Eur. F.111/223–225), Salisbury to Curzon, 23/9/01.

24. *Salisbury*, I, p. 50, Cecil to his father, April 1855; Lansdowne P. (L (5) 53 and 49), Salisbury to Lansdowne, 26/10/96, Lansdowne to Salisbury, 29/10/96, Salisbury to

Lansdowne, 9/6/1900; E.M. Spiers, *The Late Victorian Army* (Manchester, 1992); W.L. Guttsman, *The British Political Elite* (London, 1963), p. 82, table iv, figures for those with military and naval careers.

25. Lansdowne P. (L (5) 49), Salisbury to Lansdowne, 9/6/1900, (L (5) 27), Lansdowne to Lord George Hamilton, 23/12/97, (L (5)114), Hicks Beach to Lansdowne, 26/1/1900; HHM/3M/E, Long to Salisbury, 17/12/99, urging the employment of Indian light cavalry in South Africa.

26. Lansdowne P. (L (5) 49), Salisbury to Lansdowne, 3/12/99: "I have always thought the Cabinet rather underrated the Boers"; (L (5)114), Devonshire to Lansdowne, 4/12/99, 23/1/1900.

27. *4H*, lxxviii, 26–35 (30/1/1900).

28. *Ibid.*, and lxxix, 547–50 (20/2/1900); EWH/D. (48676), 2/2/1900; E.M. Spiers, *Haldane: An Army Reformer* (Edinburgh, 1980).

29. *4H*, lxxviii, 26–35 (30/1/1900); Russell, *MacColl*, pp. 386–8, Spencer to MacColl, 26/1/02.

30. EWH/D. (48679), 14/7/02; Russell, *MacColl*, pp. 230–31, Salisbury to MacColl, 18/11/01.

31. *Ibid.*; and Lansdowne P. (L (5) 49), 3/5/1900; Magnus, *Kitchener*, pp. 157–9.

32. Lansdowne P. (L (5) 49), Salisbury to Lansdowne, 25/9/96, undated [December 1899], 12/4/1900.

33. Balfour P. (49707), Selborne to Balfour, 14/12/99; Jackson, *The Last of the Whigs*, pp. 308–9; G. Douglas and G. Ramsay (eds), *The Panmure Papers* (2 vols) (London, 1908) for a selection from Palmerston's correspondence as a war premier.

34. HHM/3M/A, "The occupation of Delagoa Bay", memorandum by Salisbury, 27/12/99; Lansdowne P. (L (5) 49), Salisbury's minute of 15/12/99, Salisbury to Lansdowne, 14 and 17/9/1900; Taylor, *The Struggle for Mastery in Europe*, p. 387.

35. Lansdowne P. (L (5) 114), Devonshire to Lansdowne, 6/2, 1/3/1900 and (L (5) 46), Hicks Beach to Lansdowne, 10/9/1900; M. Howard, *The Continental Commitment* (Harmondsworth, Middlesex, 1974), 13: "in 1902 . . . the British Empire was isolated, not particularly splendidly, in a world of highly armed states".

36. EWH/D. (48677–8), 6/1/01, and a conversation with Michael Herbert of the Diplomatic Service, 10/3/01; *D.D.F.*, vol. 16, pp. 558–9, Cambon to Delcassé, foreign minister, 19/12/1900; *ibid.*, pp. 25–6, note by Delcassé, 1/12/99; G.W. Monger, *The End of Isolation: British Foreign Policy, 1900–1907* (London, 1963) on Salisbury, the cabinet and policy-making after he left the Foreign Office in October 1900.

37. *P.E.A.*, XX, pp. 237–45, Wolff-Metternich to von Bülow, 1/6/01; XVII, p. 217, memorandum by von Bülow, 13/1/00; XVIII, pp. 23–4, Wilhelm II to the Prince of Wales, 23/2/1900; *D.D.F.*, vol. 16, pp. 29–31, Cambon to Delcassé, 1/12/99.

38. *P.E.A.*, XVIII, pp. 33, 66–70, 71–2, 137–41, Wolff-Metternich, minister in the embassy, London, to Hohenlohe, 28/2/1900, Wilhelm II to the Queen of Holland, 27/3/1900, Wolff-Metternich to foreign ministry, 28/3/1900 with the Emperor's marginal comment.

39. *Ibid.*, Wolff-Metternich to von Bülow, 24/6/1900.

40. *D.D.F.*, 2e série, I, pp. 147–50, Noailles (Berlin) to Delcassé, foreign minister, 1/3/01, quoting Wilhelm II; *P.E.A.*, XX, pp. 251–4, memorandum by Holstein, 14/6/01; XVII, pp. 140–45, memorandum by von Bülow, Windsor, 24/11/99; XVIII, p. 33, Wolff-Metternich to Hohenlohe, 28/2/1900; Marsh, *Chamberlain*, pp. 478–80.

41. *P.E.A.*, XXI, pp. 143–4, Wolff-Metternich to foreign ministry, 21/12/01; XVIII, pp. 137–41, von Bülow's marginal comment on Wolff-Metternich to von Bülow, 15/6/1900; XVII, pp. 140–45, memorandum by von Bülow, Windsor, 24/11/99; XVIII,

pp. 113–14, 118–22, von Bülow to Hatzfeldt, 28/5/1900, Hatzfeldt to von Bülow, 1/6/1900, with the latter's marginal comment.

42. EWH/D. (48677), 4/2/01; HHM/3M/E, Hicks Beach to Salisbury, 21/10/01 and, class B, memorandum on "Food supply in time of war" by C.T. Ritchie, 9/6/98; Selborne P. (Bodleian: MS. Selborne 26), Salisbury to Selborne, 27/2, 18/6 and 3/7/01.

43. St Aldwyn P. (D2455/PCC/9), Salisbury to Hicks Beach, 14/9/01.

44. Curzon P. (MSS Eur. F.111/160), Lord George Hamilton to Curzon, 6/6, 17/10, 29/11, 4/7/01; quotations from the first letter.

45. Marsh, *Chamberlain*, p. 510, Chamberlain to Hicks Beach, 2/10/01; Gooch and Temperley, *British Documents on the Origins of the War, 1898–1914*, II, pp. 76–9, memorandum by Lansdowne, 11/11/01; Curzon P. (MSS Eur. F.111/160), Hamilton to Curzon, 13/6/01.

46. Curzon P. (MSS Eur. F.111/160), Hamilton to Curzon, 4/7/01 and (F.111/159 and 158), Salisbury to Curzon, 17/10/1900, 21/4/99.

47. *P.E.A.*, XX, pp. 62–4, Holstein to Hatzfeldt, 11/2/01; pp. 251–4, memorandum by Holstein, 14/6/01; Rich and Fisher, *Holstein Papers*, IV, p. 219, Holstein to von Eckardstein, 2/3/01.

48. *P.E.A.*, XX, pp. 62–4, Holstein to Hatzfeldt, 11/2/01; Curzon P. (MSS Eur. F.111/160), Hamilton to Curzon, 6/6/01, and (F.111/158 and 159), Salisbury to Curzon, 21/4/99 and August 1900.

49. Taylor, *The Struggle for Mastery in Europe*, pp. 396–7; *P.E.A.*, XX, pp. 212–14, Hatzfeldt to foreign ministry, 15 and 16/5/01; XVII, pp. 140–45, memorandum by von Bülow, Windsor, 24/11/99.

50. *Ibid.*, and XX, pp. 26–7, von Eckardstein to foreign ministry, 29/1/01, on Wilhelm II, Edward VII and Lansdowne at Osborne; pp. 217–18, Hatzfeldt to foreign ministry, 17/5/01; XXI, pp. 156–7, Wilhelm II to Edward VII, 30/12/01; Gooch and Temperley, *British Documents on the Origins of the War, 1898–1914*, II, pp. 68–9, memorandum by Salisbury, 29/5/01.

51. *P.E.A.*, XX, pp. 291–2, von Eckardstein to foreign ministry, 29/7/01; XXI, pp. 153–6, memorandum by Wolff-Metternich, 28/12/01; and pp. 7–10, memorandum by Wilhelm II, 23/8/01.

52. Herwig, *The German Naval Officer Corps*, pp. 13–14; Selborne P. (Bodleian: MS. Selborne 5/67–68), Salisbury to Selborne, 13/3/02; *P.E.A.*, XX, pp. 28–32, Wilhelm II, at Osborne, to von Bülow, 29/1/01.

53. *T.T.*, 14/2/01.

54. *Ibid.*, and 27/6, 14/5/01.

55. *Ibid.*, 8/5/02.

56. *P.E.A.*, XX, p. 43, von Bülow to Wolff-Metternich, 3/2/01; A.J.P. Taylor, *Europe: Grandeur and Decline* (Harmondsworth, Middlesex, 1967), ch. 20, "Holstein: The Mystery Man"; Gooch and Temperley, *British Documents on the Origins of the War, 1898–1914*, II, pp. 84–6, Holstein to Chirol, 3/1/02.

57. Lansdowne P. (L (5) 34), Salisbury to Lansdowne, 23/3/01.

58. HHM/3M/B, memorandum by Salisbury on the proposed Anglo-Japanese agreement, 7/1/02; Nish, *The Anglo-Japanese Alliance* is the standard work.

59. Balfour P. (49727), memorandum by Balfour on proposed Anglo-Japanese alliance, and Lansdowne to Balfour, both 12/12/01; Monger, *The End of Isolation*, pp. 58–60.

60. Balfour P. (49727), minute by Salisbury on Lansdowne's memorandum of 17/3/02; V. Cromwell, "Great Britain's Treaty Obligations in March 1902", *Historical Journal* (1963), pp. 272–9.

61. Balfour P. (49727), memorandum by Balfour, 12/12/01; *P.E.A.*, XXI, pp. 244–6, memorandum by Prince Lichnowsky, foreign ministry, Berlin, 17/2/02.

62. HHM/3M/E, Salisbury to Lord Northcote, 9/8/02; *T.T.*, 14/6/02; Taylor, *The Struggle for Mastery in Europe*, pp. 511–13, M.G. Brock, "Britain Enters the War", in R.J.W. Evans and H. Pogge von Strandmann (eds), *The Coming of the First World War* (Oxford, 1991), shows how hard it was for the Liberals to break with their diplomatic inheritance from Salisbury and go to war in 1914.

63. HHM/3M/H, Salisbury to Bishop E.S. Talbot of Rochester, 7/12/01.

64. Marsh, *Discipline of Popular Government*, p. 316, memorandum by Salisbury, 17/12/01; EWH/D. (48678), 27/11/01; Morgan, *Lloyd George: Family Letters*, pp. 131–2, Lloyd George to his wife, 24/3/02.

65. Lowell, *The Government of England*, II, chs xlvii and xlviii; J.E.B. Munson, "The Unionist Coalition and Education, 1895–1902", *Historical Journal* (1977), pp. 607–45; HHM/3M/H, Talbot to Salisbury, 4/12/01. The by-election was in Leeds North, scene of "a Nonconformist explosion", Pelling, *Social Geography of British Elections, 1885–1910*, p. 293.

66. Jackson, *The Last of the Whigs*, pp. 313–17; Marsh, *Discipline of Popular Government*, p. 319; K. Young, *Arthur James Balfour* (London, 1963), pp. xix, 179–80.

67. *4H*, xci, 659–63 (29/3/01); Curzon P. (MSS Eur. F.111/161), Hamilton to Curzon, 20/3/01.

68. HHM/3M/E, note by Salisbury, 3/5/01, on a request from the Associated Chambers of Commerce for a royal commission on Empire trade, and McDonnell's reply; Marsh, *Discipline of Popular Government*, p. 520.

69. EWH/D. (48679), 20/4/02; *4H*, xc, 1011–16 (8/3/01); *T.T.*, 14/3/01; Daunton, *House and Home in the Victorian City*, pp. 191–2.

## The Balance Sheet

1. *T.T.*, 13/10/84, Dumfries.
2. *Ibid.*, 19/5/92, Hastings.
3. *Ibid.*, 12/10/63, quoted in *P. and L.*, p. 138.
4. Mill, *Utilitarianism: Liberty: Representative Government*, p. 261 n1 (ch. vii of "Considerations on Representative Government").
5. Curzon P. (MSS Eur. F.111/158), Salisbury to Curzon, 17/10/1900.
6. *T.T.*, 5/4/88, at the Colonial Conference.
7. *Q.V.L.* (3), I, pp. 272–3, Salisbury to the Queen, 10/2/87.
8. *T.T.*, 14/4/82.
9. Robinson and Gallagher, *Africa and the Victorians*, p. 256.
10. The Rev. Edward Lyttelton to Lady Gwendolen Cecil, 6/12/1921, cited by Hugh Cecil in Harcourt Williams, *Salisbury–Balfour Correspondence*, p. xxiii.

# Index

ALLEYN'S SCHOOL LIBRARY